TEXTILES

Mary Schoeser

TEXTILES

The Art of Mankind

1,058 color illustrations

For Terry McLean and his wise council

Mary Schoeser is a leading authority in the field of textiles and is Honorary President of the UK Textile Society. As an adviser on historic textiles and wallpaper, she has worked with organizations such as English Heritage, the National Trust, Liberty in London and the Metropolitan Museum of Art in New York. Schoeser has organized many textile exhibitions, including a collaboration with the Design Museum at the University of California, Davis, to highlight elements of their collection researched in connection with this book. Her previous publications include *International Textiles*, *World Textiles*, *Silk*, *Norma Starszakowna* and *Rozanne Hawksley*.

First published in 2012 in hardcover in the United States of America by Thames & Hudson Inc., 500 Fifth Avenue, New York, New York 10110

thamesandhudsonusa.com

Library of Congress Catalog Card Number 2012932518

ISBN 978-0-500-51645-4

Printed and bound in China by C & C Offset Printing Co. Ltd

On the cover Lamy et Giraud, *Brocaded silk cannetille* (detail), 1878.

Title page English professional embroiderers, *silk embroidered and faux-quilted linen coverlet*, *c.* 1700–10. In 1910 this coverlet was in the collection of Sir Trehawke Kekewich, a barrister and judge who served as Recorder of Tiverton, Devon.

Opposite Reiko Sudo and Hiroko Suwa for Nuno, *Polygami*, 2010. Lengthy trial-and-error experimentation to see if woven structures could emulate Nuno's patented 'origami pleat' process finally yielded this origami weave technique, which allows the company to weave folded pleat patterns. This example is composed of 90% polyester and 10% cotton.

p. 6 Jacques-Louis de la Hamayde de Saint-Ange, *brocaded cannetille* (detail), 1824–30. This silk upholstery cloth was woven for King Charles X of France, probably in Lyon.

p. 7 Grand Frères for Cartier et Fils, *brocaded metal and silk liseré satin* (detail), 1808–15. Tassinari et Chatel, who took over from Grand Frères in 1871, wove this design in blue for the White House during the Kennedy Administration.

p. 8 Angelika Werth, *Madeleine, Boxing, Marie Antoinette*, 2002–10. One of a series of twelve felted merino wool and silk dresses made for historical figures and their imaginary engagement in athletic activities. Werth references Pliny the Elder's suggestion that wool felt treated with vinegar would resist iron and fire: 'The Madeleines are like that too, made of the strongest stuff.'

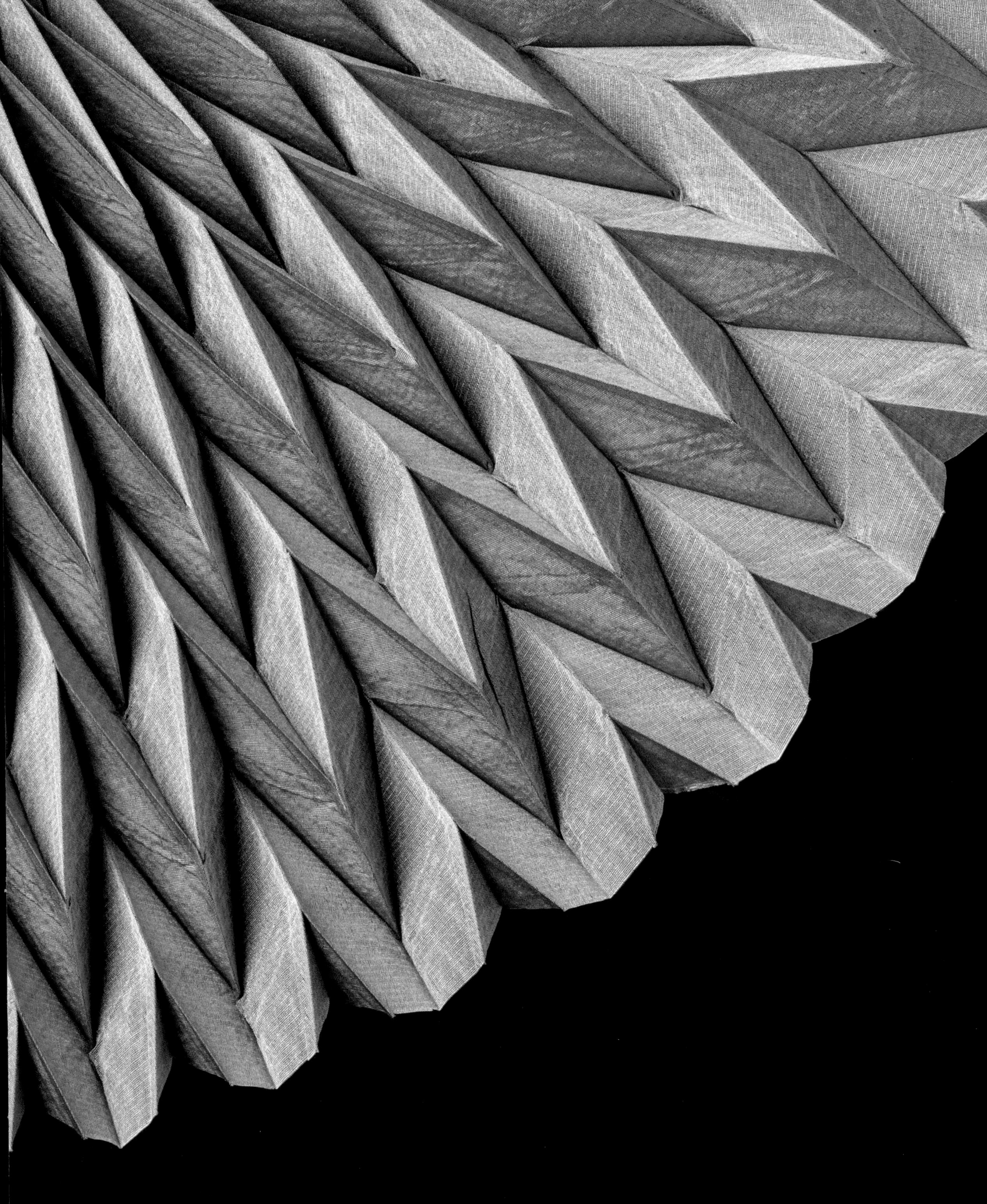

CONTENTS

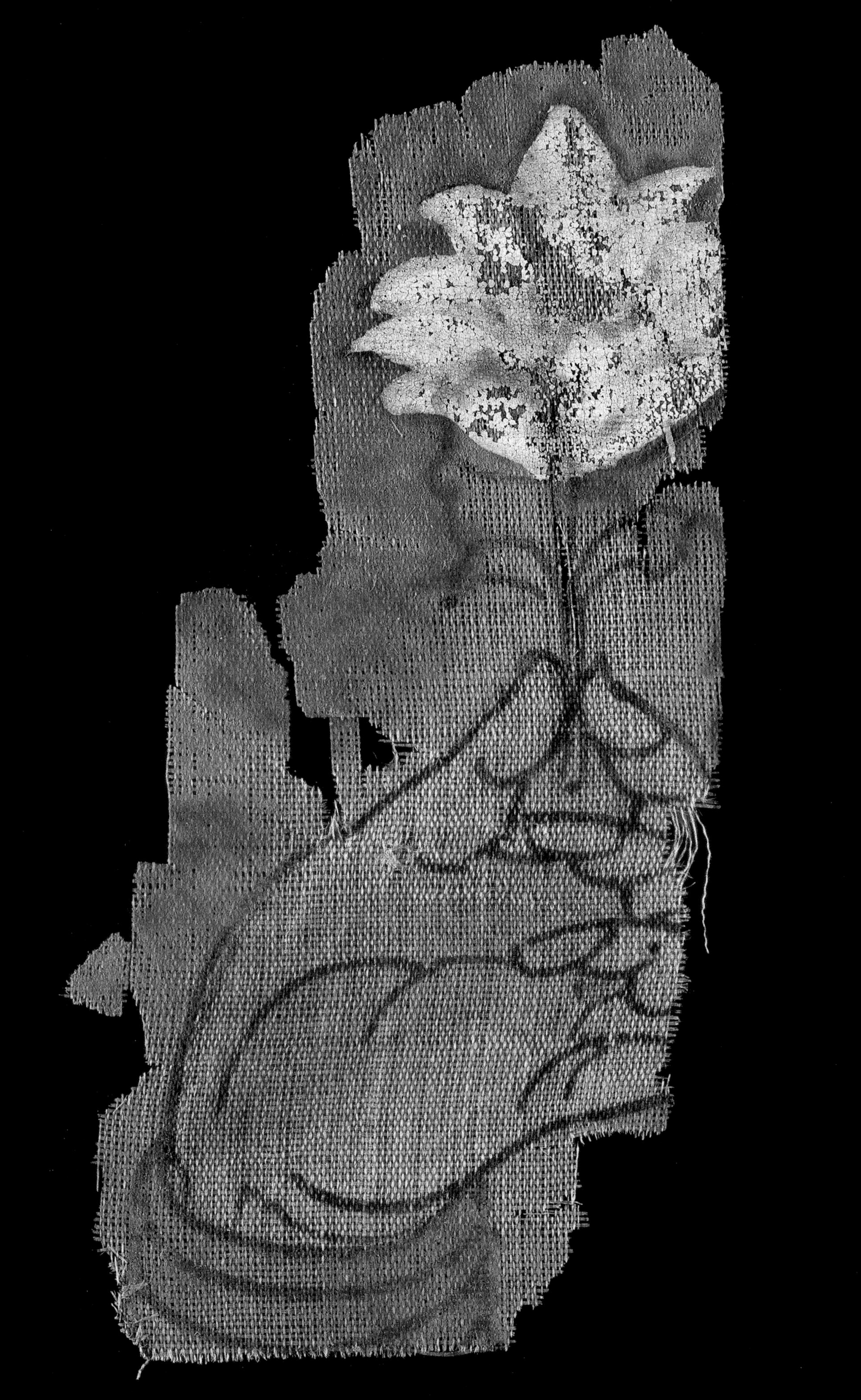

INTRODUCTION

From ancient textiles to those of the 21st century, there exists a continuum of creativity, handed down from generation to generation and inspired anew by exposure to the work of past makers. There have been moments in this story when many feared that the art of textiles would become submerged in a monotonous stream of yardage produced by machines, which began to replace the action of human hands with the invention of William Lee's stocking frame in 1589. Automation was gradual at first, and for centuries textile production still required human intervention. By the 1830s, however, much of this work had taken the form of 'machine-minding'. Fifty years later members of the European and North American Arts and Crafts movements were united, decrying the increasing industrialization as soulless. Part of their artistic response to mechanization was to investigate handmade textiles from other cultures or earlier eras, collect them, reintroduce their manufacturing techniques, and hold them up as standard-bearers. This ensured that, from the 19th century onwards, art textiles continued to be produced alongside developing technology for mass production. Beginning in the 1960s, entirely new machines began to emerge that were hundreds of times faster and, ultimately, controlled by computer. Never has it been easier to introduce new textile designs than in the 21st century: scan, load and press 'go'. Yet textile artists have once again chosen to turn away from the logic of mass production, with the result that today there are countless individuals and small enterprises that create extraordinary textiles in very limited numbers.

This is not to imply that machines have been rejected. Far from it: many new technologies are at the heart of artistic invention today. Equally, many man-made materials have been modified in response to aesthetic demands, whether from designers and makers, or from those who wear and use textiles. The knowledgeable consumer is very much a part of today's renaissance in textile arts. My hope is that this book will contribute to this knowledge, for above all its focus is how to look at textiles – or, rather, how to look at and really *see* them. Over the past forty years, the first-hand sight of hundreds of thousands of examples has convinced

Central Asian artist, *Painted silk fragment*, 8th–9th centuries. This fragment was found in the Toyok caves, in the Xinjiang Uygur Autonomous Region of China – a place where the Buddhist culture of the Turfan Plains and that of western regions converged along the ancient silk routes.

me that textiles are beautiful, inventive, expressive, and more. They reveal the human compulsion to engage with texture, colour and storytelling. They record our ever-changing feelings of play, joy, wonder and profound thoughtfulness. They preserve skills, encourage creativity and represent continuity.

The cultural significance of textiles through the ages is reflected in the fact that so many were produced and, even more remarkable given their relative fragility, that so many have survived. A large proportion of the very earliest textiles exist today because they were buried as grave goods. They show not only extraordinary technical sophistication, but also the important role textiles have always played in ritual. Possessing real monetary worth and exchange value in this life, they represented wealth and power, were given as gifts, used to pay taxes, and were exchanged for other goods or services, even for peace. Alliances were sealed, allegiances sworn and passages to heaven bargained for with textiles. Religious sites, such as tombs and monasteries, and religious garb, whether Buddhist robes, Hindu saris or Christian vestments, preserve what were judged at the time to be the finest cloths. By extension, belief in the divine right to rule ensured that the repositories of kings and caliphs overflowed with exquisite textiles. The homes of aristocrats and, later, of magnates made wealthy through the Industrial Revolution also boasted impressive textile legacies, as items were preserved or handed down from generation to generation; even relatively humble householders bequeathed garments and furnishing fabrics to their heirs. Among many cultures, cherished textiles are passed along lines of descent: cloths constitute an important part of a woman's dowry and represent her lineage. Although this practice is today associated with non-Western traditions, this belies the fact that ancestors' textiles are equally prized by many in the West.

Some textiles, passing through the auction houses or the hands of dealers, ended up in the ownership of collectors – a group whose tastes and passions preserved large quantities of textiles long before museums as we know them began to emerge, in around 1850. Dealers and collectors have continued to amass knowledge and to enrich the many institutions that preserve cloth within their walls. Curators, too, have exercised their own tastes through acquisitions and the acceptance of donations. The text that follows features many contemporary

Edouard Benedictus (attributed), *Furnishing fabric* (detail), *c.* 1925–27. The incorporation of man-made fibres into furnishing fabrics was given a boost in 1925 when this influential French designer began to collaborate with Brunet, Meunie et Cie., a Parisian firm specializing in cloths made of what was then called artificial silk. Benedictus also collaborated with Tassinari et Chatel in the making of matt cotton and shiny fibranne (viscose) cloths, the fibres shown combined here.

textiles, but also chronicles a few of these collectors and collections, primarily those that I have come to know well.

Contemporary textiles are displayed alongside historical examples to demonstrate the persistence of skill and creativity, as well as the remarkable range of possibilities offered by the same or very similar techniques. The majority of the textiles discussed and illustrated here are handmade, and those that are not show the inventive exploitation of machinery's capabilities – an 'attitude of the hand', as it were. In grouping objects together to highlight certain approaches and themes, I have been encouraged by the words of the designer Jun-ichi Arai, and his desire to make 'a small amount of things, and being able to make a great variety of them in a limitless way .... Each individual has a different fingerprint. I think that's the kind of variety that I'm looking for. But it's not something that you can do yourself. You need the collaboration of hundreds of thousands of people.' I have been fortunate to have such collaborators, among whom I count the unnamed makers of many of the textiles illustrated within these pages. The extraordinary visual richness of this volume has also been made possible by the many contributing named textile artists, who have further demonstrated their generosity by providing websites and email addresses (see 'Resources') where possible. And realizing this project would have been impossible without the support of three people associated with the Design Museum Collection at the University of California, Davis: senior lecturer emerita Jo Ann Stabb, curator Adele Zhang, and photographer Barbara Molloy.

By focusing on superb textiles from around the world, irrespective of their age, my aim is to inspire textile artists, those who are new to collecting, and those whose choices will shape the future of textile arts.

Jun-ichi Arai, *Untitled* and *Volution*, 2006. Renowned for his juxtaposition of ancient and new materials and techniques, here Arai also demonstrates his reverence for textiles in the broader cultural sphere. He has created a central form of aluminium-coated polyphenylene sulphide (pps), pleated by compression, and a sweeping wall-hanging using a 'melt-off' technique. This is his own patent, related to devoré, which removes the metal elements of a pps slit-film cloth (also his own patent).

1

I.

IMPACT

I.

IMPACT

The ongoing debate about whether textiles have artistic clout has gained momentum over the last fifty years. Some still recognize divisions between textile art, design and craft, distinguished as conceptual, mass-produced and handmade. Yet the very nature of textiles defies such boundaries. Their imagery ranges from abstract to pictorial and, however made, their artistic message is not limited by their end use; rather, it is often enhanced by the roles textiles play. This was once understood. In the 17th century it was more prestigious and costly to own a fine silk garment or tapestry than a painting by Sir Peter Lely.[1] Industrialization, with its consequent gentrification of a burgeoning middle class, and the 20th century's Modern art movement – which pushed decorative arts into a subcategory labelled 'frivolity' – solidified the tenet that textile arts were feminine and thus less important. Subsequent and serious financial investments in painting and sculpture further rendered the status of textiles questionable. Restored appreciation has been emerging slowly since the 1960s, when two things occurred. First, the International Tapestry Biennial was founded in Lausanne, Switzerland, in 1962, and until 1995 it showcased autographic, as opposed to reprographic, tapestries, as well as three-dimensional fibre works. And second, as temporary art installations and the use of non-monumental and often impermanent materials flourished, the breakdown of traditional distinctions between the various arts was recognized.[2]

Writing in 1972, the critic Hugh Kenner captured the significance of this period: 'Then suddenly the strategy shifted. Instead of art that could only go into museums, art began to be turned out that museums couldn't get at. Earthworks, for instance, [and] a kinetic sculpture of dyes dropped into a stream .... Having goaded the museum into a frenzy of acquisitiveness, the artist's new ploy is to taunt it with the non-acquirable.'[3] The most famous examples of 'non-acquirable' textiles in art are the landscapes and buildings 'wrapped' by Christo and Jean Claude: the first appeared in 1961, and the largest, *Running Fence*, lasted for fourteen days in 1976 **[3]**. By this time, feminist artists often confronted the subjugation of women by consciously incorporating textile techniques into their

1. Eun-Kyung Suh, *100 Floating Fears*, 2008. Chiffon 'pods' suspended at the end of 76 cm (30 in.) music wires move gently, creating intersecting shadows.

2. Naseem Darbey, *If Your Heart is Not Nailed to Cliffe Hall 3*, 2010. For this installation, Darbey used free machine embroidery over double layers of a water-soluble pliable clear film, sculpted over a Styrofoam base prior to the film's removal, to create what the artist calls a 'hollow drawing'. The site-specific exhibition, at Cliffe Castle Museum, West Yorkshire, was inspired by letters written by Mary Louise Roosevelt Burke Butterfield, the American wife of Henry Isaac Butterfield, a West Yorkshire textile magnate and owner of Cliffe Castle.

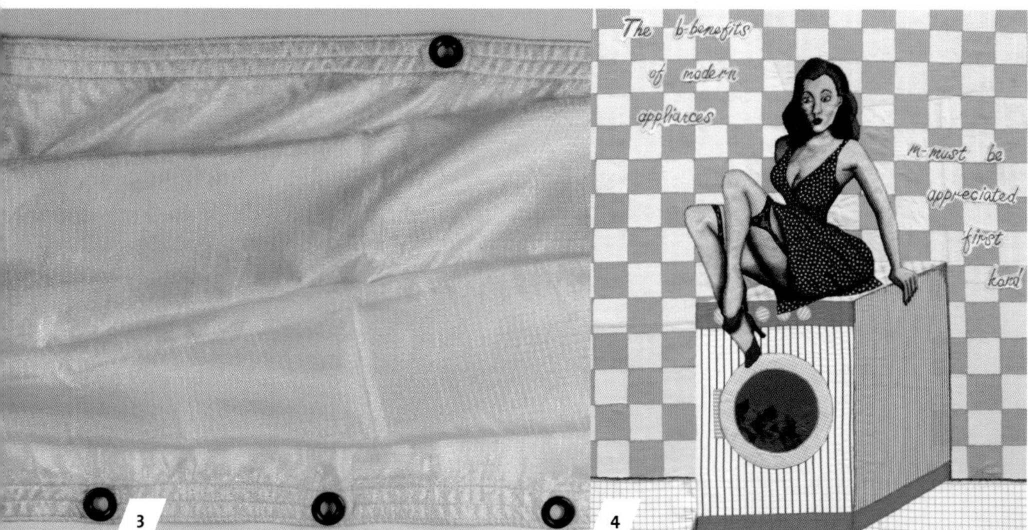

artworks, most notably Judy Chicago with her renowned *Dinner Party* (1974–79).[4] Textiles remain an important reflection of the feminist view, although the usage today is frequently more ironic, as demonstrated by Sass Tetzlaff's visual jab at the objectification of women in 1950s advertising **[4]**. Spurred on by this questioning of acquisition as artistic validation and a re-evaluation of 'female' domestic tasks as valueless, definitions of 'high' and 'low' art have gradually broken down. Textile arts are powerful tools for communication, and they contributed to this democratization within the arts.

Context

Textiles are, in a way, a form of guerrilla art. They are often invisible by virtue of their ubiquity and yet, in certain contexts, can suddenly leap out to capture our interest. Fabric manufacturers have long depended on a recognition of something special when introducing artist-designed textiles, and that is an essential part of their function: to garner attention. But artist-designed mass-produced cloths also stand as evidence of the manufacturer's commitment to a high standard and to what, for the past hundred years, has been termed an 'art into industry' initiative. I have written elsewhere that the art of textiles rests in contradictions.[5] Here the dilemma arises when fabrics from the hands of professional designers are of equal aesthetic quality to those promoted as artist-designed. Are the former any less artistic? If the design is sensitive to the material and captures the essence of the times, then the answer is no. And because many of these fabrics – whether their creators are called artists or designers – have been handmade in small workshops, generally by the originator of the designs themselves, they are often lumped together under the term 'craft'. That textiles can be produced in quantity as well as in limited editions rather stumps those who wish to categorize things, and such categories have more to do with the eventual price of the object than with its intrinsic value. Yet in my numerous interviews with collectors, not one has spoken of their passion for collecting textiles as a financial investment, or of any prescribed 'hierarchies of taste'. This is evident in the words of Lloyd Cotsen, the former chairman of the Neutrogena Corporation and a collector who

3. Christo and Jean-Claude, *Running Fence* (detail), 1972–76. At 5.5 m (18 ft) high and 39.4 km (24.5 miles) long, the 2,050 fabric panels were composed of 200,000 m^2 (2,152,780 sq ft) of leno woven nylon air-bag fabric, little of which survives.

4. Sass Tetzlaff, *Benefits*, 2011. A machine-embroidered figure clad in appliquéd fabrics presents a spoof on expectations of women in the 1950s. Its irony is driven home by the construction of the remainder, from machine-stitched, pieced men's business shirts.

5. Chinese embroiderer, *Double-sided wall hanging* (detail), c. 1760s. Probably made for export to the West – if not for a pavilion in Beijing's Rococo folly, Yuan Ming Yuan – this silk-embroidered silk satin panel includes three interlocking rings balanced on the vases's rim, signifying *Sanyuan*, or 'Three Firsts' in the civil service exams.

has worked meticulously to find the right institutions to receive donations of his treasures. In the appropriately titled *Extraordinary in the Ordinary* he explains: 'People often ask me how I could amass such a collection over the course of thirty-five years and then give it away. I do not think I am giving it away – instead I feel I am sharing it with more people. Yes, every object, every textile, every piece of folk art was personally selected by me ... each has a special place in my heart. It matters not whether these pieces were made by a famous artist or an unidentified craftsman. To me they speak volumes ... of extraordinary beauty with an inner capacity to bring a sense of joy and fulfillment.'[6]

Nor do many collectors reject textiles that are not in perfect condition, because it is the ability to handle, use and study these objects that is paramount. Roderick Taylor began collecting as a boy in India, where life, as he recalls it, was always surrounded by textiles. Eventually he became an authority on Greek and Ottoman embroidery, although he purchased textiles without any agenda, simply because he had the opportunity to do so. Taylor's collection is diverse – his first purchase was a carpet – and that, too, is characteristic of many collectors.[7] Hans Schmoller, one of the 20th century's greatest typographers, summed it up perfectly, writing in 1983: 'To be too rigid in one's definition of what to collect would deprive one of a great deal of pleasure in decorative design, which gives free rein to the old and powerful human urge to adorn bare space.'[8]

Thus the artistic value of any object also depends on the attitude of its owner. This is not just a matter of the ancient saying 'beauty is in the eye of the beholder', or, perhaps more appropriately, of Shakespeare's declaration in *Love's Labour's Lost* that 'Beauty is bought by judgement of the eye, Not utter'd by base sale of chapmen's tongues.' The ability to form an independent judgment, unswayed by the pressures of marketing campaigns, is a characteristic of creative people. As a result, their personal juxtapositions of the textiles they collect – whether displayed in the home or worn – provide an aesthetic that in itself can turn something simple into something remarkable. It is easy to appreciate the artistry in an 18th-century Chinese panel made for a palatial setting **[5]**, and placing it in a minimalist interior only accentuates its striking beauty. It is more challenging to accept as art a cushion featuring a whimsical, colourful and wittily ironic smoking-jacketed dog **[7]**, but a work such as this embodies precisely the idea of art as anti-art that the Dadaists proposed in the early 20th century.

Everything depends on the setting. Textiles, arguably, are the most accessible means of engaging with the transformation from humble object to treasured artwork. And since manipulated textiles – such as appliqué and patchwork – so often involve creating carefully judged juxtapositions, the principles of collage are a long-established element of textile arts. As its title suggests, Dawn Zero Erickson's *Displays of Possessions and of Emotions* **[6]** encompasses the themes of collage and collecting. Its form testifies to the antiquity of these co-joined activities, in its homage to the Buddhist banners typically made from precious scraps of silk. So, too, does Erickson's technique of joining these pieces using the Korean patchwork method of *chogak po*, itself used in the past to make Buddhist textiles. Adopting these features establishes an historical context, and this additional resonance is of great value to the viewer who is conversant in the language of textiles.

6

7

The 'dialects' of textiles are many and varied. This does not go unnoticed, and some artists play on the paradoxical meanings that can arise from means of fabrication and choice of materials. Jackie Langfeld does so through the incongruous elements of her life-sized *Paper Warrior I* **[10]**, using seemingly ephemeral stitches and cardboard that turn her warrior into an image of human frailty, but leaving the work 'open to a complex and individual reading, provoking discussion on many levels'. Sonja Andrew goes further in her work, exploring the post-structuralist debate regarding authorial intention versus viewer interpretation. Andrew created *The Ties That Bind II* based on the experiences of her great-grandfather (a Quaker who was imprisoned during the First World War as a result of his status as a conscientious objector) and sought viewers' interpretations of the work, asking about the influences that informed their readings **[83]**. Cheryl Bridgart, in her freestyle, machine-embroidered dream-like images, simply 'allows the audience ... to interpret my work with their own stories'. Conversely, narrative is an essential complement to the work of many, whether through its direct incorporation into works such as *The Time I'm Taking* by Rhiannon Williams **[8]** and *Script 2* by Carole Waller **[80]**, or activated through the artist's gestures, as in Martha McDonald's performance piece *The Weeping Dress* **[89]**. Naseem Darbey was so inspired by the narrative of a scorned woman that she created an entire installation **[2]**. Based on letters written from Paris by the American wife of a 19th-century West Yorkshire textile magnate and the owner of Cliffe Castle, the installation's centrepiece was inspired by one letter addressed to her 'Dear and ungrateful husband', pleading 'at least write to me if your heart is not nailed to Cliffe Hall'. Narrative, so central to the creation and use of textiles, is considered in more detail in Chapter VI.

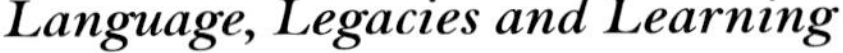

Language, Legacies and Learning

Text and textiles share substrates and much more. The intersection of text and textiles engages so many, both within and without the field of textiles, that an internet search combining these terms produces millions of 'hits'. Notable among these is the Electronic Text and Textiles Project, based in Riga, Latvia, which examines 'the position of text and textiles within the constantly shifting technological reality', builds its web-based journal via 'threads', and declares that the 'weaving of literary and cultural texts becomes a process, as much a patchwork as a network'.[9] Textile metaphors are abundant in every language, confirming that the very process of thinking is an interweaving, whether it involves following the thread or spinning a yarn. It seems impossible to discuss the mind's processes without reference to actions and characteristics fundamental to textile-making. In the words of the author Marilyn Ferguson, 'Making mental connections is our most critical learning tool, the essence of human intelligence: to forge links; to go beyond the given; to see patterns, relationship, context.'[10] Ilka White articulates this in relation to her work *Entanglement* **[11]**: 'Thinking about ... all the myriad forms of connection, subtle to vast. Like when your chest feels ripped apart by the sky's eloquence. The mind extends way out beyond the skull .... As the quantum physicist tells us, we live in an entangled universe.'

6. Dawn Zero Erickson, *Displays of Possessions and of Emotions*, 2003. Silkscreen printed and dyed *chogak po*-stitched silk and hemp. Erickson, who is well travelled, has observed that 'art is our common language and a link to our shared humanity'.

7. Indian embroiderer, *Pillow*, acquired 2003. This cushion cover is worked in appliqué and embroidery. Its humour appealed to Jo Ann Stabb, a collector and teacher, who purchased it in Davis, California for $25.

8

9

10

Sherry Tuckle, a professor in social studies of science, has made the argument that tools catalyse changes in how we think.This supports the convictions of several anthropologists and ethnographers who believe that, millennia ago, the very development of the human brain was stimulated by the emergence of basketmaking techniques.[11] The cognitive scientist Donald Norman tells us that we blame ourselves when we cannot make a gadget work, when in fact the non-communicative gadget is just badly designed.[12] We have no such problem with textiles: they are communicative even when the techniques and machinery involved in their manufacture is complex. Textiles long ago became essential models of cognitive processing, providing pathways to robotics (in the human finger replacements provided by the latches in a late 16th-century knitting frame) and computing (via the early 19th-century Jacquard punchcard weaving mechanism). Subconscious understandings allow us to intuit a vast range of concepts from mathematics to psychology, the latter clearest in the notion of comfort blankets. Textiles speak to our ability to grasp these big ideas. In her series of works 'Finding Home' **[13]**, Christine Atkins explores 'the soul-search for a place of meaning and belonging', using her handmade 'nesting box' books to highlight the human need to make emotional connections. Eun-Kyung Suh's tenuously attached *100 Floating Fears* **[1]** speaks to the same impulse to visualize that which is fervently felt, and we must wonder what lurks in the shadows. To appreciate such works we call upon haptic perception, for which textiles provide the most abundant lessons, training not only the fingers, but also the eyes. And there is ample evidence that, should scientists care to look for it, they would find a gene that identifies those who could be said to think with their fingers and are destined to manipulate materials. Michael Brennand-Wood **[141]** and Kay Sekimachi **[14]**, for example, are both artists who, long into their careers, discovered ancestors who were also involved with making textiles; it seems that the requisite skills are valuable enough to be passed along genetically.

The visual vocabulary of textiles demonstrates long 'conversations' that reach back thousands of years and connect different civilizations around the globe. The roundel form containing depictions of animals or people is an excellent example of this connection, and we can trace its historical voyage. The ancient Egyptian hieroglyph for 'eternal protection' was a shen ring, a circle on a horizontal line that represented a stylized loop of rope, and expressed the enclosing and encircling nature of textiles and their structures. Occasionally the shape was elongated into a cartouche to 'guard' a royal name, which was expressed through stylized figures and animals. Although the use of hieroglyphs was nearly extinct by the early Christian era, surviving Egyptian textiles demonstrate that the pictorial roundel remained in circulation, typically in the small tapestry-woven woollen insertions in linen garments **[112]**. Similar roundel patterns characterize the roughly contemporary silks associated with Sassanian Persia (224–642), which are the first known examples of pictorial loom-woven lengths of cloth, created by employing different coloured wefts that almost entirely cover the warp, in a compound twill structure called *samitum* or samite. From Persia and Islamic Soghdia in Central Asia (or Sogdiana, centred on Samarkand), these silks **[12]** were dispersed as gifts and trade goods along the Silk Road as far north as Scandinavia **[111]**, and were brought to Eastern Asia

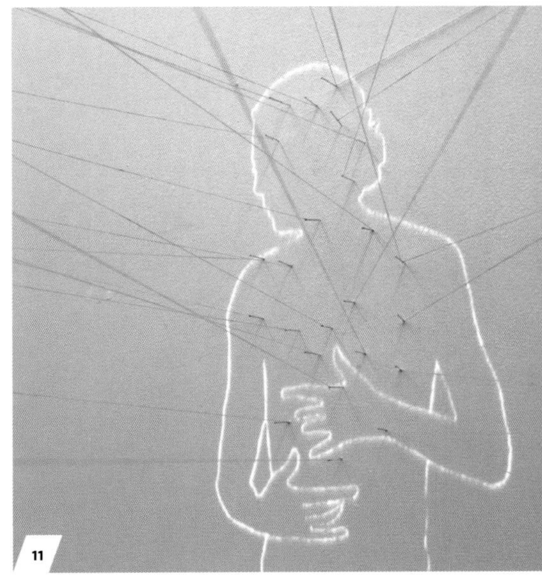
11

8. Rhiannon Williams, *The Time I'm Taking: Proust Pile* (detail), 2008. One of seven patchworks sewn from each of the volumes of Marcel Proust's *In Search of Lost Time*. Williams expects that it will take fourteen years to complete the series, which is part of a larger body of work – 'Critical Cloth' – that critiques capitalist culture through its 'slow-time' approach.

9. Judith Scott, *Twins*, undated. The intuitive manipulation of fibre is epitomized by Scott, an untrained, deaf artist who had Downs Syndrome. From 1987 until her death in 2005, she created armatures of bamboo slats or other discarded materials, wrapping these forms with lengths of knotted cloth or yarn.

10. Jackie Langfeld, *Paper Warrior I*, 2008. One of five life-size figures made of cardboard, string, paper cording, willow and steel. The ironic title reflects the artist's view of 'the position of man on this planet, his frailty and his vanity, and his inescapable mortality ... [despite] bigger weapons at this disposal'.

11. Ilka White, *Entanglement* (detail), 2008. Projected light, thread, steel pins and space are the artist's materials, used in an installation exploring connections and the 'mutual exchange between the body and the brilliant world'.

13

14

by Soghdian weavers relocated to Tang dynasty China (618–907). There, the roundel aligned with Buddhist wheel or cycle-of-life symbols, becoming an iconic image of court and church, not only in China **[108]**, but also in countries from Japan **[113]** to India **[12, 115]**. The roundel was slowly modified by silk weavers into the curved ogee arrangement that typifies Italian Renaissance patterns (themselves influenced by silks from regions where Islamic caliphs banned depictions) **[104–5, 107]**, yet its distinct appearance retained its status as a sign of continuity and survival in all sorts of other textiles, from appliqué to embroidery. Ultimately, the encircled eagle, once emblematic of the Holy Roman Empire, transferred to North America, where it became the Great Seal of the United States and appeared – together with other pictorial and decorative roundel forms – on countless woven and appliquéd coverlets, and on samplers **[116]**. Often the figures within the roundel were paired and facing, or 'confronting', each other (an arrangement also found in dynastic Egyptian art), and this arrangement became equally widespread **[92–103, 107]**.

Similarly, one can trace even more complex exchanges, for example in the case of Indian chintzes, from the 17th century traded in both the East and the West, and designed to suit each different market. Originally created with coloured grounds, chintzes were produced with a white ground to cater to particular customers, such as the British and French, whose own silks, embroideries, and prints soon adopted Indian characteristics **[136, 137, 139]**.

Jane Graves, the cultural historian and psychoanalyst, argues that 'pattern is the universe writ small', but points out that the impact of industrialization destroyed understanding of ancient patterns, the result being that, 'unfortunately,

12. East Indian weaver, *Silk samite*, 15th to early 16th centuries. Small winged felines, each 8.5 cm (3³/₈ in.) wide, adorn one of a rare and important group of Indian draw-loomed silks discovered in Tibet. Pre-dating the earliest surviving silks of the Mughal period, the theme of inhabited roundels had already appeared for a thousand years in draw-loomed silks woven elsewhere in Asia.

13. Christine Atkins, *Finding Home*, 2009. Composed of compressed Guildford Grass (part of the iris family), this hand-constructed book incorporates mica, hand-dyeing, cotton thread, machine- and hand-stitching, and etched brass. The base of the door reads 'Calm Outlet Strength of a tree'.

14. Kay Sekimachi, *Mini Basket*, 1993. Black and grey cotton cord, split-plied. Sekimachi began exploring split-ply techniques in 1976, inspired by camel girths from India, made by men and usually black and natural in colour. As she says, 'The technique is portable and all you need ... is plied yarn and ... a crochet hook.'

pattern makes sense – but not meaning'. Patterns such as the roundel were consciously revived by Arts and Crafts designers seeking pre-Renaissance inspiration **[114]**, as were the bosses (circular Japanese motifs indebted to the roundel as well as the Buddhist *enso*, a circle associated with Zen **[91]**) favoured by Aesthetic Movement designers **[106]**. Textiles from India were once again widely consulted, notably by William Morris **[132]**. This aspect of textiles implies that it was admiration rather than cultural domination that induced such appropriations. Thus Graves can conjecture that 'as we battle through the mirage of modernism and post-modernism it seems we are still looking for new possibilities through ecology and our engagement with other cultures. Pattern may yet do a lot for us.'[13]

Today's textile vocabulary is often concerned with cultural and personal memories and their transformation through time, as in the work of Marie-Laure Ilie **[79]**, for whom 'one of the most important factors inherent to fabric is its historical and sociological links with the human body', a statement echoed by many other textile artists. While Ilie's work employs modern technology to capture pictorial imagery, expressions of memories are often not pictorial. The use of vintage textiles is a case in point. Louisa Jane Irvine describes herself as from a family of strong women; this, together with wide first-hand experience of traditional women's textile crafts in indigenous cultures, results in work 'created using hundreds of pairs of my grandmother's old silk and nylon stockings, or large amounts of fabrics [that] have been found or used in some way and hold memories' **[82]**. Kim Schoenberger's untitled quilt, made from thousands of recycled teabags, was stitched on a treadle sewing machine, a reflection of the past that is invisible to the viewer **[84]**. Each teabag evoked a memory of a different conversation over a cup of tea with her late mother. This autobiographical detail should be invisible too, but there is nevertheless something in the seemingly damaged, tender surface of the work that conveys a deep and loving emotion. Resonances of the past are natural in textiles, whether or not they use recycled materials, since all begin with the creation of the very yarns and structures that provide the textile artist's palette: this, as Lars Preisser puts it, 'speaks of an *origin* or a *before*'. Denise Stanton's untitled, ghostly hand-felted figure plays precisely on this fracture between past and present **[88]**, having been created for Woodchester Mansion, a Victorian gothic masterpiece mysteriously abandoned mid-construction in 1873.

Cultural pasts are questioned by many textile artists, often in relation to the human impact on the environment. This topic is of direct relevance to textiles, since the field not only incorporates fibres such as cotton – notoriously dependent on pesticides for large crops – but has also employed many toxic chemicals in printing, bleaching and other finishing processes. Sustainable, natural fibres cannot clothe the world because there are simply not enough to go round, which means that manufacturers of petroleum-based synthetics (such as polyester and acrylic) have developed means of recycling these chemically modified products. Partnerships with consultancies such as TED (Textiles Environment Design, at the University of the Arts London) result in 'upcycled' and sustainable textiles and fashion design **[18]**. At the leading edge of this search for sustainable fibres is Carole Collet, Reader in Textile Futures at Central Saint Martins College of

15

15. Oei Khingi Liem, *Batik sarong* (detail), *c.* 1910. Modern batiks were conceived by Indonesian batik artists from Dutch postcards, wallpaper designs and printed cottons. In this sarong, the water iris, so fashionable in Northern European design a decade earlier, is set against a traditional ground of slanting lines.

16. Felix Aubert, *Iris d'Eau*, 1897–98. Water irises became closely linked with this French designer's work, illustrated here by a velveteen roller-printed by the prominent Alsatian manufacturer Scheurer Lauth & Cie. Through its emphasis on a symmetrical arrangement rather than the whiplash curve associated with Art Nouveau, the pattern aligns with Northern European tastes.

Art and Design, London. Through her BioLace project, designed to 'probe the potential of a biological manufacturing future by exploring the cellular programming of morphogenesis in plant systems', she 'imagines the creation of a hybrid strawberry plant that would produce at the same time both strawberry fruits and lace samples from its roots'.[14]

Whether by creating an environment, commenting on the environment, interacting with the natural environment, or humanizing the built environment, artists such as Silke Bosbach, Anne Field, Amy George, Mandy Gunn, Sheila Klein, Heike Reul, Nalda Searles and Evette Sunset **[127–31]** are among those asking us to contemplate and rethink our actions and expectations in relation to the world as a whole. Clyde Olliver's small stack of cord-secured slate, *Little Cairn* **[125]**, is a reminder that even the most rural areas in many parts of the world have been managed and significantly altered by humans to suit their own needs.

17. Peruvian weaver, *Textile fragment with border of standing figures* (detail), 1000–1476. From Chancay, on the central coast of Peru, this cotton open-work net, 51 cm (20 in.) wide, is embroidered in alternating squares. It has an attached camelid-fibre (wool) weft-faced slit tapestry band, with sections of weft becoming the warp-faced tapestry-weave fringes.

Colour and the Global Vision

Colour is perhaps the most visible yet least 'seen' aspect of textiles. Long-perfected fibre colourants ensure that textiles need not be pictorial to be striking, as illustrated by the examples included within this chapter. Earliest among these are bold geometric patterns found in many ancient Peruvian textiles, which began to be excavated, initially by German archaeologists, in the 1880s. The Modernist weaves associated with the Bauhaus, especially its Weimar (1919–25) and early Dessau (1925–32) periods, arguably reflect admiration for these ancient textiles. At the Weimar Bauhaus Johannes Itten instituted two cornerstones of Modernism: the foundation course, and what is still regarded by many as the most important colour theory of his century – the first to define methods of coordinating colour according to each hue's contrasting properties, including intensity. Itten clearly had an interest in weaving, and in 1924, after his departure from the Bauhaus, he established the Ontos Weaving Workshops near Zurich with the help of the Bauhaus graduate Gunta Stölzl. She returned to the school a year later, becoming master of the weaving workshop in 1927 **[23]**.

The Modernists' search for a universal grammar that communicated the 'essence of things' resulted in a philosophical understanding of the 'connectedness of colour and emotional energy'. (Itten's departure from the Bauhaus was the result of his Mazdaznan Zoroastrian philosophy, and many pioneers of Modernism – including Robert Delaunay, Marcel Duchamp, Wassily Kandinsky, Paul Klee and Piet Mondrian – were Theosophists, studying Vedic, Taoist, Buddhist, Jewish, Christian, Zoroastrian and Islamic traditions.) The London-based textile collector and dealer Esther Fitzgerald argues that the same colour relationships are also found in striking late 19th- and early 20th-century abstract ikats from Islamic Sumatra and Uzbekistan, as well as in earlier Chinese and Tibetan Buddhist ritual patchworked textiles. Fitzgerald offers these works as material evidence that 'Modernism was nourished by elements from the common pool of mystical ideas.'[15] While it has not been established whether such Asian textiles were a direct influence on Modernist colour theory **[22, 23]**, what is certain is that the Bauhaus artist Anni Albers, trained by Itten, among others, and renowned for the impact of her teaching at the progressive Black Mountain College in North Carolina from 1933–49, illustrated cloths by Peruvian weavers and cited them as her 'great teachers' in her book *On Weaving* (1965).

Albers was not the first in the United States to suggest the relevance of non-Western textiles to the modern designer and artist. Beginning in 1915, this agenda had been promoted in New York by a group of individuals representing museums, schools of design, textile manufacturers, retailers, and the magazine later known as *Women's Wear Daily*. But their remit was broader: textiles indigenous to the Americas, Africa and Oceania inspired abstract patterns for all types of textiles and, beyond that, all types of art. By 1933, when the MoMA exhibition 'American Sources of Modern Art' juxtaposed a collection of Pre-Columbian art (including textiles) with modern artworks, the relationship between early Abstract Expressionism and 'the primeval past' was made clear.[16] For weavers, Agnes Myrtle Nelson had already written *Analysis of Peruvian Weaves: Their Inspiration to the Teacher of Textiles* for the University of California (1926). This book appears to have contributed to the largely uncharted early development of a distinct West Coast formalist approach to weaving, clearly evident by the time the textile designer Dorothy Liebes established her first studio in San Francisco in 1934.

There were a handful of other 20th-century weavers who, like Liebes, excelled at handweaving prototypes for industrial production that managed to retain the lively character of handwoven cloth – in other words, its emotional content. Among those in Britain were Bernat Klein, Margaret Leichner, Tibor Reich and Marianne Straub, all born and, at least in part, trained in Europe. In North America, European-born and -trained weavers were also influential, among them Albers's fellow Bauhaus student Marli Ehrman and the Finnish weaver Marianne Strengell. Liebes, too, apprenticed with Paul Rodier, the great French handweaver, and visited Italian weavers. These mid-century functionalist weavers, whose juxtapositions of bold colours and unexpected materials or textures Ed Rossbach described as 'Contemporary', preserved the legacy of the 'truth to materials' concept of the Arts and Crafts Movement. At the same time they transformed it by injecting a sound understanding of non-Western cloth construction into their work while eschewing imitation of the patterns themselves. Liebes, for example, had studied anthropology as well as art, and spent time with Guatemalan and Mexican weavers to hone her skills. Rodier collected from the then French colonies, especially Cambodian *sampot*, the long retangular cloth worn around the lower body, traditionally of silk, twill-woven and ikat-patterned.

One could provide other examples, but the impact of Peruvian textiles seems key here. Albers collected them, as well as textiles from Mexico; Straub collected them too, acquiring many before the Second World War from the Swiss collector Fritz Iklé. His own Andean textile collection featured among those analysed in Raoul d'Harcourt's seminal work *Textiles of Ancient Peru and Their Techniques* (1924, republished as recently as 2002), and with Iklé's other textiles has been housed at the Museum für Völkerkunde (Museum of Cultures), Basel, since 1945.[17] Earlier, museums across Europe had acquired examples of Andean textiles, and the Metropolitan Museum in New York had received a gift of

18

18. Melanie Bowles and Kathryn Round, *Trash Fashion*, 2010. A crêpe de chine dress digitally printed with a vintage garment demonstrates an approach to sustainable design inspired by emotional durability. The dress was created for the exhibition 'Trash Fashion: Designing Out Waste' at the Science Museum, London, and was designed within the Textiles Environment Design (TED) project at London's University of the Arts. TED explores how designers can create textiles with low environmental impact.

Peruvian antiquities as early as 1882. It is clear, then, that Modernist weavers in Europe and North America could read about, see and even own Peruvian textiles, which are admired equally for their ingenious use of weave structures and for the fact that so many examples are between 2,000 and 4,000 years old.

In the 1970s, the Los Angeles County Museum of Art (LACMA) – already on its way to holding the largest textile collection in the western United States – acquired one hundred Peruvian textiles from John Wise, a New York collector-dealer known for his exceptional examples covering over 2,000 years of Pre-Columbian weaving, the earliest from the 5th century BC. The timing was perfect, coinciding as it did with a maturing interest in ethnographic textiles and the flourishing West Coast fibre art scene. Ed Rossbach preferred the term 'fiber-works' and dubbed this period 'post-Contemporary', in other words unconcerned with functionality per se, but with exploration without bias towards producing multiples or useful cloths or baskets. This in turned signalled the demise of hierarchies. Slowly dissolving thereafter were the differentiations between artists, designers and skilled artisans, urban industries versus rural workshops, traditional approaches versus the most modern, all of which ensured that first-hand engagement with world textiles became a significant aspect of what it means today to be a textile artist.

The designers' prerogative to explore all possible results has again allowed textiles to become what they always used to be: everything from intimate pieces of jewellery to monumental installations. And just as the vocabulary of textiles once venerated church or state, now it often values integrity, through a mode of working that results in 'slow' textiles – artisanal, sensual and intensely reflective – as well as through the interrogation of the status quo.[18] Brennand-Wood explores the illusionary space between two and three dimensions in *Vase Attacks San Francisco USA* **[141]**, which at first sight is beautiful, but upon closer examination reveals darker references to mines, military cap badges, uniform insignia, war games and skulls. In much of her work, Rozanne Hawksley, an official British War Artist, considers the plight of the individual caught in the crossfire; in *Surgeon's Equipment* she comments on the catastrophic consequences of battle as well as the role of stitch in putting a damaged body back together **[85]**. More overtly political are works representing endangered species or cultures, as exemplified by textiles referencing Tibetan tiger rugs **[121–23]**. It has been argued that the emancipation of art has a negative side: 'The contents to be expressed, the forms to be chosen to fit them, the materials to be used and the genres to be kept or newly named, all of these matters have to be groped for from now on ... art has totally become a rootless existence.'[19] For textile artists, however, it is clear that textiles themselves form a firm foundation, a network linking a regard for the past, questions about the present, and exhilarating ideas for the future.

19. French embroiderer, *Pair of appliqué and embroidered hangings* (detail), 1630–40. Separately prepared in silk *gros point*, floral columns were applied to a wool felt ground, after which the edgings and floral bunches were embroidered. With a height of 2 m (79 in.), these panels would have been very costly and were probably worked by professionals.

20. Indonesian artisans, *Warp-ikat tube/wrap skirt* (detail), *c.* 1976. Vivid colours on golden and minty-green grounds were selected to appeal to the Western market, in this case to be imported by Thousand Flowers, San Francisco, in 1977. Note the weft ikat forming a border on the lower edge.

21. Chinese embroider, *Child's collar*, 20th century. This striking and semi-rigid collar is composed of embroidered silk satin and damask sections interlined with paper and edged with black cotton braid.

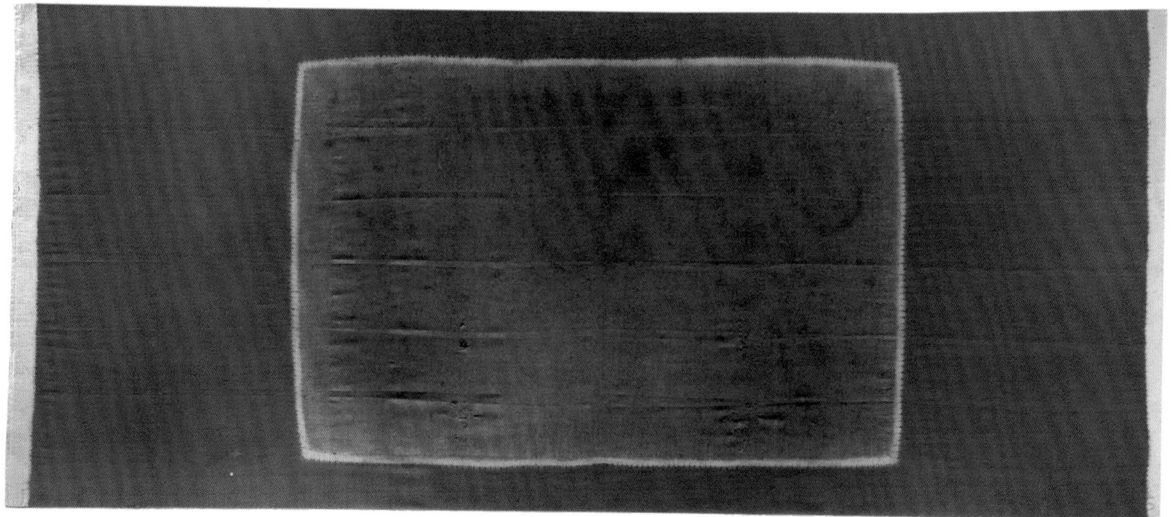

22. Palembang artisans, *Three handwoven lowans*, mid- to late 19th century. From Sumatra in Indonesia, these ceremonial cloths would have been presented to the wife at her marriage ceremony. Each is approximately 81 × 200 cm (32 × 79 in.), and they were woven with indigenous silk and resist-dyed using the *tritik* (stitch and gathered resist) process.

23. Gunta Stölzl, *Untitled*, 2011, from a design painted *c.* 1927. This is from an edition of fifteen rugs each 2.45 m (8 ft) square, hand-knotted in hand-spun wool and mohair for Christopher Farr, London.

24. Banni artisan, *Odhni* (detail), *c.* 1900. A limited colour palette highlights the striking geometric forms on this Gujarati woman's silk twill veil-cloth or head-covering. It is embroidered with running stitch and *abhala*, buttonhole stitching that keeps the *shisha* mirrored glass pieces in place.

25. Erica Grime, *Celebrations*, 2009. A doublecloth construction allows for vivid tonal juxtapositions in this cotton and linen weave, made malleable through the inclusion of wire.

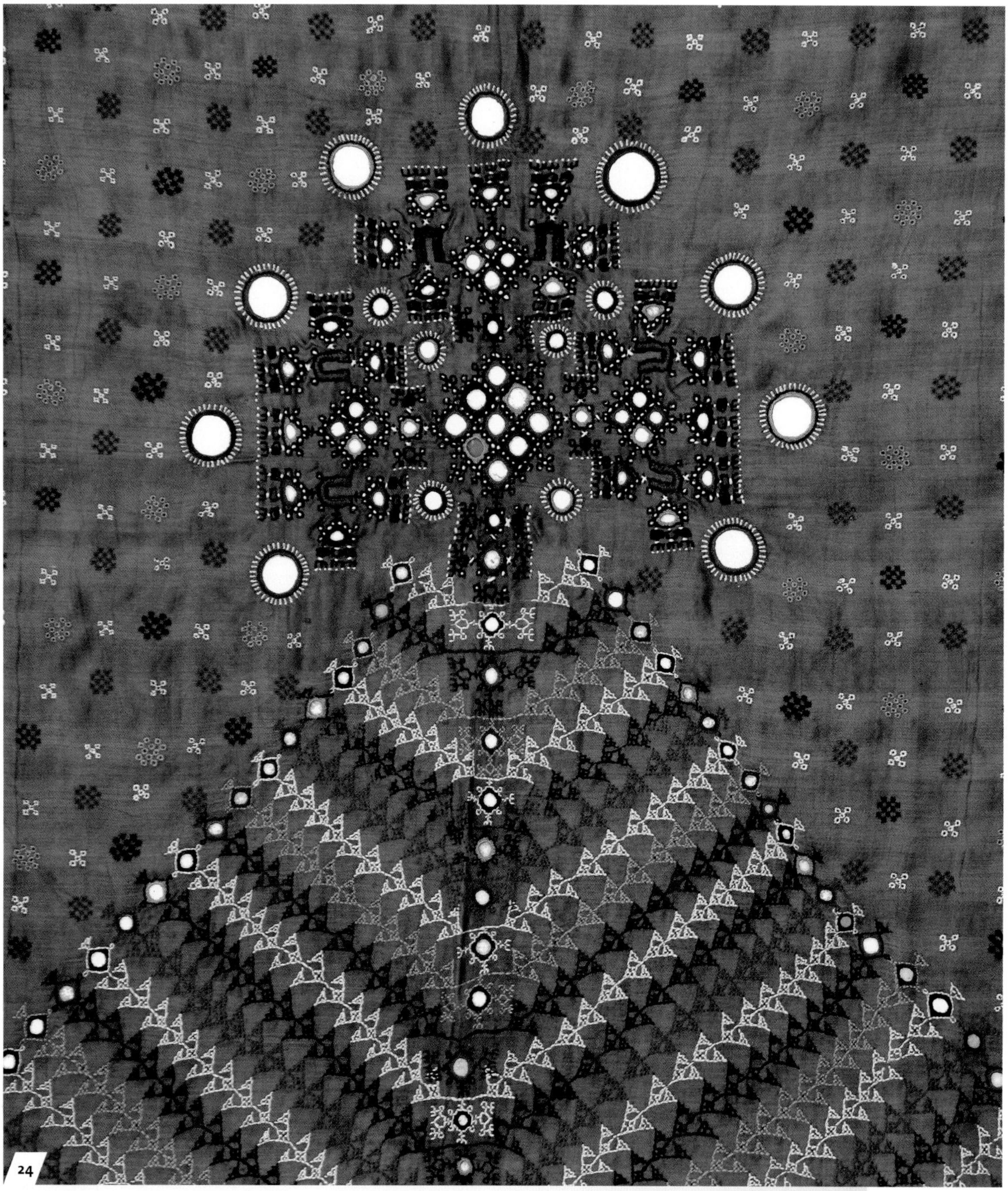

24

26. Uzbekistani artisans, *Pieced panel* (detail), 1920s. The bold juxtaposition of colours within each diagonally pieced silk strip is enhanced by subtle sections of very light ikat-dyed red.

27. Ewe weaver, *Strip-woven cotton cloth* (detail), 1920–40. Similar striking chequerboard designs were also woven by the Inca, who controlled a large stretch of western South America from 1438–1533, during the same period when the Ewe people migrated to the south-east corner of Ghana, on the African coast.

28. Laotian weaver, *Yardage* (detail), 2002. Acquired in the Vientiane morning market in Laos, this cloth with supplementary weft decoration was handwoven with hand-dyed silks of primary colours. It was then over-dyed in a golden-hued dyebath to appeal to Western tourists by making the tones more mellow.

29. French artisans, *Hand-printed cotton damask*, *c.* 1925. Overprinting of a damask creates broken tones of colour, which have been hand-printed by blocks or an early form of screen printing.

26
27
28
29

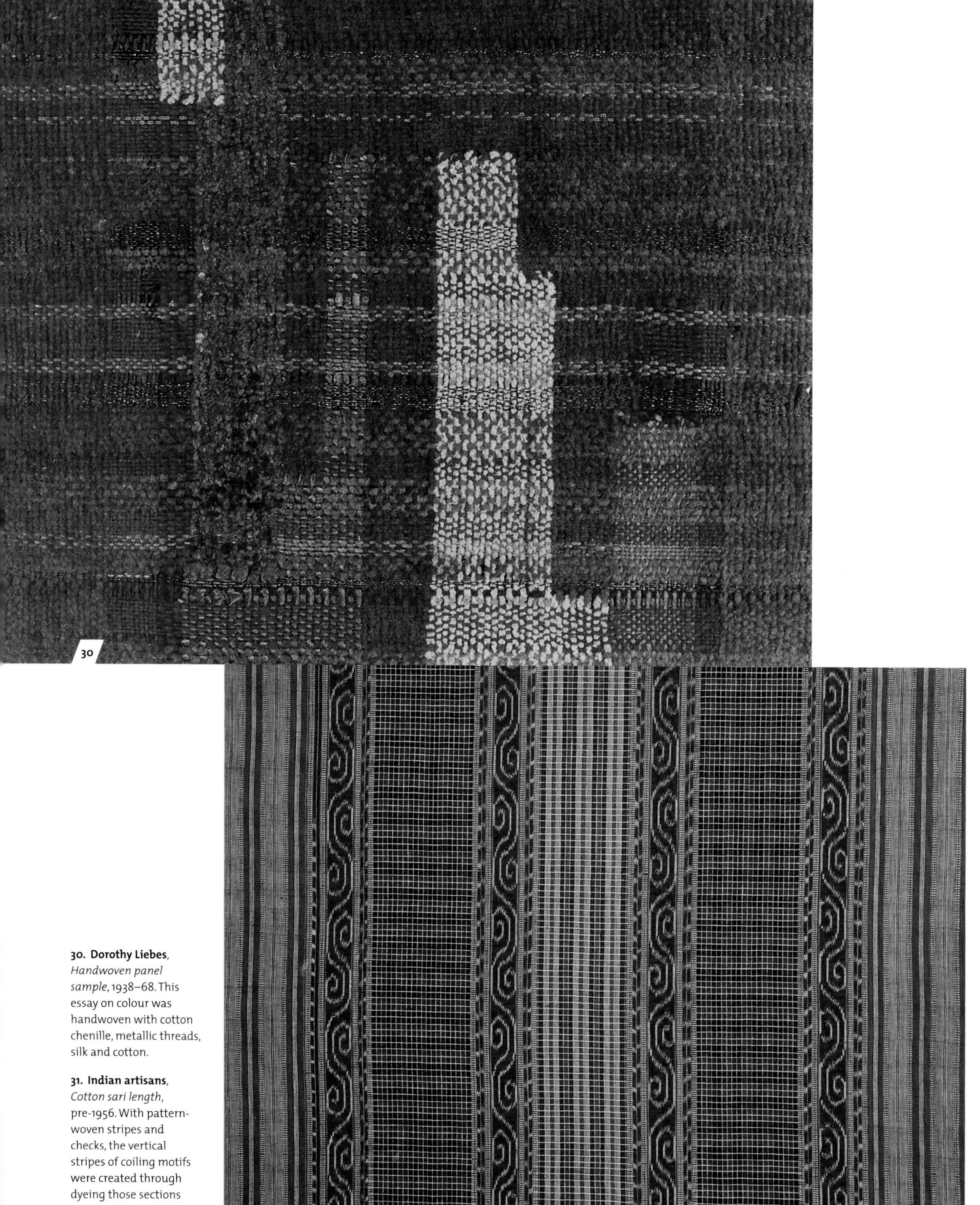

30. Dorothy Liebes, *Handwoven panel sample*, 1938–68. This essay on colour was handwoven with cotton chenille, metallic threads, silk and cotton.

31. Indian artisans, *Cotton sari length*, pre-1956. With pattern-woven stripes and checks, the vertical stripes of coiling motifs were created through dyeing those sections of the warp prior to weaving, a process known as 'ikat'.

32. Chinese machine printer, *Pha sin* (detail), 2002. This was purchased in the Muang Sing market, Laos, where the desire for colourful woven cloths has led to the production of these printed polyester imitations. This cloth simulates tubular skirts with *mat* (ikat) and supplementary weft decoration.

33. Oaxacan weaver, *Fiesta* huipil (detail), 1968. Handwoven on a back-strap loom, this girl's fiesta blouse incorporates vivid shades of cotton in tapestry stripes alternating with leno-interworked bands decorated with a supplementary weft chicken motif.

34 and 35. Unknown machine printer, *Yardage* (details), 20th century. These printed cloths imitate the vivid colours and complex reverse-appliqué technique typical of the molas from the San Blas Islands of Panama.

36. Zandra Rhodes, *Top Brass*, 1964. Rhodes, now internationally known for her fashions, designed this mélange of medals for Heal's range of screen-printed furnishing fabrics in the year of her graduation from the Royal College of Art, where she studied textile design.

37. Doreen Dyall, *Doll's House*, 1962. Doreen Dyall is among the many graduates of London's Royal College of Art textile department who, during the 1950s and 1960s, brought the influence of Pop Art to bear on furnishing fabrics. This example was screen printed for Heal Fabrics, London, known in this period for avant-garde textiles.

38. William Crozier/ Dovecot Studio, *Easter Day*, 2008–9. This tapestry, with its many tonal variations, is the result of a collaboration between Crozier and the weavers of the Dovecot Studio in Edinburgh: David Cochrane, Naomi Robertson, Jonathan Cleaver and head weaver Ronald Grierson.

39. Uzbekistani artisans, *Silk and cotton ikat*, c. 1900. The deep yellow colour comes from the vegetable dye, saffron.

40. Margo Lewers, *Orange Came Through*, 1975. Painted dye on linen intended to 'isolate the feelings which one has experienced or the impressions one has garnered and to re-express them in form and colour'. Lewers was an Australian Abstract Expressionist painter who had studied textile design with John Farleigh in London in the early 1930s.

41. Indian hand-printer, *Scarf* (detail), *c.* 1990. Brilliant colours obtained from synthetic dyes distinguish this cotton voile, which was made for export, in this case to Cost Plus World Market, a chain of American stores founded in San Francisco in 1958 to provide a 'global bazaar'.

42. Patan family, Patola *swatch*, *c.* 1978. The Indian term *patola* refers to the double-ikat technique in which both warp and weft are dyed prior to weaving. This example was acquired in 1978 when only two families continued this complex traditional method.

43. Ptolemy Mann, *Three Pieces to Dress a Wall – (After Albers)*, 2010–11. This triptych of stretched woven panels echoes the geometric tension of Albers's early wall pieces of 1925. Mann aims to 'evoke timelessness in their aesthetic [and] pay homage to a modern textile icon ... to readdress my own origins as a weaver'.

44. Uzbekistani artisans, *Ikat fragment*, early 20th century. A silk and cotton warp ikat.

45. Preeti Gilani, *Silk scarf*, 2008. Traditional handweaving techniques combine with computer technology and hand-dyeing to give Gilani the means to show colour with lustre, sheen and softness, to highlight the luxurious qualities of silk.

41

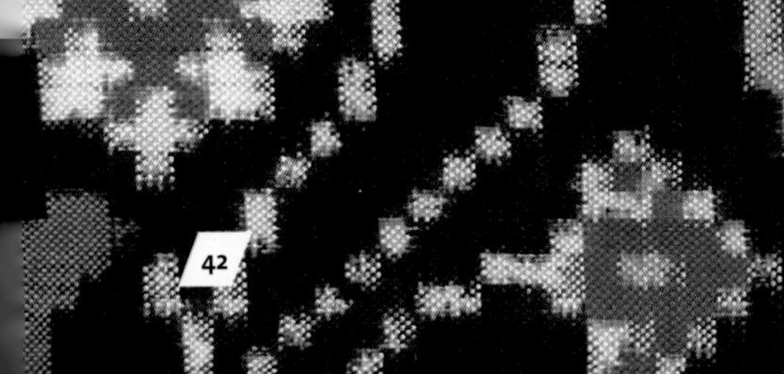

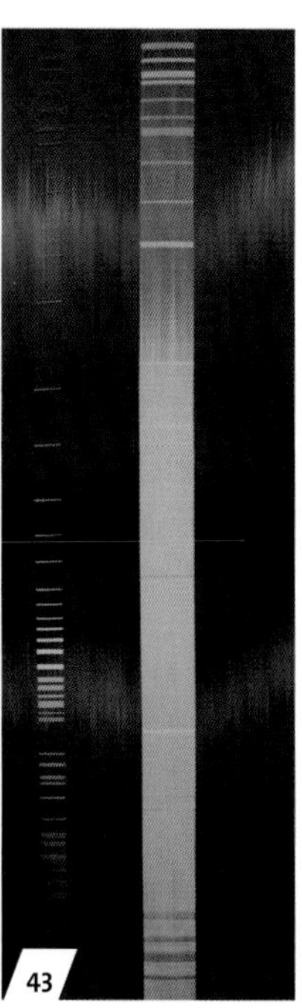

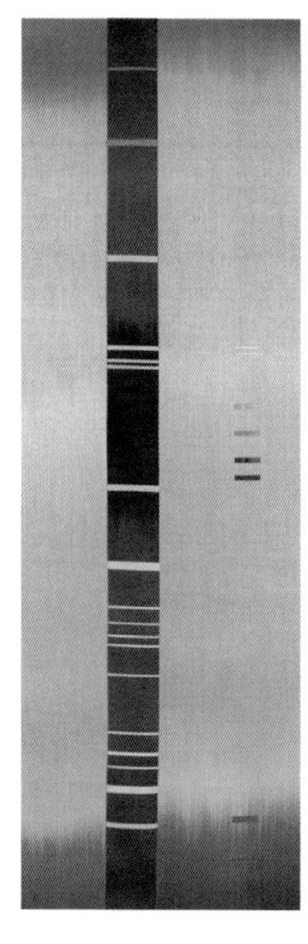

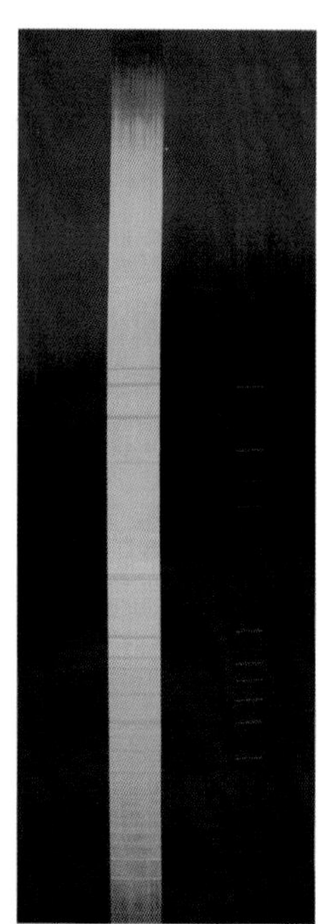

46. Sibyl Heijnen, *Theatre curtain*, 2006. Cutting, twisting, curving and rolling were the experimental processes used to produce a synthetic fibre curtain for the stage of the Theatre de Spiegel in Spinhuisplein, in the Netherlands, composed of almost 100 segments. Each segment can rotate individually, creating slow changes in form and colour, the latter including 23-carat gilding.

47. Mary Restieaux, *Untitled ikat*, 1980. Spun silk ikat, woven in a warp-faced plain (tabby) weave. Acid dyes were used to colour both the plain and ikat stripes, the ikat created by dip-dyeing the yarns prior to weaving.

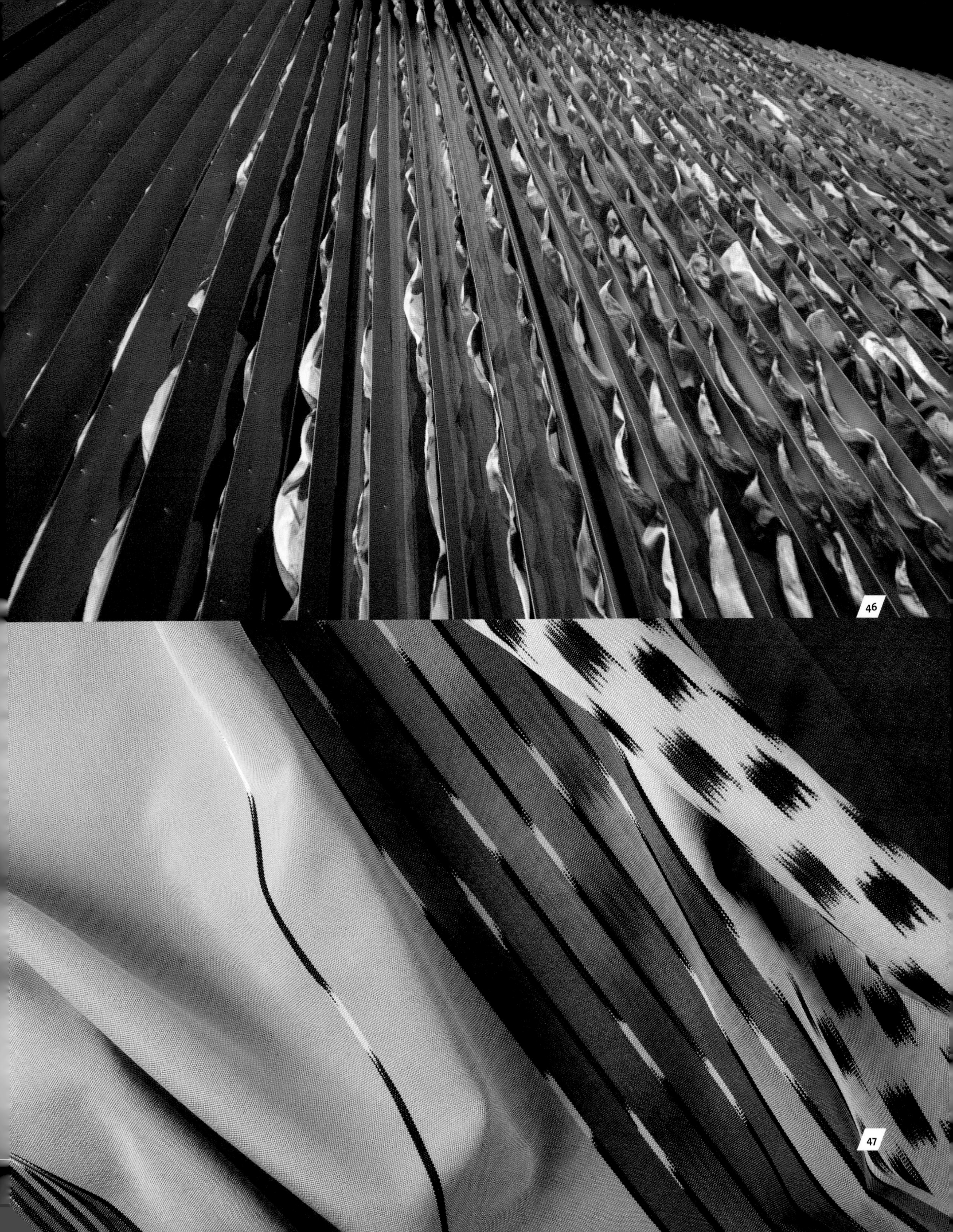
46
47

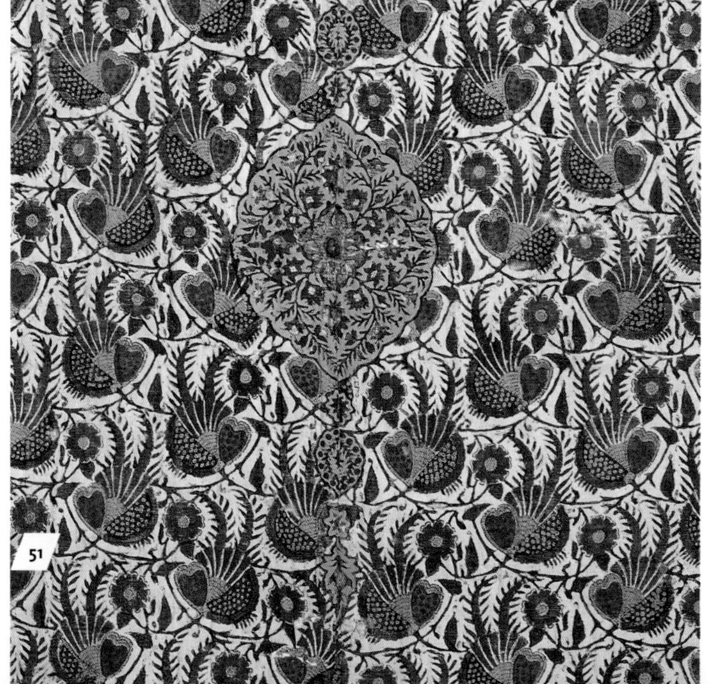

48. British embroiderer, *Panel for the Royal Reception Room, Glasgow International Exhibition* (detail), 1888. This panel, by an unknown embroiderer and designer, possibly associated with the Royal School of Needlework, London, was stitched with arrasene (a chenille-like thread) and gold work on blue silk satin. It displays the 'art needlework' colouration associated with the Royal School.

49. Uzbekistani artisans, *Suzani* (detail) 1860s. From the Bokhara district of Uzbekistan, this dowry embroidery is worked in vivid silks on cotton.

50. Chinese weaver, *Ming dynasty kesi* (detail), late 17th century. In the lower border of a silk tapestry-woven panel are imperial dragons and three animals representing courage, bravery and strength.

51. Indian artisans, *Bedcover* (detail), early 18th century. Displaying the rich colouration that made Indian chintzes sought after in both the East and West, this cotton bedcover was mordant painted and printed.

52. Lewis Jones, *Warner hand-screen printed furnishing fabrics*, 1937 and 1938. A designer at the Silver Studio, London, from 1910–53, Jones used a vivid background hue to play to the screen's capacity to deliver solid as well as subtly shaded colours. The glazed finish enhances the lacquer-like effect.

53. English amateur embroiderer, *Feltwork panel* (detail), mid-18th century. Hundreds of pieces of petal-shaped felted wool, dyed in ombréd shadings and gradated colours, have been appliquéd and embroidered to create a richly toned three-dimensional effect.

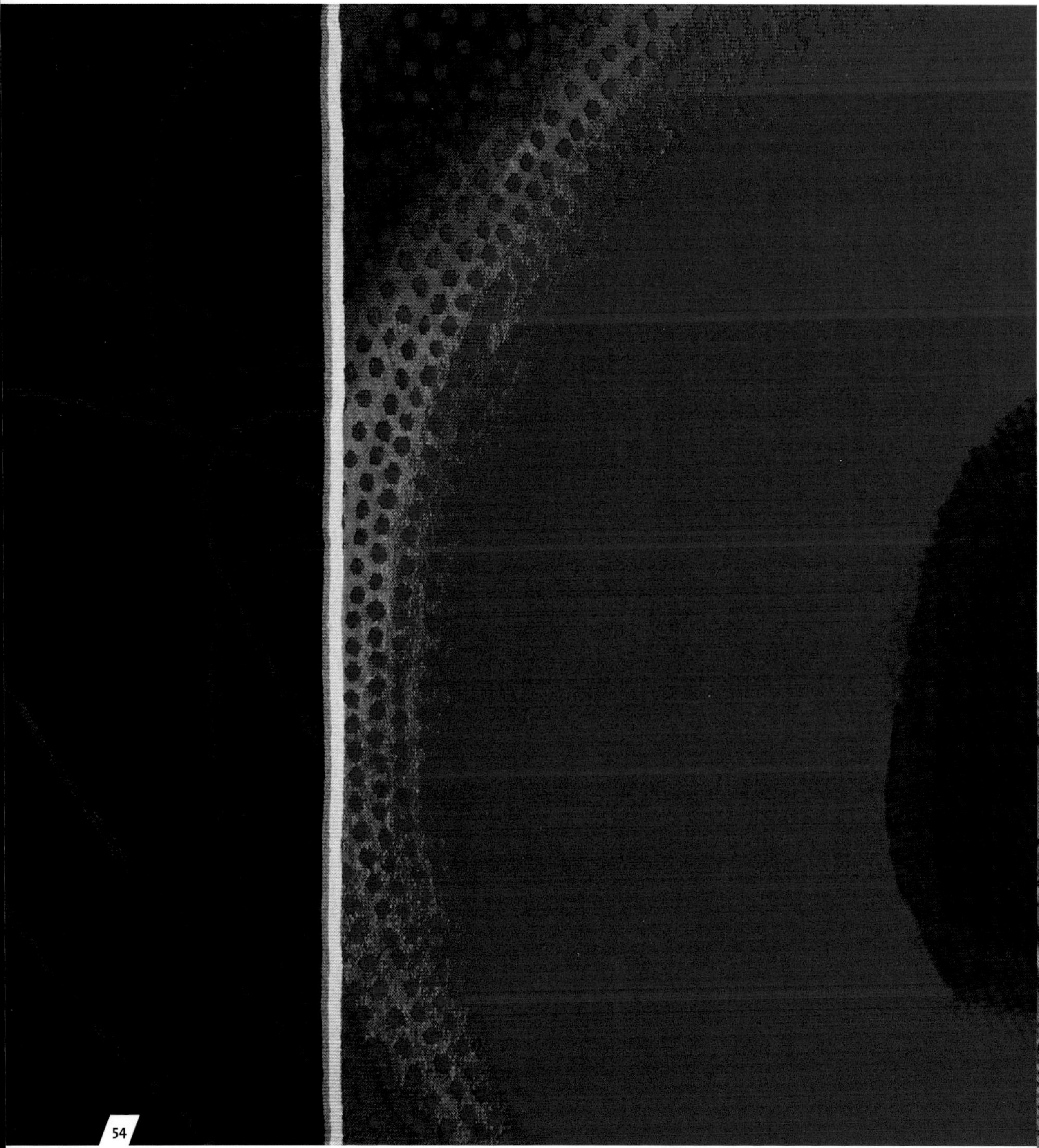

54

55

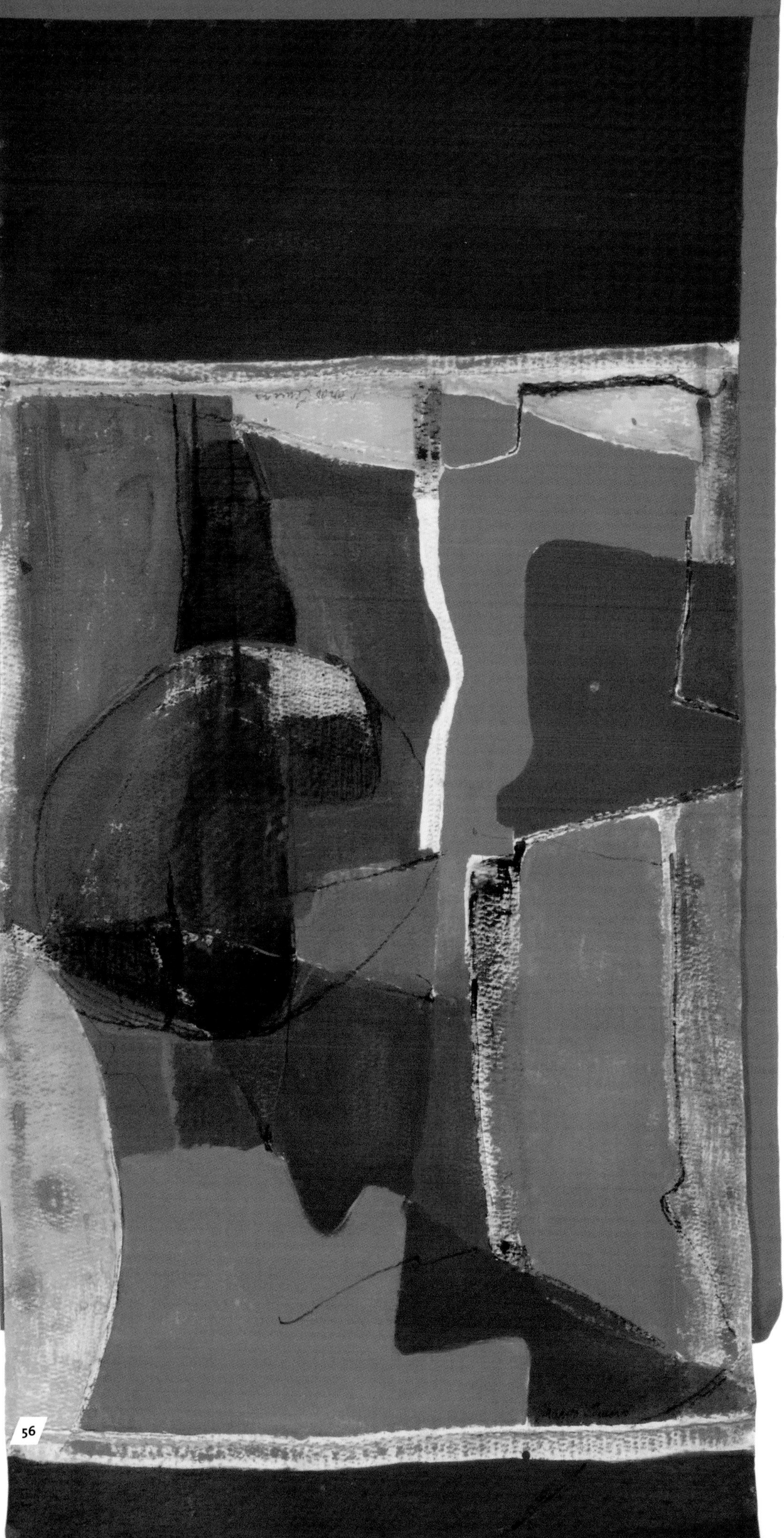

54. Jo Barker, *Vermillion Glow*, 2008–9. Barker works freely with photography, collage, printmaking and drawing before slowly realizing, in tapestry form, her interest in the emotional impact of colour.

55. Lanvin New York – Paris, *Necktie* (detail), *c.* 1970s. Probably hand-block printed, the vivid colours of this silk, used to make a necktie, gave a 'far out' update to a traditional Indian pattern.

56. Margo Lewers, *Orange and Red*, 1975. At the age of 67, Lewers created a series of works based on early watercolours, experimenting with overlaying transparent colour, painting with dye onto raw silk and terylene. In 1981 Lewers's home and collections became the Penrith Regional Gallery and The Lewers Bequest in New South Wales, Australia.

57. Chinese weaver, *Northern Song dynasty* kesi *fragment*, 10th–11th centuries. Rare surviving silk tapestry fragments, such as this one, still preserve aspects of their original brilliance.

58. Robert Hillestad, *Meadowlark in Fiber*, 2007. Yarns of silk and synthetic fibres have been hand-knitted with a loop technique, and incorporate bias streamers of silk fabric. The work captures the flash of vibrant yellow in the breast of the Western Meadowlark.

59. Janet Stoyel, *Experiment* (detail), 2007. Stoyel, the pioneer of laser printing and cutting, experiments here with laser and ultrasound treatments on silk. The silk is then sandwiched in glass and kilned to produce iridescent colours.

60. Anne-Marie Wharrie, *Aunt Marie* (detail), 2010. Joyously coloured cotton reels, from the artist's family's factory where her aunt worked, are combined with vintage beads, crochet and wrapping.

61

61. British amateur maker, *Sweetmeat purse*, *c.* 1600–30. This purse, worked in fine tent stitch on canvas, features an atypical pastoral scene. Filled with lavender, these purses were stored with clothing and linens; filled with pomanders or coins, they were expensive gifts.

62–70. Various makers, *Bags and pouches*. Bags have long been a means of expressing identity, a fact preserved in such phrases as 'diplomatic bag' and acknowledged in today's 'status bag'. The use of such an accessory as a 'badge of office' means that it need not be functional, as is the case with the ceremonial mid-20th century Tunisian stuffed, velveteen hand-shaped bag (68), embellished with silk and gold foil, sequins and beads. Elaborate examples, such as the drawstring purse woven with silk and silver gilt-wrapped thread, probably made in England *c.* 1700 (70), were 'endowing purses', given by a groom to his bride. Equally diminutive is the Japanese 20th-century ikat-patterned hempen pouch (63). Slightly larger is the Indian evening bag couched with glass seed beads and plastic sequins, made in 2003 (65). At about 23 cm (9 in.) high are: the bag fronted with glass seed-beads (69) and woven bag with inlaid wool weft (62) typical of Western Plains Native Americans in the late-1800s; a Guatamalan 1920s' example of looped grass with crocheted rim (67); and a Peruvian tasselled cotton bag from the 1950s, with supplementary weft decoration (64). The Iranian wool felted bag (66), from the 1960s, is the largest at 40 cm (16 in.) high.

62
63
64
65
66
67
68
69
70

71

71. Ethiopian artisans, *Crocheted hats*, *2010*. Striking variations are created largely through the selection and juxtaposition of differently coloured bands. Jayne and Joss Graham are well-known London collectors and dealers, who travel the world searching for textiles. This gathering of hats was photographed by Jayne in California.

72. Tatyana Yanishevsky, *Cavernous Rage*, 2010. Welded and soldered steel and LED lights are animated by being enfolded in hand-knitted yarns in this work, which is 91.5 cm (36 in.) high.

73. Anne Field, *Fragments 2004 AD*, 2004. Handwoven cotton, partially destroyed by fire, on pottery fragments by Harvey Bray: the result is likened to 'left-over lives found in archeological digs. Textiles are rare finds so I made this work in honour of those early weavers … who lived, loved and died, just like us.'

74. Vicki Mason, *Mixed Floral Bouquet*, 2011. Powder-coated brass, copper and sterling silver; hand-dyed PVC; polyester, rayon and viscose thread. Mason's combination of remnant pedestrian plastics from the upholstery and stationery industry with textile and metalworking techniques creates 'a cross media/material discourse' challenging classifications of 'what jewellery and textiles should be'.

76

77

78

75. Rowland Ricketts, *Nine Objects No. 7*, 2004. Maple seeds and indigo-dyed wool form a contemplative work, the making of which for the artist 'challenges me to better define for myself the substantive meaning of the plants and processes that I use'.

76. Jennifer Falck Linssen, *Beauty in the Deep* (detail), 2006. Handcrafted basket of *katagami*-style handcarved paper (originally used to make printing stencils) and stitched construction with continuous coil looping and exposed-core coiling. Materials include sterling silver, fine silver, archival cotton paper, indigo, monofilament, waxed linen, paint and varnish.

77. Della Reams, *Qatar Flora*, 2009. Wool and mixed-fibre yarns are worked in hyperbolic hand crochet, with hand- and machine-knitted stems. These 'blooms', set in purchased bases, symbolize the rapid evolution of Qatar since the discovery of oil, particularly the 'growing array of people from different cultures [and] increasing colors and patterns adorning the Qatari women's traditionally black *abayas* (outer garments)'.

78. Melanie Siegel, *Vessel*, 2009. Free-motion machine embroidery, with metallic threads. Accepted by the jury at the Musée Jean-Lurçat et de la Tapisserie Contemporaine, Angers, France, for the XXI Triennale International des Mini Textiles travelling exhibition, *Avec ou sans Eau?*

79

80

79. Marie-Laure Ilie, *Belles de Jour/Belles de Nuit,* 2009. Incorporating silks painted and heat-transferred with images of ancient statues to 'evoke a sense of both permanence and deterioration … petrified body shapes bring to mind enclosures, physical as well as mental [and] a whole range of timeless human feelings'.

80. Carole Waller, *Script 2,* 2011. Hand-painted dye on a silk organza garment. Waller's label reads: 'I'm No Walking Canvas', meaning that the fluid movements of both cloth and body are equal ingredients in her wearable art.

81. Paula Martin, *Memory Horizon No. 2,* 2003. Cylinders incorporating painted muslin and bamboo evoke the artist's mountainous bushland home and her interest in the ephemeral patterns of natural processes. At over 2 m (7 ft) long, the shadows play a part equal to that of the piece itself.

82. Louisa Jane Irvine, *Column,* 2010. Mixed-media sculpture incorporating plaster-stuffed stockings, intended to nudge the viewer 'out of their comfort zone to encounter feminine corporeality in a new and subtle space, a space where repulsion and attraction meet in silence'.

83. Sonja Andrew, *The Ties That Bind II,* 2008. Composed of flocked, appliquéd and stitched cotton printed digitally, by screen and via heat transfer, this triptych reflects on the consequences of the artist's great-grandfather's Quaker beliefs. The panels represent the start of the First World War, his imprisonment as a conscientious objector, and the continued hostility towards objectors and their families thereafter.

84. Kim Schoenberger, *Quilt* (detail), 2010. Hand- and treadle-machine stitched recycled teabags, which, 'like life, are delicate yet strong, fragile yet resilient, stained with the spreading of warm comfort'.

85. Rozanne Hawksley, *Surgeon's Equipment* (detail), 2003. This piece is part of a multimedia installation called *The Seamstress and the Sea.* Surgical needles and stitches that might keep a sailor alive at sea are shown to be the same as domestic needles and stitches, which, through their employment, kept the seamstress alive on shore.

81

82

83

84

85

86. Anne Jackson, *Witch Hunt Maleficium (In Memoriam)*, 2007. The persecution of witches across Europe began in earnest shortly after the Gutenberg printing press allowed widespread publication of treatises warning that witches were a threat to be feared and eradicated. This knotted tapestry cotton linen depicts woodcut images from early publications, including the *Malleus Maleficarum*, and alludes to the 'witch hunts' in the modern-day sensationalist press.

BEATOS PUTO
QUIBUS DEORUM MUNERE
DATUM EST AUT FACERE
SCRIBENDA AUT SCRIBERE
LEGENDA, BEATISSIMOS VERO,
QUIBUS UTRUMQUE.
HORUM IN NUMERO AVUNCULUS
MEUS ET SUIS LIBRIS ET TUIS
ERIT.
QUO LIBENTIUS SUSCIPIO
DEPOSCO ETIAM, QUOD INIUNGIS.

ERAT MISENI CLASSEMQUE
IMPERIO PRAESENS REGEBAT.
NONUM KAL. SEPTEMBRES
HORA FERE SEPTIMA MATER MEA
INDICAT EI APPARERE NUBEM
INUSITATA ET MAGNITUDINE ET
SPECIE.

USUS ILLE SOLE, MOX FRIGIDA,
GUSTAVERAT IACENS
STUDEBATQUE. POSCIT SOLEAS
ASCENDIT LOCUM, EX QUO
MAXIME MIRACULUM ILLUD
CONSPICI POTERAT.
NUBES, INCERTUM PROCUL
INTUENTIBUS, EX QUO MONTE (
VESUVIUM FUISSE POSTEA
COGNITUM EST), ORIEBATUR,
CUIUS SIMILITUDINEM ET
FORMAM NON ALIA MAGIS
ARBOR QUAM PINUS
EXPRESSERIT.

NAM LONGISSIMO VELUT
TRUNCO ELATA IN ALTUM
QUIBUSDAM RAMIS
DIFFUNDEBATUR, CREDO QUIA
RECENTI SPIRITU EVECTA, DEIN
SENESCENTE EO DESTITUTA
AUT ETIAM PONDERE SUO VICTA
IN LATITUDINEM VANESCEBAT,
CANDIDA INTERDUM,
INTERDUM SORDIDA ET
MACULOSA, PROUT TERRAM
CINEREMVE SUSTULERAT.
MAGNUM PROPIUSQUE
NOSCENDUM, UT ERUDITISSIMO
VIRO, VISUM.

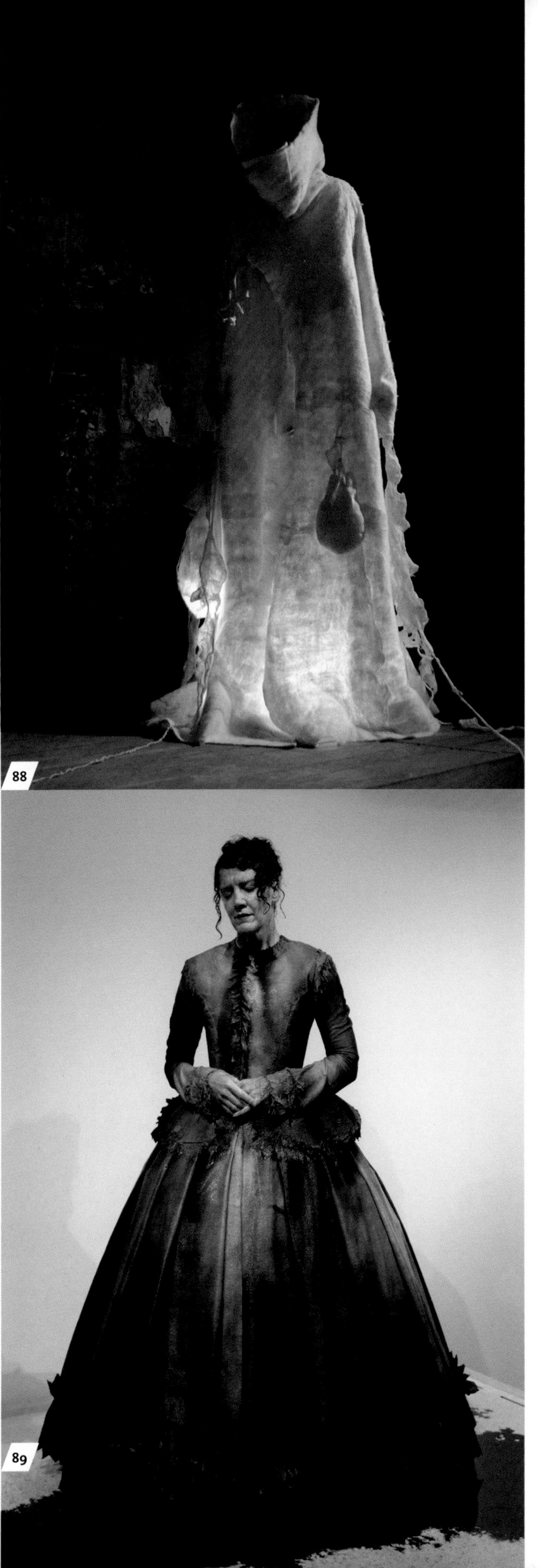

87. Els van Baarle, *Plinius' Letter*, 2010. Inspired by antiquity and the remains of structures ravaged by wind and weather, van Baarle's work of layered waxes and dyes reveals 'a treasure of details when observed up close'.

88. Denise Stanton, *Untitled 3*, 2008. This hand-felted sculptural installation was made in response to an unfinished 19th-century mansion in Woodchester Park near Stroud, Gloucestershire.

89. Martha McDonald, *The Weeping Dress*, 2011. McDonald performs in this Victorian-style dress made of crêpe paper, singing a mourning lament while the dress is sprayed with water. The paper 'weeps' away its colour in order to express McDonald's 'longing for home, and larger ideas of impermanence and temporality'.

90. Chinese weaver, *Sengijazhi*, 1644–1700. This Buddhist priest's *sengijazhi* (mantle) was created by a *kesi* (tapestry) weaver using silk and metallic foil-wrapped yarns, with the motifs arranged into squares to represent the patchworked mantles of discarded cloth that originally represented a monk's rejection of worldly values. Both mantles shown here were collected by Bella Mabury.

91. Japanese weaver, *Kesa*, 1775–1825. Here silk yarns and *lamella* (metallic foil strips) have been brocaded on a silk twill ground, with an ikat-dyed warp creating the alternating blocks of colour. The stepped block pattern is characteristic of a *kara-ori* No theatre costume, and this Buddhist priest's *kesa* (mantle) is thought to have been made from one that was donated to a temple.

92. Professional English embroiderer, *Forehead cloth, cross-cloth or crosset*, c. 1610. Confronting birds, stitched with silk and metal-wrapped threads are set amid silver sequins and coiling stems composed of silver-wrapped threads secured in a variation of compound loop-stitching. Such cloths were worn with coifs, of which an exact match to this example is in the Museum of London.

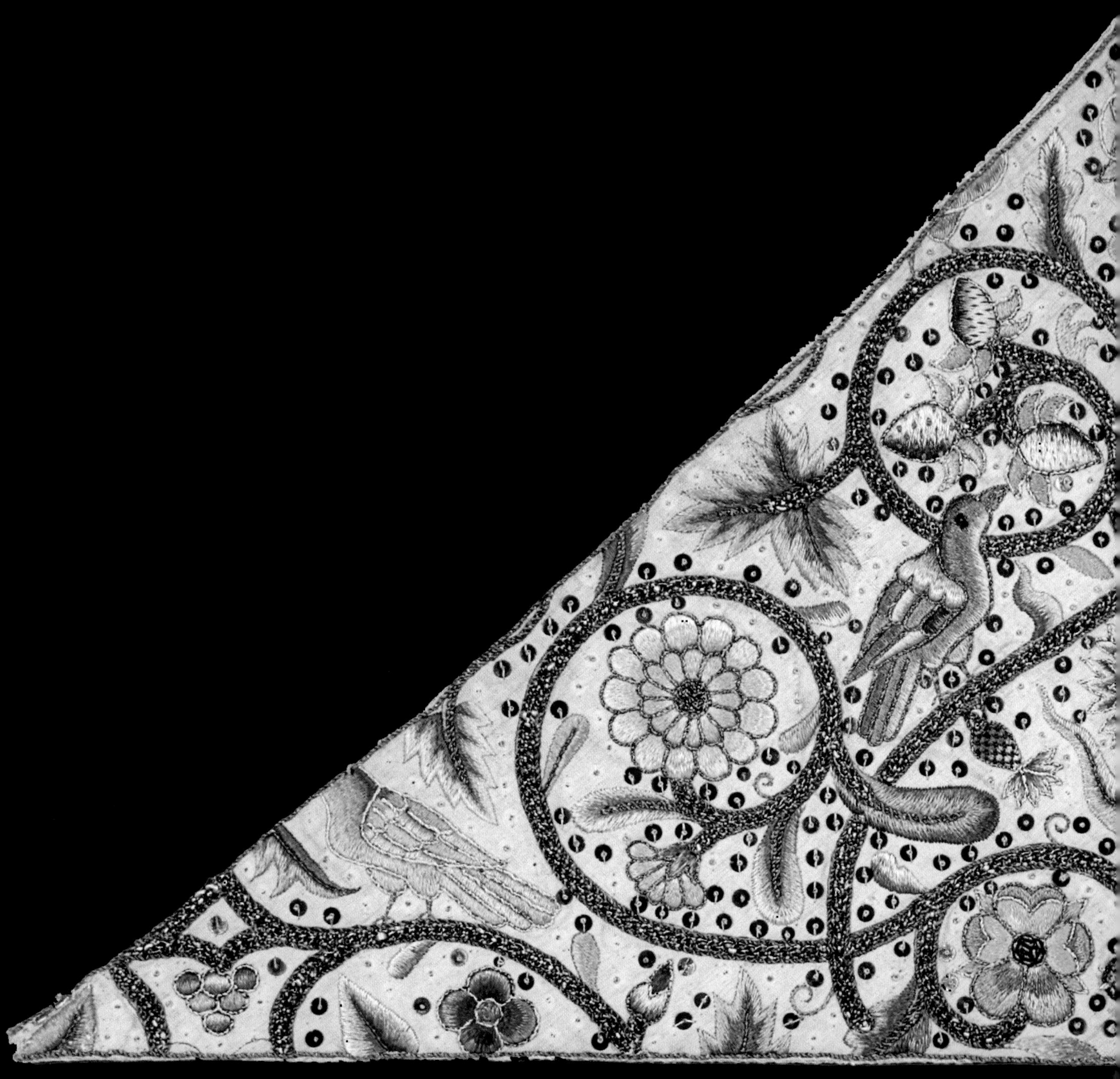

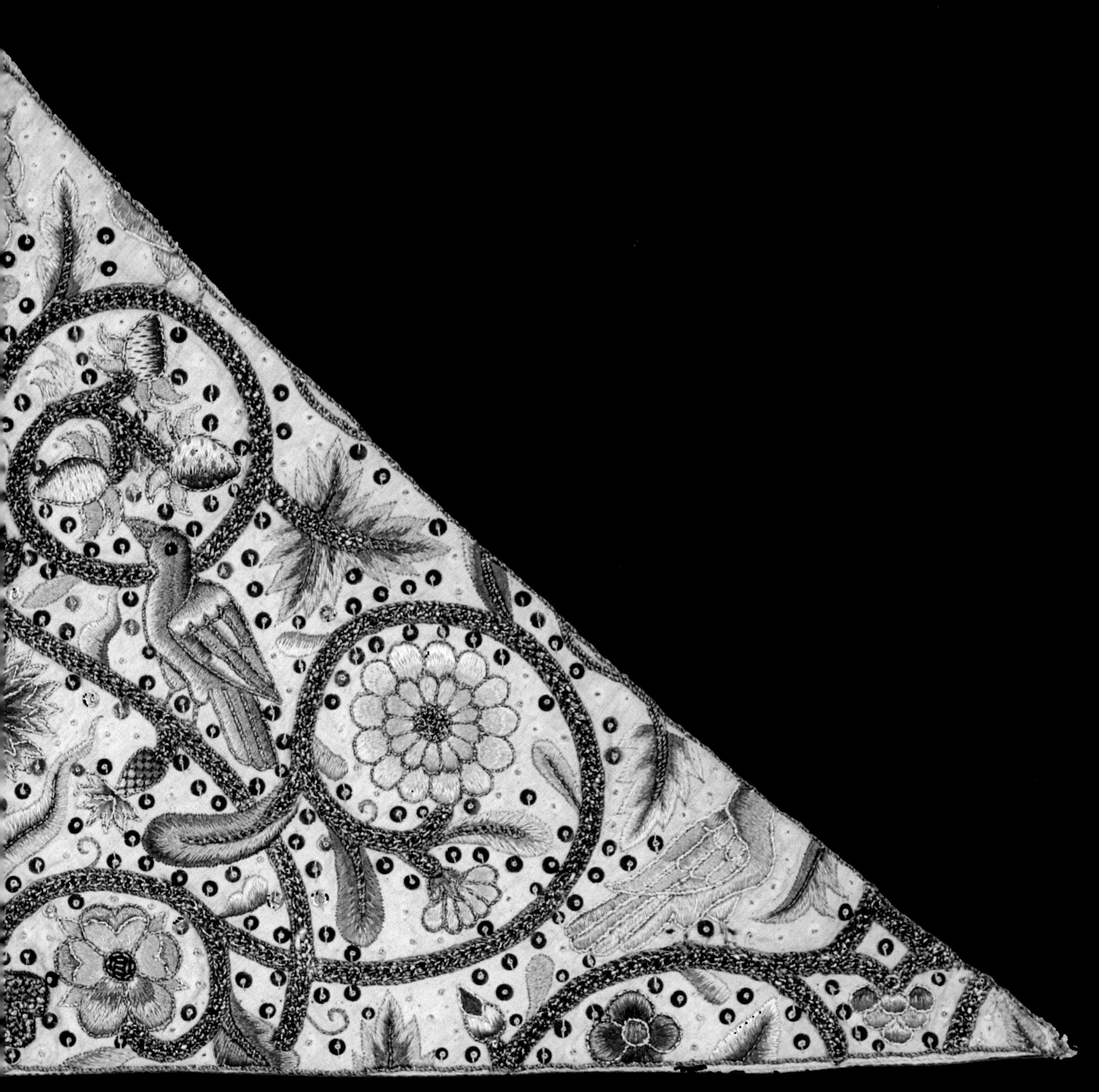

93
94
95
96

93. Umbrian weaver, *Towel* (detail), *c.* 1550–1600. Linen towels such as this, the ends decorated with indigo-dyed supplementary cotton wefts, are called 'Perugian towels' after a principal Italian centre of production. The motifs are thought to derive from Mamluk weaving, and are combined with those from Gothic Europe, where hunt themes were equally popular.

94. Guatemalan weaver, Huipil *panel* (detail), 1950s. This cotton cloth, patterned with indigo-dyed supplementary wefts, is symmetrical along both the vertical and horizontal axis, a more complex arrangement typically associated with Sunni Muslims as well as the Mudejares – Moors who remained in Spain and Portugal after the Christian reconquest.

95. Spanish or Italian weaver, *Fragment*, *c.* 1600. Woven with silk and metallic threads, this compound weave depicts confronting uncrowned rampant lions of the sort associated with Habsburg rulers.

96. Sumba artisan, *Hinggi kaworu* (detail), late 19th century. This indigo-dyed cotton warp ikat carries a pattern adapted from Indian *patola*. It would have been worn by elite Indonesian men as a waist and shoulder cloth.

97. Gujarati beadworker, *Panel*, late 19th century. From the Saurashtra region of western India, this panel of confronting birds and symmetrical trees is worked with seed beads in a technique called 'net-like weave'.

98. Indian embroiderer, *Embroidered coarse cotton* (detail), mid-20th century. This embroidered Indian cotton, possibly a cradle cloth, was collected by Ed and Katherine Rossbach in the second half of the 20th century, as were the pillow cover (100) and the example of block printing (101).

99. H'mong embroiderer, *Panel*, 1990s. Cross-stitched cotton panel with pieced frame, about 20.5 cm (8 in.) square, made in the H'mong region of China or in Thailand.

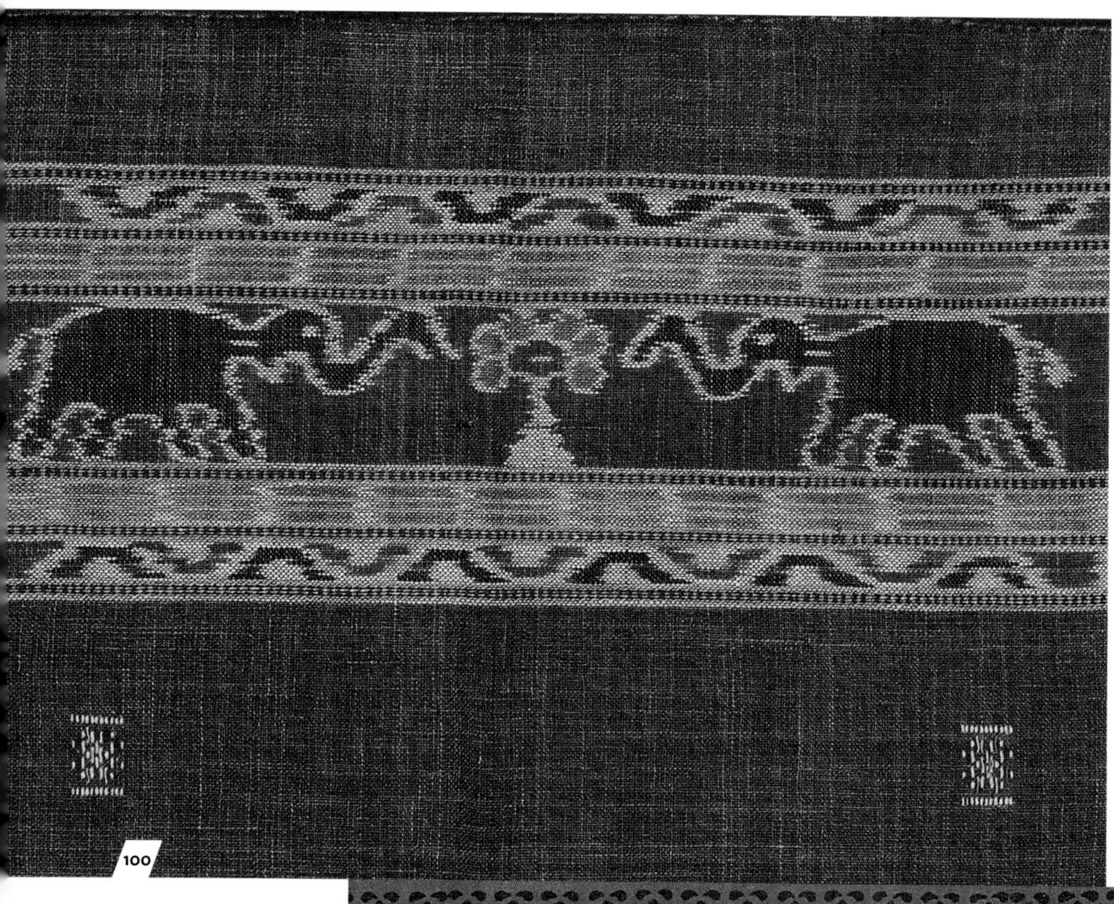

100. Indian weaver, *Orissan ikat pillow cover* (detail), mid-20th century. Symmetrical bilateral patterns, mirrored in the vertical or warp direction, are readily made on the loom but are also found in all other types of textiles, since bilateral symmetry is prevalent in nature and in human faces, and thus has significance in many societies and religions. Orrisa weavers are known for their ikat technique, as exemplified by this cotton pillow cover.

101. Indian manufacturer, *Machine print*, mid-20th century. This machine print, imitating block printing, also depicts confronting, bilaterally symmetrical animals.

102. Azemmour embroiderer, *Decorative band* (detail), *c.* 1820. The imagery on this coastal Moroccan linen cloth with a ground of rugina (rust-dyed) silk plaited stitch is of a type found throughout the Mediterranean. As elsewhere, it symbolizes rituals and narratives that bind the natural and spiritual worlds.

103. Laotian weaver, *Door panel or coffin cover* (detail) *c.* 1995. Handwoven, the red cotton ground is embellished with silks used as both continuous and discontinuous supplementary wefts.

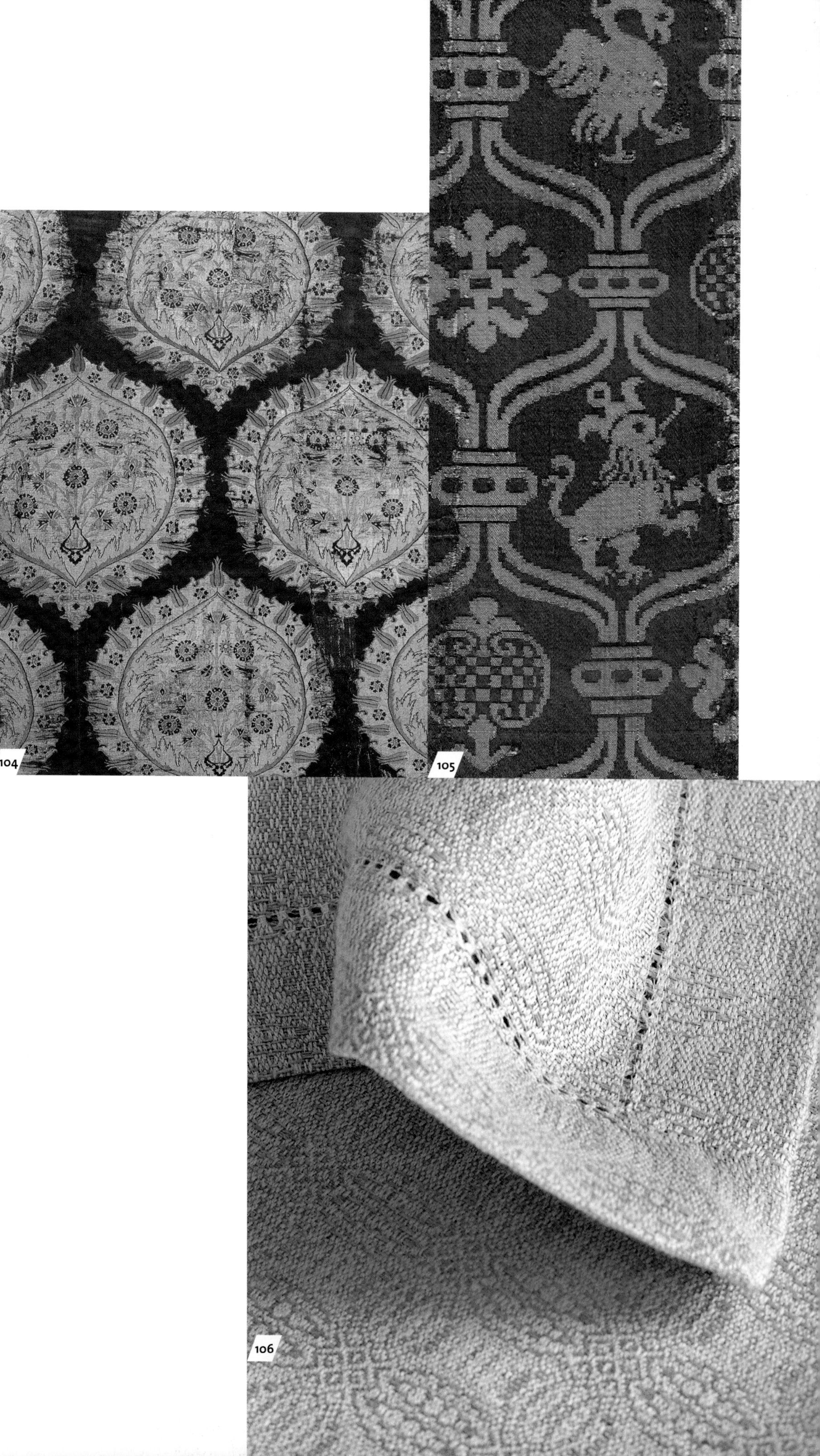

104. Turkish weaver, *Brocaded silk*, *c.* 1570–1600. This rare and particularly fine example of Ottoman weaving incorporates tulips. These flowers are symbolic of the empire's Central Asian roots, as well as of the word 'Allah', with which it shares the same letters in Arabic. The silk expresses diverse Persian concepts including universal monarchy, renewal, peace, mystical intoxication and earthly power.

105. Spanish weaver, *Silk damask fragment*, 1500–50. The ogival network containing animals in profile and stylized rosettes harks back to earlier roundel forms.

106. Mungo Design, *Cloverleaf Napkin*, 2011. Inspired by a deep respect for handweavers who produced complex designs for centuries, Stuart Holding founded Mungo Design in 1998 to revive traditional weaving crafts. This example, based on interlocking roundels, was woven on a shuttleless Dornier loom on a farm in South Africa, with locally produced linen yarn.

107. Mudéjar weaver, *Silk lampas*, late 15th century. Rampant crowned lions confront each other under split palmette leaves in this Andalusian compound-weave silk, probably woven in Granada, famed since the 14th century for its high-quality silks. Originally woven at the end of a long period of Muslim Nasrid rule (1232–1492), such patterns were made for several further decades for the new Christian patrons.

108

109

108. Chinese printer, *Silk panel* (detail), 1950s or earlier. The roundel here is composed of a five-clawed dragon, a symbol of the emperor in many Chinese dynasties. This cloth was once in the textile collection of the San Franciscan textile and performance artist Kaisik Wong.

109. Japanese manufacturer, *Furoshiki* (detail), 20th century. The crane motif, representing longevity and good fortune, is one of a number of circular crests found on this imitation cotton batik wrapping cloth.

110. Walter Crane, *The Four Seasons* (detail), 1893. Machine-printed on Japon silk by Thomas Wardle & Co. for Liberty of London, Crane's use of an ogee-shaped roundel, typical of Renaissance patterns, nevertheless retains the suggestion of a shen ring rope.

111. Swedish weaver, *Skåne* röllakan (detail), *c.* 1850–1900. This handwoven linen runner's roundel pattern, interwoven in wool, was in use in Scandinavia by at least 1500. These panels were earlier painted on cloth with a lime-based covering.

112. Coptic weaver, *Garment fragment*, 6th century. Known for their funerary portraits, which had a soul-searching gaze, early Egyptian Christians, or Copts, also wove integral wool tapestry panels into linens for garments, typically employing the roundel for its protective connotations.

113. Japanese manufacturer, *Machine-woven brocaded rayon* (detail), 1988. Appearing in Eastern textiles by the 7th to 10th centuries as a result of the eastwards migration of Soghdian weavers, ancient roundel patterns still retain their currency in modern Japan.

114. Liberty of London, *Liberty Art Fabric fragment*, *c.* 1895. Hand-block printed on tussah silk, this roundel pattern is indebted to the 'pearl roundels' found in Chinese textiles, which are in turn derived from Central Asian Soghdian roundels.

LYNA
"LIBERTY" ART FABRICS
Nº B954
Width 28 ins.
Price 4 per yd
110
111
112
113
114

115

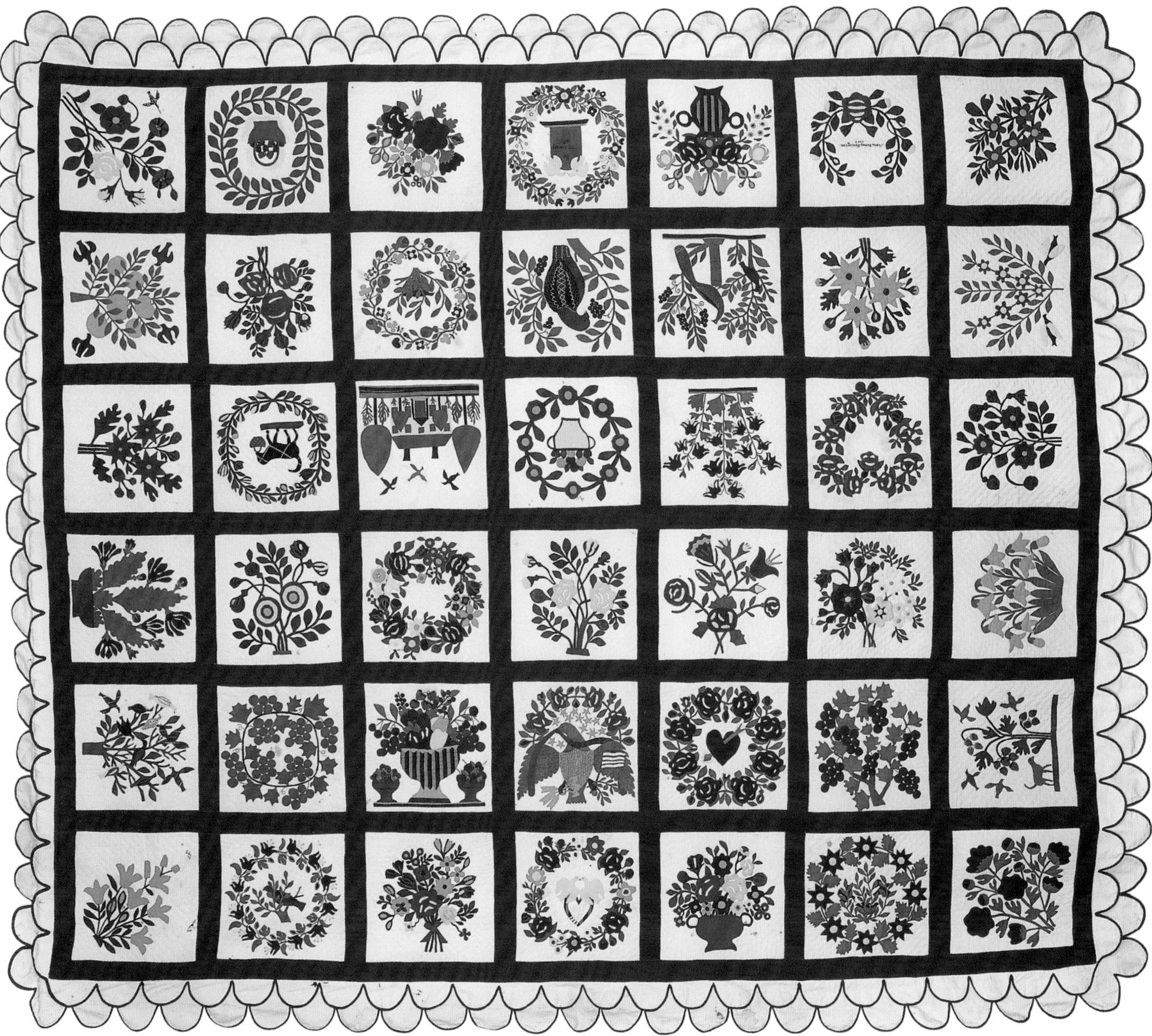

116

115. Indian weaver, *Silk samite* (detail), 15th century. Samite is a weft-faced compound twill in which the main warp threads are completely hidden by the floats of the ground and patterning wefts, with only the binding warps visible. A weave structure first associated with Sassanid Persia, the pattern is indebted to the same culture.

116. Anna Putney Farrington, *New York State quilt*, 1857. Many of this quilt's forty-two appliquéd blocks show continued use of the roundel. A block in the centre of the second row from the bottom depicts the American eagle surmounted by the vestige of a roundel.

118

117

117–119. Katherine Maxwell, Scottish maker and Tunisian maker, *Various plaids.* The plaid pattern, as seen in a Tunisian painted and strip-applied leather ceremonial cushion cover (119), made *c.* 1970, has often alluded to the hunter-warrior. The popularization of Scottish tartans by Queen Victoria made such patterns appropriate for a young boy's dress in the 1880s (detail, 118), and their use transferred to the American West via Scottish cowhands and ranches – an allusion suggested in a detail of Katherine Maxwell's *Man's Tailcoat* (detail, 117), 2010–11, made of recycled cotton/Modal and hand-loom knitted in the artist's Santa Fe studio. Maxwell leaves yarns dangling to help the wearer appreciate how these textiles were made.

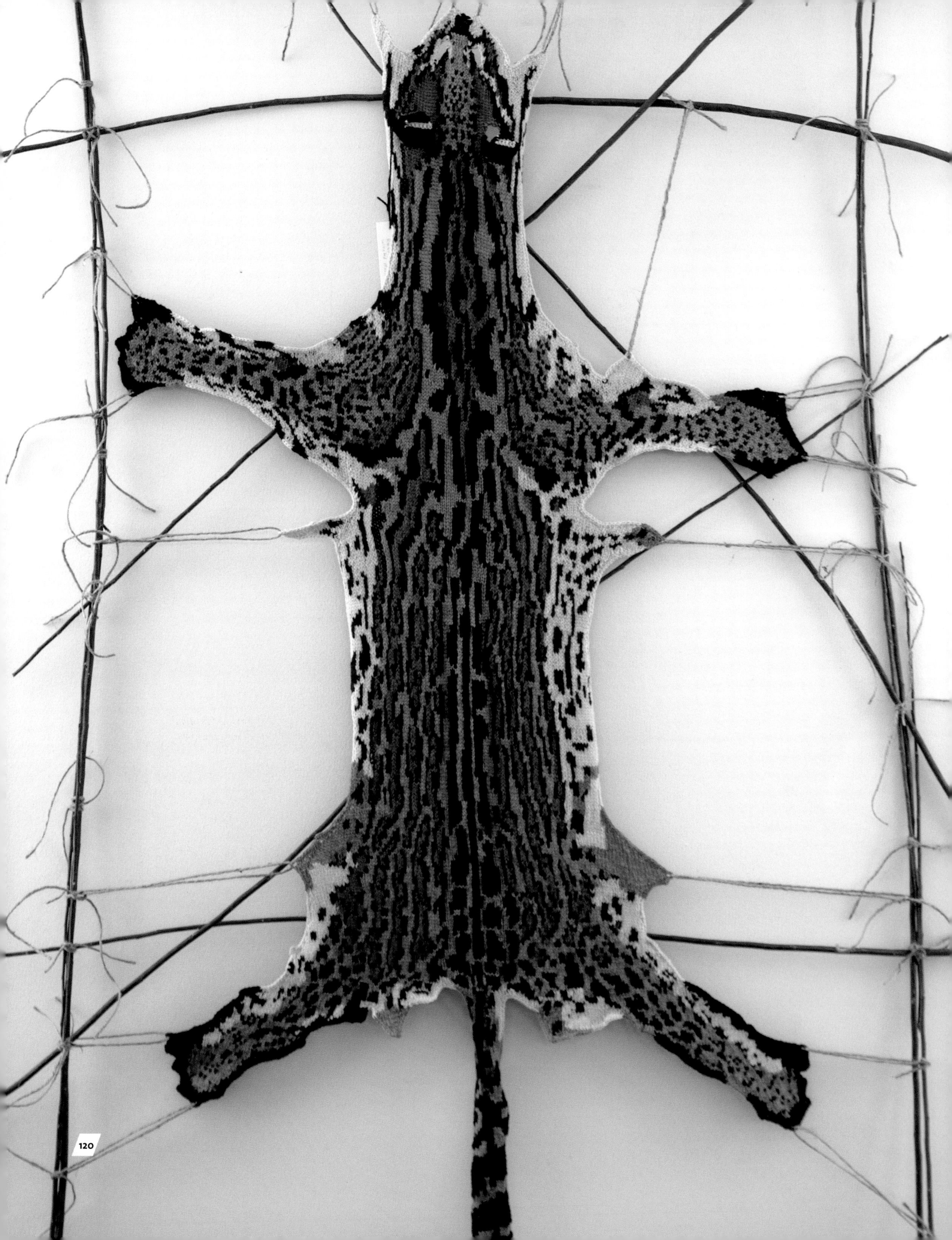

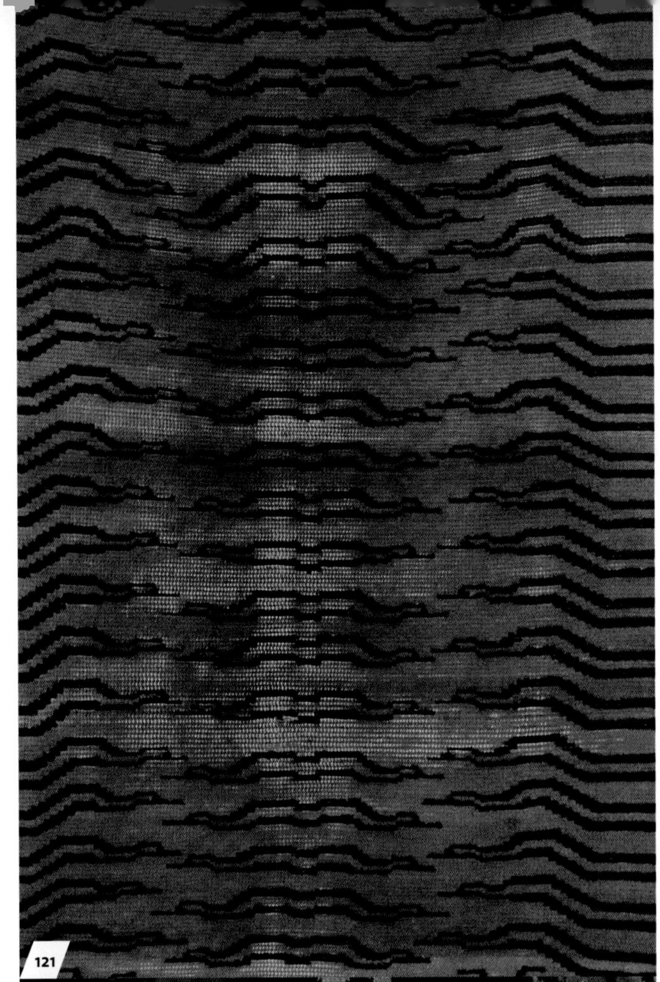

121

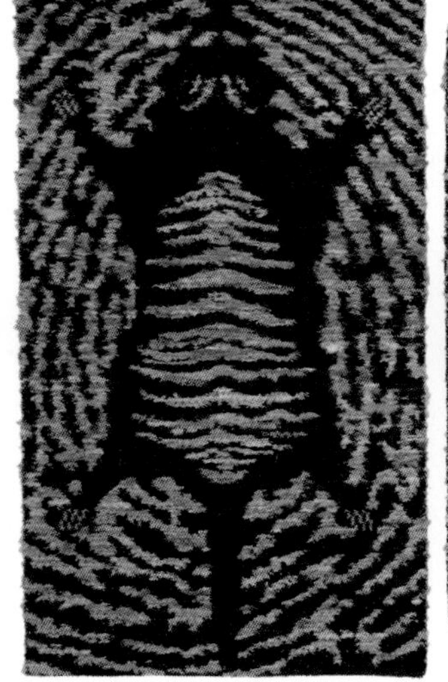

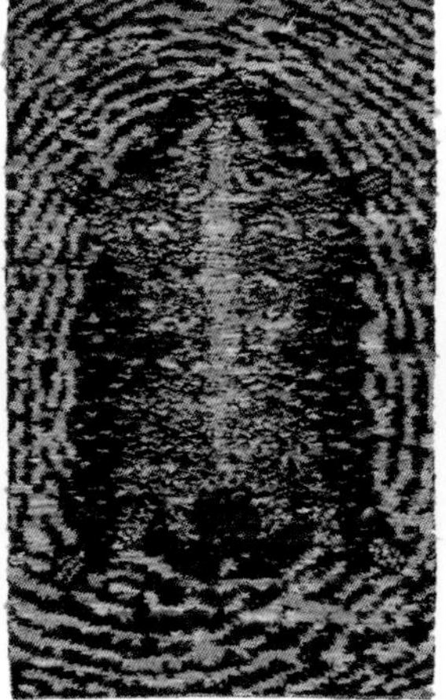

122

123

120. Ruth Marshall, *#4 Ocelot*, 2010. A hand-knitted textile interpretation of a female ocelot, based on the study of an actual pelt collected from Venezuela in 1929 and now in the American Museum of Natural History.

121. Tibetan artisans, *Rug*, 1880s. This rare rug, 115 × 84 cm (61 × 33 in.) in size, has a wool pile hand-knotted in a manner unique to Tibet, where the depiction of tigers and tiger skins is believed to give strength or expresses power. Tibetan tiger rugs were unknown to Westerners until 1979, according to Mimi Lipton, an authority on the subject who once owned this example.

122. Beth Hatton, *Tasmanian Tiger, Hairy Nosed Wombat, Quoll (Extinct and Endangered Species, 5th Series)*, 2001. Woven in block weave using shaft switching from kangaroo skin offcuts, wool and red cotton thread on a cotton warp. Consciously echoing the format of a Tibetan tiger rug, thought by many to have arisen to avoid the use of real tiger skins, the incorporation of fingerprints alludes to mankind's responsibilities, while the use of culled kangaroo skins 'imparted another knowledge, through my hands ... conflicting feelings about this material drove my work for ten years and still disturbs me'.

123. Janet Lipkin, *Tibetan Tigers* (detail), 1990. A wool and silk machine-knitted and dip-dyed coat.

124

124. Evette Sunset, *Skygate Rooftop Walkform, Synagogue Place, South Australia, 2003*. For this rooftop walk, fruit-wood prunings were placed on the ground as a warp, and long vine cuttings as wefts were wrapped and caught over, interlocked using previous layers and dry tendrils.

125. Clyde Olliver, *Little Cairn*, 2010. Cumbrian slates topped with a sisal-tied sandstone pebble stand approximately 9 cm ($3\frac{1}{2}$ in.) high. They allude to the English Lake District, where the rocky landscape provides the artist with both materials and inspiration.

126. Nalda Searles, *Kangaroo Couple in the Bush*, 2008. Heads of common meadow-hay fibre top figures dressed in recycled garments (the brown base dress was made by artist's the mother in 1975), vegetable-dyed and overstitched with *Xanthorrhoea preissei* bracts. Searles is today known as an innovator in the use of native fibres and found objects from the environment.

125

126

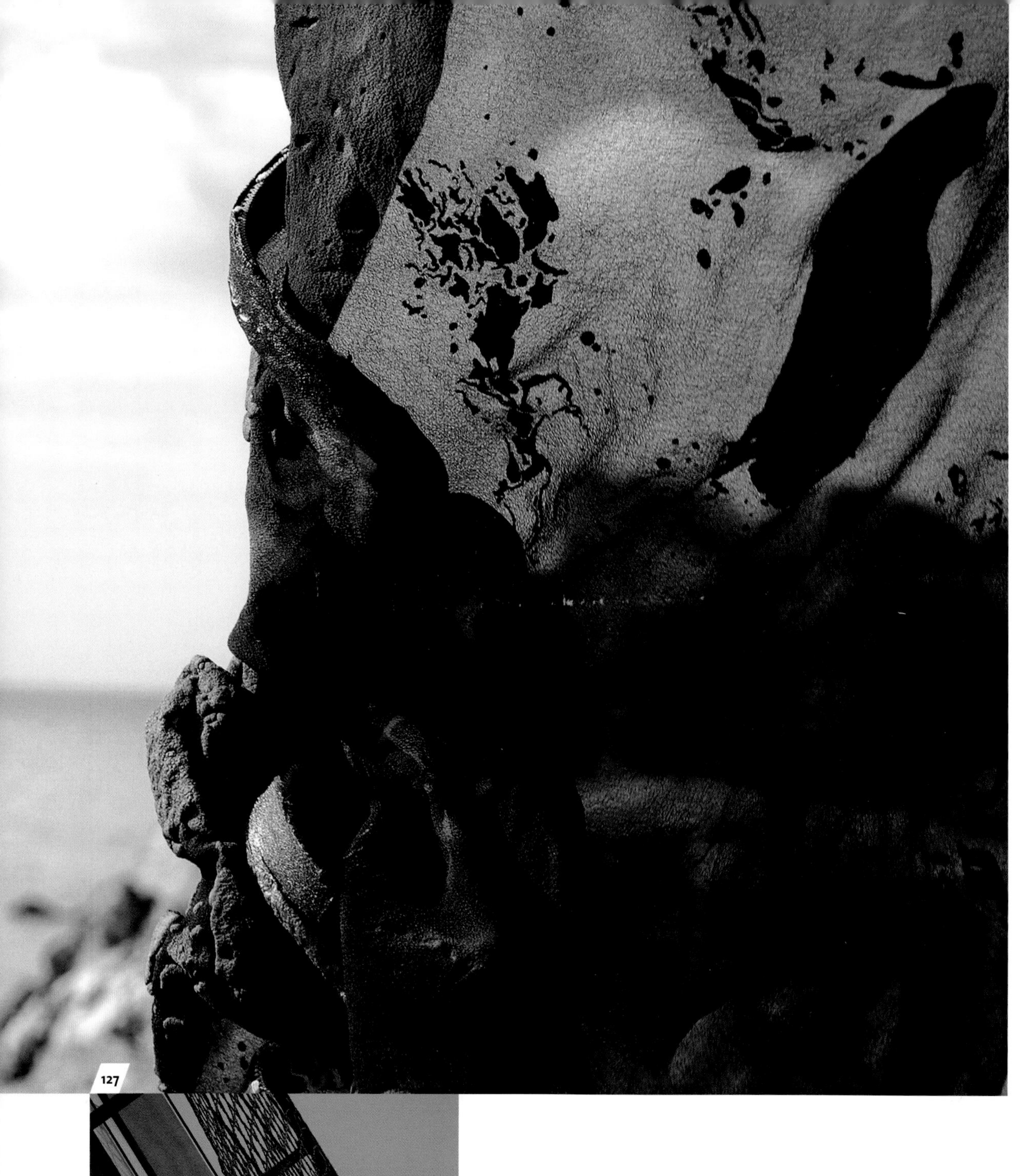

127. Amy George, *Oleaginous Extremis*, 2011. In response to the 2010 oil spill from BP's Deepwater Horizon platform, George screen-printed black expanding puff-binder ink onto silk crêpe georgette. Water is central to George's work, whether she bleeds out digital prints or makes textiles waterproof.

128. Sheila Klein, *Comfort Zone*, 2004 (detail). Recalling blankets, shawls and other domestic textiles, permanent 'curtains' were crocheted from stainless steel yarn, custom-made in Belgium, for the exterior of Harborview Hospital, Seattle, Washington, to comfort both it and the users of the building, and to reference porch infills that once graced the site.

129. Silke Bosbach, *Textile Land Art*, 2011. Bosbach's 'textile land art' is produced in and with nature. Here she employs paper yarn woven *in situ* to symbiotically connect the landscape to the material itself.

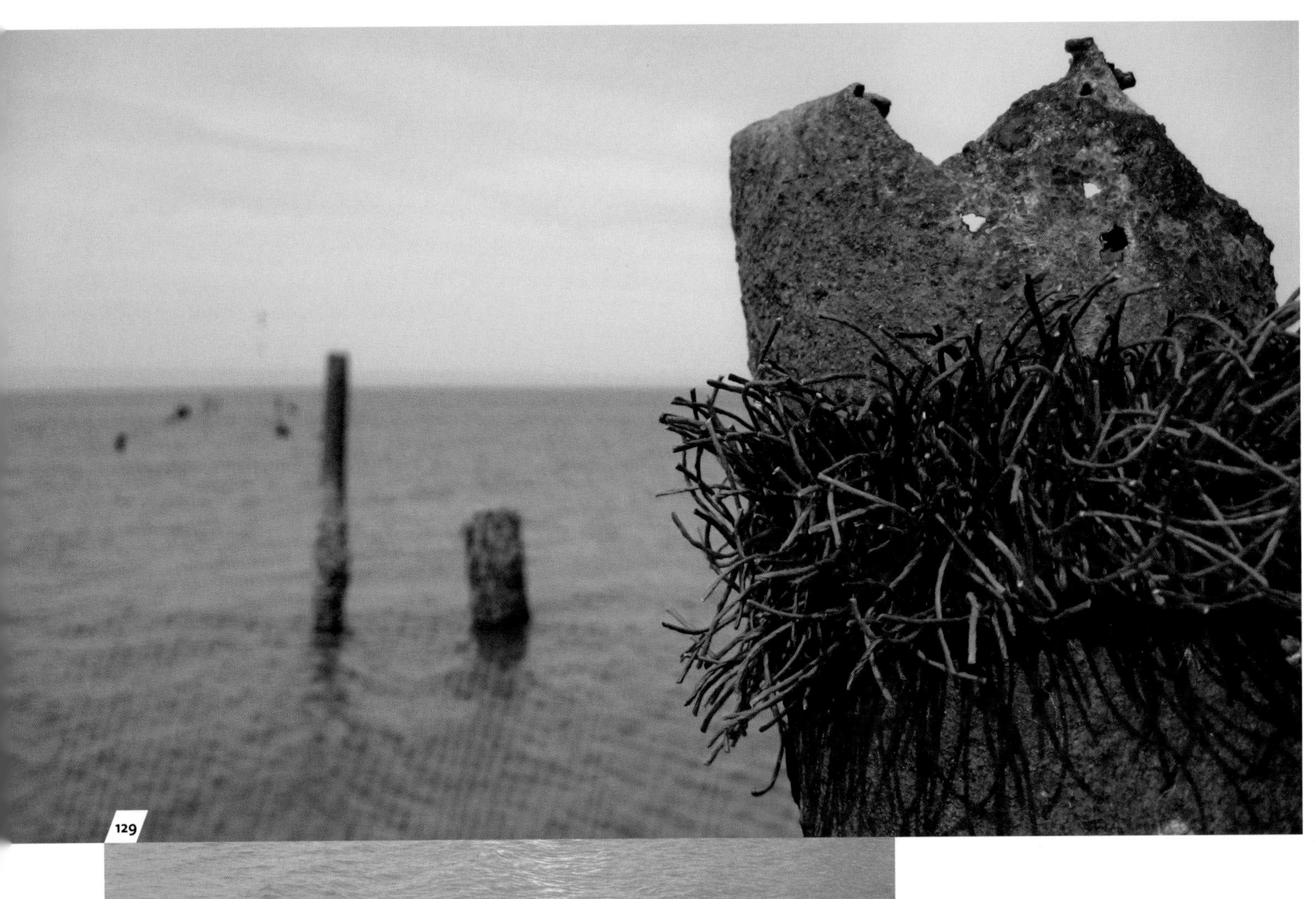

130. Mandy Gunn, *Surge*, 2009. Installation at The Floating Land, a climate change art event held in Noosa, Australia, where attendees included Tuvalu Islanders, whose land is being lost to rising waters. Bracken sticks were harvested and woven by being twined into lengths of 10 m (33 ft), then twisted or floated on the water, simulating encroaching waves and drowning lands.

131. Gaurav Jai Gupta, *Aqua Crush Scarf*, 2009. Handwoven silk scarf from Akaaro, the studio from which Gupta produces sustainable cloths for fashion and interiors, all intended to revive appreciation for contemporary Indian textiles.

133

134

135

132. William Morris, *Cray*, designed 1884. A furnishing fabric requiring thirty-four wood blocks to print, 'Cray' was continually produced for five decades in numerous colourways. With its combination of sinuous lines, delicate vines and exotic blossoms, it is indebted to Owen Jones's theories expressed in *The Grammar of Ornament* (1856), and to Indian textiles.

133. Gujarati embroiderer, *Deccan coverlet* (detail), 18th century. Made for export to Europe, this cotton coverlet is embroidered in silks with a vigorous floral design, which like no. 139 includes a bifurcated tree, a motif often seen on Indian palampores (bed covers). The blossoms and leaves with detailed internal patterns greatly influenced European designers, both at the time this was made and later during the Arts and Crafts Movement.

134. Annabelle Collett, *Merge*, 2008. A camouflage pattern embroidered with William Morris's 'Chrysanthemum' design is embedded with tweed fabric and, according to the artist, 'explores the way the body and its coverings act as resonators of social histories, gender attitudes and personal commentary ... [and] conceal or reveal, to proclaim or disguise'.

135. The Silver Studio, London, *The Fintona*, c. 1902. This hand-knotted wool pile carpet, designed by The Silver Studio and made in Donegal, Ireland, by Alexander Morton & Co. for Liberty & Co. of London, employs a bifurcated tree to organize the principal pattern. This and the curling leaves in the border are both characteristic of the period and inspired by Indian patterns of two centuries earlier.

136. English or Continental artisans, *Painted silk* robe à la française (detail), c. 1740. The many-coloured exotic plants and flowers depicted on this silk moiré gown, formerly in the possession of the 27th Lord and Lady de Clifford of Cliff House, Leicestershire, pay homage to imported Indian chintzes, while the gleaming white ground is a Northern European preference.

137. English printer, possibly Bromley Hall, *Copperplate-printed cotton*, 1770s. Printing with engraved copper plates allowed for fine line details previously unobtainable with block printing – a feature highlighted by the inclusion of feathery leaves. These and the stylized flowers on sinuous stems are indebted to Indian textiles and their Chinoiserie variants.

138. Ottoman embroiderer, *Pillow cover* (detail), 17th–18th centuries. In a type of work associated with Turkey, fine linen has been densely embroidered in silks, gilt-wrapped silk thread and flat gold metal strips. The design itself is indebted to Mughal antecedents.

139. Indian artisan, *Painted and dyed cotton palampore*, early 18th century. Made on the Coromandel Coast for export to Britain or America, such coverlets were highly prized for their wash-fast colours. Prompting European printers to pirate Indian printing methods, palampore patterns also influenced other European textiles of all types.

137

138

140

140. Janet Cooper, *Monkey Dress*, 2009. From the 'Party Dresses' series, which explores the artist's 'unconventional love and attachment to the discarded ... combined with my disdain for proper dress and "correctness" ... The figure is vacant and no personality is intentionally suggested.' Fabric swatches, newspaper corsages, ruffles of plastic bags, flea market cast-offs and crocheted flowers intermingle with a treasured collection of monkey images.

141. Michael Brennand-Wood, *Vase Attacks San Francisco USA* (detail), 2009. An installation utilizing computerized machine-embroidered blooms, acrylic paint, glass, wire, wooden forms and collage on a wooden base.

1

II.

INGREDIENTS

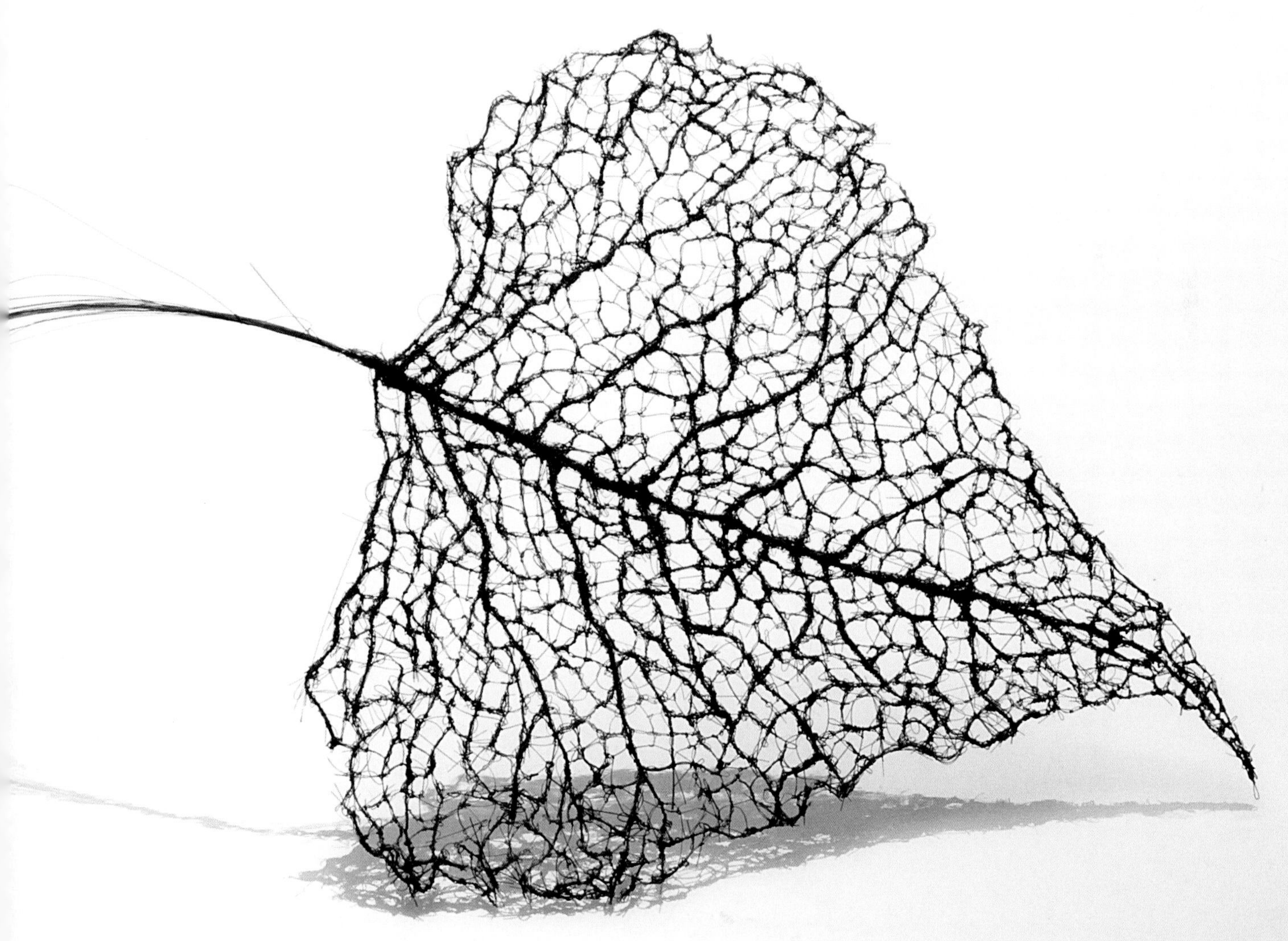

II.

INGREDIENTS

Textile production involves a uniquely complex chain of processes that begins with the gathering or making of ingredients, and ends with finished items. The importance of the ingredients used is embedded in the word 'material'. In all Western decorative arts this term is used to denote substances that can be manipulated, but only in textile arts is it also the term for an intermediate product, namely cloth. Etymologically, 'material' relates to 'matter'. Thus, in a literal sense, just as facts that matter are 'material', cloth is very much about substance or content. Form typically – although not always – comes later, when materials are transformed into clothing, furnishings or objects for use, admiration and contemplation. This chapter explores these various substances, lingering over the behaviours of the ingredients that ensure 'material', in the textile sense, really does matter.

We are subconsciously aware of many characteristics of textile ingredients through a lifetime of acquaintance with their surface and visual qualities. Authorities on the history of consumption, consumer behaviour and the psychology of textiles seek to unravel our perceptions of such qualities, because they tell us about patterns of influence, marketability and human behaviour. Far from making it simpler to identify textiles, however, our perceptions are the very features manipulated by fibre manufacturers and finishers when aiming to make one substance ape another. The use of one material to imitate another is a striking feature of the development of man-made and synthetic fibres since the mid-20th century, but it is also an ancient practice, which, over time, has contributed to changing judgments about any one fibre's suitability and desirability. To appreciate this point, let us begin with the simplest but most important aspect of ingredients: their natural capacity to inspire invention.

1. Jenine Shereos, *Leaf (Brunette)*, 2011. Strands of human hair have been wrapped, knotted together and stitched into a water-soluble backing material. At each point where one strand of hair intersected another, a tiny knot was made, allowing the entire piece to hold its form.

2. Andrea Eimke, *Home* (detail), 2008. Free-form machine-sewn lace – composed of paper, mulberry barkcloth, lemon hibiscus bark fibre, polyester thread, soluble stabilizer and wire – is shaped into a spiralling form.

Invention

The field of textile arts embraces any natural or synthetic material that can be manipulated as a strand, whether by wrapping, stitching or knotting. All of the historical evidence indicates that string was a principal springboard for significant human advancement. From sewing to seafaring, thread, yarn, cord and rope

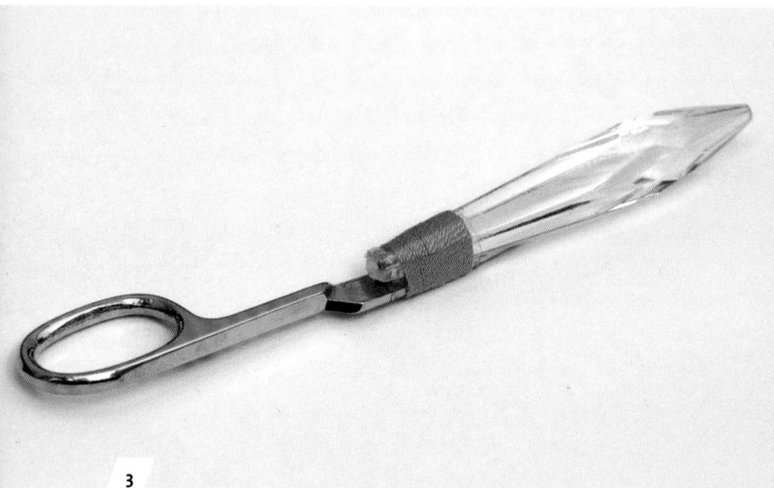
3

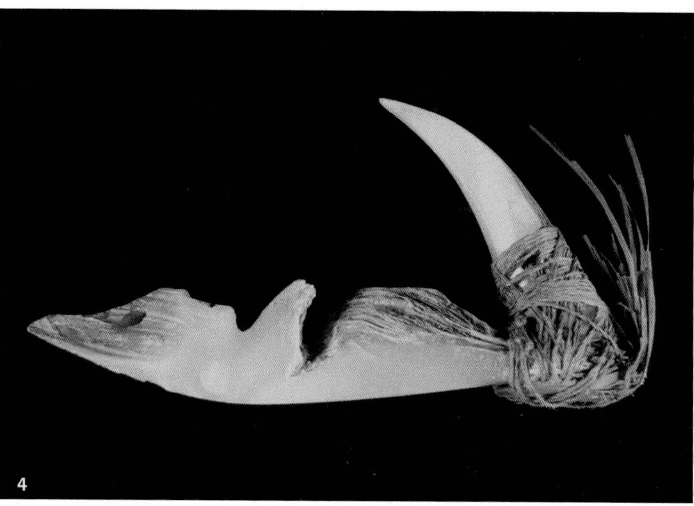
4

were fundamental to the very formation of societies, making possible efficient hunting and herding, shelter and storage, exploration and migration, and the aesthetic expressions vital to cultural cohesion, namely individual adornment and outward affirmations of group beliefs and identity. From the finest of threads to the most robust of ropes, the key to their usefulness is that all provide strong yet flexible binding or pulling power by virtue of twist. Twist greatly increases the tensile strength of any material, and can be readily observed in nature in the load-bearing capacity of twisted vines and, among man-made objects, in the powerful resilience of tennis racket strings, traditionally made of twisted animal gut. Although needles survive from only about 23,000 BC, and cordage from about 16,500 BC, evidence of their use – in the form of strung or stitched beads of stone and teeth – date from about 38,000 BC.[1] Together these artefacts prove just how early humankind was taking its first inventive steps towards everything from tool-making to personalized decoration. And 'everything' is the truth of the matter: the Bronze Age, with its associated development of metalworking, did not arise until around 3,200 BC.

Such long precedents have ensured continuity. Millennia later, textile artists continue to find inspiration in prehistoric techniques to fasten or attach, such as hafting. Vanda Campbell's *Clear Cut* **[3]** wittily evokes both literal and textual joining: so many tools were made by binding stone to stick that 'haft' also means 'handle'. From Barbara Shapiro's 'Power Garment' series, *Young Hunter* **[5]** deploys the fastening power of twisted strands while recalling the myriad objects, found and made, that have embellished textiles in every era and culture, whether as talismans of physical prowess, indicators of social standing or protection from real or imagined evils. The long-standing tradition of embellishing items with cowry shells, beetle wings and feathers **[19, 20, 26, 28]**, significant as emblems of the power of nature as well as having inherent exchange value, is echoed in contemporary pieces by Nalda Searles and Kay Sekimachi, who respectively incorporate bracts (specialized leaves) unique to Australia and sea urchin spines into wearable works **[21, 23, 24]**. Man-made objects, such as buttons, sequins and glass beads, continue to be used as embellishments around the world, although in the West these trinkets have lost their magical connotations, a point

3. Vanda Campbell, *Clear Cut*, 2010. A found scissor handle and cut-glass finial are bound with thread. Campbell based the work on historical chatelaines, the decorative chains that women or housekeepers wore around their waists to hold their keys and household objects. She has managed to strip the ideas, media and context to their purest form.

4. Native American maker, *Awl-type piercing or inscribing tool*, late 19th–early 20th centuries. This abalone or oyster-shell mother-of-pearl awl is similar to Crow, Nez Perce and Cheyenne tools. The handle and separate sharpened curved 'beak' are lashed together with dried sinew shredded into fibres. It may also have served a dual purpose as an amulet.

addressed by Catriona Faulkner in her surprising inclusion of utilitarian brass safety pins amid otherwise decorative elements in much of her work. The more unexpected the embedded object, the more significant the commentary. Take, for example, *Cradle to Grave*, from the 'Pharmacopeia' series by Susie Freeman and Dr Liz Lee in collaboration with the video artist David Critchley **[32]**. In this work, pocket-knitting holds a lifetime's worth of pills in a silent testament to modern-day shamanism, for these, too, are talismans of physical prowess, indicators of social standing or protection from everyday life.

Curiosity, experimentation and play have provided an intuitive understanding of the complex underlying physical principles at work in what we have come to call spinning (or, in silk processing, throwing). And the core thought processes that induced this leap from observation to construction, from the found to the man-made, remain central to the material arts. An excellent illustration is an account by the weaver and teacher James Bassler of the genesis of *Shop* **[6, 70]**, which perfectly exemplifies the human capacity for invention. Bassler arrived on the first day of a new term with the goal of teaching his students the importance of textile arts in early human history. 'I posed the question "What technology was discovered in order to make a yarn?" None of them knew until they looked closely at the yarn I passed out. "It's spun!" I then asked them what material do we have readily available to us, to create a yarn. To answer that question, I spotted a Trader Joe's [paper shopping] bag on a table ... I told them that their first assignment was to cut and spin yarn from [a paper] bag and I demonstrated what it takes to do this. The following class revealed varied results but the majority were quite good. Two or three were better than mine (no wonder, I am not a spinner).' Bassler then proceeded to weave with the brown paper yarn. It was only as he wove that he had the idea to mimic the form of the shopping bag, not in order to create a utilitarian object, but 'to draw attention to the adaptability of handweaving to create three-dimensional form [and especially] to celebrate the beauty of a hand-made object,' as well as 'the honesty and beauty of a simple, and readily available, material'. He is not alone in valuing the readily available: among other artists who do so are Nithikul Nimkulrat, whose ethereal work *Seeing Paper* **[69]** also employs paper yarn, and Jackie Abrams, whose thoughtful basket, *Wisdom* **[137]**, incorporates recycled dry cleaning bags and videotapes.

Bassler also created *Shop* in order to highlight the significant role that vessels played in ancient history, as they still do today. In terms of materials alone, their influence was significant because vessels – including those constructed using the basketmaking techniques revitalized in the second half of the 20th century and considered in Chapter III – can incorporate the widest variety of found ingredients in both their decoration *and* construction. Jackie Langfeld's *Fool's Gold III* **[7]** and Denise Stanton's untitled installation **[8]** illustrate the range of possible materials, from DIY and packing-paper detritus to felt. Despite their striking differences, both of these works employ vessel forms that visually express compression. The choice of materials is apt, since paper and felt are made through the application of pressure, in paper to fermented cellulose (the primary component in tree barks and plant stalks, including papyrus and esparto, as well as in cotton and linen), and in felting to moistened wool and other hair fibres. Both felt and paper are ancient materials: felting dates from

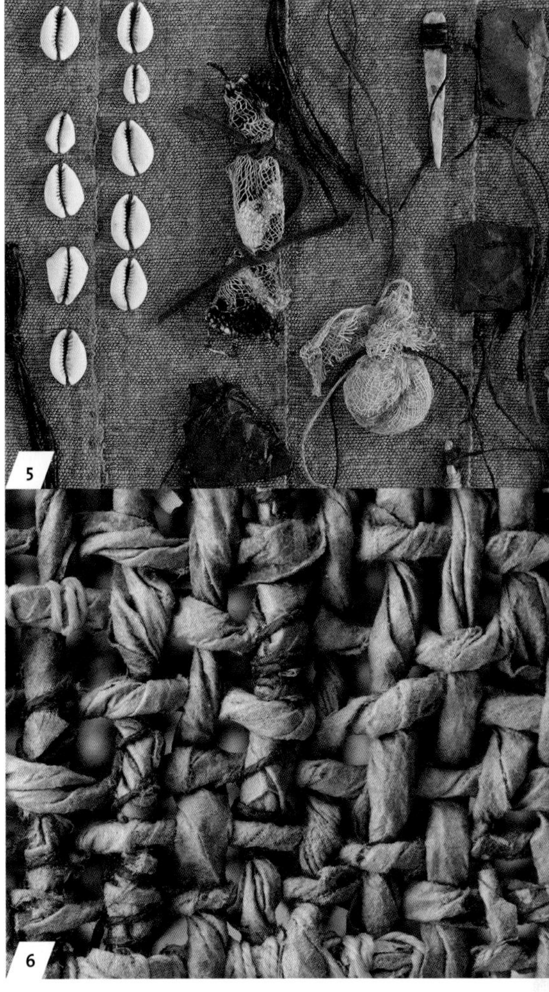

5. Barbara Shapiro, *Young Hunter* (detail), 2003. This T-shaped shirt was inspired by those worn by hunters in Mali. Composed of handwoven silk strips, it has cowry shells, found objects, and bundles treated with acid dyes and pigments bound to the surface.

6. James Bassler, *Shop* (detail), 2009. Bassler's bag was woven from approximately eight paper shopping bags. It took two to three intermittent years to complete, and Jennifer Mayeta, one of Bassler's students, assisted in creating many of the tightly spun balls of brown paper yarn.

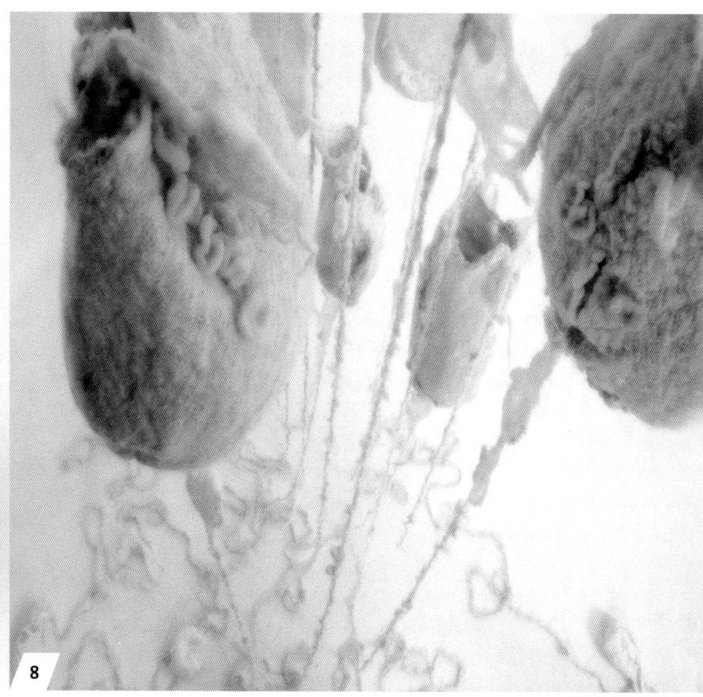

possibly as early as *c.* 6250 BC, although the earliest certain surviving example, from Beycesultan in Anatolia, dates from about 3,000 years later, by which time the Egyptian use of papyrus is also documented. Chinese rag paper survives from about 150 BC. Their mechanical methods of production emerged from the observation that most mammal hair mats naturally, and that wet cellulose (plant) fibres eventually form a malleable mass. Both also share the ability to integrate colour and additional elements, such as leaves, seeds or threads, while remaining a cohesive material. In addition, they can deploy the same range of decorative techniques, from coiling, interweaving and stitching to printing and embossing. These two materials thus have a common history, sharing innovations in mark-making and production techniques that have enriched creative life for centuries. In 1994 Polly Blakney Stirling and her assistant Sachiko Kotaka built upon these ancient concepts to develop nuno (fabric) felting in their workshop in New South Wales, Australia, illustrated here by *Deep Into the Abyss*, a work by Dana Connell and Elena Shandalov **[9]**. In this technique a loose, fine fibre, usually wool, is compressed into a sheer, open-weave material such as silk gauze, cotton voile, organza, muslin or nylon. Often incorporating several layers of loose fibres laid at right angles (the way papyrus paper was made), the resulting cloth has a fluidity absent from pure wool felt, making it well suited to shaped clothing, which can even be seamless if the component pieces are felted when still wet.

Intentions

Despite the fact that one is of animal origin and the other is derived from vegetables, the link between hair and paper resides in their fibrous character. The inclination of all natural fibres to bind or tangle together allows them to be transformed into long flexible strands – a characteristic mimicked in man-made

7. Jackie Langfeld, *Fool's Gold III*, 2010. Cardboard hand-stitched with paper cording is embellished with glass gemstones and imitation gold leaf. The work is deliberately made of cheap materials to represent the fooled and the foolish.

8. Denise Stanton, *Untitled II*, 2007 (detail). This installation, which explores the textural possibilities of hand felting, poises seemingly weighty forms upon fine stems, creating an ethereal impression.

and synthetic fibres and cables. The fibres described as 'man-made' are composed of regenerated plant materials; they are cooked, stirred or extruded in various ways and share features with all cellulosic fibres, such as cotton and linen. In concept, man-made fibres relate closely to felt and paper. Synthetic fibres, on the other hand, are generated chemically from polymers – usually petrochemical – that cannot be harvested from nature and must be especially modified for fibres such as polyesters and acrylics. Whatever their origin, the greater their fibrosity, the more cohesion between the strands, hence the use of highly fibrous wool in felts, and less fibrous silk and fine, smooth synthetic threads when passage through construction or cloth needs to be easy, as in embroidery. This can be seen by comparing the muted delineations, visible as tiny crimps along the surface, created by the human hairs in Jennie Haard's knotted *Leaf (Brunette)* **[1]**, with the freely undulating audio cables in Lars Preisser's *Weaving With Sound of its Own Making* **[10]**.

The type of strands used is not dependant on physical characteristics alone, since the artists' intentions are reinforced by their careful choice of material. For example, Haard alludes to the fall of both hair and leaves, to 'the natural systems of transformation, growth and decay'. Pressier uses stereo cables handwoven into the fabric and linked to headphones so that the listener can hear him weaving: this echoes the creation of his work, in which sound waves emanating from his loom generated a series of patterns, each a response to the rhythm and pace of the machine as he wove the previous pattern. In *Transparency?* **[58]**, Ulla de Larios uses the differing degrees of transparency and impenetrability of silk and wool to comment on transparency in government: 'silk and wool, subjected to an identical [weaving] process, parallel the impact the different administrations have on the state of the country: the silk retains its structure and is transparent, the wool narrows and collapses into a dense mass of impenetrable fibres'.

In some cases artists use found cloths for their evocative nature. Paddy Hartley's choice of fabric was essential for *Emancipation 'His'* and *Emancipation 'Hers'* **[13, 14]**. In these two works, instruments used in dissection are held within cloths sourced from the artist's family: blue fabric from workman's overalls, worn for many years by the artist's mechanic father, and a red-checked cloth, reminiscent of a rustic tablecloth, from Hartley's home. These dependable, trustworthy woven cottons are in startling contrast to the murderous intent of the tools they encompass. Jean Cacicedo's selection for *Reveal* **[15]** of a heavy coating 'melton' wool, found in a fabric store many years ago, alludes both to the traditional fabric used for jackets and, because it is a warming fibre, to a living being. That sense of life is essential, too, in Mary Elizabeth Barron's use of recycled cloths **[97]**, predominantly from her own old clothes and those of her family and friends: 'they are embedded with their memories and shared experiences. Both the physical form and the emotional memories guide and inspire the form.' Marty Jonas, who describes herself as a formalist concerned with process and technical problem solving, manipulates found fabrics and draws on her memories to spark the viewer's imagination and their own memories **[98]**. She says, 'My mother taught me to knit, crochet and sew while my father taught me to hammer, saw, solder and drill. I cannot remember a time when I was not doing something creative, using threads and cloth, with my hands .... Fiber is an extension of my voice.'

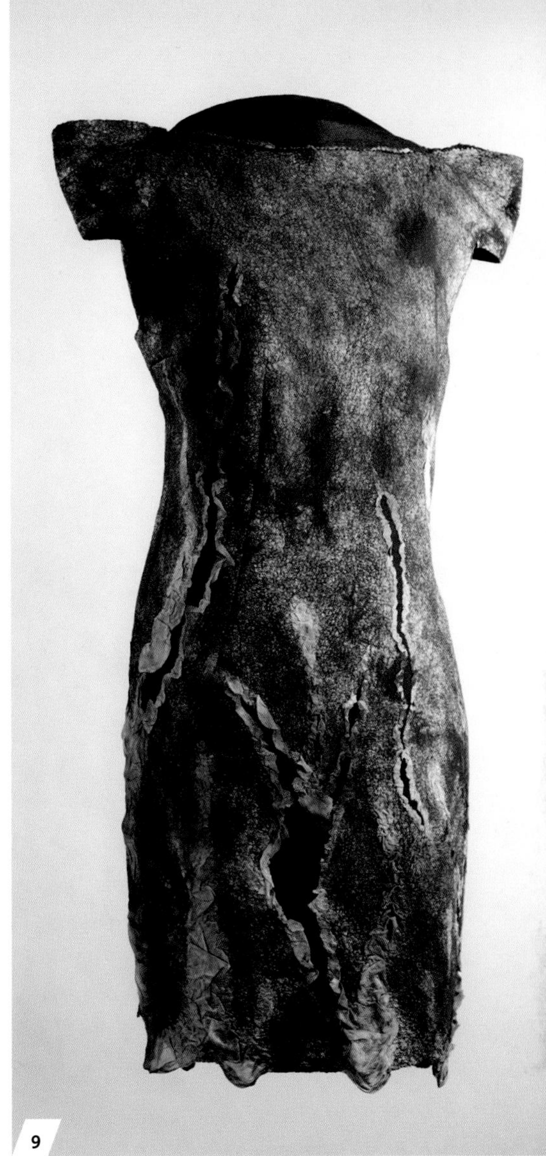
9

9. Dana Connell and Elena Shandalov, *Deep Into the Abyss*, 2011. Nuno-felted fabric designed and made by Connell is employed in a dress designed and sewn by Elena Shandalov.

In contrast, many simple and very beautiful cloths are made in celebration of the unique qualities found in natural fibres and dyes. As Tim Parry-Williams explains, 'It is often hard to describe the fruits of personal labour, and the development of "product" can be slow. But, for me, the approach is as important as the outcome. My thoughts about the process of weaving were once beautifully echoed by an Japanese friend who described "listening to the voices of the materials, and constructing a song or story".' Mika McCann, who was born in Tokyo and resides in Hawaii, uses indigenous plants **[11]**, saying, 'Ideas begin with the material. When I touch it I see the images there, in the air. The vision comes automatically from the fiber.'[2] Todate Kazuko, head curator of the Tsukuba Museum of Art in Ibaraki, Japan, makes the same point in relation to the work of the master indigo dyer Fukumoto Shihoko: 'A *some* (dye) artist is always highly attuned to the nature of the fabric. This is because cloth is not simply a kind of canvas onto which colors are placed – it is only when the substance that is dye functions as a cooperative whole with the material of the fabric, that a new realm is created. Thus it can be said that the artist of *some* dye, that in some ways utterly Japanese art, has a unique sense of the materials when viewed against the very different Western sensibility that produces the print, where pattern is simply imposed on cloth.'[3] The artist herself says that the 'nature of indigo synchronizes with my nature. My senses are developed through the process of indigo dyeing. Indigo allows me to interact with nature.'[4]

10

Indigo belongs to a class of unique natural dyes, in that it is insoluble and must be fermented, dissolved and deposited around the fibres in an oxygen-reduced state, in a cold dye vat. Lifting the cloth out repeatedly to reintroduce oxygen returns the dye to an insoluble state, revealing its colour. This means that patterns must be created by painting or printing a resist paste (or wax, in batik), or by physical resists known as 'shibori', the widely accepted Japanese term for resist pattern-dyeing by binding, stitching, folding, twisting or otherwise compressing cloth prior to immersion. (In the West the first of these methods is known as 'tie-dyeing'.) Carol Anne Grotrian works with indigo, and through shibori depicts the five principal natural sources of this colorant **[100, 101]**, all of which were eclipsed by synthetic indigo after it became available in 1897. However, in recent years natural indigo has gained renewed appreciation throughout the world. This development has been aided by Jenny Balfour-Paul, an Englishwoman who has lived and worked in the Middle East and North Africa, and who has researched, written about and worked with indigo for over two decades. Balfour-Paul says, 'Each year I love growing my own Japanese indigo and combining it with natural indigo from other parts of the world to make an international fermentation dye vat.' She additionally represents the widespread rise in the exploration of other plant dyes, extracted in hot dye baths, commenting that 'It is fun to contrast the indigo with other natural dye colours, whether rust shades from West African cola nut, rich pinks of Mexican cochineal, or yellows from home-grown weld' **[106]**.

What many would class as inks (although they often *are* dyes; see Chapter IV) have re-entered the arena too. In *Healing Sutras* **[128]**, Erin Endicott uses walnut ink to stain vintage cottons that have been passed down by women in her family. The stains represent psychological wounds, their origins, and the

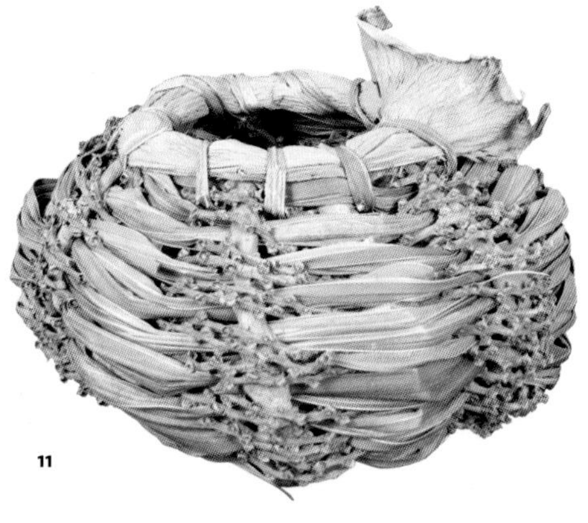

11

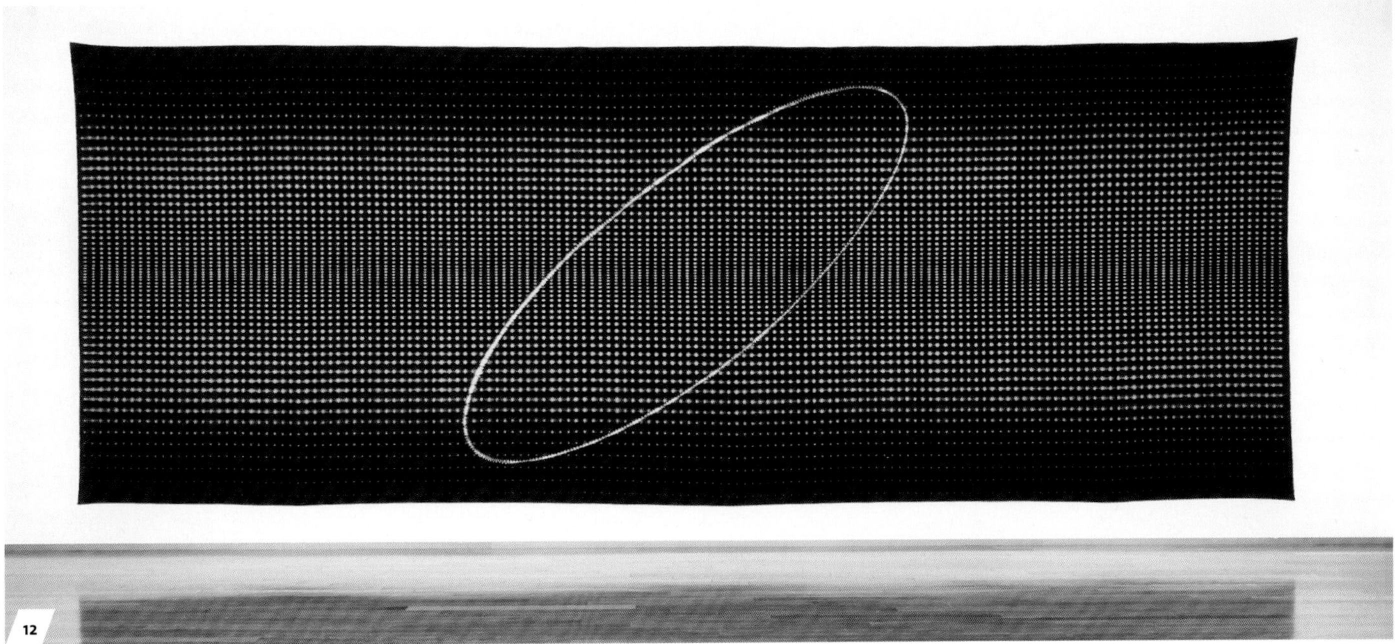

way that making visible, visceral objects can be part of the healing process: 'Ink on fabric has a mind of its own – it takes the control away from me and does its own thing. It is magical to drop the ink onto damp fabric and literally watch the "wound" grow and take shape before my eyes ... it's quite the opposite of the degree of control I have over the stitching.' Although Jun Tomita uses synthetic dyes, painting or tie-dyeing his warps prior to handweaving **[127, 129]**, his skilful interpretation of the art of *kasuri* (ikat) shows a similar sensibility towards the serendipitous: 'I am inspired by the color I see around me in the fields and forests, and by the changes that time has wrought upon the walls of old houses. Life as seen upon a wall is not manifested in any grand way as is expressed in the words of history or tradition. It is a simple layering of time and the accidental staining that paints the wall, giving ... depth and mood.'[5]

Artists' choices are also determined by the availability of local materials, particularly those that are not distributed globally. Hilary Buckland uses zamia palm and cotton native to Australia as a metaphor for the two strands of her history. As a child in Lancashire, England, she was familiar with the region's historical significance during the Industrial Revolution, when local mills processed imported raw cotton, producing the vast majority of the world's finished cotton cloth. Later, as an emigrant to Australia, Buckland learned to spin, weave and dye with native plant species, and she gins cotton as it was done for centuries before Eli Whitney's introduction of mechanized ginning in 1794. In *As We Sow ...* **[51]**, the materials create a parallel between Buckland's own story of migration and the dispersal of cotton cloth and clothing 'around the globe over centuries, and with it many of the practices and production that are unsustainable, environmentally damaging and inequitable. This echoes the migration of Western ideas, industrialization and globalization.' As a European outsider in a close-knit Polynesian island community, Andrea Eimke also uses materials to express subjective experiences and ambiguous feelings regarding cultural identity **[2, 36]**.

10. Lars Preisser, *Weaving With Sound of its Own Making* (detail), 2009. Handwoven fabric composed of cotton, wool and audio cables, with attached headphones and CD players. The fabric, suspended over a sheet of perspex, bends into an arch under its own weight.

11. Mika McCann, *Basket*, 1988. Known as one of Maui's foremost basketmakers, McCann has twined Hawaiian philodendron, watsonia, wattle and coloseed, highlighting their varied textures and colours.

12. Fukumoto Shihoko, *Ginga (The Galaxy)*, 1998. Indigo shibori and discharge on cotton cloth, folded and stitched.

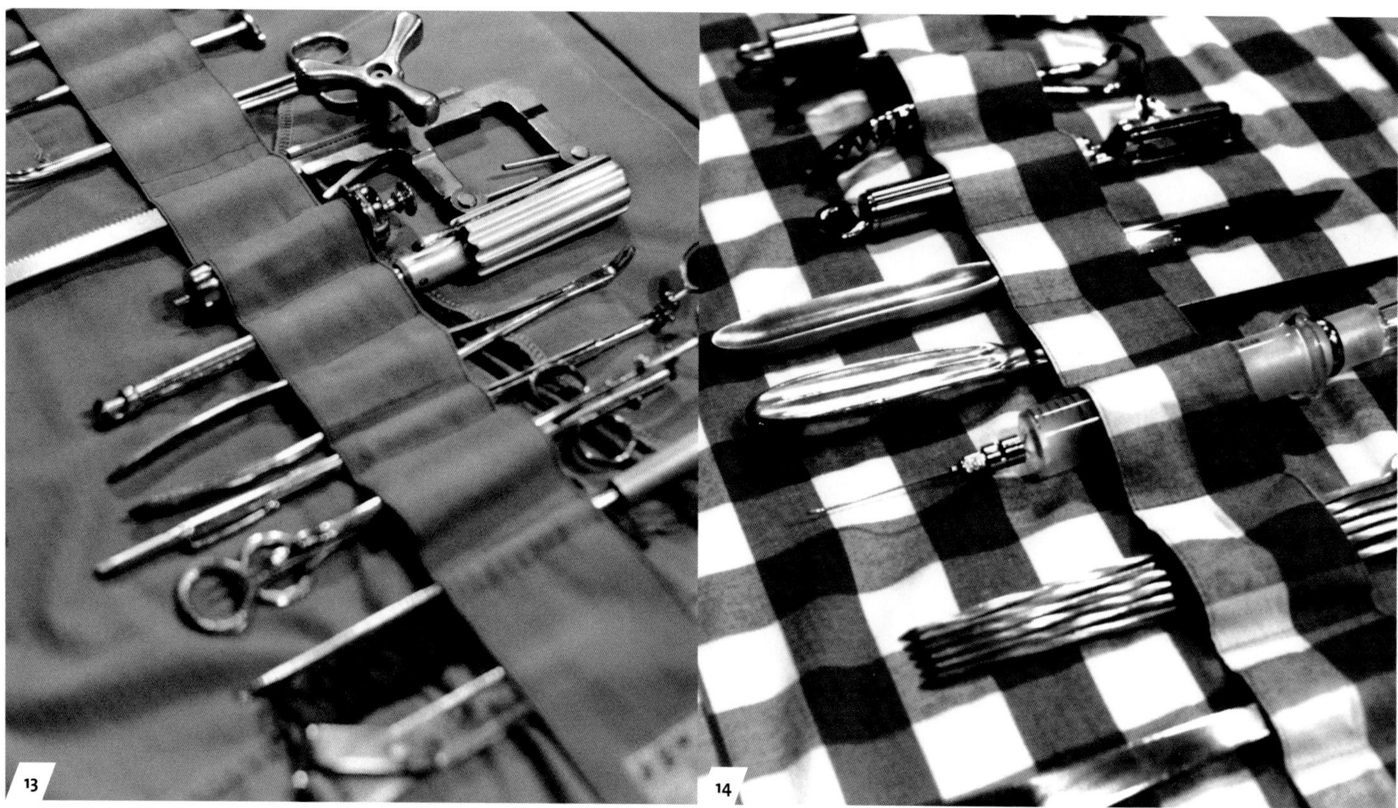

13 14

Home offers a 'shell around an imaginary space of contemplation ... created as a comfort zone', melding tapa (barkcloth) and *kiriau* (bark fibre) indigenous to Polynesia with synthetic non-woven materials such as soluble stabilizer, interfacing, and threads from her 'techno-cultural' background. Of the bark material, Eimke explains, 'Tapa has low tensile strength but good moulding qualities when wet. It is a strong and somewhat stiff material when dry. It can easily be ripped in the direction the fibres grow, but needs cutting in the other. If beaten thinly, it resembles lace. In ancient and modern Polynesia it is the material itself and the way in which it is employed that defined its resulting purpose, and not messages that may be contained in its decoration.' Her use of lace 'alludes to the sensitivity with which an intercultural position needs to be approached [and] hints at the vulnerability of an outsider's position'.

13 and 14. Paddy Hartley, *Emancipation 'His' (Dissecting Set)* and *Emancipation 'Hers' (Dissecting Set)* (details), 2000. The oversized surgical wrap in no. 13, made from overalls worn by the artist's father, holds tools from his father's garage alongside surgical and postmortem tools. These grisly implements include bone-nibblers, saws and a tonsil guillotine. Produced as part of a residency at The Royal Armouries, Leeds, in response to participants' encounters with violence and conflict in the home, this work (tongue firmly in cheek) plays 'with the notion of escaping the marital bonds through foul means'. The gingham tablecloth (14) holds kitchen tools, including a vegetable peeler that closely resembles a skin-grafting tool.

Alchemy

Despite advances in science, there remains something seemingly magical in the transformation of plants into dyestuffs, gold and silver ores into threads, the soft into the rigid, or a 'perfect' cloth into one rusted or partially destroyed. The incorporation of precious metals into textiles can be traced as far back as 2300 BC, to ancient Troy, where gold beads were found among loom weights, suggesting that they were interwoven just as Native American *wampum* belts incorporated interwoven shells. The earliest example of pure gold wire treated as thread comes from Anatolia and dates to 1800 BC. Thereafter, and to the present day, the most prized of textiles have been embellished with narrow strips of gold and silver, beaten flat (*lamella*) or wrapped around a fibre core for a more flexible yarn, or applied with gold leaf or paint **[76, 77, 94, 95]**.

Long experience with such materials has contributed to the development of 'smart fabrics' or 'intelligent textiles', such as those that are electrically conductive, or that incorporate fibres and yarns of brass, stainless steel, aluminium, copper or nickel. The range of results is diverse: from electrically active polymeric materials that contribute to artificial muscles, to optical fibre sensors and thermally sensitive fabrics that assess their wearer's needs. (Not limited to metallic fibres, such developments are often based on well-established techniques such as knitted scaffolds for tissue engineering.[6]) Straddling the science and art of techno-textiles, Frances Geesin uses industrial shielding and thermoplastic nonwoven fabrics and geotextiles – permeable fabrics that, when used in association with soil, have the ability to separate, filter, reinforce, protect or drain – that she electroplates. Her 'Torso' series **[91, 92]** was created by heat-fusing polypropylene to a dress form and applying conductive paint prior to electroplating, during which the slowly built-up metal became self-supporting. Geesin's 'Frozen Charlotte' series **[16]** revolves around small, found porcelain figures embedded in a range of materials, ranging from sari fabric to industrial shielding, all rendered conductive and electroplated with metals such as copper, zinc and nickel. The originator of this and several related techniques, Geesin says of her explorations, 'I work intuitively. It's play, really.'

15

There is a sense of play in many textiles, especially those that contain elements of the unexpected: Carole Waller's glass-encased panels **[146]**, for example, or Debra Rapoport's hat **[139]** made from a repurposed crinoline. At Jakob Schlaepfer, a speciality Swiss firm specializing in couture fabrics and directed by Martin Leuthold, every season brings forth something astonishing, from fabrics coated with copper to laser-cut, feather-laden sheers **[131, 132]**. The co-founder of Nuno, Reiko Sudo, is known for her combination of traditional techniques, the most modern manufacturing processes, and ecological awareness, yet the resulting cloths always have a light, joyous touch **[35]**. Norma Starszakowna's surfaces are an amalgam of seemingly random layers of imagery, which appear casually burnished. Yet these, as with fabrics by Schlaepfer and Nuno, are the result of extensive, controlled experimentation. Starszakowna combines shibori, dye and print processes, both 'the filmic, glazed translucent digital image and the qualities achieved by screen-printed media, including embossed effects obtained through synchronous imagery screen-printed with heat reactives and subsequent patinated erosions'. This has resulted in 'a new genre of textile, one whereby layers are accumulated, almost as part of the physical continuum'. In all of these examples, there is no haste to embrace or discard a technique or media; rather, ideas are nurtured, often over long periods of time and with considerable eventual impact.

A notable example is Starszakowna's deployment of rust and crush processes **[17, 120]**, which she began to develop in 1990 for the fashion designer Issey Miyake. At a time when pigment printing (as opposed to shibori-crush and patterning techniques) was considered an inferior method in Japan, this 'effectively bridged the divide between Japanese tradition and a "Western" aesthetic, making experimental print acceptable'. Preparing the way for a focus on

15. Jean Cacicedo, *Reveal*, 1999. A witty play on the clothed torso, this bag is constructed from dyed and stitched wool, jesso and polymer. Cacicedo found the wool in a New York fabric store many years before she made this piece.

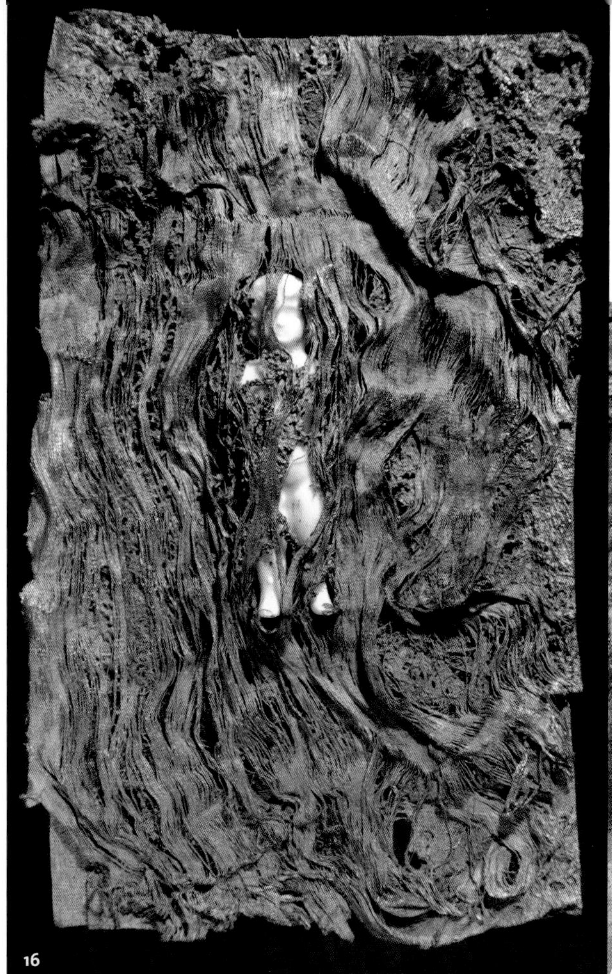

printed textiles at Nuno from 1992 on, Starszakowna's crush-print technique was later to influence designer Yoshiki Hishinuma, and in 2006 made its way into the Prada spring collections, where, as Starszakowna is content to point out, 'it is probably perceived to be a Japanese concept'. The textiles produced in her studio – often worked on both sides with heat-reactive pigments, iron oxides, embossing and patination fluid – remain too complex for a commercial printer to replicate in bulk. I asked for her views on new materials and techniques: 'Aaargh!', she began, 'this depends on how they are used. There is a wealth of as yet unexploited opportunity in technology, for example in the use of nanotechnology and micro-encapsulation to produce sensory textiles that provide material and health benefits, etc.' True to her own oeuvre, however, she added this admonition: 'Technology is only a tool, and since machines are by nature mechanical, one has to ensure that purpose is not over-ridden by awe of method. In this respect, the Japanese are past masters at subverting the machine to produce the idiosyncratic rather than the uniform, perfect product.' [7]

Jun-ichi Arai, who co-founded Nuno in 1984, is the ultimate Japanese master. Since there are too many innovations to his credit to recount, Matilda McQuaid, head of textiles at the Cooper-Hewitt, National Design Museum in New York, summarized his achievements thus: 'His primary legacy is this belief in experimentation, which is embodied in all of his work, whether it is destroying surfaces to create something that is much more beautiful than the original textile, or using traditional methods with new materials.'[8] Those traditional textiles are not solely Japanese: in 1968 Arai visited Central America, Eastern Europe and South-East Asia as technical instructor in fabric manufacturing, which may

16. Frances Geesin, *Frozen Charlotte 3*, 2002. This is one work from a series of twelve. Each features a found porcelain figure embedded in fibres and fabrics that have been metallized by electroplating.

17. Norma Starszakowna, *Rust Rune Wall* (detail), 2011. Heat-reactive and stable pigments, including puff binder paste and oxidized rust, have been screen-printed onto silk organza. Starszakowna's materials and processes reflect 'early experiences in a highly textured, politically charged environment', capturing the 'inevitable erosions of time'.

account for the 'humanity' seemingly embodied even in his cloths interwoven with fine stainless steel and aluminium yarns **[99]**. As Arai says, 'There are expressions that have been used to describe me – one is "dream weaver". But a dream is not something spontaneous, not something that can be quickly achieved. You have to keep seeing that dream, and you have to keep at it for a long time. And you need to have some consciousness of that dream; it's not just an unconscious thing. If you make a conscious effort, sometimes it comes to you. I set things up, and I don't know what's going to happen, but I keep seeing the dream of how I want things to happen [and] it comes to me.'[9]

Others dream too. Imagining the transformation of the urban landscape gave rise to the company Tactility Factory, and to the Girli Concrete range of designs, based on patented technology developed by Trish Belford, a textile designer, and Ruth Morrow, an architect, working together within the University of Ulster, Belfast. They offer a bespoke design and crafts service, as well as working in partnership with concrete prefabrication manufacturers to produce larger quantities: 'The secret to the Girli Concrete ranges lies in designing fabrics to combine with the concrete in such a way that the textiles remain on the surface of the concrete and are fully integrated within it,' without peeling away. The yarns must tolerate the harsh alkaline environment of the concrete, which is why they use linen, although the material is also important to Belford and Morrow because this bast fibre, from the inner bark, or phloem, of certain trees and herbs – in this case flax – has played a key role in the textile heritage of Northern Ireland. Inspiration from antique textiles, gold leaf and flocking are also incorporated, resulting in extreme alterations in the expected visual and tactile qualities of concrete **[87–90]**.

To alter expectations of a different sort was the aim of a project initiated by the Swiss embroidery company Forster Rohner. This high-end firm conducted a joint research project with the Hochschule für Technik Rapperswil and the Interstate University of Applied Sciences of Technology in Buch, Switzerland, to create a fashionable alternative to the usual messenger-type bags, with integrated thin, flexible solar modules. The result was the Solar Handbag **[18]**, produced by Diffus Design in Copenhagen, home to the designers Hanne Louise Johannesen and Michel Guglielmi. In addition, the Alexandra Institute and the Center for Software Innovation, both in Denmark, helped in the development. Through miniaturization of the photovoltaic material (monocrystalline silicon) into oversized 'sequins', the Solar Handbag could be made using traditional techniques, its surface embroidered with an integrated combination of normal embroidery and conductive embroidery. This harvests energy from the solar sequins to a rechargeable lithium battery. Aside from being able to charge a mobile device, opening the bag at night or in dark surroundings activates optical fibres attached to the inside, which produce a diffuse glow so that keys and the like can be located easily **[138]**. With its stitched-on platelets, redolent of those found on a saddlecloth at Pazyryk in the Altai Mountains and dating from *c.* 400 BC, the Solar Handbag is emblematic of the continuity of creativity that informs most techno-textiles – a concept metaphorically captured in its elliptical shape, which resembles 'the relationship between the sun and moon – between light source and enlightened'.[10]

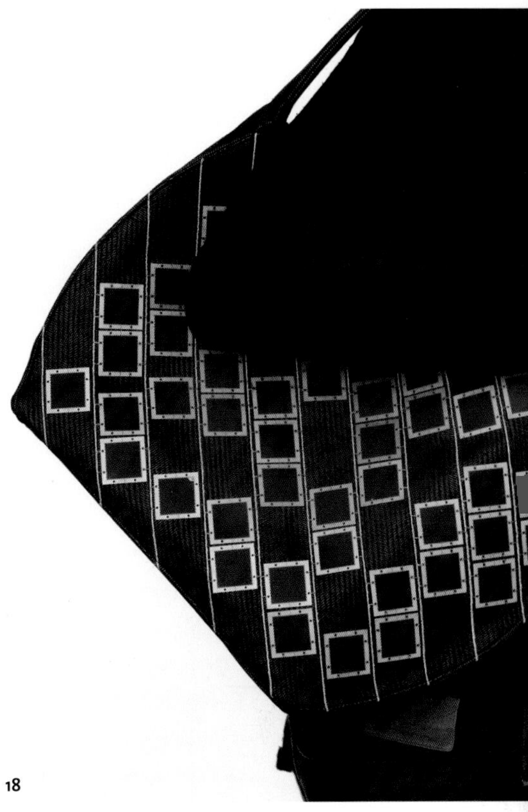

18

18. Forster Rohner and Diffus Design, *Solar Handbag*, 2011. Combining solar plates with traditional embroidery, Diffus Design assistants Stine Lagefoged and Yasamin Zafar created a solar energy-harvesting surface that is highly efficient and offers maximum design freedom.

19. Romanian hatmaker, *Young man's hat*, 20th century. Wool felt hat with a *rotta de panni*, or five concentric rows of peacock feathers attached with wax under black cotton knit cords. This is a style worn by young men in Nasaud, northern Transylvania.

20. Indian embroiderer, *Evening dress fabric* (detail), 1845–50. Made for export, in this case to England, delicate muslin glistens with gold sequins, twisted threads and iridescent wings harvested from 'jewel' beetles.

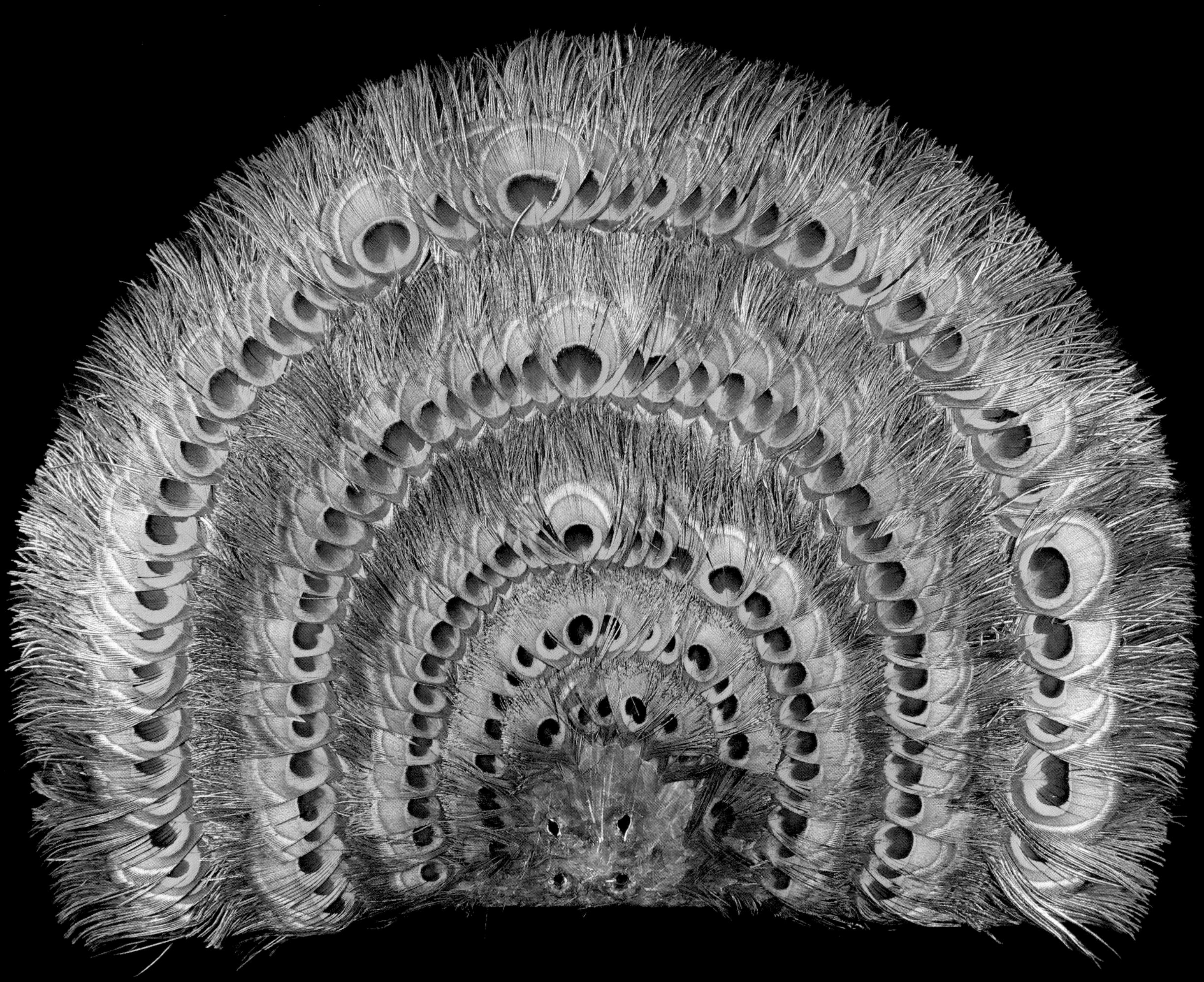

20

21

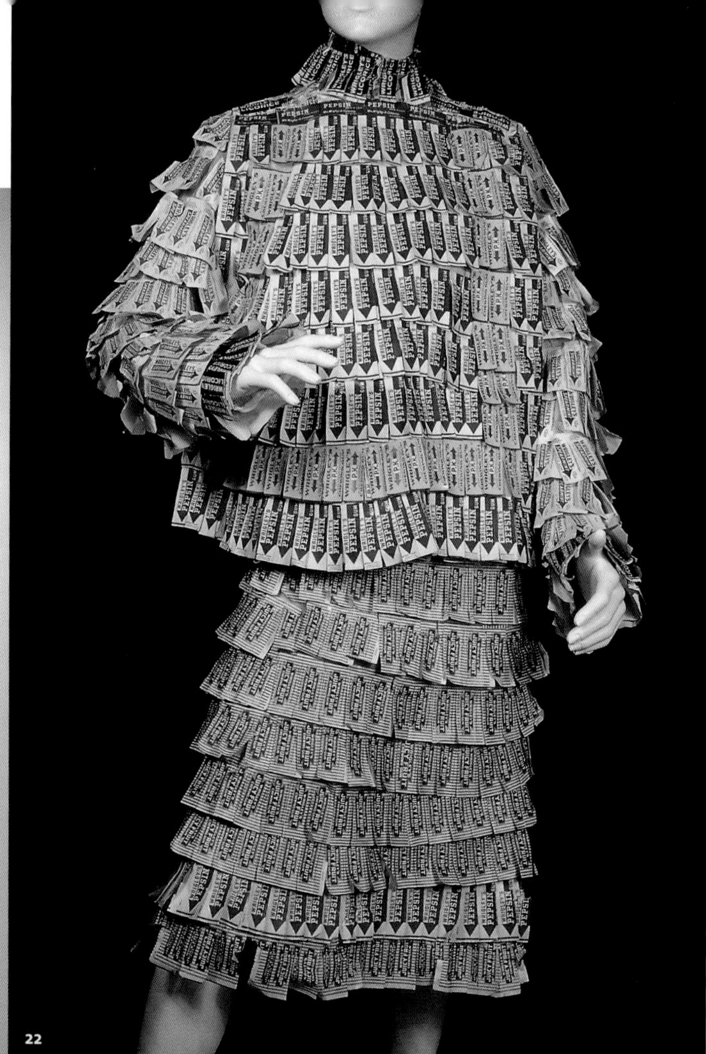

22

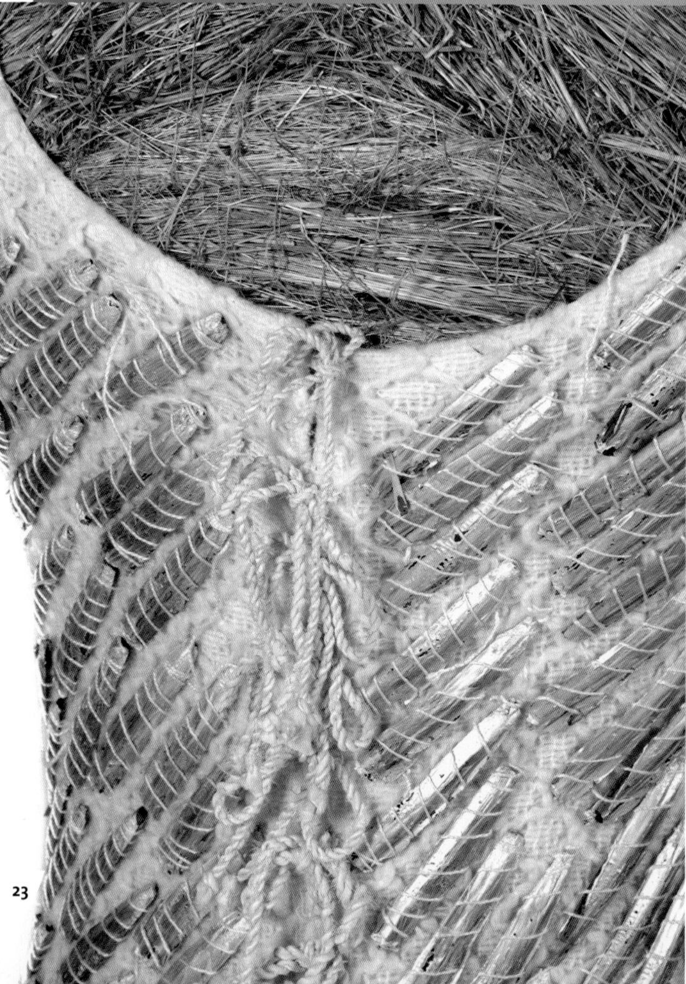
23

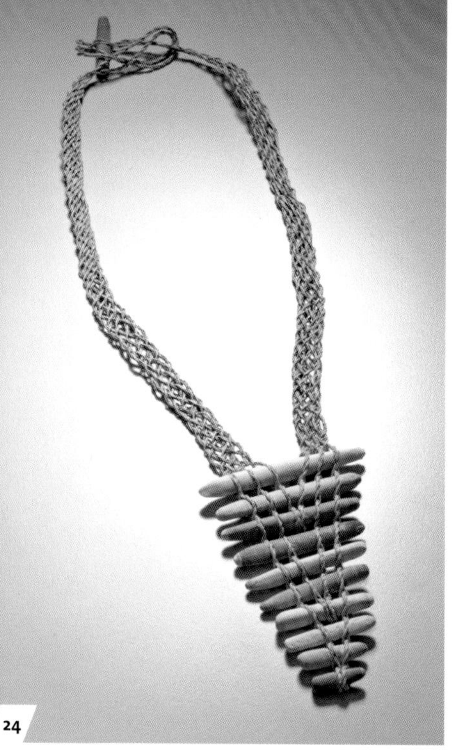
24

21. Nalda Searles, *Mallee Leaf Jacket*, 1997. A recycled woven plaid jacket with leather buttons has natural mallee leaves from the *Eucalyptus platycorys* stitched individually onto the front and back of the jacket using linen thread. The leaves were taken from a storm-broken branch.

22. American artisan, *Novelty dress*, 1930s. Decorated with an assortment of Wrigley's chewing gum wrappers glued to a cheesecloth underdress.

23. Nalda Searles, *Kanga Dress* (detail), 2008. A white woollen Paris-labelled vintage dress 'beaded' with *Xanthorrhoea preissei* bracts coated with acrylic paint and tied with silk string from a salvaged silk shirt, the kangaroo section of common meadow hay fibre.

24. Kay Sekimachi, *11 Spines*, 2011. A necklace 40 cm (16 in.) long is composed of eleven sea urchin spines and two-ply paper cord, employing the split-ply technique.

25. Sadhana Peterson, *The Tea Party* (detail), 2011. In bringing together machine lace, plastic toys, tea bags, paper, expanding foam, recycled curtains, table cloths and a wedding dress, the artist was inspired by a child's tea party and 'the joy of making mud pies. Here the child is so immersed in her play that her "brewing thoughts" turn her into a tea party.'

25

26

27

28

26. Banja Ra artisan, *Woman's ornamental back panel*, *c.* 1960. Prized for their translucent sheen (the word 'porcelain' derives from *porcellana*, the old Italian term for the shell), cowries have currency value and are full of meaning in many cultures, representing power, fertility and spirituality. Such bags have long been made, changing only in the threads used.

27. Filipino artisan, *Piña-cloth tabard* (detail), *c.* 1960. Flowers composed of iridescent pink sequins with red glass stamens sit on top of a mass of red embroidery and needlelace that secures red bead-centred sequins and glass bugle beads.

28. Pwo-Karen artisan, *Singing shawl* (detail), purchased 1991. This cotton shawl, of the type made and worn by young Karen girls at funeral ceremonies, was acquired at the weekend market in Chautuchak, northern Thailand. Its edge is decorated with a network of iridescent green and silver beads, and glass and plastic buttons that also embellish each intersection. Attached by knotting to the fringe are hard wings of the beetle *Sternocera aequisignata*.

29. Afghan artisan, *Kutchi dress* (detail), before 1990. This black cotton woman's dress is embellished with silk embroidery, mother-of-pearl and plastic buttons, brass rondels, and glass and metal beads.

29

31

32

33

30. Egyptian artisan, *Siwa Oasis wedding kaftan*, 20th century. Nylon interwoven with gold metallic stripes, decorated with silk embroidery and embellished with mother-of-pearl and coloured plastic buttons, coloured glass 'stones' set in silver with attached silver bells, cowry shells and tassels.

31. Sara Nordling, *Tribute*, 2010. One of a set of four weavings commemorating photographic slides at Indiana University that were converted to digital images and then discarded. Fascinated with the slides as objects, Nordling was 'saddened by the loss … as it spoke to the ending of an era [and] all the hours of labor in making the slides and keeping the catalogs'.

32. Susie Freeman, Dr Liz Lee and David Critchley, *Cradle to Grave* (detail), 2003. One individual's pill diary of 24,000 pills entrapped in a nylon monofilament pocket-knitted armature. The 1.5 × 13 m (4.9 × 43 ft) installation was commissioned in 2003 by Dr Henrietta Lidchi for the British Museum collection and was displayed in 'Living and Dying', an exhibition at the Wellcome Collection, London.

33. Janet Lipkin, *Untitled*, 2005. This small reverse-appliqué panel, 17 cm (6¾ in.) high, is composed of painted and stitched canvas over a supplementary weft-striped cotton, framed with paillettes of various sizes, some embellished with beads and fragments of cloth.

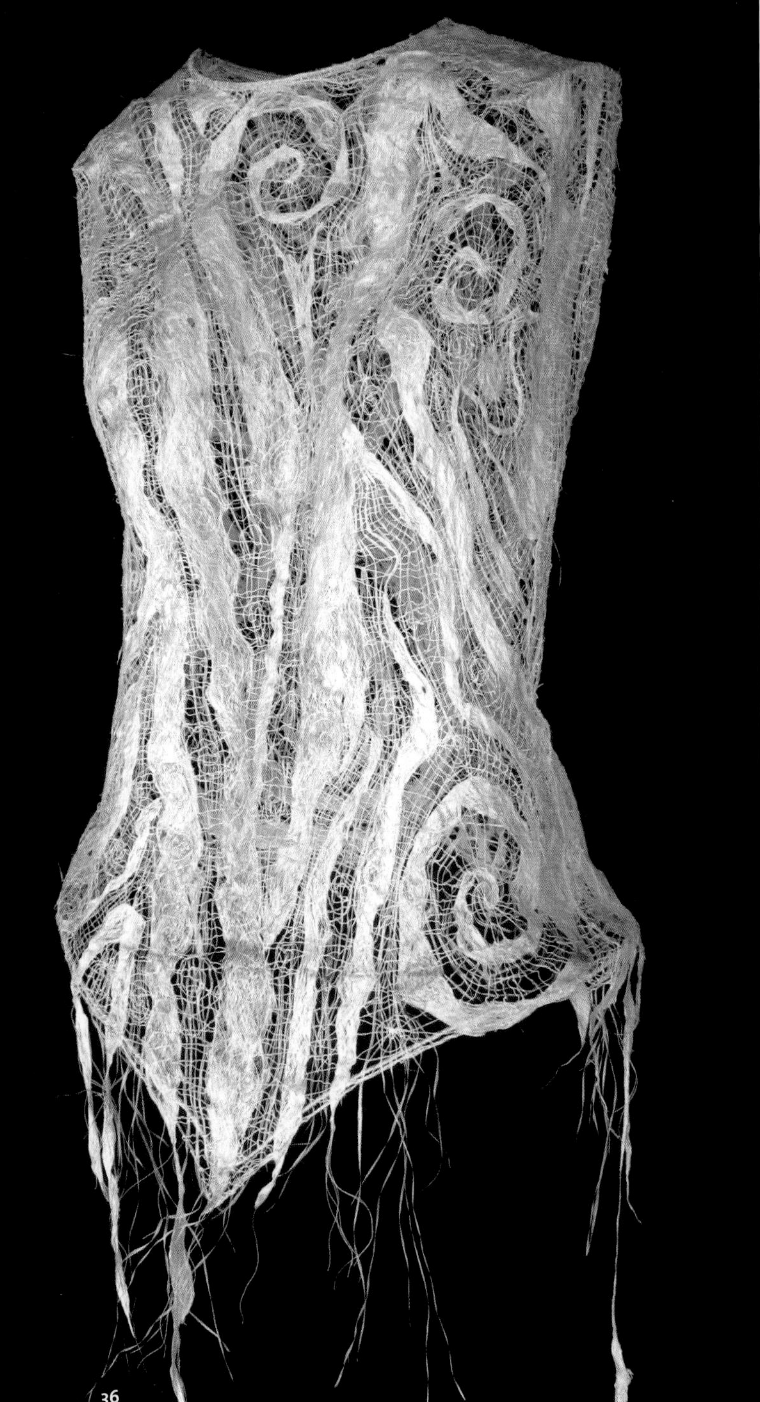

36

37

34. Janice Appleton, *Best Before*, 2006. A bedside mat, 39 × 66 cm (15.35 × 26 in.) in size and constructed from plastic bread tags wired together using backstitch, is the artist's wry expression of her feelings about the demise of her heterosexual marriage.

35. Reiko Sudo, *Tubular Baby Hairs* (detail), 2006. In a work composed of cotton (75%) and Saran, which is flame-resistant and highly water-absorbent, threads of the latter fibre were impregnated with strontium aluminate, a phosphorescent pigment that stores sunlight and shines in the dark, more typically associated with safety garments and devices.

36. Andrea Eimke, *Home*, 2008. Free-form machine-sewn lace made of paper mulberry barkcloth and lemon hibiscus bark fibre, the beaten cloth 'deconstructed, tied, intersected, fused, and laced together with non-woven synthetic fibre materials like soluble stabilizer and polyester thread. By doing so, elements can interact with each other, overcome the limits of their materiality, and extend beyond the potential of the individual substances.'

37. Joanne Circle, *Butterfly into Leopard*, 2009. Inspired by the butterfly signature in a Jack Shadbolt painting, the artist incorporated handmade felted shibori-dyed tendrils into a felted vessel inlaid with horsehair and cotton and silk threads, dotted with wool and coloured with walnut and aniline dyes. It was formed to suggest 'a balance of male and female energies'.

38
39
40
41

42

43

44

38. Cameroonian artisan, *Tse Nteng* (detail), 20th century. This ceremonial hat, possibly from the Bandjoun kingdom, has dyed raffia bundles plaited through a looped cloche form composed of thick yarns of natural raffia, twisted for strength.

39. Hawaiian basketmaker, *Basket with handle* (detail), before 1990. The entire basket is composed of four sections of plaited palm leaflets with ribs.

40. Rathcrona haymaker, *Bundle of Cordage*, before 1973. This hay, called 'sugawn' in the Republic of Ireland, was a gift to Ed Rossbach from Susan Ropenberg Thompson, a former student who collected the rope when living in the west of Ireland, in Rathcrona, Kilmaley, County Clare.

41. Raffia strands. From the leaves of tropical raffia (raphia) palms – historically associated with Madagascar but also grown in tropical Africa and Central and South America – raffia is tough and one of the few natural fibres that are used unspun.

42. Helen von Ammon, *Hat*, c. 2000. Knitted with large needles using garter stitch and short lengths of yarns (thrums), with ends hanging off the surface as a fringe (rather than being knotted to the preceding length of knitting yarn). Von Ammon spins on an Anthony Cardarelle spinning wheel, marrying exotic fibres such as baby camel down from Mongolia, silky alpaca from South America, the softest cashmeres from the Himalayas, and cultivated and wild silks from Italy and India into one-ply, two-ply, crêpe-spun and bouclé yarns.

43. British embroiderer, *Chair-back upholstery panel*, late 18th century. With a border worked in *gros point*, the *petit point* scene depicts country pursuits, including the harvesting and spinning of flax.

44. Otovalo spinner, Equador, *Cotton thread*, c. 1974. In a small multicoloured sisal basket are cotton threads, just off the spindle. Cotton's internal structure is spiralled, making it easy to twist. When wet, this characteristic causes minute rotations – as in a tiny spin dryer – which means that the fibres dry very quickly.

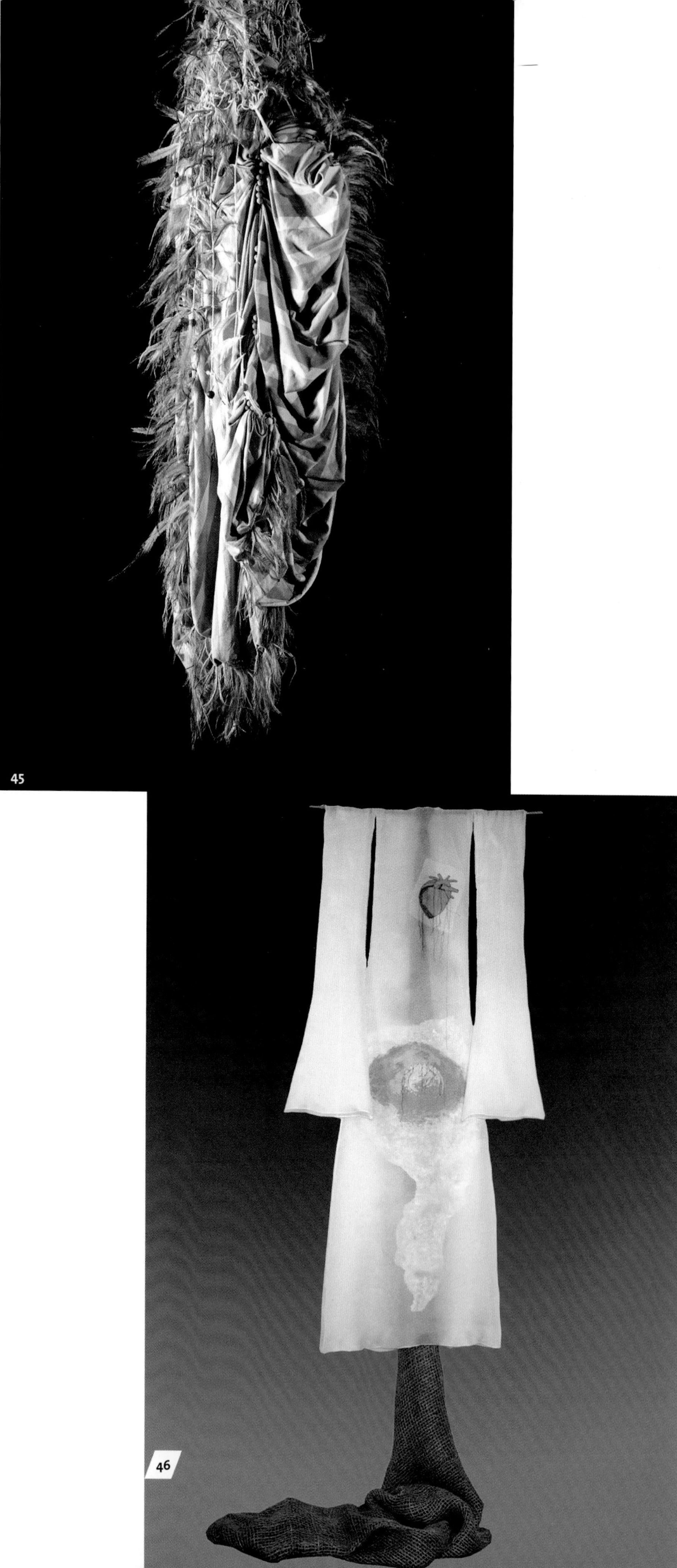

45. Margaret Barnett, *Gidgee Dreaming*, 2007. Inspired by the semi-arid Queensland landscape and made in memory of the pioneers of this region, this contemporary shibori sculpture, with hand-knotted netting capturing emu feathers, is produced from fabric made of natural-coloured indigenous cottons grown near Dalby. Barnett described it as 'wonderful fabric to work with – it draped beautifully'.

46. Maria Ortega, *Self-Portrait*, 2006. Life-sized sculpture composed of patchworked and collaged natural materials ranging from the ethereal to the robust: wild silk organza, Indian paper and thick raffia.

47. Janine McAullay-Bott, *Basket*. Queen Palm fronds and philodendron leaves were interwoven by the artist, a 'bush sculptor' whose work is dedicated to visualizing and honouring the Noongar culture of Western Australia: 'My weaves are culturally significant, ever-evolving, and my way of visualizing my people; their culture, the unique sense of humour they possess.'

48. Tibetan artisan, *Shoes*, before 1976. Slippers with the body of the shoe made of fine twined sisal and the soles of thicker sisal. The top edge has a single twining of turquoise, and the vamps have butterflies drawn in grey ink.

49. Beth Hatton, *Introducing Species*, 2007. Indigenous stitching technique using linen thread, plant materials indigenous to Lake George in central New South Wales (red anther wallaby grass and *Allocasuarina* seeds), and scotch thistle and Yorkshire fog grass, which are local weeds. Modelled on replica shoes made at a Sydney museum, this example commemorates convicts, the area's first European settlers, as 'a cheeky lot … undaunted by their lowly position'.

50. Beth Hatton, *Offering #1 (Regeneration Series)*, 2008. An indigenous stitch-coiling technique used to partially wrap an old plough disk given to the artist by George Grundy. Grundy is a farmer from Lake George, New South Wales, who, losing his topsoil to drought followed by rains, planted native grasses to sustain his cattle. The incorporation of wallaby and kangaroo grasses signify life and hope.

45

46

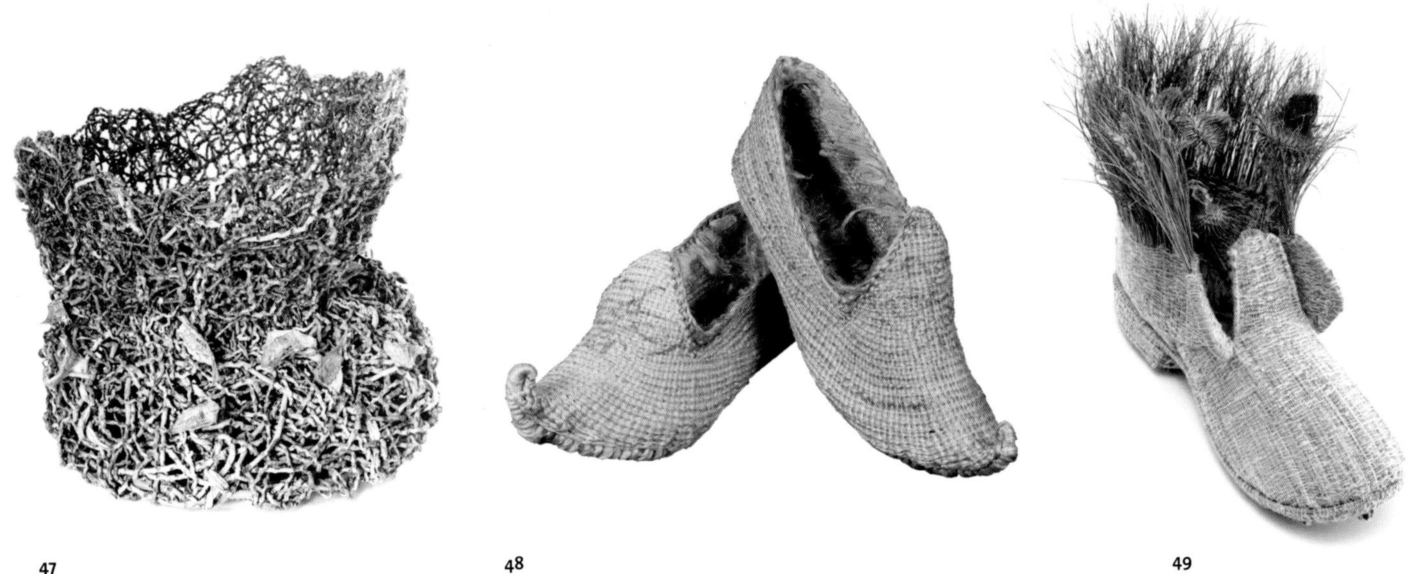

47

48

49

50

53

51. Hilary Buckland, *As We Sow* … (detail), 2011. Cotton seeds from Perth, Australia, are embedded within hand-stitched silk, in a panel 2 m (6½ ft) wide.

52. Louisa Jane Irvine, *Untitled* (detail), 2011. A mixed-media wall hanging made of pieces of calico that were torn and rouched, dipped in wax and manipulated while they hardened, prior to being stitched together. Calico tolerates this process because it is made from unbleached and relatively thick cotton yarns, plain-woven (tabby-woven).

53. Ann Richards, *Mobius Neckpiece*, 2004. A biologist turned weaver, Richards finds that living things provide inspiration, 'particularly in terms of underlying principles of growth and form. I use contrasting materials to create highly textured, elastic textiles, whose characteristics emerge spontaneously from the interplay between fibre, yarn twist and weave structure'. Here linen pleats are complemented by folds applied by hand, relying on the 'memory' of a silk/steel yarn.

54. Ikuko Ida, *Kimono fabrics*, 2012. The tones of these naturally dyed silks are enhanced by the subtle variations characteristic of handwoven cloth. Ida, a kimono-weaver who works in collaboration with Tim Parry-Williams, describes their philosophy as 'beauty in simplicity, functionality, and a balance of both; and outstanding quality of idea, but with an appeal of familiarity'.

55. Alison Morton, *Linen handtowels*, 2006–11. The long, strong fibres of linen make them ideal for all functions that necessitate frequent washing, which renders the linen progressively softer. The fibre length gives it a gleam, suiting it to texture-woven patterns (deflecting light variously to produce light and dark tones).

56. Michiko Uehara, *Rising Steam x 2* and *White and White*, 2005. Using delicate hand-thrown silks, most produced in her own garden in Okinawa, Japan, the artist creates her unique *abezuba ori* or dragonfly-wing weave. The pink *Rising Steam* is dyed with gromwell and cochineal. The dark tones come from gardenia, logwood and getto. *White* employs undyed silk and piña (pineapple fibre).

57

58

57. Yvonne Wakabayashi, *Pina Sea Anemones*, 2009. Pina fibre, manipulated in a shibori-inspired technique of tie/bind, was selected for its transparency and its 'ability to hold three-dimensional form and to appear fragile and ethereal'.

58. Ulla de Larios, *Transparency?— Malefeasance, Hope, The Last Eight, The Next Eight? and Par for the Course*, 2009. Hand-woven and -dyed, these columns – shaped by the differing reactions of silk and wool to identical weaves – explore the theme of transparency.

59 60 61

62 63 64

65 66 67

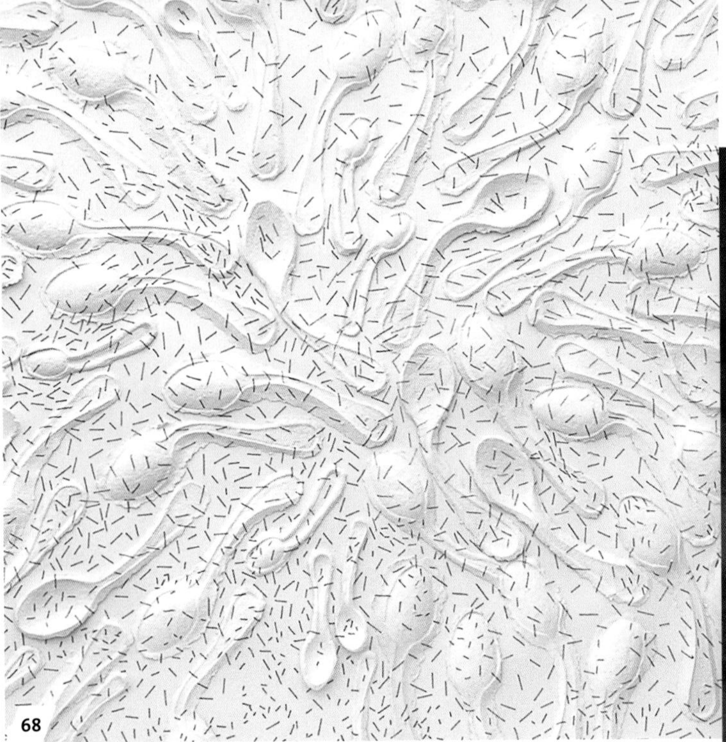
68

69

59–67. Plant materials provide a range of working strands from thick to fine, unprocessed to spun. They can be used in their natural state, as in the Korean basket composed of grasses and palm leaves with cane spokes and upper rim (60). Varying from relatively pliable to rigid when dry are rattan (61), cane (59) and bamboo (63), which are stripped of bark and leaves and split into strips; shown here are examples from the 1960s–80s, all plaited and from Sri Lanka, the Philippines and Japan respectively, the latter lined with silvered paper. More flexible still are strips made from the many widely available palm tree leaves such as date and duom, which the Fulani people of Mali plait with stripped reeds (62). The genus *Pandanus* includes about 600 species that are found from West Africa eastwards to Hawaii, represented here by coiled baskets from Pakistan (65) and Namibia (67, worked over cane). Fibres spun from the bast flax are fine and robust, making them capable of intricate manipulations as typified by needlelace, seen here in a French doily from 1917–18 (64). Finer still, and more fragile, is cotton, exemplified by a mid-20th century American crocheted doily (66). Each of these was once in the collection of Ed and Katherine Rossbach.

68. Paula Martin, *... of their feeding streams*, 2010. A stitched cast-paper panel, 125 cm (49 in.) square. 'This work,' Martin says, 'evokes the flowing swirling patterns of a stream and, at the landscape scale, valleys and hills receiving and dispensing nurturing water.'

69. Nithikul Nimkulrat, *Seeing Paper*, 2005. Paper and paper string knotted over wire make up this 1 m (39 in.) high 'floating' silhouette. This Thai artist's interest lies in the immateriality of physical materials in creative processes, and in 'making things by hand as a means for logically thinking through senses and materials in a slow and thoughtful manner'.

70

71

72

70. James Bassler, *Shop*, 2009. A paper bag woven with yarn from approximately eight paper bags. Bassler believes that making is a gateway to learning in all subjects: 'the best way to do that: get their hands actively working with materials that represented what early peoples were faced with'.

71. Jane Dunnewold, *Etude 25: For Trumpet, Choir and Elinor* (detail), 2011. Hand-dyed pongee silk and fused antique Bible pages (run through a printer to add the musical score) are resist-patterned and silkscreened using sand – 'literally sanded to knock the paper pieces back into the fabric'.

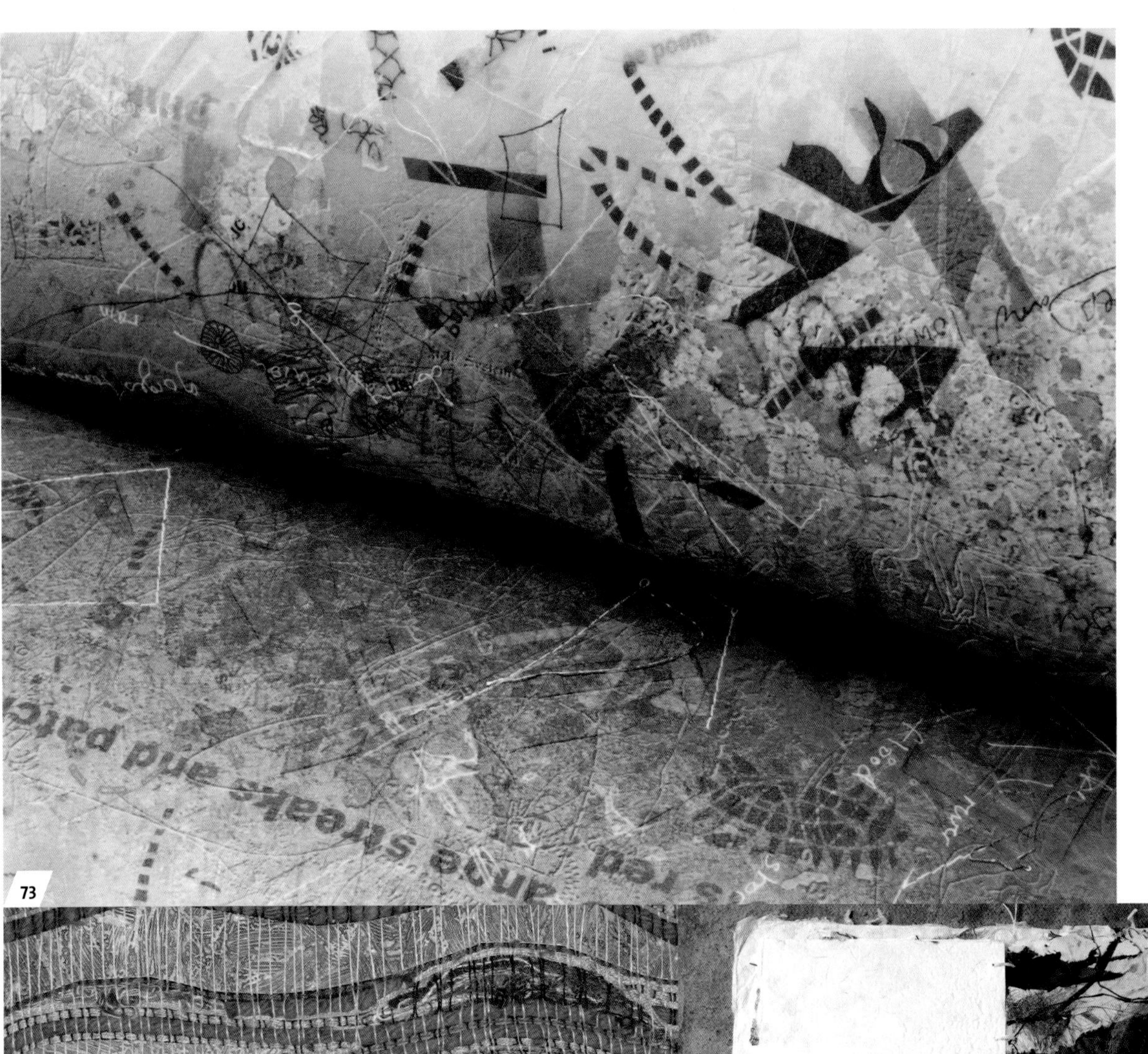

72. Japanese artisan, *Hippari*, before 1976. The back of this man's jacket of net embedded in paper is embellished with the Japanese brush and *baren* (printing pad) technique. Although also directly printed, the sleeve pattern simulates a *katagami* (mulberry paper stencil) pattern that creates white dots by depositing rice paste that acts as a dye resist.

73. Pat Hodson, *Seepage* (detail), 2010. This book is composed of paper tissue, silk and linen thread worked with wax, crayon and Epson Ultrachrome inks by mixing resist, collage, drawing and digital printing.

74. Brigitte Amarger, *Le Livre des Traces*, 2003–7. This book, handmade of paper and incorporating fibres, threads, tarlatan gauze and ink, references 'the first traces left by men ... paintings on the virgin wall like a white page ... scraps of textiles like an old testimony of the second skin which covered their naked bodies'.

75. Boisali Biswas, *Mystique* (detail), 2008. Handwoven panel with inserted strips of painted wallpaper and clumps of varied yarns. 'I have always had a deep-rooted attachment to traditional art forms of India and owe some of my stylization to the captivating traditional patterns and the rich array of colours.'

78

79

80

81

82

83

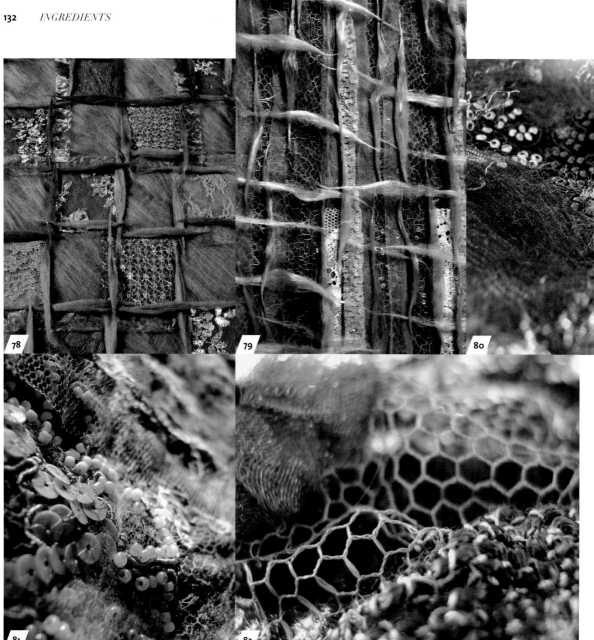

77. Algerian embroiderer, *Tanchifa* or *Bniqa* (detail), 18th–19th centuries. This head-covering, made for a wealthy woman to wear in the hammam, is of hand-spun woven linen. The ground is worked with silk and gold threads, including *lamella* and flat strips, all held to the surface of the cloth by couching with silk from underneath.

76. Bengali weaver, *Royal* jamdani *muslin* (detail), *c.* 1910. *Jamdani* (brocading), adds discontinuous supplementary wefts during weaving. Here they are of silver *lamella* (thin metallic strips) wrapped around very fine hand-spun undyed cotton yarns, which also form the ground. Silver threads also run down the warp. Bengal was long famous for its hand-spinning of the most delicate cotton threads, which came to be known as muslin.

78–82. Claudia Moeller, *Posh Wool Collection* (details), 2011. After receiving acclaim in 2001 for her evening wear collection, in part for her complex fabrics, Moeller created this independent collection. These fabrics blend naturally toned or lightly dyed silk chiffon, georgette and ribbons, superfine merino rovings (pure or blended with silk, alpaca or cashmere), and fragments of vintage laces. 'Fashion becomes another language to capture memories and to express emotions.'

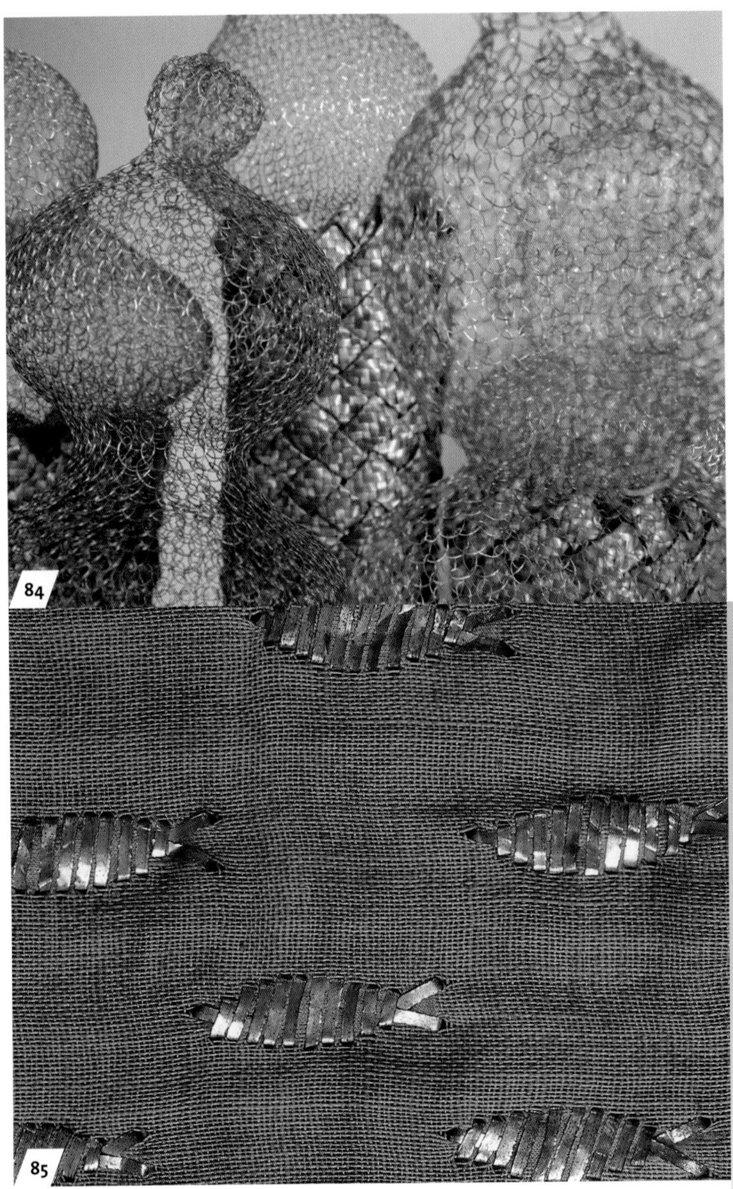

83. Fiona Crestani, *Drift*, 2009. Wire and linen pleat weave, with further development of the surface through the conscious use of rust.

84. Sara Nordling, *Hope*, 2010. Woven baskets with knitted wire forms within. The paradoxical use of materials contradicts any expectation that metal is solid and straw is light.

85. Tunisian artisans, *Dohlja* (detail), late 19th century. Just a handful of the many motifs embroidered in *tai* (flat gold or gold-plated metal) on this cotton wedding tunic from Monastir.

86. Ursula Gerber Senger, *Present Day Nomads*, 2011. Bronze net and copper coloured with heat (oxidation) and partly melted. 'The figures represent cravings of the uprooted wanderers of today where more people move between different beliefs, cultures and countries.'

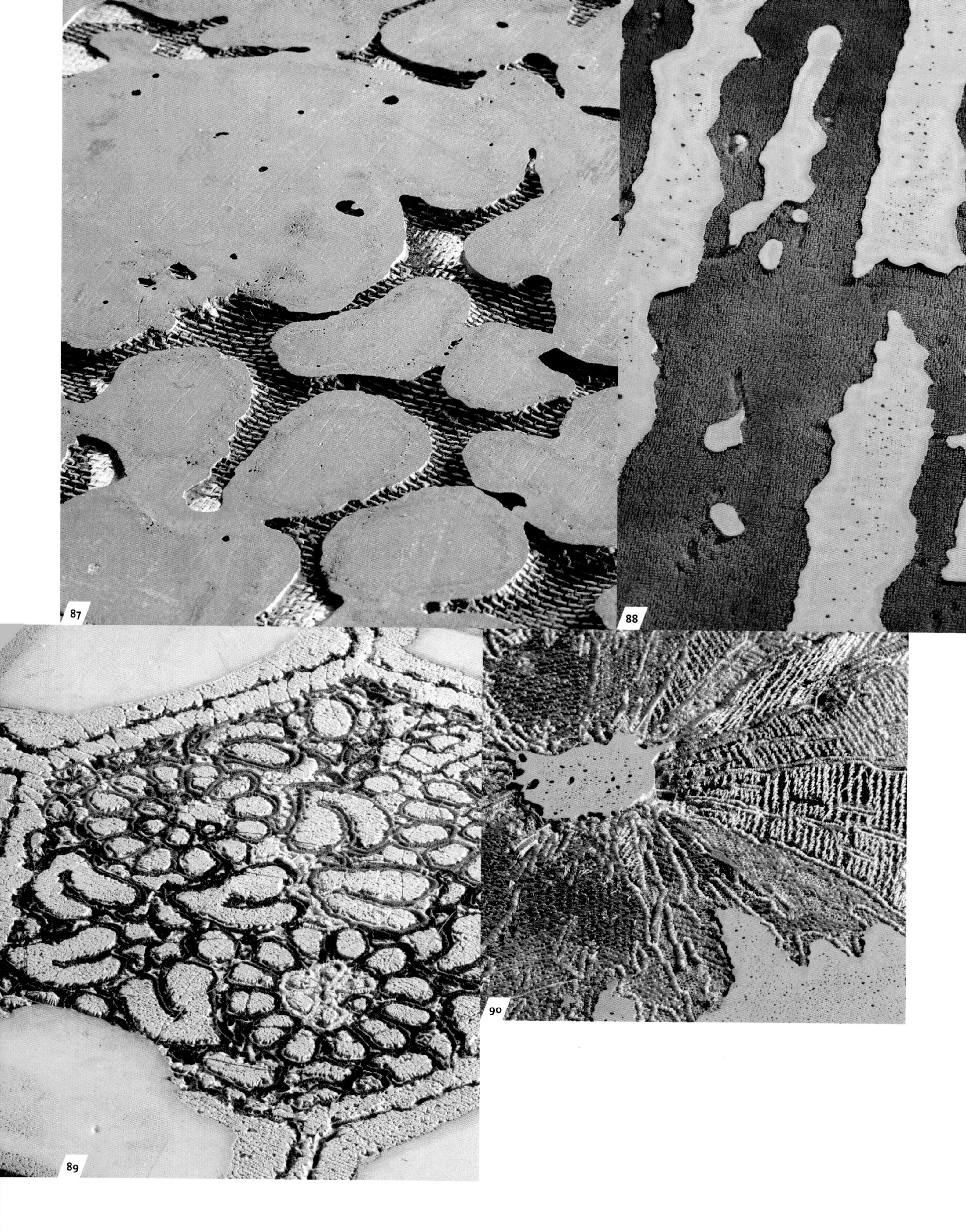
87
88
89
90

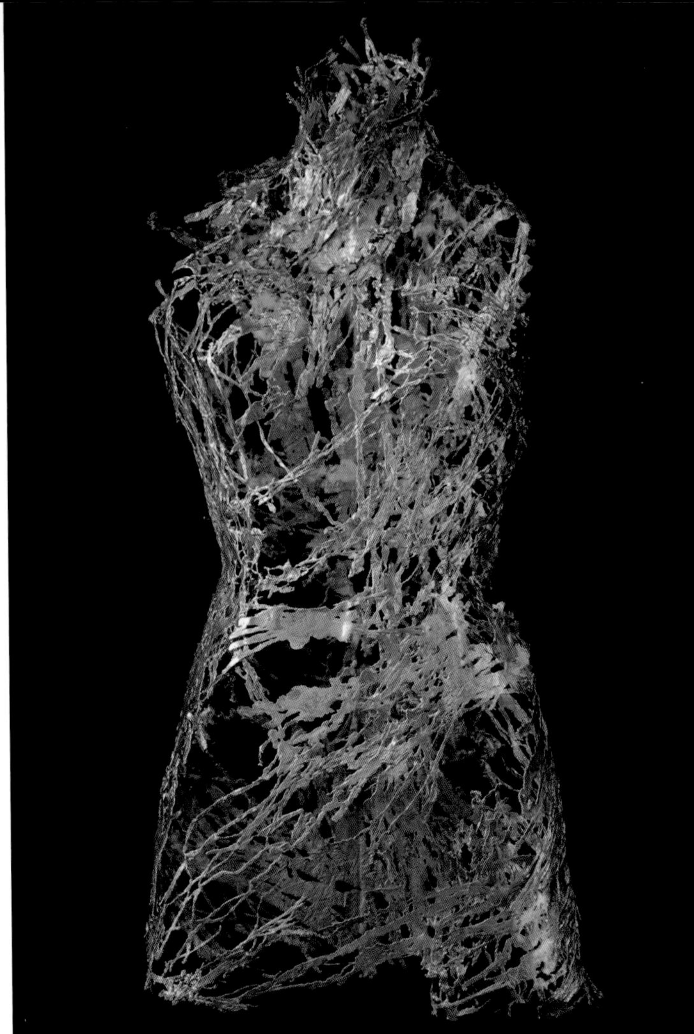

87–90. Trish Belford and Ruth Morrow, *Girli Concrete*, 2009–11. Belford and Morrow direct The Tactility Factory, a research and development unit within the University of Ulster. They integrate fibres into concrete through stitched surfaces (89, 90), combine stitch, gold leafing and linen – the latter selected because it tolerates the alkaline environment of concrete (87) – and incorporate hand-dyed velvet, seen here (88) as installed in a restaurant in Belfast.

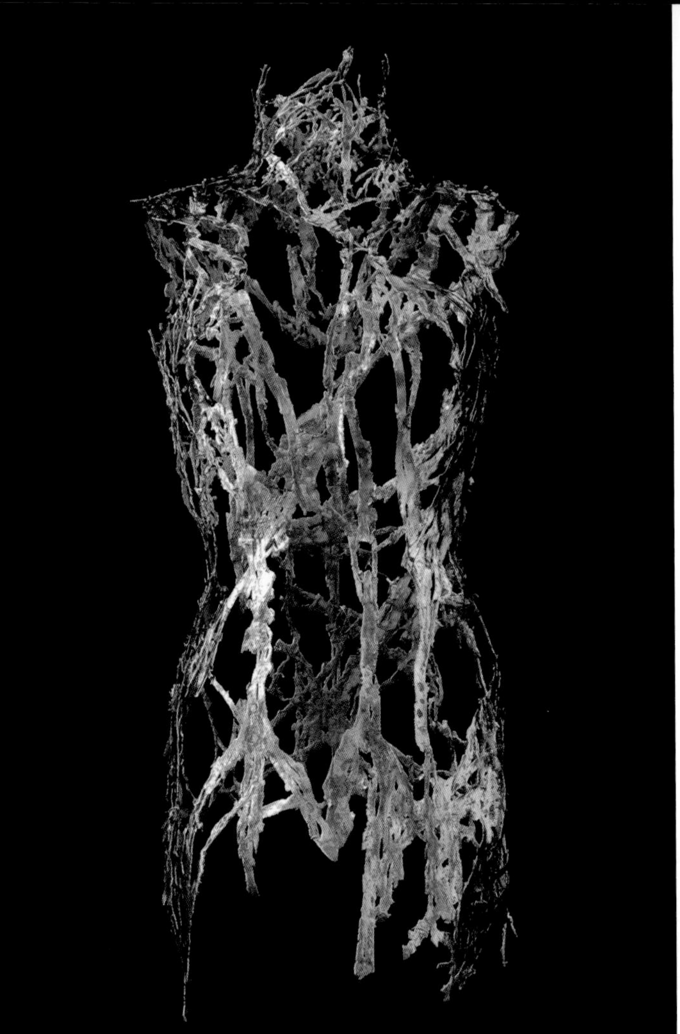

91 and 92. Frances Geesin, *Torso 5 and 6*, 2002. Two from a series of six torsos created by fusing polypropylene to a dress form, cutting through it and then electroplating the themoplastic material by applying conductive paint. This process, which the artist describes as 'drawing with metals and describing form with fibre', makes the forms self-supporting.

93. Lucy Arai, *2004.11 Close Up* (detail), 2004. Sumi ink, indigo pigment and gold gilding on heavy handmade paper are intermingled with *sashiko* stitching (literally, 'little stabs') – a form of decorative reinforcement stitching traditional in Japan.

94. Bengali artisans, *Royal* jamdani *muslin with applied gold decoration*, *c.* 1910. Cotton plain weave with discontinuous supplementary patterning wefts (brocading) in different colours, lavishly couched with gold *lamella*: one of a number given by the king of Nepal to George V when he visited India in 1911.

95. Turkmen artisans, *Chador* (detail), before 1977. This coat or robe worn by Turkmen tribal women was purchased in Herat, Afghanistan. Of black cotton twill, it is densely worked with appliqué, back-stitched zigzag embroidery and cotton cords couched in self-colours or with gold- and copper-wrapped threads.

96. Unknown artisan, *Embroidered textile fragment*, 19th–mid-20th centuries. This 4 cm (10 in.) high panel is worked with gold silk embroidery on brown cotton, with the diagonal rows of motifs done in long running stitches separated by lines of back stitches.

97. Mary Elizabeth Barron, *Seams – Twists & Turns*, 2008. Seams cut from old cloths acquired predominantly from family and friends are coiled with knitting cotton and polyester threads into baskets: 'In their first life they were clothes, utilitarian and practical, and their purpose in this first life helps to inform their second life as art.'

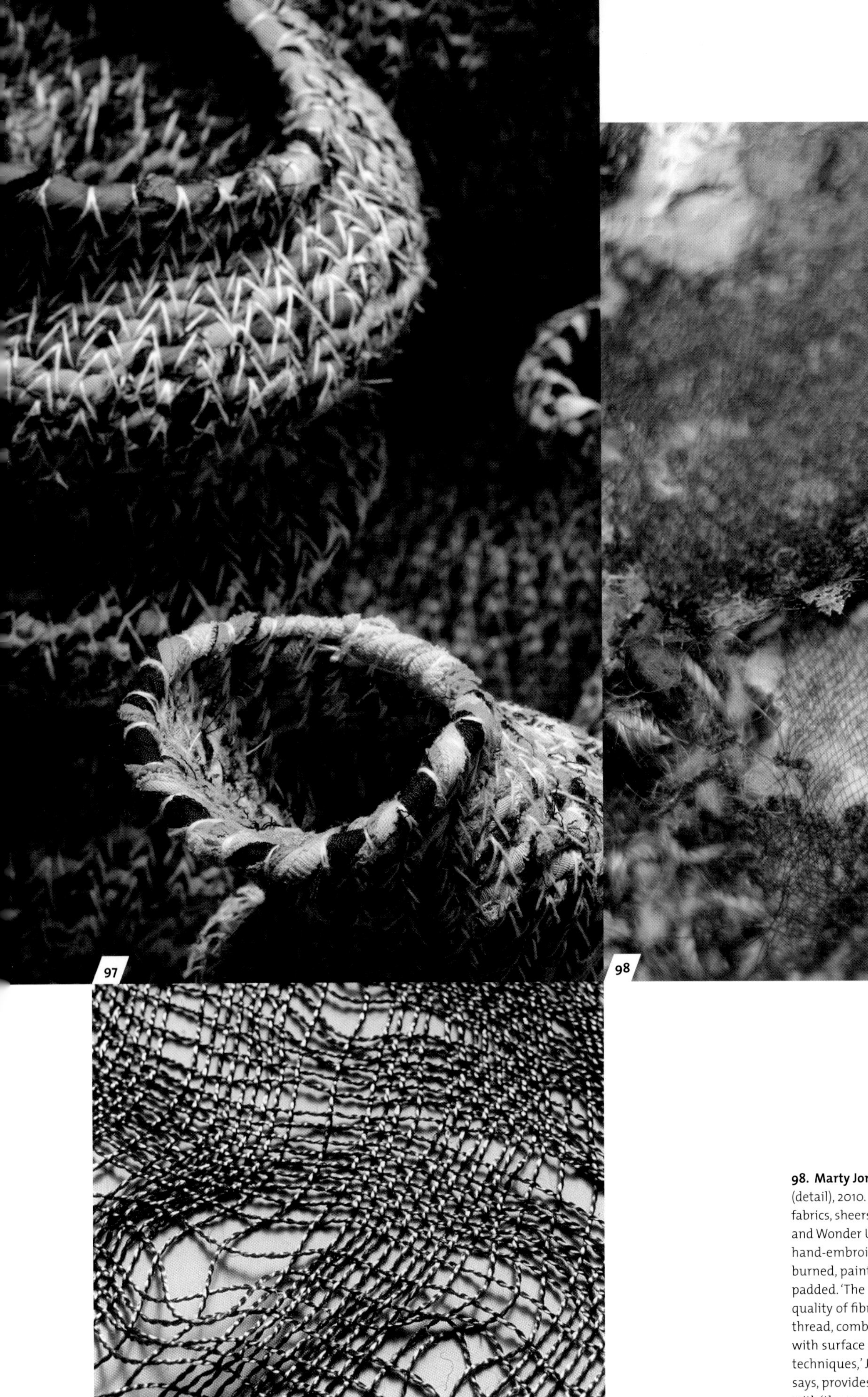

97

98

99

98. Marty Jonas, *Pebbles* (detail), 2010. Cotton fabrics, sheers, netting, and Wonder Under are hand-embroidered, burned, painted and padded. 'The tactile quality of fibre and thread, combined with surface design techniques,' Jonas says, provides her with 'the opportunity to speak visually'.

99. Jun-ichi Arai, *Stainless Steel Weave*, 1980s. In 1955 Arai, a textile engineer, developed a revolutionary means of weaving metal thread, based on traditional methods of weaving gold and silver lamé. He was the first to explore weaving with macrogauze, a yarn that looks like silk but is actually a stainless steel microfilament.

100

102

100 and 101. Carol Anne Grotrian, *Indigo and the Murex* (detail and whole), 2008. A whole cloth quilt of cotton fabric and batting, indigo-dyed and with *sashiko* stitching. Each of the outer panels represents a major source of indigotin, the plant constituent that produces indigo dye. From left (in 101) they are: *Indigofera*, the plant that travelled from India and Africa to the New World; *Isatis* or woad, important for centuries in Europe; the murex shellfish, an ancient source of a purplish-blue dye; *Strobilanthes cusia* from subtropical Asia; and *Polygonum* (also visible in no. 100), favoured in Japan.

102 and 103. English printer, *American blue resist bedcovers* (details), 18th century. With their white areas preserved by a block-printed resist, such indigo resists are associated with the Hudson River Valley, Long Island and western Connecticut. They were made in England especially to suit American tastes.

104. Japanese artisan, *Furoshiki* (detail), 20th century. The shibori bird motif on this wrapping and carrying cloth was stitched and gathered, while the parallel lines and those denoting the bird's wing were folded and then stitched, all prior to immersion in an indigo dye bath.

105. Balinese artisan, *Kain panjang* (detail), late 19th century. Indigo and morinda red create all the colours on this cotton *kain*, an ankle-length batik. Traditionally the entire surface of this cloth is decorated, often with borders at both ends; it is considered more formal than a sarong and is worn by both men and women.

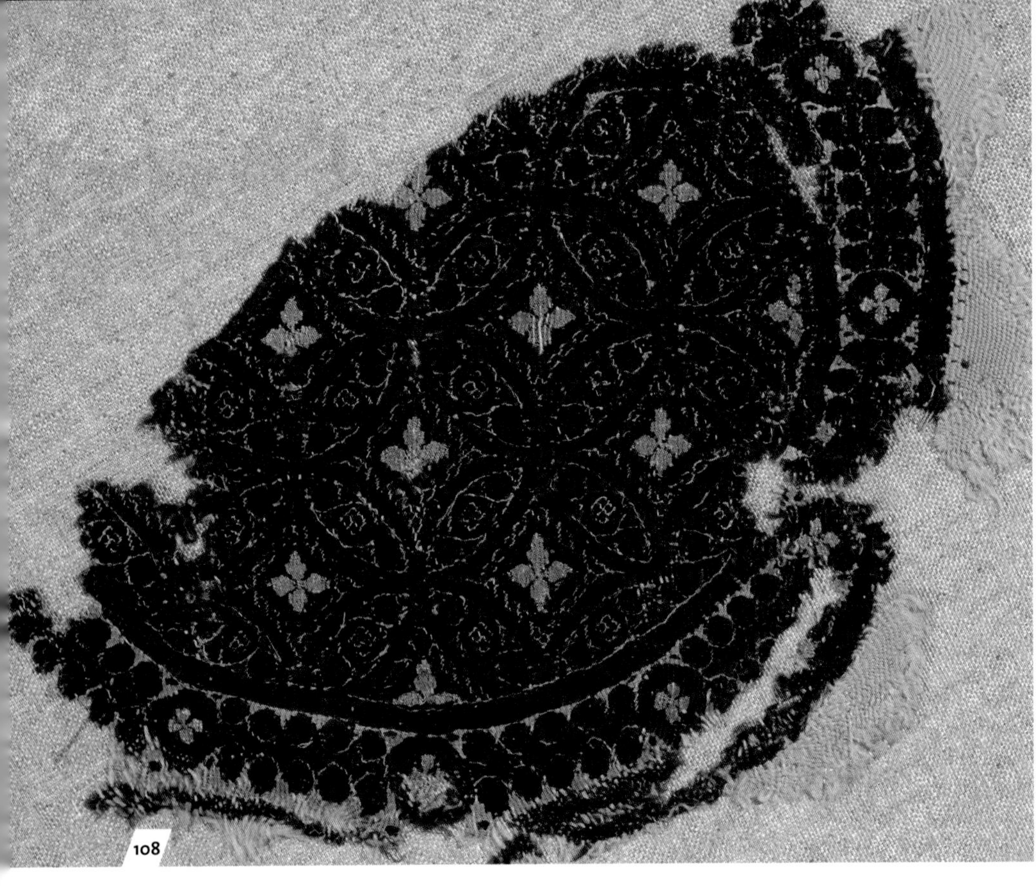

106. Jenny Balfour-Paul, *Just Dyed*, 2011. Drying on the line are the results of dyeing with natural indigo from Bangladesh and El Salvador, and with Mexican cochineal.

107. Barbara Shapiro, *Mali Basket* (detail), 2007. Coiled indigo-dyed raffia on wired paper rush.

108. Egyptian artisans, *Roundel fragment*, 2nd–3rd centuries. This fragment is one of the few textiles from late antiquity in which Tyrian purple, from the murex shellfish, has been identified. It also is interwoven with a decorative metal thread made of pure gold.

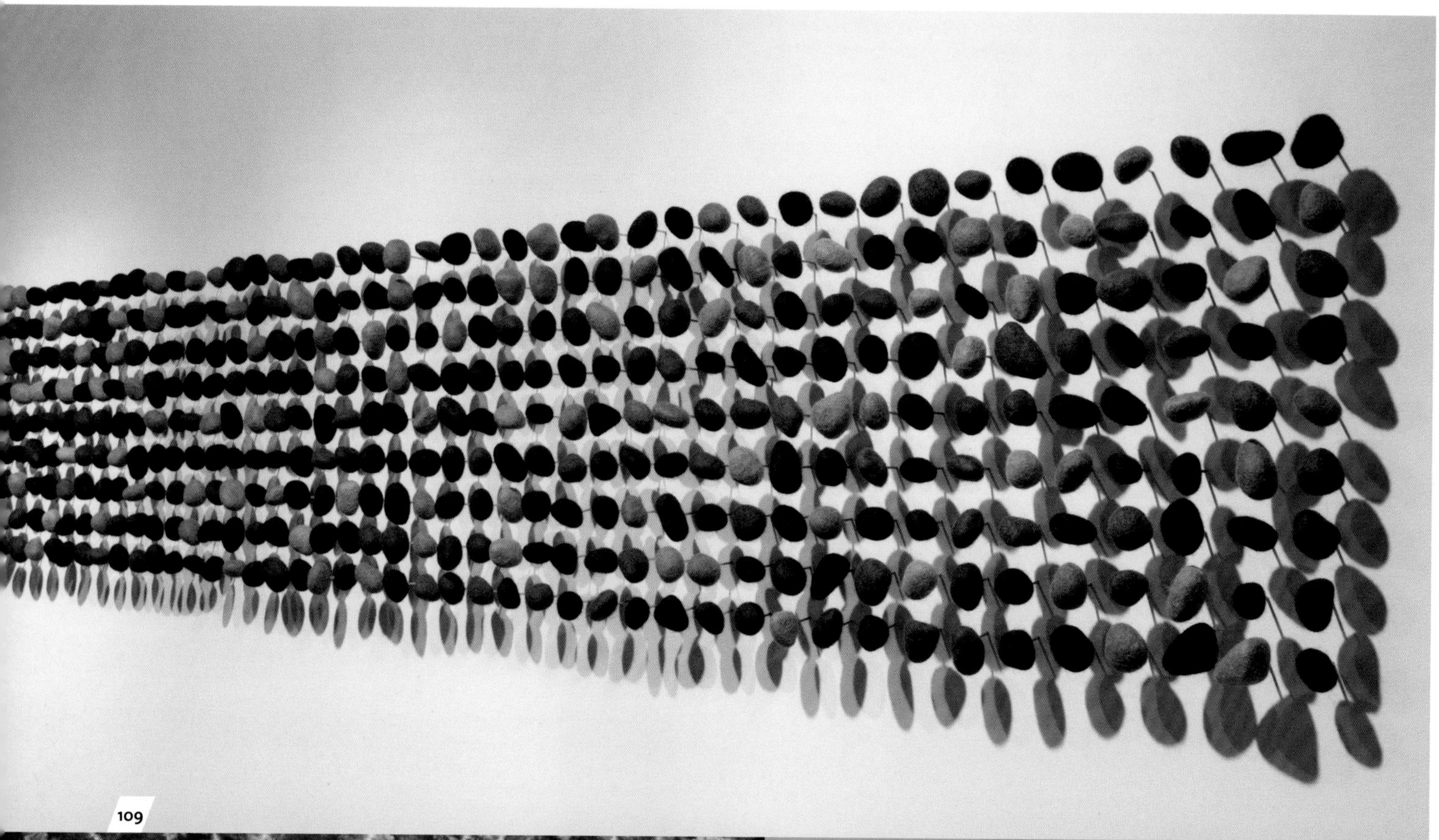

109

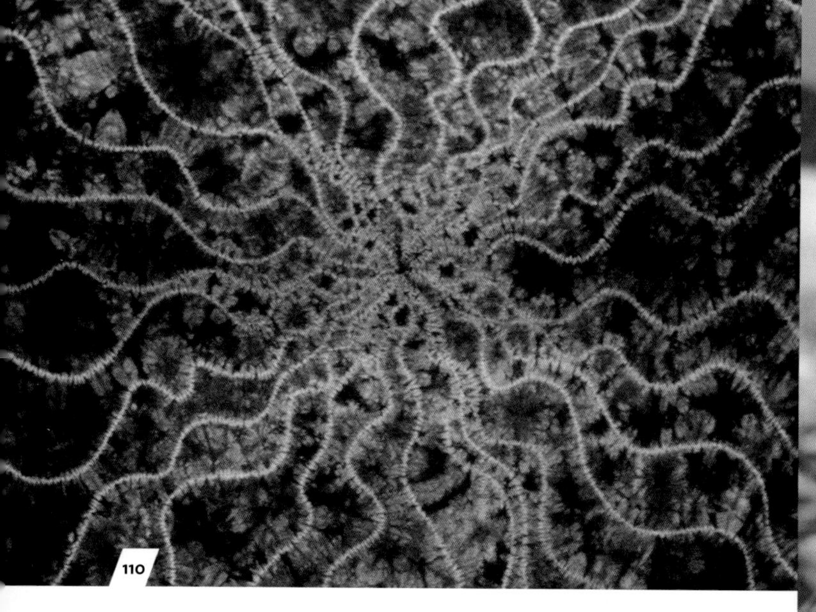

110

111

109. Rowland Ricketts, *Untitled (after te-lta)*, 2009. Stones wrapped with varying shades of indigo-dyed karakul sheep's wool, traditionally used for the finest Persian rugs because of its strength. Wool's affinity for dye is second only to that of silk.

110. Jenny Balfour-Paul and Lucy Goffin, *Spin-off*, 1997. This piece was stitch resist and dyed in an indigo fermentation vat made with natural Nigerian indigo. As the makers explain, 'Stitch resist and indigo are made for each other; indigo dye oxydizes, creating the myriad of shades and marbling effect when the resist stitches are removed.'

111. Rowland Ricketts, *Immanent Blue* (detail), 2009. In the foreground of this installation are dried indigo plants. The piece also incorporates panels of indigo-dyed *kibira*, a loosely woven hempen cloth that is translucent and often used for doorway dividers in Japan.

112. Japanese artisan, *Rectangular textile* (detail), 20th century. Cotton patterned using paste resist with *katagami* (stencils) prior to dyeing with indigo. The lighter blue shades were created through fewer immersions, meaning that these areas were covered with paste once the desired tone had been achieved.

113. Japanese dyer, *Paste-resist swatch*, 1980s. Vivid touches of colour enliven this indigo resist cotton, purchased from Kasuri Dyeworks in Berkeley, California, established by Yoshiko Wada in 1975 as a folk art gallery and shop specializing in Japanese textiles and crafts.

114. Ainu embroiderer, *Chikarkarpe*, late 19th century. A checked cotton Japanese kimono is embellished with applied bands of indigo-dyed cotton and pale indigo chain stitch in traditional geometric motifs intended to ward off evil spirits.

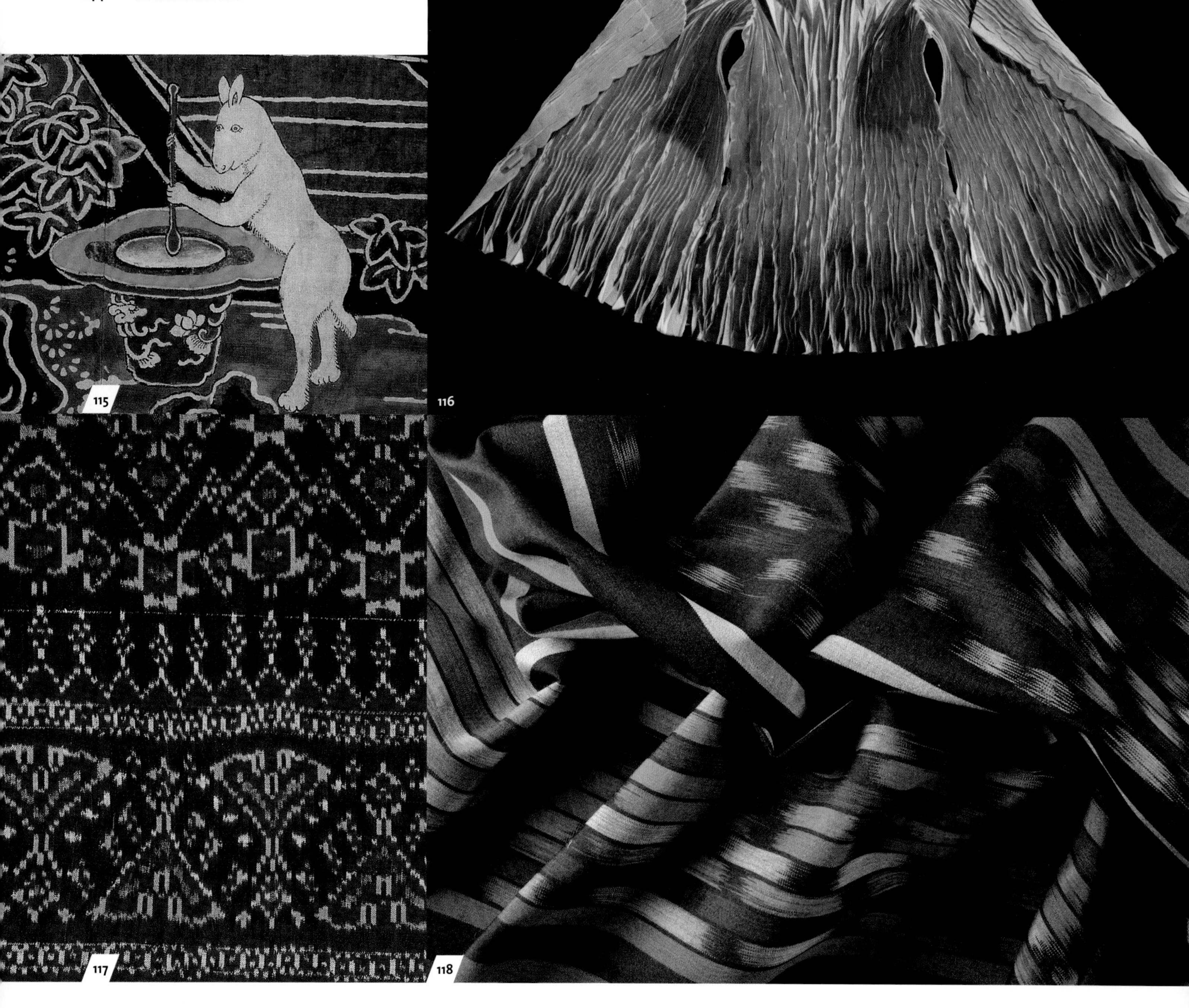

115. Chinese artisan, *Wedding cloth* (detail), before 1939. For this cloth, most probably obtained in Foochow, a hand-painted paste resist has preserved the white areas during indigo dyeing, and the remaining colours were hand-painted. Extracting red dyes requires a hot vat such as the one represented here.

116. Ana Lisa Hedstrom, *VEST*, 2008. Shibori-manipulated polyester felt subtly-shaded through dye sublimation transfer printing. 'I think of fabric as conversation. It can be subtle, bold, witty, seductive. The shibori resist dye techniques create intricate patterns which may be perused as a language or script.'

117. Kampuchean artisans, *Tubular silk ikat* (detail), 1975–79. The overdyeing of morindin (red from the root bark of the morinda tree) and indigo blue to create black is found in many Asian ikats and is associated with auspicious occasions. The touches of green in this Cambodian example are the result of the overdyeing of indigo and a golden-toned dye. This ikat came from Ken Ballard in Chiang Mai, Thailand.

118. Mary Restieaux, *Spun silk ikat*, 1978. Restieaux believes that nothing matches the brilliance of warp-dyed colours and that, 'painstaking though the process might be, it has excitement and an unpredictability as the warp moved when wound onto the loom'. The feathering between the colours, combined with their intensity, has been her preoccupation and enthusiasm ever since.

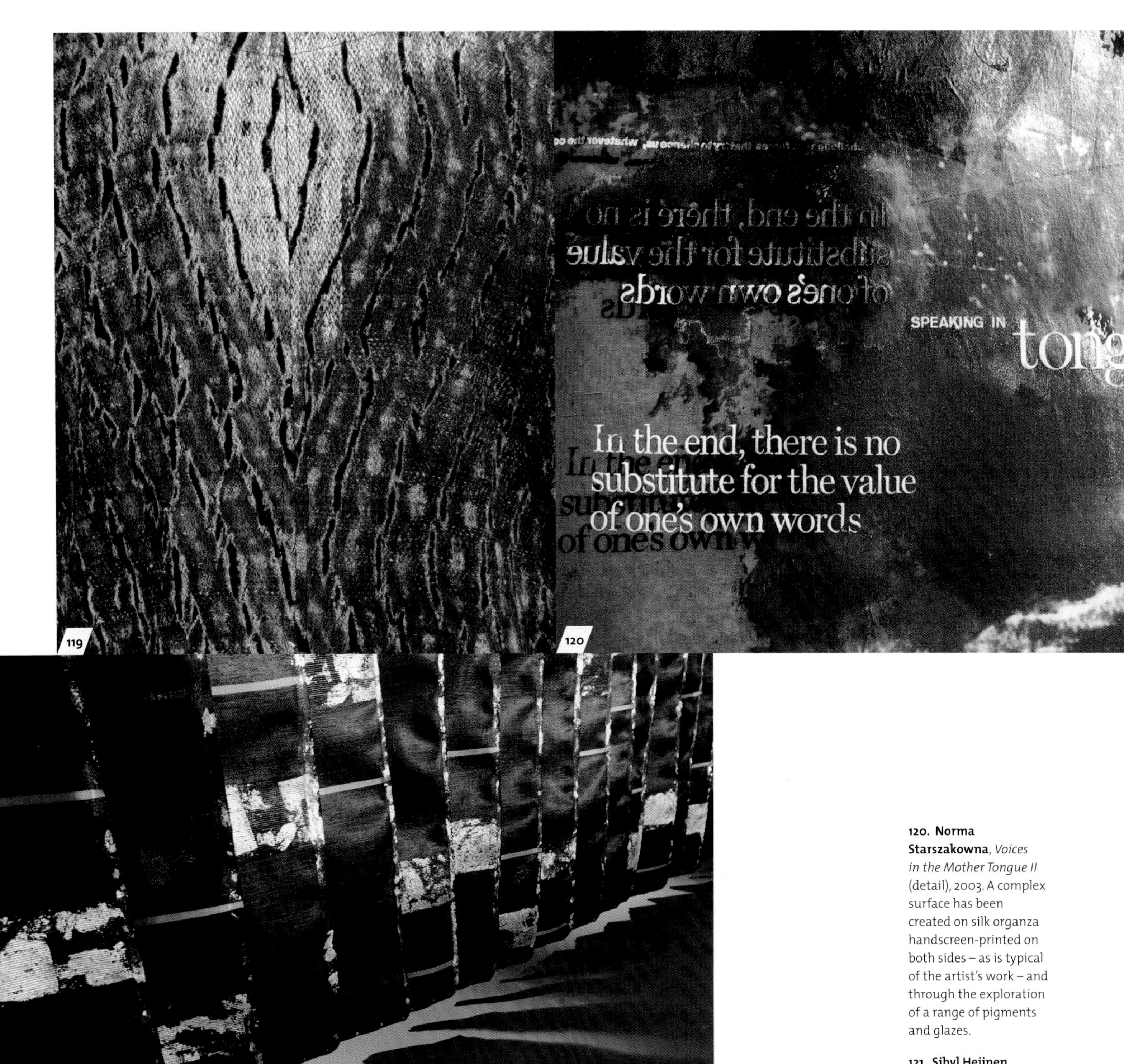
119
120
SPEAKING IN
In the end, there is no
substitute for the value
of one's own words
121

119. Candiss Cole, *Sleeveless tunic/vest* (detail of back), *c.* 2004. Custom-made for Jo Ann Stabb, this garment's cloth was hand-woven with hand-dyed raw silk and multicoloured yarns, after which it was embellished with shibori resist and additional overdyeing.

120. Norma Starszakowna, *Voices in the Mother Tongue II* (detail), 2003. A complex surface has been created on silk organza handscreen-printed on both sides – as is typical of the artist's work – and through the exploration of a range of pigments and glazes.

121. Sibyl Heijnen, *Magic Wall Room Divider* (detail), 2008. Specially designed for the meeting room at Royal TenCate's headquarters, this work is composed of woven synthetics gilded with aluminium. It is based on a louvered system that allows the vertical panels to swivel and the entire structure to be folded away.

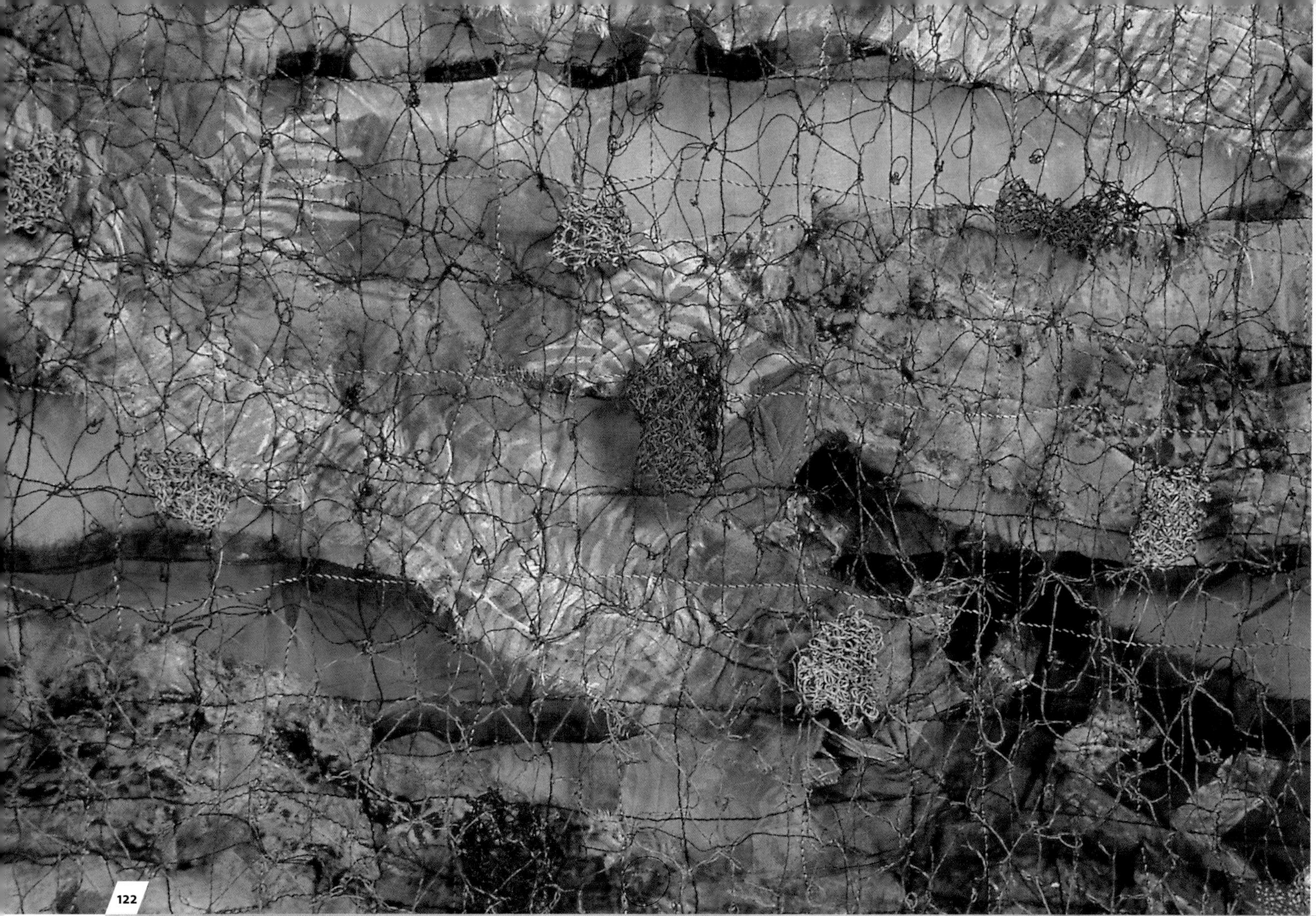

122

123

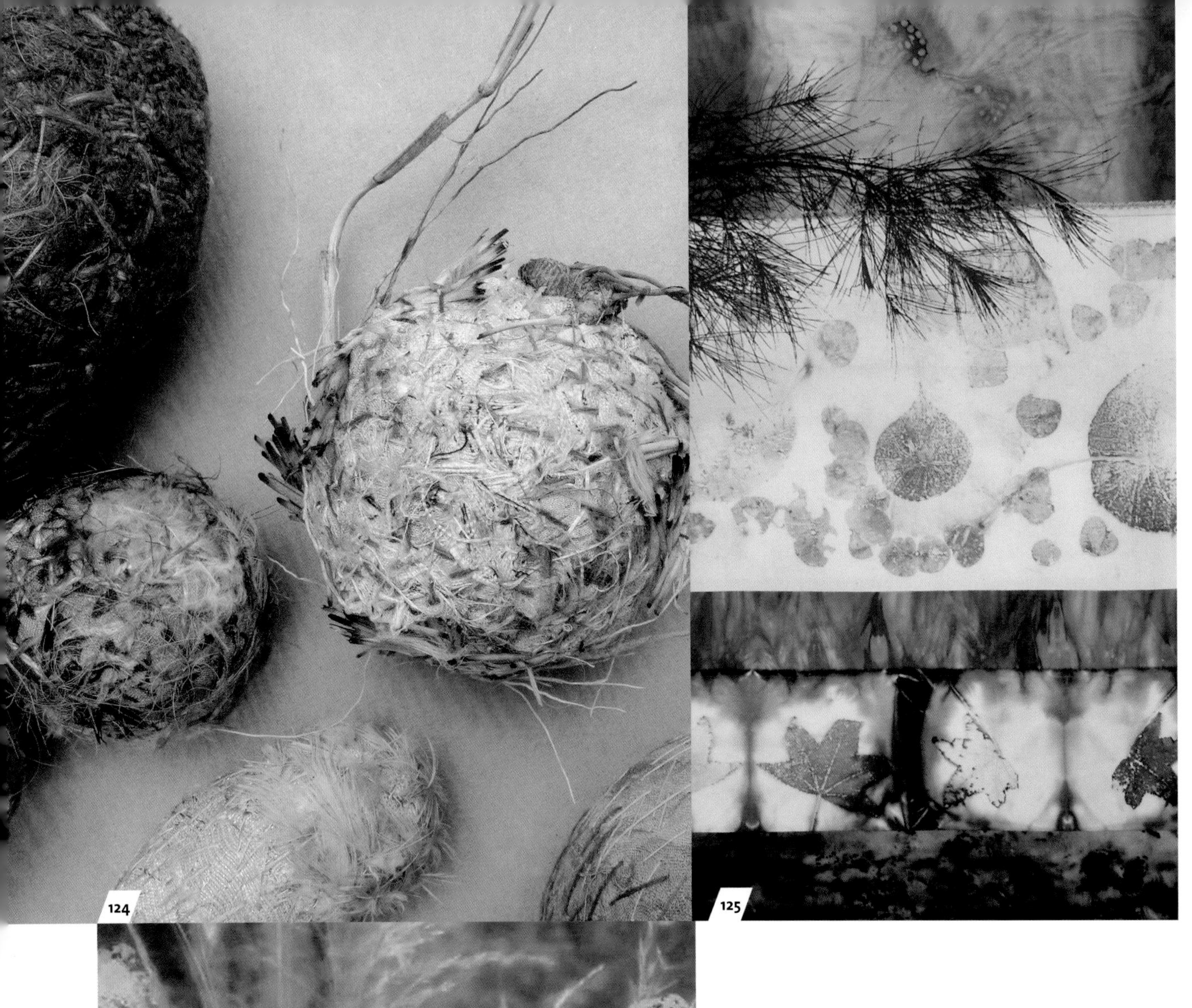

126

122. Susan Taber Avila, *Aqueous Zone* (detail), 2002. This close view of a large panel highlights the subtle variation of tones in the hand-dyed silk organza remnants, which are encased in a machine-stitched web.

123. Kath Wilkinson, *Earthly Delights*, 2007. In this panel, 60 cm (24 in.) high, silk threads coloured and stained with reduced eucalyptus tea, tree and wattle dyes, ochres and soil were machine- and hand-embroidered as well as appliquéd.

124. Ilka White, *Desert Life (Under, Inside, All Around ...)* (detail), 2006. Hand-stitched *Spinifex* budgerigar and other feathers, silk, camel hair and cloth dyed over a fire with the leaves of eucalyptus evoke the artist's response to Australia's Newhaven Reserve: 'Life is condensed in the heat of the Tanami but it's far from barren. Subtle colour and rhythm accompany a powerful stillness here, which is felt as much as seen.'

125. Anne Leon, *Autumn Beach Dreaming*, 2011. The need to implement ecologically sustainable practices has impelled the artist to explore plant dyeing techniques and water-based screen printing, resulting in nuances of mark-making with leaf imprints, each unpredictable and individual.

126. Marie-Therese Wisniowski, *Warrawee – Travellers' Meeting Place* (detail), 2011. The artist's signature MultiSperse Dye Sublimation technique employs disperse dyes on satin, hand-printing multiple resists and overprinting with numerous plants native to Australia. 'Warrawee' indicates a favourite resting place for indigenous peoples to meet when on a 'walkabout'.

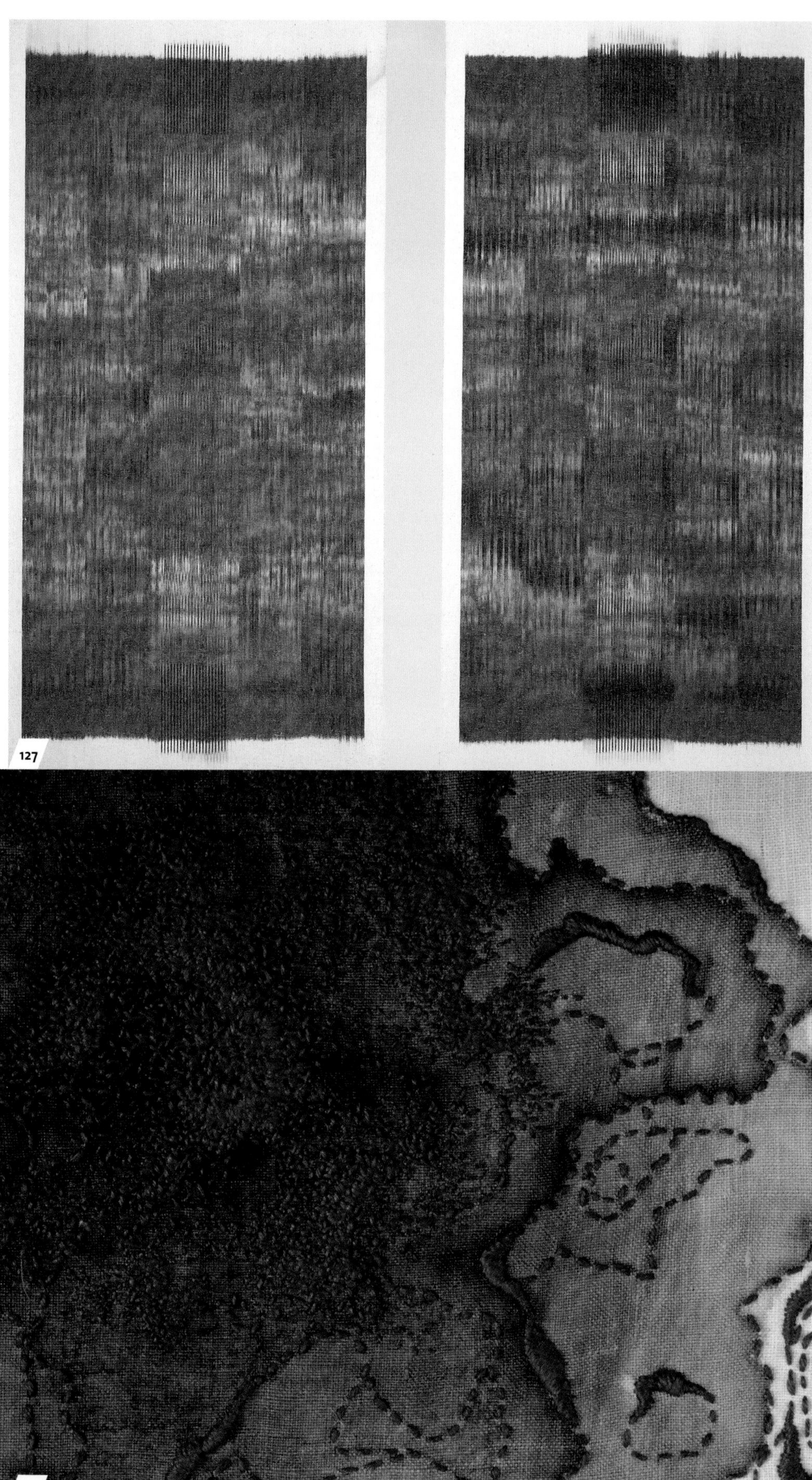

127

128

129

127. Jun Tomita, *Kasuri No. 38-1 Red and White, 1986*. Linen warp and silk weft *kasuri* (ikat). The warp was hand-painted with synthetic dyes.

128. Erin Endicott, *Healing Sutras* (detail), 2011. Hand embroidery on antique fabric stained with walnut ink. The stitched marks symbolize veins, roots, cellular structures or seeds: 'One stitch at a time, hour after hour ... this is where the healing lies.'

129. Jun Tomita, *P. Kasuri No. 206 Red and White*, 2008. At just over 2 m ($6^{1}/_{2}$ ft) high, this silk, whose warp is hand-painted with synthetic dyes, expresses the artist's intention 'to create a space and a time in which the observer can experience solitude – something similar to what I feel when I am before nature, where I can feel a time and space filled with peace'.

130. West African artisan, *Stamped strip cloth* (detail), *c.* 1990. The dyed ground of this handwoven coarse cotton strip cloth was derived from *Cola nitida* (the kola nut), with the pattern itself impressed with a dye derived from a compost of leaves and iron-bearing river mud. The stamp was carved from raffia palm.

132

131

133

131. Jakob Schlaepfer, *Malevich*, 2011. This ultra-light polyester fabric is coated with aluminium and inkjet printed. It is intended for interiors.

132. Jakob Schlaepfer, *Embroidery samples*, 2010–11. Various embroideries for haute-couture purposes, double-layered, including several filled with feathers in different sizes and colours.

133. Izabela Wyrwa, *White-Black*, 2005. Wire, metal mesh and thread are seemingly animated in this work, which measures 300 × 250 × 200 cm (118 × 98 × 79 in.).

134. Izabela Wyrwa, *Something in the Air*, 2010. Wire, metal mesh and plastic are secured together in a structure 3 m (118 in.) high. They not only appear weightless, but also defy traditional expectations regarding textile materials and techniques. This work was awarded a silver medal at the 13th International Triennial of Tapestry at the Central Museum of Textiles in Łódź.

135. Daniela Bauer, *Orbit*, 2010. This hand-sewn hat is the artist's visualization of the cyclic, even-tempered movement of nature, as exemplified by a planet's orbit. From a base of sinamay, a straw-like fibre made from the *Musa textilis* or abaca plant of the Philippines, swirls of crinoline rise around an orange ostrich-feather spine.

134

135

136. Fiona Crestani, *Untitled*, 2010. Exploiting a gauze weave, the artist has utilized fishing line and silk to create a light and fluid form.

137. Jackie Abrams, *Wisdom* (detail), 2011. Coiled with pearl cotton thread is a foundation of recycled dry cleaning bags, videotapes and silver ribbon. 'Sitting in my studio, with materials in hand, is always a source of fulfilment, meditation, frustration and satisfaction … . Journeys, especially in Africa, have had a profound influence … . I am learning to simplify things, to state what is important.'

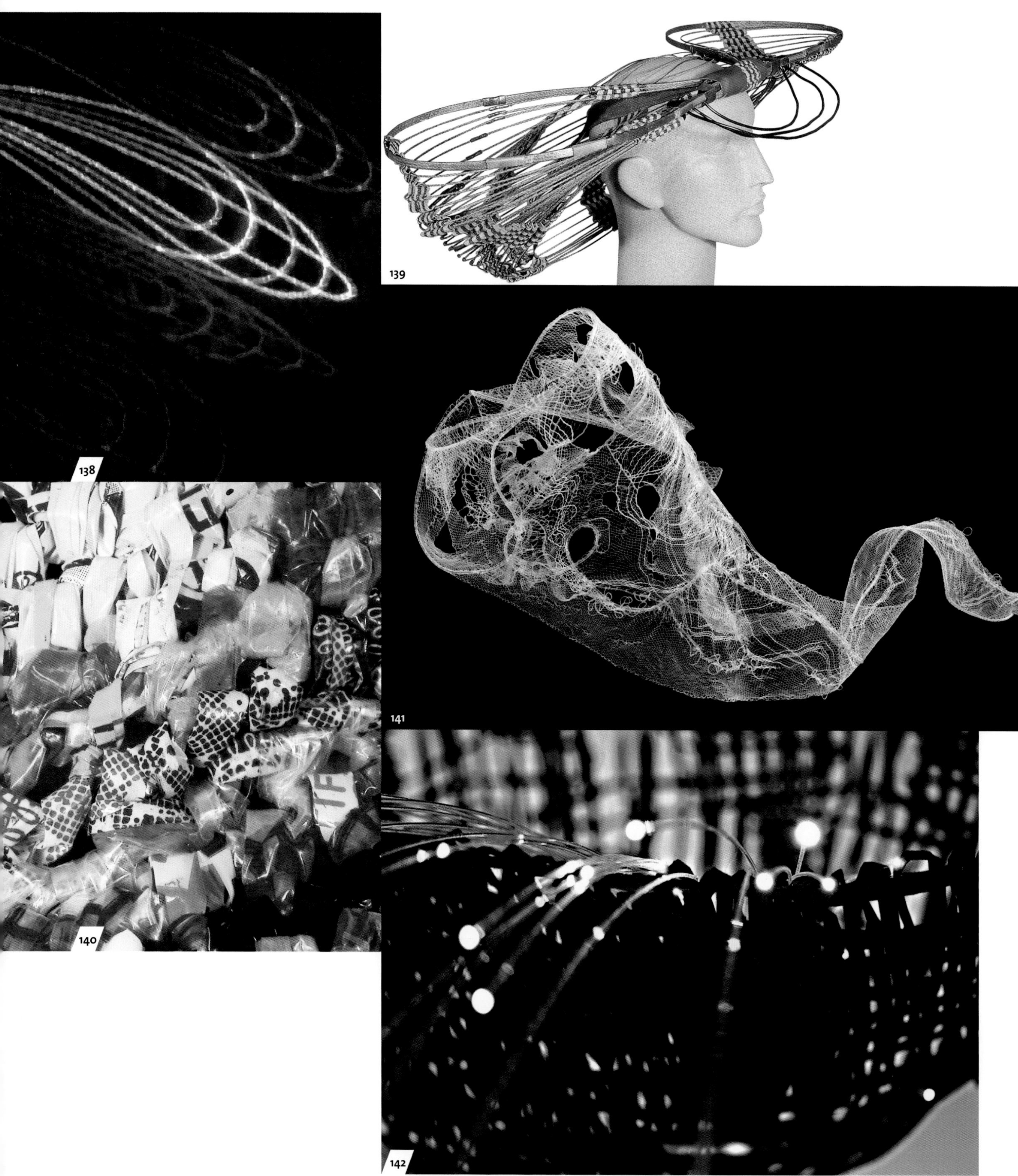
138
139
140
141
142

143

138. Forster Rohner and Diffus Design, *Solar Handbag* (detail of interior showing solar-powered light), 2011. The design team focused on textiles, computer-generated systems and sensor technology in the field of solar energy, soft circuits and low-energy light. This light, incorporated into the bag's lining, is a unique solution to the problem of finding contents buried within a handbag.

139. Debra Rapoport, *Hoop Hat I*, 1985. A skirt hoop – made of brown and white thread-covered wire and flat metal strips threaded through and anchored to brown and white cotton bands with silver-toned metal studs – has been folded, manipulated and bound with ribbons to form a hat with two flanges either side of the head. The original waistband fabric and flat metal strip have been painted with gold and rose paint.

140. American maker, *Circular mat* (detail), 1960s–1980s. Strips of plastic bags have been manipulated by single and double crochet into concentric bands emerging from a central point. Donated to the UC Davis Design Collection by Ed and Katherine Rossbach, this may have been made by them or one of their students.

141. Gabriele Grohmann, *Rauch*, 1996. Part of the 'Zigarre' collection from CMPdesign, Berlin, and intended to be either worn or placed in a room, this work is composed of fishing line of various colours and diameters, and combines bobbin lace techniques with new structures, all intended to translate the appearance of cigar smoke into lace.

142. Marieta Toneva, *Light Movement* (detail), 2010. Interwoven optical fibres and paper twine create a large illuminated form, 240 cm (94½ in.) wide. 'The character of the specific material is also very important to me. It speaks its own language even though it is part of a work of art that expresses an idea.'

143. Rozanne Hawksley, *White Mirror* (detail), 2004. Giving new life to discarded objects is a lynchpin of the artist's approach to materials. Here cherished polished bones are stitched with pearls, sequins, feathers and a variety of fabrics, threads and cords to give new life to a mirror, itself alluding to the proposition in *Orphée*, Jean Cocteau's surrealistic film of 1950, that life comes and goes through a mirror.

144. Pat Moloney, *London Met Project* (detail), 2007–8. Hand-manipulated weave using a knotted rug technique incorporating rubber, plastics, reflective materials and optical fibres with a colour-changing sequence. 'I recognized that by being alert to the unexpected and the unforeseen, opportunities can be created for the interchange of ideas between the hand, the mind, and the digital aesthetic.'

145. Jennifer Shellard, *Project 1*, 2007–10. Investigations into light-responsive and light-reactive materials resulted in this textile handwoven in silk and stainless steel with elements of fluorescent material, seen here under UV light.

146. Carole Waller, *Colonnade*, 2005. Created for the Chelsea Flower Show in London, paintings in dye on a cloth of mixed silk and viscose are laminated between glass. The combination of protein and cellulosic fibres allows use of the devoré process (which 'devours' selected areas of viscose only) and renders the imagery ambiguous, with the sheer and opaque areas of cloth moderating the intensity of the brushed-on dyes.

147. Sibyl Heijnen, *Water (Helen Keller)* (detail), 1999. Transparent plastic rolled, cut to about 20 cm (7 7/8 in.), tied up together and standing on Plexiglass. The entire piece is 1 m (39 in.) square. In its invitation to feel and see the plastic as water, it plays both to 'knowing fingers' and to haptic sensibilities, asking the eyes to 'touch'.

1

III.

STRUCTURE

2

III.

STRUCTURE

Textiles, even lengths of yardage, are three-dimensional objects. The third dimension, depth, results from the fact that all textiles are created through the forming of connections, whether hair-scale to hair-scale in felting, looping in knitting, or interworking in weaving. The fibres' character and dimensionality, too, are dependent on connections made on the material's surface or on a cellular level. The flexibility and strand diameter of the material employed, together with its density of placement, determine both the rigidity and the thickness of the final product. As a result, the selection of ingredients and method of making are interdependent. This chapter highlights that interplay, while focusing on the nature and range of connections employed when creating textiles.

Aside from felting, knitting and weaving, there are many other ways to form a textile, methods that are all contained under the umbrella terms 'construction' and 'structure'. Both allude to an 'architecture' of cloth, itself an apt description since many ancient forms of dwellings – such as tents, wooden huts and wattle-and-daub houses – employ either textiles or textile-making techniques. If one bears in mind such freestanding examples of textiles and textile structures, it becomes easy to see that, in the absence of a rigid, permanent support, some form of anchoring is required. However fluid the end result, the same is true when one makes any type of textile. Anchoring can be provided in many ways. Felt requires a firm resting place during compression. All other textile structures need at least one component with sufficient rigidity, a characteristic that might be present only temporarily when tension is applied by hand or machine, or could be permanent owing to the nature of the material itself. The techniques that do not require the aid of a loom make this distinction most clearly, and that is where we begin.

Non-Tensioned Techniques

Basketmaking provides the primary examples of non-tensioned techniques, incorporating, as it does, at least one material firm enough to manipulate in a free state. The interlocking of a basket's elements can thus be done by hand. The

1. Tim Parry-Williams, *Large Opera Wrap (Olive Green Check)*, 2010. Handwoven raw silk and natural dyes. Likening a scarf to a good piece of jewellery, Parry-Williams nevertheless aims for his subtle surfaces and textures 'not to stand out too much and to lend quality to the whole appearance of the wearer'.

2. Mo Kelman, *Darkside*, 2009. Shibori-patterned elastic fabrics are stretched and tethered between a lashed bamboo structure and the wall. The dyeing method is *mokume* (meaning 'woodgrain'), achieved by tightly gathering multiple rows of stitching, which in the heat of the dyebath sets a 'memory' of this compressed form. 'My sculptures are tensile structures, seeking a point of balance that is tentative, a state of tension that is temporary.'

earliest surviving baskets are Egyptian and date from 10,000 to 12,000 years ago, but evidence of their manufacture predates that by another 8,000 years. No machine has replaced the practice of making baskets by hand. This fact contributed to their reassessment in the 1960s and 1970s, led to a large degree by Ed Rossbach, then professor of design at the University of California, Berkeley. His 1973 book *Baskets as Textile Arts* remains the seminal publication on 'the aesthetic quality of baskets as it relates to process and material and human impulses'.[1] Rossbach, a weaver, was by then already known for his combination of unconventional materials with traditional basketry techniques – wickerwork and twining, plaiting, and coiling **[6,188]**. His work, which eventually encompassed nearly every textile-making process, was inspired by his observation of baskets preserved by anthropological surveys or still being made around the world. Rossbach became an avid collector, remarking some dozen years later: 'Our house is full of baskets. They're stored everywhere in the place. They're in the clothes closets, kitchen cupboards, cedar chests, and, mostly, in cardboard cartons. I am obsessed with them; they are oppressive, and yet my wife [Katherine Westphal] and I keep buying more, and I keep making more. They seldom depart the premises once they get inside, and if they do, for an exhibition, they almost always return to find their places have been taken by other baskets. But they must be taken in. They are like the sentimental characters in a poem by Robert Frost.'[2]

Some of the hundreds of baskets Rossbach and Westphal collected are illustrated here **[3, 8, 53–55, 62–69, 71–75]**, including two – a bird's nest and a French 'nest' basket **[4, 5]** – that demonstrate his delight in their essence: 'Who cannot respond to the joy of transforming some familiar vegetal material into a utilitarian container requiring no tools, no machines, only skillful manipulation ... ? So direct, so spontaneous, so straightforward ... .'[3]

The closest cousins to the nest basket are twined and wickerwork examples, which differ only in that the horizontal (weft) 'entangling' is arranged as a controlled enclosing of a vertical element, called a 'stake'. In basic twining, a twist of two wefts occurs either side of each stake **[75]**. In wickerwork, the wefts run over and then under, alternately working behind and in front of the stakes as each horizontal pass is made **[3]**. Thus enclosed, stakes are held into place. However, for all the simplicity of the concept, the results can vary considerably depending on the density of placement and the width of the materials used. In wickerwork the weft's scale can be very broad; over widely spaced stakes the result is a fairly smooth surface **[62]**. Narrow wefts create a ridged surface that follows the profile of the vertical stakes within the structure. The insertion of splints curving over the surface adds contrapuntal movement. In twining, varying the rise of wefts to the surface, by spanning two, three or more stakes as each row progresses, produces textural patterns composed of straight diagonals ('twills') or, when reversed back and forth, zigzags and similar geometric designs. Changes in the weft colour make these patterns more apparent, and greater elaborations in texture and design are possible by twining with three rather than two wefts **[71, 74, 83, 164, 166]**. By adding or removing stakes, changes in form can be created in wickerwork and twined objects from very small to very large. Twining is often incorporated into wickerwork at points where such changes occur, to secure the addition or removal of stages.

3. American basketmaker, *Fishing Creel* (detail), before 1988. This basket is wickerwork of bamboo and wood, with a sliding carved wooden bolt and reed loop closure.

The passage of wefts – twisted or over–under – is identical in the process of weaving, so much so that some basketmakers refer to the stakes as 'warps'. Yet both the ability to leave sizeable open stretches and to sculpt as the making progresses is unique to the materials associated with twining and wickerwork, such as split bamboo, rattan cane, split willow rods, and other resilient yet sturdy grasses and branches. The over–under technique in wickerwork is also characteristic of plaited basketry, which, in its simplest form, employs two elements intersecting at right angles **[63–68]**. That said, as Rossbach explains, there 'is no distinction between the elements, as warp and weft, or as foundation and binder. All elements perform the same function; all are equally active.' These elements are typically flat, ribbon-like, flexible and cohesive. So although two-element plaiting resembles wickerwork interweaving, both plaiting elements 'must interact in the structure; none can remain static and inflexible while others move around it' **[170]**.[4] This eliminates most materials suitable for the stakes that give such stability to all wickerwork and much twining, which is why plaiting is associated especially with tropical climates, where there is a plentiful supply of rattan skins, as well as the flat, flexible leaves of many other palms and of pandanus plants. It also means that plaiting forms a lighter, more malleable and seemingly more fragile basket than stake-based basketry techniques, yet in fact it is remarkably resilient.

To modern basketmakers, plaiting suggested the innovative introduction of other non-load bearing materials such as folded newspaper, cardboard, polyethethylene film tubing and bags, polystyrene (Styrofoam), and other forms of plastic and paper strips **[60]**. (Leather strips had long been plaited and are widely used in shoe, belt and bag design.) Twining, with its need for a flexible weft, invites the use of a similar range of non-traditional materials, and can also easily incorporate strands with a round profile, such as cable and fine-gauge wires **[55]**, which have also found use as wickerwork wefts, although to a lesser extent. While wickerwork uses few variations on the over-one, under-one technique, and twining accommodates many variations in the passage of the weft, in both cases the weft traverses in an essentially horizontal direction – even if that means working a basket on its side, as in the familiar 'hooped' willow baskets that, once

4 and 5. Ed Rossbach Collection. This bird's nest (4), constructed from grass, twigs, paper, mosses and string, illustrates the natural prototype for baskets, which are epitomized by a French nest basket of twigs, branches, wire and nails (5), made before 1988.

finished, show stakes in graceful curves radiating out horizontally from beneath either base of the handle. Plaiting, in contrast, can deviate from this right-angled plan through the introduction of more elements – as many as six, which form a complex arrangement based on hexagonals.

The similarities between the different basketmaking techniques have long inspired makers to combine them in one piece, or cross-fertilization among the styles. Thus the basketmaker's ingenuity can test the observer's skills. Nevertheless, among the three techniques, the typical flatness of plaiting materials makes plaiting the easiest to 'read'. Examination of two-element plaiting reveals the plain, twill and zigzagged interlacings identical to those used by a weaver, but (since the weaver's threads are significantly finer) they are far less evident to the naked eye.

The interest in materials and techniques that informed the first wave of basketry's revival in the 1960s and 1970s was driven by weavers investigating basketry; not surprisingly, it was paralleled in other fibre arts. This formalist approach led naturally to the breakdown of distinctions by end use. Baskets became non-functional, their techniques served makers of large-scale hangings and installations, and the vessel form emerged as an important vehicle for textile artists whose methods bear little relationship to those customarily used. Basketry's continuity since antiquity – as well as the continued production of traditionally made baskets – was further appreciated as Postmodernism developed in the 1980s, and with it a restored respect for both the 'ordinary', and the allegorical and metaphorical content of everyday things. This made baskets and their concepts ideal means by which to express an individual's relationship to

6. Ed Rossbach, *Wagner's Rhine Journey*, 1987–88. Ash splints, rice paper and heat transfer printing were the artist's media and his method of image-making, resulting in a polished form that reflects Rossbach's early background in ceramics as well as his preference for making 'personal-sized' art.

7. Silvia Japkin Szulc, *Seeds of Space Historia-1* (detail), 2010. Splint-like parallel strips of photographic images are manipulated in groups in a unique method that derives from a basketmaker's arsenal of techniques.

society, as well as, in the more holistic sense, society's relationship to the natural world. Silvia Japkin Szulc takes the latter approach, in work that transforms the real world into a three-dimensional spherical structure whose surface is modified by the manipulation of splint-like strips of photographic images **[7, 45]**. She says that, quite often, 'the deconstruction and reconstruction of the proposals in contemporary visual arts has manifested itself by the disintegration of the material elements', but in her own work, 'after their metamorphosis, I reintegrate anew the changed elements into the original structure ... a sphere,' adding, 'I want to signify in part our unadaptation and readaptation to the world.' By using an organic method that appears familiar – akin to, but moving beyond, traditional wickerwork – Szulc pushes the viewer to consider nature, past and future. Drawing upon the very core of basketmaking, namely its reflection of geographical distinctions in its vegetation, she probes our largely unconscious ability to interpret materials as modern or traditional, unorthodox or expected.

Szulc's structures also suggest coiling, the fourth main basketmaking technique, and one that is also relatively easy to read. It, too, is based around one element holding another in place, but the firm element – in coiling called a 'foundation' rather than a stake – occupies the horizontal, not the vertical, position. Spiralling continuously outwards from the centre, foundations can be a single heavy reed, one or more sapling rods, bundles of lightweight reeds, grasses or other flexible materials, including flax, hemp and related bast fibres, or indeed anything that can be compressed into the required tubular shape. The uppermost foundation element is tightly bound to the foundation below by means of a binding strand that wraps while simultaneously catching through the wrapping below or piercing the lower bundle itself. Although changing the pace and angle of the interlocking binding make numerous options for textural and colour-based patterning, the spiralling route of the foundation is always clearly visible **[8, 61, 69, 73, 105, 168]**. The wrapping material itself must tolerate a tensioned tug, so a cord or yarn is required, or raffia or other palms that have sufficient tensile strength without the addition of a twist. Both the option of yarn as a binder and the nature of the wrapping process – no different in its course from the overhand linking stitch called 'overcasting' or 'whipping', which reinforces or joins cloth or leather – are another reminder that only a handful of motions create a myriad of textile types. Rigid when completed, a coiled basket is still a sewn construction. Take the foundation away, and the binders would reveal interlinked rows that, with looping and lacing, form the basis of many other off-loom techniques.

8. Unknown maker, *Coiled tray with zigzag edging* (detail), before 1988. The foundation is wrapped and bound with natural and green- and pink-dyed palm. It was collected by Ed Rossbach.

Looping, Knotting, Lacing and Twisting

Look carefully at a decorative Italian basket, with its shape defined by a wire frame **[9]**. The openwork areas are plaited, the dense areas are wickerwork, and around the wires is the same overhand stitch as used in coiling, but here secured by being passed back around itself before it makes the next overhand loop. Some coiled baskets incorporate this knot, called 'half-hitch' in rope-work **[151, 152]**. In sewing and embroidery this is a buttonhole stitch, widely used, as its name implies, to stabilize and strengthen buttonholes and any other edge that requires reinforcement. More importantly in this context, it is the principal stitch in needle lace, which originated in the Venetian Republic early in its dominion of Dalmatia (1420–1797), on the eastern coast of the Adriatic Sea. Needle lace evolved from cutwork in which holes cut in cloth, typically linen, are edged with a whipped or buttonhole stitch and, often, the open areas linked by buttonholed bars, called 'brides' **[143]**. Related techniques are pulled threadwork – a fine mesh openwork ground made by alternatively removing some threads and strengthening neighbouring threads with buttonhole stitch – and *reticello* ('little net'), in which the framework of threads increases to one-half to three inches (1.3–7.5 cm). In pulled threadwork the design appears as solid cloth on an enmeshed ground; in *reticello* the open frames are filled with closely worked buttonhole stitches forming both solid and openwork patterns. *Punto in aria*, the first true needle lace, dispensed with the cloth as a starting point **[153]**. Instead, selvedge threads are tacked to parchment (on which the design is drawn) to provide tensioning points from which buttonholed motifs are created. Once these have been linked by brides, the selvedge thread is removed, freeing the parchment to be used again. Italian in name and in origin, *reticello* and *punto in aria* ('stitches in the air') are but two examples of how a single means of making connections appears in many diverse applications, in this case used by the mariner, basketmaker, seamstress, lacemaker and embroiderer.

Look again at the Italian basket and its wickerwork and plaiting. Both techniques occur in bobbin lace, which uses thread-wound bobbins to provide tension as the threads are worked around pins to build up the design **[10]**. The over–under passage of elements common to wickerwork – and weaving – creates solid areas appropriately called 'toile' (French for 'cloth'); in between are brides or meshes (*réseau*, also found in needle laces) built up by braid-type plaiting, twisting or knotting **[148]**.

Here I must interject a passage about terminology. 'Plaiting' has two related meanings. The first is as basketmakers use it, to indicate the interweaving of two or more elements that need not share a common starting point, as is easily understood by observing a caned chair seat often worked with as many as eight elements. The second meaning refers to what can be distinguished as 'braiding', in which three or more elements are diagonally interlaced in the same direction, from a common starting point. Some authorities describe all plaiting as braiding, notably the eminent curator Irene Emery, who also termed this structure 'oblique interlacing'. In contrast, Pat Earnshaw, an influential collector and scholar of lace, refers to one-directional braiding as plaiting, but notes early in her comprehensive volume on the identification of lace that there are many alternative and contradictory uses of terms. Earnshaw highlights 'needlepoint', an often-used descriptor for needle laces (the 'point' meaning 'stitch' in French) and the confusion this causes in America, where needlepoint is a generic term for several varieties of embroidery.[5] On the subject of needle laces' buttonhole stitch, Emery is engagingly frustrated by the plethora of optional names: 'The technique of *simple looping* has been adapted to so many different fabric requirements in the course of centuries of use in many parts of the world that descriptions of the structure are especially diverse in terminology. There are a number of expressions like "quarter knot," "single Brussels stitch," "*point de tulle simple*," "lace stitch," "needle hitching," "loop stitch," "single-loop technique," "buttonhole coil," and

9

10

"cos-combing" which being of limited reference and use are also of limited usefulness. Other expressions like "coil-without-foundation," "knotless netting," and "lace coiling" are indirect references at best, although they are sometimes used with the apparent intention of indicating the *simple loop* structure.'[6] Much confusion regarding terminology, as Earnshaw notes, arises because scholarship on textiles has grown exponentially since the mid-19th century, much of it propelled forward by collectors who, like the lace authority Mrs Palliser (who donated her samples to the Royal Albert Memorial Museum, Exeterm, in 1869) 'had to be largely independent in her attributions and nomenclature, having no other extensive collection to refer to.' Earnshaw describes 'the originality of some of her identifications' as 'now rather irritating, and it might appear that many of her examples were named simply from the places where she bought them'.[7]

One might expect today's collector to be better able to categorize their treasured textiles, but the global trade in artisanal production seldom reveals technical information, and the internet's ready supply of images of vintage and antique textiles often depends on general descriptions rather than precise identification. Indeed, that can be part of the fun for the collector, or even the curator. As Dilys Blum has put it, in her role as the Jack M. and Annette Y. Friedland Senior Curator of Costume and Textiles at the Philadelphia Museum of Art, 'it's like being a detective: you know you've got something remarkable or rare, and the enjoyment is in tracking down every possible clue.' A good starting point is the textile's structure, which together with its material can point to certain centres of production. And while many collectors focus on a particular end product, there is equal satisfaction in taking a structural approach. For example, my own interest in lace – necessitated by a stint cataloguing it for Christie's South Kensington, London – arose from my knowledge of basketmaking, which I had learned from James Bassler some five years earlier. It was fascinating to observe already familiar structures, but at the minute scale allowed by fine linen threads, silk strands and – in European pieces made after about 1833, once they had been spun fine and strong enough – cottons. Subtle variations in the *réseau* often distinguish one type of lace from another, and here, too, it was interesting to find that the ideal form was hexagonal, the most efficient shape to create a stable yet flexible arrangement, especially in openwork **[11]**. Among the precedents to true needle lace, the square mesh of Buratto is twined; that of pulled work is made by bundling and wrapping sets of threads in a plain woven cloth – actions producing a remarkable range of delicate geometric patterns, yet paralleled in coiling, which is gigantic in comparison. On the square meshes of Buratto and filet (the second, also called lacis, distinguished from the first by its knotted ground) **[149, 158]**, designs are run in with a needle, filling pattern areas with what in lace, embroidery and sewing is called 'darning', an over–under construction that we have already met in wickerwork and two-element plaiting.

To create lace and related textiles, all that is needed is a needle or a bobbin, or another form of small shuttle, together with tension, whether provided by the temporary selvedge threads in needle lace, pins for securing a starting band in bobbin lace, or a frame for the embroidered or needle-run laces. For all other forms of linking, looping, twisting and knotting, only one fixed edge is required. In macramé, this was originally provided by cloth, from which the

9. Italian basketmaker, *Basket with wire handles and armature* (detail), before 1971. Wickerwork and plaited natural and red-dyed split raffia palm leaves. The scalloped edges and handles are covered with buttonhole stitch. This basket was purchased on Ischia by Ed and Katherine Rossbach.

10. Gabriele Grohmann, *Rauch* (detail), 1996. Various dimensions of fishing line are shown in the process of being manipulated by bobbins wound with surplus line. Using traditional and new bobblin-lace *réseaux*, or meshes, including a six-sided mesh called 'droschel', the work is held in place by pins as it progresses.

11

dangling warp threads at either end were rendered secure by being knotted into diagonally linked patterns [82, 146]. In tatting, a more delicate form of knotting, thread wrapped around the hand provides the base for working with a shuttle, although a firm edge can also be supplied by a needle similar to the type used in hand-knitting (itself a form of weft interlooping). Crochet is also secured with the hand, but worked with a hook to create interlooping that connects both to the previous row, as in knitting, and to loops in the same row [12, 102, 110, 147]. As will be apparent by now, there are many variations possible in each of these categories. Other techniques can readily form equally disparate results: for example, braids can be solid and flat, or tubular and three-dimensional. The effects created with these techniques can be decorative treatments of cloth [136, 144] or edges of cloth; equally, they can form separate edgings altogether, or – in the case of macramé, crocheting and knitting – can be constructed as ready-shaped garments [129] and accessories including hats, stockings, leggings, gloves and bags. The same range of items can be made by netting, which was already in use 29,000 years ago in the present-day Czech Republic. Provided the material is strong, netting is firm yet flexible, whether linked (think of a chain-linked fence) or looped, and can be very closely worked or widely spaced, always retaining its inherent elasticity [57, 77, 145].

Of course, these techniques can also be used to make sculptural forms, wall-hangings and installations [101, 102, 109, 128, 173–78], and it is the constant rethinking of structures that plays an important role in textile arts. Ply-splitting, for example, is a form of braiding in which the plied cords that are used can be untwisted enough to insert the crossing element through them, rather than in front or behind. Long associated with the making of animal trappings in Rajasthan and with decorative darning in the eastern Mediterranean, Nepal, India and Japan, it is a technique that since the mid-1980s has been explored by Errol Pires, coordinator of textiles at India's National Institute of Design, who learned it in Jaisalmer from Ishwar Singh Bhatti (subsequently the recipient of a Master Craftsperson Award). Pires makes objects ranging from garments to vessels **[14, 58, 59]**. Jewellery and many other objects are also made from this technique – and not only in those regions where it is indigenous. Key to this transmission from East to West was Peter Collingwood's 1998 publication *Techniques of Ply-Split Braiding*. Collingwood, who learned the braiding method in India, had already published *Techniques of Sprang: Plaiting on Stretched Threads* in 1974, which has become the standard book on sprang. This is an ancient tensioned-warp technique for making a stretchy structure in which adjacent threads are twisted and – since it grows towards the centre – are locked in place with a single central weft **[13]**. (Leno weaving, or gauze weaving, first found in ancient Chinese textiles, uses the same principal but locks each warp twist with a weft and is not elastic **[91, 127]**.) Before the development of knitting at least 1,000 years ago, sprang was the quickest way to make an elastic form, and its employment of parallel threads fixed at both ends qualifies it as loom-woven despite its distinctive use of only one binding weft.

Loom-Weaving

While there are many variations among looms, all serve the same basic function: to hold the warp threads in parallel and under tension while the weft threads are inserted. The passage of the weft, with a few exceptions **[94]**, is straight through

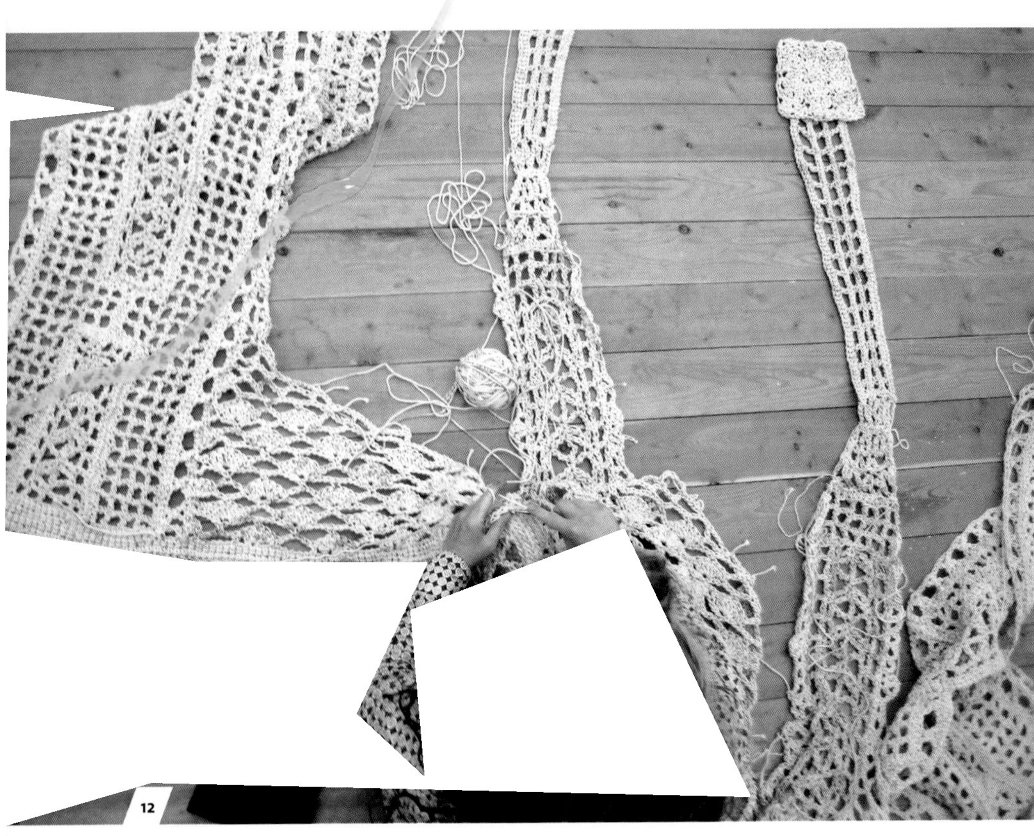

12

11. American maker (attributed), *Embroidered lace choker* (detail), *c.* 1900. Embellished with gold and silver metallic-thread chain stitch, gold and clear seed beads and seed pearls, this choker is composed of recycled tulle, a machine-made six-sided mesh. Tulle was first made by machine in Nottingham, England, in 1768, and its mechanized construction was perfected and patented by John Heathcoat in 1809. After his Loughborough factory was attacked by Luddites in 1816, he removed to Tiverton, Devon, and also established a steam-powered factory in Tulle, France – a location that gave its name to this net.

12. Sheila Klein, *Textile Wallah* (detail), 2008. Here the artist is in the process of crocheting with tea-dyed cotton sein twine. 'When travelling through Rajasthan, India, in 2008, I found the perforated lacy window walls to be so much like crocheted architecture – formed by a series of posts and interstices creating a geometric hierarchy.'

a 'tunnel' or shed of warp threads in which some are raised and others lowered or stationery to allow the weft to go under and over the warps. It is the sequence of the warp-thread positions that determines the texture and pattern of the cloth. We have already encountered two basic patterns via basketry. A regular over–under passage is called 'plain' or 'tabby' weaving **[114]**, while over-three and under-one creates a 3/1 twill weave **[65]**. Many other configurations are possible, but my purpose is not to describe them all. Rather, it is the significance of the shed control itself that deserves emphasis. As Désirée Koslin explains in her authoritative account of the nature of looms: 'The application of a shedding device to the warp was momentous, and is indicated clearly in the Neolithic. When it was introduced, weaving took off with a mega-leap in the production of surplus value *vis a vis* its then rivals in fabric-formation, which continued to be laboriously made loop-by-loop, link-by-link, or knot-by-knot. The mechanized shedding was a breakthrough because multiples of hundreds or thousands of warp threads could be raised or lowered with a single movement by means of a shed rod and a heddle rod.'[8]

Thus the Neolithic's development of shedding enshrined cloth – albeit still handmade – could be described quite literally as the fabric of life. For millennia, cloths were not only functional and ritual objects that far outnumbered any other man-made alternatives, but they were also easy to transport. (This distinction is still clear in the French word *meuble*, denoting moveable furnishings – and especially textiles – as opposed to *immeuble*, or fixed property.) Textiles perfectly suited nomadic lives as well as exchange, trade and hoarding for unforeseen needs. Until the Renaissance's development of easel painting (itself usually on a textile base, canvas), pictures were created directly onto a wall and thus were fixed in their position. Until the introduction of colour in films and on television, textiles remained the most abundant source of 'moving images'. Little wonder that many incorporate depictions of people and animals – snapshots, as it were, recording the features of life's transitory existence and rendering it seemingly permanent, as epitomized by Cecilia Blomberg's tapestry *Lucas II* **[183]**.

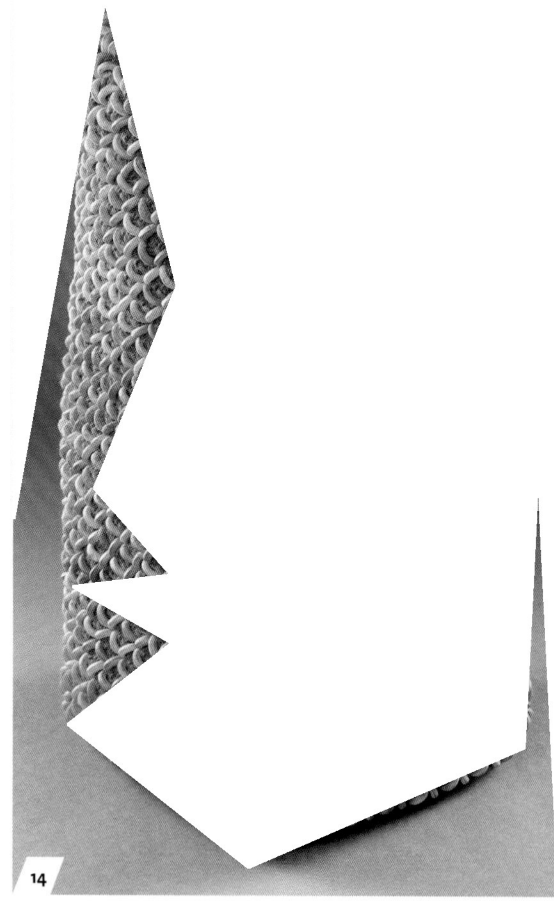

14

Tapestry is the weaving technique most closely aligned with picture-making, since one can 'draw' with individual wefts plain-woven solely where each colour is needed. The earliest surviving example was found in Sampul in the Tarim Basin (present-day Western China), in a mass grave from the 3rd to 2nd centuries BC.[9] It depicts a centaur and a soldier. Thought to be Hellenistic and thus early proof of contact between Greek culture and China, it had been made into a pair of trousers, which gives some idea of the fineness of its structure. By the time tapestry-making began to flourish in Northern Europe in the early 1300s (having existed there since at least the early 11th century), tapestries were more substantial, blanketing walls with a barrier whose densely packed woollen wefts offered warmth as well as vivid decoration, often with touches of gold thread **[156]**. For peripatetic householders, such as the nobility of the period, they were as symbolic of wealth and comfort as the private jet is today. Typically using a linen weft, this linen/wool combination has become standard worldwide for tapestries but has never been the only option. In China silk was the fibre of choice – and of necessity, since wool was not available, and the weft had to be a dye-absorbent fibre. This method of making pictorial panels was used as

early as the Tang dynasty (618–907) and called *kesi*. In India, where the related twill-tapestry weave was introduced from Central Asia and Persia **[16, 163]** in the 15th century, it was used to make fine Kashmir shawls, and at the same time *kesi* itself began to be used for garments. A painstaking technique that eschews all but the tensioning and most basic hand-selected shedding offered by the loom, tapestry evolved independently in the prehistoric American South-West and remains associated with Navajo rugs, in which the imagery is abstract but no less meaningful than pictorial weaves. From the Balkans to the Indian subcontinent such rugs are called 'kelims'.

As tapestry demonstrates, simple equipment is no barrier to complex patterning (it just takes much longer to create), and tapestry-making has never been industrialized. Nevertheless, the urge to depict images through weaving – but more quickly – is mirrored in the development of other types of looms. Building patterned areas into a length of fabric as it was woven on the loom depended at first on the weaver's memory and their skill in introducing extra wefts, either running from selvedge to selvedge (supplementary weft **[20, 26, 27, 30, 131, 157, 162]**), or inserted only where an additional colour was needed (brocading **[17, 137]**). This could be done, and still is, with a shed rod and heddle rod, and forty or more 'darned-in' pattern sticks charting each successive pass of the weft in one complete pattern, to be removed and replaced at the back of the set as weaving progresses. Speedier was the use of heddles (frames suspended mid-warp, through which pre-determined sets of warp threads were securely threaded), but even quicker and less cumbersome was to divide the task into two by using a draw-boy, whose task was to control the patterning warps while the

13. Indian artisan (attributed), *Belt* (detail), before 1986. Mercerized cotton sprang belt shown relaxed (closed) and stretched open. The uneven tone of the blue colouration suggests it was dyed with natural indigo.

14. Errol Pires, *Rings of Peace*, 2008. Vase form 45 cm (18 in.) high, created with ply-split braiding of four-ply dyed linen cord and inserted wooden rings.

15. Peruvian Highlands weaver, *Doublecloth textile* (detail), before 1974. This true doubleweave shows the same pattern on both sides, reversed in coloration. Handmade in Cuzco of alpaca coloured with natural dyes, the symbols are visual metaphors representing the relationship that the Quechua people have with their physical and spiritual worlds.

16

weaver's manipulation of heddles created the ground cloth. Of unknown origins, but certainly Middle Eastern or Asian, and possibly employed as long as 1,400 years ago, drawlooms were essential for the creation of an abundance of fabrics with sumptuous patterns such as those found in Chinese, Persian, Ottoman and European silks **[17, 125, 134]**. The loom was gradually refined and ultimately replaced by the punchcard-controlled mechanical Jacquard over the course of the 19th century **[159, 184]**, and by computer-controlled looms in the 1980s **[113, 126, 130]**, but the concept of ever more economical management of thousands of patterning threads was central among the many developments that shaped a wide range of hand- and, later, power-driven looms. Parallel developments in the West in patterning and faster production occurred for knits, nets and lace **[179]**. There now exist thousands of hand-operated and machine-powered loom types differing in the resulting cloth construction, equipped for particular fibres, simpler for smaller patterns – and each 'an ever-mutating organism, fitted and adapted to new demands and functions', and a subject in themselves.[10]

17

Despite the plentiful supply of patterned weaves, cloths that are essays on colour and structure have carved out their own niche **[84–94]**. A great number of these are hand-woven, and many weavers speak not only of the satisfaction of investing time and care in the preparation of yarns and exploration of cloth structures, but also of the commitment derived from knowing they are preserving and enriching a craft that has such a long and significant history. As Tim Parry-Williams puts it, 'We live in a culture increasingly disconnected with the making of useful things and, in particular, woven textiles. Industrialization has long since put the making of cloth somewhere "over there", carried out by someone else, and available quickly and therefore cheaply without much regard.'

Such concerns parallel the voices petitioning for 'slow food'. This grassroots movement, founded in Italy by Carlo Patrini in 1986, has become a global phenomenon focused on quality of life and environmental issues. The concept of what can today be called 'slow textiles' **[60]** is much older. For weavers, foremost among its proponents was Ethel Mairet **[19]**, who, as the wife of the geologist A. K. Coomaraswamy, had from 1903–7 travelled in India and lived in Ceylon, where she taught and revived traditional Ceylonese embroidery. On her return to England, Mairet established Gospels, a weaving workshop where hand-spinning, weaving and natural dyeing were undertaken. Her publications – *A Book on Vegetable Dyes* (1916) and *Hand-Weaving Today* (1939) – influenced more than one generation of weavers, as did many of her apprentices. Visiting weavers were numerous and included Peter Collingwood, who, while serving as a doctor during the Second World War, had 'discovered a lifelong passion for textile structures from around the world after receiving a gift of a Bedouin tent hanging, which remained a treasured possession'.[11] Among the structures Collingwood studied was tablet-weaving, also called card-weaving, because this ancient process involves a set of square cards aligned under tension, with warp threads running through holes at each corner. Rotating the cards creates a shed, and the resulting narrow bands can range from highly complex to subtly textured **[18, 43, 115]**, as Collingwood demonstrated in his comprehensive book on the subject. Written in 1982, it remains a standard reference and has inspired many to take up the tablet-weaving technique.

16. Persian weaver, *Royal tapestry*, c. 1524. This twill-weave tapestry – woven with silk and metallic threads – has at its centre the young boy prince Shah Tahmasp, who succeeded to the throne in 1524. The tapestry probably celebrates this event, as the boy's image is surrounded by auspicious motifs, including angels, birds and winged men bearing gifts.

17. Lyonnais weaver, *Brocaded silk*, 1730–32. In the style of the designer Jean Revel (1684–1751), this silk is brocaded with coloured silks and silver threads. It demonstrates a then new mastery of texture and shading achieved by designers and drawloom weavers of the period.

Collingwood, like Rossbach, Albers and Mairet, became one of a handful of internationally known weavers renowned not only for their own work, but for facilitating the exploration and reinvigoration of traditional techniques. Of equal importance were Jack Lenor Larsen's books on interlacing, weaving, dyeing and, in 1986, two volumes (co-authored with Mildred Constantine) on *The Art Fabric*. All of these individuals drew their knowledge from first-hand observation, and became astute – and ultimately generous – collectors. Rossbach and his wife donated to the Design Collection at the University of California, Davis; Collingwood's and Mairet's collections are both at the Crafts Study Centre in Farnham, Surrey; Anni and Josef Albers set up a foundation with their work in Bethany, Connecticut; and Larsen donated his work to LongHouse Reserve in East Hampton, New York, which he established in 1992.

These weavers were all highly skilled in the observation and analysis of structure. Epitomizing this outlook is Collingwood, of whom it is said that, among his books, his 'personal favourite – and the one that gives the most insight into his inquiring mind – is *The Maker's Hand* (1988), in which he analyses, with diagrams and photographs, 100 woven structures from around the world'.[12] The structures Collingwood considers in the book range from the springs of a US Army Jeep seat to Botswanan beer strainers. Clearly Collingwood – and the others – believed that it was essential to embrace world culture. Many contributors to this volume share the same view. Candace Crocket, for example **[43, 80, 115]**, recalls being 'drawn to textiles as a means of artistic expression because of their tactile quality and their historic connection to all peoples and to all cultures'. They would all undoubtedly also agree with Larsen's statement that 'experiencing art in living spaces [is] a unique learning experience'. It is telling that the LongHouse website, in describing the organization's 'art focus ... on ethnographic objects and handcrafts', stresses both as 'areas of collecting with aspects for every purse', reinforcing the point that textiles are all-inclusive and not elitist.[13]

18. Saxon weaver, *Tablet-woven fragment*, 9th century. This British silk ribbon, interwoven with gold metal thread and edged with narrow silk braids and metal hemispheres, was once part of a set of ecclesiastical garments. Such small wares were often used to reinforce seams or edges, and were the only form of highly decorative woven textiles available to all but the most privileged until the 18th century.

19. Ethel Mairet, *Handwoven fragment*, *c*. 1925–35. This simple checked cloth typifies the work produced by Ethel Mairet at Gospels, her workshop in Ditchling, East Sussex, before the influence of visiting weavers, many from Europe. It is of hand-spun eri silk, used both in its natural colour and hand-dyed with indigo, madder and other vegetable dyes.

20. Guatemalan weaver, *Handwoven textile* (detail), 1950s or earlier. Densely packed supplementary wefts on an indigo-coloured cotton weft-faced ground ensure that the weft floats form the design on the front of the fabric only. This piece was collected by a home economics instructor, Ms Farrar, in the 1950s.

21. Sigmund von Weech, *Upholstery Fabric*, 1929. Handwoven at the Handweberei Sigmund von Weech, which the artist and his wife had founded in 1921 in Schaftlach, Germany, this fabric incorporates chenille threads and most probably was intended for use on the tubular steel furniture also designed by von Weech.

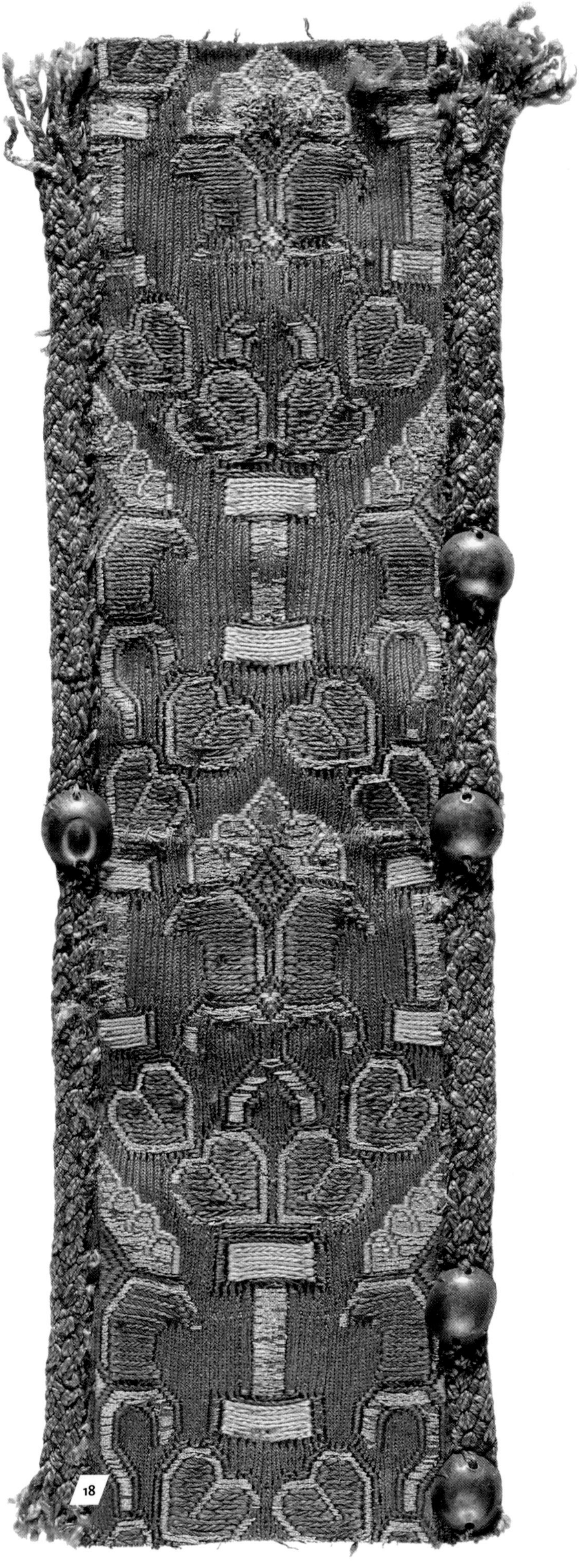

19

18

3150.
3159.
3161.
3163.
3160 A.
Rothbodige
breitgestreifte Cuttni.
3130.
1528. B.
2083.

23

24

22. Mende weaver, *Kpokpo* (detail), early 20th century. This large strip-woven cotton cloth, over 4 m (13 ft) long, required virtuosity in the juxtaposition of bold designs with subtle variations in patterns and hand-dyed colours, as well as a knowledge of the long-standing traditions of Sierra Leone weaving. Such specialized production was typically commissioned for events such as state ceremonies and funerals as displays of wealth and social position.

23. Elizabeth Calnan, *The Fruits and Seeds of Life* (detail), 2011. Double weave incorporating warp ikat and solid-dyed silks.

26

24 and 25. European weaver, *Striped swatches*, *c.* 1815–35. Possibly made in Norwich, a centre for this type of weaving with worsted yarns, these cloths survive in two pattern books compiled at the time for salesmen and together containing over 1,000 swatches. Here the elaborate floral supplementary warp stripes are based on a satin weave, itself created by employing far fewer wefts than warps, which thus dominate the surface.

26. Malagay weaver, Lamba akotifahana, *c.* 1900. In these textiles, used to clothe the living and to wrap the dead, the rich supplementary weft patterning in bright silks combines vertical striped bands with geometric designs that reflect the status of the cloth's owner. This example relates to one of the *lamba* given to President Grover Cleveland by Queen Ranavalona III of Madagascar in 1886.

27

27. Guatemalan weaver, *Rectangular textile with four selvedges* (detail), 20th century. The cotton ground is covered with white continuous supplementary wefts and brightly coloured discontinuous supplementary wefts, the latter the true brocading technique that simulates embroidery. The reverse of the cloth shows the bright cottons worked only in the areas where they are needed.

28 and 29. Laotian weavers, Vientiane, Pha sin (details), 1940 or earlier. Tubular silk ikat skirts with a deep hem border, one of red and black cotton (which appears plum-coloured, right) and the other of red, green, plum and black silk, both with gold metallic supplementary weft geometric motifs. That the hem border is woven rather than embroidered indicates that this skirt pre-dates the Second World War.

30. Laotian weavers, Vientiane, *Rectangular textile* (detail), 1990s. Possibly a shoulder cloth, this textile has geometric motifs of alternating solid, striped and discontinuous supplementary wefts. Only the black is dyed commercially: the other colours are derived from barks and berries. This was collected by Cynthia LeCount, who led a Research Expedition Program from the University of California, Davis, to Thailand and Laos in 1999.

31. Sally Weatherill, *Pocket-woven ties*, 2011. These silk ties carry abstract patterns in colour combinations that either emphasize or disguise the designs, and interact with the embossed effect created by the pocket weave. Jacquard-woven by hand, such complex patterns echo the effects of brocading but are produced at greater speed.

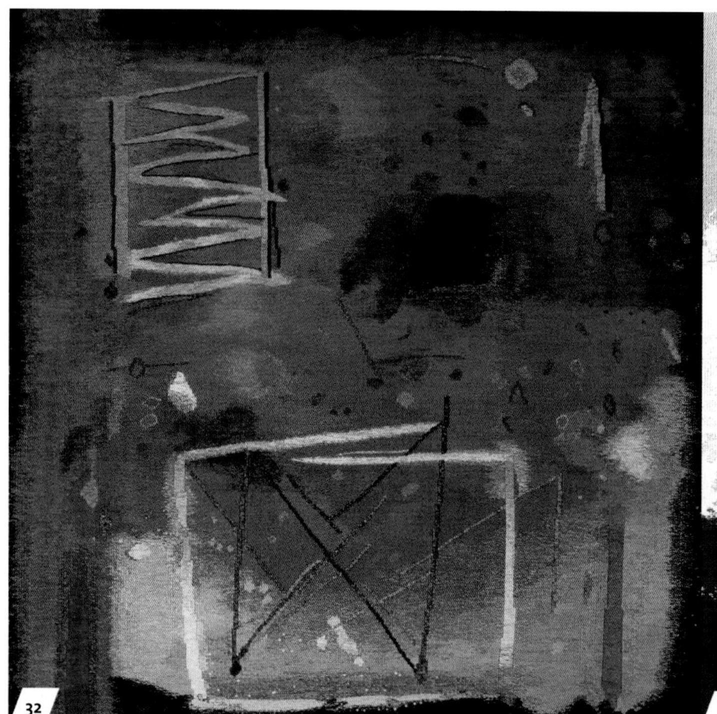

32. Gerda van Hamond, *Wall Talk 1*, 2010. Cotton-warp, wool-weft tapestry, 138 cm (54 in.) square. Noting that it takes between 500 and 700 hours to produce the larger tapestries, usually over a period of three to four months, the artist comments that 'imagination has to be developed and nurtured. ... I do a lot of walking. For me it is the pace at which to observe, to notice the grandiose and the miniscule.'

33. Sara Brennan, *Broken White Band with Pink*, 2005. Tapestry-woven wool, cotton and linen. This relatively small work, approximately 81 cm (32 in.) square, 'takes its initial inspiration from landscape, responding with a very simplified and reduced use of form. It is an expression of a whole and a personal response.'

34. George-Ann Bowers, *Canna White II*, 2005. Loom-woven panel employing cotton, wool, rayon and silk, with areas of texture created both by the weave structures and the incorporation of bouclé yarns.

35. Alex Friedman, *Bound*, 2007. Incorporating shadow effects and breaking away from a traditional rectangular shape, this three-dimensional work is nevertheless weft-faced tapestry. The artist chooses 'not to rely on extra scaffolding devices so the results are more in the bas relief mode'. She uses 'tension as the main guide for this effect'.

36. Christina Frey, *Magma III*, 2008. This small mounted tapestry, only 13.5 cm (5¼ in.) high, was woven with silk and linen.

37. Marc du Plantier, *Aubusson tapestry*, 1950s. At just over 3 m (10 ft) in height, this abstract study of volume, colour and texture was commissioned by Pinton Frères, which was founded in Aubusson, France, in the mid-19th century. It is handwoven using the slit-tapestry technique.

38 and 39. Ulla de Larios, *Crossing #11*, 2005. The artist explores her status as an immigrant, having moved from Sweden to California: 'Through the weaving process, time becomes evident in the slow progression of threads … warped, dyed, threaded, sleighed and shot across. The loose weave structure shows the ambivalence of the position "In-between". The little petroglyph humans in the panels' middle are obvious reference to the large part of the world's population that is uprooted each year.'

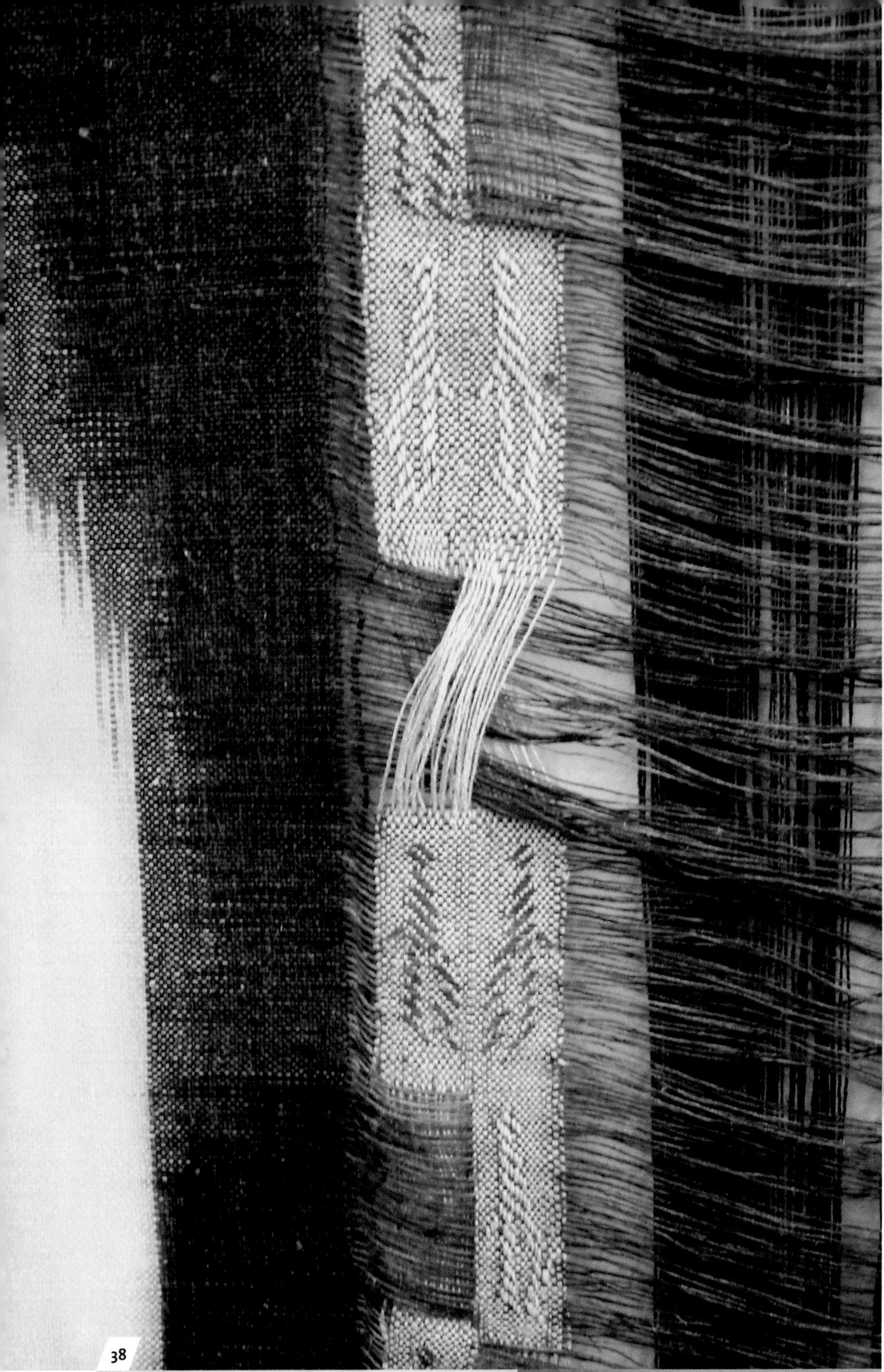

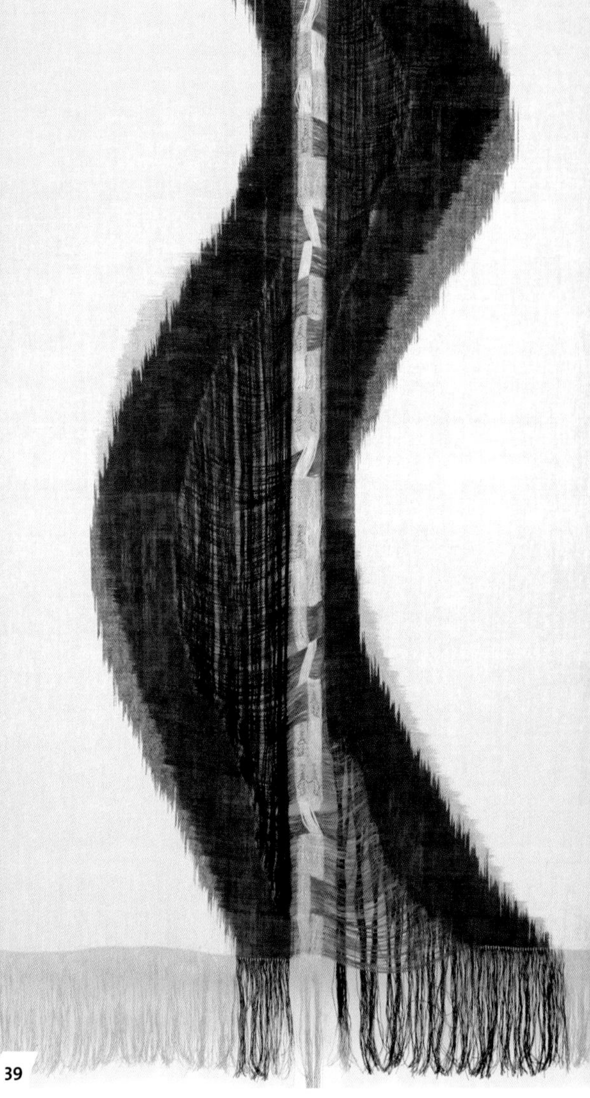

38

39

40

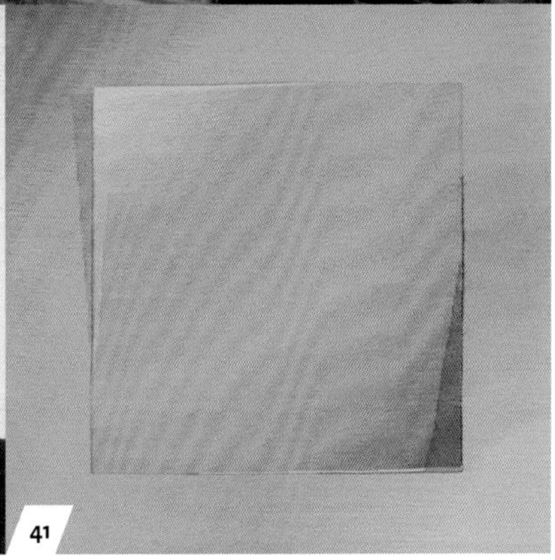

41

40 and 41. Hillu Liebelt, *Blue on White* and *Into the Unknown*, 2008 and 2010. Both works are rayon and cotton tapestries 60 cm (24 in.) square, but *Blue on White* also incorporates silk and brushed aluminium. 'Colour for me is almost always the starting point .... Sometimes I just begin by choosing yarns from my shelves and leaving them grouped together [until they] feel all right after a week has passed .... In the process of designing, the aim is always to condense the initial sketch, eliminate the unnecessary, to refine and structure.'

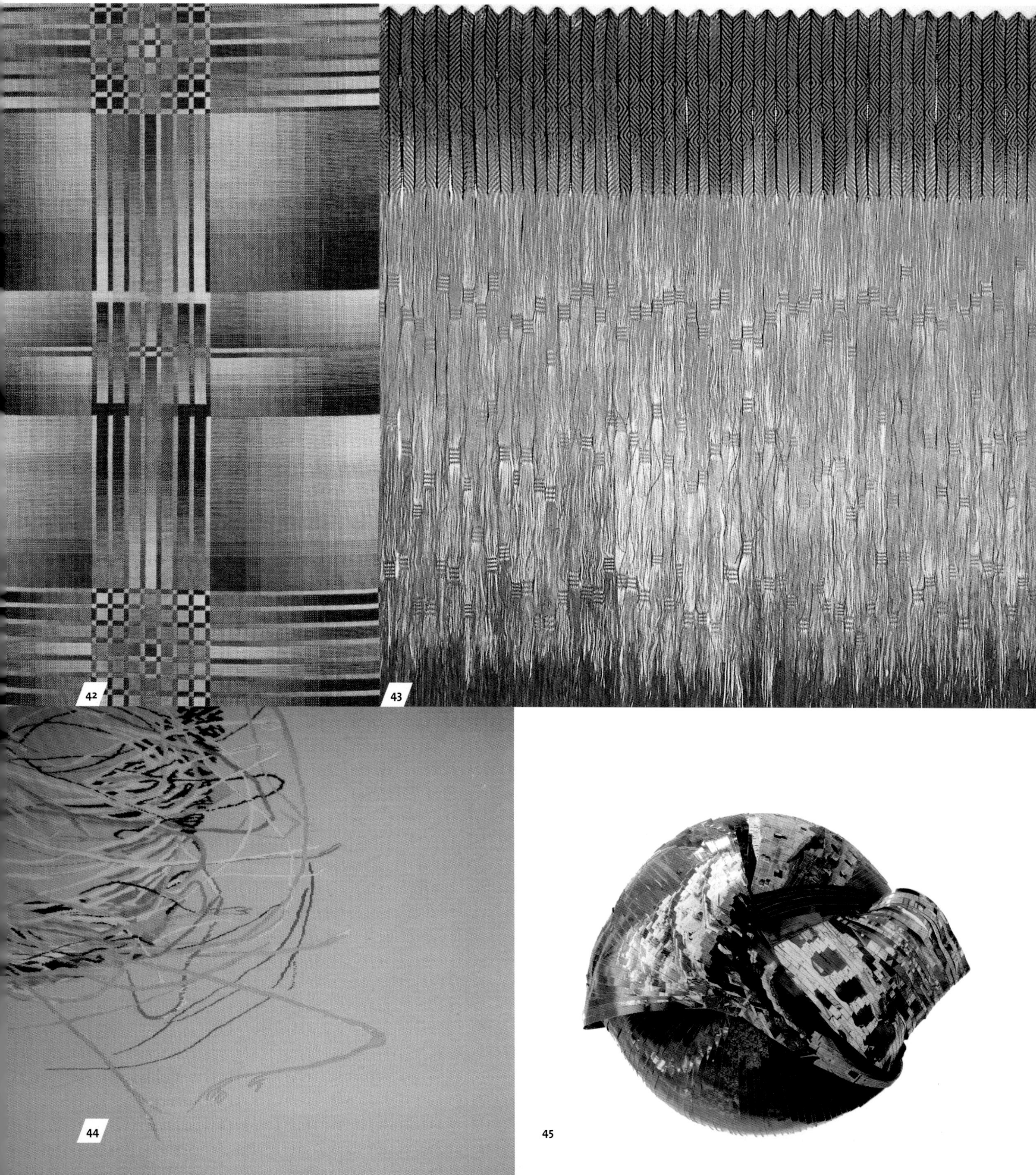
42
43
44
45

46

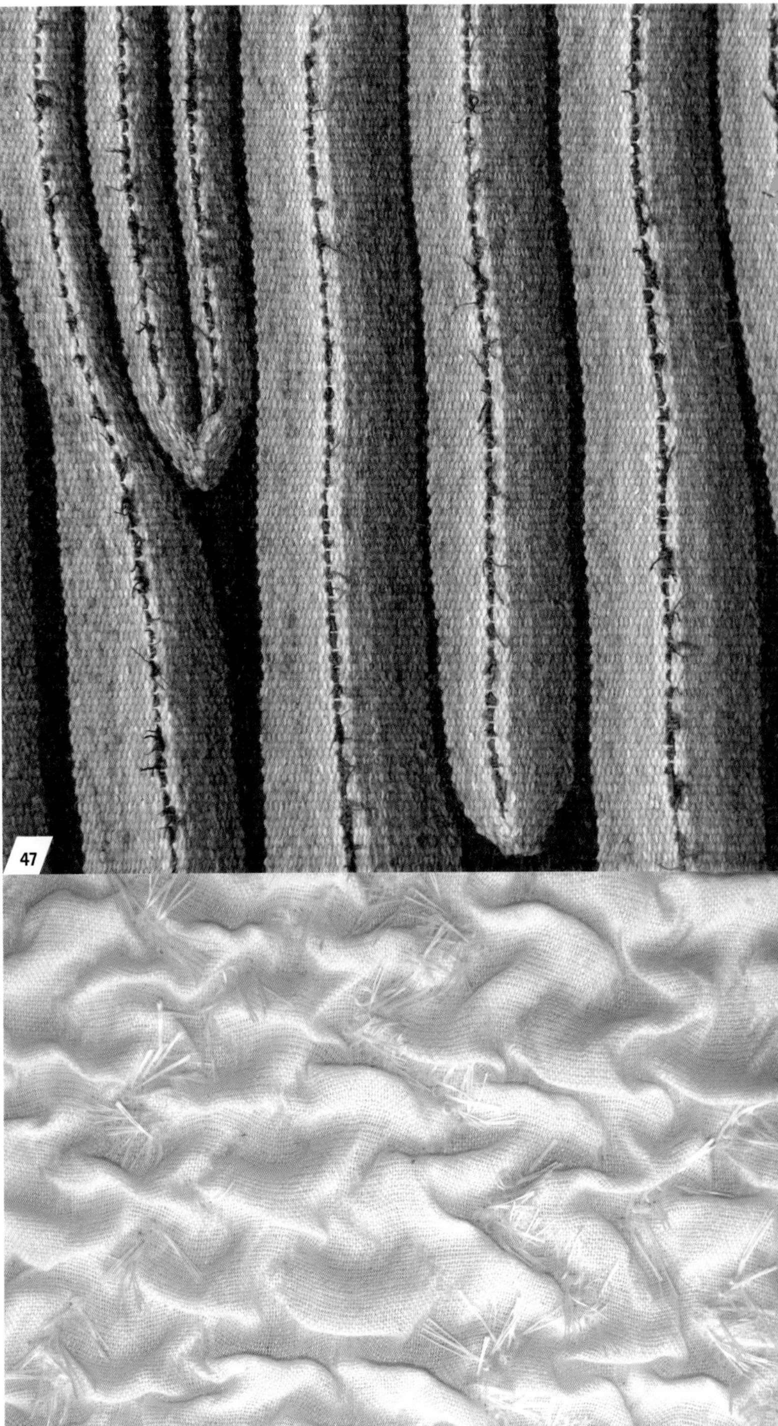

47

48

42. Nancy Middlebrook, *City 5*, 2010. In this small panel, 66 cm (26 in.) high, a double weave allows controlled and subtle variations of perspective and colour. The hand-dyed cotton yarns take inspiration from the artist's chosen palette, so that they 'speak to each other within a grid'.

43. Candace Crockett, *Water #3*, 2008. This panel 134.6 cm (53 in.) wide is composed of some sixty bands of card-woven cotton and linen, both dyed and painted by the artist, who is an authority and author on card-weaving.

44. Inge Norgaard, *Nesting 02*, 2009. One from a series of tapestries intended to capture the 'motions and orderly randomness of the lines of a nest, pared down to the minimum.'

45. Silvia Japkin Szulc, *Seeds of Space Historia-1*, 2010. Using strips of photographs reassembled into a sphere, Japkin creates a symbolic representation of the world, as well as of the deconstruction and reconstruction of discourse in today's visual arts, which is often expressed in the disintegration of material elements.

46. Margaret Crowther, *Fandango*, 2007. With a diameter of approximately 1.3 m (51 in.), this piece was woven in sisal 'to convey a feeling of exuberance and excitement ... weaving without using any sort of loom or frame. The freedom of this "hands-only" technique resulted in some impromptu decisions and unexpected developments.'

47. Lyn Hart, *Saguaro Oscuro*, 2010. This small tapestry is a colour-value study of the fleshy ribs of a giant cactus that grows near the artist's studio in the American South-West. It was hand woven in linen, linen fishnet coated with persimmon extract dye, and natural- and synthetic-dyed wools, all on a linen warp.

48. Stacey Harvey-Brown, *Snowfield*, 2011. Handwoven on a 16-shaft loom, this stitched double cloth with embellishment is a response to a snow-covered hay field, as well as to a 'yarn challenge – to incorporate a yarn that felt very like dental floss'.

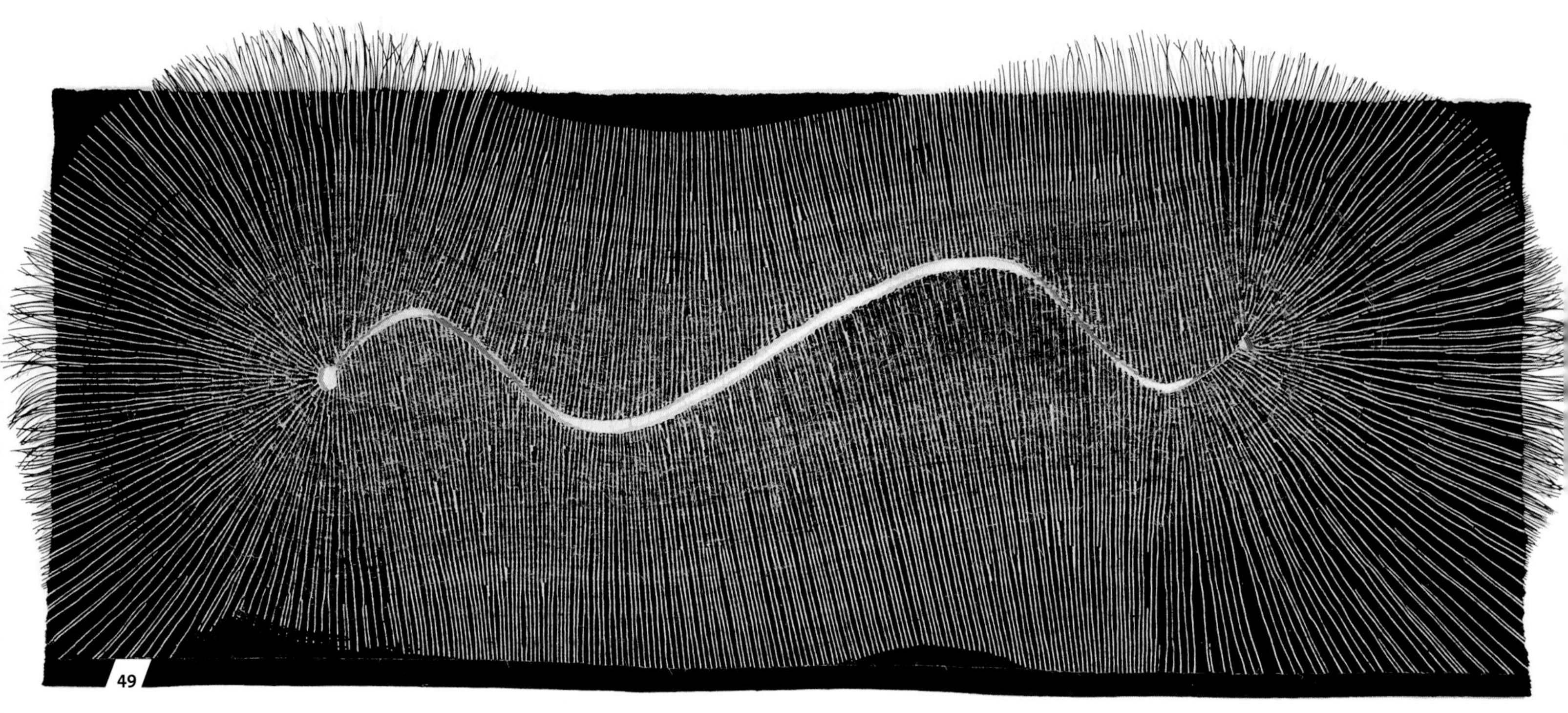

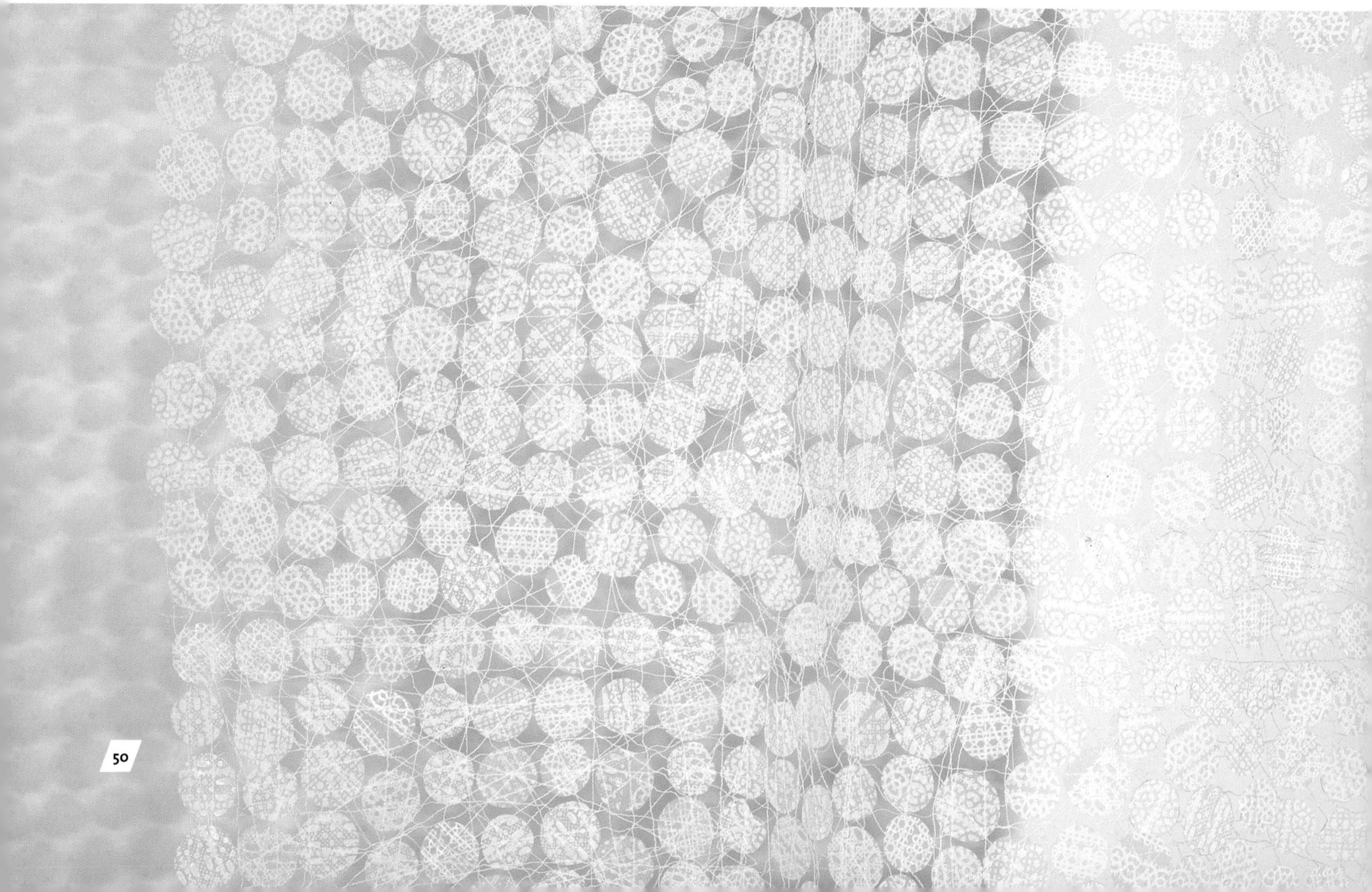

50

51

49. Cygan Wlodzimierz, *Orbitrek, Grand Prix Lodz*, 2007. This 3 m (10 ft) wide wool and sisal circular weaving represents the artist's 'attempt to establish or discover the existing meanings of woven objects .... I have given up using the loom for the sake of the frame,' he says. 'I don't want to feel restrained. I invent and construct simple devices that let me use my warp freely.'

50. Cecelia Heffer, *Contemporary Lace: White Shadow*, 2006. Through machine-stitched silk on a soluble substrate, Hefner references 16th-century Venetian lace. She explores 'the notion of linking people to historic ties through the integration of memory, pattern and technology'.

51. George-Ann Bowers, *Striation*, 2005. Employing cotton, wool, rayon, silk and silk charmeuse fabric, this kimono form was created using a triple-weave pickup technique with warp painting, or ikat.

52. Stacey Harvey-Brown, *Dry Stone Wall*, 2010. A computer-controlled Jacquard handwoven single and double cloth, whose three-dimensional qualities are the result of combining yarns with differential shrinkage during finishing.

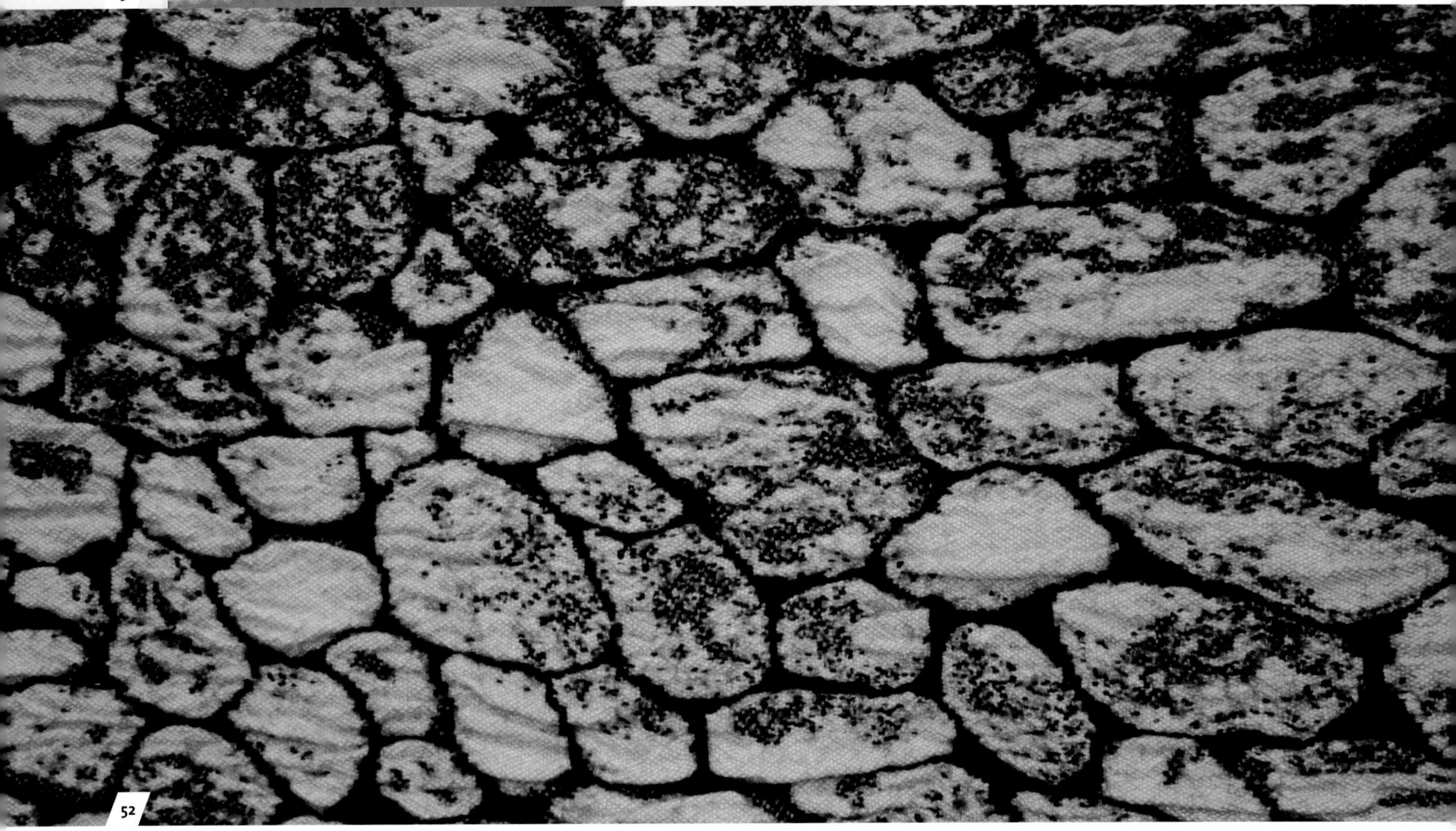

52

53

54

55

56

57

53. Miriam Plotnicov, *Wickerwork basket*, c. 1960–75. Willow from Ohio was used in this wickerwork basket by Plotnicov, who was an authority on the beads of indigenous peoples from different parts of the world, as well as a curator of crafts.

54. Italian basketmaker, *Scalloped plaited basket*, before 1975. Machine-stitched plaited strips of dyed purple cane were moulded to create this basket's scalloped shape.

55. Sicilian basketmaker, *Fishing basket*, before 1971. Diagonally overlapping cane warps are anchored by wire wefts lashed to the cane at intersections. The reinforced rim is of cane bundles wrapped with cotton string.

56. Nazca artisan, south coastal Peru, *Feather fan*, c. 600. This rare fan has feathers bound and secured by interweaving.

57. Brazilian artisan (attributed), *Expanding netted carrying container*, before 1986. Knotless netting of plied and plaited sisal rope.

58 and 59. Errol Pires, *Peace Container* and *Tripodod Container*, 2008. Both created by ply-split braiding, the white vessel is 15 cm (6 in.) high and constructed from four-ply cotton cord made from undyed cotton kite string, and its companion, three times the size, is worked in four-ply dyed cotton cord.

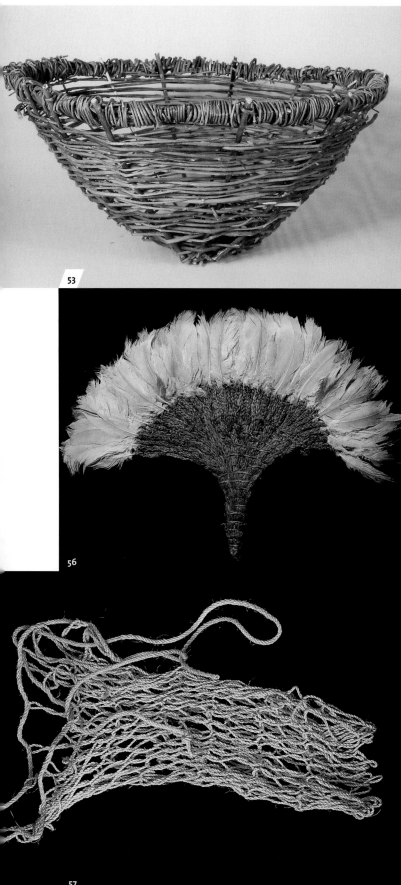

60. Lois Walpole and Kate Green, *Rapid Eye Basket*, 1987–98. Strips of plain and printed corrugated cardboard were overpainted by Walpole and her husband, and then woven by outworkers – in this case the artist Kate Green – as part of a 'mini industry' for sustainable basket production. As Walpole explains, 'consumer products and packaging still have many years of life left . . . . These materials, which already have their own history, ... intrigue, amuse or otherwise stimulate the viewer or user.'

61. Karyl Sisson, *Tape Measure Vessel*, c. 1998. Coiled, recycled cotton tape measures secured with polymers and thread are topped with a vintage Bakelite lid. 'My focus has been the transformation of these familiar objects through the building of form and the development of structures that suggest living organisms, indigenous architecture or ceramic vessels. These collectibles serve as building materials while any number of basketry and needlework techniques provide the method of construction.'

58

59

60

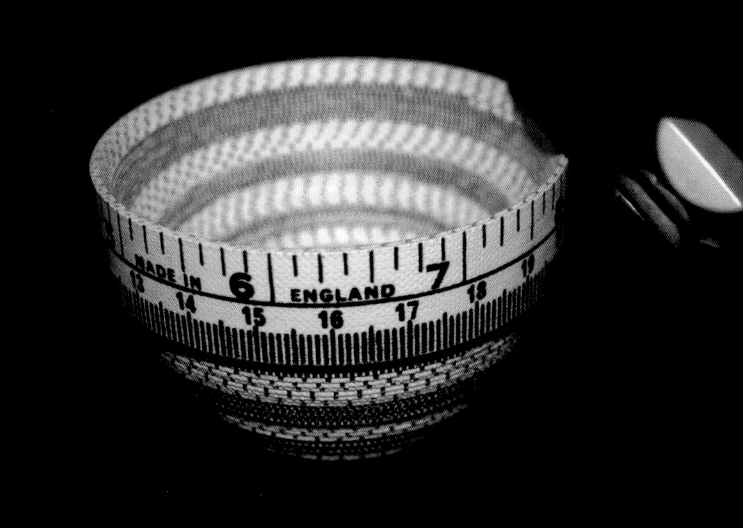

61

62–68. These details of baskets reveal structures also used on the loom. The basic over–under passage of wefts around a stake (warp) is seen in a wickerwork tub basket of grass cord and natural and painted wood (62), and more complex arrangements are shown in the remaining examples, all of which are plaited. These include two Colombian baskets employing a patterned 3/1 twill in palm (65); a reverse twill in bamboo, made by Tukano Indians (64); and two Indonesian examples employing checked patterns, one of red- and black-painted bamboo (66), and the other of natural and dyed palm (68). The multicoloured twilled-check example in fine natural and dyed straw is from Madagascar (63). A variation on the houndstooth pattern, in which both the warp and the weft consist of alternations of two natural and two dyed palm 'ribbons', can be seen in the Sri Lankan basket (67). All were collected by Ed and Katherine Rossbach, several being illustrated in Ed Rossabach's *Baskets as Textile Arts* of 1972.

69. Nubian basketmaker, *Coiled basket with lid,* before 1971. Yellow-, brown- and black-dyed palm in geometric patterns is coiled with natural-coloured palm on a foundation of reeds.

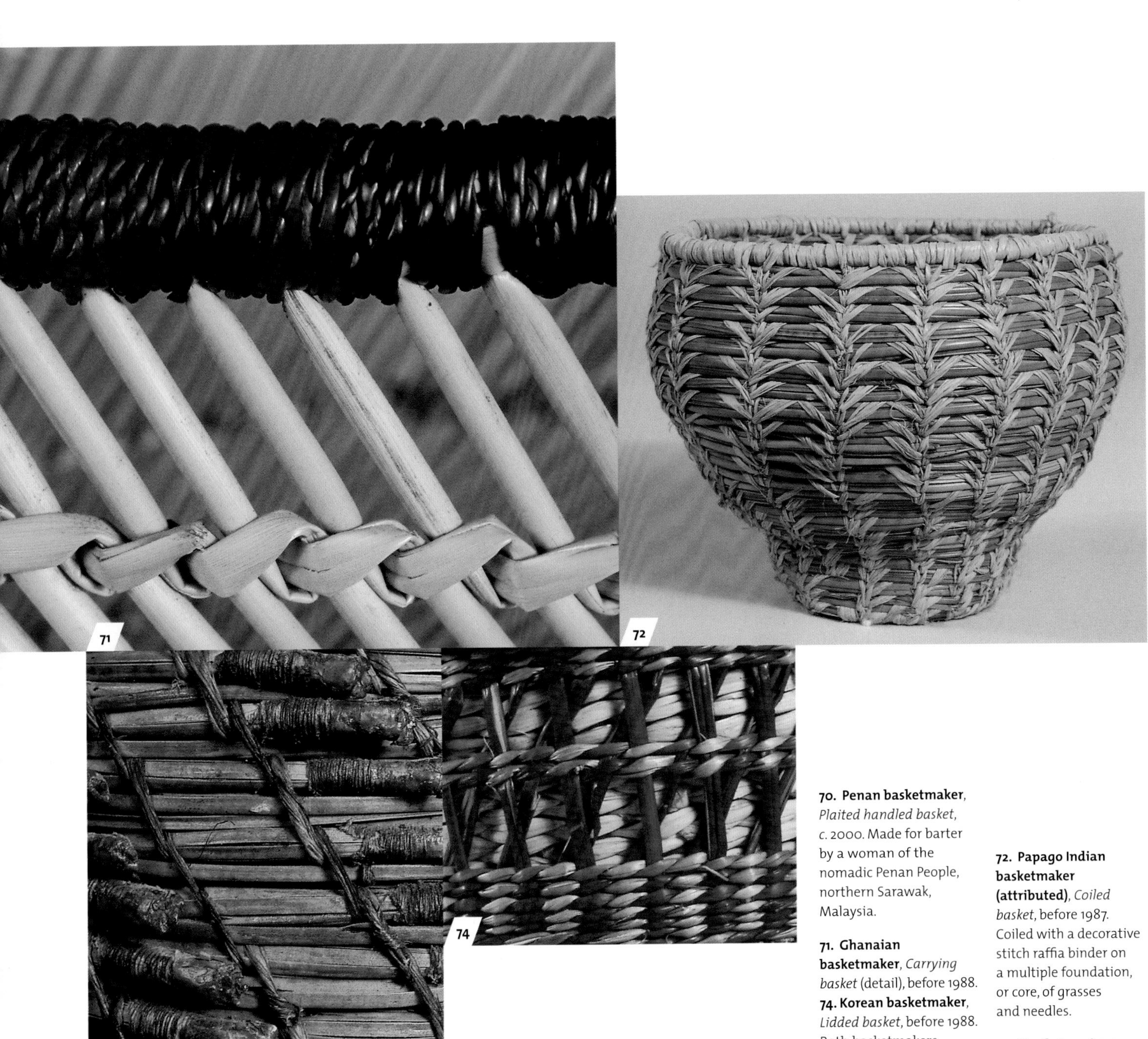

71 72 74 73 75

70. Penan basketmaker, *Plaited handled basket*, c. 2000. Made for barter by a woman of the nomadic Penan People, northern Sarawak, Malaysia.

71. Ghanaian basketmaker, *Carrying basket* (detail), before 1988.
74. Korean basketmaker, *Lidded basket*, before 1988. Both basketmakers and weavers employ weft-twining, in which paired wefts are twisted between each warp, as seen in a Ghanaian carrying basket of natural and dyed fibrous cord, and a Korean double-walled lidded basket of natural seagrass. On the loom weft-twining takes the material completely around a warp and, in *soumak*, around several warps. These concepts rotated 90 degrees lead to warp-twining and gauze weaves.

72. Papago Indian basketmaker (attributed), *Coiled basket*, before 1987. Coiled with a decorative stitch raffia binder on a multiple foundation, or core, of grasses and needles.

73. North American basketmaker, *Coiled cylindrical basket*, before 1988. With a foundation of pine-needle bundles, the widely spaced twine binder runs on the diagonal, accentuating the wrapped heads of the bundles.

75. Ghanaian basketmaker, *Openwork twined and wrapped basket* (detail), before 1988. A twined basket of straw, with a reinforced rim wrapped in natural and dyed cord.

76. Mandy Gunn, *WeAVE*, 2003–4. Secured with rivets along the edges, old rusted steel mine strapping was cut and woven into a coiling installation 5 m (16 ft 5 in.) long. 'By reusing well-known materials, I feel I am drawing attention to our wasteful society ... but I also like the inbuilt history of the material and the way this can contribute ... and often become the subject matter of the work.'

77. Columbian artisan, *Expanding knotted carrying container* (detail), 1968. Hand-knotted, dyed two-ply sisal cord.

78. Guatamalan weaver, *Cinta* (detail), before 1984. This headwrap is made of long tassels topped with pom-poms. Rows of rayon thread, cut and applied to resemble feathers, hang at the bottom, and hold loops of heavy, white rayon cord. Wrapping secures these and the rayon-thread fringes. Of a type produced in Totonicapán by both men and women, to be sold all over Guatemala in tourist markets, these textiles are also used as belts and hat bands, and were more popular with Maya women between the 1930s and 1960s than they are today.

79. New Mexican lacemaker, *Colcha coverlet border*, c. 1820–50. This type of multicoloured, scalloped wool and plaited-lace border is a distinctive feature of *colcha*. These self-couching stitched coverlets, curtains, altar frontals and other interior textiles were made in a territory that today is in the United States, but from 1821 to 1846 was part of Mexico.

78
79

80

81

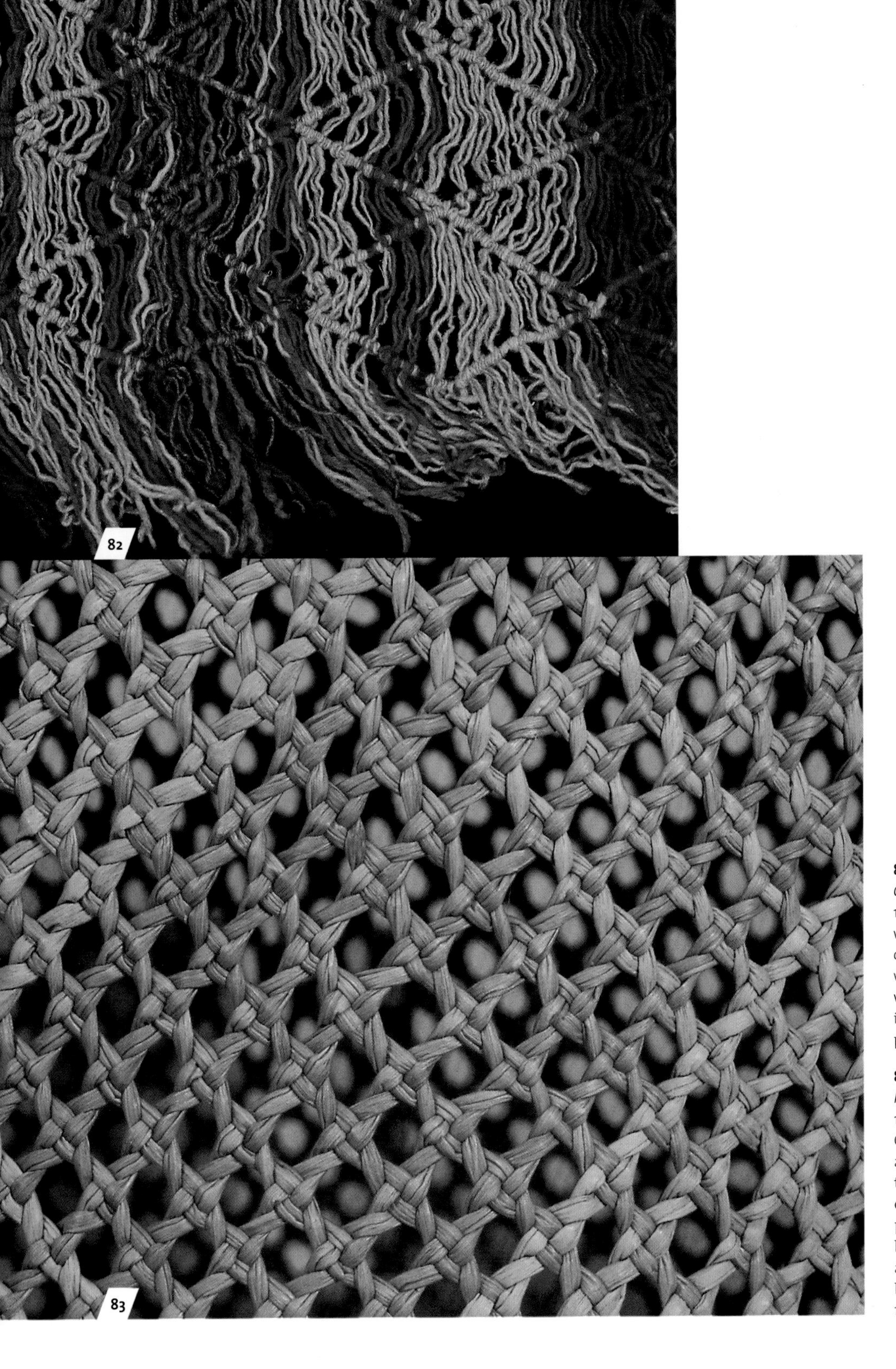

80. Candace Crockett, *Ceremonial Bag* (detail), 1975. Loom-woven body with wood buttons and card-woven additions of wool, with knotted and wrapped tassels laid in as the card-weaving progressed.

81. Peruvian weaver, *Poncho* (detail), before 1974. Woven in the Cuzco Highlands from alpaca, the fringe on this poncho is composed of individual strands passed through and looped to a narrow braid and then twisted. The braid is secured with feather-stitching.

82. Mexican weaver, *Rebozo* (detail), before 1986. The fringe of this wool shawl is composed of the warp elements, extending 18 cm (7 in.) beyond the end of the *rebozo* and macraméd, illustrating the traditional function of this knotting technique.

83. Ecuadorian artisan, *Twined basket* (detail), before 1989. Penwork diagonal twining in orange and green raffia illustrates the close conceptual relationship between this knotless technique and that of macramé and other similar knotting methods.

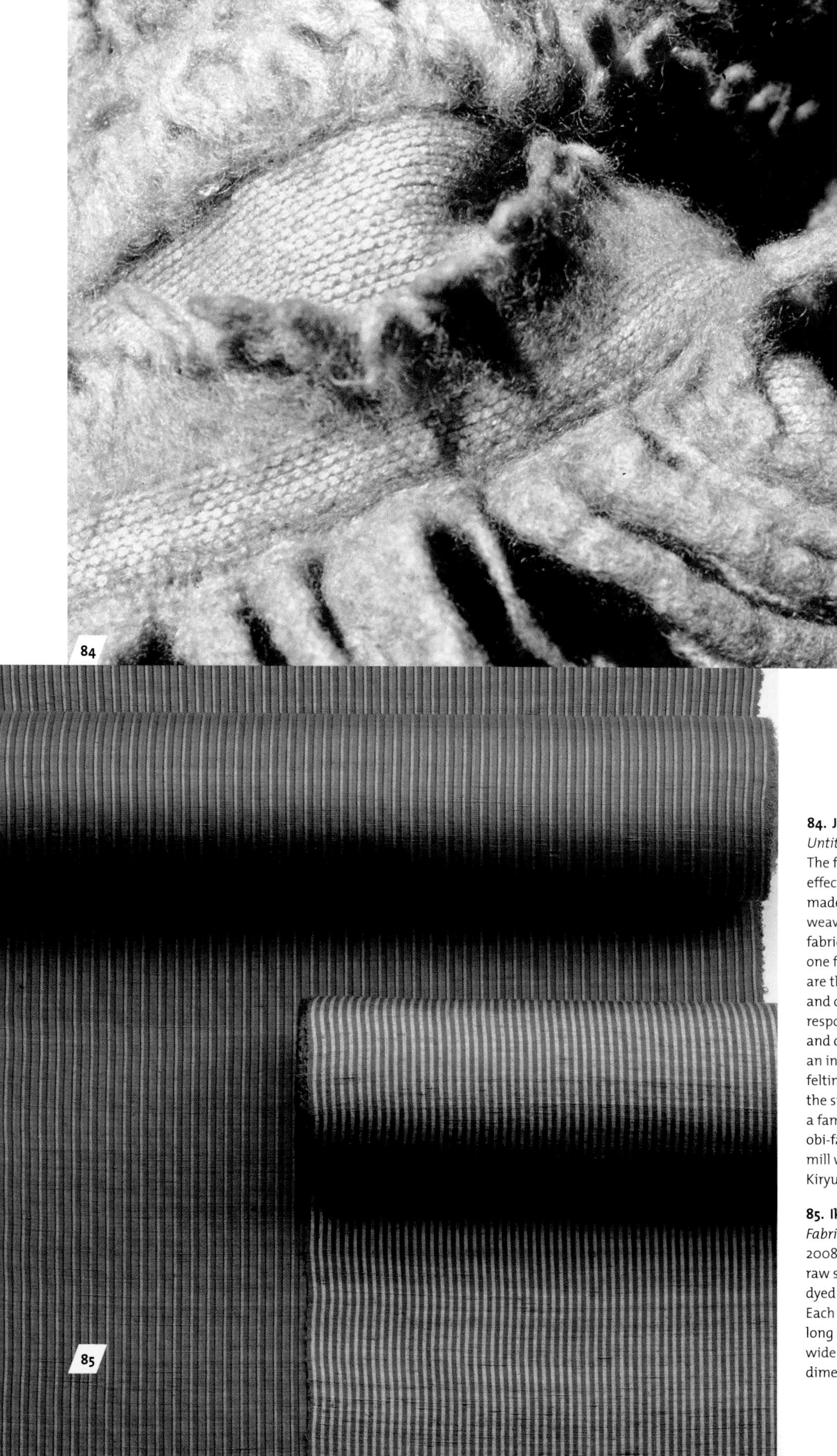

86. Christine Keller, *Scarf Breeze, Hauchschal*, 1997–2001. While working as the principal designer for Handweberei Rosenwinkel in Germany – a small handweaving unit known for its employment of differently abled staff – Keller developed mercerized cotton and merino wool handwoven and hand-felted fabrics. This scarf developed by accident: 'One of the weavers wove a sample fabric too loosely, and during the felting the texture came apart .... Our director ... cut off this piece of fabric and wrapped it around her neck.' Keller refined the technicalities, and the result was this award-winning design.

87. Tim Parry-Williams, *Cloth 3* (detail), 2009. This was handwoven from spun silk and linen, and coloured with acid and direct dyes. Emerging from a 'Future Craft' research project, it represents a very particular philosophy, 'deeply informed by my industrial ... experience and understanding (systems of production, design methodologies, cycles etc.) ... expressed through a deliberately handwoven cloth'.

84. Jun-ichi Arai, *Untitled*, c. 1987–93. The frayed and knotted effects in this cloth, made using a tricot weave in which a knitted fabric is worked from one fully threaded warp, are the result of cutting and of the differing responses of its wool and cotton yarns to an intense milling (or felting) process. Arai is the sixth generation of a family of kimono- and obi-fabric weavers whose mill was established in Kiryu, Japan, in 1900.

85. Ikuko Ida, *Kimono Fabrics (Checked)*, 2008–10. Handwoven raw silk and floss silk, dyed with natural dyes. Each piece is 12 m (13 yds) long and 39 cm (15¼ in.) wide – the traditional dimensions.

88. Marianne Straub, *Warner powerwoven upholstery fabrics*, 1952–68. All of these cloths began as handwoven prototypes that exploited Straub's knowledge of vegetable dyeing and hand-spinning. Arranged with the earliest on the right, they were sold through British firms, including Warner & Sons Ltd, Heal's, Parker Knoll and Ercol Furniture.

86
87

89
90
91
92
93

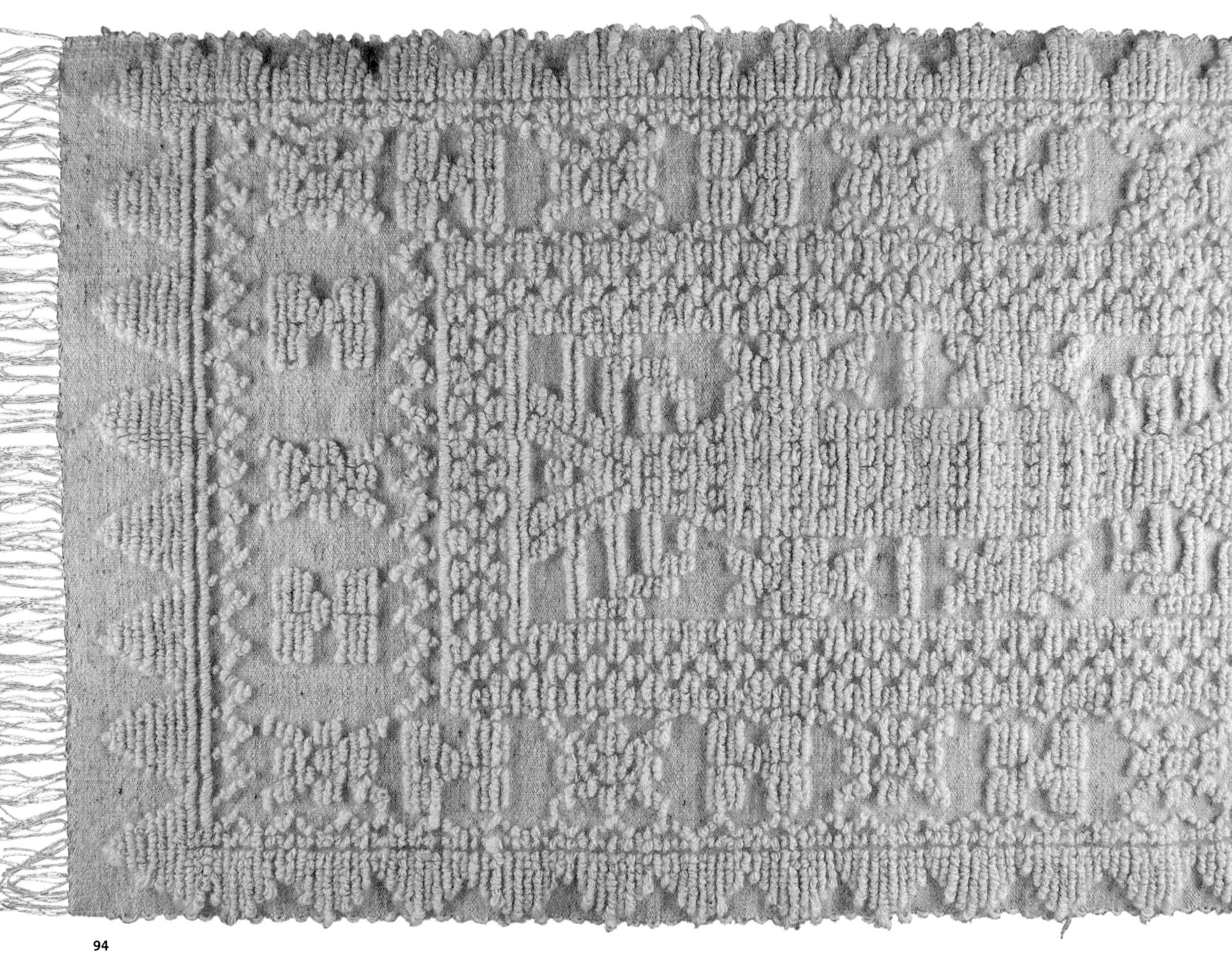

94

89. Alison Morton, *Linen hand towels*, 2008–11. Luxury bed, table and utilitarian linens are prized for the subtle coloration of undyed flax and their increasing softness with each wash. From the top, these examples were handwoven in herringbone (with a handspun weft), huckaback, and canvas weaves, while in the background is a plain or tabby weave.

90. Tim Parry-Williams, *'Denims' collection*, 2009. Handwoven samples employing various sizes of cotton and linen yarns, and natural dyes. 'Sources of inspiration have varied from the Roman ruins at Herculaneum and Oplontis, to Japanese Shinto shrines. More often it is the colour of a shadow or the texture of a wall where the tiles have been removed.'

91. Sally Weatherill, *Frost*, 2004. Viscose scarf woven in a leno technique with fine white silk and a delicate viscose yarn. 'Leno, while twisting the yarns securely at intervals, also allows them freedom to move,' explains Weatherill. 'In this way the beauty of each individual yarn can be fully appreciated.'

92. Chinami Ricketts, *Kimono yardage*, 2011. This play on a check pattern suggests broad, horizontal near-white bands through ikat dyeing of the indigo blue and natural-brown cotton warp stripes.

93. Sara Nordling, *Textures*, 2009. Highly twisted wool and acrylic yarns hold the grid formation created by spaced placement of the plain-woven warp and weft.

94. Cretean weaver, *Looped rug* (detail), before 1986. This wool and cotton rug was made by the 'confetti' technique, in which the shed is opened, a knitting needle is inserted, and the wool weft is wrapped around it; the next weft is beaten down to hold the loop in place. Using an indented rod instead of a needle is how velveteen is made, the indentation holding the blade that cuts the loop open.

95

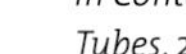

95. Nithikul Nimkulrat, *My Old Lady*, 2002. This is one of five human-sized sculptures, made of multilayered woven Thai silk, from the artist's 'Dress Party' series.It presents 'dresses that require no wearer and cannot be worn'. The garments are intended to represent 'humans at each stage of their life'. Nimkulrat urges people 'to realize the value of things and people they usually neglect'.

96. Mariana Minke and Sara Forzano, *In Context – Woven Tubes*, 2009. Tubular garments change their form depending on their dimension, the type of woven pattern, the openings (which are integral to the form) and the finishing treatment. *Second Skin* (on the left) is made of cotton, elastane and silk in a double-weave warp ikat with de-coloured weft, and *Reflection* is a doubleweave and plissé of cotton ribbon, copper thread, linen and PVC tubes. Both are handwoven and 'born, developed and expressed directly on the loom'.

96

97

97. Deirdre Wood, *Interlocking Woven Rings*, 2010. These linen, wool and ikat-dyed silks are strip-woven. Curving strips emerge from the linen and silk, enabling the artist to produce woven rings. By calculating the width of a strip needed to produce a circle of a given diameter, Wood can weave rings of different sizes that, when sewn together, fit exactly inside each other.

98. Margo Selby, *Wool scarves*, 2009. Selby is influenced by various artists, such as Bridget Riley and M. C. Escher, who inspire her graphic and optical patterns, and the pointillist painter Georges Seurat, whose colour mixes stimulate Selby's approach to mixing yarn on the loom.

99. Reiko Sudo, *Rice Straw*, 2008. The city of Tsuruoka in Japan is located in a rare silk production area, where everything from raising silkworms to weaving is undertaken. Made of earth-friendly *Tsuruoka* silk, rich in natural moisture-retaining amino acids, as well as cotton, this fabric was inspired by the local Yamagata landscape, its racks of windblown rice straw depicted by weaving in nubby *tsumugi* (plied silk yarn), which was then hand cut.

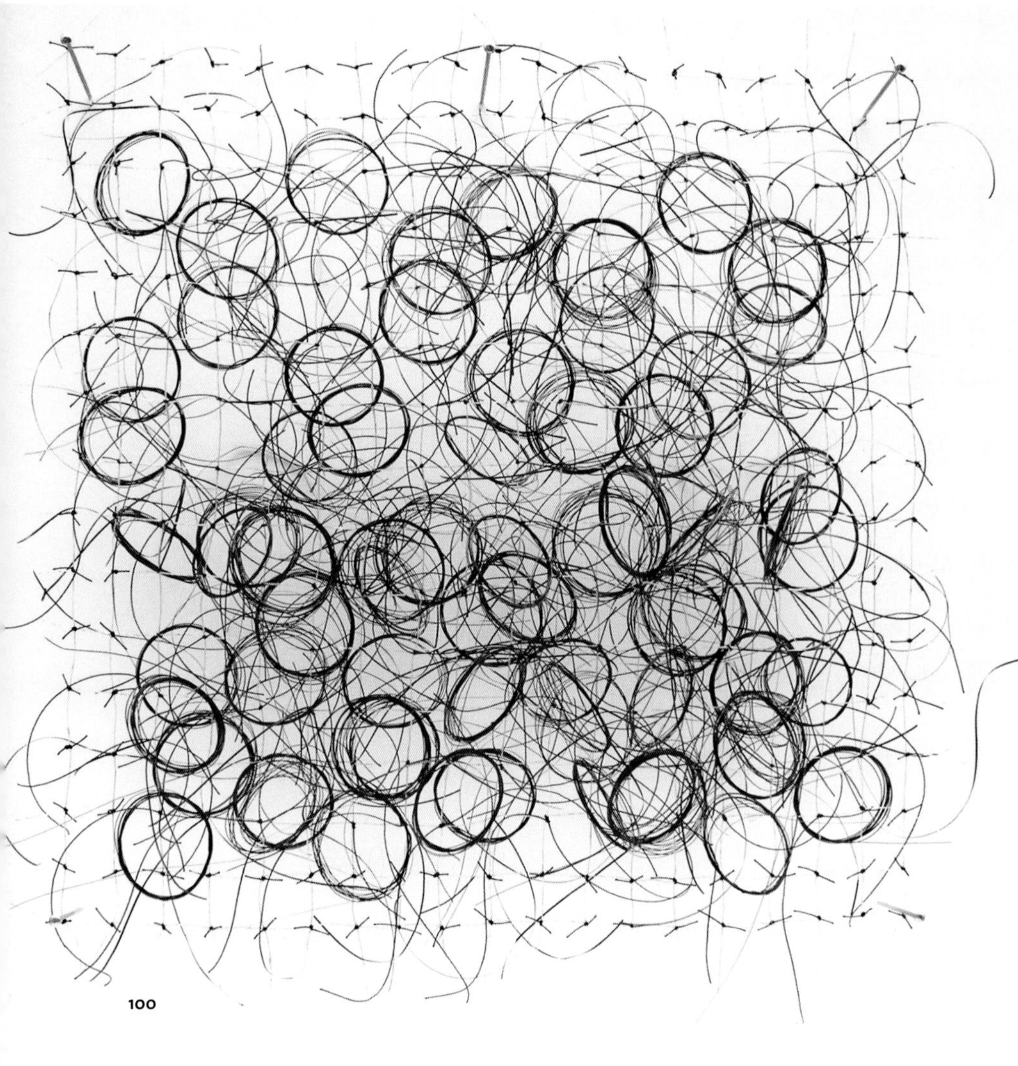

100

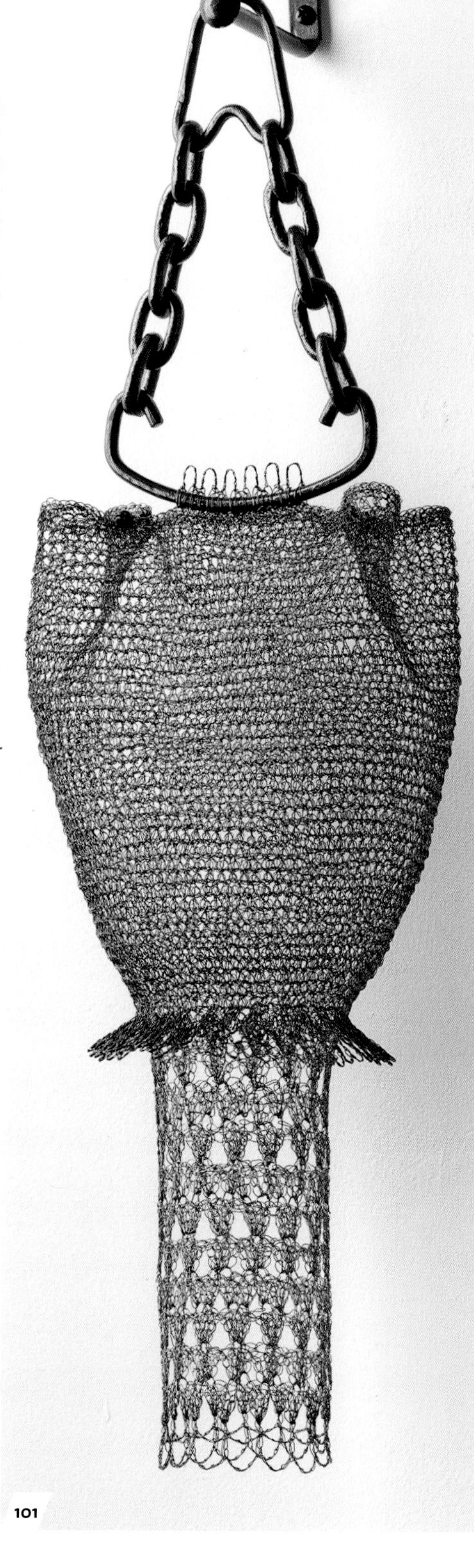

101

100. Linda Green, *Buoyancy*, 2009. 'Drawing' directly with knotted wire and monofiliment, the artist here expresses her interest in chance versus order and the illusion of depth and translucency.

101. Tracy Krumm, *Lure (Pouch)*, 2011. Crocheted nickel, forged steel and found objects are given a resin patina to create an interplay of delicacy and strength.

102. Tracy Krumm, *Double Chain (Sleeve)* (detail), *c.* 2009. Creating intricate pattern and texture with crocheted copper wire, and incorporating forged steel and found objects, the completed work was treated with a patina resin.

103. Flora Sutton, *Vinculos (Ties)*, 2005. Argentinian artist Sutton uses her own techniques to manipulate wire and iron to form a sculpture standing 150 cm (59 in.) high.

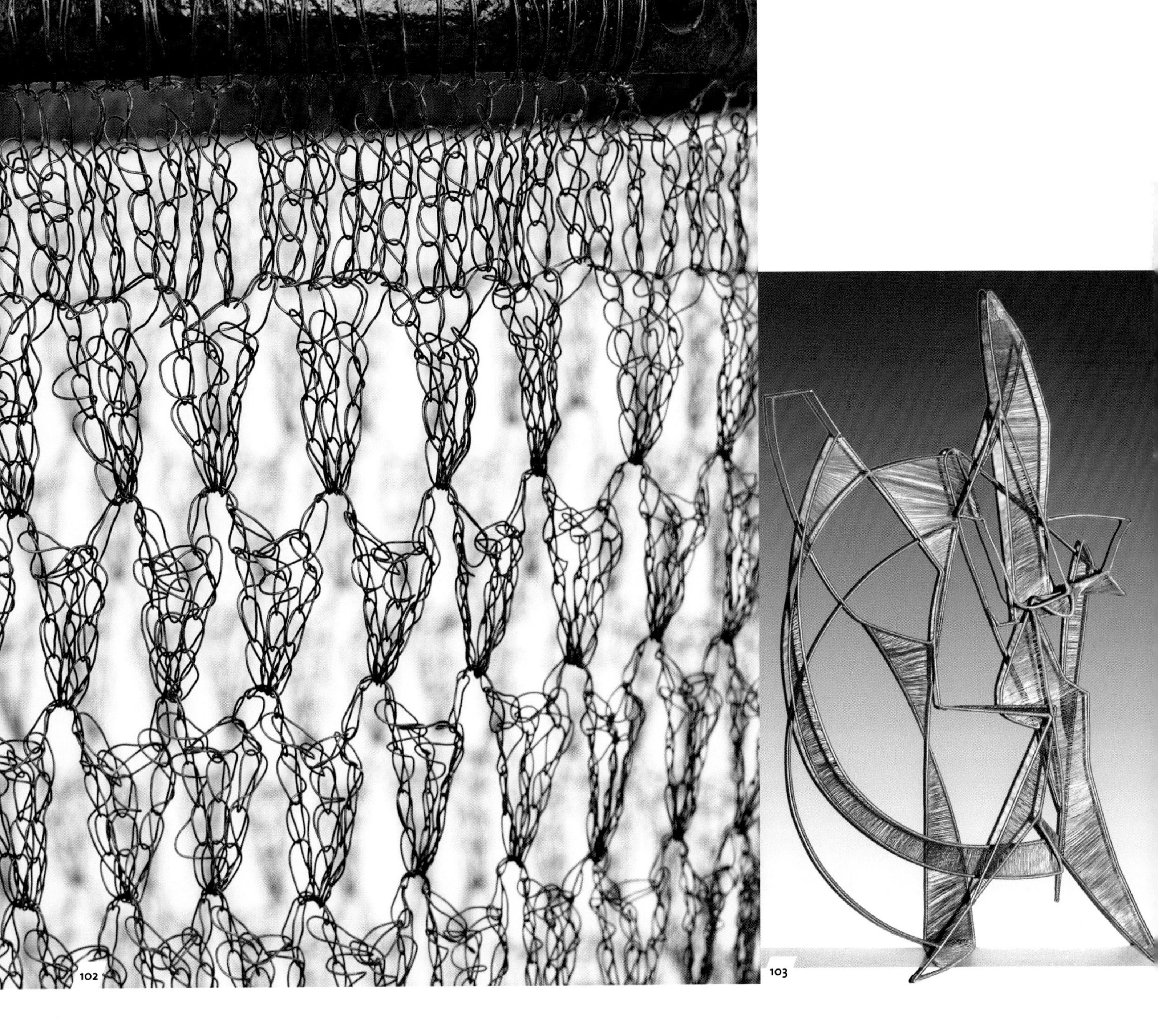

102

103

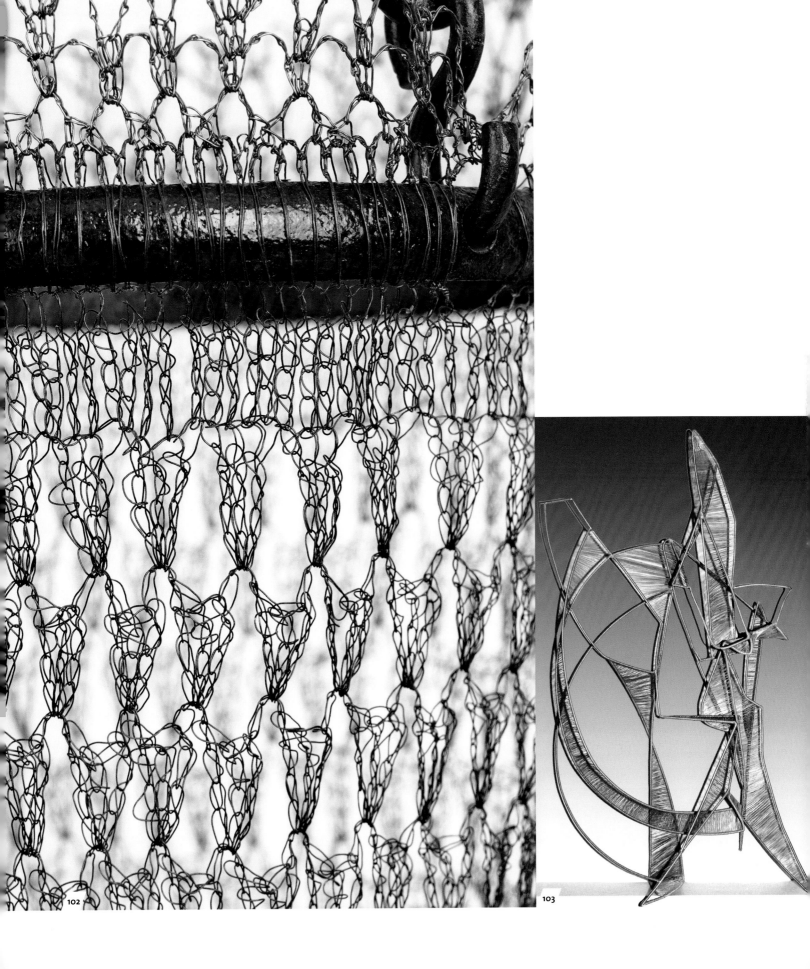

105

104. Mary Elizabeth Barron, *Small Family Tree 1*, 2008. Old clothes predominantly belonging to the artist and her family are coiled with cotton and polyester thread: 'Our clothes are very personal and intimate and ... they embody the work with these qualities. ... Both the physical form and the emotional memories guide and inspire the form.'

105. Jackie Abrams, *Grounded*, 2011. Coiled scraps of fabrics and threads: 'Sitting in my studio, with materials in hand, is always a source of fulfilment, meditation, frustration and satisfaction.'

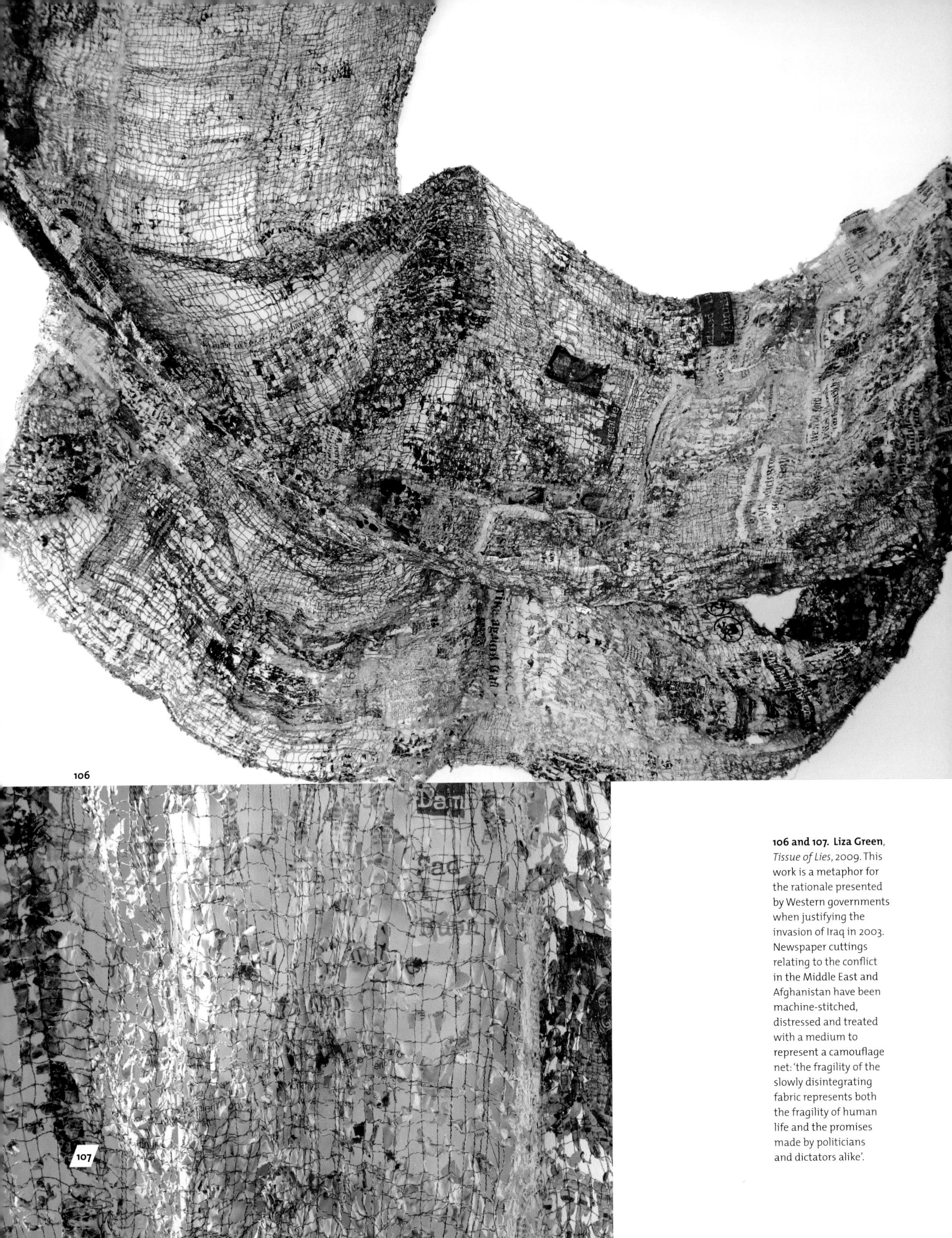

106

107

106 and 107. Liza Green, *Tissue of Lies*, 2009. This work is a metaphor for the rationale presented by Western governments when justifying the invasion of Iraq in 2003. Newspaper cuttings relating to the conflict in the Middle East and Afghanistan have been machine-stitched, distressed and treated with a medium to represent a camouflage net: 'the fragility of the slowly disintegrating fabric represents both the fragility of human life and the promises made by politicians and dictators alike'.

108

109

110

111

112

108. Havva Halaceli, *Festival* (detail), 2009. Linen, cotton and elastane woven on a Jacquard loom.

109. Havva Halaceli, *Body Dress*, 2008. Copper wire and polyester thread are knitted and crocheted into a form suggestive of both a body and a dress.

110. Janet Lipkin, *Spiral* (detail), 1973. Detail of the back of a short jacket hand-crocheted in wool and glitter-polyester yarn. Lipkin trained as a painter and sculptor at the Pratt Institute, New York, where she began to execute her artwork in crochet. This example is now in the collection of the Oakland Museum in California.

111. Christine Sawyer, *Yesterday's 'Must Haves'*, 2011. At approximately 135 cm (53 in.) square, this worsted and cotton tapestry addresses waste and over-production.

112. Erica Grime, *Organic Moods*, 2011. A triple weave of cotton dissolvable yarn, linen, wire and elastic yarn.

113

114

113. Cynthia Schira, *Etymon* (detail), 2010. Woven with a warp of white Egyptian cotton and a black cotton weft, this damask panel measures 3 × 9.1 m (10 × 30 ft) and was constructed on an electronic Jacquard loom at the Oriole Mill in North Carolina. Reflecting the artist's long-standing interest in notations, codes and cyphers, the patterns are abstractions from thirty-nine online digital images of objects within a single museum collection.

114. Egyptian weaver, *Tiraz (inscribed textile) fragment*, 11th century. Bands of silk tapestry on plain-woven linen alternate between decorative motifs and Arabic script, the incorporation of which was initially associated with caliphate workshops but spread widely. Calligraphy had a higher status than painting in Islam at this time, and it remains regarded by many as this culture's most prominent art form.

115. Candace Crockett, *Dress Series, Ghost Dress* (detail), 1991. Of loom-woven linen, cotton and cotton fabric, this panel, approximately 124.5 cm (49 in.) square, is reminiscent of the ancient Andean *khipu* – or *quipu* – which employed a series of knotted cords that were used to store information.

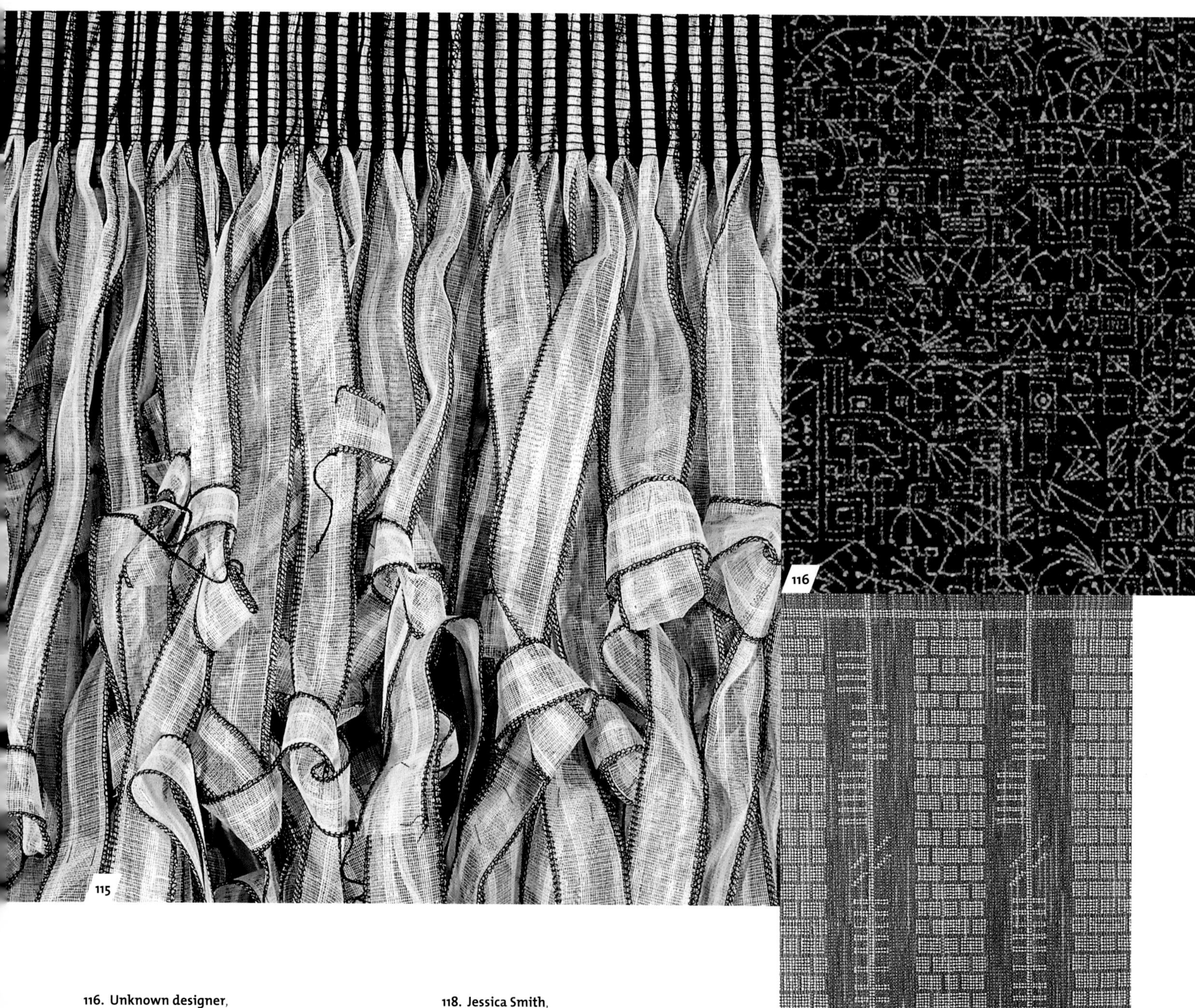

116. Unknown designer, *Automotive textile*, 1959. Woven for Chrysler and incorporating turquoise lurex, this diminutive pattern makes reference to printed circuit boards, which, with laminated copper pathways to conduct electricity, became common in consumer electronics in the mid-1950s and subsequently facilitated information-transmission systems, including those associated with computing.

117. Karin Schaller, *Cuinas gan uaigneas (Quietness without loneliness)*, 1995–96. From the artist's 'Ogham Alphabet' series, this 115.5 cm (45½ in.) high panel was handwoven in silk, rayon, cotton and metallic threads employing the 'summer and winter' structure.

118. Jessica Smith, *Elephant and Mossie*, 2004. A matelassé structure (a variant of double cloth) woven on a dobby loom, this polyester and silk piece, 30.5 cm (12 in.) long, is also embroidered with French knots. The artist alternates between drawing on paper and on the computer to 'design, produce and "place" narrative patterns. These patterns have a historical reference, contemporary message and a subversive twist.'

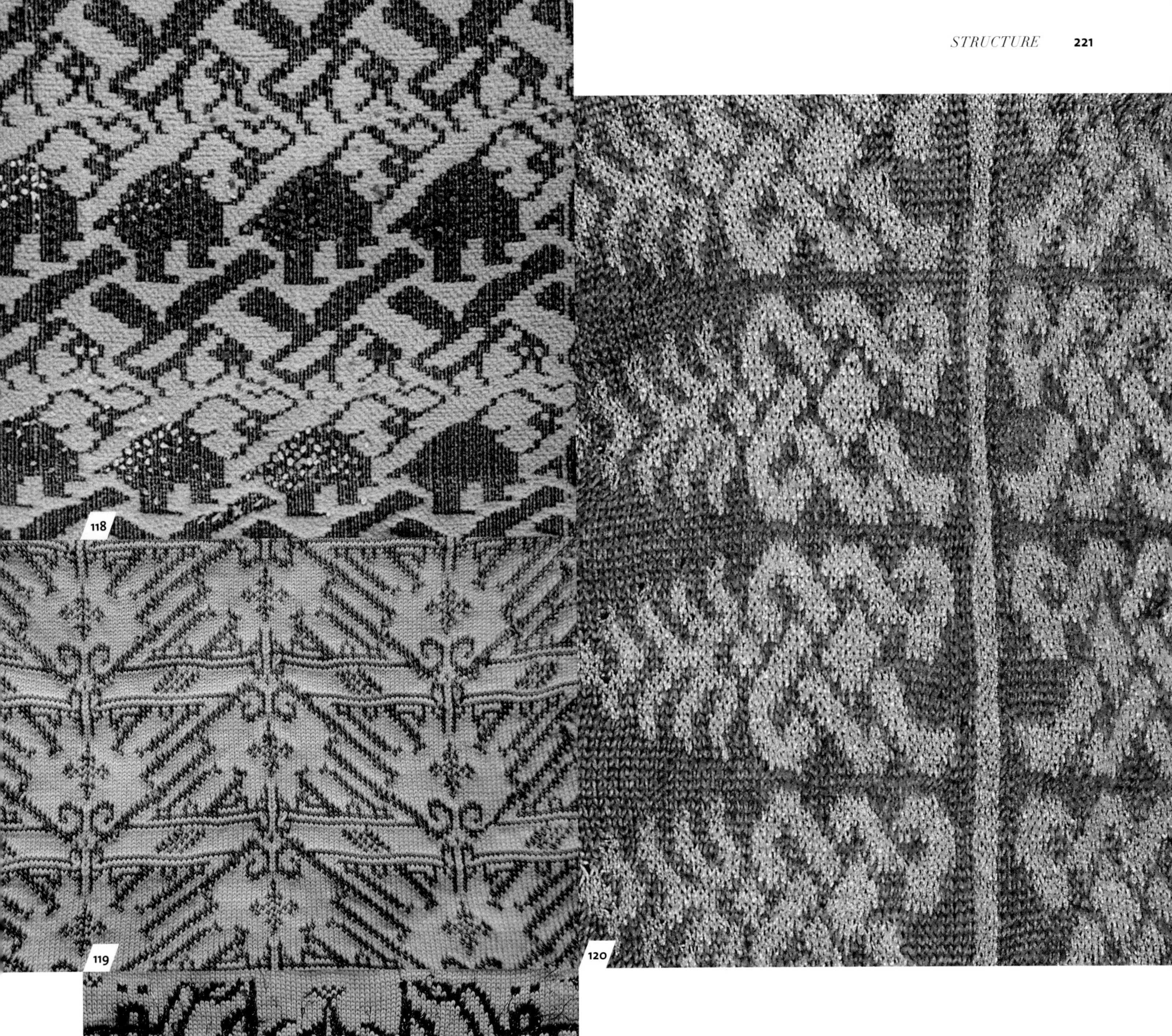

119. Della Reams and Fatima Al-Najar, *Fatima 2*, 2011. Digitally designed, this pattern was realized in merino wool and rayon yarns on a hand-operated knitting machine by Reams and her Qatari student, whose name is represented in the work in Arabic calligraphic form. Reams refers to the long-established Arabic practice of wearing script-embedded textiles, and to 'soldiers wearing prayers woven into the fabric closest to their skin.'

120. European knitter, *Man's knitted silk jacket* (detail), early 17th century. Displaying hispano-moresque pseudo-calligraphy, this garment reflects the transmission of Middle Eastern knitting to Spain, and thence to the rest of Europe, via Muslim knitters employed in the 13th century by Spanish Christian families. It was most likely made in Spain, Italy or the Spanish Netherlands.

121. Della Reams and Maryam Al-Thani, *Maryam fabric*, 2011. Silk-cashmere and polyester sparkle yarns worked on a hand-operated knitting machine to render the name of another of Reams's students in Arabic. In both of these examples the adaptation from design to knitting machine was undertaken by Reams.

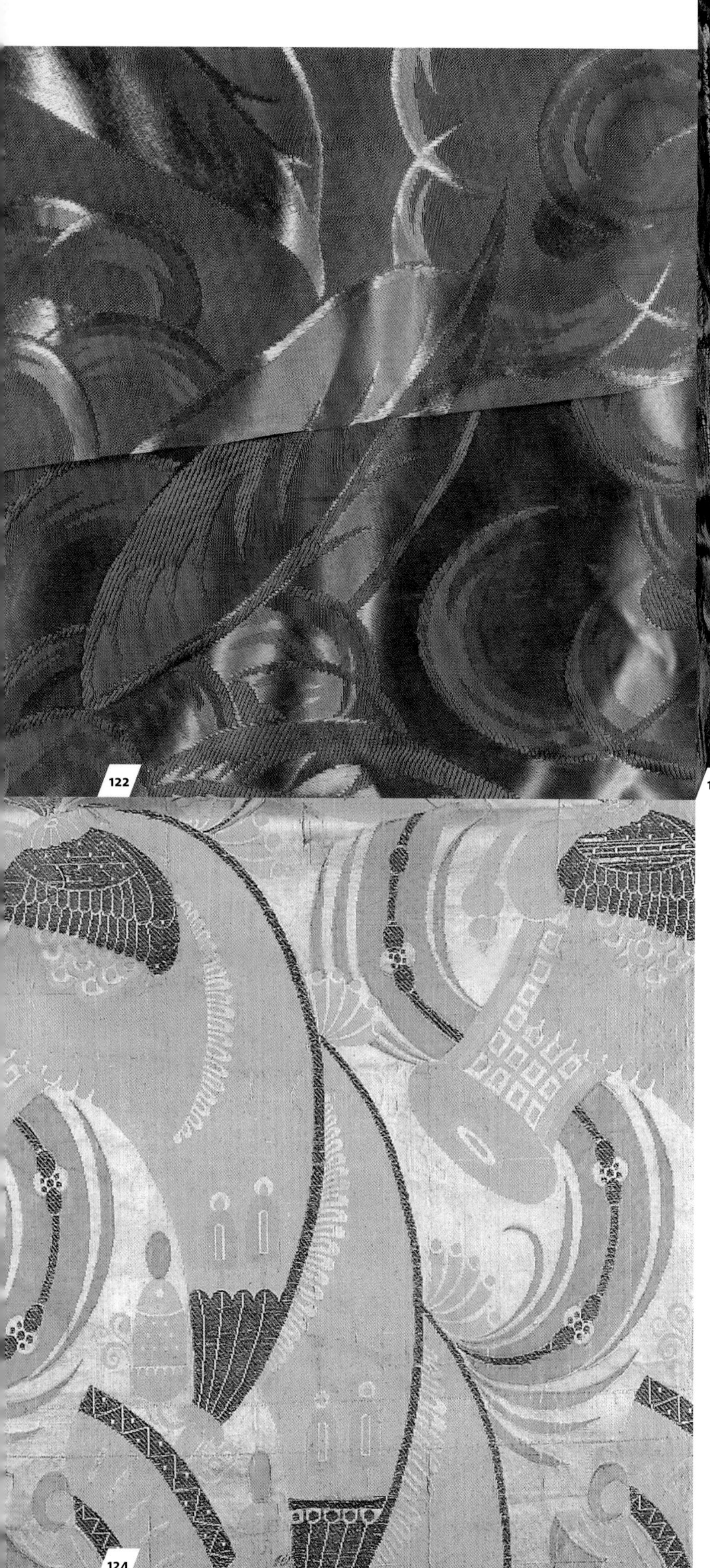

122. Kaisik Wong, *Trousers* (detail), *c.* 1960s–89. Based in San Francisco until his death in 1989, Wong was a pioneer of the wearable art movement, known for his extraordinary combination of fabrics, often vintage. Here he has used both the face and back of a rayon damask from the 1930s.

123. French weaver and Indian tailor, *Dinner jacket/coat* (detail), early 1930s. Made for the Maharaja of Darbhanga (1907–1982), probably in Calcutta. The French silk and metallic-thread handwoven lampas (meaning that it has multiple wefts and/ or warps) combines exuberant Art Deco styling with the influence of the 'bizarre' silks of some 200 years before.

124. French weaver, *Bizarre silk fragment*, *c.* 1710–30. Bizarre silks are characterized by large patterns of stylized or abstract shapes with a diagonal emphasis. The motifs were thought to be exotic and oriental in origin, and the colour combinations were considered strange, hence their description as 'bizarre'.

125. Lyonnais weaver, *Brocaded silk*, *c.* 1734–40. This formal dress silk juxtaposes areas of plain weave (tabby), satin and brocading to create a wide range of textural and three-dimensional effects – novelties attributed to the French designer and entrepreneur Jean Revel (1684–1751). Epitomizing the opulence of Rococo style, the areas brocaded with silver metallic-wrapped threads carry forward the earlier 18th century taste for lace-like and 'bizarre' styles.

125

126. Heather Macali, *Warped (Panoramic View)*, 2009. Handwoven double weave made on a TC-1 (Thread Controlled) loom in metallic yarns and hand-dyed cotton and Tencel – a brand of cellulosic yarn obtained by an organic solvent spinning process that has the generic name 'lyocell'. Beginning with hand-drawn patterns, Macali describes their conversion to the digital, dyeing and weaving stages as 'intense, laborious, repetitious and utterly consuming'.

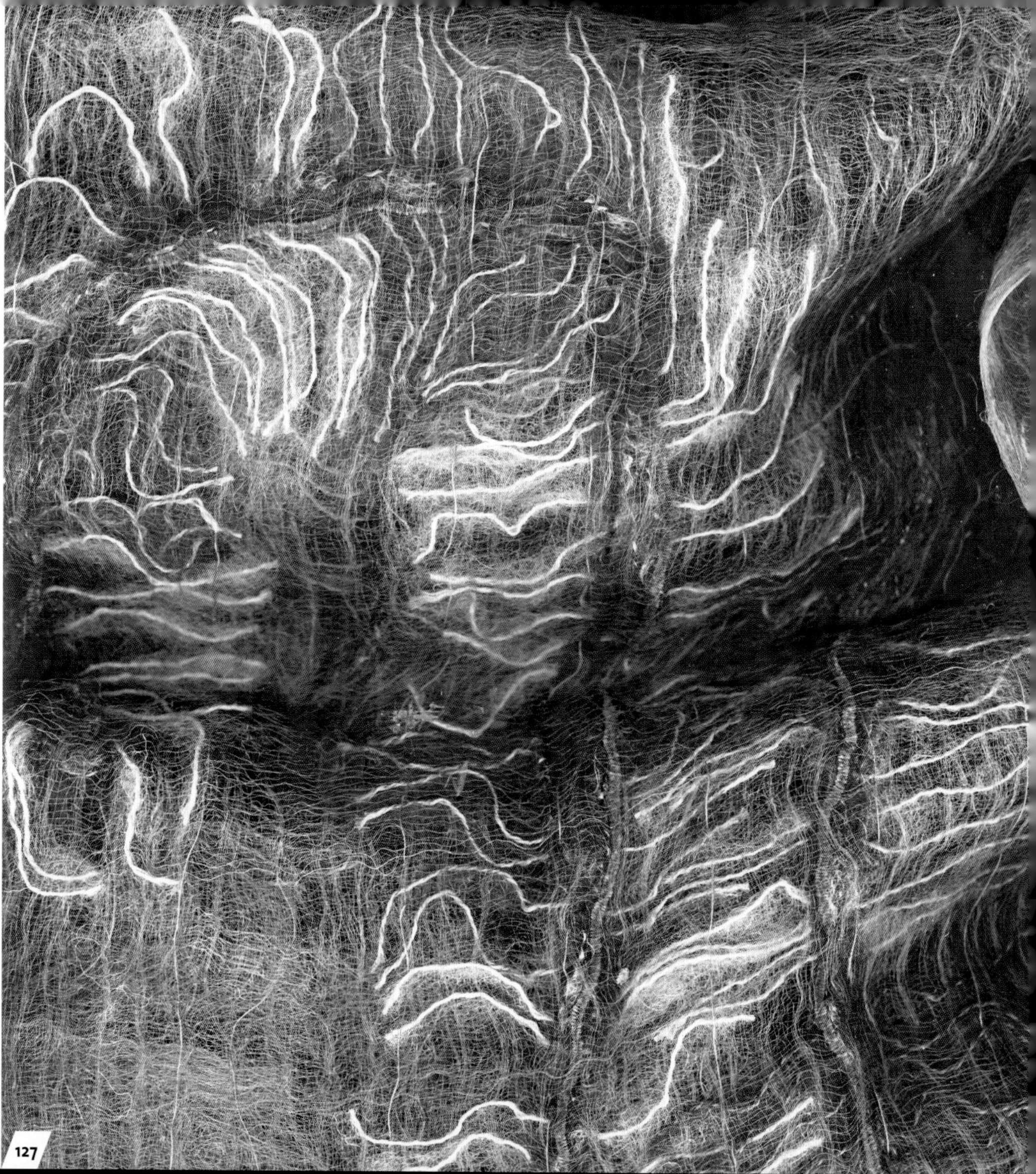

127

126

127. Elegant Additions, Inc., *Fleurs scarf* (detail), 2010. Handwoven in India, this scarf employs inlaid hand-dyed silk yarns caught in a silk leno gauze weave. The company, headed by Chandresh Sheth, is based in Newark, Delaware.

128. Rosmarie Reber, *Cascade* (detail), 2009. This exterior installation includes eighty strips of differing lengths, each 10 cm (4 in.) wide, knitted by fingers with copper thread. Under changing daylight or electric lights its appearance is moderated, alluding to the constant variations seen in falling water.

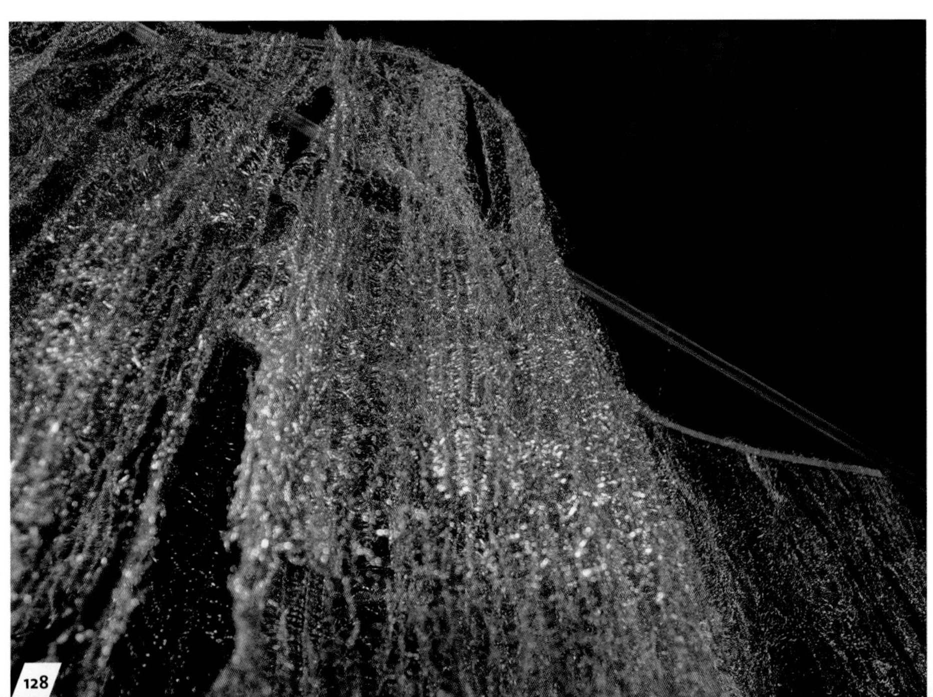

129

130

129. Janet Lipkin, *Mexico in Midday*, 1987. A wool coat intarsia machine-knitted with an ikat-like background created by the incorporation of hand dip-dyed yarns, shibori-resisted while in skein form.

130. Jane Freear-Wyld, *Euphorbia*, 2011. At 124 cm ($48\frac{3}{4}$ in.) high, this tapestry, woven with a wool weft on a cotton warp, was developed digitally and is an experiment using a pixellated design technique on representational subject matter.

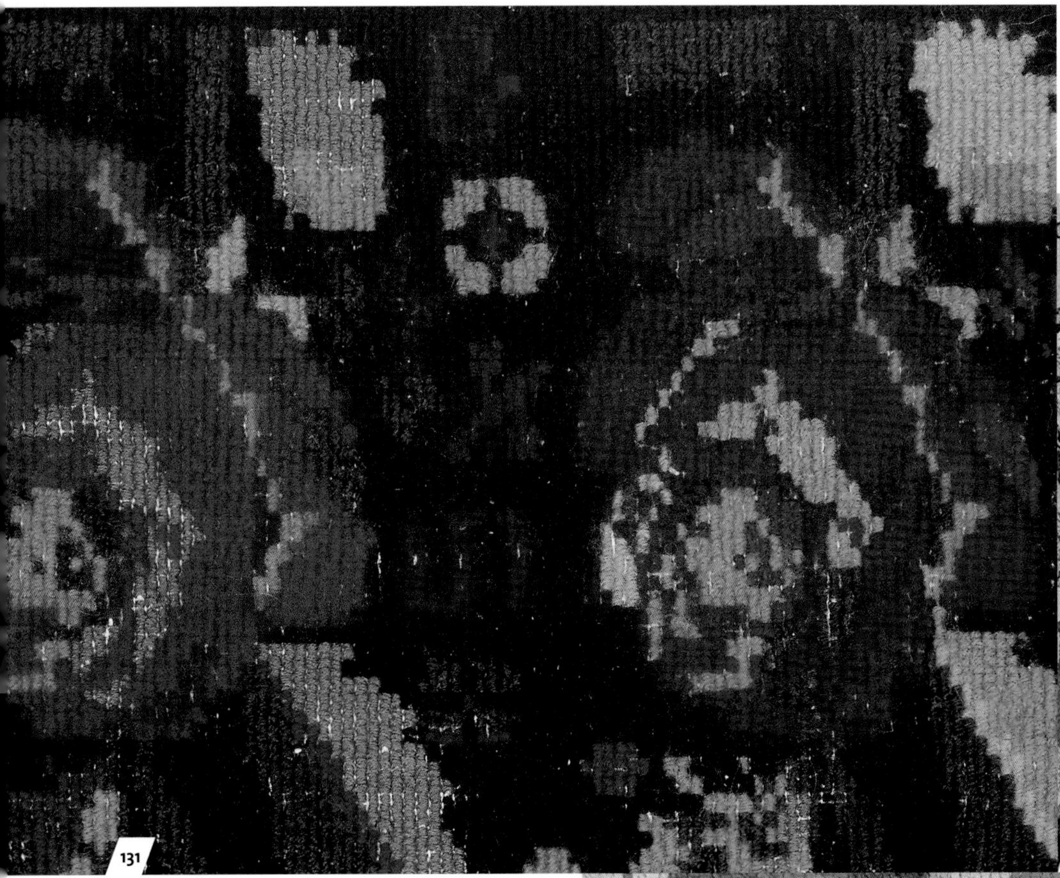

131. Guatemalan weaver, Huipil *panel*, 1960. Roses of multicoloured wool supplementary wefts are handwoven into a cotton weft-faced rep (ribbed) ground.

132. Sabine Parge, *Panama*, 2007. Mixed fabric, ranging from cotton jersey to panne, makes up this velvet rug created through a hooking technique.

133. Guatemalan weaver, *Handwoven textile*, before 1988. This vivid cotton, woven with supplementary warps, was collected by Kaisik Wong and acquired from his family by Jo Ann Stabb in 1997. It epitomizes the influence of Latin America textiles on the Californian wearable art movement.

134. Chinese weaver, *Ch'i-fu* (detail), *c.* 1900. Brocaded with silks and gold metallic thread, the *ch'i-fu* was a full-length, semi-formal coat worn in court or in the service of the Manchu government during the Qing dynasty (1644–1911). The dragon is the paramount symbol of this period, and such garments are often called 'dragon robes'.

135. Chinese weaver, *Rank badge* (detail), before 1850. Silk floss in seed ('forbidden') stitch and couched gold thread form a central bird among stylized clouds rising out of a wave. It was most likely worn by a civil servant of the eighth rank, which was identified by the quail symbol.

136

137

138

139

140

141

142

136. Indian embroiderer, *Decorative band fragment* (detail), *c.* 1900–70. Mustard-yellow silk satin is embellished with multicoloured cross-stitch silk embroidery, with each horizontal stripe edged with couched metallic plaited cord.

137. Ahmedabad weaver, *Salwar* (detail), c. 1840. Brocaded *boteh* decorate this silk in a rare combination of gold and silver coloration called *ganga-jamuna*. The loose trousers made from this cloth were worn by Khengerji III, the Maharaja of Kutch.

138. Italian weaver, *Chasuble*, c. 1450. A cut and uncut silk and gold metal thread velvet with a large stylized pomegranate pattern, of the sort that were prized across Europe. The central orphrey panel is woven, with over-embroidery in couching stitches – a method associated with Northern Europe, particularly Germany.

139. Italian weaver, *Chasuble fragment* (detail), mid-16th century. Made of a two-coloured silk giselé velvet (i.e. having cut and uncut loops), this small contrapuntal coiling-stem pattern also became fashionable among Northern European embroiderers. This and no. 140 are two among the many textiles that passed through the hands of the textile authority and dealer Kay Robertson.

140. Italian weaver, *Brocade* (detail), 17th century. Brocaded with silk and metal threads, this panel was in Adolph Loewi's private collection during the 1930s and 1940s, when it was purchased for the Los Angeles County museum service by Bella Mabury.

141. Persian weaver, *Silk fragment*, late 18th–early 19th centuries. Silk brocaded with wool and gold metallic-wrapped threads.

142. Aleppo artisans, *Sidriyeh* (detail), *c.* 1860–70. Bedouin men often commissioned workshops in Aleppo to make such overgarments, woven in slit tapestry from shoulder to waist level and at the hem with floral motifs on a ground of gold metal thread. Completed with couched gold threads and gold braid, this would have been worn belted over a floor-length robe and trousers.

143. Filipino artisans, *Cut and drawn-work abaca and ramie band*, *c*. 1917. Decorated with added white cotton, abaca and ramie embroidery thread. Abaca is a coarse, strong and durable fibre from the trunk of the abaca plant, *Musa textilis*, which belongs to the same family as the banana and is native to the Philippines. Ramie is a strong, soft, slightly lustrous fibre from the inner bark of various species of the *Boehmeria* genus.

144. English knitter, initials A. O., *Whitework sample*, 1863. Cotton yarns have been finely knitted into thirty-two designs bordered with sawtooth edging in a sampler band that measures 186.7 cm (73½ in.) long. The making of such openwork patterns, or knitted lace, demanded great skill and was highly fashionable in the mid-19th century.

145. Egyptian artisan, *Asyut shawl* (detail), *c*. 1980. Netting with run-in motifs of *badla*, a flat metallic yarn typically silver-plated.

146. Ecuadorian artisans, *Rebozo* (detail), 1971. This woman's long cotton shawl has a warp-ikat patterned centre, 136 cm (53½ in.) long, with knotted white cotton end bands and fringe, each 80 cm (31.5 in.) long. The indigo dyeing was done in a village south of Cuenca, and the fringe was knotted by women from a nearby southern Ecuadorian town, Gualaceo. The women rely on memory for the designs, which are taught to them when they are young by elder women in the family.

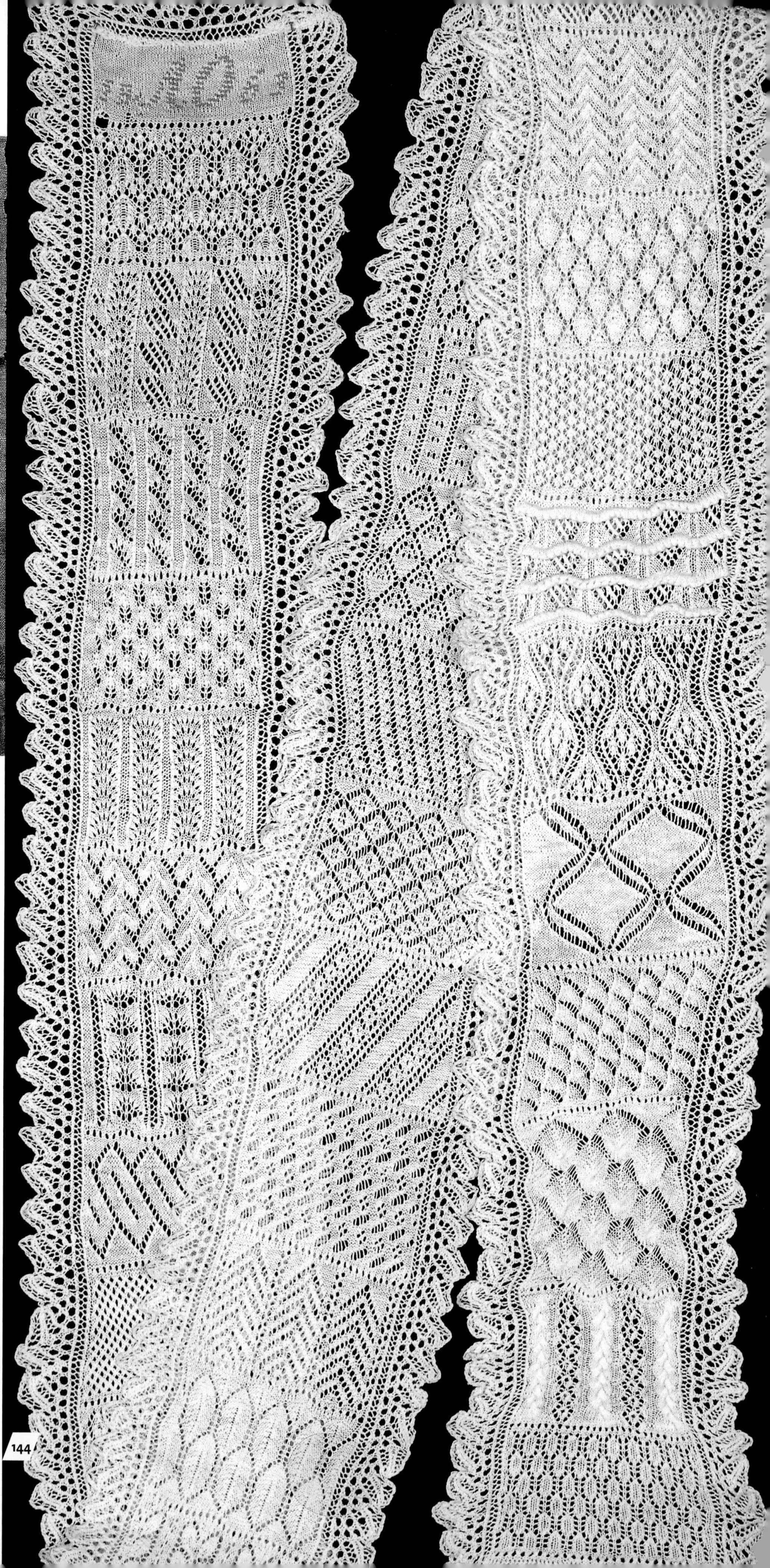

147. Irish artisans, *Irish crochet collar* (detail), *c.* 1870–80. By the mid-19th century crochet had become a significant means of supplementing income in famine-ravished Ireland. Different women specialized in individual motifs, which were then assembled and connected by brides, in imitation of needlepoint laces.

148. Belgian lacemaker, *Lace trimming* (detail), early 1880s. This band 8.9 cm (3½ in.) wide combines Brussels bobbin and Duchesse needlepoint lace techniques. At 4.2 m (13¾ ft) long, it would have been enough to embellish one woman's gown of the period only modestly.

149. German artisan, *Lacis bethrothal panel*, 17th century. Lacis, an ancient form of knotting used to make fishing nets and other utilitarian objects, had become decorative by the Middle Ages. Made from linen threads, here the solid areas are of cloth stitch, or interweaving, and the textural sections are in various single-ply filling stitches. Outlines are in a twisted or twined darning stitch, and the border is of bobbin lace.

150. Reiko Sudo, *Watchspring*, 2009. To create this cotton (80%) and polyester (20%) textile suggestive of a coiled-steel watchspring, the design was embroidered onto a water-soluble base fabric that was then dissolved away. It was made by Nuno Corporation, the Japanese company co-founded by Sudo in 1984 and renowned for its innovative functional fabrics.

147

148

149

151
152

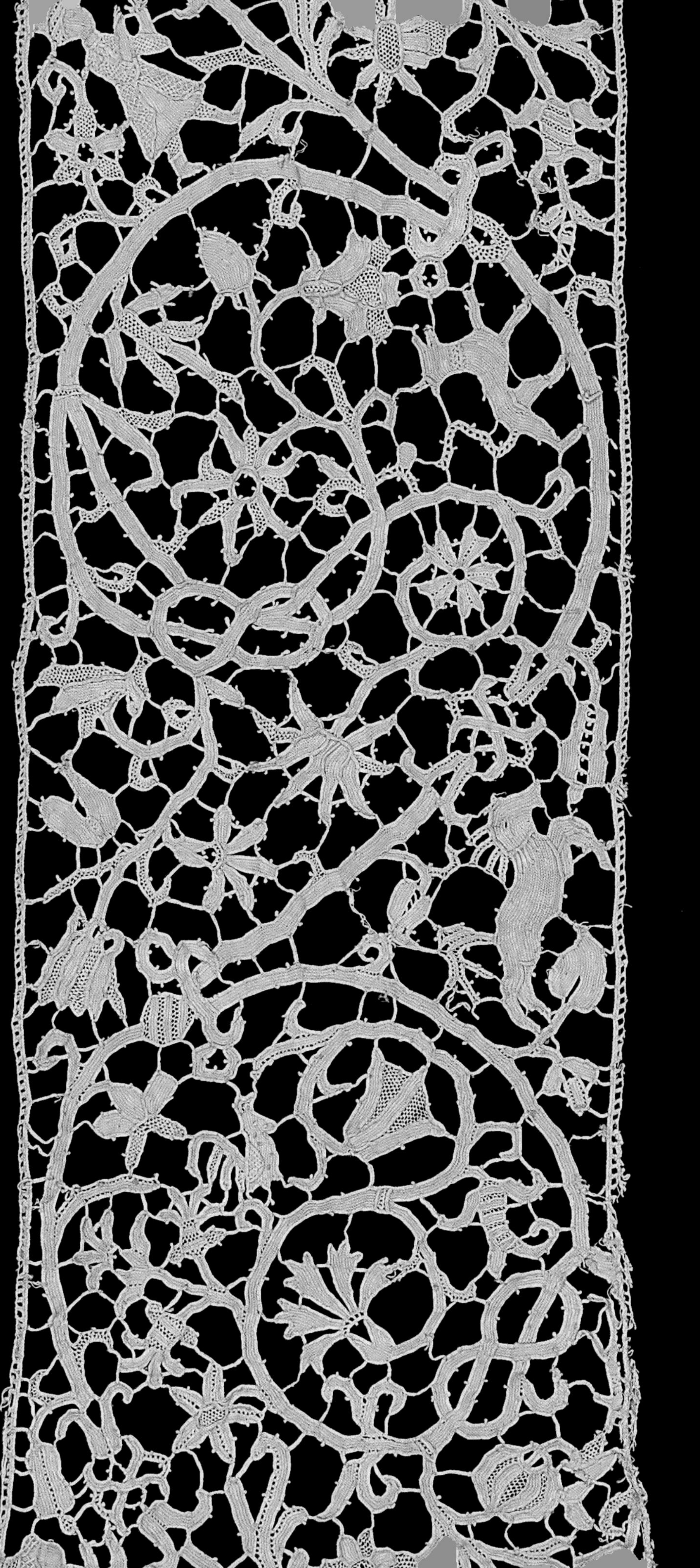

153

151. Nithikul Nimkulrat, *The Chandelier No 2 – The Octopus* (detail), 2011. This chandelier, made of half-hitch knotted paper string and halogen bulbs, reflects the artist's questions about the boundaries between functional and aesthetic objects.

152. Nithikul Nimkulrat, *The Birch Tree* (detail), 2008–10. Knotted paper string forms a tree 1 m (39 in.) high – the artist's response to Iceland's attempt to reinstate forests. The paper string in this conceptual work is a product of Finland, the artist's former home, and represents 'forests in a treeless land'.

153. Venetian lacemaker, Punto in aria *band* (detail), early 17th century. Linen threads couched over a pattern drawn on parchment form the design foundation, which is then overcast or buttonholed. The solid areas are of buttonhole stitch, worked into each other row by row, after which connecting bars, or 'brides', are also buttonholed.

154. Schleswig-Holstein weaver, *Beiderwand*, late 17th century. This is a rare example of Danish *beiderwand*, a form of weaving that combines areas of double cloth, here the linen figuring, with a tied-down ground, in this instance of indigo- or more probably woad-dyed blue wool. The scene represents Christ entering Jerusalem.

155. Sardinian weaver, *Hanging* (detail), early to mid-20th century. Loom-embroidered cotton chenille on heavy khaki cotton depicts lively imagery, including decorative roundels that reflect Sardinia's history – in particular its occupation by the Moors, and then by the Spanish, the latter from 1323 to 1720.

154

156. Flemish tapestry-weaver, *Verdure tapestry* (detail), 1640–65. Woven in Brussels with coloured silk and wool wefts, this tapestry was made by Jan van Leefdahl, a merchant-weaver who would have owned the workshop, taking commissions, employing weavers and controlling the designs that were used. He was mentioned as a dean of the craft in 1644.

157. Ban Chiang weaver, *Door hanging* (detail), 1997. A panel of handwoven cotton from Thailand, with multicoloured silk and gold metallic-wrapped thread supplementary weft motifs.

158. Italian lacemaker, *Filet lace runner* (detail), before 1975. Darning stitch creates the motifs on this ecru linen filet lace, distinguished by its knotted netting ground.

159. W. Craig, *Double-cloth coverlet* (detail), 1857. Handwoven using a Jacquard loom attachment, this signed and dated coverlet was woven in Greensburg, West Virginia.

160. European weaver, *Damasquette fragment*, 18th century. This two-colour hunting scene was woven as a damask, but with an additional weft to maintain the clarity of the motifs' colour.

161. Laotian weaver, *Hom* (detail), 1997. Of coarse cotton woven with extremely long weft floats, this large shawl was purchased in Chiang Mai market.

158

159

160

161

162. Silver Studio (attributed), *Liberty Art Fabrics sample BX6479* (detail), *c.* 1905. This tussah silk furnishing tissue (woven with continuous supplementary wefts) may have been the work of John Illingworth Kay or Harry Napper, who under the direction of Rex Silver produced many designs in the British Art Nouveau style.

163. Middle Eastern weaver, *Shawl fragment* (detail), 19th century. Twill tapestry-woven in fine wool, this high-quality cloth is perhaps part of a Kashmir shawl or, because of the depiction of cattle, one from Afghanistan or Iran.

164

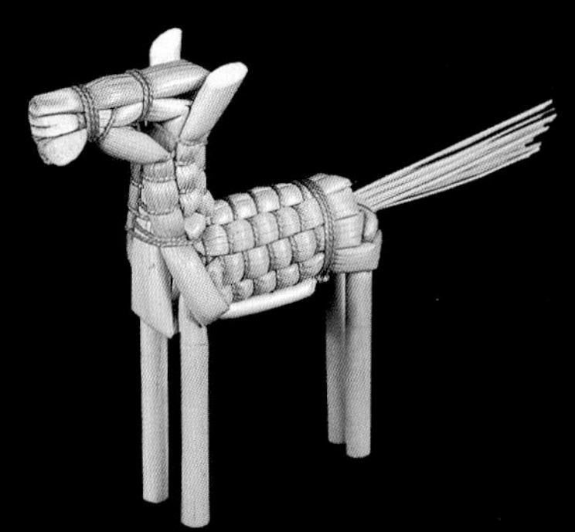
165

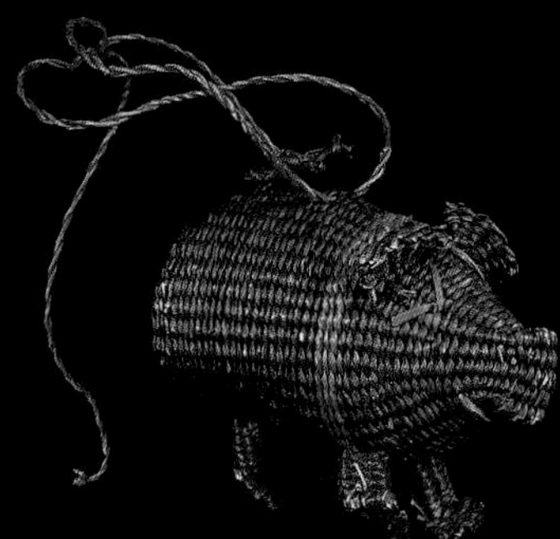
166

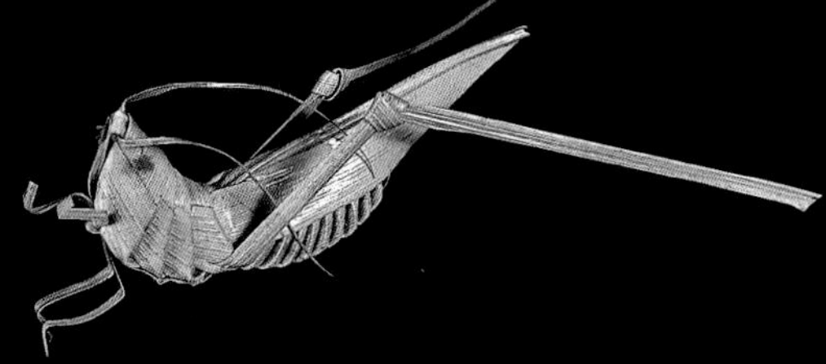
167

168

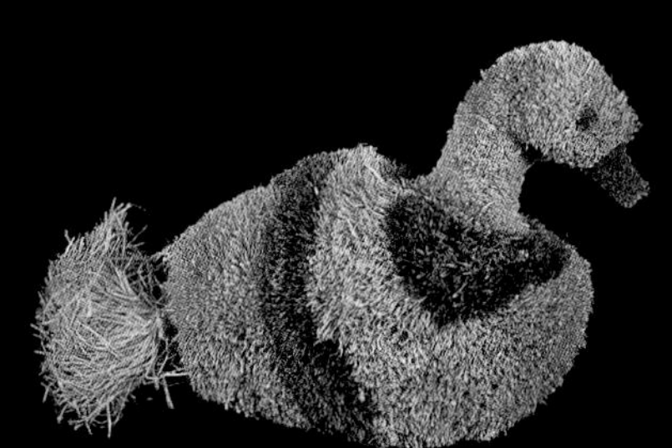
169

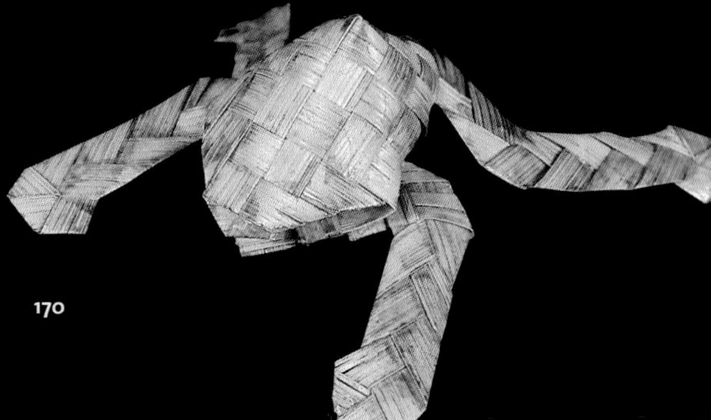
170

171

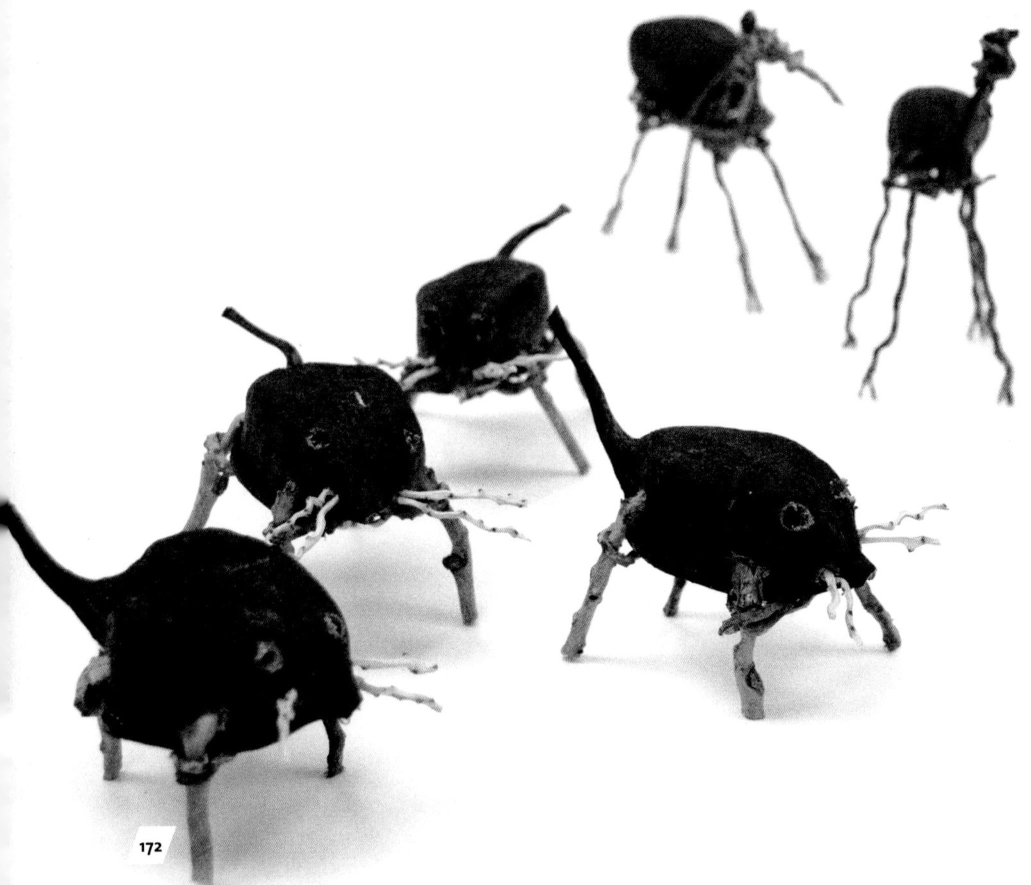

172

164–170. Miniatures formed with basketry techniques are made around the world. From Ecuador are the twined straw figure and the purple pig (164, 166). The miniature horse (165), from Kanuma City, Japan, is made of plaited and wrapped millet straw and brown silk thread. This folk art form was devised in 1964 by Yukio Aoki, a broom-maker and craftsperson, using remnants from brooms. The cricket (167) is Chinese, of plaited palm leaf with coral cotton-thread tufts for eyes. The duck-shaped, lidded basket of grass coiled with raffia, with attached pine cone segments (168), was made in North or South Carolina, while the duck-shaped brush in natural and dyed grasses (169), held together in the centre with paper-covered wire, is of unknown origin. The plaited frog (170), of varnished flat straw, is from Thailand.

171 and 172. McAullay Bott, *Turtles* and *Bush Rats – Bush Rat Pack*, 2010. Working with kurrajong seed pods and Queen Palm fronds to create animal forms – the largest of which is a turtle 23 cm (9 in.) long – the artist aims 'to convey to the public the beauty of the Noongar peoples of the south-west of Western Australia: my mother's people, my ancestors'.

173. Adrienne Sloane, *Truth to Power*, 2007. Sloane uses wire knitting for her works. As she says, 'By moving the context of knitting from clothing geometry to sculpture, knitting becomes a medium with a link to a rich and complex fibre tradition that has the power of history behind it.'

174. Adrienne Sloane, *No Strings Attached*, 2006. In an installation nearly 120 cm (48 in.) wide, linen warp-knit figures reflect the sense that knitting 'has long been considered a woman's medium. I aim to … dissolve those boundardies. I knit to rejoin the frayed and unravelled places around me.'

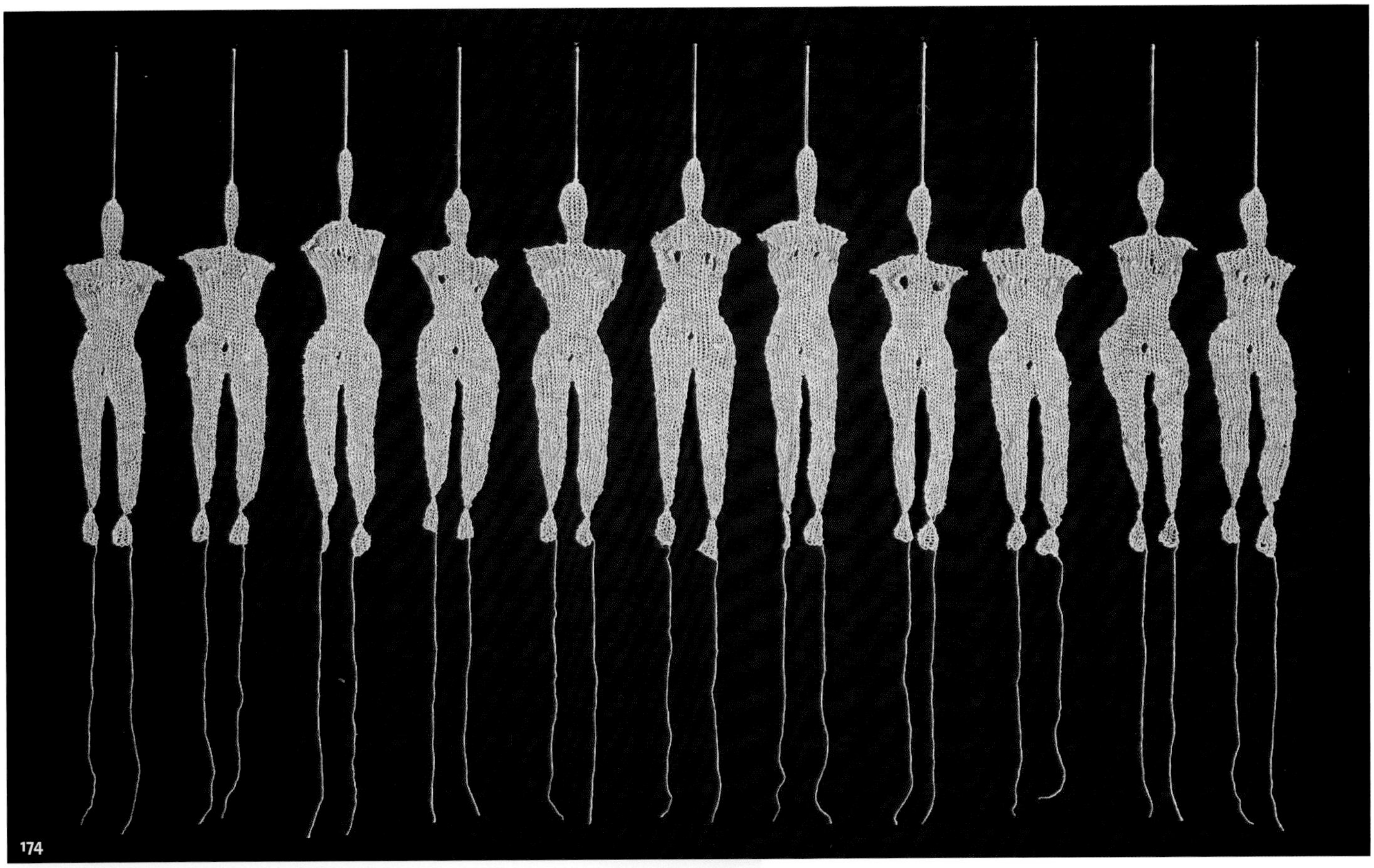

174

175

175. Cecilia Heffer, *Chile*, 2010. This small machine-stitched assemblage, 20 cm ($7^7/_8$ in.) high, incorporates rusted cloth, natural dyes and digital transfers of an 1860 photograph of a Mapuche Indian taken in Chile by Odber Heffer. It 'draws from the past and reinterprets memory as a textile narrative through the combination of traditional and new textile technologies'.

176. Adrienne Sloane, *Body Count*, 2007. Knitted wire forms, assembled onto chicken wire, merge unconventional materials with traditional craft while using familiar ancient forms – gloves and stockings – as an expressive platform equally suggestive of amputated legs and forearms.

177. Brigitte Armager, *Femmes* (detail), 2011. One of an installation of three life-sized figures composed of X-ray blue transparencies with découpage cutting, machine embroidery and appliquéd black lace.

178. Kiyoko Sakurabayashi, *Courtesan IV*, 2005. Part of a series made over several years, the courtesan was chosen to epitomize 'the indomitable power of the human spirit to survive and carry on'. First knitted in many different colours and materials to reflect the woman's life before she became a courtesan, and then dyed black to represent life afterwards, the sculpture's many hidden colours are 'still there, but submerged, suggesting the surviving inner life and spirit'.

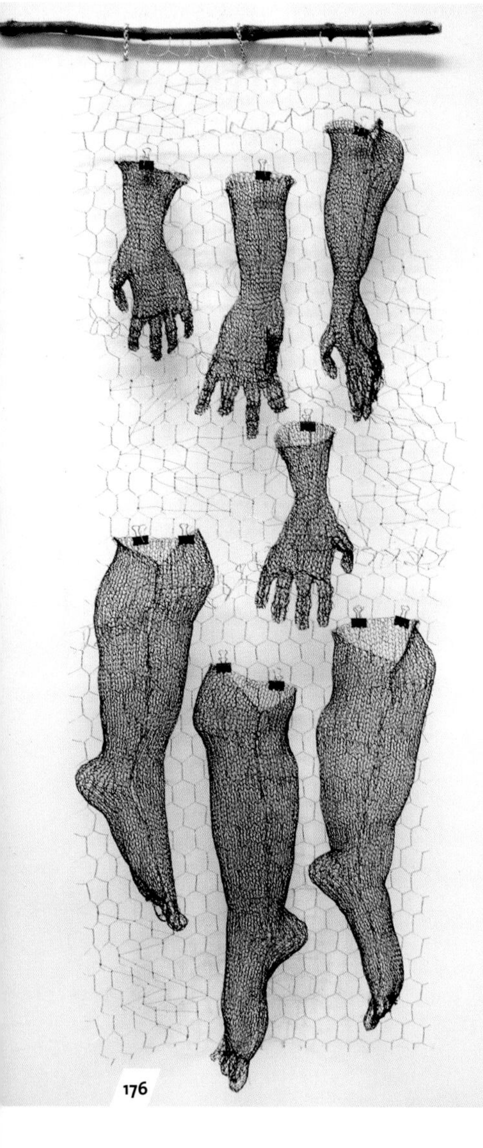

176

177

179. Sandy Black Original Knits, *Leopard scarf* and *Siamese Cat scarf*, 1982. Both pieces are entirely of angora. The leopard was knitted by Jacquard and intarsia, using a manually operated knitting machine, with embroidered detail. The Siamese cat was knitted plain with intarsia and embroidered details.

180. Chinese artisans, *Hanging scroll* (detail), thought to be early 20th century. This *k'o-ssu* (tapestry) has details such as the hair, jewelry, facial details and areas of clothing that are hand-painted.

181. Persian weaver, *Textile fragment with standing figure*, 16th century. A silk satin with figuring in samite, or weft-faced twill. The outlines are in gold metallic thread. Although this type of weaving had become widespread by this period, it had long been strongly associated with Persia.

182. Patricia Armour, *Coming Home Soon – 'Windows of the Soul' series*, 2009. The artist says of her tapestries, 'I draw inspiration … from the haunting Neolithic sites and the great tapestries of Europe. Celtic legend, my own spirituality and ancient history also have a strong influence.'

183. Cecilia Blomberg, *Lukas II*, 1987. This wool and linen tapestry integrates the artist's two decades of specialization in tapestry with her work as a muralist and illustrator.

184

185

186

184. Christine Keller, *'Die Prinzessin auf der Erbse' (The Princess on the Pea)*, 1997. Five editions in different colours were Jacquard-woven into panels 3 m (10 ft) high. One is now in the private collection of the Fairytale Museum, Bad Oeynhausen, Germany.

185. Christine Paine, *Sand Woman*, 2010. Paine's work is concerned with transient moments and our alienation from the natural world. For this piece, woven with a cotton warp and a wool and linen weft, the inspiration was prehistoric female figurines. The artist developed her drawing using mud and sticks, 'seeking to interpret the gestural and instinctive marks in woven tapestry'.

186. Margaret Crowther, *Mask and Man*, 1988. A continuous length of paper yarn was looped and manipulated to draw the life-sized facial forms, which were then held by tying with a finer paper yarn.

187

187. Persian weaver, *Mother and child*, 1600–25. This luxuriant silk is a cut velvet with voided areas revealing a satin ground. Technically it is consistent with Safavid Persian royal production, but the features, costume and subject matter are not typical, and it is thought it may have been woven in an Indian workshop staffed by Persian weavers. It came out of Tibet in the 1980s.

188. Ed Rossbach, *Faiyum Basket*, *c.* 1988. Rossbach echoes the evocation of life found on painted mummy cases by encasing plaited rattan in heat transfer-printed and painted paper. Although his title suggests that the work was inspired by an example from Roman Egypt, the imagery itself more closely resembles mummy cartonnages of about 700 BC.

188

1

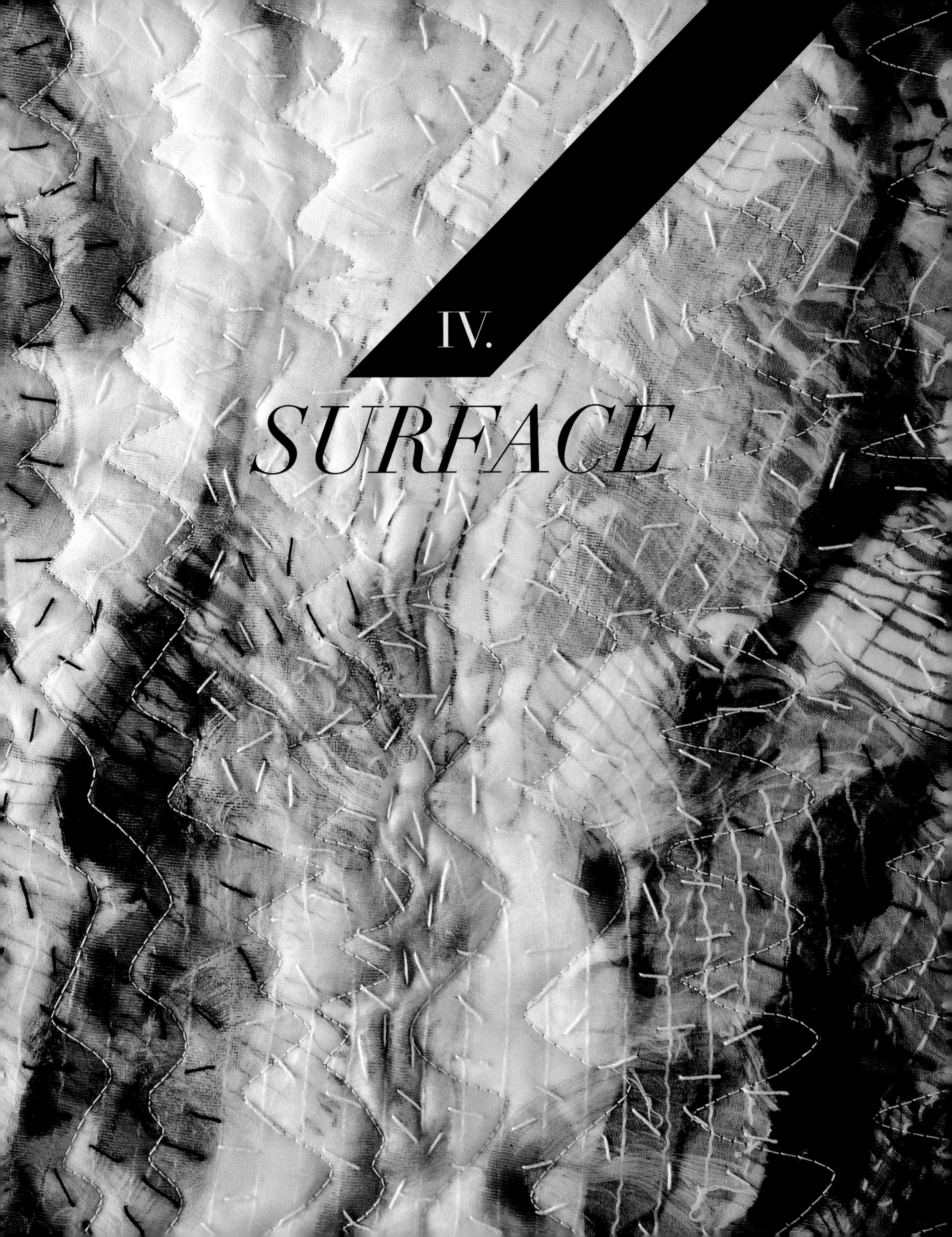

IV.

SURFACE

IV.

SURFACE

Over the last two decades, studies of the analogies that can be drawn between cloth and skin – furred, pierced or tattooed – have been central to the reassessment of textiles and their significance in playing a 'pivotal role as idiom of personhood and identity'. This is particularly true for anthropologists, who until some twenty years ago 'repeatedly ignored the often ephemeral and highly fragile cloth in favour of the theorisation of male dominated exchange and ritual'.[1] Being much closer to the subject, historians of dress had been highlighting the 'idiom of personhood' for some time, taking as a core text Ernest Fluegel's *Psychology of Clothes* (1930), which studied the implications of what today we would call discretionary consumption. Marilyn J. Horn's 1968 interdisciplinary study of clothing, *The Second Skin*, took the behaviourist's route, itself chronicled by Horn as originating within the American field of home economics in 1948.[2] Nevertheless, all of these studies, whether examining garments of uncut cloth, minimal tailoring, or the most complex examples of the couturier's skill, are about textiles as worn. An alternative is to examine textiles as *made*, exploring their surface qualities and treatments as extensions of the physical world. Legend suggests that the term 'surface design' had been coined by Jack Lenor Larsen prior to his appearance as keynote speaker at a seminal conference on the topic in 1976: 'Larsen felt the loom relegated fabric to uniformity and that surface designers are more interested in fabric as geography, which provides unlimited options for dimensional and structural enhancements, greater possibilities for opening interior spaces, and more opportunities for experimenting with color, texture, and design.'[3]

With this in mind, one can argue that all cloth, when not cut up or folded, crimped or otherwise manipulated, is embellished in ways that align directly with our understanding and treatment of mammal topography – that is, both pelts and the epidermis. There is the very texture of cloth, which can range from fur-like to (these days) the smoothest of skin. Then there are the meaningful marks that are stitched (pierced) or painted and printed (tattooed). This rather self-evident observation is helpful only so far as it stresses the importance of the interaction

1. Pauline Burbidge, *Under the Waterfall* (detail), 2004. Layers of transparent, painted and pleated cloth, hand- and machine-stitched. Now in the collection of Coats Crafts UK.

2. Ilka White, *Dune* (detail), 2007. A side view reveals seabird feathers piercing a silk and cotton panel, evoking the wind moving the dunes, as well as a 'communion with a little dry flap of penguin skin lying on the sand, pierced all over with hundreds of minute feathers ... an alarming reminder that this underwater swimmer is still a bird'.

between the structure of a cloth and its surface. If the end result is to have integrity – both literally and aesthetically – the surface treatment must be sensitive to the ground cloth, whether covering it or leaving areas exposed, or melding with rather than obliterating the structure to create a cohesive whole, which will be like a skin: resilient, individualistic and 'alive'. That said, surface treatments *are* free from structural constraints, and this is what presents the makers of piled, stitched and printed textiles with unique challenges, which have been widely explored by educators and artists since the mid-1970s. At the beginning of this period the field lacked the formal mechanisms for comparison and communication that characterized exhibitions and other vehicles serving structure-oriented work. It was to fill this gap that the University of Kansas held the first Surface Design Conference in 1976, and a year later the Surface Design Association (SDA) was formed. The SDA has since extended its focus to include constructed textiles, and its international membership and influence have ensured the perpetuation of the term 'surface design', which is the principal subject of this chapter.

3. Ayrshire weaver, possibly Alexander Morton & Co., *Liberty of London C864 swatch*, *c.* 1880. The loose spinning of dyed cotton yarns accentuates their clipped edges in this Scotch leno madras – a method of weaving associated with south-western Scotland employing continuous supplementary wefts that are sheared away where not interwoven into the leno ground.

Yarns

As noted in the introduction to Chapter III, the character of a textile arises from the interplay between construction and fibres, but beyond that a great range of textures possible in cloth are dependent on the nature of the yarn or threads employed. Generally speaking, initial developments in spinning (and throwing, for silk) appear to have been aimed at producing a result that was as uniform as possible and, from about 1500 onwards, more quickly made. In fact, the making of yarns – whether continuous strands of textile fibres, filaments or other materials – has been central to the progress of textile manufacture, so much so that there is a direct parallel between the spinning capacity of a region and its overall economic might and consequent global influence. From the Renaissance alone, one can trace this impact in Italy's dominance of European silk-throwing, for example. British imperial power was closely linked to the introduction of mechanized cotton-spinning in Britain the late 18th century. Twenty years ago it was clear that China was the rising economic star, having the highest number of spindles in operation. Recently that position has been taken by India, which produces over one fifth of the world's yarns: 'In the world textile scenario, it is the largest producer of jute, second-largest producer of silk, third-largest producer of cotton and cellulosic fibre/yarn, and fifth-largest producer of synthetic fibre/yarn.' In addition, about sixty per cent of the world's looms (over 5.5 million, and more than half of them hand-operated) can be found in India, where there is recognition that the diversity and self-sufficiency of its textile industry are 'coupled with its close linkage with our ancient culture and tradition'.[4] One of these traditions was the unequalled quality of the finest Indian hand-spun cotton threads, which formed the foundation of some of the world's most desirable cloths for several centuries until about 1820, when British machine-spinning overtook India's hand-spinners. Among the traditional Indian cotton cloths were the gossamer-light muslins, but even an opaque cotton cloth made an important contribution, enhancing the clarity of drawn and stitched imagery in the chintzes and silk embroideries that were so highly sought after **[4]**.

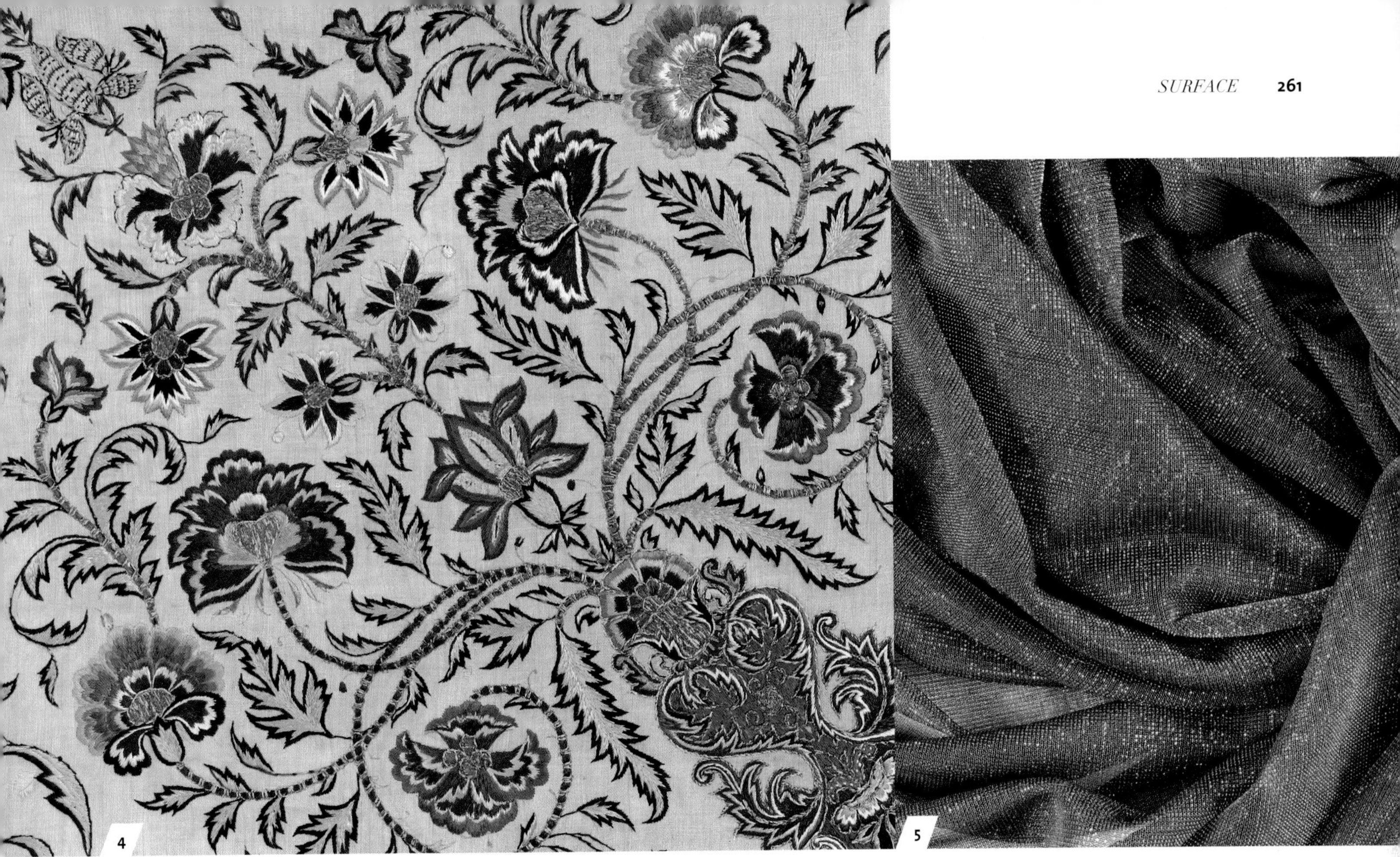

The interplay of more substantial threads in cloths composed of, or incorporating, finely spun yarns is one way in which today's textiles, such as those by John Parkes and Ulla de Larios, explore the ancient fascination for delicate threads **[40, 41]**. There are many more options now, since there are hundreds of variations of man-made and synthetic fibres, including microfibres, that are less than one denier and yet strong and very soft to the touch; and specialist monofilament (extruded) yarns, such as those of metallic fibres, which not only sparkle, but also minimize static electricity **[5]**. In contrast, many others textiles demonstrate what is, historically, a more recent interest, namely yarns that appear to be imprecisely or barely spun, either to give them bulk and the appearance of a hand-spun yarn, or to produce a yarn that stretches. (However, many textile artists avoid the use of some textured synthetic filament yarns – especially those made by the false-twist process, which is the cheapest means of adding bulk and stretch to a yarn, but achieves this only by utilizing spindle whirls at such high speed that the resulting intense pitch is a danger to health and hearing.) Enthusiasm for the aesthetic of hand-spun yarns re-emerged slowly as a result of the Arts Crafts Movement **[3]**. Its appreciation of the natural irregularities of fibres was initially most apparent in the adoption of Indian tussah silk for what became associated with Liberty Art Silks, a trend made possible by the work of Thomas Wardle, who, at dyeing and printing works in Leek, Staffordshire, overcame the resistance of this wild silk to dyeing **[83, 84]** – and also taught William Morris how to dye.[5]

Of equal long-term importance was the rugged texture produced in plain power-woven cloths by Donald Brothers of Dundee, Scotland, between 1896 and 1916. These were the 'craftsman canvases' promoted in North America by

4. Deccan embroidery workshop, *Floorspread* (detail), 1750–90. Summer carpet worked in satin-stitched floss silks and couched metal-wrapped thread on a ground woven of fine hand-spun cotton, for which this region in India was known. It was made for courtly domestic use or for the export market.

5. American or Chinese manufacturer, *Knitted fashion fabric*, late 20th century. This jersey-knitted fabric incorporates a metallic monofilament fibre that is fine, strong and soft, and also minimizes static.

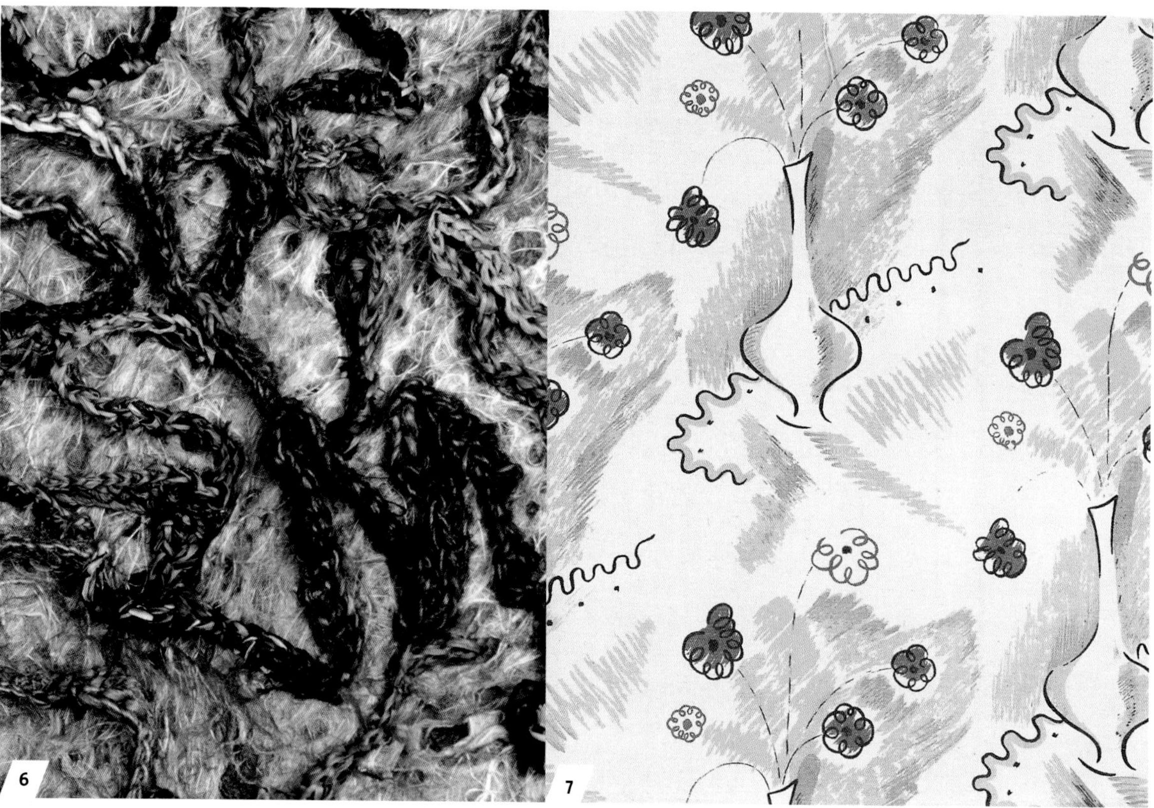

Gustav Stickley. The key to their unique character was the use of blended jute and linen yarns, which absorbed dye differently, resulting in subtle variations of tone. This effect was a conscious aesthetic that 'came to signify a naturalness and individuality of character in fabric to create with other materials such as wood and stone a continuity between the outside and inside of the house, manifesting the picturesque desire for simple living close to nature'.[6] These plain-woven rugged cloths, which began to be printed after the Second World War **[7]**, contributed – together with the work of weavers themselves (see Chapter I) – to the widespread association of mid-20th century modernity with textured grounds. To this day, a yarn that is textured, however subtly and of whatever ingredients, is seemingly more 'natural'. A close look at Tricia Smout's *The Cycle of Life* **[6]** illustrates how the deliberate choice of natural-fibre yarns that are not (as they could be) tightly spun underscores her commentary on the cycle of birth, growth and decay, both in nature and in 'human civilizations, cultures and fashionable trends in our artforms'.

Texture is integral to piled surfaces, which may be hand- or machine-made and, either way, strongly suggest nature because they are redolent of fur. Pile carpets, once rare and perhaps the most extravagant of all objects destined for the interior, have long been of primary interest to both antique collectors and historians, but for different reasons. For the collector, carpets made of a silk warp and weft, with a knotted pile of wool, are remarkably strong and thus have a long useable life. For the historian, large pile carpets signify the presence of a highly organized urban workshop, such as the one, probably in Tabriz in Persia, that wove the famous pair of Ardabil carpets, each originally approx 5.35 m wide

6. Tricia Smout, *The Cycle of Life* (detail), 1999. Employing crocheted script in yarns of cotton, jute, hemp and raffia, this wall hanging is composed of three leaves incorporating handmade Japanese paper, each representing a cycle of nature, human life, cultures and fashions in the arts. This, the central leaf, reads: 'Nature speaks in signs and symbols.'

7. Grace Peat, *Burlesque* (detail), 1938. This furnishing fabric, hand-screen printed on linen by Donald Brothers of Dundee, typifies the lingering appreciation for softly textured grounds. It was still being sold in 1951, through Dan Cooper, a New York designer-manufacturer of avant-garde textiles.

and 10.5 m long (17½ x 34½ ft). Completed in 1539–40, they were commissioned by Shah Isma'il, founder of the Safavid dynasty (1501–1722), for a mosque in Ardabil in north-western Iran. One of the carpets, now in the Victoria and Albert Museum, London, has a pile with about 5,300 knots per 10 cm square (340 knots per square inch), or over 25 million knots in total. The other **[8]**, given to the Los Angeles County Museum of Art by J. Paul Getty, is smaller as a result of having been used to repair its partner in the mid-19th century, but it is even more densely knotted. Their making would have required several years and many hands.

It is easy to see why alternative and less labour-intensive methods of creating the same effect had been sought long before, in the form of an extra set of warp threads drawn up into loops, each row of loops being secured by ground wefts and then slit open to form the pile. The Han tombs at Mawangdui, in Hunan Province, China (170–140 BC), preserved cloths made by this method. Loops can be left uncut, and can also be drawn up from supplementary wefts **[37]**, as in the Spanish looped coverlets called *felpa gallega* ('plush Galician') that have been made in northern Spain for well over 1,000 years. When the making of warp-looped piled cloths was eventually introduced to the West via Italy at the beginning of the 13th century, they became known as 'velvet', from the Latin *villus*, meaning 'shaggy hair'. Kay Robertson, whose considerable knowledge of early velvets began in Venice at the knee of her father, the highly influential antique furniture and textile dealer Adolph Loewi, recalls being taught in the 1930s to recognize pre-1500 velvets by feeling them **[45]**: 'like kitten fur,' she says, whereas velvets from the 16th century and later are 'just a little more bristly'.[7] (This description perfectly captures the impact of Leonardo da Vinci's invention

8. Safavid royal carpet workshop, *Ardabil carpet*, 1539–40. Made in Tabriz, in modern-day Iran, this carpet, with a finely knotted pile in wool on a silk foundation, was given to the Los Angeles County Museum of Art by J. Paul Getty in 1953.

of the winged or fly spindle, which preformed simultaneous stretching, twisting and winding operations on silk strands, making them more taut.[8])

Another way to suggest fur is to include frayed strips of cloth, which are not uncommon additions to baskets from many continents, and are the basis of rag rugs. These uses for recycled strips are not necessarily 'poor cousins' to alternative forms of decoration: both can create treasured tokens of exchange and a renewed existence for old cloths **[42]**. Chenille ('caterpillar') yarn is made specifically to appear 'furry' on all sides, yet it, too, is cut from cloth – in this case a leno designed for the purpose, with crossed warps spaced out so that, once it is woven, slitting through the gaps results in the very narrow cut lengths, twisted to become yarn **[33, 34]**. And of course, fur itself can be introduced in strip form. Beth Hatton uses kangaroo-skin offcuts, from animals culled under the supervision of the Australian National Parks and Wildlife Service **[46]**. She does this to denote native fauna in works that speak about the impact of colonization: 'Rather than becoming extinct or endangered due to settlement, some species such as the kangaroo grew in number.' The black areas in her rugs are wool, 'signifying introduced species that had a disastrous impact on native mammals even while being vital for the early economy'. Here, then, is the resilience of cloth and its components likened to the resilience of species and, as the curator and writer Michael Newall observed, to indigenous cultures and skill-based crafts, which 'have managed to maintain continuity and identity while adapting to colonialism, industrialisation, modernity and now global capitalism'.[9]

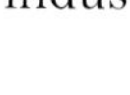

Stitch

Stitches can also create intensely textured surfaces, employing the piercing of cloth with a needle-led thread to develop essays in colour, form and imagery that are not limited to a right-angled construction (as in most weaving) and are dimensionally stable (which knitting is not). The scope is endless: the scale can range from minute to gigantic, techniques are wide-ranging, and the combination of hand and tool can create signatures with all the individuality of handwriting, as the distinctive abstract work of Robert Hillestad demonstrates **[10]**. Just as hand-knitting results in different tensions, so each person has a unique rhythm when they stitch, and thus produces a characteristic surface. This distinct pace and tension is central to the energy of works such as Betty Levy's *Into the Maelstrom* **[98]** and Carolyn Nelson's *Fragment of a Love Story II* **[100]**, with the first capturing the power of natural forces, and the second, of emotions. Nelson, in addition, alludes to a stone bench where 'my first lover and I left red threads as messages for each other in 1967 and ... again in 2008'. Meaning and the pace of stitches also align in the mixed-media pieces created by Lucy Arai **[99]**, who learned the revered Japanese craft of *sashiko* from her uncle in Tokyo when she was a girl. This embroidery and quilting technique is distinguished by white running stitches of complex patterns hand-sewn into deep indigo-dyed cotton fabric, and is associated with the darning of worn fabrics, flourishing as 'the humble stitch' of northern Japan's farmers and firemen from 1615 to 1868. *Sashiko* demands an even stitch; of acquiring this skill, and the skill of *termari* (embroidered balls) from her mother, Arai has said: 'My experience in a master and apprentice relationship

9. Jun-ichi Arai, *Untitled cloth* (detail), 1960s. In an ingenious variation on the principles of velvet weaving, here floated sections of red woolly nylon, interwoven with a saran curl yarn, have been cut to form tufted balls on a plain woven polyester ground.

10. Robert Hillestad, *Textiles Study #52*, 2004. In a specific group of his collages, inspired by the tendency of certain abstract painters of the 20th century to use their media as subject matter, Hillestad manipulated threads of assorted fibre content to emphasize their inherent characteristic as media. In doing so he drew less visual attention to the techniques of couching, machine stitching and overlays of net through which the threads are held in place.

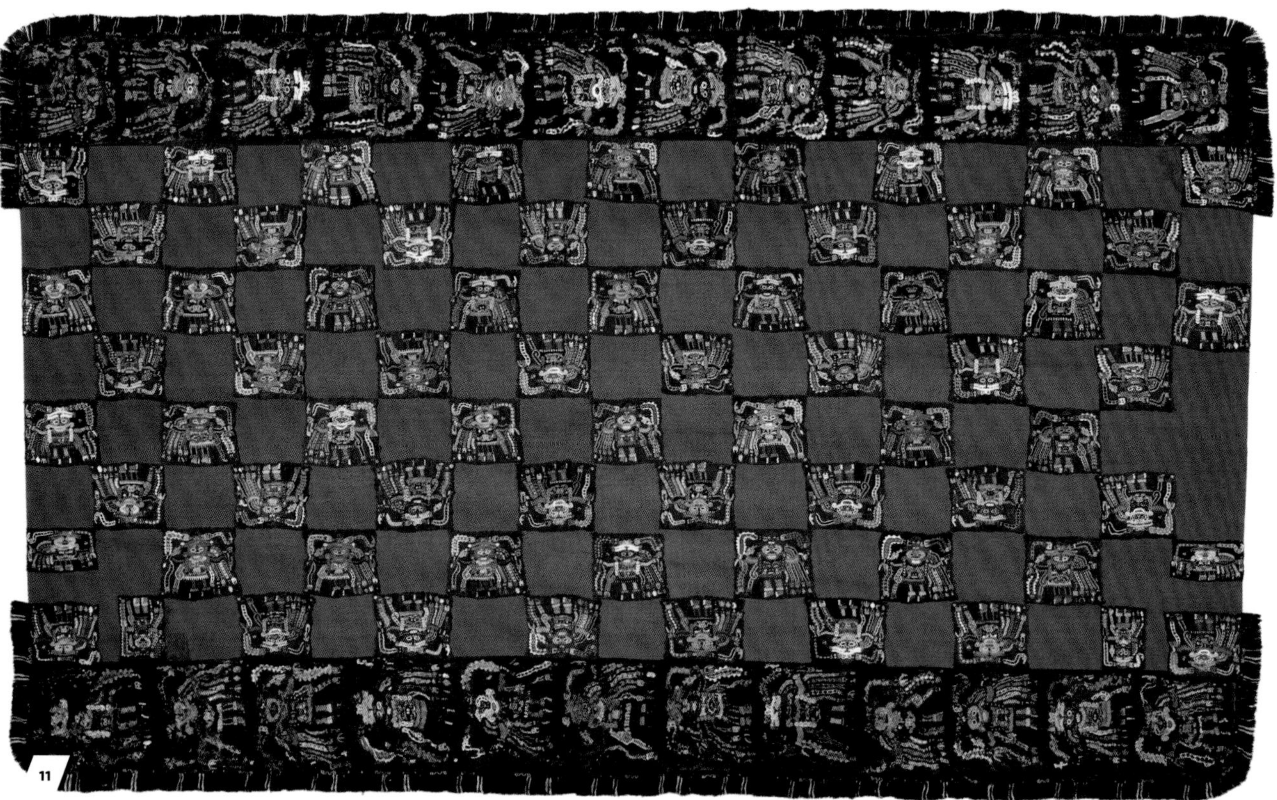

established the developmental process of my art: practice, achieve technical proficiency, practice more, refine the execution, practice, play, innovate, practice altered techniques ... practice, refine, practice, play, innovate, practice.' Arai's eloquence with stitch is combined with what she calls her 'naive and experimental handling of ink' in the ancient practice of *sumi-e*, a type of painting in which the ink on white paper 'was thought to reveal a person's humanity, their aesthetic, moral, intellectual and emotional character', as stitch manifestly does as well.

The relationship between text and textiles has already been discussed in Chapter I, where the focus was on their metaphorical resemblances. Because one can draw freely with embroidering, even examples over 2,000 years old from Egypt, Northern Europe, the Andes **[11]** and China convey in their patterns (as do other types of textiles) ideas about ideology, cosmology and self-image.[10] However, stitch can make such textual comparisons literal in the form of samplers, which can include names, phrases or alphabets. Although the latter two were not typically incorporated into samplers until about 1650 – some 150 years after stitch-only named and dated examples **[12]** can be documented – the inclusion of a religious or moral quotation has come to epitomize sampler embroideries **[187–88, 193–95]**. Because the stitches are placed to correspond with the structure of the ground cloth, one might expect the 'handwriting' to be uniform among examples of similar types or dates. But it is not, and to examine samplers for their subtle variations in colour, scale and arrangement is highly rewarding.

The sampler's long association with 'good girls' – as a demonstration of literacy, as well as skill with a needle – today makes it a potent symbol of the subjugation of women. One cannot touch upon this topic without mention of

11. Peruvian artisans, *Mantle*, 100 BC – AD 200. From a Paracas mummy bundle, this mantle, plain woven with camilid fibre, is embroidered in stem stitch showing conventionalized anthropomorphic beings or shamans.

12. German embroiderer, initials M. H. L., *Spot sampler*, 1685. Some twenty patterns are recorded in this silk sampler, worked in tent, rococo, cross, long-arm cross, satin and Algerian eye stitches. Several relate to designs illustrated in pattern books by Helena Rosina Fürst, which were first published between 1660 and 1676 in Nuremberg.

the feminist, art historian and, later, psychotherapist Rozsika Parker (1945–2010), whose 1983 publication *The Subversive Stitch: Embroidery and the Making of the Feminine* was seminal. It was the catalyst for two related exhibitions in Manchester in 1988, as well as for the direction taken since by many textile artists – men among them. As Parker's obituary in the *Guardian* newspaper put it, 'In all her work is a stitching-together of the themes that occupied her: women's struggle for recognition within the art establishment; a challenging of the division between fine art and the decorative arts; the tensions, sometimes productive, sometimes destructive, in women's creative work. She was keenly observant of the ambivalences of domesticity and of motherhood. In writing that was assertive without being aggressive, she tackled the pressures on women, especially young women, to have perfect bodies.'[11] These very themes are central to Janice Appleton's cross-stitching of a poem written by her husband 'just before the sex reassignment operation that ended our heterosexual marriage'. Appleton 'deliberately chose the style of a traditional sampler to stitch this ... because of the historical relationship between women and this form of textile and the cultural role of the sampler in educating for rigid sexual roles'. The changing letter forms and the sampler's large scale also contribute to the meaning of the work **[189]**.

Scale is also critical in Linda Behar's depiction of her Chinese grandmother, whose account of her marriage is rendered whisper-like by being contained within an embroidery that measures only 24.8 x 21 cm (9¾ x 8¼ in.) **[190]**. At the other end of the spectrum is Susan Taber Avila's *Garden Wall* **[191]**, which, at 2.7 x 9.1 m (9 x 30 ft), is a veritable 'shout' of words describing 'things people want and desire, as well as spam subject lines for life improvement and email scams that prey on greed' – and all a play on the Garden of Eden metaphor. For over twenty years Avila has explored the possibilities of the simultaneous development of structure, surface and content through stitch worked on the water-soluble fabric PVA (polyvinyl alcohol), which is subsequently dissolved away. The principle of a 'disappearing' fabric is also explored in the work of Vishna Collins **[35]** and Josette Luyckx **[13]**, who exploit the freedom of free-motion machine embroidery in different ways. It is an old technique, invented in 1883 for the making of what was called 'chemical lace' – an imitation lace created by machine embroidering with cotton threads on a silk ground that was subsequently burnt away in a bath of chlorine or caustic soda. (Devoré is a related technique, in which a cloth composed of two fibres is selectively printed with a corrosive to remove areas of one of the fibres **[143–44]**.) Vanishing muslin, a saltpetre-treated cotton that crumbles when ironed, became available a century or so ago as an alternative (and as a stabilizer) and remains in use, together with other vanishing films and fabrics removed by hot or cold water that are appropriate for the small studio. Such a shift – from aids destined for the commercial workshop to those suitable for home use – typifies the progress of stitching machines, too. Their development began with the first practical hand-embroidery machine **[15]**, invented in 1828 by a Frenchman, Josué Heilmann (who sold the patent rights to Henry Houldsworth & Company of Manchester a year later), and ends, thus far, with computerized embroidery machines.

In the history of machine stitching, key moments include: the invention of an improved sewing machine in 1846, with its lock stitch; the patenting of the versatile Cornely machine in 1865, which produced chain and moss stitch; the

12

13

13. Josette Luyckx, *Orange Grove Bolero* (sleeve detail), 2009. Rayon threads free-motion embroidered on a soluble base (ground), and tulle (applied leaves). The vines are hand-stitched, and the unseen body of the garment is of fabric hand-dyed and -woven by Luyckx's collaborator of sixteen years, Marie Payne.

multi-needle lock stitch-based Schiffli, invented two years earlier but dormant until the 1880s **[128, 160]**; and domestic sewing machines with built-in cogs producing fancy stitches, available from the 1950s. Examples of these machines are studied and preserved at Manchester Metropolitan University (MMU), where machine embroidery has been a speciality since the 1960s, for much of the time under the leadership of Anne Morrell **[96–97]**. There one can examine the back of fabrics, an essential aid to identification **[15]**. Judy Barry, who taught at MMU from 1967 to 2005, explains why this is necessary: 'The development of mechanically made stitching has a vast and complex history, which is further confused by the fact that today we tend to think of "machine embroidery" as being worked on a sewing machine. Historically, though, embroidery machines and sewing machines developed along quite different lines, and for very different purposes.'[12]

The reason for this confusion is a deliberate strategy, developed as domestic sewing machines became widely available. The machine- and thread-makers from the late 19th century onwards recognized the importance of individuals as consumers of their products, and promoted 'art' (or free-motion) embroidery on the sewing machine. Singer issued a book on the topic in 1911, and from 1916 employed a series of skilled machinists in London to demonstrate possibilities both to those working at home and as educators. By the 1930s this job belonged to Rebecca Crompton, who also advised on the influential Needlework Development Scheme, initiated in Scotland in 1934 by the thread-maker J. & P. Coats and run until 1961. Providing educational materials and short courses for teachers, Crompton promoted free exploration and the use of the needle (including the sewing machine's) as a drawing implement. After the Second World War, J. & P. Coats, Singer and a few others funded touring exhibitions incorporating examples of work – by Crompton and others – that were seen throughout North America and in Italy, Africa, Australia, New Zealand and Hong Kong. The legacy of machine- and thread-makers sponsoring exhibitions and promoting innovative artists continues **[1]**, as does exploration of machine stitching, as shown in many of this chapter's illustrations. Alice Kettle **[16]** goes further, challenging the accepted scale of embroideries as well. The difficulty in distinguishing hand from machine stitching demonstrates the creative possibilities that result from long experience with a technology; powered stitching thus provides a model of inventive subversion, redirection and lateral thinking.

Yet in many cases the function of the stitch is to provide an unseen attachment for surface embellishments, which may be in the form of other threads (called 'couching'), but may also range from the most delicate of beads and feathers to robust, large-scale baubles, buttons and, yes, bows **[26–33]**. In sewing, stitching, too, is often invisible. Nevertheless, as the primary means of connecting materials together, it is essential because structural stitch is durable and flexible, and can sculpt with more finesse than gluing, tacking or stapling. The consequent freedom of movement in garments not only enhances their performance, but also does make them a 'second skin'. (Only tubular knitting offers a similar body-friendly form.) And because it can join very different materials together, the field of 'stitch' creates the greatest range of effects; today it is defined less by a group of techniques than by common a point of view. The huge range of resulting work even allows for the inclusion of welding, as in the

14

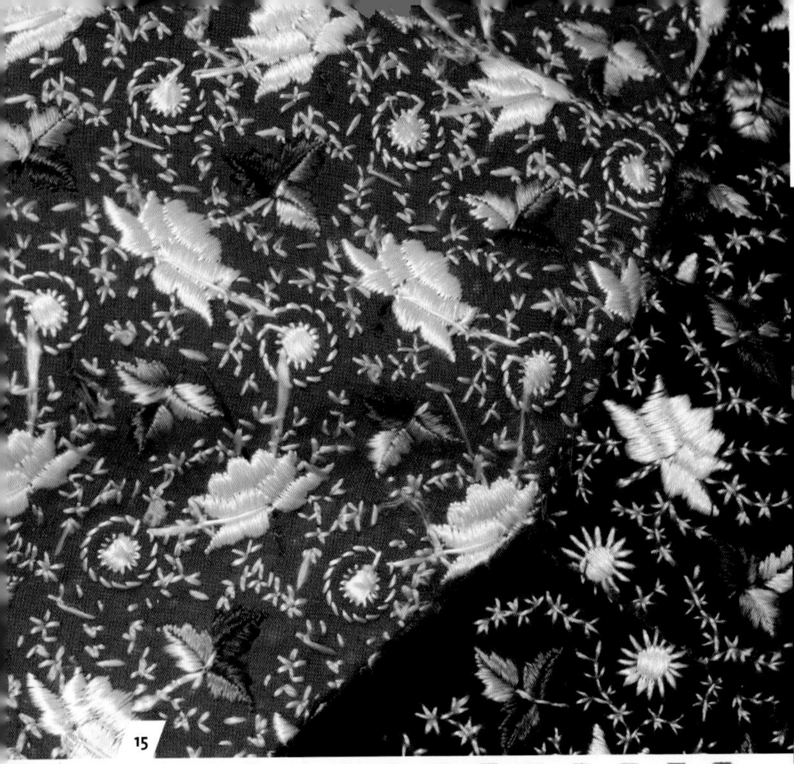

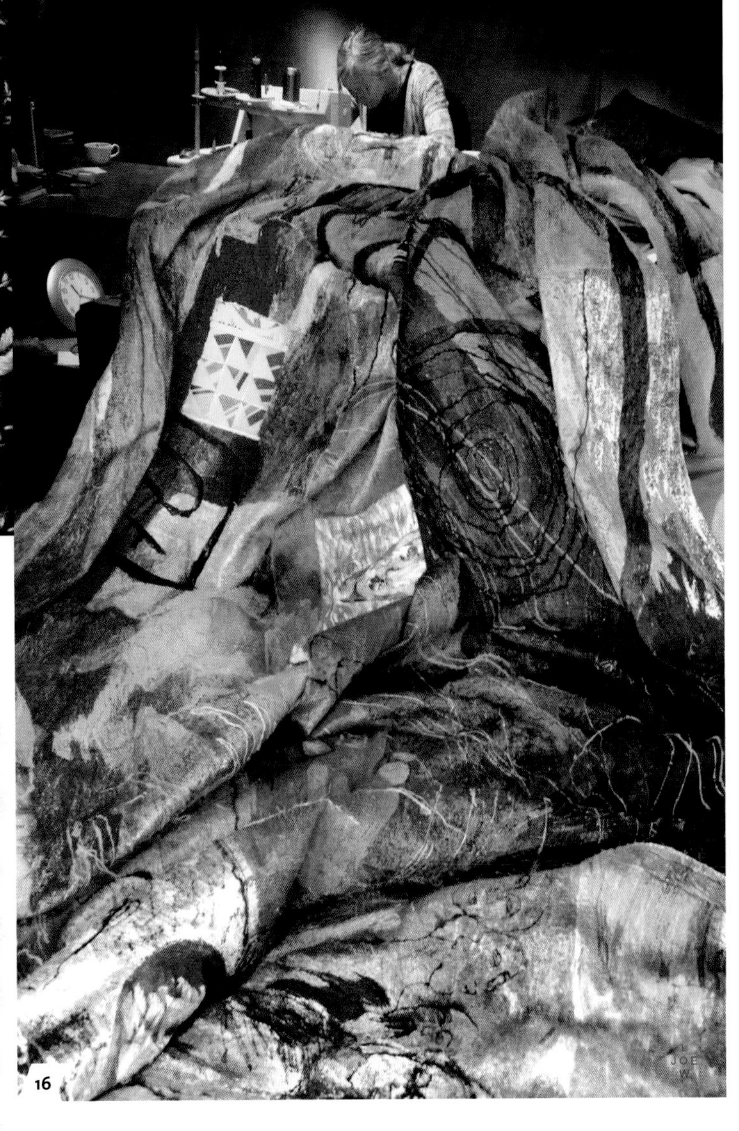

14. Michael Brennand-Wood, *Archive*, 1984. This construction, 60 cm (23.6 in.) high, broke new ground with its combination of thread, fabric collage, graphite, wire and wood, contributing to the breadth of the present-day field of 'stitch'.

15. Houldsworth's, Manchester, *Embroidered dress fabric*, 1880s. Through its connecting strands of silk floss and the fact that it displays the same amount of thread as on the front, the reverse of this silk fabric reveals that it was embellished using a multi-needled hand-embroidering machine. The machine was invented by Josué Heilmann in France, who sold the patent rights to Houldsworth in 1829.

16. Alice Kettle, *Looking Forwards to the Past*, 2007. This enormous piece, 3.5 × 16.5 m (120 × 650 in.) in size, was made in nine sections using free machine stitch, Omni stitch, computerized stitch, Cornely stitch and an embellisher, with patches and other pieces made by others as part of a collaborative project for the Winchester Discovery Centre, Hampshire.

work of Julia Griffiths Jones, who is inspired by her study of Central European embroidery **[17]**. Michael Brennand-Wood, a textile artist who has consistently pushed the boundaries over the past thirty years, utilizes a breadth of materials in his sculptural forms, yet he also references traditional textile structures, and in doing so has often gone against theoretical trends **[14]**. This brings us back to the relationship between stitch and body piercing, both literally and as a metaphor for the anti-fashion or radical stances embraced within the field.

Painting and Printing

Skins, tattoos, paintings and prints on fabric are a fascinating quartet of interconnected processes and materials. To keep them soft and pliable, leathers are treated with tannic acid from the bark and leaves of certain trees. The very same acid is an important constituent in dyes – making cottons, for example, much more receptive to dyestuffs, and polyamide yarns less likely to stain or fade when dry cleaned. Tannic acid was also present in ancient inks, such as gallnut black, the ink used for intaglio (engraved copperplate) printing, which had developed in Germany by the 1430s and allowed thin plain silks – as well as paper and, later, cotton and linen cloths – to display broadsheets, maps and other illustrations and information **[118]**. Whether applied to a cave wall, barkcloth, linen or the skin, early paints were most often composed of iron oxide earths (ochres), which remain in use – on body and cloth – in many regions today **[19]**.

Indeed, the complex developments that have led to modern dyestuffs can be viewed, put simplistically, as the Western chemists' gradual understanding and replication of the colouring actions of substances that were used intuitively millennia ago, and still are. In addition, the oldest and most direct means of marking – using pigment on a finger, stick, stamp or brush (the earliest example is a painted linen from el-Gebelein, Egypt, dating from 4000–3500 BC) – has followed a labyrinthine course. Superseding dyeing, or immersion of the entire cloth in a

17. Julia Griffiths Jones, *Shirt of a Lad* (detail), 1997. Inspired by Central European textiles and tinkers, who themselves duplicated the effects of lace and knitting, as well as prose and poetry, the artist captures the fluidity of fabric in mild steel wire, spot-welding while composing, brazed for final stability and finished with one or more layers of paint.

18. Malian artisans, Bògòlanfini, 20th century. The *bògòlonfini* (literally 'mud cloth') is associated with several ethnic minorities of Mali, West Africa, but especially with the Bamana peoples. The cloths' black coloration is the result of a reaction between a yellow dye and fermented river mud; the white areas result when the yellow alone is discharged.

19

vat, printers by the 19th century returned to direct mark-making via a machine, which employed chemical colorants that could be fixed onto cloth without needing to submerge it. In contrast, the creation of a pattern using the dye vat can be done by putting something on the cloth – either a painted or stamped mordant to attract the dye to certain areas and fix it to the material, or a substance that prevents the uptake of dye. The first is the technique known as 'colour-fast block-printing' **[21]**, which Europeans adopted from India in the 17th century. The second technique is generally known by its Indonesian name, batik, though it was widely used **[70]**; examples found in Egypt and the Crimea have been dated as far back as the 4th century BC. One can also bleach a pattern out, creating white on a coloured ground, by stamping or drawing a discharging agent **[18]** – a technique related to devoré, which removes certain fibres to create the desired outcome and is well illustrated by the work of Lesley Richmond **[143, 144]**. (A fourth, ancient, means of patterning by wrapping or clamping selected areas of cloth is known by its Japanese name, 'shibori', and is discussed in Chapter V.)

Although a more precise understanding of dyes and the use of machine printing, by rollers of engraved metal or carved wood, was well established in Europe by the 1820s – and roller printing, with its crisp delineations, was to remain the dominant method of production until the Second World War – the same period is characterized by explorations of alternative means of printing and patterning that resulted in more faithful representations of the handmade mark. Some of these experiments, such as the use of lithographic techniques in the second half of the 19th century, were cul-de-sacs, but others bore fruit. Batiks from Indonesia inspired the reassessment of this technique, initially by the Dutch, and by the 1920s it was being used by textile artists across Europe and in North America. An interest in stencilling probably arose from the reopening of Japan to the outside world in the 1860s. This technique piqued several inventors' interest in the 1870s and 1880s with the availability of more synthetic dyes, which could be printed directly rather than applied in a dye vat, and led to the closest

19. Malian artisans, *Shirt*, before 1981. Dyed yellow with leaves of the *n'gallama* tree, this shirt was hand-painted with fermented mud to draw the figures and decorative bands. The mud reacts with the dye, rendering a permanent colour. It was made by a woman on brown cotton strip-woven hopsacking, itself produced by a man.

forbear of hand-screen printing, patented by Charles Nelson Jones of Michigan in 1887 for printing flour sacks. However, it was only in the early decades of the 20th century that screen printing began to be explored for its artistic possibilities: for example, Fortuny patented a related continuous stencil machine with a photographically produced print-media barrier in 1910. Meanwhile, hand block-printing, never extinct, was redirected in many cases towards artist-designed textiles, such as those emanating from the Wiener Werkstätte (1903–32) in Vienna, Paul Poiret's Atelier Martine in Paris (1911–29), the Omega Workshops in London (1913–19) and Stehli Silks, the giant independent American subsidiary (1897–*c.* 1950) of the still-extant Swiss firm Stehli Seiden, known in the 1920s for designs by Ralph Barton, Clayton Knight and others. Over 10,000 Wiener Werkstätte designs are documented, many by its co-founders, the architect and designer Josef Hoffmann, and the artist Koloman Moser. The far smaller Omega Workshops produced designs by Roger Fry, Vanessa Bell and a handful of others; some were stencil-printed, and the workshop's approach to involving artists in textile design had lasting impact in the UK **[87]**. The advantage of the hand techniques was that far, far less space or investment was necessary; in comparison to machine printing, it was a 'kitchen sink' activity, especially when undertaken for limited editions. Thus in its initial exploratory stages avant-garde hand-screen printing was primarily driven forward by women, such as Ruth Reeves in America **[61]**, while lino block-printing was explored by several who had trained under Noel Rooke in the book production department at the Central School of Arts and Crafts, London, among them Joyce Clissold **[2, 149–57]**.

20. Althea McNish and Colleen Farr, *Liberty screen-printed dress fabrics*, 1959 and 1964. Top and left are 'Nicotea' (1959) and 'Trinidad' (1964) by Althea McNish; bottom right is 'Cherokee' (1959) by Colleen Farr. All show the use of wax-resist (batik) and watercolour in the design development.

21. Joyce Clissold, *Footprints* (detail), *c.* 1926–31. In 1925 Elspeth Little, Gwen Pike and Celandine Kennington founded Footprints in Hammersmith, London, to supply block-printed textiles to Little's shop, Modern Textiles. This block-printed linen depicts Footprints' activities, including printing, hand-painting and vat-dyeing. Clissold apprenticed there in the mid-1920s, took over in 1929, and maintained Footprints until 1982. In 1931 it moved to Brentford, Essex.

By the early 1930s, hand screens were being adopted by manufacturers who mimicked the artistic approach of small studios, and commercial hand-printers were learning to make imprecise imprints to retain the desired appearance of spontaneity, typically using textured ground cloths to underscore the craftsmanship involved. The capacity of the screen to capture a hand-painted mark was soon widely understood **[24]**. The influence of independents also spread. It was a period during which the role of freelance printed-textile designers became established, and well into the 1950s many designs were created by artists who are no longer associated with textiles, such as Graham Sutherland. (Freelance design for woven fabrics was much rarer, because until the development of computerized looms a thorough understanding of cloth construction was required.) In the wake of the requisitioning of copper for war purposes, roller printing declined and mechanized screen printing soon took its place, first on a flat bed, and then as a rotary process. But the impulse to suggest the handmade mark remained, and the ever more sophisticated photo-engraving of screens made it possible. One result was the use of wax resists – drawing with wax crayon and water-based paints – a technique used by the sculptor Henry Moore, who learned batik as a schoolboy and used wax-resist for his drawings (his textile designs are now well documented). It is illustrated here with fabrics designed by Althea McNish and Colleen Farr for Liberty **[20]**.[13]

At first applied largely to stable fabrics such as woven silks, cottons and linens, advances in screen printing allowed for the printing of jersey knit, as seen in *Ulisse* **[77]**, produced in 1966 by the Milan-based fashion house Ken Scott.[14] Their records indicate that the jersey was of Ban-Lon nylon, that nine

22. Nigel Cheney, *Commonwealth (For Linda)* (detail), 2011. A digital print on cotton panama, embellished with hand and machine embroidery, and free machine quilting.

23. Hil Driessen, *Drift 23*, 2005. For this prototype panel for the University of Literature/Drift 23 project at the University of Utrecht, a machine-stitched trapunto image of a tree was photographed, scanned into a CAD program, enlarged and printed on a TreviraCS ground (a fire-retardant polyester) using a Stork inkjet printer.

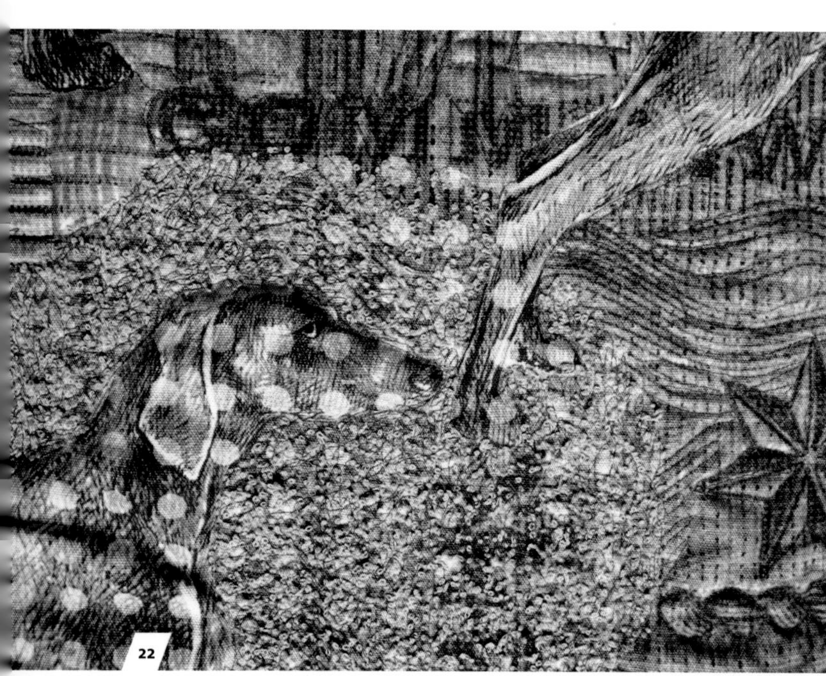

screens were used, and that the photo-engraver was Fasoia. Such detail, typical of manufacturers' and designers' archives, is invaluable in charting the nuances of the history of printing, as it is for every other type of textile. Printed jersey was rarely collected by museums until about thirty years ago. An early entrant into this area was the museum that collected *Ulisse*, The Museum at the Fashion Institute of Technology (MFIT), established in 1969 at the Fashion Institute of Technology, New York, to inspire students as well as designers. Being closely connected to New York's fashion and textile businesses, the museum acquired background histories of the companies and designers whose work was deposited in its collection. The importance of this archive is summarized by MFIT's curator of textiles, Lynn Felsher Nacmias: 'Most textiles are the product of designers or artists whose names are not usually known by the general public. From the over-the-counter textile not usually given much thought by the public to the one-of-a-kind or specialty cloth ... that textile has interest and meaning that engages the viewer. There are times when one sees a textile and thinks – extraordinary!'

24

Commercial digital printing became available in 1993 but was initially limited to applications where the mass-production standards of colourfastness did not have to be met. This hurdle was crossed early in the present century; today fabrics ranging from the sheerest of silks to heavy velvets, including Lycra and other stretch materials, are printed with all available dyestuffs and pigments, as well as through sublimation (transfer) printing. Hil Driessen turned to digital printing for a large panel to be installed in an historic building at the University of Utrecht in the Netherlands **[23]**. She scanned in a machine-stitched trapunto (stuffed quiltwork) image of a tree, which was then enlarged and printed. This perfectly suited her interest in illusionist designs and in 'dematerializing the textile', as well as her belief that one medium leaves marks on another. And, as Driessen's work illustrates, other advantages of the digital process include an unlimited image size and colour range. While many textile artists take advantage of these possibilities alongside the ability to use digital photographs, few use them on their own. Pat Hodson **[73, 75]** speaks for many when she describes her working method, 'in which the computer is exploited for its potential for unending improvization of an idea – a continual fragmenting, deconstructing and reusing of the digital file to make new work'. Hodson adds that the screen image is only half the story: 'The idea is never fully realized until image encounters tactile materials .... The 'virtual' marks and textures drawn on computer interact with hand-drawn marks and patterns; dye colour with digital colour.' Andrea Ellis, whose interest is in 'traces' or 'imprints', uses a devoré-treated digital top layer above other layers treated by dyeing, screen printing, mono printing from casts of digital embroideries, and discharging **[165, 167]**. Others combine digital printing with hand-printing or stitch, or both – such as Nigel Cheney, whose wall hangings incorporate free machine quilting **[22, 146]**. Such multi-processing sits firmly within the craft tradition, and for Cheney the exploration of both hand-operated and computer-driven machinery 'places the work in current debates around the role of technology', a point iterated in his playful banknote-based imagery, which reflects upon 'value, pedigree and speculation'. In addition, multiple approaches fully exploit the range of surface characteristics that bring textiles to life, underscoring that parallel between cloth and topography.

24. Unknown designer, *Furnishing fabric*, c. 1950. Found in a Parisian market, this glazed cotton is screen-printed, showing the capacity of this technique to convey the impression of both watercolour painting and engraved lines.

25. Dirkje van de Horst-Beetsma, *Folded* (detail), 2009. Dense overworking with free machine stitching on canvas is combined with hand-dyed fabric from Els van Baarle, a fellow Dutch textile artist who specializes in batik.

26. Nadia Albertini, *Embroidery* (detail), 2010. On a tulle base, tiny wool balls, rhinestones and clasped diamonds are hand-embroidered for haute couture purposes.

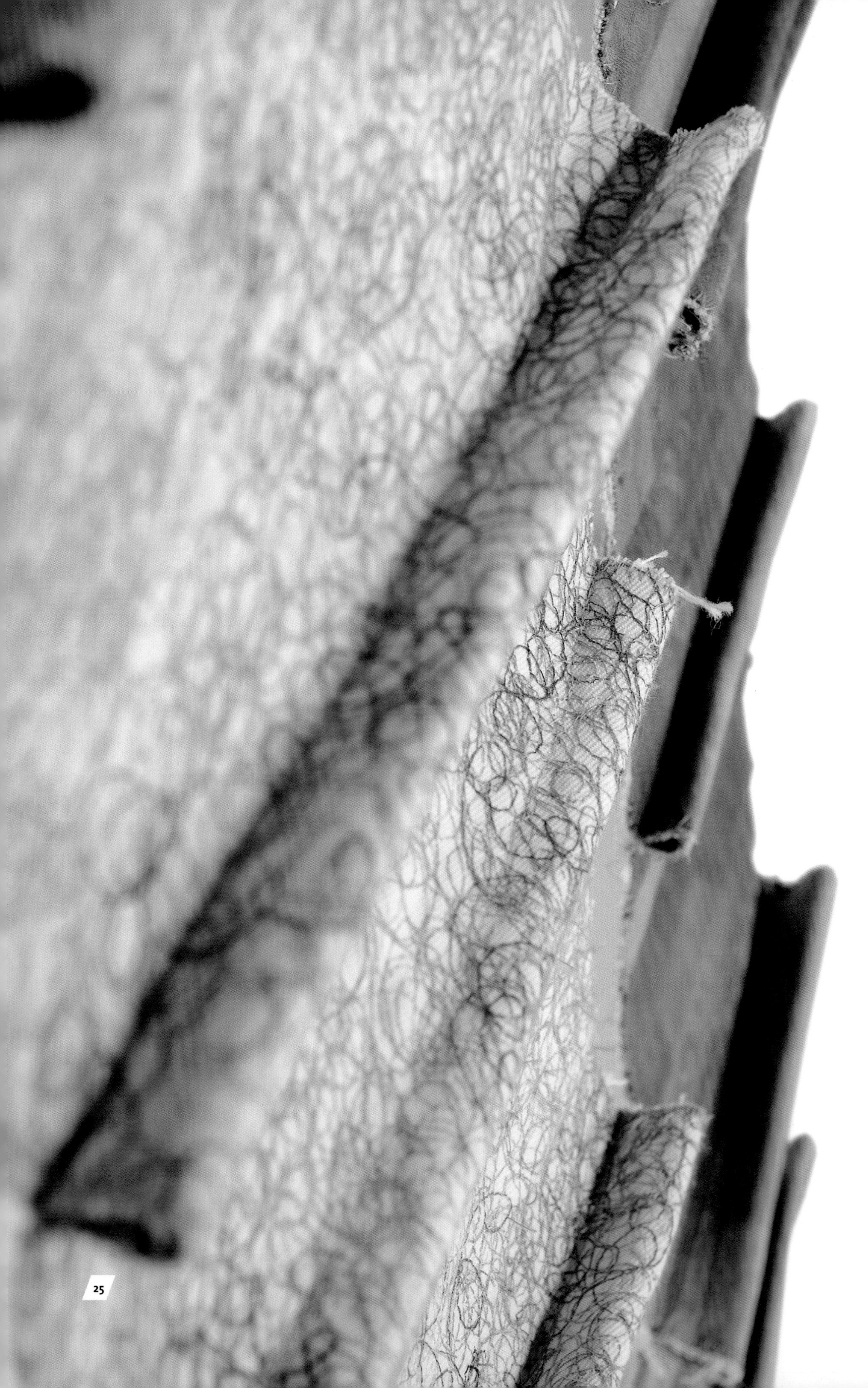

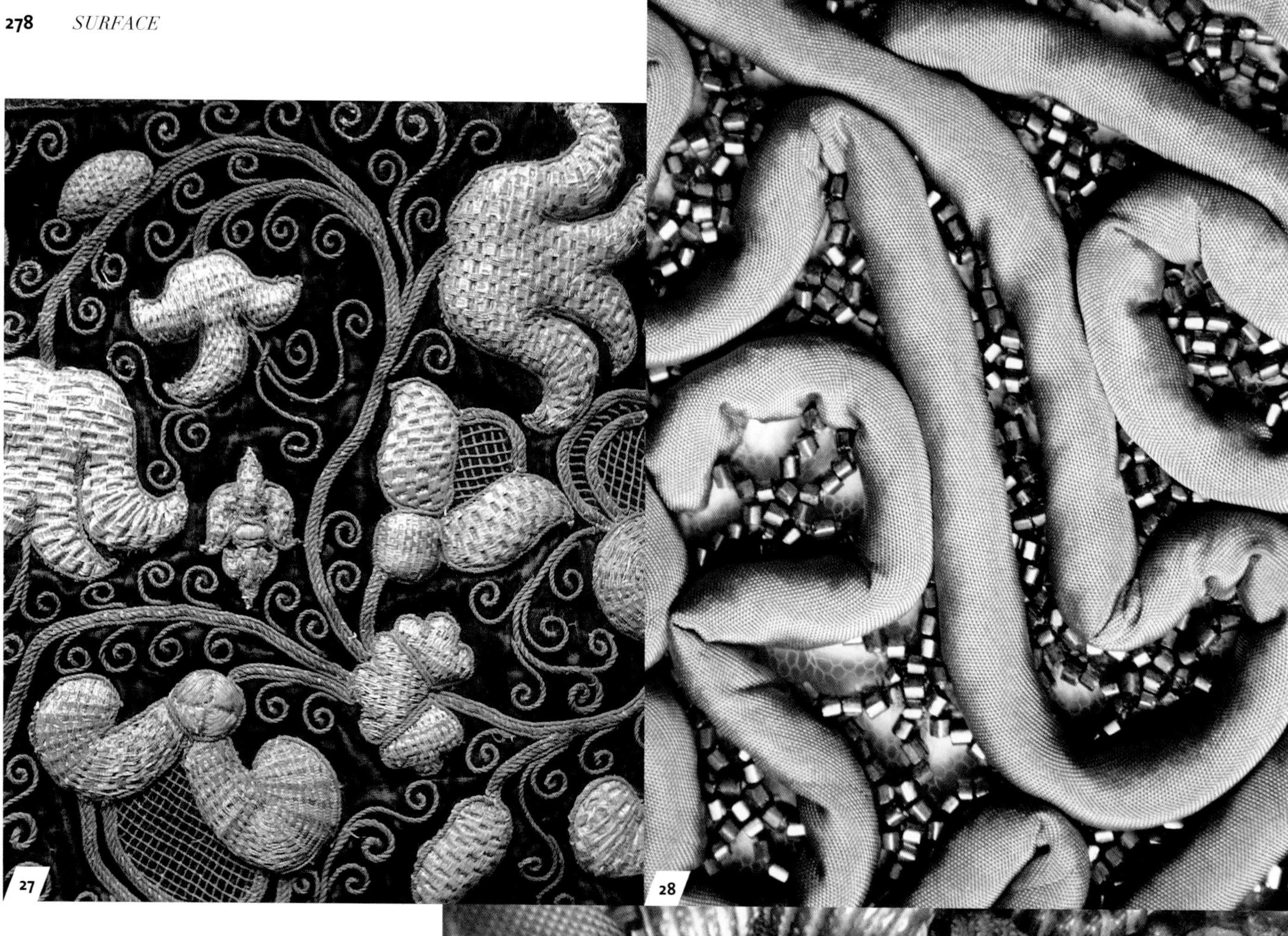

27. Spanish professional embroiderer, *Bullion work panel* (detail), *c.* 1650–1700. Couched cords and raised work of gold and silver metal threads swirl across a silk velvet ground in a panel made for a Spanish wedding; unseen is a rose within a coat of arms, meaning that the pope sent a witness.

28. Nadia Albertini, *Embroidery* (detail). Worked on a tulle base, wool-stuffed budelinis made of silk satin meander around metallic beads, and plastic sequins define the undulations of the tulle ruches.

29 and 30. Hand & Lock, *Embroidery samples*, *c.* 2010. Hand & Lock was established in 2001 with the merger of two London bespoke embroidery companies, S. Lock (founded in 1898 as C. E. Phipps & Co.) and M. Hand (founded in 1767). These two examples hint at the range of hand- and machine-embroidered effects carried out in their workshops for military, fashion and couture uses.

31

32

33

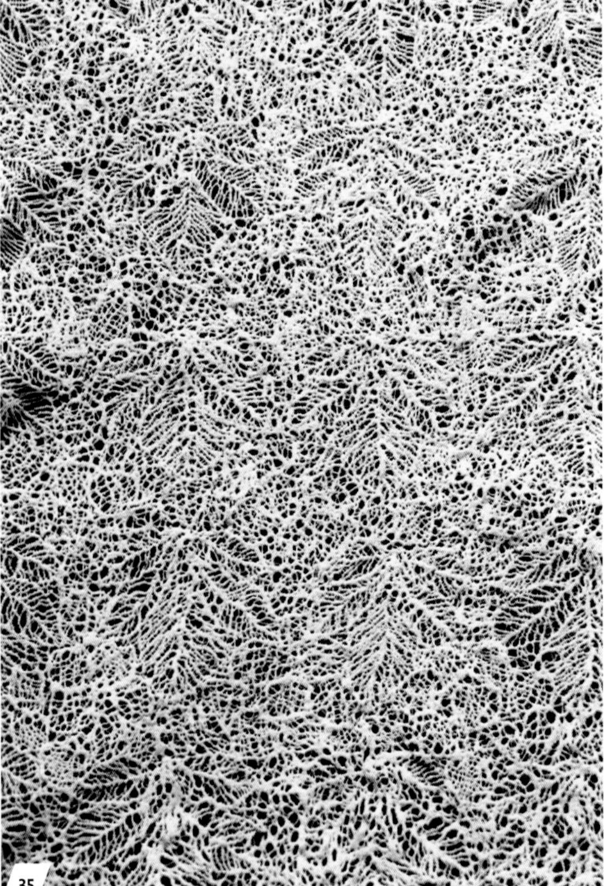

31. Hand & Lock, *Ricardo San Martini slippers for Tom Ford* (detail), *c.* 2010. Black velvet hand-embroidered with matt purl (tightly coiled gilt wire) and smooth purl (coiled, flattened gilt wire).

32. Italian embroiderer (attributed), *Dalmatic* (detail), *c.* 1600. Velvet applied with silk-embroidered silk satins and couched with gilt threads forms this bold design. This technique, called *taillure* (meaning 'cut' in French), was used on the Russian Steppes as early as the 5th century BC for felt saddles and horse trappings.

33. European embroiderer, *Court suit waistcoat* (detail), *c.* 1725. Several types of gilt and silver-gilt metal threads, paillettes and beads are couched amid strands of couched blue silk chenille. This interweaving technique was called *rapport* by French embroiderers.

34. Tadek Beutlich, *Stole* (detail), 1948–52. Handwoven by Beutlich during the period in which he ran Ethel Mairet's Gospels workshop, the lively surface is the result of yarns rather than weave structure. Undyed chenille, undyed continuous filament rayon, and machine-spun dyed cotton slubbed wefts, some looped and cut, are plain woven on a spaced warp (held thus by the loom's reed) of dyed and undyed machine-spun cotton.

35. Vishna Collins, *Jedna Mlada* (detail), 2001. The Croatian saying *Jedna mlada, pet rada* means 'one bride, five embroideries'. In an homage to her grandmother and the traditional dress of her homeland, Collins has used crochet and pearl beads to enhance free-form machine embroidery on vanishing cotton, in total requiring 40 km (25 miles) of spun polyester sewing thread.

36

37

38

36. Martin Appleby, *That Darned Jumper* (detail), 1964–. In an ongoing creation, natural and synthetic yarns and shoelaces now completely darn a plain green sweater knitted by Appleby's mother when he was a student of engraving at the Central School of Art and Design, London.

37. Spanish weaver, *Alpujarra carpet*, 17th or 18th century. Made with a looped woollen pile on linen in the Alpujarra region, which had been the last stronghold of the Spanish Muslims, or Moors, until their expulsion in 1609. This technique remained characteristic here and in other formerly Islamic regions such as Crete and Sardinia.

38. Edwina Straub, *Ripples* (detail), 2011. As if drifting over the surface of this large panel are machine-stitched forms made with gold thread, monofilament and cotton threads, hand-dyed with fibre-reactive dyes. 'Like the transformation of sensory awareness into experience, the manipulation of yarn transforms its essence … . Through the projection of their shadows the ephemeral character of my art emerges.'

39. English or American printer, *Roller-printed dress fabric* (detail), mid-1880s. This lightweight open-weave cotton for a summer day dress has a self-coloured stripe, highlighted where overprinted with black. Such printed mulls, as these cloths were called, were highly fashionable at this date.

40. John Parkes, *Veil/unveil* (detail), 2010. Silk georgette and cotton voile cloths dyed with natural and synthetic dyes hand- and commercially applied, hand-stitched with linen threads.

41. Ulla de Larios, *Transparency #4* (detail), 2009. Silk, with a spaced warp creating distortions within a tabby weave.

39

40

41

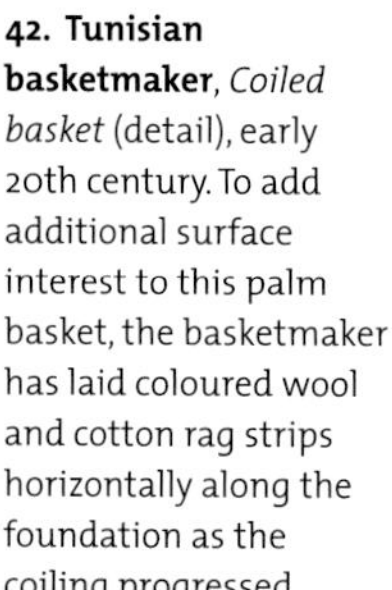

42. Tunisian basketmaker, *Coiled basket* (detail), early 20th century. To add additional surface interest to this palm basket, the basketmaker has laid coloured wool and cotton rag strips horizontally along the foundation as the coiling progressed.

43. Indian weaver, *Sari cloth* (detail), c. 1965–85. The silver metallic-thread fringed diamonds embellishing this crepe-chiffon cloth are made with a supplementary warp, clipped away near the edges of each motif.

44. European artisans, *Stamped velvet* (detail), 16th century. Impressing a pattern on plain silk velvet using wooden blocks and other tools was a technique known in France as *goffrata* and later, *gauffrage*. Such cloths were significantly cheaper than loom-patterned velvet.

45. Italian weaver, *Two-pile velvet fragment* (detail), *c.* 1450. Among the most luxurious of Renaissance textiles were silk velvets such as this, with two heights of cut pile and brocading with gold metal thread.

46. Beth Hatton, *Selection #2 (Cattle)* (detail), 2001. Woven in block weave using shaft switching, from kangaroo-skin offcuts and wool on a cotton warp. The black stencil markings spell out 'cattle' – animals introduced to Australia – while the names of displaced native species are spelled backwards by the kangaroo-skin tufts.

47. American mill, *Yardage* (detail), 2001. In this rapier loom-woven double weave, the weaving elements cross to form two separate layers and patterns of squares. The repoussé effect is accentuated by the use of soft cotton yarns with a flannel finish.

48. Indian dyer and weaver, *Double-ikat panel*, 1990s. A stained glass-like grid has been created in this cotton double ikat or *patola*, in which the yarns used in both warp and weft directions are pre-dyed.

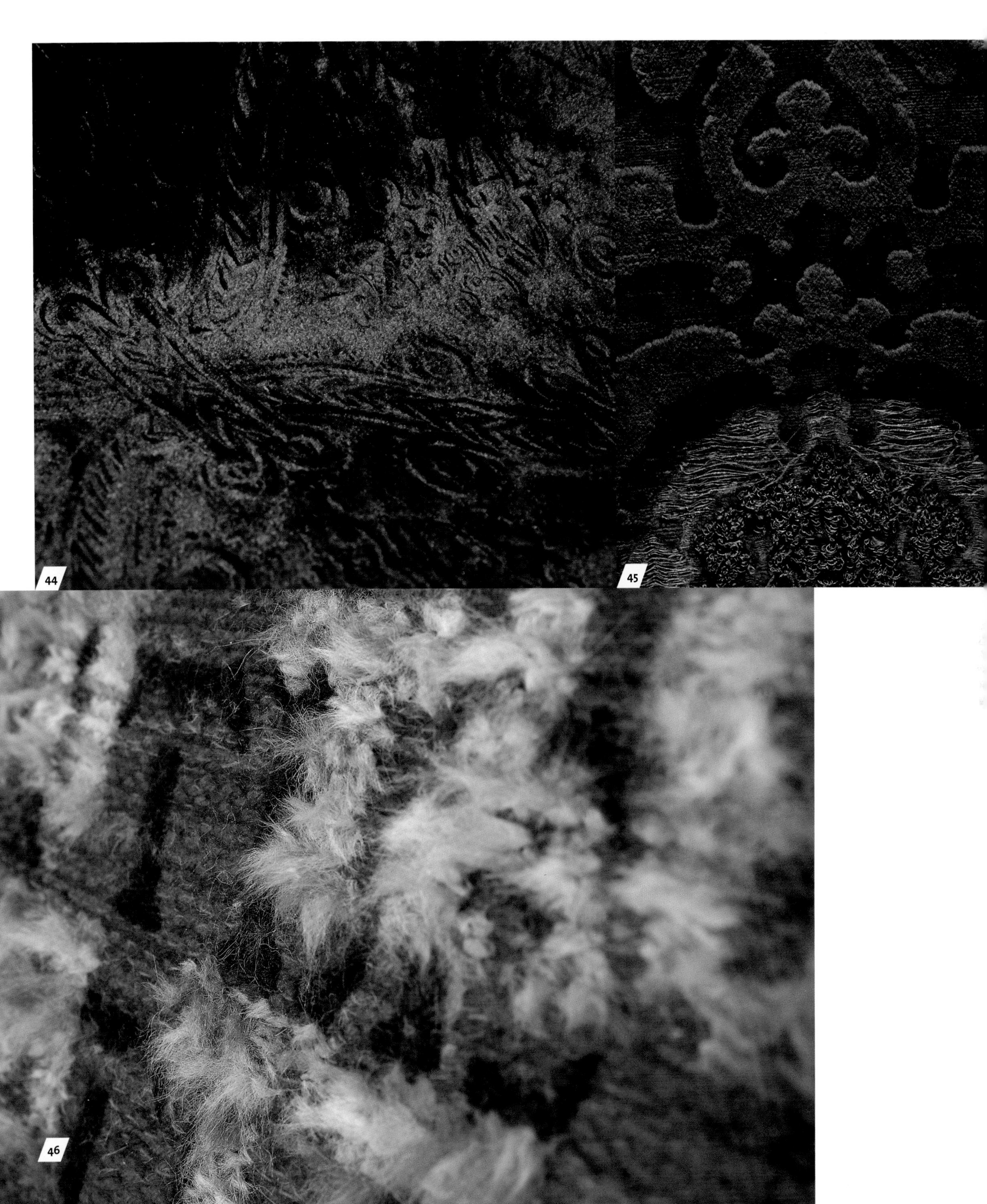
44
45
46

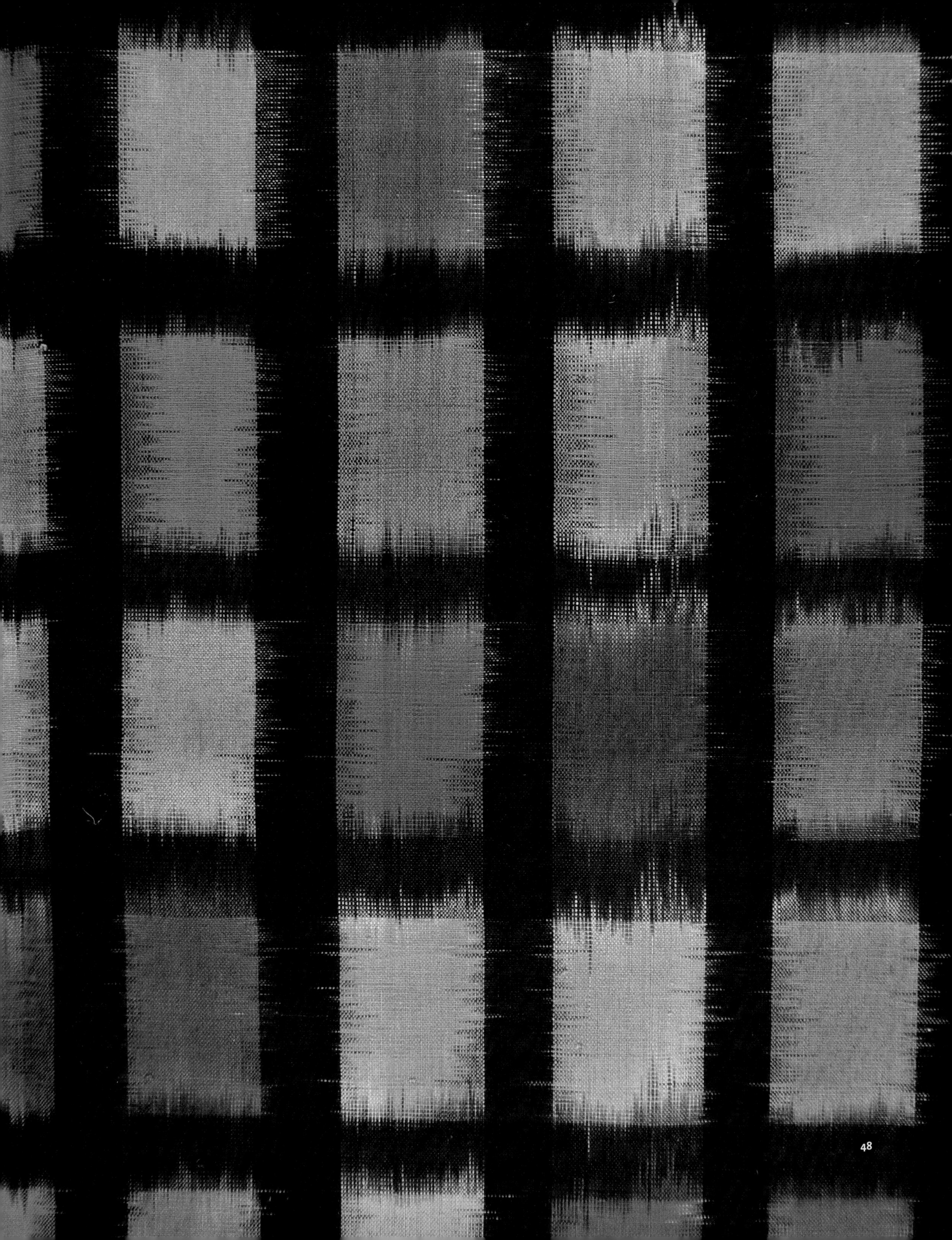

49

50

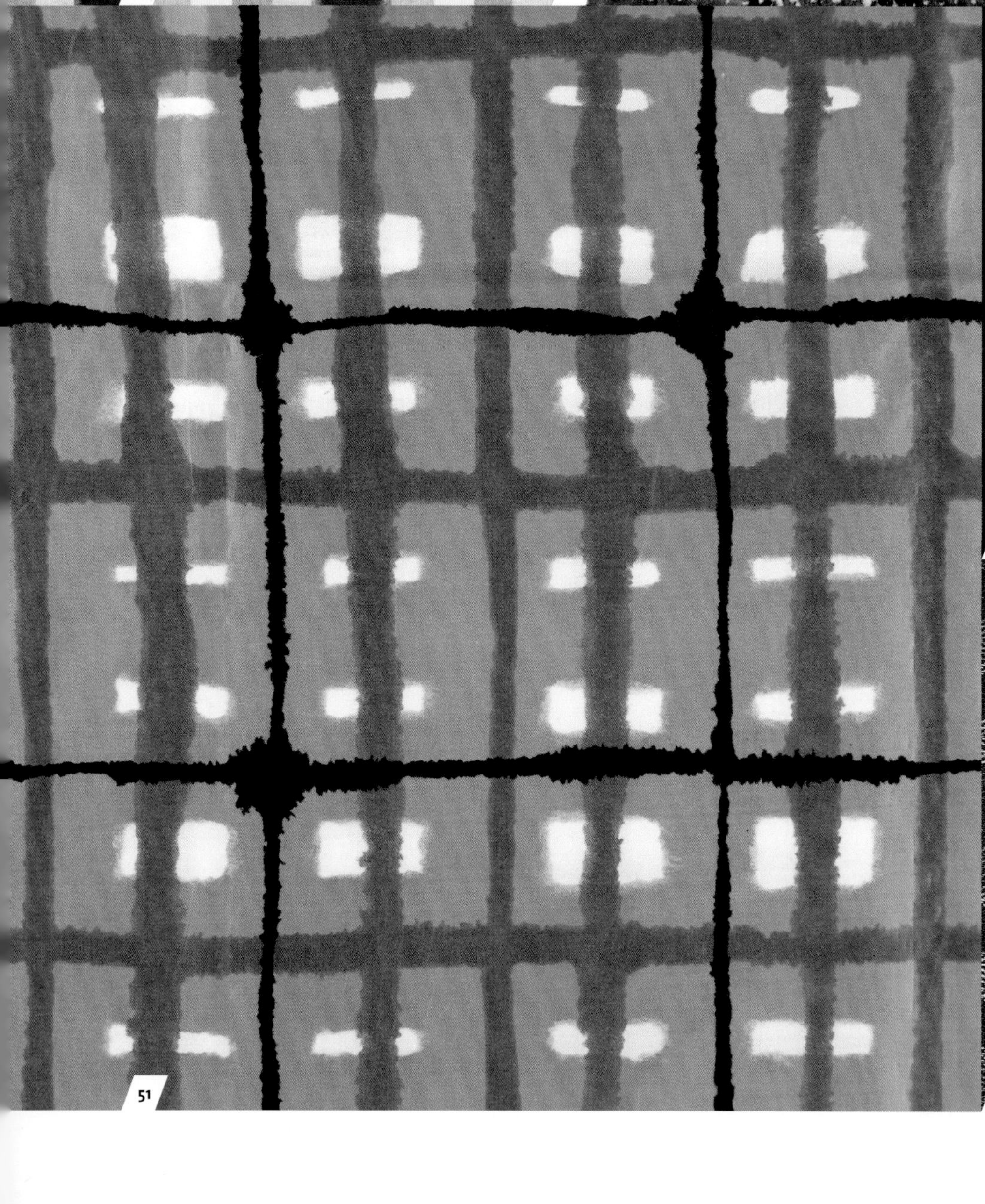

51

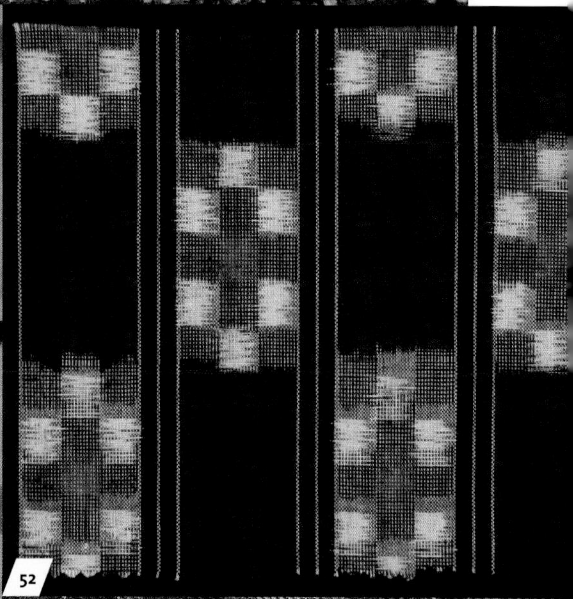

52

53

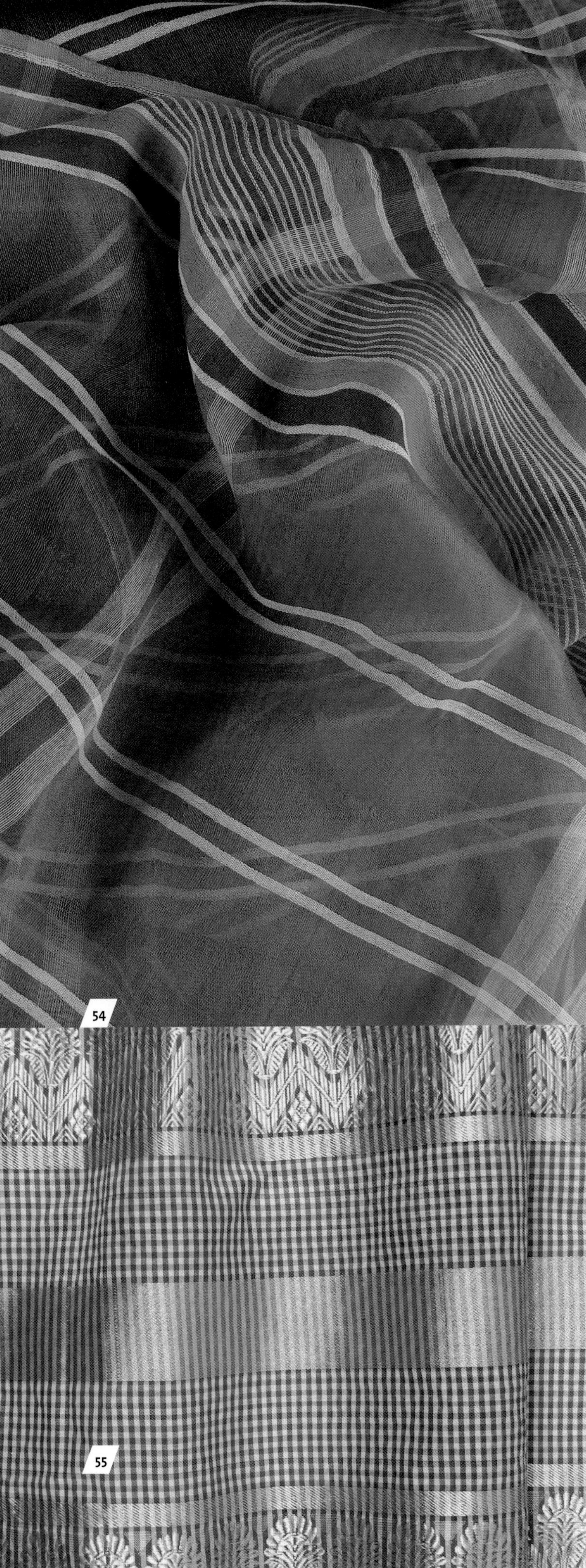

49–55. The choice and treatment of yarns create much of the impact of all these cloths. Two are cotton double ikats, one made in India in about 1960 (49), and the other some twenty years later in Japan for the Kasuri Dyeworks Berkeley, California (52). Much thicker wool yarns make up two Peruvian handwoven cloths. The first (50) is a *frasada* (blanket, detail shown) made in 1970 in Huasta, and is plain woven with an undyed cream wool warp and dyed wool wefts, the brown yarns dyed in walnut leaves. The second is a 2/2 herringbone twill plaid fabric called *jerga* (53), in which the warp threads are more tightly spun than those of the weft. Produced in Aija in the Cordillera Negra, this type of cloth was used to make sacks. Fine synthetic yarns created the two sari cloths woven in India between about 1965 and 1985. The chiffon incorporates satin weft and warp stripes and gold metallic-thread brocading (54) and the other (55) has a striped warp with a border of alternating striped wefts (creating gingham) and gold-coloured wefts in plain and patterned weaves. The final example (51) is printed in imitation of ikat, on a fine, smooth cotton sateen cloth. It was manufactured by Fuller Fabrics of New York, probably in the 1960s, not long after the firm became famous for designs by such artists as Picasso, Miró and Chagall.

56 and 58. Cross-stitch embroidery is widely used among ethnic groups in southern China, northern Laos, Thailand and Vietnam. Above (56) is a detail of a Miao silk sleeve piece from *c.* 1985, and to the right (58) is a detail of a contemporary trouser leg, worked by a woman of the Yao (Mien) northern hill tribe of Thailand, where very fine silk cross-stitch embroidery in geometric motifs is carried out on indigo-dyed homespun cloth.

57. Laotian weaver, near Vientiane, *Shawl* (detail), 2002. Handwoven by a woman in silk with geometric supplementary wefts that are almost twice as thick as the dark brown-black warp threads, this cloth emulates textural effects characteristic of embroidery. Solid bands using gold-coloured silk weft threads produce a shot effect.

59. French printer, *Foulard patterns*, mid-19th century. This selection of two-colour patterns, block-printed onto a fine cotton ground, probably in Rouen, was created to show the factory's selection of designs. All were intended for neckerchiefs and imitate woven patterns.

38
39
40
94
42
32
49
45
67
87
90
89
59

60
61
62
63

60. Taiwanese artisan, *Taipei tapa* (detail), *c.* 1970–75. Tapa cloth is made from the thin fibrous bark of the paper mulberry and the *Pipturus albidus plant*, and is decorated in several ways. Here a dye-covered pad has been rubbed over the cloth, itself placed against a carved pattern. Hand-painting then darkens the principal motifs and grid.

61. Ruth Reeves, *Guatemalan Document* (detail), 1935–40s. Reeves' use of ethnographic materials as inspiration began early in the 1920s, and in 1934 she studied the textiles of Guatemala under the auspices of the Carnegie Institution, designing this cloth a year later and continuing to hand-screen print it on linen until about 1950.

62. Ling Po, *Prototype for 'Design No. 102'* (detail), 1954–55. One of several designs for F. Schumacher & Co.'s range of Frank Lloyd Wright 'Taliesin Line' woven and printed textiles, this pattern was created by a Fellow at Wright's Taliesin West studio in Scottsdale, Arizona. It illustrates Wright's interest in Maya carving, most evident in his details for the Ennis House, Los Angeles, of 1924.

63. Teresa Paschke, *Ceah 4* (detail), 2009. Incorporating 'shadows' of lace and stylized motifs from Latin American textiles with other imagery, all developed from digital photographs, this cotton canvas was wide-format inkjet printed and completed with hand embroidery.

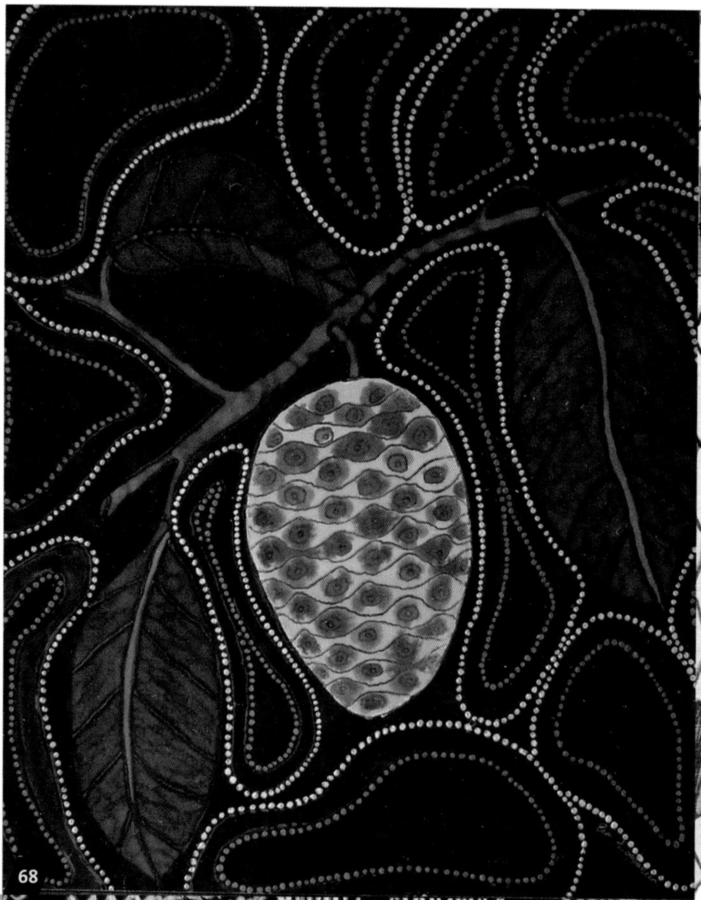

68

69

70

71

68. Eva Wanganeen, *Meyak* (detail), 2003. Inspired by the culture of her ancestors, the native people of Australia, the artist depicts a tree used for medicine in traditional Australian and Malaysian practices. Wanganeen has painted on silk with acid dyes and gutta-percha, a natural latex produced by this type of tree.

69. Mariska Karasz, *Skein* (detail), 1952. This screen-printed furnishing linen was released by F. Schumacher & Co., New York. It is a *trompe l'oeil* depiction of knotted netting, and is adapted from one of the artist's own embroideries, an art form the Hungarian-born former fashion designer took up in the late 1940s.

64. Italian printer, *Block-printed linen* (detail), 16th century. Probably produced in Florence, this is a rare surviving example of European block-printing prior to the influence and understanding of Indian dyed printing in the late 17th century.

65–67. Three 10- to 15-year-old students at the Central School of Art and Design, London, *Warner & Sons block prints for Fortnum & Mason, London*, 1937. Commissioned by H. G. Hayes Marshall of Fortnum & Mason's furnishing department, these linens were deliberately 'badly' printed by Warner's professional block printers to create a naïve, spontaneous and historical look.

70. Hawaiian artisan, *Batik shirt* (detail), acquired 1961. Complex freehand-drawn patterns in wax resist cover the surface of this batiked cotton cloth, which was made into a shirt labelled 'Reyn's Menswear, Catalina Island, Honolulu'.

71. Mary White, *Cottage Garden*, *c.* 1955. Heal's Wholesale and Export Limited produced this screen-printed furnishing cotton for its famous London shop as well as for other retailers. Its limited number of colours reflects lingering post-war restrictions, as does its relatively small repeat size, which minimized wastage.

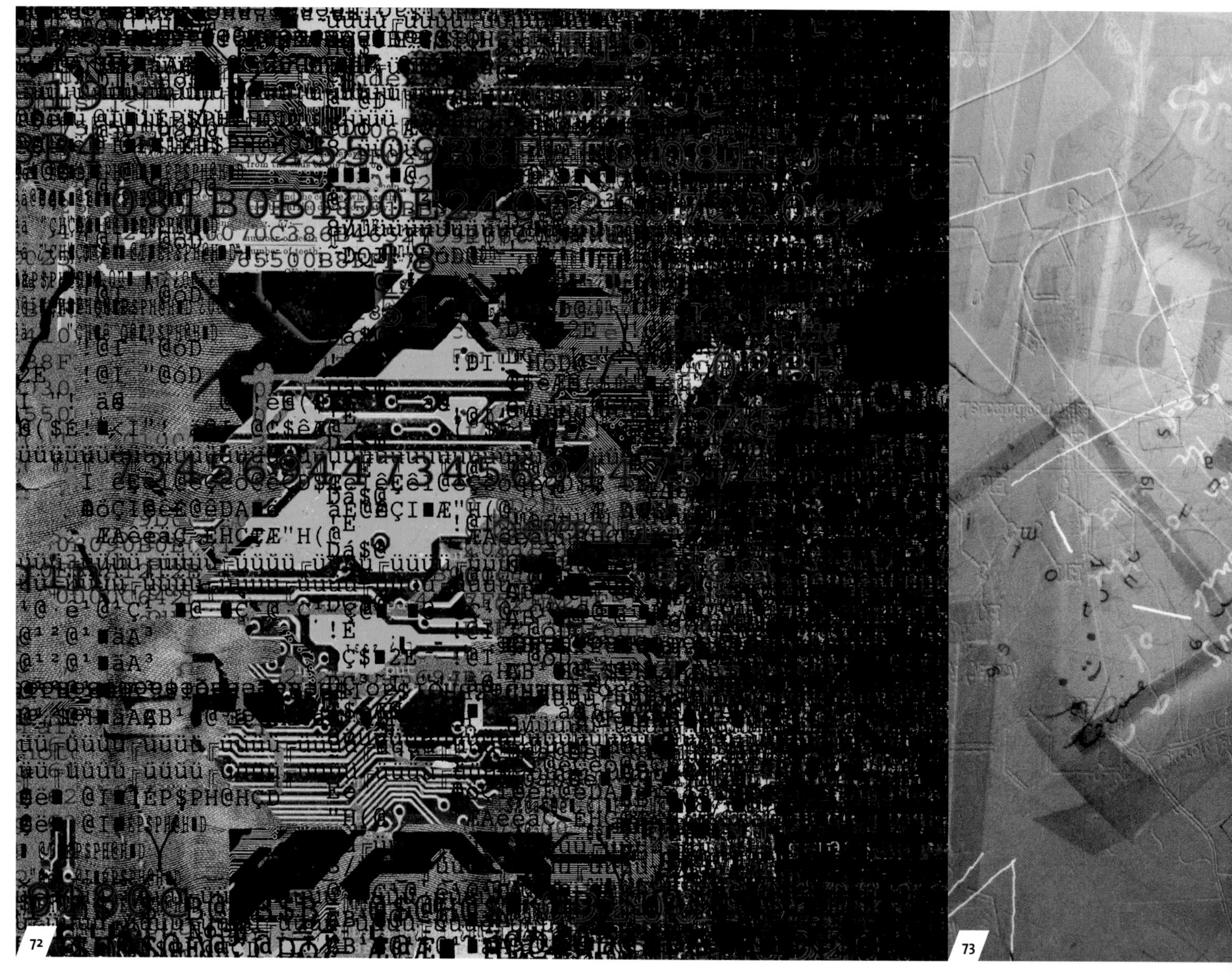

72. **Neil Bottle**, *Silk scarf* (detail), 2011. From the artist's TechnoCraft collection, developed after a period of time in India, Egypt and the United Arab Emirates. A complex combination of hand and digital techniques was used to express inspiration drawn from the history, culture, climate, landscape and peoples of these regions.

73 and 75. **Pat Hodson**, *Shadows – Blue* (whole and detail, 73), 2007. Using paper tissue, silk, linen thread, wax, crayon and Epson Ultrachrome inks, Hodson combines resist, collage drawing and digital printing to reference 'darkness made visible, shadows of memory, glimpses of light'.

74. **Peter Campbell**, *Capulet*, 1961. Silk headscarf, hand-screen printed at Liberty's printworks in Merton, a suburb of London where William Morris's printworks had been located. Alongside his oils, watercolours, drawings, calligraphy, and wood- and linocuts, the designer's expertise in enamelling is evidenced in the brilliant tones.

74

75

76

77

78

79

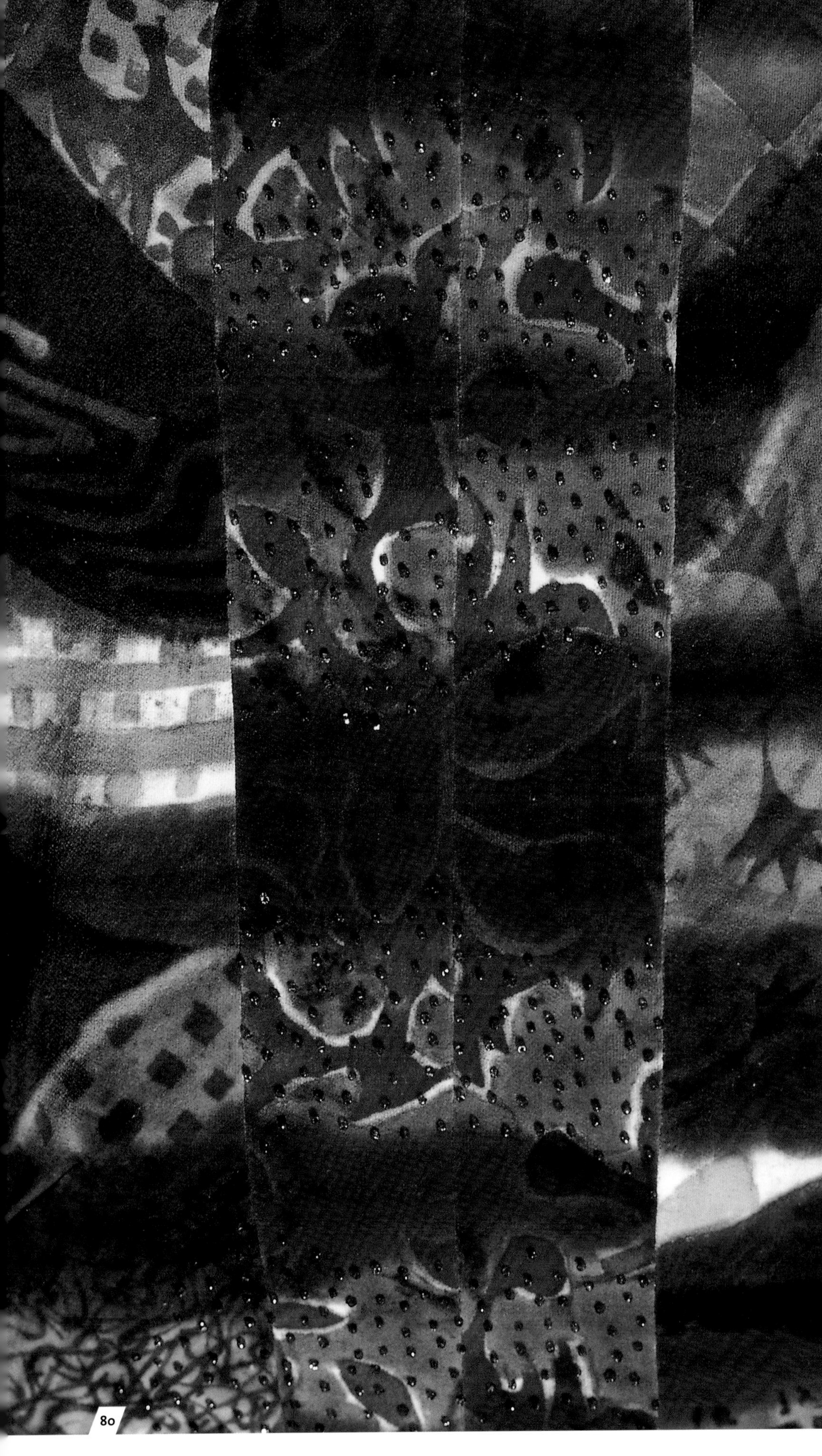

76. Maija Isola, *Medusa*, 1967. This screen-printed cotton from Marimekko was among the designs that made this Finnish company a trend-setter. Founded in Helsinki in 1951, Marimekko was first introduced to the United States by the architect Benjamin C. Thompson, who in 1953 founded the D/R (Design Research) store chain in Cambridge, Massachusetts, where this piece was purchased.

77. Ken Scott, *Ulisse*, 1966. This vivid printed jersey knit of Ban-Lon nylon was printed in Italy at the height of Scott's global influence as an American-born fashion designer established in Milan. He was known for such floral fabric designs and for developing fashion shows.

78. C. J. Pressma, *Bull and Other Friends*, 2008. This machine-quilted panel is formed from the artist's photographs collaged and inkjet-printed on cotton.

79. Japanese dyer, *Furoshiki*, 1969. This wrapping and carrying cloth, woven in hand-spun slub cotton yarn, depicts dried abalone strips called *noshi*. It was created using the *tsutsugaki* technique of a rice-paste resist applied to the surface with a cone-shaped tube.

80. Katherine Westphal Rossbach, *Sheath dress* (detail), 1970. Cotton velveteen, paste-resisted and stencilled with multiple colours of Inko dye, this dress cloth was created when the artist taught textile design and history at the University of California, Davis. She was widely influential in her exploration of colour and different print media and techniques, here taking inspiration from Japanese *noshi*.

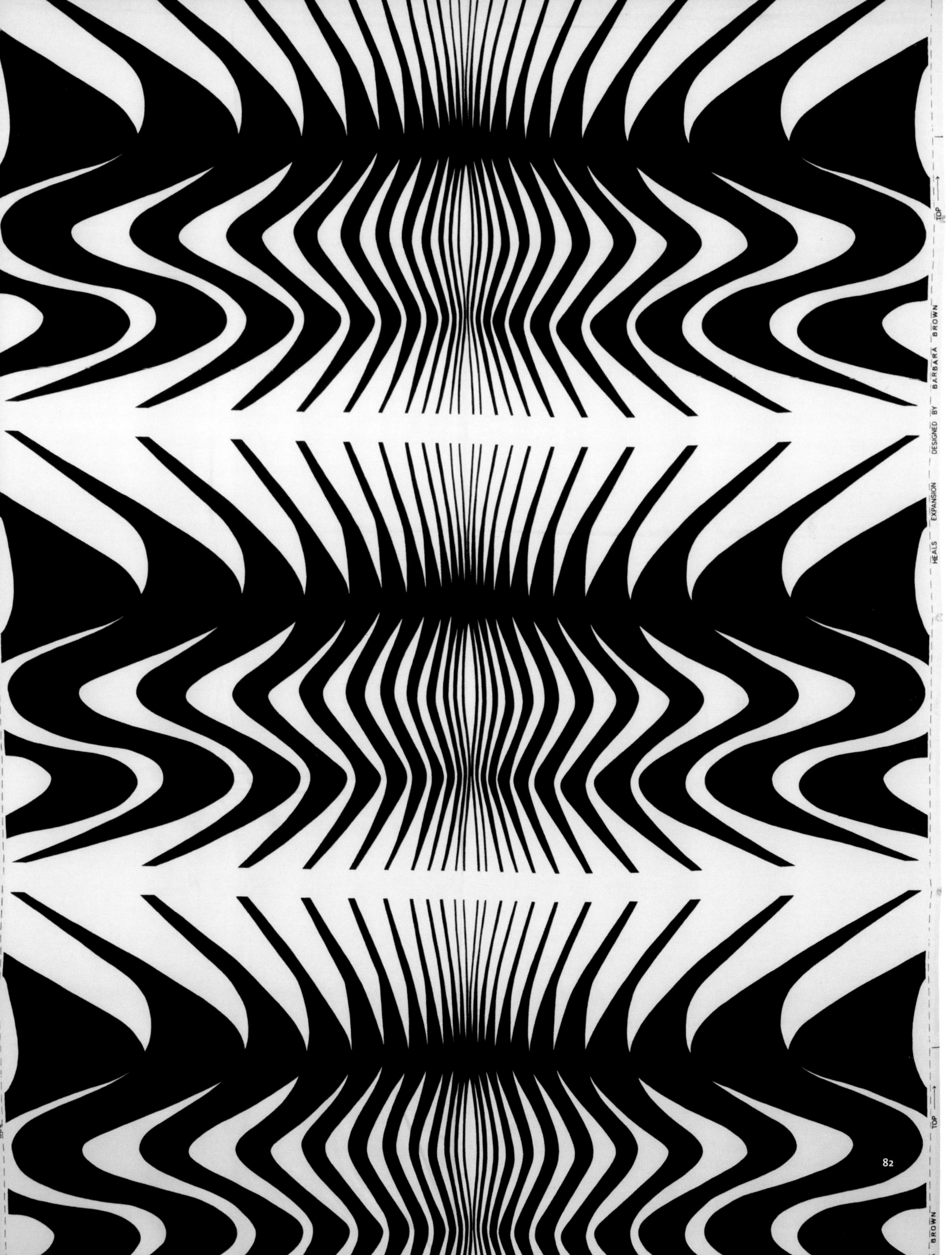
HEALS EXPANSION DESIGNED BY BARBARA BROWN
TOP

83
84

85

81. Angelo Testa, *Sportsmen's Blues*, 1942–47. One of the most influential of 'New Bauhaus' designers, Testa designed this hand-screen printed cotton while still a student at what is today the School of Design, Chicago, but did not produce it until he founded Angelo Testa & Co. in 1947.

82. Barbara Brown, *Expansion*, 1966. Brown's striking Op Art design was produced as a screen-printed furnishing fabric by Heal Fabrics Ltd, London.

83. By or after C. F. A. Voysey, *Sirang* (detail), *c.* 1906. Voysey was an influential and prolific designer who sold his work many British manufacturers, among them Liberty, which stocked this silk, and Thomas Wardle & Co., who pioneered the printing of tussah silks such as this.

84. Unknown designer, *Liberty Art Fabric*, *c.* 1890. Arthur Lasenby Liberty founded his 'art emporium' in London in 1875 and promoted the use of tussah silks, both plain woven and printed. This example, probably printed by Thomas Wardle & Co., Leek, Staffordshire, illustrates the warmth lent to the coloration by the unbleached tussah ground.

85. Wolf Bauer, *Collage*, 1967. Screen-printed on cotton velvet by Pausa AG in Germany, this was one of four designs created by German-born Bauer for Knoll International Ltd. Bauer was a multi-disciplinary designer, and this example was developed as a collage of torn paper pieces, representing *trompe l'oeil* columns.

86. Zandra Rhodes, *Untitled* (detail), *c.* 1965. Shortly after her graduation from the Royal College of Art, London, and inspired by both Roy Lichtenstein and comic books themselves, with their crude printing in black and red half-tone dots, Rhodes produced a series of designs with explosions and enlarged dots, drawn with crayons. Having just established her own print studio, she produced some in house, but this example was sold to Heal Fabrics Limited who screen-printed it on a furnishing-weight cotton satin.

87. Vanessa Bell (attributed), *Maud*, 1913. The handful of printed linens designed by the Omega Workshops (1913–19, London) had lasting influence, combining for the first time in European textiles the appearance of spontaneous hand-painting with vivid colours. All Omega cloths were produced in France, and this particular pattern is stencil-printed.

88. Jakob Schlaepfer, *Secret Garden* (detail), 2011. Ultra-light polyester fabric coated with bronze was inkjet-printed to create this furnishing sheer.

89. Marion Stoll, *Hill*, 1938–48. This panel was embroidered in fine and expensive wool, dyed in Austria, by Stoll, an American-born artist who lived in Europe from 1900 to 1931. Writing about modern techniques in embroidery in *The Studio* in 1927, Stoll noted that 'in colour-work, a very striking characteristic of the new embroidery is its radical simplification of stitchery … the general effect is obtained by the simplest means. Complicated "fancy" stitches are seldom, if ever, found in modern embroidery in colours: the needle is a means to an artistic end, not an end in itself.'

90. Stephanie Schulte, *Flaunt – Body Gesture 2*, 2009. Machine embroidery and 'the use of images, materials and practices associated with women's art and traditional models of feminity' are employed by the artist to 'bring to light the various parallels between new domesticity, the resurgence of craft and re-codification of feminine iconography'.

91. Eleri Mills, *Meirch yn y winllan (Ancestral landscape with horses)*, *c.* 2009. Paint, hand-stitching and appliqué on cloth.

92

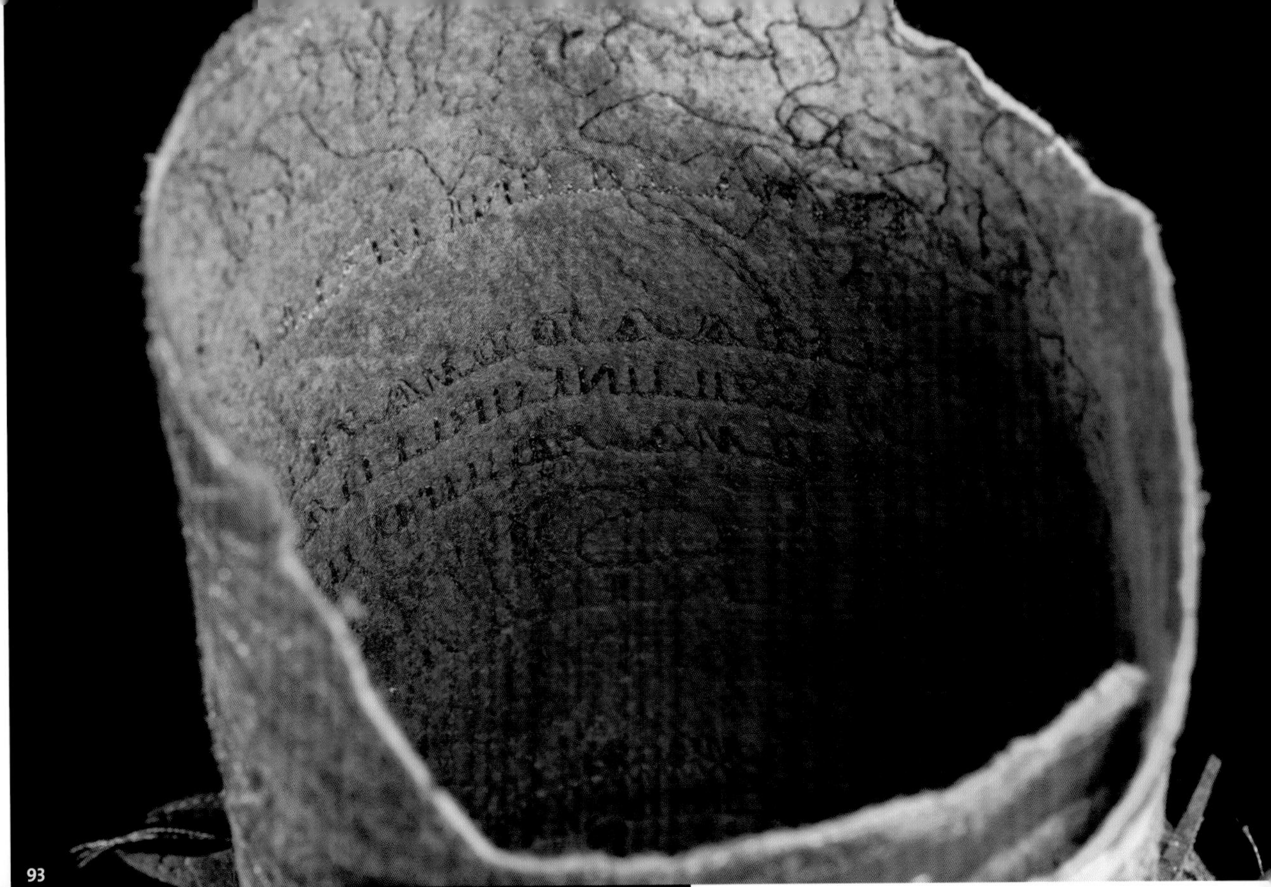
93

94

92. Nicki Ransom, *Whisper Within*, 2010. This charcoal drawing on cotton fabric has hand-stitched details.

93 and 94. Anni Hunt, *Headline News*, 2009. This vessel has a base of wool and rayon felt that was hand-dyed and copper-foiled, after which a series of painted and stamped papers were collaged onto the surface with layers of newsprint. The surface was then stitched with a secret alphabet and other hand-stitching. Hunt calls it 'a container for all those moments one wants to shout about from the rooftops! All the "secrets" are on the outside.'

95

96

95. Vincent Malta for M. Lowenstein & Sons, Inc., *Iliad*, 1953. This dress fabric of discharge-printed cotton has a linocut-inspired design resembling sgraffito. Printed on the selvedge is 'A Signature fabric, "Illiad" created by Vincent Malta of Associated American Artists'. Lowenstein was founded in New York City in 1889 and, after nearly a century of extraordinary expansion, was purchased by Springs Industries in 1986.

96 and 97. Anne Morrell, *Overshadow* (whole and detail), 2008. Cotton fabrics were sprayed with colours before and during the interlacing of patterns in a running stitch and appliqué. 'I look to make pieces that work through words,' says Morrell: 'words with different outcomes and meaning in the work. The word "bias" is always there – as in "stitching on the bias" – and the word "Incline", a slope.'

98. Bette Levy, *Into the Maelstrom*, 1999. Using silk thread on a black silk noil ground, Levy has developed a personal language of stitches that is often based on her own photographic studies and is frequently employed on a small scale. It is seen here in a panel 7.8 cm (20 in.) high.

97

98

99

100

99. Lucy Arai, *2006.02* (detail), 2006. Mixed-media *sashiko* (Japanese running-stitch embroidery) on handmade paper is worked with sumi ink, acrylic, indigo pigment, 18-carat gold and thread.

100. Carolyn Nelson, *Fragment of a Love Story II*, 2009. This small textile collage is composed of hand-dyed and mono-printed silk organza, metallic organza and a hand-stitched web of hand-dyed organzine thread.

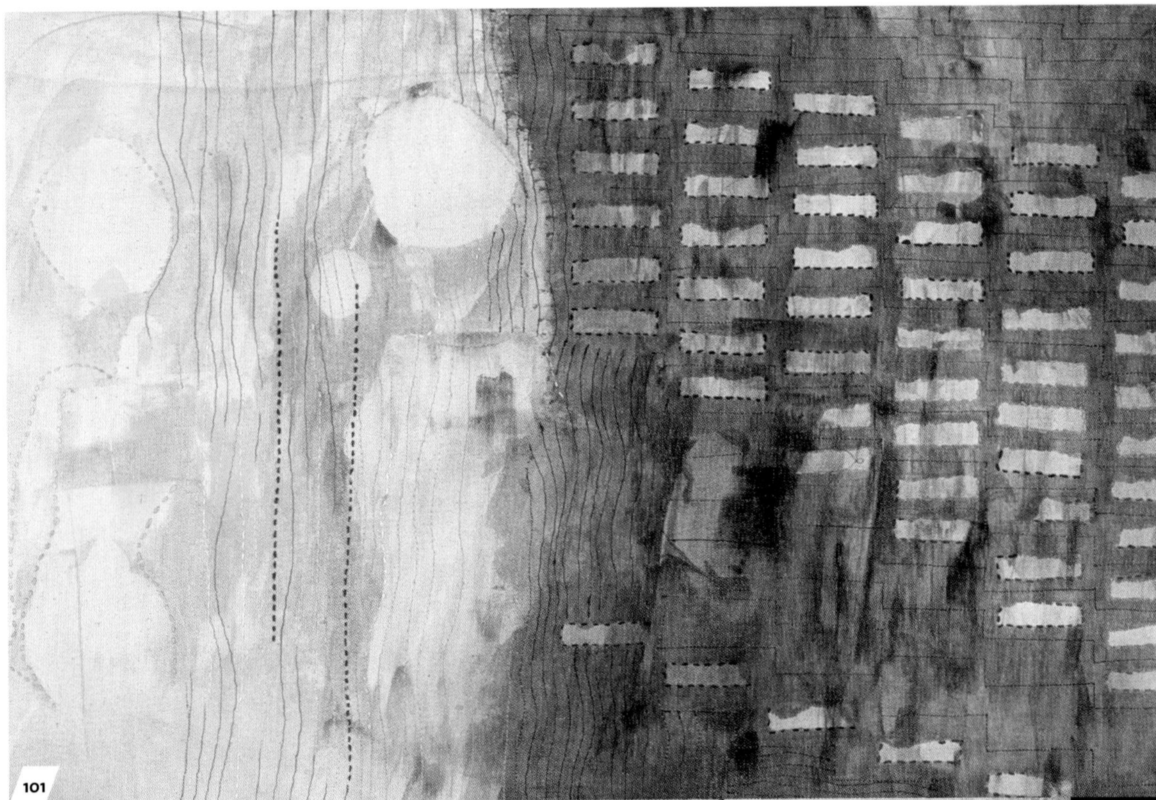

101. Clairan Ferrono, *Last Conversation*, 2007. Ferrono combined hand-stitching and machine quilting over a painting on canvas created in 2001 and stitched six years later as part of a dialogue with her mother: 'The piece resonated with the conversations my mother and I had … as she was dying. We never knew which conversation would be the last, so each one had to count.'

102. Teresa Paschke, *Cherry Blossom*, 2010. This hand-embroidered panel, 152.4 cm (60 in.) wide, is cotton canvas, printed with a wide-format inkjet printer. Paschke is 'interested in finding relationships between seemingly unrelated things', and uses layering 'through stitched marks, images or the cloth itself … to express psychological fragmentation, memories that are barely visible yet always present'.

103. Sue Hotchkis, *Ardwick* (detail), 2011. Black Bondina cotton screen-printed with a heat-expanding print medium has also been treated with Procion dyes, transfer paints and a discharge medium. It forms the background to kunin felt coloured, distressed and stitched by hand and free-motion machine.

104. Caroline Brown, *Sorsele, Sweden* (detail), 2009. Reflecting an experimental approach in this working sample, found objects from a riverbank in Sorsele were sealed in melted plastic and then used to print on painted silk. The piece was then hand-embroidered with silk and rayon threads.

105. Unknown maker, *Quilted grey wool petticoat* (detail), 19th century.

106. Anne-Marie Stewart, *Maya Memory*, 2006. Black-dyed cotton face and back, with cotton wadding between, was free-machine quilted with black thread, and discharged with painted fabric lizard motifs sewn and appliquéd, to capture 'the essence of carved stone worn away by caressing hands, acid rain, tree roots and looters' cuts'.

107. Mark Hearld for St Jude's Fabrics, *Doveflight*, 2006. This screen-printed cotton displays the artist's admiration for the English printmakers Edward Bawden, John Piper and Paul Nash, all of whom also designed influential textiles between *c.* 1923 and 1963. Here Hearld captures the energetic lines associated with the British School of linocuts.

103

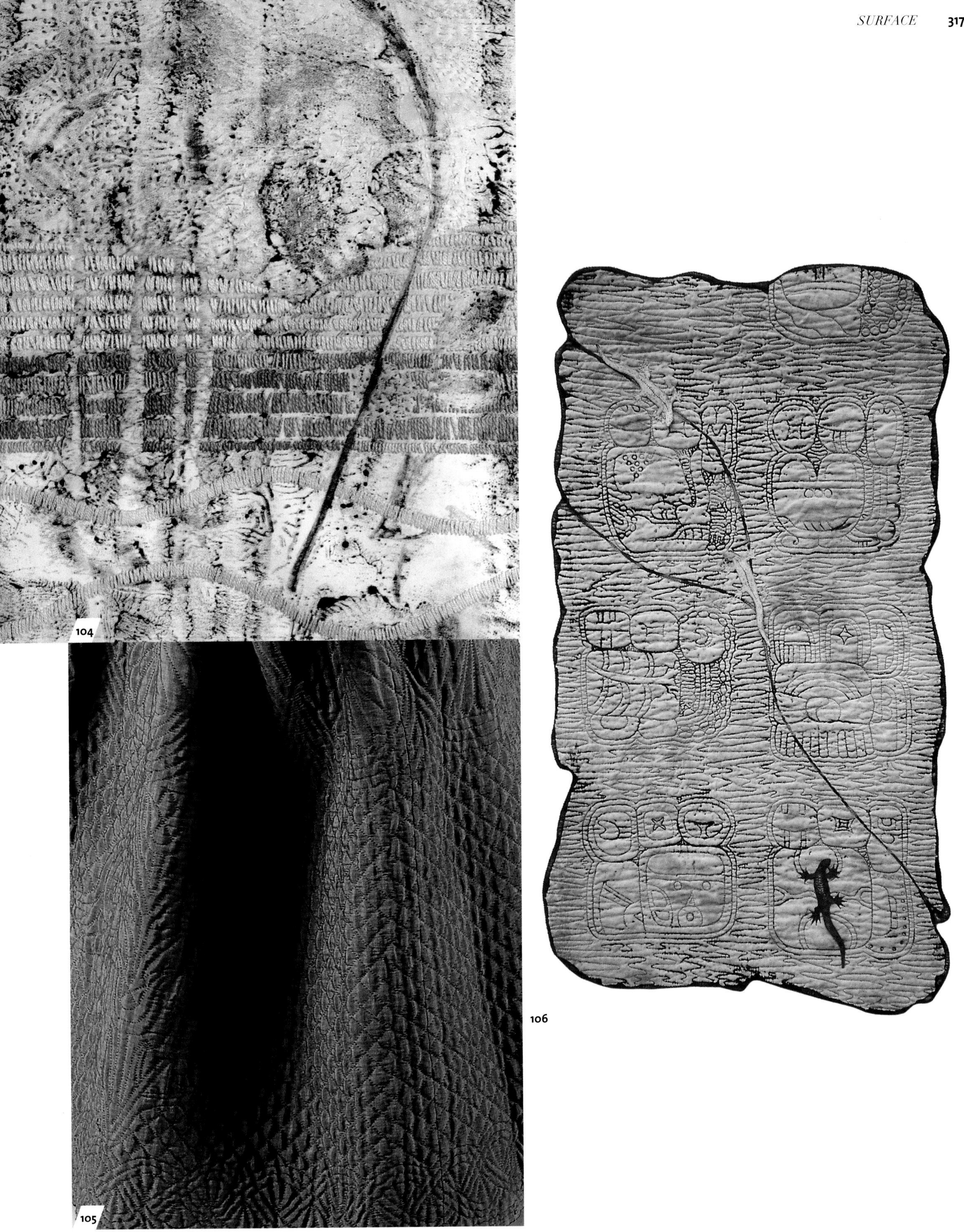

104

105

106

108. Sarah Campbell, *Spotted Creatures*, 2010. This one-off hand-painted silk scarf was created with silk paints and resist. Revealing the artist's knowledge of ethnographic textiles, it also captures the free-drawing style associated with the influential design studio Collier Campbell, which Campbell formed in the 1970s with her sister Susan Collier.

109. Bogor, Java, Indonesia, *Man's headscarf*, before 1964. This batik utilizes reds, soga brown, light blue and indigo on an indigo background. Soga brown is a unique Javanese colour from the bark of the *Pelthophorum ferrugineum* tree. Silver threads are couched around each border.

110. German embroiderer, *Panel* (detail), mid-15th century. Embroidered with Gobelin and surface satin stitches in polychrome silk floss and two-ply white linen thread on a painted linen background, this type of work was a speciality of Lower Saxony from about 1300 until about 1600.

111. Martin Bradley, *Cockpit* (detail showing two colourways), 1957. Bradley was 26 years old when Liberty commissioned this design for one of their hand-screen printed cottons, intended both to cater to the younger clientele and to support up-and-coming artists.

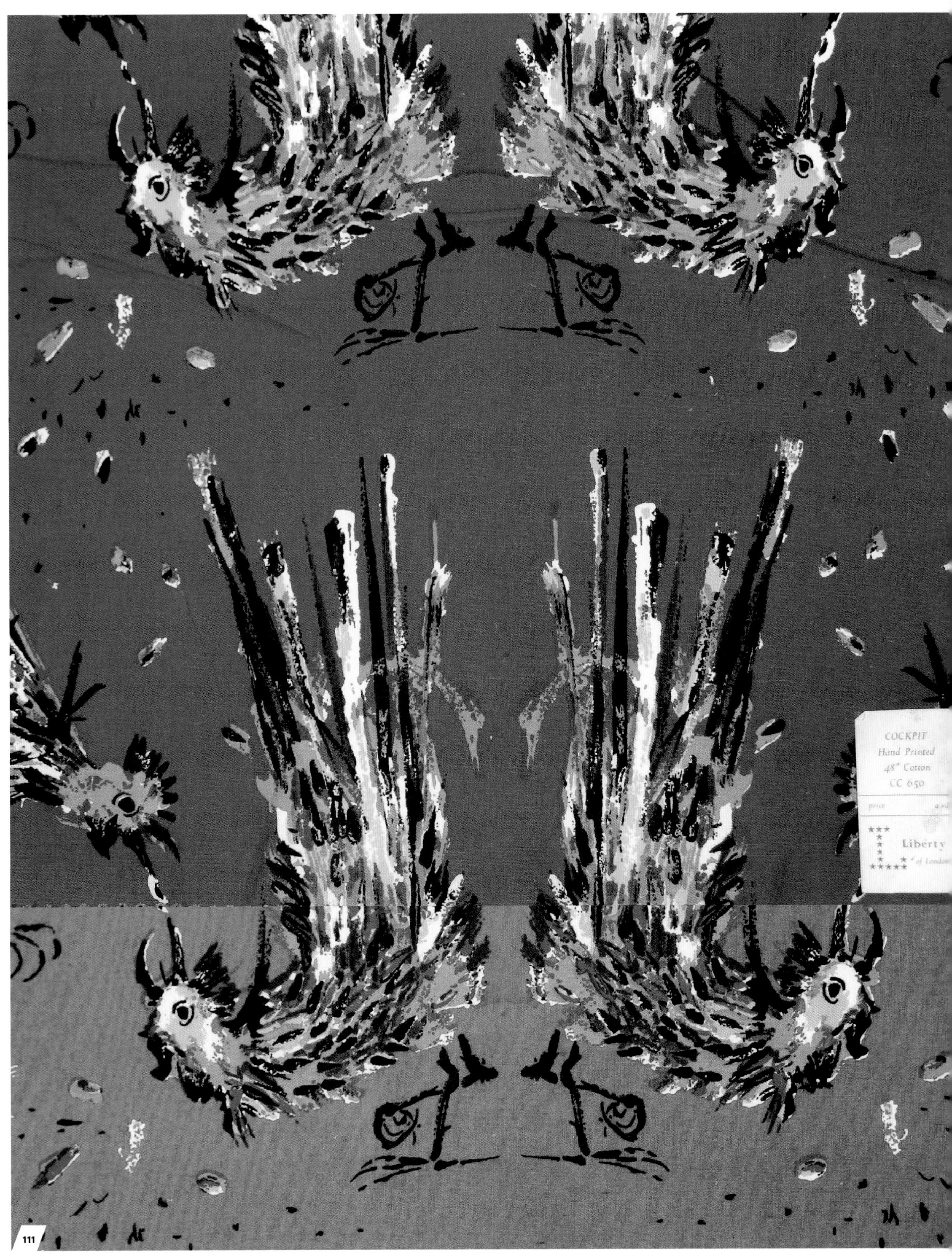
COCKPIT
Hand Printed
48" Cotton
CC 650
price
Liberty
of London
111

112. Maya Culture weaver, Huipil (detail), before 1978. Woven on a backstrap loom, this tunic has very dense double-faced brocading through the use of unplied cotton threads. It was originally acquired by Margot Blum Schevill during fieldwork in the village of San Antonio Aguas Calientes, Sacatepéquez, in the highlands of Guatemala.

113. Indian hand-printer, *Rectangular scarf* (detail), *c.* 1990. This vividly printed cotton voile scarf was purchased by Ed and Katherine Rossbach at the import chain Cost Plus, which was founded by William Amthor at Fisherman's Wharf in San Francisco, California, in 1958.

114. Lamy et Giraud, *Brocaded silk cannetille* (detail), 1878. This Lyonnais firm won a silver-gilt medal at the 1878 Paris Exposition Universelle with a silk of this design, probably by Eugene Prelle, their chief designer. Its impact partly derives from the textures within the many-coloured brocaded areas and the markedly twilled cannetille ground.

115

115. English embroiderer, *Apollo*, early 18th century. Surrounding Apollo are animals in the already traditional style of heraldry: the lion meaning sovereignty, the leopard indicating English adherence to the monarchy; and the hare representing man's eternal soul. The great variety of silk stitches indicate that this was a skilled amateur's work.

116 and 117. Fran Gardner, *Reddish Egret* and *Piping Plover*, 2010. Two of eight stitched images of birds made after the Deepwater Horizon oil spill in the Gulf of Mexico in 2010. These works reflect the artist's response to the destruction of the birds' habitat: 'Thread represents the delicacy of this ecosystem – beautiful if observed untouched, but easily disturbed or broken.'

118. I. Penn, *Copperplate-printed cotton* (detail), *c.* 1780. Designed and engraved by Penn in London, this image of a parrot was derived from Francis Barlow's *Diversae Avium Species* of 1658. Barlow is the earliest-known British-born animal painter, and his paintings of birds had a sustained influence on textile imagery for well over a century.

119. English embroiderer, *Apron* (detail), 1728. Dresden work, with its contrasting opaque and open-work areas on a delicate ground of hand-spun and hand-woven cotton, animates the depiction of peahens.

120. Madras (Chennai) embroiderer, *Panel* (detail), mid-19th to early 20th centuries. Silk satin with a muslin backing is finely embroidered in silk satin stitch and couched gold metallic-wrapped thread. Bronze, silver and gold metallic crimped wire (purl) is used on the flowers and the rooster, which are padded with cotton thread.

121. Elizabeth Pococke, *Knotted whitework coverlet* (detail), 1749. Couched knotted cotton threads of differing dimensions add varying textures to the flowers and foliage in a design that is probably French in origin. Regarded as a pastime appropriate for gentlewomen, knotted whitework was at this time associated with Mrs Delany (1700–1788), who was a friend of the maker.

122. By or for Elizabeth Smith, *English stencilled and painted cotton velvet panel* (detail), *c.* 1825–50. Theorem painting, or painting on velvet, was fashionable in Britain for much of the 19th century, as was an interest in botany and horticulture.

123. Turkish manufacturer, Bursa, *Silk stole* (detail), 2011. This textile is woven in silk with alternating bands of opaque twill and sheer slub-embedded organza, and the floral pattern is printed over all. This is one of many silks imported into England by The Silk Route, established by Hilary Williams in 1989.

124–127. Bianchini-Férier, *Paper impressions of block-printed designs*, 1974–80. Founded in Lyon in 1888, Bianchini-Férier began producing dress silks for Givenchy, Balenciaga, Cardin, Chanel, Dior, Féraud, Laroche, Nina Ricci, Yves Saint Laurent and Scherrer in the early 1960s. Their vast post-war archive was recently acquired by the Design Library, based in New York and London.

124
125
126
127

128
129
130

128. British manufacturer, *Schiffli embroidery (reversed)*, *c.* 1885. This detail of the reverse of a Schiffli-embroidered dress fabric shows the characteristic linking shuttle threads and the lower proportion of thread on the back, as well as a slightly 'untidy' appearance.

129. Ottoman embroiderer, *Panel* (detail), 1600s. In Bokhara couching or Bokhara stitch, a multi-stranded silk thread is self-couched with many tiny crossing stitches, which may be aligned from row to row to produce patterns.

130. Rhodian embroiderer, *Pillowcase* (detail), 1820–25. This linen pillowcase is embroidered with thick strands of silk dyed in the Dodecanese islands, giving the leaf motifs their distinctively warm tones.

131. Indian embroiderer, *Coat* (detail), 2003. Black wool is embroidered all over with multicoloured silk chain stitch in a floral style known as 'Japanese Garden'.

131

132
133
134
135
136
137
138
139

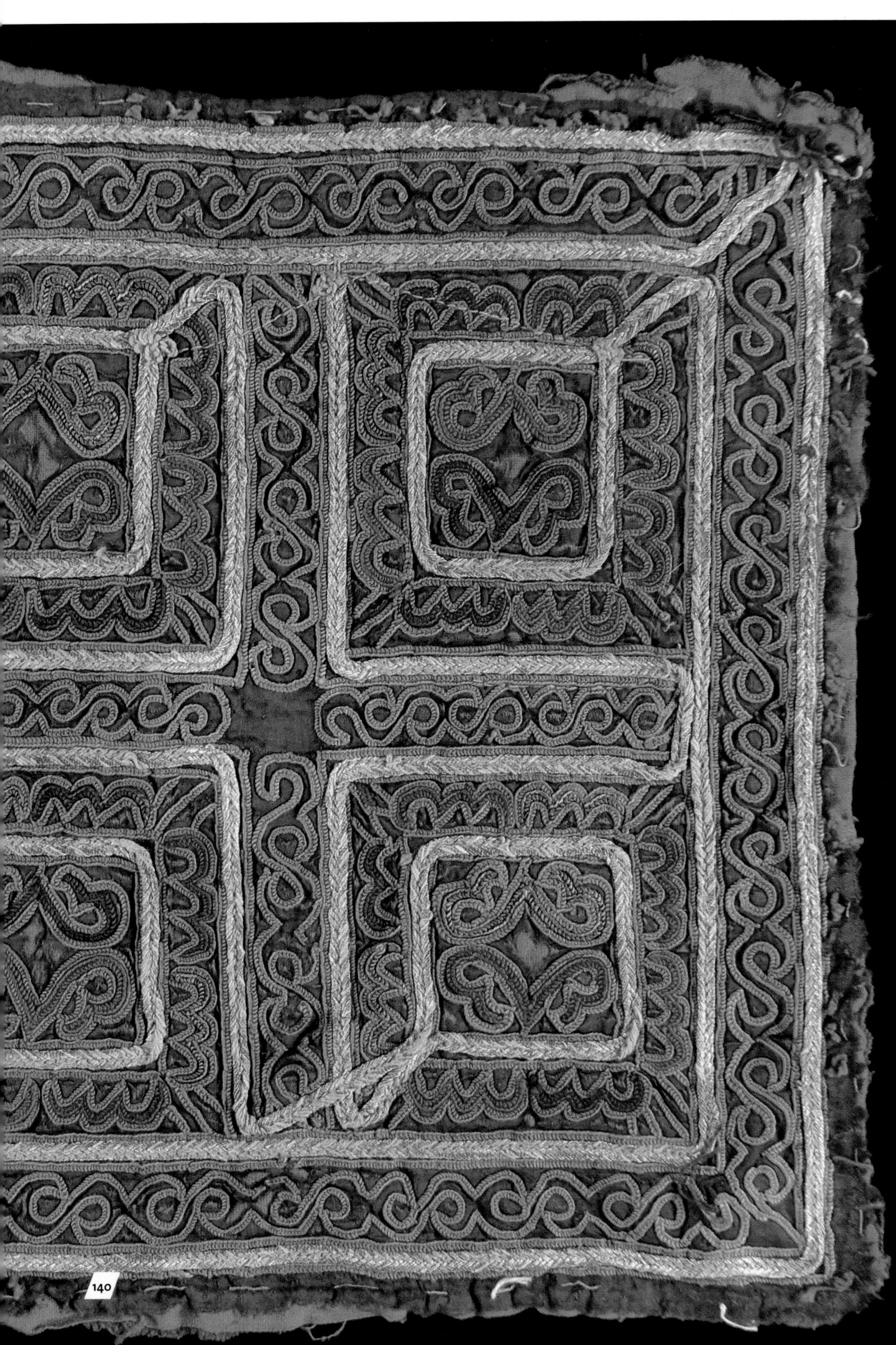

132–140. Afghan embroiderers, *Dress fronts and other panels*, before 1977. Purchased in Kabul, these pieces show variations on related motifs and stitches. One panel (140) is composed of layered silk and cotton fabric worked with ladder (square chain) stitch, mirrorwork embroidery using cretan stitch, and silver metallic-wrapped thread braid, the latter anchored with machine stitching.

141. Elizabeth Hinkes, *French Garden* (detail), 2008. Celebrating the box of scraps that can become a piece of work, the artist uses pieces of felt and threads 'usually too short to bother with'. These are couched, appliquéd and sewn using free stitch and more formal stitches.

142. Michael Brennand-Wood, *Pretty Deadly* (detai), 2011. This square panel is densely collaged with machine-embroidered blooms, badges, toy soldiers, fabric, resin and glass.

143 and 144. Lesley Richmond, *Distant Forest*, 2011, and *Winter Forest* (detail), 2009. Both of these works are devoré on cotton/silk fabric with a heat-reactive base. The earlier work, *Winter Forest* (144), is finished with acrylic paint, and *Distant Forest* (143) is finished with a rust patina. Richmond chooses her approach to 'simulate the growth forms of organic substances by changing the structure of the fabric rather than imposing a design on the surface of the cloth'.

143

145

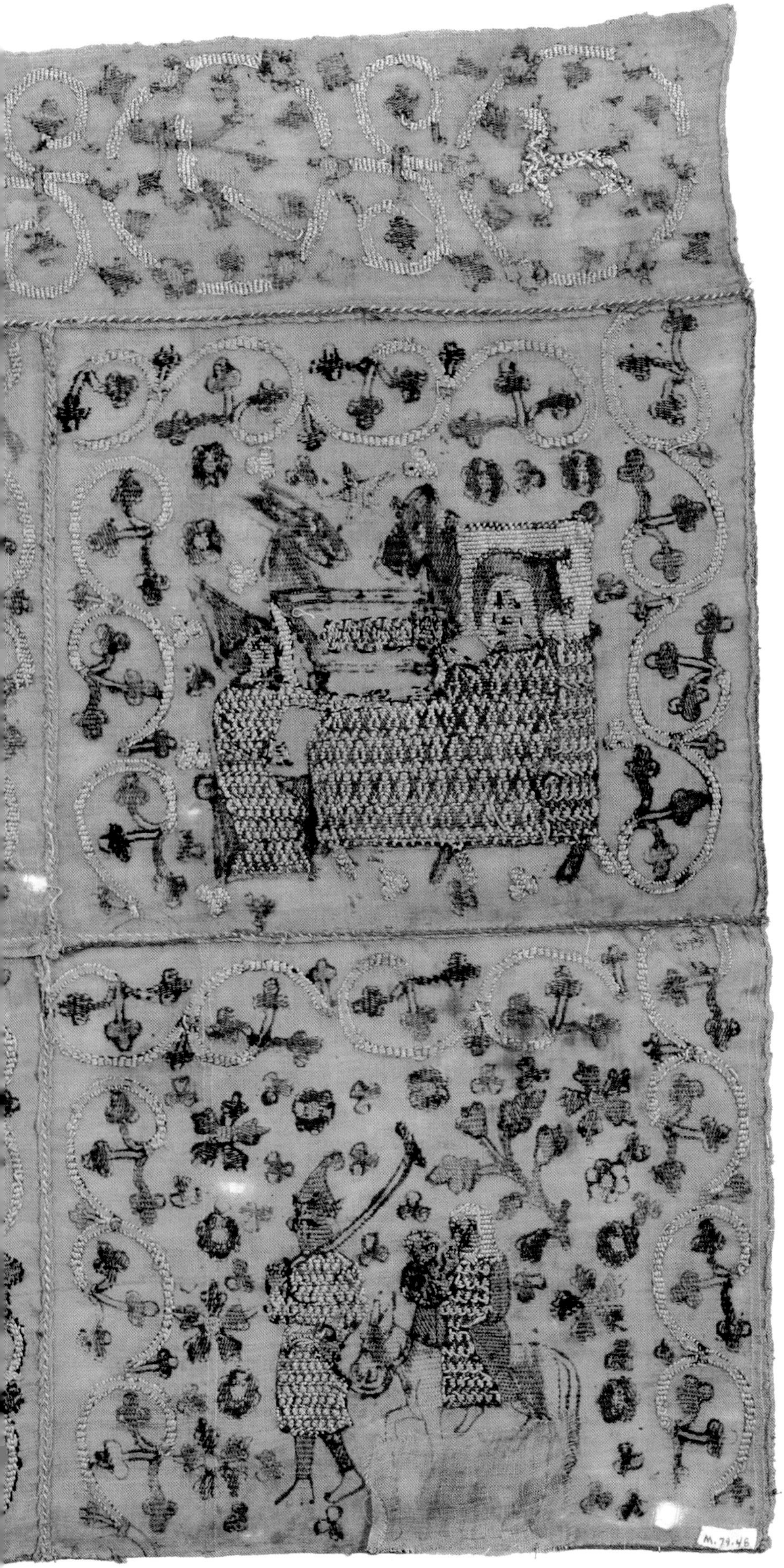

145. German embroiderer, *Altar frontal*, *c.* 1380. Worked on local linen cloth in Lower Saxony, the Nativity and other scenes from the life of Christ are embroidered in silk and undyed linen. In the scene on the lower right, the drawing intended to guide the embroidery can be clearly seen. This rare frontal is 108 cm (42½ in.) wide.

146. Nigel Cheney, *Commonwealth (For Linda)*, 2011. From a series of six panels 1.5 m (5 ft) square, this example shows the complex surface of a digital image before it was printed on cloth. It was created with Adobe Photoshop-altered scans of decommissioned bank notes and original ink drawings. A detail of the completed work can be seen on p. 274.

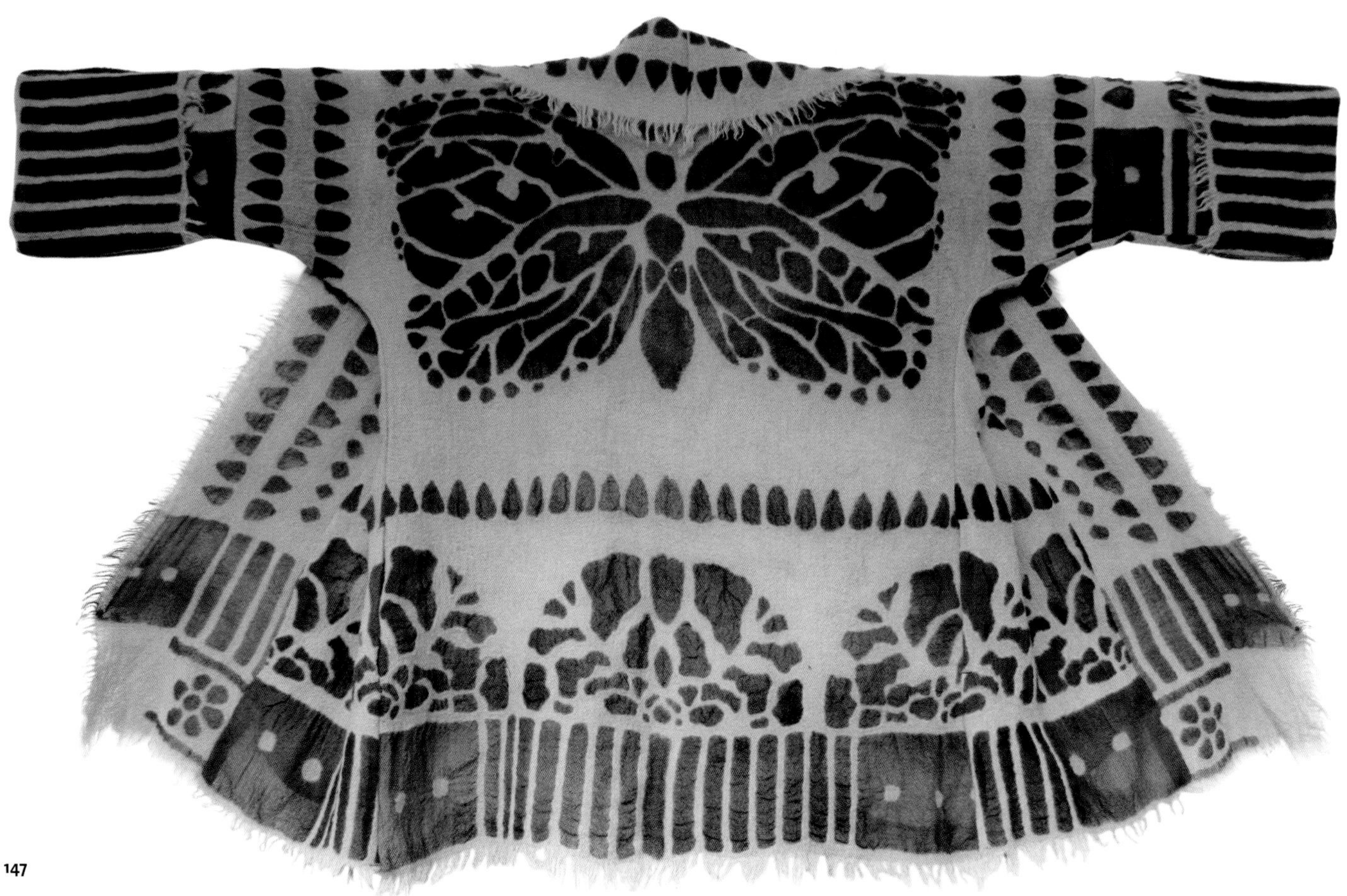

147

147. Jean Cacicedo, *Tattoo Transformations*, 2011. Cacicedo made this woman's jacket out of fulled woven wool, which she resist-paste printed and dyed.

148. Timorous Beasties, *Brick Moth*, 2011. Founded in Glasgow in 1990 by Alistair McAuley and Paul Simmons, Timorous Beasties uses a range of techniques, mixing advanced and traditional methods to achieve both soft and hard imagery. Here the fabric was digitally printed and then embroidered.

149
150
152
153
155
156

149–157. Joyce Clissold, *Footprints swatches*, c. 1933–37. All from the same small sample book, these patterns were hand-printed with synthetic dyes on a variety of textured cottons that add additional surface interest. All of these swatches were lino-printed.

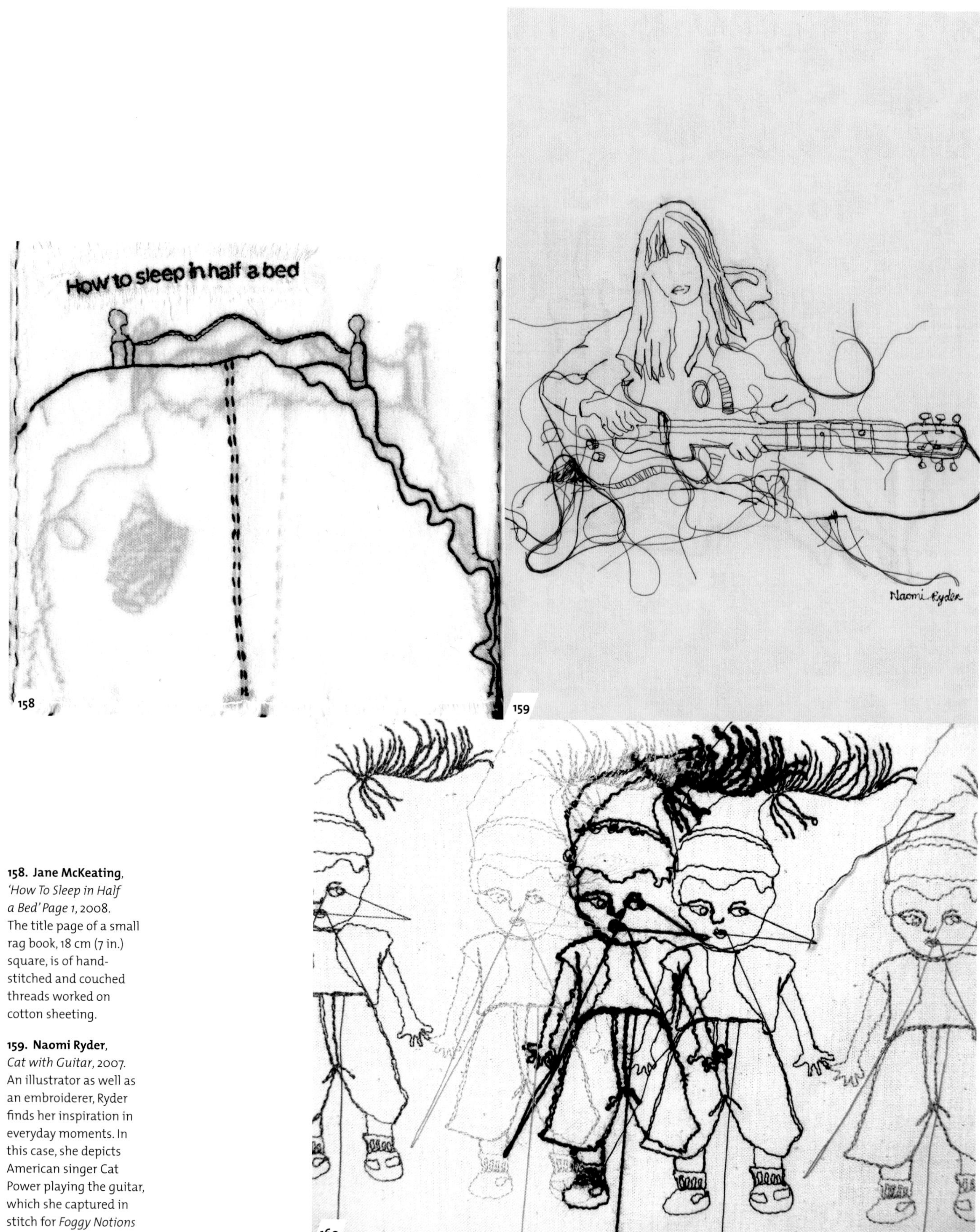

158

159

160

158. Jane McKeating, *'How To Sleep in Half a Bed' Page 1*, 2008. The title page of a small rag book, 18 cm (7 in.) square, is of hand-stitched and couched threads worked on cotton sheeting.

159. Naomi Ryder, *Cat with Guitar*, 2007. An illustrator as well as an embroiderer, Ryder finds her inspiration in everyday moments. In this case, she depicts American singer Cat Power playing the guitar, which she captured in stitch for *Foggy Notions* magazine.

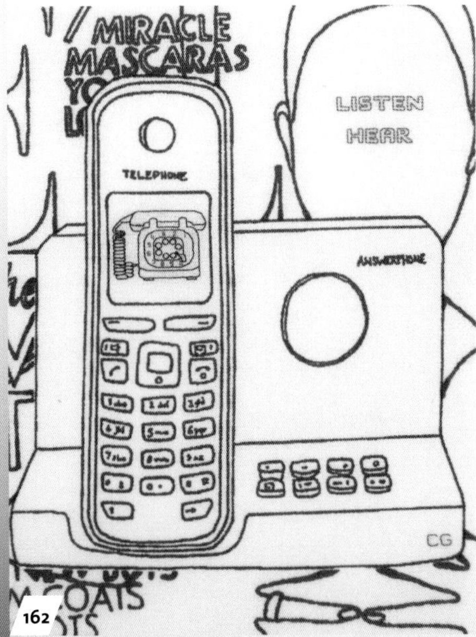

160. Melanie Miller, *Costume Nation* (detail), 2006. Featuring various threads on calico, stitched using the multi-needle Schiffli machine, this piece is part of a series that explores how a mass-production embroidery machine can be used as a drawing tool. It also raises questions about the globalization of clothing production.

161. Naseem Darbey, *Find My Handsome Short Lace Camisole*, 2010. This machine-stitched drawing on soluble Romeo Aquatics film was part of an installation at Cliffe Castle Museum in West Yorkshire, where the artist had a one-year residency.

162. Caren Garfen, *It Rang a Bell* (detail), 2010. Silk threads are hand-stitched onto a silkscreen-printed cotton depicting a life-sized telephone.

163. Astrid Polman, *Voortbordurend (Embroidering onwards)*, 2008. A pencil drawing enhanced with red embroidery shows the artist's sensitivity to mark-making, as well as the power of thread to animate imagery.

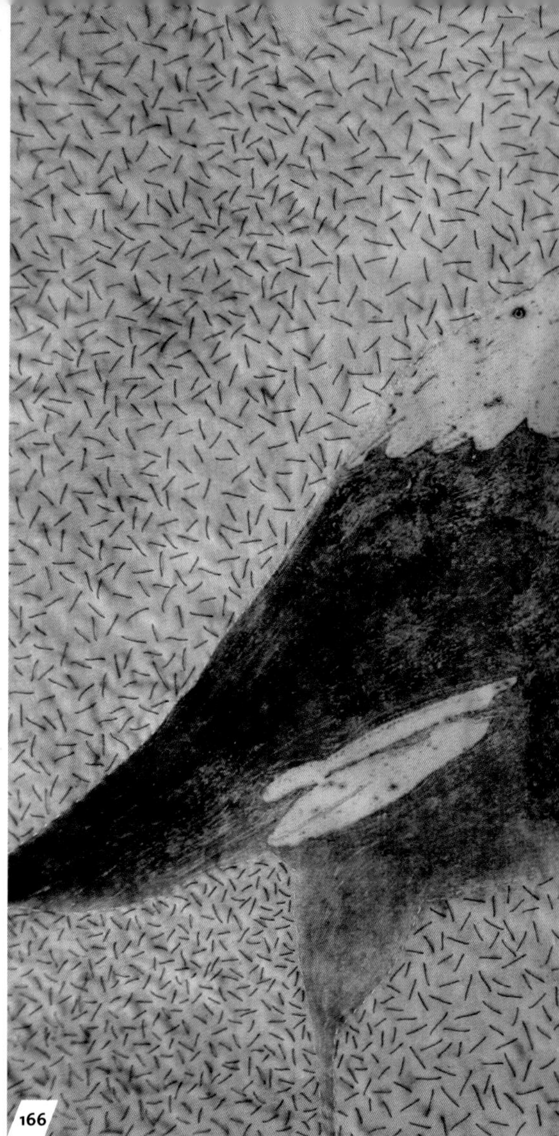

164. Japanese dyer, *Festival banner* (detail), before 1987. Thought to depict a samuri legend, the imagery has been created using the *tsutsugaki* technique (freehand rice-paste resist) on finely woven undyed cotton cloth.

165. Andrea Ellis, *Miss Taken*, 2009. In this work, a panel of silk/viscose treated with acid and reactive dyes, discharge and devoré is superimposed over a painted photograph. Digital images held no interest for Ellis until she discovered that she could 'destroy the "perfect" top layer to reveal other images below'.

166. Hilary Peterson, *Magpie Garden* (detail), 2009. Silk treated with plant dyes, collagraph prints and stitching records the artist's exploration of the coastal area where she lives. As Peterson says, the 'plant dyes secure the fabric in time and place, as the plant gives up a different shade of colour depending on the season, weather conditions and soil type'.

167. Andrea Ellis, *Edo Girl*, 2008. Fascinated by the idea of traces and imprints, Ellis has created this ethereal image by using the devoré technique, which eats away some areas of a polyester/linen/viscose cloth, and layering the result over a photograph and cloth printed with reactive dyes.

167
168

170. Jessica Watson, *Toy Man*, 2007. This silk and cotton embroidery on hemp is from the artist's 'Sketches from Rio' series. Based on Rio's charismatic beach hawkers, these works question the value of an image based solely on the complexity of its technique. Watson asks: 'Is there more to the work, just as when we meet a person, are they their job or is there more to them?'

171. Tilleke Schwarz, *Free Recovery*, 2010. Embroidered mainly in cross stitch and couching in silk, cotton and rayon threads on linen, this work records the Dutch artist's visit to the UK. It includes, at top right, the message: 'Free recovery, await rescue'. Of such phrases, she says: 'I like them a lot as they are so optimistic and full of trust'.

168. Joan Beadle, *Artist's Book: Cut One On Fold* (detail), 2009. This book, created as an edition of five, comments on unintentional yet valued mistakes in sewing. It closes with a complex fold, and employs layered and cross-purposed, rephotographed digital images. The book also features methods used in sewing: pressing, creasing, ironing and stitching.

169. Sue Stone, *Loaves and Fishes*, 2010. An array of textiles and baked goods are portrayed in this portrait of Stone's grandparents. The title refers to their Methodist beliefs and to her grandfather's job as a baker, as well as to the fact that their home city of Grimsby in Lincolnshire was then the world's busiest fishing port. The partly obscured 'closed' sign signals the end of this way of life.

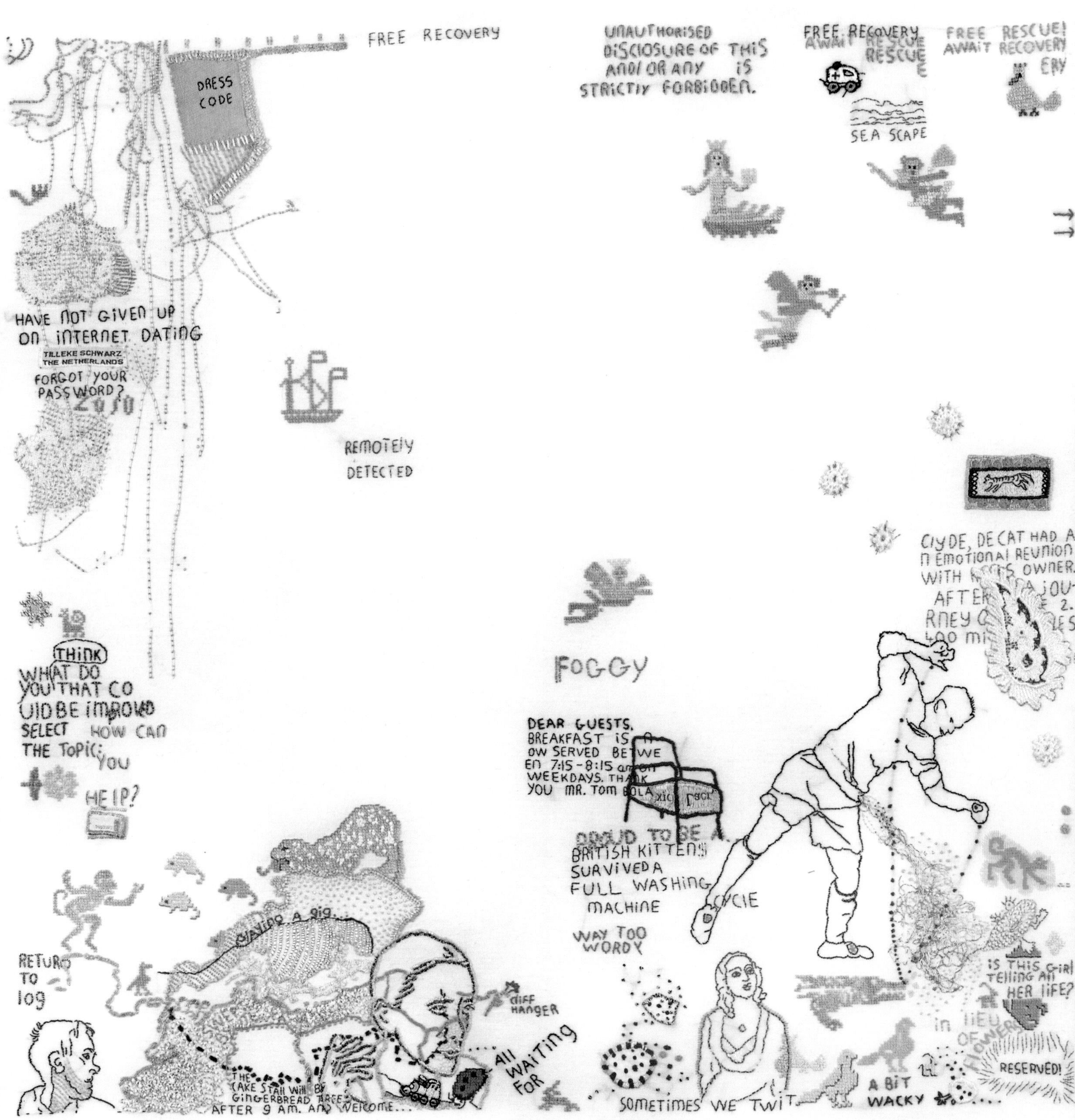
FREE RECOVERY
DRESS CODE
UNAUTHORISED DISCLOSURE OF THIS AND/ OR ANY IS STRICTLY FORBIDDEN.
FREE RECOVERY
FREE RESCUE!
AWAIT RECOVERY
SEA SCAPE
HAVE NOT GIVEN UP ON INTERNET DATING
TILLEKE SCHWARZ
THE NETHERLANDS
FORGOT YOUR PASSWORD?
REMOTELY DETECTED
THINK
WHAT DO YOU THAT CO ULD BE IMPROVED
SELECT THE TOPIC:
HOW CAN YOU HELP?
FOGGY
DEAR GUESTS. BREAKFAST IS N OW SERVED BETWE EN 7:15 - 8:15 am ON WEEKDAYS. THANK YOU MR. TOM BOLA
BRITISH KITTENS SURVIVED A FULL WASHING MACHINE
WAY TOO WORDY
RETURN TO LOG
CLIFF HANGER
ALL WAITING FOR
AFTER 9 AM. AND WELCOME...
SOMETIMES WE TWIT
A BIT WACKY
IS THIS GIRL TELLING ALL HER LIFE?
RESERVED!

171

172. Sue Stone, *David as Dalí* (detail), 2010. This work is from the artist's 'Weekend in Barcelona' series of hand- and machine-stitched panels portraying herself and her husband. The surreal compositions include local cod and haddock, and have background images of the Gaudí mosaics and tiles seen in the Park Güell in Barcelona, as well as imagery from Grimsby, their English home.

173. Anton Veenstra, *Blond Boy with Bike*, 2005. This large panel, 150 cm (59 in.) high, is an experiment by an experienced tapestry weaver, using vintage buttons stitched with upholsterer's thread onto stretched canvas. The image is based on a photograph taken by the artist's parents when they had finally been released from a migrant camp at Cowra, Australia, where Veenstra was born. As the artist says, 'the bicycle represents the potential freedom and mobility of citizen status after the restriction of internment'.

174. Marguerite Zorach, *Made for Selda and Ralph Jonas*, 1926–27. This portrait of the Jonas family is the work of one of America's leading Modernist embroiderers. At 122 cm (48 in.) square, it took the artist more than two years to complete, working in wool yarns on a linen ground. Trained and active as a painter, Zorach produced fewer than twenty embroideries, having adopted stitch as a medium during her child-rearing years.

175. Raymond Duncan, *Untitled dress panel* (detail), *c.* 1920s. In 1911, at the age of 37, the American-born Duncan and his Greek wife, Penelope, founded the Akademia in Paris, which offered free courses in their areas of specialization: dance, arts, and crafts. (The pair later opened a similar school in London.) They supported themselves through two shops in Paris, selling items including hand-painted and -dyed textiles, which were worn as scarves, tunics and capes.

176. Susie Vickery, *Rebti Mandal, Artist* (detail), 2005. Vickery's experience of rural and refugee development projects for women, particularly in the area of handicrafts and costume in Nepal, Tibet and India, is the inspiration for her embroidered textile pieces, which draw on issues of iconography, identity, gender and Asian art. Rebti Mandal is an artist in a women's handicraft project in Janakpur in the south of Nepal.

177. Susie Vickery, *Mahendra Shah: Rickshaw Wallah* (detail), 2005. Hand embroidery and appliqué using old saris. Mehendra Shah is a rickshaw driver in Janakpur, Nepal.

176

177

178–181. Liberty has long been famous for its fine printed 'conversationals', of which four are shown overleaf: Pru Roskrow's *Debden* (178), 1990; Jack Prince's *Camile* (179) and *Lady Penelope* (180), both 1992; and *Maria's Fan* (181), 2005, by Circle Line, a London design studio owned by Jeremy Somers.

182. Langfield Fashions, *Cotton dress* (detail), *c.* 1958. This roller-printed fabric depicts the cut of the dress for which it was used.

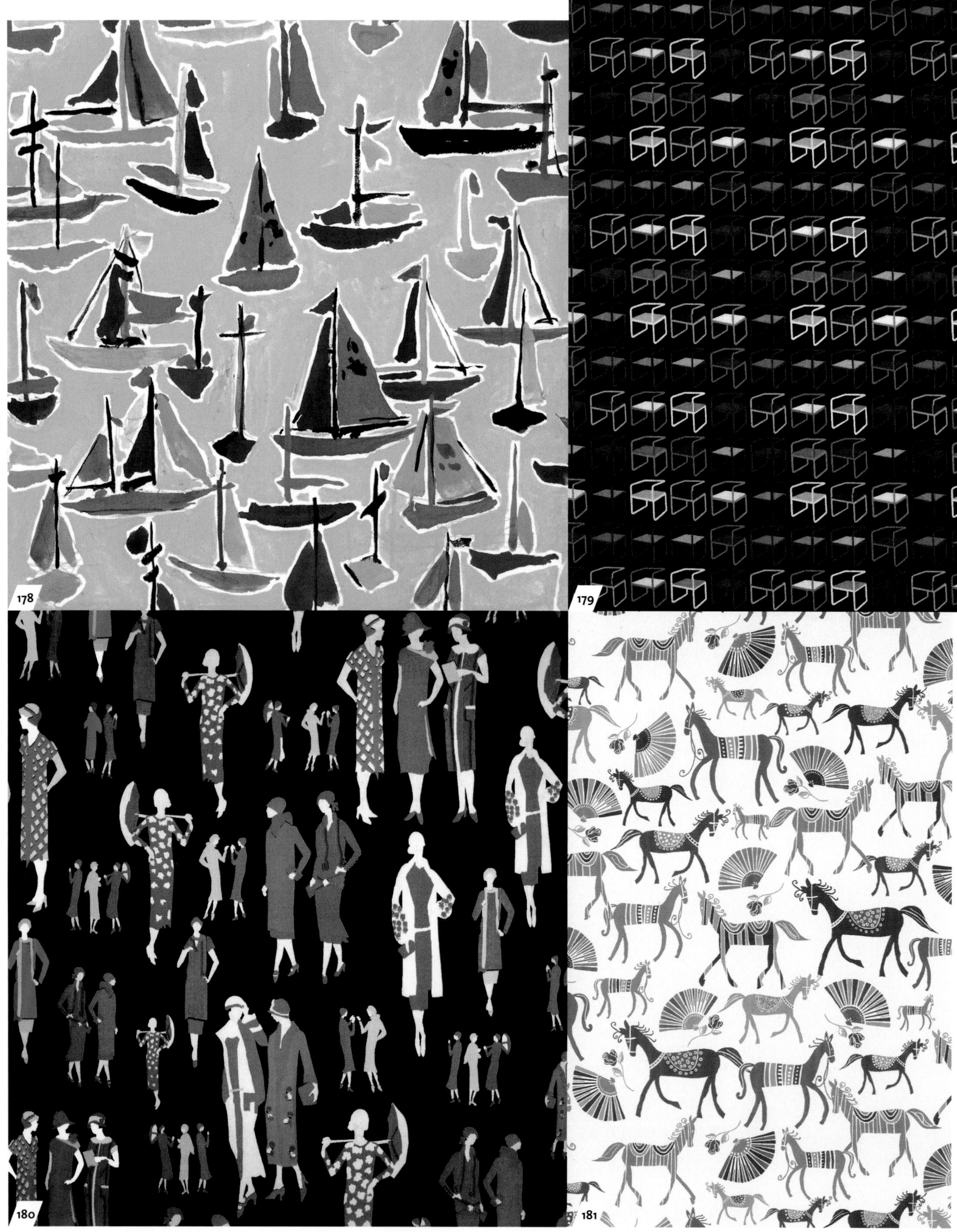

178

179

180

181

183. Japanese maker, *Girl's kimono* (detail), 20th century. This multicoloured printed silk *chirimen* (a 'wrinkled' crepe made by justapoxing threads with opposing twists) incorporates simulated *kanoko shibori* (tie-dyed) dots.

184. Raymond Honeyman, *Teapots* (two colourways), 1990 and 2011. Selected and recoloured by Kaffe Fassett for his Craft Fabric Collection, the design by Honeyman came from the archive belonging to Liberty Ltd.

185. E. A. Seguy, *Butterflies* (detail), 1926–28. This velveteen, printed with densely placed butterflies, was designed by Seguy, a prolific French designer who also produced folios of pochoir-printed design ideas, including *Papillons* in about 1925. The cloth may have been patterned with the pochoir method, in which black outline prints were hand-coloured with the help of a thin zinc or copper cut-out stencil guide.

186. Jean Patou, *Scarf* (detail), 1964–66. A hand-screen printed silk twill, this scarf depicts three flower pots with circular blooms composed of letters, with the darker letters spelling out the designer's name and 'Paris', seen here. This design shows a knowledge of the *Letters* of Pliny the Younger (AD 62–110), in which the writer describes the garden of his villa in Tuscany, where topiary took the shape of names.

187. British amateur embroiderer, *Crewel-embroidered workbag*, 1675. While the real and mythological creatures featured here would have been drawn from bestiaries and needlework pattern books, the range of infill and shading stitches were the choice of the maker, whose intials are worked on the reverse.

188. Domita Duncan, *English sampler*, signed and dated 23 June 1738. Worked largely in tent stitch, this sampler is unusual in its use of black wool in the background of the letters and numbers, which were typically set against the natural tone of the linen fabric on which they were stitched.

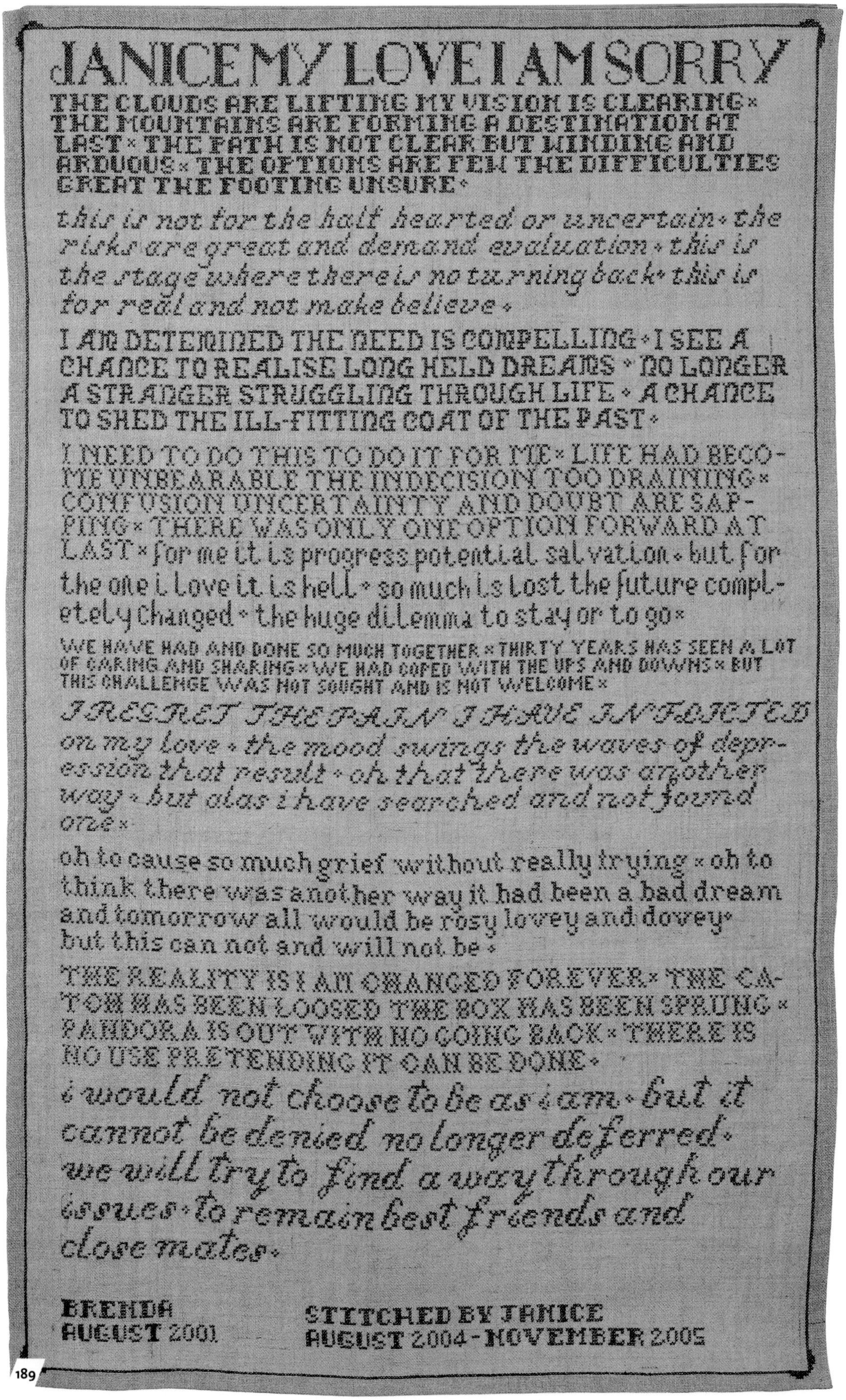

JANICE MY LOVE I AM SORRY
THE CLOUDS ARE LIFTING MY VISION IS CLEARING × THE MOUNTAINS ARE FORMING A DESTINATION AT LAST × THE PATH IS NOT CLEAR BUT WINDING AND ARDUOUS × THE OPTIONS ARE FEW THE DIFFICULTIES GREAT THE FOOTING UNSURE ×
this is not for the half hearted or uncertain • the risks are great and demand evaluation • this is the stage where there is no turning back • this is for real and not make believe •
I AM DETEMINED THE NEED IS COMPELLING • I SEE A CHANCE TO REALISE LONG HELD DREAMS • NO LONGER A STRANGER STRUGGLING THROUGH LIFE • A CHANCE TO SHED THE ILL-FITTING COAT OF THE PAST •
I NEED TO DO THIS TO DO IT FOR ME × LIFE HAD BECO-ME UNBEARABLE THE INDECISION TOO DRAINING × CONFUSION UNCERTAINTY AND DOUBT ARE SAP-PING × THERE WAS ONLY ONE OPTION FORWARD AT LAST × for me it is progress potential salvation • but for the one i love it is hell • so much is lost the future compl-etely changed • the huge dilemma to stay or to go ×
WE HAVE HAD AND DONE SO MUCH TOGETHER × THIRTY YEARS HAS SEEN A LOT OF CARING AND SHARING × WE HAD COPED WITH THE UPS AND DOWNS × BUT THIS CHALLENGE WAS NOT SOUGHT AND IS NOT WELCOME ×
I REGRET THE PAIN I HAVE INFLICTED on my love • the mood swings the waves of depr-ession that result • oh that there was another way • but alas i have searched and not found one ×
oh to cause so much grief without really trying × oh to think there was another way it had been a bad dream and tomorrow all would be rosy lovey and dovey • but this can not and will not be •
THE REALITY IS I AM CHANGED FOREVER × THE CA-TON HAS BEEN LOOSED THE BOX HAS BEEN SPRUNG × PANDORA IS OUT WITH NO GOING BACK × THERE IS NO USE PRETENDING IT CAN BE DONE •
i would not choose to be as i am • but it cannot be denied no longer deferred • we will try to find a way through our issues • to remain best friends and close mates •
BRENDA
AUGUST 2001
STITCHED BY JANICE
AUGUST 2004 - NOVEMBER 2005

189

189. Janice Appleton, *Janice My Love I Am Sorry*, 2005. This cross-stitched cotton on a hessian ground recounts the contents of a letter written to the artist by her husband as he recognized his need to be a woman. This large work (92 × 121 cm, 36 × 48 in.) plays with the traditional scale of samplers.

190. Linda Behar, *Chinese Grandmother*, 1995. This small work, 24.8 cm (9¾ in.) high, uses fabric paint with cotton and polycotton thread embroidery to replicate a photograph of the artist's grandmother and to preserve an extract from the story of her grandmother's marriage and life in Hawaii, dictated to an uncle who translated it into English.

got married at the age of eighteen
n the 20th day of the ninth moon
f 辛丑 (1901). People all talked that
he man was from the Land of the
old Mountain (America) and had
a brand-new house.
Though I found
my sisters-in-
law to be
friendly and
affectionate,
my husband's
disposition
was without
one bit of a
loving heart.

190

191

192

191. Susan Taber Avila, *Garden Wall* (detail), 2009. This installation of hand-dyed, printed and laser-cut fabric remnants, machine-stitched and assembled in three layers, carries words and phrases over its surface.

192. Alice Kettle, *Looking Forwards to the Past* (detail), 2007. A close look at a small portion of Kettle's narrative panel reveals the complex surfaces developed by the artist, who is known for her large-scale hangings. It is based on free machine stitching worked from the back of the cloth – a method that preserves the spontaneity of her original sketches.

193

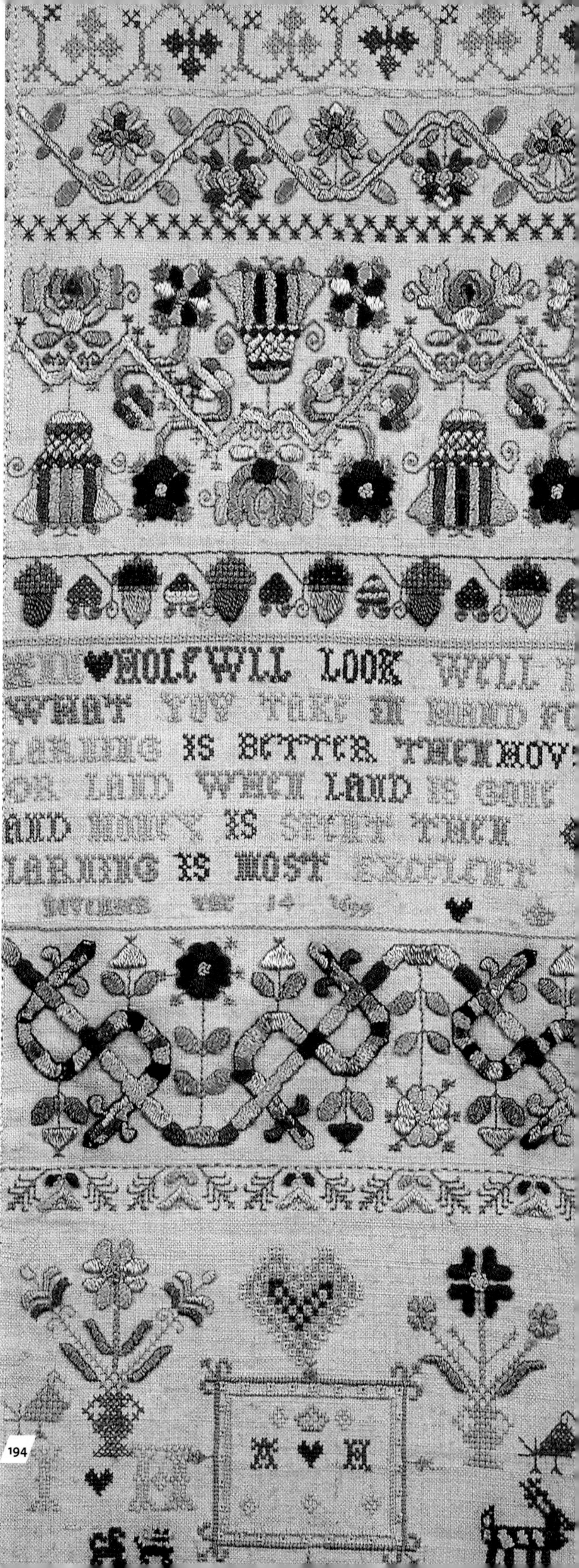

193. Mexican embroiderer, *Sampler*, *c.* 1785. Silk and metal thread embroidery of individual animals and heraldic and religious motifs occupy one-third of this linen sampler, with the remainder worked in multicoloured drawnwork and self-coloured needlelace.

194. Ann Holewil, *Judith Hayle sampler*, 1699. There are eleven known English samplers worked under the guidance of Judith Hayle between 1691 and 1710. This example of highly skilled schoolgirl needlework is typical of the period, a time when samplers ceased to be unorganized records of stitches and became well-composed demonstrations of skill.

195. Hannah Hicks, *Ackworth School sampler*, 1790. Ackworth School was a Quaker institution in Yorkshire, founded in 1779. Worked in polychrome silk threads and using cross stitch throughout, the roundels, or medallions, are similar to motifs on German and Northern European examples, while the 'frame' of half-medallions is characteristic of this school. Both this and no. 194 are about 36 cm (14 in.) high.

194

Hannah Hicks 1790
A TOKEN OF LOVE

1

V.

ADDED DIMENSIONS

2

V.

ADDED DIMENSIONS

Once cloth has been woven, it may be printed or stitched, but it may also be cut up and manipulated in myriad ways, or joined to companion lengths to create a larger whole. This versatility is the beauty of textiles, but also complicates their categorization. The distinct identity that quilts have attained derives partly from their definition as having at least three layers stitched together. That said, quilts might be quilted only (a 'whole cloth'), composed of shaped and joined pieces (patchwork) or stitched with additional cut-out pieces of cloth (appliqué), or might include a combination of all three. Each of these quilting techniques is an ancient one. Tradition has it that they developed as a means of repair or reinforcement, or to make items out of many small pieces of cloth, either recycled or new. An example of the latter can be found in places where narrow looms are typical, such as Africa, where cloth is cut as little as possible, if at all; the resulting lengths are sewn together, side by side, to create 'strip cloths'. Slightly less narrow are traditional Japanese cloths, which are also cut as little as possible and therefore dictate the essentially untailored form of the kimono. Fabrics used as they are found or formed on the loom also invite pleating and gathering, which can produce varying results, from the traditional pleated indigo resist-dyed skirts of northern Laos and China's Guizhou Province to the Scottish kilt and cloth tubes densely amassed at the waist, forming full skirts that are found worldwide.

In the continuum between craft, couture and art, ethnographic and historic examples have provided both inspiration for many recent fashion statements and a springboard for artists whose medium is textiles. This can be readily seen in the relationship between art quilts and Buddhist monks' robes, *kasaya*. Originally assembled from old patches of cloth and worn as a sign of humility, *kasaya* began to be constructed of new materials of the highest quality (given as gifts from supplicants), just as Western patchwork, initially a form of necessary recycling, now 'petitions' for the artistry of finely judged assemblages. Such aesthetic and contextual similarities aside, the dialogue between past and present frequently pivots around the creative challenges presented by a handful of characteristics. The capacity of textiles to act as a support for non-fibrous

1. **British amateur embroiderer**, *Chintz appliqué border*, 1842. This panel would originally have formed part of a large coverlet. The array of English printed dress cottons dates from the 1820s and 1830s, and feature appliqués of figures, animals, hearts, diamonds, spades and clubs.

2. **Japanese artisans**, *Kesa* (detail of a corner), 19th century. This pieced Buddhist monk's stole is composed of borders and inner strips of a silk and gold metallic brocaded cloth with rectangles of a silk brocaded matelassé (woven to suggest quilting) at the four inner corners.

adornment and to carry imagery has already been considered; its ability to denote culture, place or point of view has arisen as well (and these topics will be considered more fully in Chapter VI). This chapter looks at all of these attributes anew, against a background of cloth's greatly varied plasticity and weight, which is known as 'handle', as well as its tendency to invite the use of multiple techniques and complex manipulations. The impact of much greater accessibility to ethnographic and historical material, which has been a defining characteristic of textile arts in the past four decades or so, will also be considered.

Letting the Cloth Speak

The manipulation of cloth by seaming strips together is technically straightforward, but it results in a remarkable array of visually arresting cloths, whether as a result of supplementary-weft patterns or simply the subtle variations of stripes, checks and the muted fluctuations within indigo-dyed yarns. Strip cloths have a long and continuous history in many cultures in West Africa, where those constructed with a balanced or warp-faced plain weave were employed as a currency – a use documented by the 11th century that lasted into the 20th.[1] Admired and collected around the world today, such cloths, known as *kente* and made by both the Asante people of Ghana and the Ewe people of Ghana and Togo, are traditionally worn toga-like by men, and as an upper and lower wrapper by women **[35–38]**. From the Indian subcontinent to Asian Pacific regions, cloth has long been worn in the same way. Leaving aside saris, sarongs and other similar garments (which are of a single length of wide-loomed cloth), the seamed cloth appears throughout this vast area too: in Bhutan, for example, where women wear a *kira* composed of three silk-brocaded cotton panels, each about 46 cm (18 in.) wide and thus some six times wider than *kente* strips **[3]**. On the other side of the world, in the Americas, the whole-cloth or simply seamed garment also characterizes native cultures. The work of anthropologists, ethnographers and, since the 1980s, scholars of material culture has ensured that all of these textiles, whether strip cloths or whole-cloths, are now widely understood as significant within indigenous ritual, social and economic domains.

What makes such traditional cloths of wider interest is the fact that the high regard in which they are held by their makers is not lost on outsiders – even when they lack an in-depth understanding of their meaning. These cloths 'speak' on many levels: of fine craftsmanship to the initiated; of complex and ancient patterning to those attuned to symbolism; and of finely balanced compositions of colour and texture to the artistically minded. On a more prosaic level, cloth panels display well. For over a century these factors have ensured a place for ethnographic textiles in Western museums, and in good numbers.[2] Many came through the hands of archaeologists, ethnographers and others with a professional interest, and for private collectors they were rare and often expensive things. In the 1970s, however, this began to change, as global travel became easier and political dynamics shifted. One result was the 'discovery' of textiles by the Miao – a linguistically related ethnic minority in southern China, some of whom had migrated to South-East Asia and, after the communist takeover of Laos in 1975, to Australia, France, the United States and elsewhere **[4–5]**.

3

3. Kurtö woman weaver, Bhutan, *Kira*, *c.* 1900. This cotton strip-weave *kira* (a woman's overwrap garment) was woven on a backstrap loom with areas of *thrima* and *sapma* (brocading resembling chain stitch and satin stitch embroidery). Its design has intellectual and religious meanings in Bhutan, where artistic pursuits and the contemplation of colour are forms of spiritual exercise.

4. **H'Mong woman,** *Jacket*, late 20th century. Of black rayon velvet, this modern Blue H'Mong jacket has front edges of bright polychrome acrylic cross-stitch embroidery on white loose-weave cotton, edged with rayon-ribbon stripes and fine triangular appliqués of rayon ribbon. These are secured with machine stitching; the appliquéd and embroidered sunburst motifs are hand-stitched. Purchased in Anusarn Market in Chiang Mai, Thailand, in 1997.

5. **H'Mong woman,** *Skirt* (detail), 1980. Traditional skirt consisting of three horizontal panels including an upper hip panel of white cotton that is unseen. The remaining skirt is indigo resist-dyed, pleated and overstitched.

John Gillow, a collector, dealer and author, recounts being among the first to enter the Miao region after 1975, describing himself as 'a young English guy on my third overseas trip, buying off the backs of Miao women', struck by the beauty of their simply constructed jackets and densely pleated skirts (they are composed of three rectangular cloths: a flat piece folded over at the upper hip; the attached knife-pleated panel; and a lower band of batik, cross stitch, appliqué or other embellishments). The appetite for these textiles was clear on Gillow's return trip six months later, when highly literate women had taken over responsibility for their sale, and even more noticeable another year on, when textiles were coming into central markets from hundreds of kilometres away. Gillow says that he went trekking for textiles because 'they're easily portable and highly valuable; I could be on an Indian train with a couple of duffle bags worth £10,000.' He recalls that, within a decade, he and other trailblazers had popularized ethnic textiles to such an extent that specialized textile tours proliferated: 'people go, buy, bring their finds home and love them'. By the mid-1990s this was an industry of such importance that it was scrutinized by scholars, who could study 'the political economy created by a public eager to buy and collect textiles'.[3]

Such was the money textiles were attracting that magazines such as *Fiberarts* (1973–2011) emerged, not only to highlight post-Contemporary developments, but also to chronicle textile-art collectors, detailing why they collect, how they got started, how they acquire objects, and how they display their collections. The same consumers also supported the rise of wearable art – the American term for experimental textiles in garment, scarf or hat form. Among those captivated by Miao kilted skirts was the textile artist Ellen Hauptli,

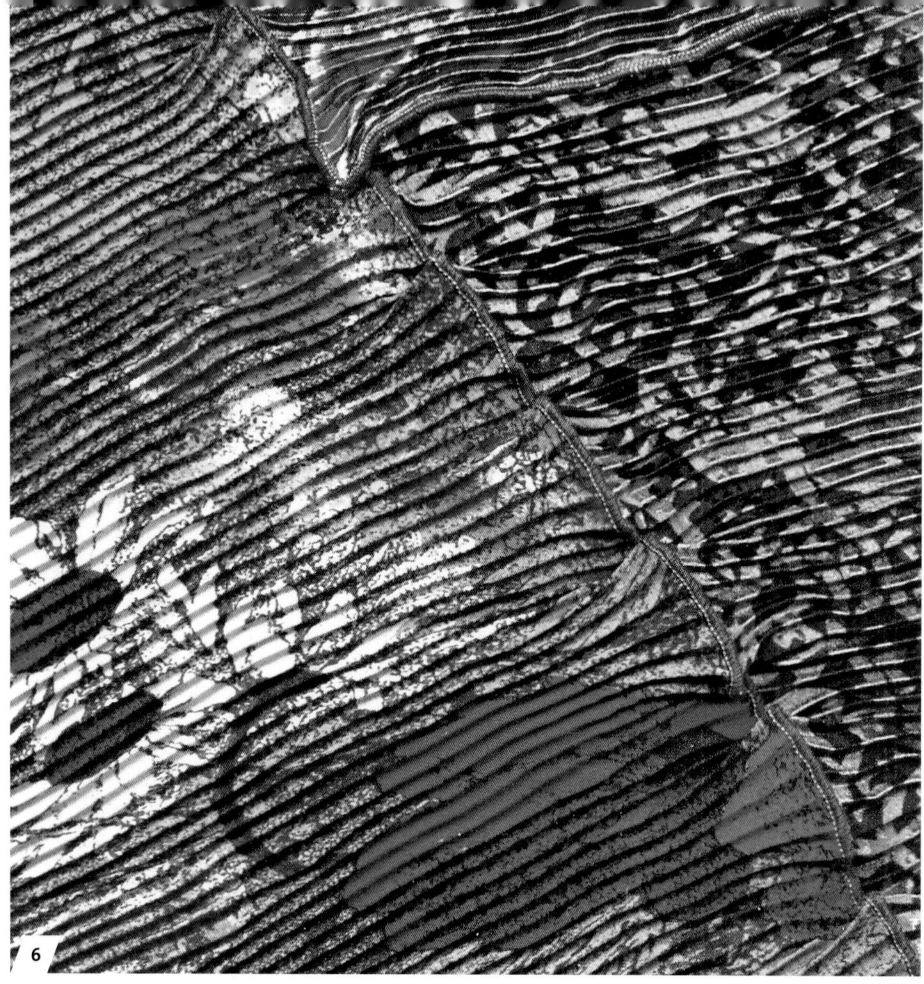

whose pioneering work in pleated clothing began in the 1970s [6, 25, 32]. Hauptli's concepts were unique in American wearable art at the time, as they embraced synthetic rather than natural fibres. Ultimately incorporating pleated and stitched polyester cloths in a mix of manufactured prints, overdyed by airbrushing, her garments sculpted the cloth around the body, a feature later associated with the Pleats Please collections by Issey Miyake [54]. Miyake, who presented his first examples in 1989 and launched the named range in 1993, also makes use of lightweight polyester jersey, but creates his signature look by cutting and sewing together pieces two-and-a-half to three times larger than the finished garment, and then using heat to permanently set the pleats. Miyake's is an industrial process, although the garments must be hand-fed into the press, and allows texture and form to be created at the same time. Vertical, horizontal and zig-zag pleating is used to create varying effects and architectural shapes. While many others continued to explore methods of pleating – including those produced on the loom – Hauptli meanwhile transferred her signature 'thread trails' (zig-zagged seams left dangling) to simply shaped garments constructed from the thick quilted *ralli*, long made in the Sindh province in Pakistan and western India [32]. In their original form, *ralli* consisted of recycled cloths secured with *kantha* (running stitch) to a base sheet of dark fabric or an old *ajrak* (a cloth 2.5 to 3 m long, stamped with ancient Indus Valley patterns) to create a bedcover. These began to circulate during the 1980s, and globally so after about 1995.

The increasing availability of ethnographical textiles and garments in Western markets suggested other directions for textile artists. Some, such as the decorative emphasis on seams (vital when the cloth is either very thick or

6. Ellen Hauptli, *Being In the Green Forest ensemble* (detail), 1996. Pleated and stitched polyester in a mix of manufactured prints, airbrush-overdyed, forms a skirt, top and jacket, and demonstrates the evolution of Hauptli's pioneering work in pleated clothing begun in the 1970s. It was inspired by her research on Chinese pleated skirts.

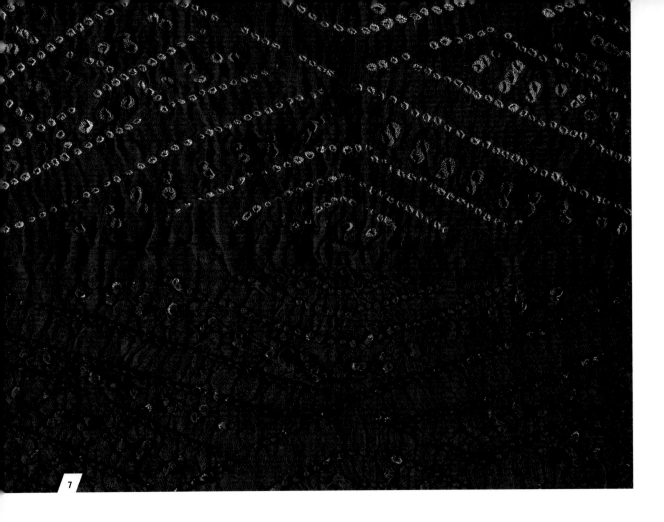

very thin) and the use of appliqué in other potential areas of wear, can be readily observed **[22]**. Others need to be studied carefully. Physical resists to dyes, by folding, pleating, wrapping or clamping, fall into the latter category. These complex methods of creating a pattern by manipulating a whole cloth have been used around the world for well over a 1,000 years, each known by local names and indicating a specific method. *Bandhani*, for example, is the Indian word for plucking and binding cloth into small points **[7]**. Such resist techniques gained a new following during the 1960s, when a handful of artists such as Marian Clayden taught themselves what English-speakers then called 'plangi', adopting the Malay–Indonesian term for gathering and binding cloth. Clayden, who relocated from Australia to California in 1967, built up an enviable reputation – and, later, a limited-edition fashion business – based around her skill as a dyer, as well as her acute understanding of economical yet creative use of cloth. Her *Shadow Kimono* of 1981 is a tour-de-force of sophisticated references to ethnographic textiles blended with the radical nuances of Western manufacturing, employing industrial cotton strapping that is branded, dyed, assembled and brush-discharged **[40]**. By this time shibori, the Japanese collective term for all physical resists, was beginning to gain ground, and its near universal use was settled with the first International Shibori Symposium, held in Japan in 1992. This event was organized by the World Shibori Network, founded by Yoshiko Iwamoto Wada, rightly described as 'this art form's most ardent and influential promoter'.[4] Shibori remains a specialist's technique. Among the first to take Wada's classes – taught with Donna Larsen at the influential Fiberworks Center for the Textile Arts in Berkeley, California, from 1975 until its closure in 1987 – was Ana Lisa Hedstrom

7. Indian dyer, *Plangi-dyed cloth* (detail), before 1988. This cotton gauze-like fabric was folded in half lengthwise and in thirds widthwise, tied and then dyed. Thread knots remain attached in the central area. With dimensions of 208 × 122 cm (6 ft 9 in. × 4 ft), it is too small for a sari and is probably an *odhani*, worn by women as a shawl or scarf.

[66, 67], who was winning prizes for her mastery of the process by the late 1980s. 'I think of fabric as conversation,' she says: 'It can be subtle, bold, witty, seductive. The shibori resist-dye techniques create intricate patterns which may be perused as a language or script. I hope my own dialogue with the process, color and piecing will ultimately speak to the viewer.'[5]

Patchwork and Quilting

The influence of personal collections has been mentioned by many of the contributors to this volume, including quilt-makers. Dianne Finnegan describes the influence of Australian Aboriginal art on her own work, with particular reference to a work she purchased from the artist Melba, of Maningrida, an indigenous community in the Northern Territory, Australia. A bark painting, it depicts a dilly bag made from string – significant because Melba's culture believes that children are carried across the sky in such bags to be sprinkled on families below **[8]**. Finnegan explains the stylization in Melba's work and its impact on her own: 'Space is divided up in Australian Aboriginal art … by the relationships of landscape elements and their formation by ancestral beings. Having learnt traditional quilting, in which most quilts consist of regular repeating blocks, this very different approach to dividing up the surface area of a work has made me rethink all aspects of my work. Concentric squares and circles as well as stripes have multiple meanings in Aboriginal art, they remind me of log-cabin and strip-piecing construction, and represent sitting-down places and pathways in my work as well as geomorphological processes. The significance of a quilt has also become more relevant: I now see the large surface as an opportunity to represent my story and my sense of place … and because I originally studied to be a geomorphologist, landforms and the forces acting to shape them are frequently expressed. *In Apartment, Apart from … A part of …* **[9]** the view is planar, the structure is loosely based on the house plan for our apartment … . Colours reflect the usage of the rooms, blues and greens for water used in kitchen and laundry, red for passion in bedroom and living room. Below the apartment, greens and browns of rocks and vegetation give way to the blues of Sydney Harbour. A piece of a library bag dyed and embroidered by my son Thomas when he was in infant school appropriately is located in the library, and favourite artists are inscribed on the spines of books in a strip-pieced row.'

On the subject of accommodation, one cannot overlook Henry Francis du Pont, an American who collected a vast array of textiles in order to furnish Winterthur, his Delaware estate, and Chestertown, his Long Island summer home. Winterthur became a museum of decorative arts in 1951, and Linda Eaton is the curator of textiles there. In *Quilts in a Material World: Selections from the Winterthur Collection*, she details du Pont's deep-seated interest in interior design during the first half of the 20th century, noting that 'he was not alone. Other wealthy collectors of folk art and Americana, including Electra Havemeyer Webb, Ima Hogg, Bert and Nina Little, Henry and Helen Flynt, Henry Ford, and John D. and Abby Aldrich Rockefeller, also began collections for the purpose of decorating.' Having furnished their own homes, these members of America's social elite went on to create 'collections that now form the basis of important museum

8. Melba, *Dilly Bag*, 2011. This piece, decorated with ochre pigments and a PVC fixative on stringybark (*Eucalyptus tetradonta*), was made by an artist of the Maningrida people of the Northern Territory, Australia. The *rrark* (an Aboriginal term for repetition) and striped and cross-hatched motifs are typical of Arnhem Land Aboriginal art. Owned by Dianne Finnegan.

9. Dianne Finnegan, *Apartment, Apart from … A part of …*, 2008. Hand-dyed and found cottons, machine-pieced and heavily free machine quilted. Each 'room' has furniture – and sometimes people – quilted in, to be discovered gradually upon close examination. The dining-room table has plates, knives, forks and even a vase of flowers.

10. American quilter, *Pieced quilt*, c. 1820. The arrangement of the one-patch blocks follows the shape of the bed, with roller-printed toiles set along the sides. This quilt once belonged to Henry Francis du Pont, who bequeathed it to Winterthur Museum, Delaware, in 1969.

9
10

holdings at Shelburne, Bayou Bend, Historic New England, Historic Deerfield, Greenfield Village, Colonial Williamsburg, and Winterthur'. When du Pont died in 1969, quilts that he had retained for his own use entered the Winterthur collection. Among these is one **[10]** that illustrates Eaton's observation that the colours and patterns of quilts in the interwar years 'were also recognized as being appropriate for use with modernist furniture'. She quotes the author Ruth Finley, writing in 1929: 'Today's taste is not shocked by such antique combinations as purple and cerise nor by composition so stark as to be geometrical.'[6]

Thus the connection between Modernism and quilts was already established – at least among decorators, collectors and, presumably, quilters themselves – when the art world discovered quilts as a result of a much-fêted exhibition of 'Abstract Design in American Quilts' at the Whitney Museum of American Art, New York, in 1971, and a year later 'American Pieced Quilts' at the Smithsonian American Art Museum in Washington, DC, the same city where the first National Quilt Association exhibition had been held in 1970.[7] Among the award-winners at the latter was Mary Schafer, whose research and work played a vital role in the establishment of modern American quilt-making.[8] It was only after this time that the making of art quilts gained wider recognition, with opportunities to exhibit and showcase developing gradually. National acceptance of quilting as an art form was promoted through organizations such as Studio Art Quilt Associates, founded by the Californian Yvonne Porcella in 1989, which now has more than 2,500 members worldwide. (However, to put this in perspective, the Embroiderers' Guild, founded in 1906 in London, has more than 25,000 members globally.) In 1997 the International Quilt Study Center & Museum opened at the University of Nebraska in Lincoln, with a founding collection donated by Ardis and Robert James. Today the collection consists of more than 3,500 quilts from the last three centuries and more than two dozen countries. In 2008, it was estimated that quilting in the United States alone was an industry worth $3.3 billion annually. It is equally vibrant globally: in Europe the largest annual event is the Twisted Threads' Festival of Quilts, held in Birmingham every year since 2003, with the support of the Quilters' Guild of the British Isles, which was founded in 1979. The festival's array of international exhibitors **[185–91]** attracts some 35,000 visitors over the space of just four days.

Many quilts remain based on a grid format, an arrangement fundamental to textiles because it is derived from the natural tendency of interweaving to create right-angled structures. As a consequence of following the structure of the cloth, many early examples of drawn and pulled threadwork, as well as cutwork, utilize the same organizational principle **[12]**. The grid can, in fact, be found in use in every type of textile and, as Hannah Higgens has argued, it is the most prominent visual structure in Western culture, ancient in origin. In addition, Higgens notes that, like grids, 'human sensory and cognitive frameworks establish a relationship between order and disorder, which is why psychologist Howard Gardner has described human intelligences in the grid-based terminology of "frames" of mind'.[9] The grid structure, shared with bricks, maps and musical scores, reminds us that pieces of cloth are building blocks, sensory landscapes and essays in tonalities of colour and texture, as well as of sound. The blocks may be set on point **[10]** – a common alternative arrangement, not only for quilts, but also for carpets and

11. Amanda Schwartz, *Sample*, 1986. Machine-stitched with an automatic pattern on a domestic Bernina using a thicker matt cotton thread, dyed cheesecloth has been layered to produce a grid-quilted surface and additional appliqué. Further texture and colour effects were added with hand-stitched running and herringbone stitches in a soft embroidery cotton.

floors – which only serves to reinforce the 'balancing act' required in the selection and arrangement of materials. When the grid is not present, the possibilities and challenges of selection and arrangement remain, as epitomized by the random piecing in the aptly named 'crazy quilts'. Martha Opdahl **[151]** cites influences from American crazy and block quilts as well as Japanese kimonos, strip weaves and pre-Columbian Andean weavings – 'variations within a limited vocabulary of motifs'. Yet she describes her drive for order and immediate rebellion against it as 'spontaneity, lyricism, freedom. In my work lines begin and disappear; patterns swirl and dissolve; a clear structure is often subverted by the movement of the background. I see these tensions as a reflection of a central conflict in real life.' And the work need not be abstract to contain the same sensibilities. Maria Holohan's figurative pieces **[162, 166]** contain 'shadowy threats, while the collage surface, quilted, scraped or raised, connotes the inability of humans to master their emotional environment'. As these last two examples illustrate, there are many who use some or all of the quiltmaker's techniques yet do not produce a quilt in the strictest sense.

12. Indian embroiderer, *Redwork panel, c.* 1600. Double running stitched worked in red silk on a linen ground forms twelve motifs dispersed at random over forty-eight squares, each surrounded by a band that has been cut away and outlined with yellow silk, also used in the interstices for the floral motifs. This rare piece may have been a pillow cover and is only about 42 cm (16½ in.) square.

Textiles Parkour

Since the 1970s, the freedom to move through three-dimensional space has increasingly provided opportunities for textile artists, who occupy a conceptual landscape in which they are at liberty to move in any direction within their textural domain. There seems no better term for this activity than 'textiles parkour'. Parkour, a non-competitive physical activity that developed in the 20th century from the obstacle course, is also described by participants as a state of mind.

Although the aim of parkour is to move quickly and efficiently through an urban landscape, one can compare it to textiles because of parkour's enhancement of spatial awareness, which encourages self-confidence and critical-thinking skills to overcome obstacles. However, the 'artful dodging' in textiles parkour takes place as if in slow motion. As the social analyst Richard Sennett writes in his book *The Craftsman*, describing the historical record as a catalogue of experiments in making things, material culture does not 'follow the rhythms of biological life . . . . The histories of things follow a different course, in which metamorphosis and adaptation play a strong role across human generations.'[10]

Thus the development in Scotland of Secessionist embroideries over a century ago contributed as much to post-Contemporary developments as did the events of the 1960s. Looking at an elegant embroidered collage (probably) by Ann Macbeth, dating to the beginning of the 20th century, it may be hard to accept at first glance that the battle for manoeuvrability had already begun **[13]**. Yet Macbeth and others associated with the Glasgow School of Art took what was then a radical approach to textiles, one that was widely disseminated through publications aimed at schoolteachers. Extreme simplicity, with expanses of plain cloth and flattened forms, resulted in a proto-abstraction indebted to Japanese, medieval and Celtic precedents. The reduction in perspective was a rejection of the accomplishments of post-Renaissance textile artists and machines, which increasingly had rendered images realistically. What is more, this approach was a statement of authenticity, a return to 'roots' that can be seen in other nationalist movements, from the American campaign for an indigenous style discussed in Chapter I, to Irish art needlework and *l'art Munichois*, the decorative style launched in Munich

13. Glasgow School of Art, possibly designed by Ann Macbeth, *Two Women in Aesthetic Dress*, *c.* 1908–16. Silk satin is embroidered with floss (untwisted) silk strands in satin stitch and French knots, with various cords couched with silk and metal threads. These and glass beads add subtle contrast to large areas of appliquéd plain silks.

14. Mary Lloyd Jones, *Barclodiad y gawres (The Apron of the Giants)*, 1983. Barclodiad y Gawres is a 4,000-year-old burial chamber on Anglesea. Using dyes and wax resist on cotton, the artist's intention was to create a positive image of women's work, incorporating references to prehistory, the land and a Welsh identity.

in 1908 and communicated through an exhibition in Paris two years later. (This style was influential on Paul Poiret's decision to found, in 1911, the École Martine: an experimental school where working-class Parisian girls sketched freely, and Poiret purchased their best drawings for use in his design studio, Atelier Martine.) Once authenticity was established as a legitimate perspective in the intellectual sense, there emerged a freer use of cloth and stitch in embroidery, often exposing raw edges and emphasizing the collage process by using layered fabrics, the uppermost transparent. However, throughout the interwar years and beyond, these works remained within established artistic boundaries, and were generally framed. It took another generation to circumvent this particular obstacle. Mary Lloyd Jones was among those rebelling against the standardized format **[14]**. In her work of the late 1970s to mid-1980s she wanted to 'create a link with women's work and the quilt-making tradition in Wales', but had an 'intuitive need to break out of the rectangle, the tyranny of the stretched and framed canvas' to make 'compositions that could fly across walls'. As a result, she took to folding, pleating, twisting, ripping, wiping and hanging, all activities with a strong domestic link. Having recently returned to this format, Lloyd Jones finds the same techniques today to be expressive of a threatened countryside and unstable global situation.[11]

Over the same period other 'rules' began to be broken. Raised work of the 17th century, for instance, was viewed in 1907 as 'that curious phase', one that was 'delightfully disregardful of any of the fettering rules of proportion and perspective', producing work described as, at best, quaint and funny, at worst, crude **[86]**.[12] Within a few years Margaret Jourdain, a collector and prolific writer on the decorative arts, was championing stumpwork, agreeing that it had previously been regarded as 'grotesque', but that the style of embroidery should now be considered 'both curious and valuable'.[13] However, it took several more challenges to the canons of taste before the point was reached – in the 1980s – when practical, instructional publications devoted to the subject began to proliferate.

Pop Art, in which the division between fine and commercial art was dismissed, played an important role in this shift, as did the Western consumer's discovery of new types of ethnographic textiles, some of which have already been discussed. One of these textiles, whose popularity reached fad proportions during the 1970s and 1980s, is the mola from Latin America **[174–81]**. These distinctive products, made by Kuna Indian women of the San Blas Islands in Panama, are intended as blouse fronts. Molas consist of reverse appliqué, meaning that the top fabric has cut-out areas revealing layers of fabric below. Variety is introduced by inserting various solid-coloured fabrics, which are additionally appliquéd to the tops. The widespread interest in these outside Panama can be traced to the fact that many were collected by Captain Kit S. Kapp while on numerous expeditions to the islands in the 1960s.[14] Kapp's subsequent book, *Mola Art from the San Blas Islands* – self-published in 1972 and in its fifth edition by 1982 – explains that molas evolved in the late 19th century from traditions of body painting, cloth painting and decorative bands sewn to hems of loose dresses. This is more than an iteration on the theme of human topography. While many other ethnographic textiles are abstract or highly stylized, molas are unashamedly decorative, more akin to stumpwork caskets, mirror frames and the like than to the reserved figuration of, say, Andean or Guatemalan textiles.

15. Fon nu artisan, Benin, *Banner* (detail), 1973. From Benin (formerly Dahomey in south-western Nigeria), this appliquéd traditionally styled cotton banner employs expanses of plain cloths and flattened images, in a form of proto-abstraction that in this case was influential in interwar France, which administered the Fon kingdom from 1892 to 1960.

16. Pilar Tobón, *Homage to the Kimono*, 2005. Tobón, founder of the World Textile Art Organization, interweaves plain, printed and bronzed silks with both closely set and freely falling silk strands.

Embracing the decorative was a risky turn, given that textiles of all sorts had for so long been dismissed as women's work precisely because they *were* decorative. Then the 1990s' flirtation with minimalist arts and interiors seemed likely to undo decades of innovation and public presence. The cessation of the Lausanne Biennales in 1995 did not auger well. Yosi Anaya captures the mood in the Americas: 'These were the moments when universities closed their textile departments and important textile biennials ceased to exist; moments in which the historic yet hushed thread of activity – mainly relegated to women – had to undergo a new adaptation because of this detour, obstacle, and closure. How to reaffirm the validity of the artistic intent in the creative production of textiles despite the fact that the hierarchic currents of artists' thought bounced it back to the home and as a pastime, in an era in which art moved and continues to move in new conceptual and theatrical level? How to vindicate and restore the creative processes implicit in the handling of materials, forms, techniques, colors, spaces and history, while textile activity diversifies in so many manifestations that it becomes almost unclassifiable?'[15] The response came in 1997 when Pilar Tobón **[16]** formed what is now the World Textile Art Organization (WTA) in Miami, Florida. As a Colombian textile artist, she recognized that Latin textile arts were unknown beyond national borders, and that even 'within them, the situation was precarious, above all for those traditional artists of ancestral culture'.[16] Biennials followed, in Latin America and Miami, with an international roster of participants. The void left by the lost European biennial was also filled: the 8th International Textiles Biennial was held in Kaunas, Lithuania, in 2011. Meanwhile, momentum was being generated by other influential membership organizations, including the European Textile Network (ETN), initiated in 1990 by Beatrijs Sterk and Dietmar Laue, editors of *Textil Forum* magazine, and formally constituted with Council of Europe patronage in 1993.

In retrospect, the 1990s marked a point when those within the field gained a self-awareness that allowed, eventually, for less concern about outside opinions. Take Mary Cozens-Walker, whose work has been compared to stumpwork **[87, 91]**. In 1993 Audrey Walker, herself a well-known British embroiderer, described it thus: 'Mary's work is "awkward" – it defies neat categorisation and challenges norms of aesthetic good taste, so that any pre-conceived notions of what might constitute "high art", "low art", "fine art", "craft", "sculpture" or "embroidery" must be set aside.'[17] In 2000 Cozens-Walker's work was said still to 'fly in the face of fashion in the contemporary visual arts'.[18] Despite that perception, many textile artists have taken this course, and are no longer concerned with labels or acceptance. Their decision appears to be related to the greater exposure now granted to the rich and diverse traditions within the history of textiles themselves. Nothing is too 'ordinary' to be dismissed. Just at the start of her career, Sam Morris describes her creations **[17]** – toys with a new take on century-old printed and stuffed animals **[18]** – as having 'a sense of humour but with added darkness, something that is appealing but also a bit gruesome too, in a comical way'.

In this game of textiles parkour, twists and turns have obliterated a single approved route to validation, offering possibilities to move into areas where the artist is unconstrained. Inspiration might come from sources that are Eastern, Western, Latin, First Nation, Jacobean or Rococo; materials might be natural

17

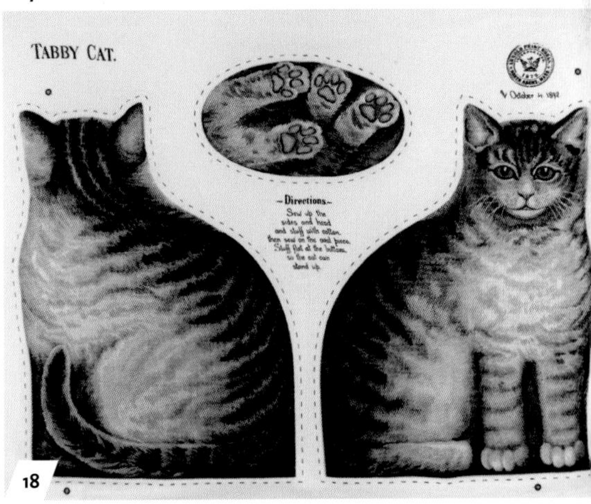

18

17. Sam Morris, *Prototype Stuffed Toy*, 2010. Aiming to create adult toys, Morris collages imagery that is then printed onto canvas to create her edgy characters, which she intends should trigger the memory of a forgotten childhood story.

18. Arnold Print Works, Massachusetts, *Tabby Cat*, c. 1892. This is one of several roller-printed heavy cotton ready-to-sew dolls and animals patented by this firm, which had been founded in 1860 and by 1905 was among the largest textile printers in the world, with offices in New York and Paris. It closed in 1942.

19. Frances Butler, *Apron* (detail), 1970s. Silk-screened cotton canvas printed by Frances Butler's textile printing company called Goodstuffs Fabric Company, based in Emeryville, California. Butler was at this time a faculty member in the Department of Environmental Design at the University of California, Davis, and remained so until her retirement in 1994.

20. Katherine Westphal, *Wall hanging* (detail), mid-1970s. Referencing the complexity of traditional textiles, a checked oilcloth is appliquéd with cotton crocheted rabbits and flowers. This sizeable panel (1 × 2.25 m; 40 × 89 in.) was made for the conference room of the Department of Applied Behavioral Sciences at the University of California, Davis.

21. Indian artisans, *Petticoat* (detail), 1750–75. Painted and dyed cotton, overprinted with gold; made on the Coromandel coast for the Dutch market.

or ultra-modern. Valerie Huggins starts with her long-standing interest in shrines, rooted in her strict religious upbringing and fuelled by travels in Greece and Mexico **[134, 135]**: 'Using strong colour, kitsch and even humour, my work challenges the viewer to question where the comfortable, familiar symbols of Christianity come from, and where myth, superstition and paganism end and organized religion begins.' In contrast, Denise Prefontaine uses 'the media of textiles and glass as well as those of light and space, combining them to create works which both respond to and interact with their environment' **[81]**. All of these artists participate in what would today be recognized as a Post-modernist melange, which, like Post-modernism itself, rests on critiques that began a century ago.

One reason for this has been the creation of study collections within university and college textile departments as opposed to established museums. These collections are less constrained by the taste of trustees, the need to take in only the best-preserved examples, and the inevitable red tape. The molas illustrated within these pages, as well as many of the other textiles, reside in the Design Collection at the University of California, Davis (UCD), and are part of a collection actively used for teaching. Jo Ann Stabb joined the UCD staff in 1968, having done her Masters at the University of California, Los Angeles, where the now pre-eminent ethnographic textile collection of the Fowler Museum (founded in 1963) was merely, as she puts it, 'wonderful stuff in the basement'. Teaching practical courses and costume history at UCD, Stabb witnessed Katherine Westphal **[20]** bring in all sorts of textiles for the students to study. Watching her and thinking of the Fowler collection in the design department, Stabb realized, 'This is how to teach', and decided that the UCD's holdings needed to grow **[167–71]**. Other teachers elsewhere have done the same, creating an influential subculture of collecting by and for textile artists. This informs works such as Stabb's *Swan Song: My Last Academic Plan Ever!* **[98]**: a coat constructed to celebrate her retirement in 2002. The joyous exterior, made of recycled silk scraps, captures both the lyrical buoyancy of feathers and the jaunty 'tabs' of a mid-1920s flapper's shift **[97]**. The hidden interior is hand stamp-printed with the University of California's long and convoluted academic planning process, and gold dollar signs are embroidered around the coat's interior hemline. Stabb wanted to articulate the fact that 'the University is compelled to run as a business with an eye on the "bottom line" to generate a substantial income/profit margin – for survival! Basically, government funding, research grants and outside institutions drive these plans. Often money speaks louder than "ideas".'

The truth in Stabb's words inspires more and more participants in textiles parkour. Textiles seem to thrive on the need for adaptation. Contradictions, questions and a refusal to be confined to a singular 'now' bring forth subversion in diverse forms. Rhiannon Willliams uses discarded (valueless) newspapers and lottery tickets in a traditional (and cost-conscious) patchwork format that critiques the desire to have it all **[99,100]**. Jennifer Vickers also employs newspapers **[103]**, but as a 'focus for contemplation on the human cost of war' in memorials that 'engage contemporary audiences in continuous relationships with historical events and people'. As Julie Montgarrett **[84]** puts it: 'By way of accidental or implied relationships, I hope to contradict the expectations of rational coherence of contemporary life, of singular dominant white settler narratives of Colonial history … . I make works informed as much by embroidery histories as by contemporary ideas, in relative exile from the often fraught domains of both art and craft, rather than, like many contemporary artists, borrowing textile mainly as material for innovative effect.' The past is ever present.

22. Russian embroiderer, *Dress* (detail), before 1930. Polychrome silk cross-stitch embroidery is on and around a pieced and appliquéd front placket made from crêpe fabrics. The shank buttons are covered with crocheted silk thread. Purchased in 1930 in Florence, where it was displayed on the wall of a Russian tea room, it was made in the western Ukraine or eastern Slovakia.

23. Sandy Starkman, *Skirt* (detail), 2006. Gathered tiers of polyester chiffons and one polyester satin (second from top) juxtapose Western and Eastern patterns, the latter including faux shibori. The Brooklyn-born Starkman creates many of his fashions in India, his second home.

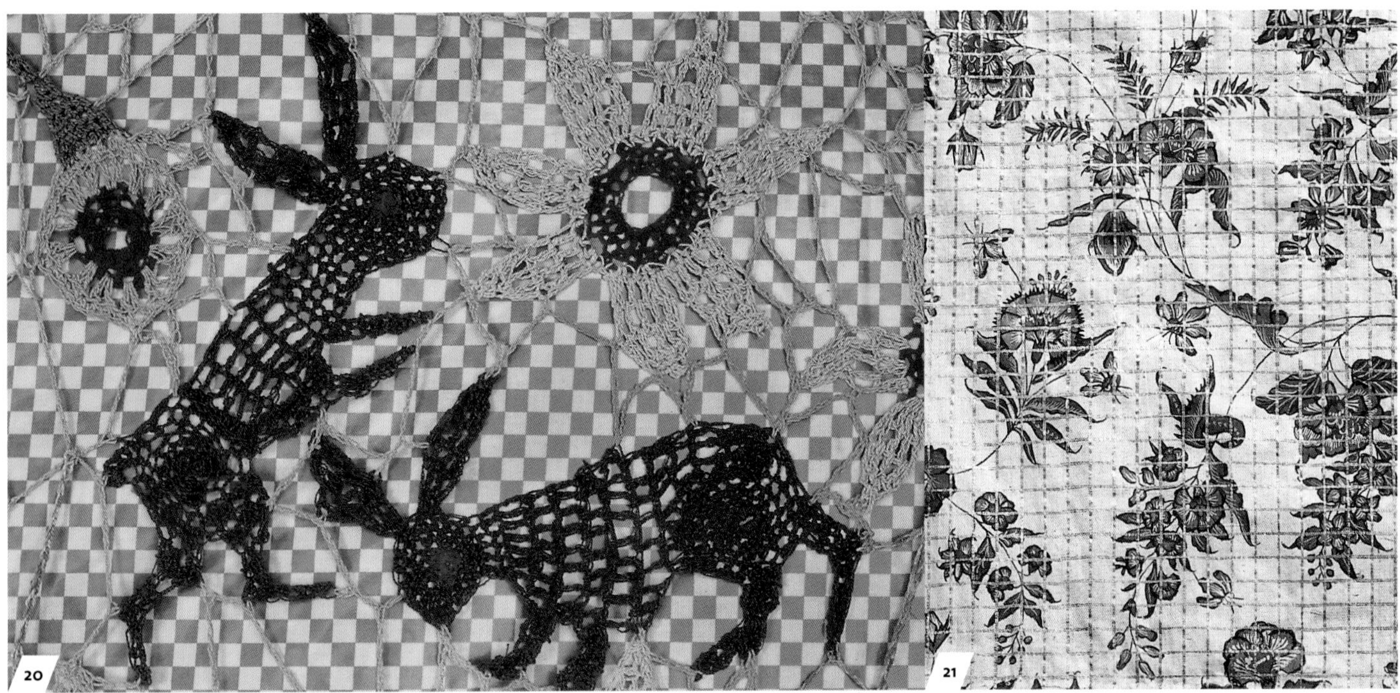
20

21

24

25

26

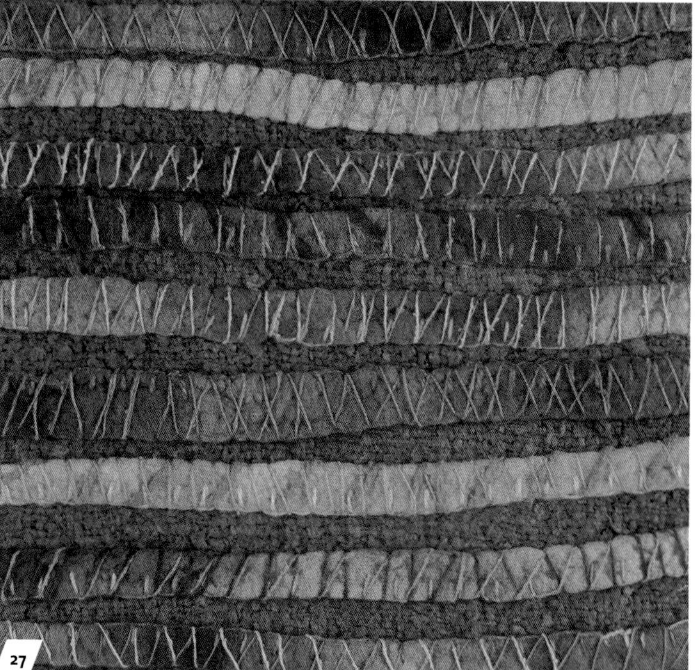

27

24. Seminole artisan, Florida or Oklahoma, *Child's gathered skirt* (detail), before 1970. On a salmon-coloured rayon satin, one inset band of typical Seminole patchwork is surrounded by rows of applied rickrack.

25. Ellen Hauptli, *Socks*, 2006. A pair of cotton jersey socks with a random brush stroke-like print has a stitched back seam and top hem in turquoise perle stitch.

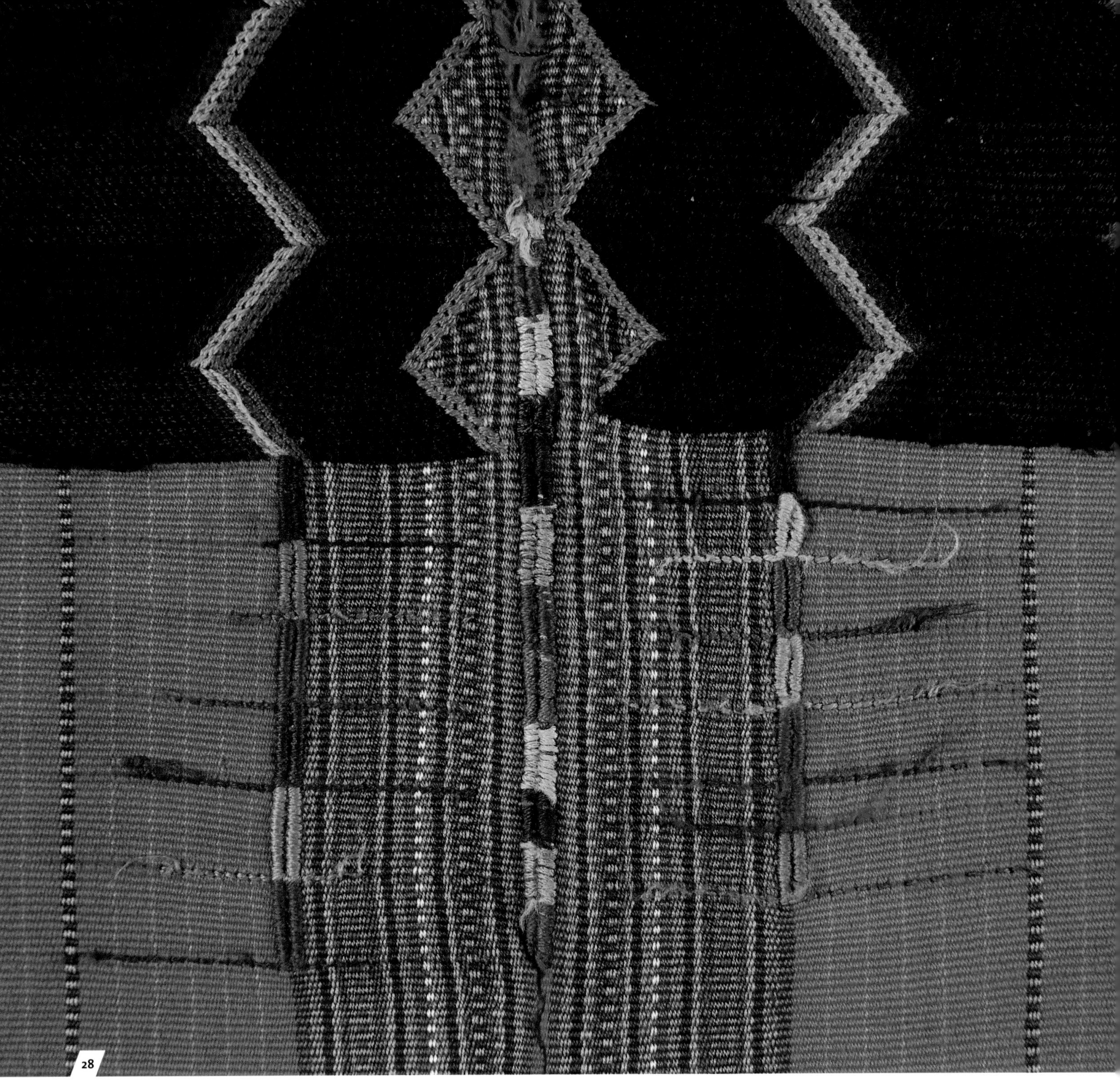

26. Turkmen maker, *Child's dress or shirt*, *c.* 1940. Constructed from a central cotton panel folded over at the shoulder with pieced side skirt panels. The sleeves and embroidered yoke are rayon. The edges are reinforced with braid, and a lining of pieced cotton floral prints – probably Russian – is attached with vertical rows of running stitches.

27. Bailey Curtis, *Waistcoat* (detail), 2006. Dip-dyed handmade wool felt strips are stitched to a dyed silk background.

28. Quiché weaver, Guatemala, Huipil (detail), before 1980. Purchased in a market in Guatemala City, this *huipil* is made from two single handwoven cotton panels. The purple yoke has blue diagonal patterns created as the weaving progressed by wrapping the red weft, in the soumak technique. The miniature tassels are thread ends.

29. Jean Cacicedo, *Tee Pee*, 1988. Inspired by the transformative properties of wool cloth when shrunk, pieced and dyed, the artist regards cloth as the primary element in much of her work: 'My sewn constructions tell stories about images collected from journeys both physical and spiritual.'

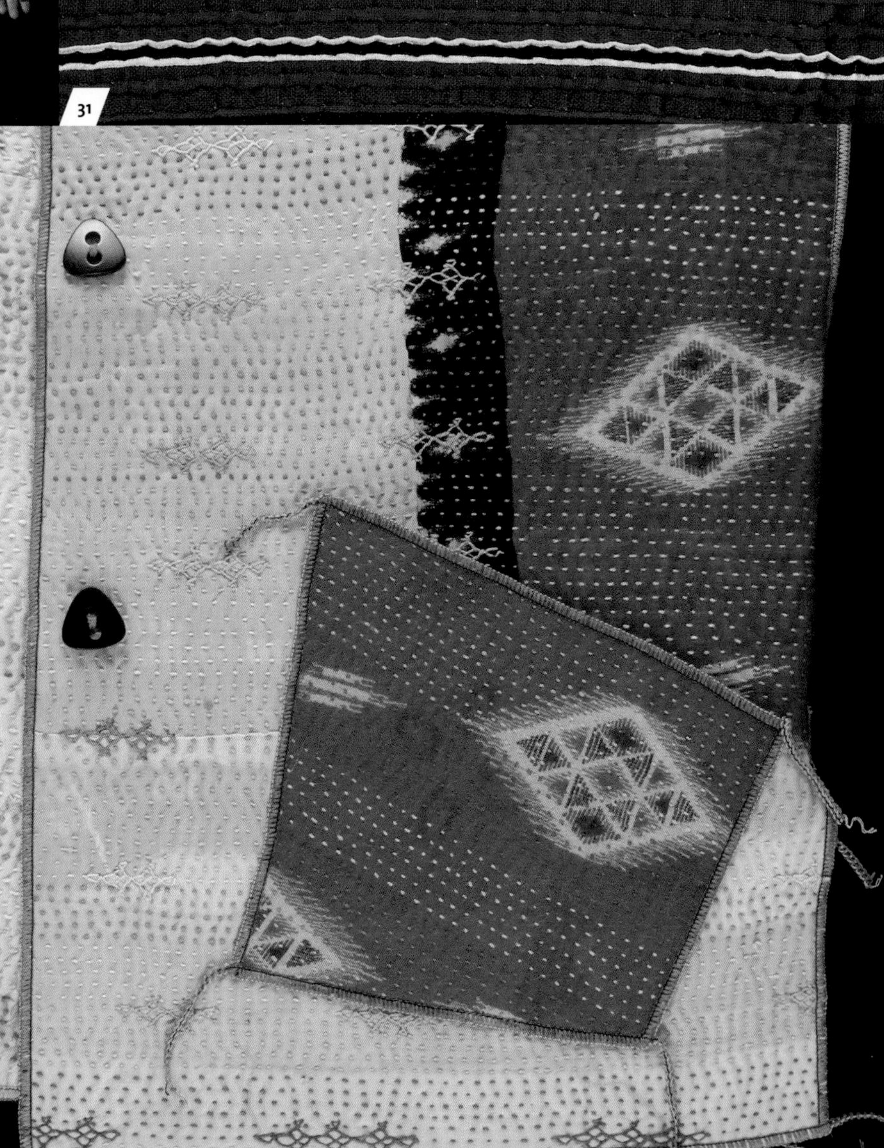

30. Catherine O'Leary, *Red Bojagi*, 2010. *Bojagi* is a traditional Korean sewing technique, typically used to create a wrapping cloth, in which small pieces of fabric are pieced together with narrow seams. Here the seams emphasize the sculptural qualities of organza and its transparent nature.

31. H'mong woman, Laos, *Jacket* (sleeve detail), 20th century. The tips of the sleeves are trimmed with narrow strips of overlapping appliqué with inserts of rickrack handmade made from folded white cotton strips.

32. Ellen Hauptli, *Jacket* (detail), 2009. Made from recycled cotton *ralli* quilts from Pakistan. The seams and pocket edges are reinforced and emphasized with Hauptli's signature machine zig-zag stitching, which extends into decorative finials.

33

33. Issey Miyake, *Jacket* (detail), *c.* 1978. The upper body and sleeves of this jacket are formed of strips of double-faced wool used vertically with each outer edge free. The reversible cloth's pattern echoes shibori effects.

34. Nigerian artisans, probably Yoruba, *Man's* agbada *robe* (detail), 1964–65. Striped indigo-dyed handwoven cotton strips, 10 cm (4 in.) wide, are machine-sewn together along selvedges and overcast by hand. Yellow crochet and decorative embroidery reinforce the neckline, and form a small pocket accessible from the top.

35–38. Ewe artisans, *Strip cloths* (details), *c.* 1950 and 1970s. Handwoven in narrow strips by members of an ethnic group in Ghana, Benin and Togo. Many Ewe cotton wrappers are characterized by the inclusion of blocks of supplementary weft patterning that are sewn together to create a chequerboard arrangement.

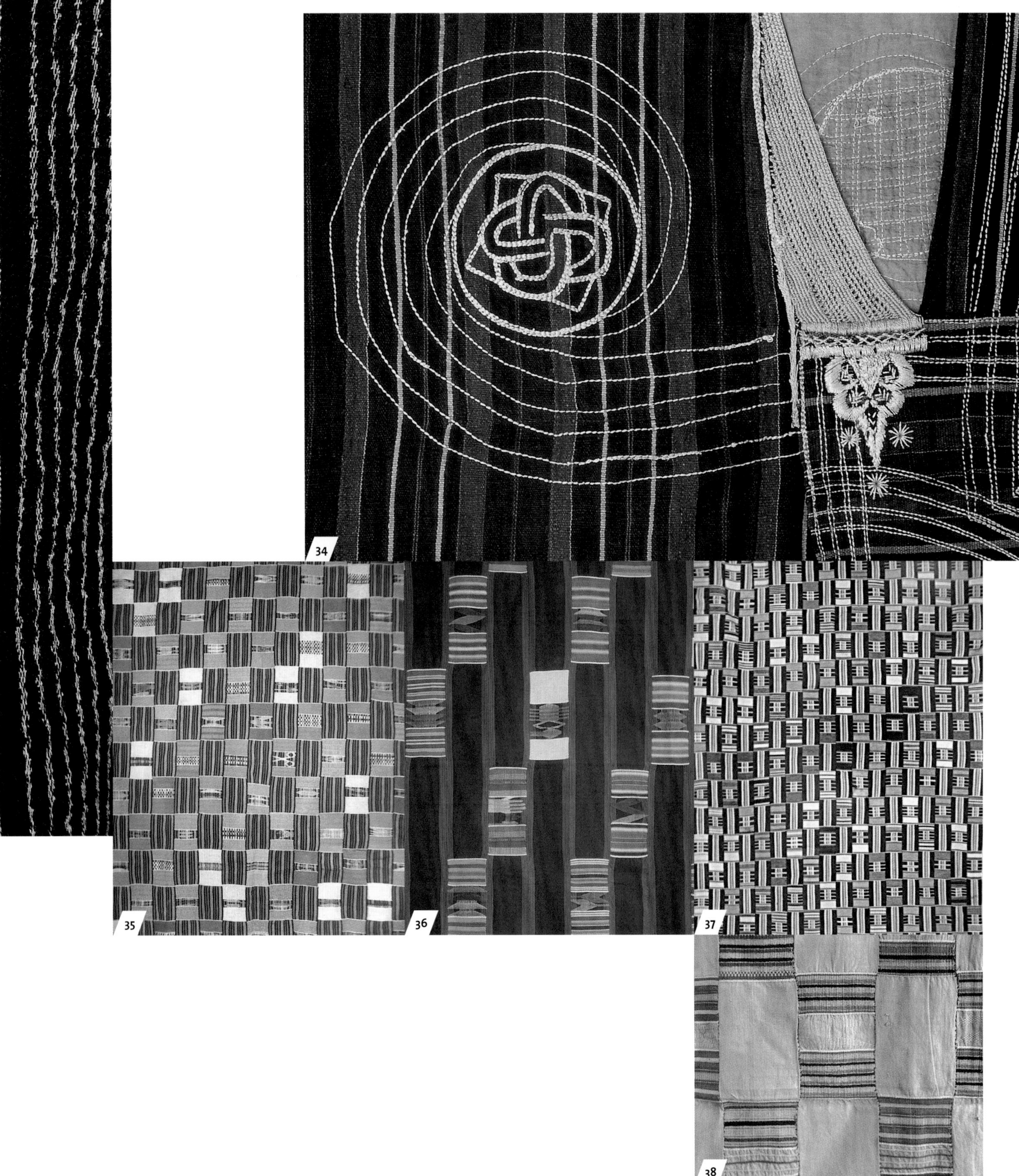
34
35
36
37
38

39. Wodaabi artisans, *Skirt* (detail), *c.* 1950. The front panel of this indigo-dyed cotton strip cloth-wrapped skirt is embroidered in chain stitch with a range of geometric patterns, for which this nomadic cattle-herding and -trading culture is renowned. Their migrations stretch from southern Niger, through northern Nigeria and north-eastern Cameroon, to the western region of the Central African Republic.

40. Marian Clayden, *Shadow Kimono*, 1981. Industrial cotton strapping has been branded, dyed, assembled and then brush-discharged.

41. Shihoko Fukumoto, *Tsushima VI*, 2009. An old handwoven *taima* (hemp) *okusozakuri* (undyed work kimono) was picked apart, some pieces indigo-dyed and all portions finally reassembled into a rectangular form 220 × 99 cm (86.6 × 39 in.) in size.

40

41

42. Loretta Oliver, *Trapped/Protected*, 2011. Prompted by the sight of the Pink Palace in Jaipur and its screened windows, suggestive of either security or imprisonment, Oliver created this piece through a wet felting technique, using wool fibres with inlays of cotton wool and hand-dyed, handwoven fabric.

43. Wari weaver, Peru, *Man's tunic*, AD 500–800. Using the scaffold technique, historically unique to the Andes, each square and S-shaped meander was woven as an independent element on the loom (the edging threads turned back on themselves), after which the scaffolding threads were removed, the freed pieces were plain-dyed or tie-dyed and all were reassembled into a new whole.

44. James Basslser, *Chueco*, 2007. In a work inspired by the Peruvian scaffold-weaving technique, hemp, silk and alpaca dyed forms were sewn to a handwoven background of interlocking warps and wefts.

45. John Parkes, *Mantle/dismantle (after Nazca)*, 2008. Pieced and quilted by hand with linen and cotton threads, the silk face cloths were hand-dyed with synthetic and natural dyes for a panel measuring 183 × 122 cm (72 × 48 in.).

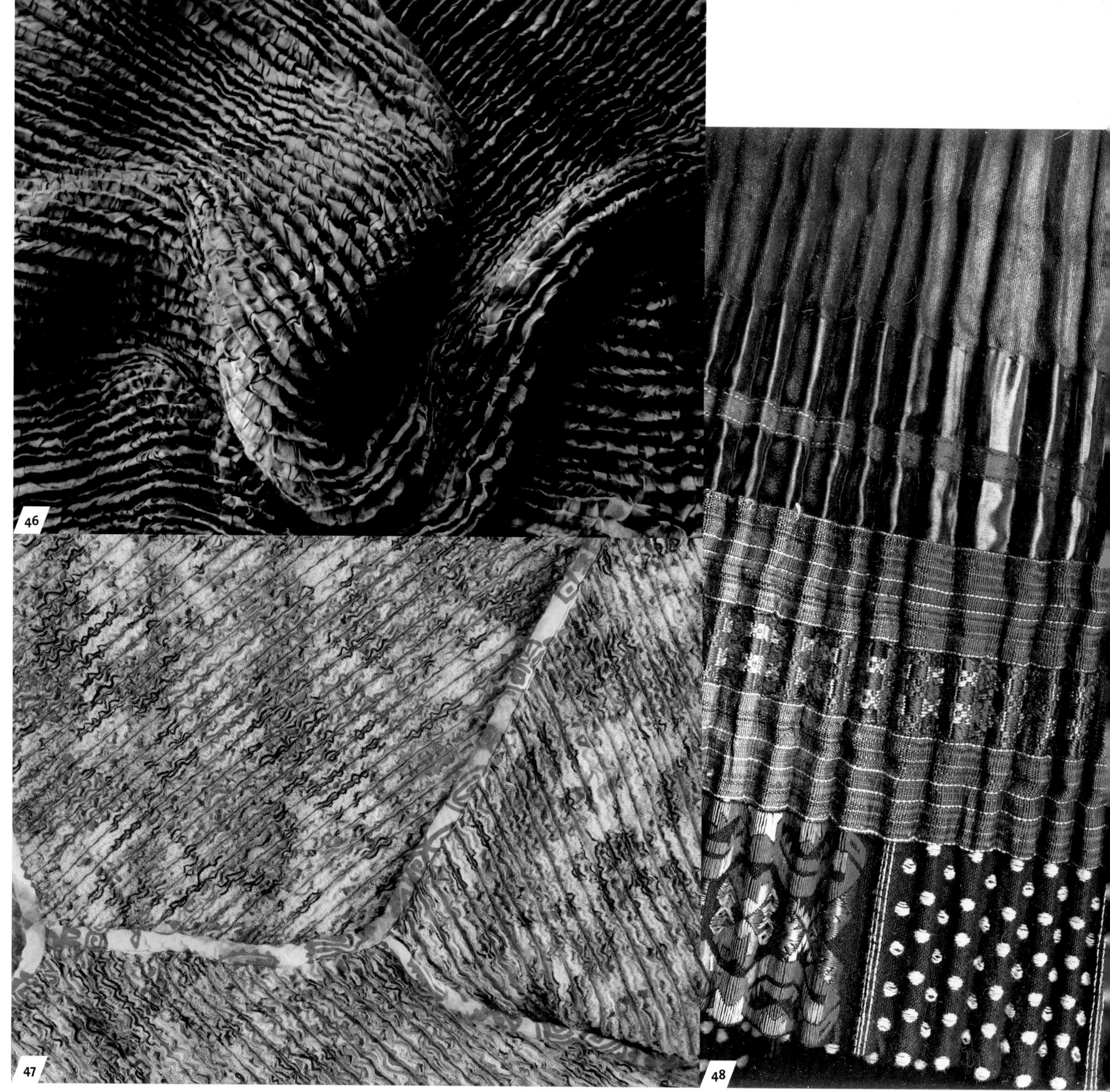

46. Mandy Southan, *Raku* (detail), 2011. Created through double *arashi* shibori and dip-dyeing, this hand-painted, double-pleated and overdyed silk has a dynamic quality: 'The elasticity of the cloth allows me to make sculptural textiles, which open and close with movement revealing and concealing the underlying pattern.'

47. Anonymous American maker of wearable art, *Jacket* (detail), 2003. This piece is made from printed rayon challis fabrics layered and stitched to the ground fabric in narrow parallel diagonal rows. The subsequent cutting open and washing of the fabric formed a chenille-like effect. This garment was acquired from Norma May International, Charleston, South Carolina.

48. Miao artisan, *Skirt* (detail), *c.* 2000. The outward-facing deep hem of this kilted indigo-dyed cotton skirt is decorated with embroidery and applied ribbons. The fading bronzed-green tone results from the application of bean starch, egg white, persimmon juice, ox-hide glue, soaked bark juices, ox blood or, more recently, gentian violet.

49. Justine Limpus Parish, *Scarf/Necklace*, *c.* 2000. Polyester with heat-set rows of zig-zag pleats, shibori-dyed, is further embellished with hand-painting of gilt pigment on the top edges.

50. Sally Weatherill, *Thames Pleat Scarves* (detail), 2010. Silk, wool and Lycra are woven on a Jacquard loom in a pocket weave, which allows the Lycra to contract and form pleats.

51. Indian maker, *Evening jacket* (detail), 2001. Overstitched seaming highlights the joining together of various devoré satin and chiffon fabrics.

52

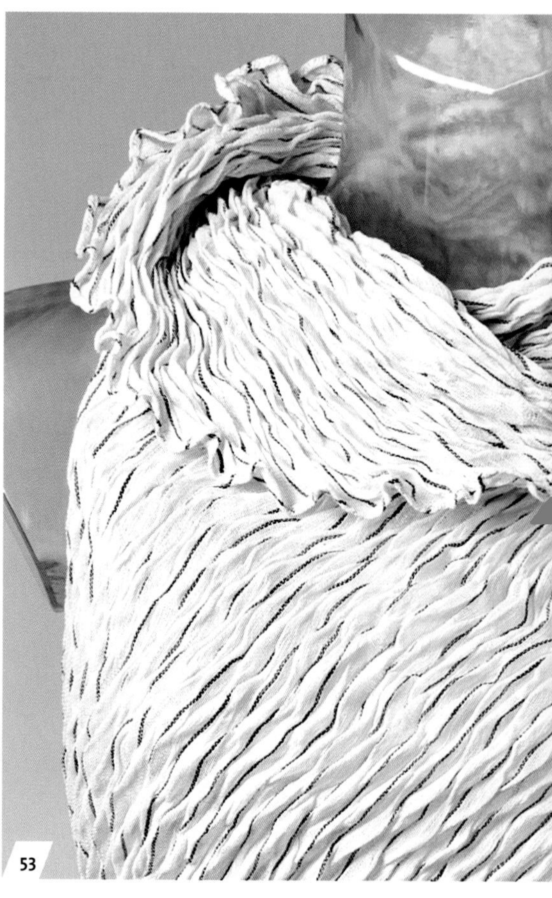

53

54

52. Jakob Schlaepfer, *Samples*, 2011. These samples are among Schlaepfer's offerings for the prêt-à-porter ranges for summer 2012. The designs make use of laser-cutting and three-dimensional ruching techniques.

53. Lotte Dalgaard and Ann Schmidt-Christensen, *Wadjet* (detail), 2011. A wool and linen plain weave has a 'shibori' weft of high-twist wool thread to form the split-level pleats, made stable by being steamed under pressure. This honeycomb pleated technique allows the web to be cut on the bias into two pieces and simply draped around the body without further cuts.

54. Issey Miyake, *Pleats Please skirt, blouse and purse* (details), 2004–5. Lightweight polyester jersey is cut and sewn together prior to heat-setting the permanent pleats, which can be straight or multi-dimensional (blouse, centre). Laser-cut motifs embellish the skirt's hem (top).

55. Neil Bottle, *Slate* (detail), 2011. Bottle explores the relationship between digital and craft techniques to show how these seemingly opposing practices can coexist – here with a digital dye-sublimation print on hand-pleated polyester. The print itself is hand-generated and digitally manipulated.

56. Anne Selby, *Fibonacci Boa* (detail), 2010. Silk, pleated and dyed with *arashi* shibori techniques.

57. Ann Richards, *Gauze Pleat* (detail), 1997. Tussah here forms a gauze (crossing) warp, which creates an open but very stable structure. The mohair weft is a singles yarn and consequently unbalanced, so it creates a 'natural' pleat during wet finishing.

58. Ann Richards, *Silk Pleat* (detail), 2001. Silk and linen form these natural folds. Trained as a biologist before becoming a weaver, Richards is intrigued by the underlying principles of growth and form in living things. She uses 'contrasting materials to create highly textured, elastic textiles that undergo a striking transformation from the smooth, flat state they have on the loom, to the crinkled or pleated textures that they assume when they are wet-finished.'

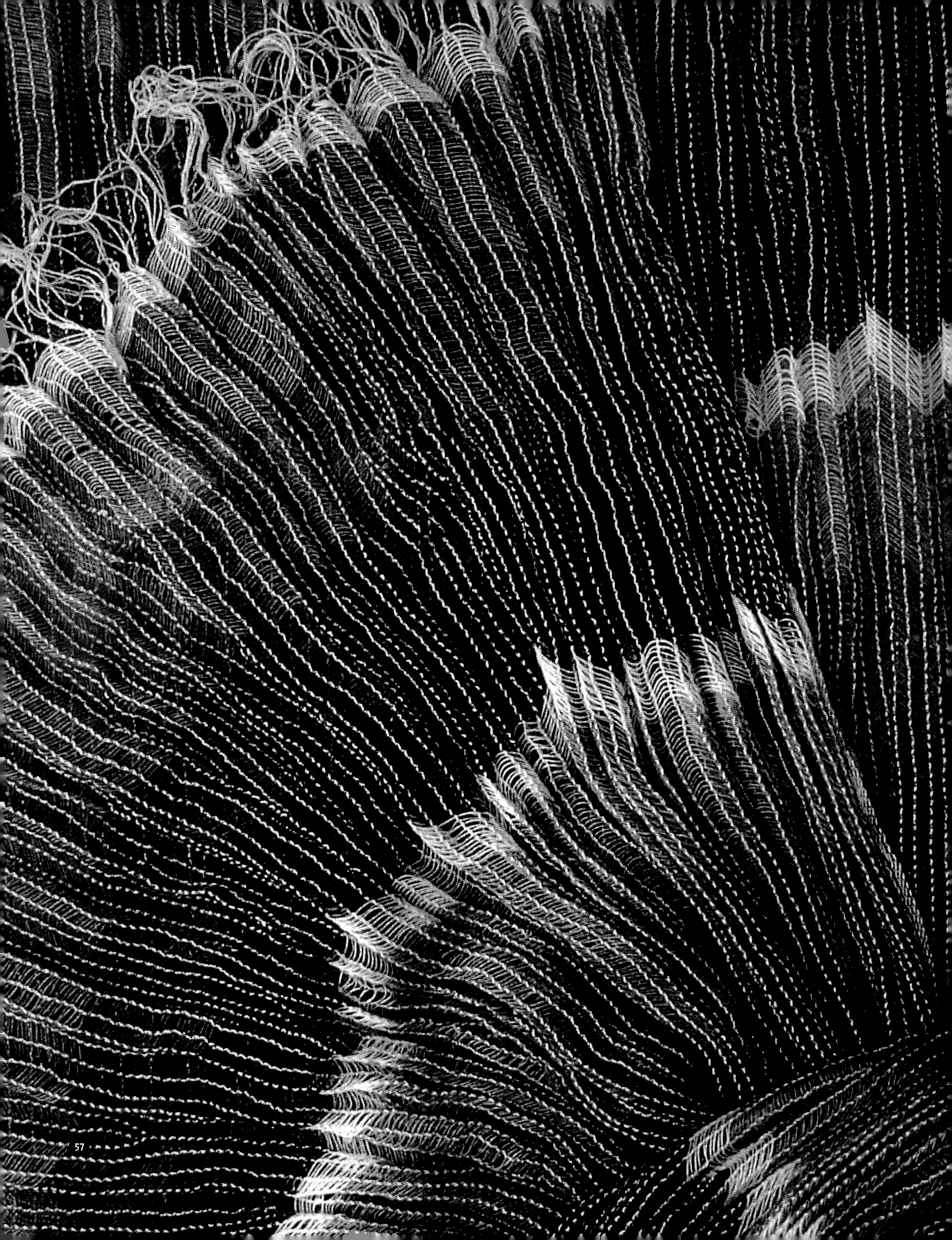

59

60

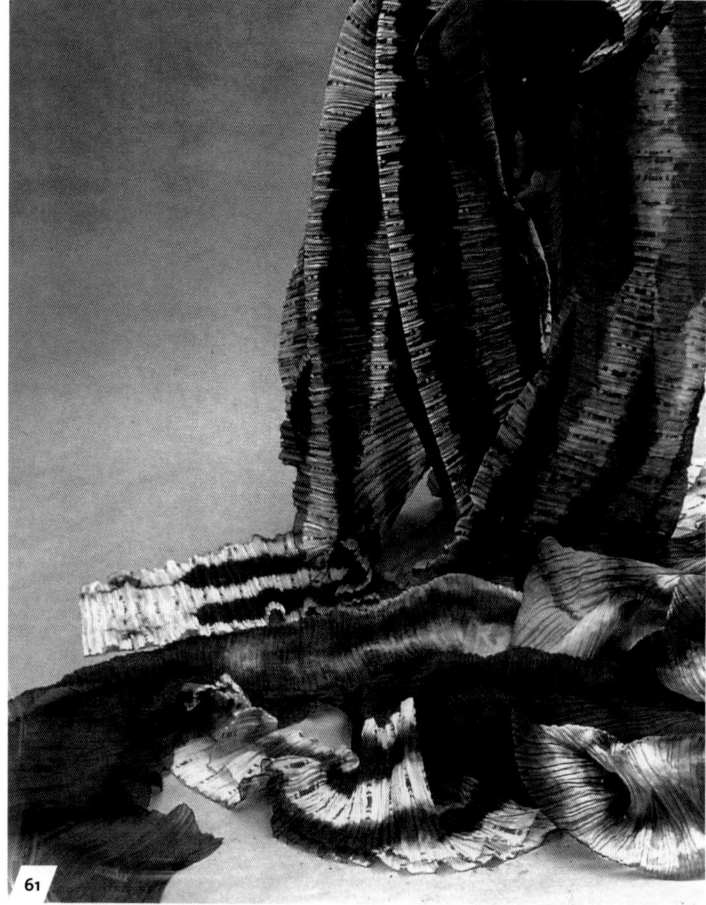

61

59. Havva Halaceli, *Black & White* (detail), 2008. This close view of Halaceli's empty dress shows her manipulation of silk with silk yarn, as if readied for shibori.

60. Silke Bosbach, *Modern Shibori – Water Object*, 2011. A modern take on the ancient shibori technique, this sculpture captures water in plastic, using metallic yarns wrapped as in *plangi* (tie-dye) to tie it closed.

61. Patricia Black, *Luminous Bardo* (detail), 1993. 'Luminous bardo' is a term from the *Tibetan Book of the Dead*, which describes the transition from one sphere of reality to another. Black's textile is marked by scintillating light patterns and shifting spectra – qualities she achieves through dyeing and discharging silk organza.

62. Barbara Shapiro, *Ndop* (detail), 2005. Handwoven silk strips, pieced and stitch-resisted against indigo dye. In technique and title it pays homage to Bamileke *ndop* cloths, which are used by the peoples of the Cameroon Grassfields both as clothing and to demarcate ritual spaces.

63. Ann Brown, *River*, 2010. An artist's book composed of indigo-dyed dupion silk, mulberry silk, stranded cotton and nylon insect mesh, *River* is accompanied by a found and altered cardboard container. Exploring the potential of stitch-resist as a drawing medium and added embroidered marks, the work references the threat to rivers posed by development.

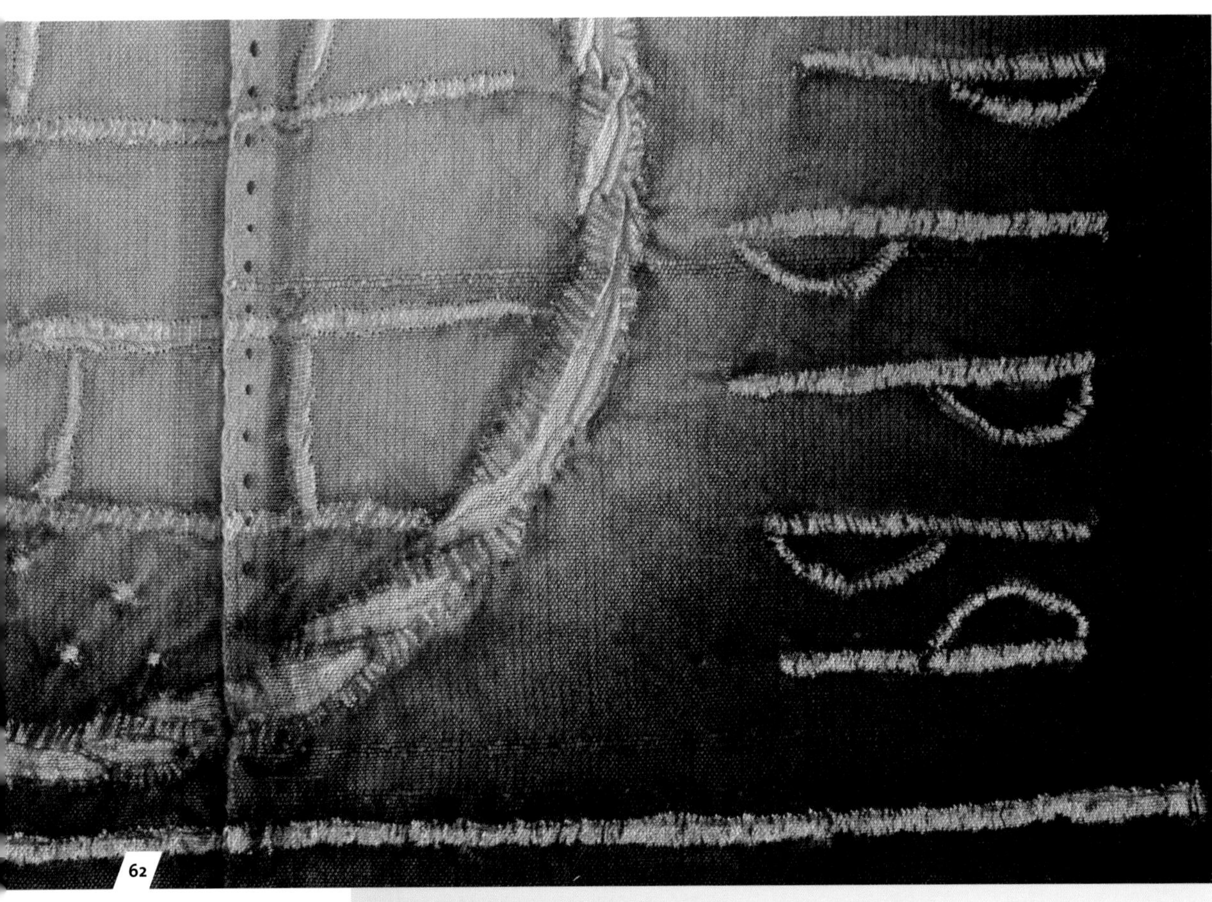
62

63

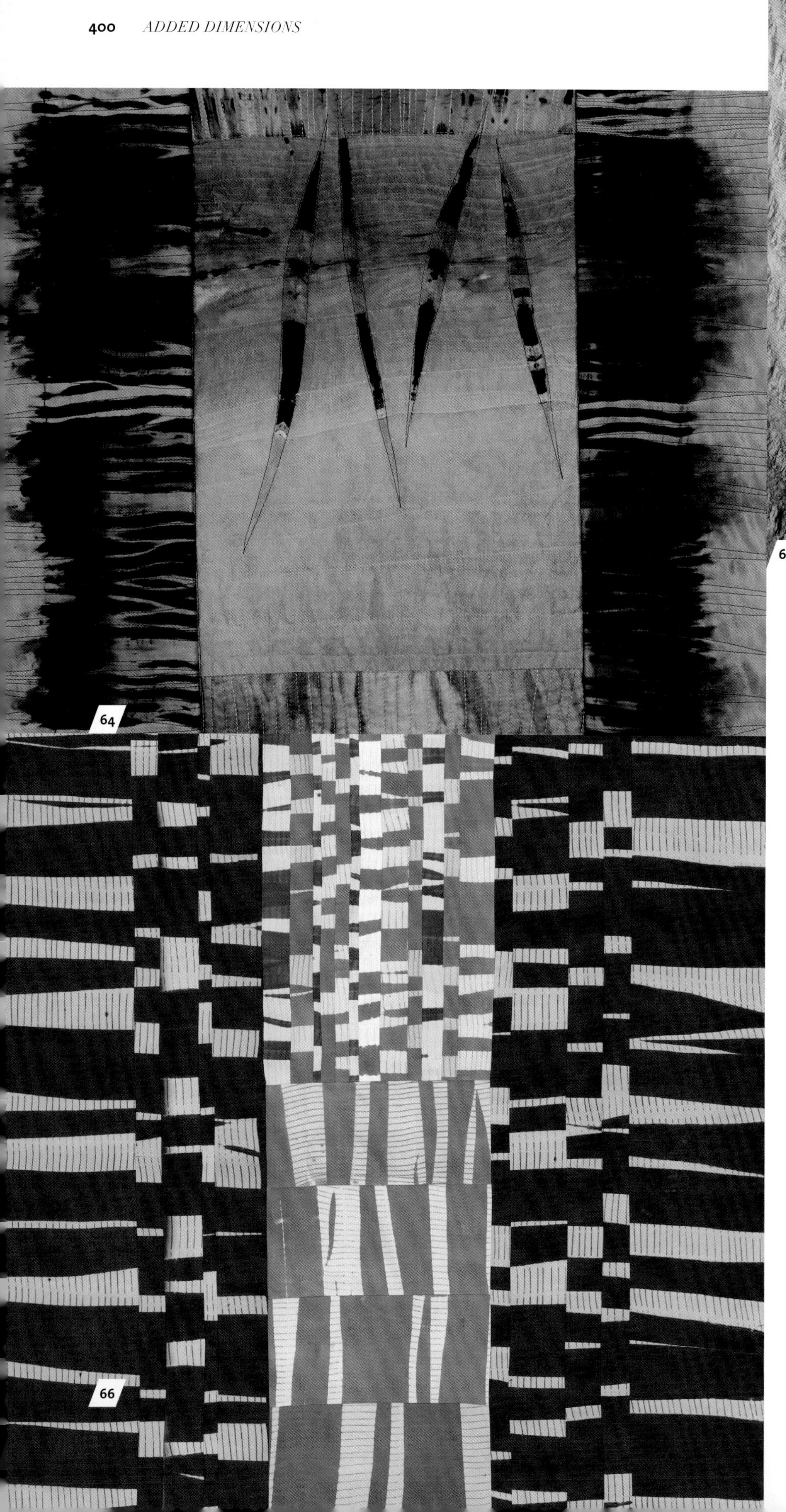

64. Judith Content, *Apparition* (detail), 2008. With a height of 185 cm (73 in.), this imposing panel of pieced silk satin, silk charmeuse and Thai silk was *arashi* shibori dyed and machine-quilted to capture the undulating reflections of ocean piers during a mid-winter dusk, when waves were 'like liquid mercury cresting with vivid reminders of the setting sun'.

66 and 67. Ana Lisa Hedstrom, *Horizontal Shift* and *Kuba*, 2009. Both resist-dyed, pieced and stitched, *Horizontal Shift* is of silk and *Kuba* of linen. The first panel is just over 119 cm (47 in.) high and *Kuba* is larger, at 203 cm (80 in.) high.

65. K. C. Lowe, *Aurora Dreaming the Sea* (detail), 2005. A nuno felt construction of Australian merino wool hand-felted through 33 m (36 yds) of silk crinkle crêpe and silk habotai, hand-dyed with Scottish crottal (caudron-dyed in Tarbert, Isle of Harris), overdyed with a combination of Scottish wode and various Alaskan dye plants, and finished with Lurex and tussah silk surface inclusions.

68

68. Ludwika Zytkiewicz-Ostrowska, *Connections*, 2007. Bringing out the tendency of this shibori-coloured and -pleated silk to roll up, the artist 'did not want to "force" objects to function in unnatural shapes .... My main intention became to seize and register this one moment which I considered as the most expressive.'

69. Mo Kelman, *It Holds What is Gone*, 2006. A sewn construction with a diameter of 61 cm (24 in.), this was created from *mokume* (woodgrain) shibori resist-dyed and shaped silk, black walnut hulls, cotton cord and nails. *Mokume* involves sewing rows of stitches over the entire cloth; gathered tightly, the stitches resist the dye while the heat of the dyepot sets the compressed form.

69

70. **Cathy Moon**, *Insect Fabric* (detail), 2011. The shibori technique of *kumo* stitching is used to create twisted peaks on silk habutai fabric. Three-dimensional shibori fabric often takes on organic forms, and this piece reminded the artist of mythical mountains, so she created larger-than-life beaded insects that 'live' upon them.

71. **Lois Hadfield**, *Good, Evil and All That Lies Between* (detail), 1990–99. Folding and clamping several times (*itijime* shibori) in order to paint on both front and back of the pleated surface, for this silk wearable fabric the artist was able to graduate the colours slowly across the surface, with a dominant colour becoming secondary, and vice versa.

72. **Mandy Southan**, *Fiji – Black Pearl* (detail), 2011. This work displays hand-painted subtleties and a depth of dyed colour that only silk can project. The white areas were maintained with gutta resist. Southan stitched the silk – designed for a dress-in-a-bag – to heat-mouldable polyester to permanently shape it through hand-bound shibori.

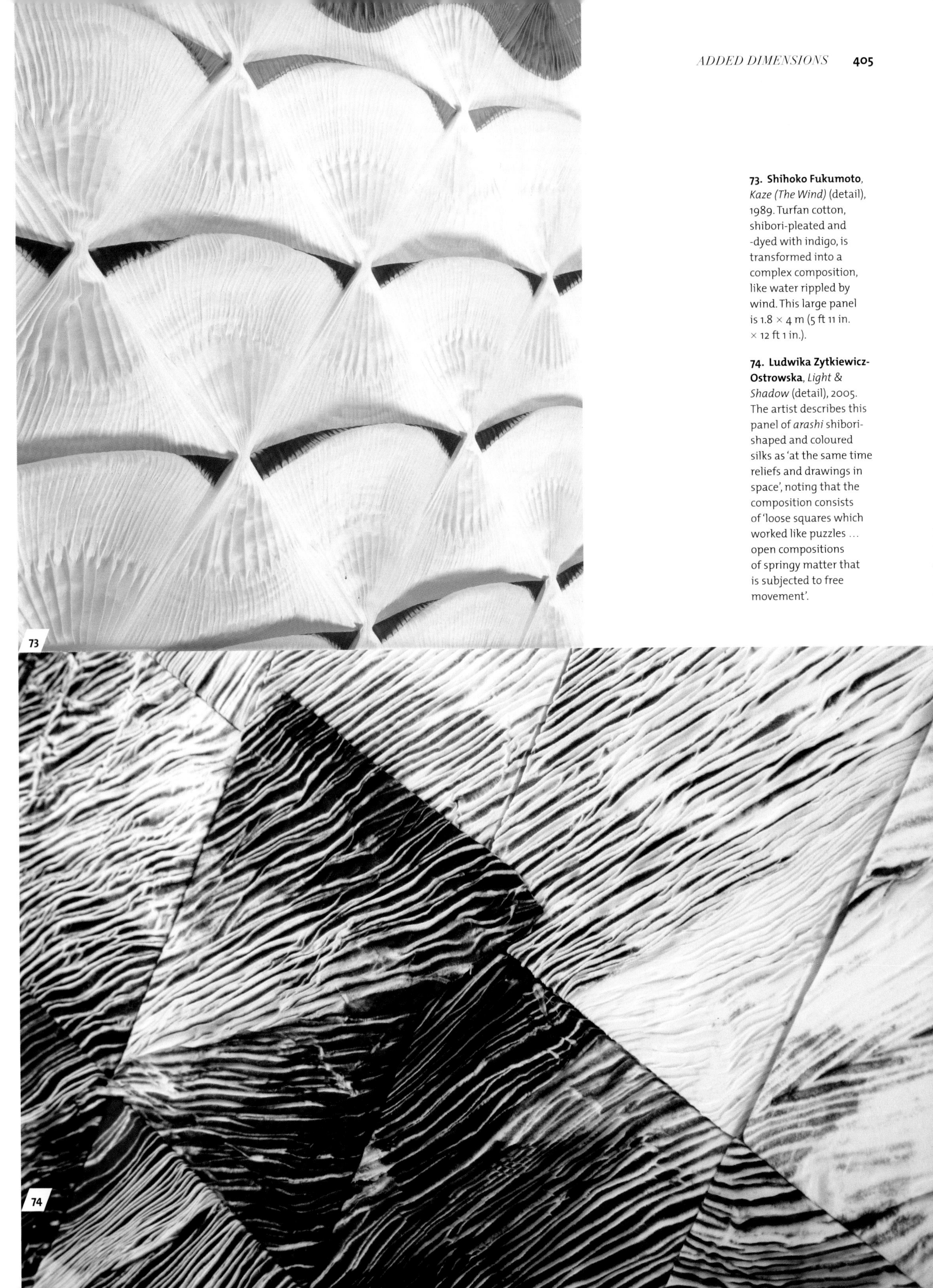

73. Shihoko Fukumoto, *Kaze (The Wind)* (detail), 1989. Turfan cotton, shibori-pleated and -dyed with indigo, is transformed into a complex composition, like water rippled by wind. This large panel is 1.8 × 4 m (5 ft 11 in. × 12 ft 1 in.).

74. Ludwika Zytkiewicz-Ostrowska, *Light & Shadow* (detail), 2005. The artist describes this panel of *arashi* shibori-shaped and coloured silks as 'at the same time reliefs and drawings in space', noting that the composition consists of 'loose squares which worked like puzzles … open compositions of springy matter that is subjected to free movement'.

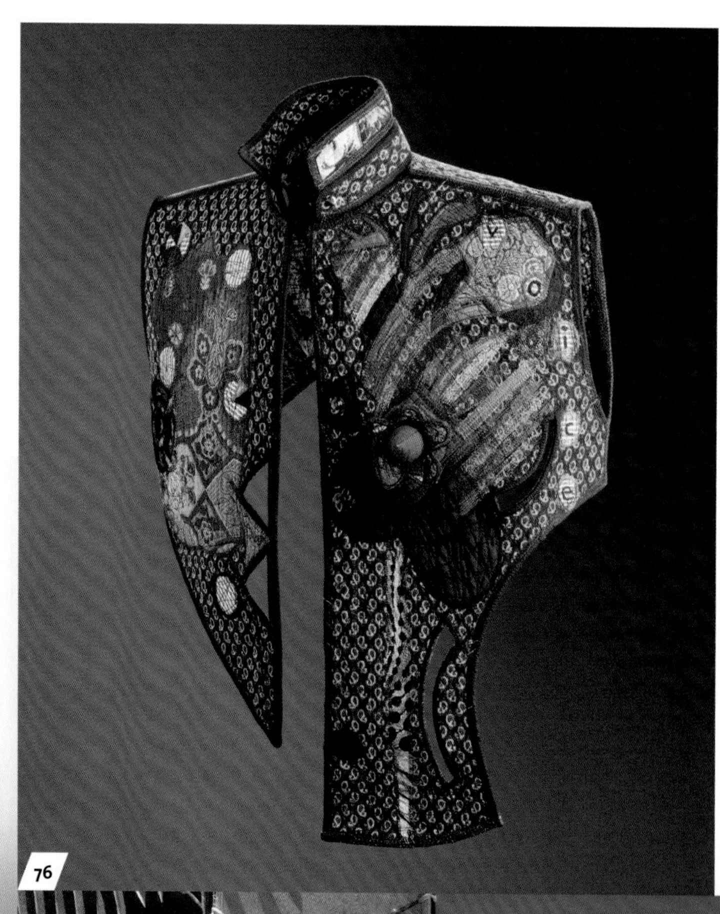

76

75

77

78

78. Ruth Levine, *Alter Aalto*, 2011. Inspired by the smooth and refined lines of Alvar Aalto's classic 1937 vase, this piece explores 'the possibility of its dark side ... alter ego/alter Aalto' through linen canvas made rough and textured with impasto gel and photographic transfer of images of Tasmania's Cradle Mountain. It is stabilized by an internal base of weighted felt.

79. Clyde Olliver, *Still Life*, 2006. Olliver's work reflects his training in textiles, stone-carving and life drawing, all begun when the artist was in his forties. Here a still life is stitched on slates resting on a slate shelf 33 cm (13 in.) long.

75. Sibyl Heijnen, *Colour View*, 1989. This standing sculpture has a height of 1 m (39 in.) and is constructed from rolled, sewn and cut cotton cloth.

76. Kay Kahn, *Voice*, 2011. From the artist's 'Armor Series' and employing both hand and machine stitching, a shirt has been deconstructed, quilted, pieced and appliquéd with silks and cottons, and finally reconstructed. Kahn describes her work as 'a mosaic of fragments, collected experiences, information, and images'.

77. Jennifer Falck Linssen, *Shelter* (detail), 2009. A handcrafted vessel of *katagami*-style handcarved paper also includes archival cotton paper, aluminium, waxed linen, coated copper wire, paint and varnish. It stands close to 50 cm (20 in.) high.

79

80

80. Anne-Marie Wharrie, *Aunt Marie*, 2010. In this work Wharrie pays homage to her aunt, who was head machinist in the family's clothing factory in post-war Sydney, Australia. A handmade wooden dummy is embellished with 'a fractured collection of significant fashion paraphernalia … illustrating my belief that "everything is relative"'.

81. Denise Prefontaine, *Patchwork* (detail), 2011. Drawn to the ephemeral, intangible and playful, the artist has bound dichroic glass with monofilament, to 'animate the inanimate and also to allow for the possibility of change', whether through the effect of wind, the sun's rays or 'dancing shadows in response to light and movement'.

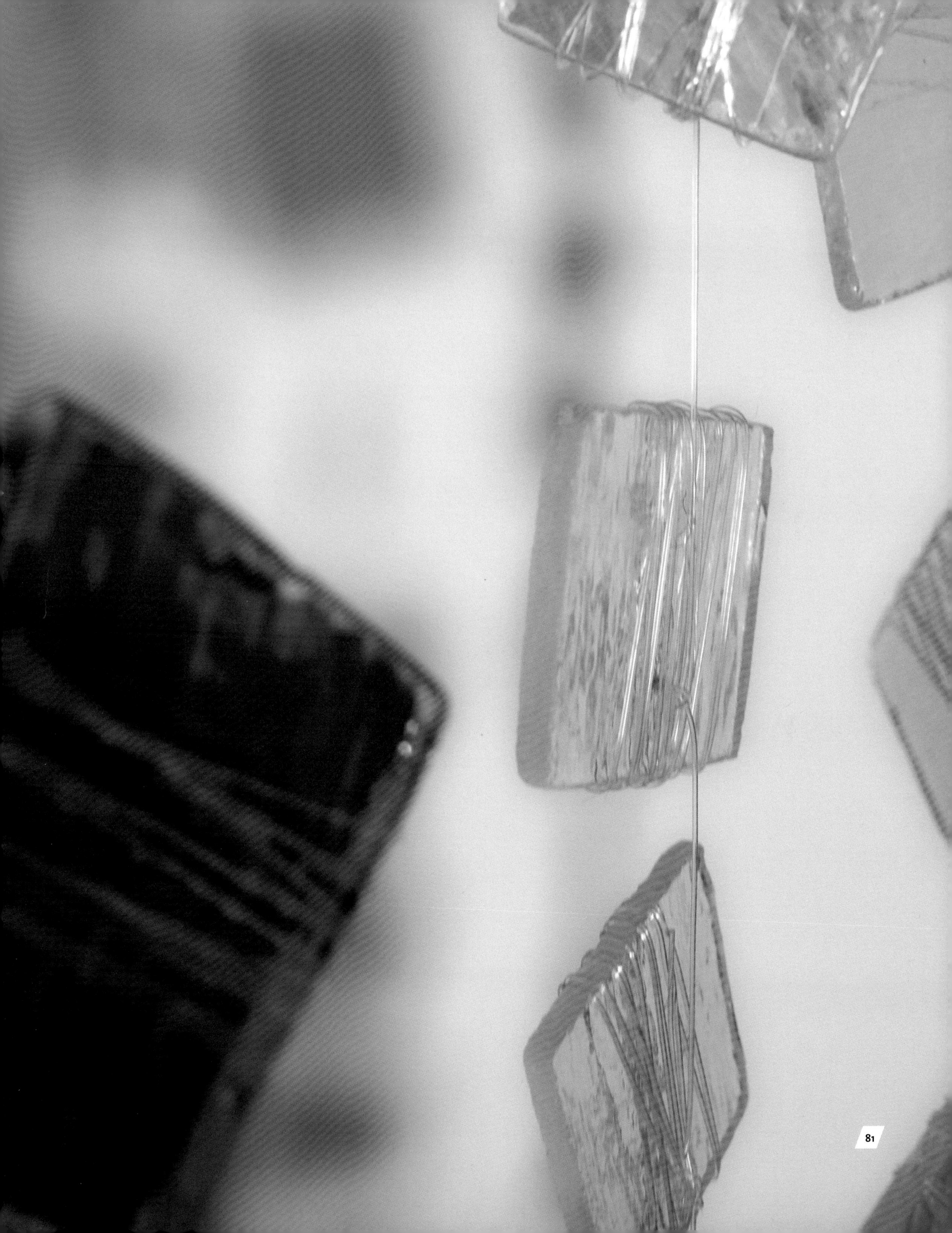

82

82. Bolivian artisan, *Oruro woman's fiesta hat*, 2002. Of stiff off-white wool felt with an acrylic woven hat band and a tin-framed mirror among the hat band decorations, this hat is lavishly enlarged with dyed feathers, acrylic fringe, and wrapped wires with beaded pom-poms and elaborate finials, all secured by the hat band.

83. Tadek Beutlich, *Figures in Cocoons 2*, 1996. Using PVA-soaked cotton wool, modelled over a woven structure of resilient esparto grass, Beutlich developed this technique late in his influential career, during which he became known for strong, sensuous, personal and original woven forms. 'Unless you are a genius, first you must see, and then you are excited, and then you think how you would interpret it.'

84

85

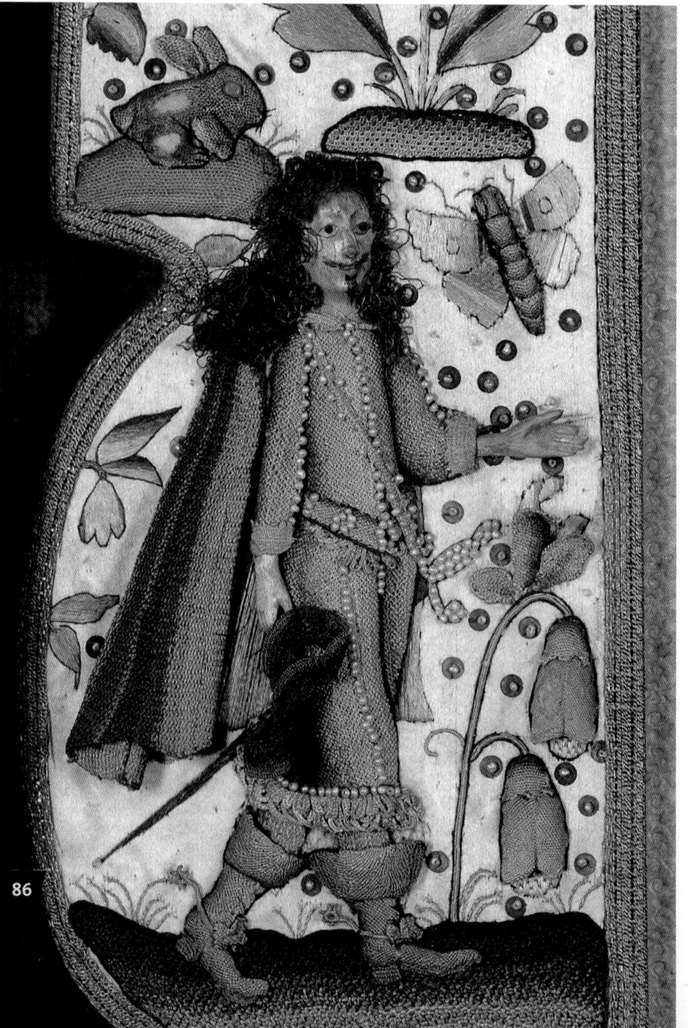

86

84. Julie Montgarrett, *Otherwise: Fragile Facts and Beautiful Fictions Hidden in Plain View,* 2011. Multiple layers of appliquéd monoprinted, screen-printed and digitally printed hand-drawn silks, cottons, polyesters and natural linens were hand- and machine-embroidered to found papers, with sections then cut away: 'like unfinished sentences that fit together ... certainty and logic are replaced by ambiguity and paradox'.

85. Primy Chorley, *Dancing Dolls,* 1986. Inspired by old dolls and toys in doll houses, these figures were stitched with crewel wools, stranded cotton and perlé threads on cotton velvet and Welsh flannel. Their height is 28 cm (11 in.).

86. English embroiderer, *Raised-work and needlework mirror frame* (detail), 1650–70. The creation of raised figures – also known as 'stumpwork' – by skilled amateurs required great skill. The figure here has a padded form and boxwood face and hands, all covered with detached buttonhole, satin and long-and-short stitches, silk-wrapped cord, seed pearls and painted silk.

87

87. Mary Cozens-Walker, *Under the Covers (Utility 5)*, 2005. The British Utility Mark spearheaded a national campaign to 'make do and mend' as part of the war effort. In keeping with this mentality, the artist has used sheets, pillow cases and a blanket from early in her marriage, emphasizing 'the intriguing shapes made by human bodies under the covers'.

88. Christine Atkins, *Convoy*, 2008. Parading over an expanse 53 cm (21 in.) long, these sculptural forms utilize a unique cloth made from Guildford grass (onion weed) and cotton thread, hand-dyed and hand- and machine-sewn to found and constructed objects. Atkins invites us to 'Look deep inside to see the hidden messages and secreted stories.'

89

90

89. Padmaja Krishman, *Precious Seconds*, 2009. One of five laptops inspired by the value of timelessness in India. The screen is of cotton scraps hand-embroidered in the tradition of *kantha*, an embroidery used in Bangladesh and Bengal, and the keyboard is stitched on second-hand cloth. Its message accords with the dialectic highlighted by the artist: 'between past and present, culture and marketing, handicrafts and technology, slow and fast … less and more, the timeless and the disposable'.

90. Janet Cooper, *Landscape of Stitches*, 2011. In a painted pine box 22.9 cm (9 in.) square, secondhand fabric, thread and faint or partly obscured words express the artist's fascination with 'the patinas of the used, the mysteries of the discarded and the themes of memory and the common place'.

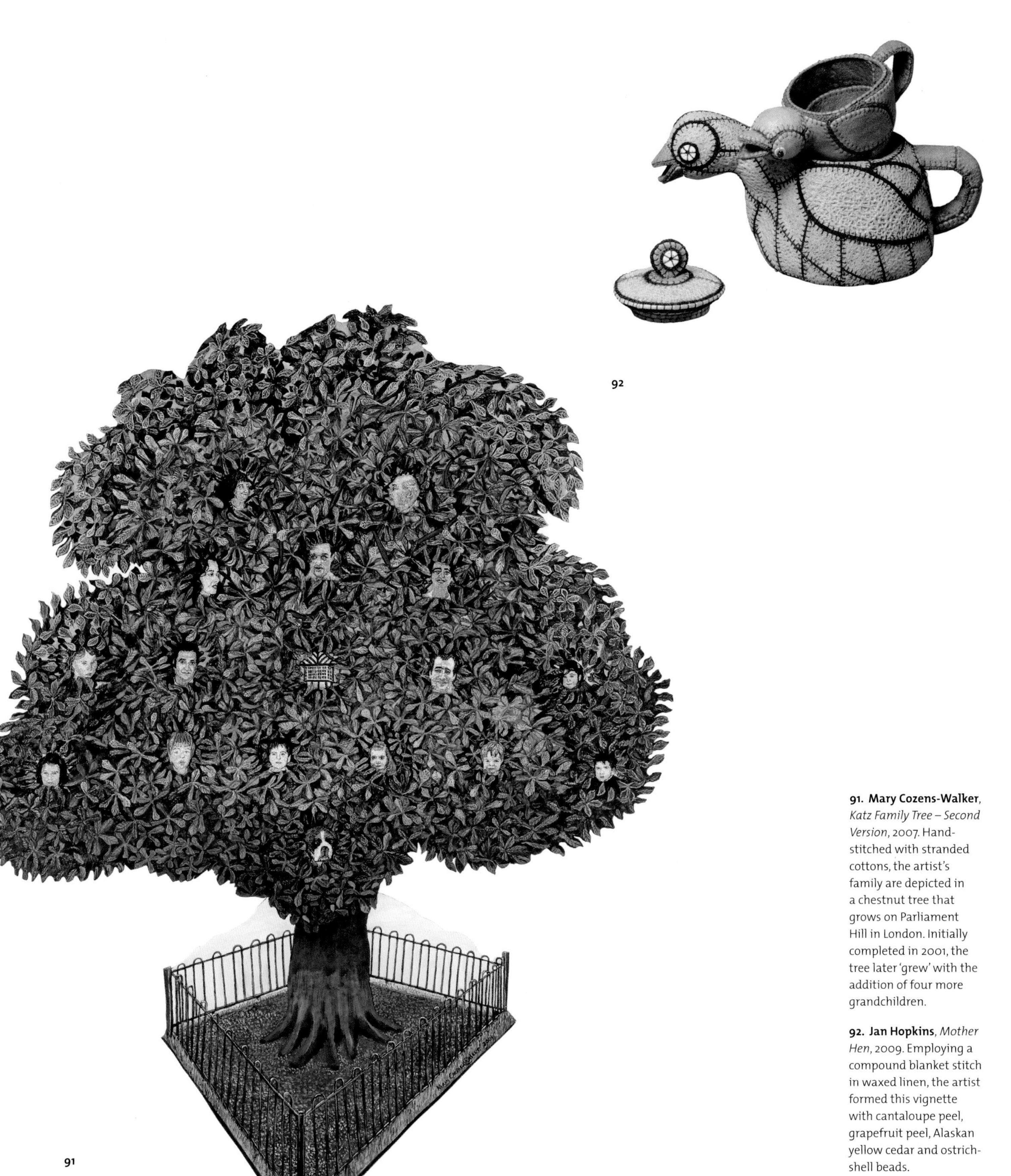

92

91

91. Mary Cozens-Walker, *Katz Family Tree – Second Version*, 2007. Hand-stitched with stranded cottons, the artist's family are depicted in a chestnut tree that grows on Parliament Hill in London. Initially completed in 2001, the tree later 'grew' with the addition of four more grandchildren.

92. Jan Hopkins, *Mother Hen*, 2009. Employing a compound blanket stitch in waxed linen, the artist formed this vignette with cantaloupe peel, grapefruit peel, Alaskan yellow cedar and ostrich-shell beads.

94

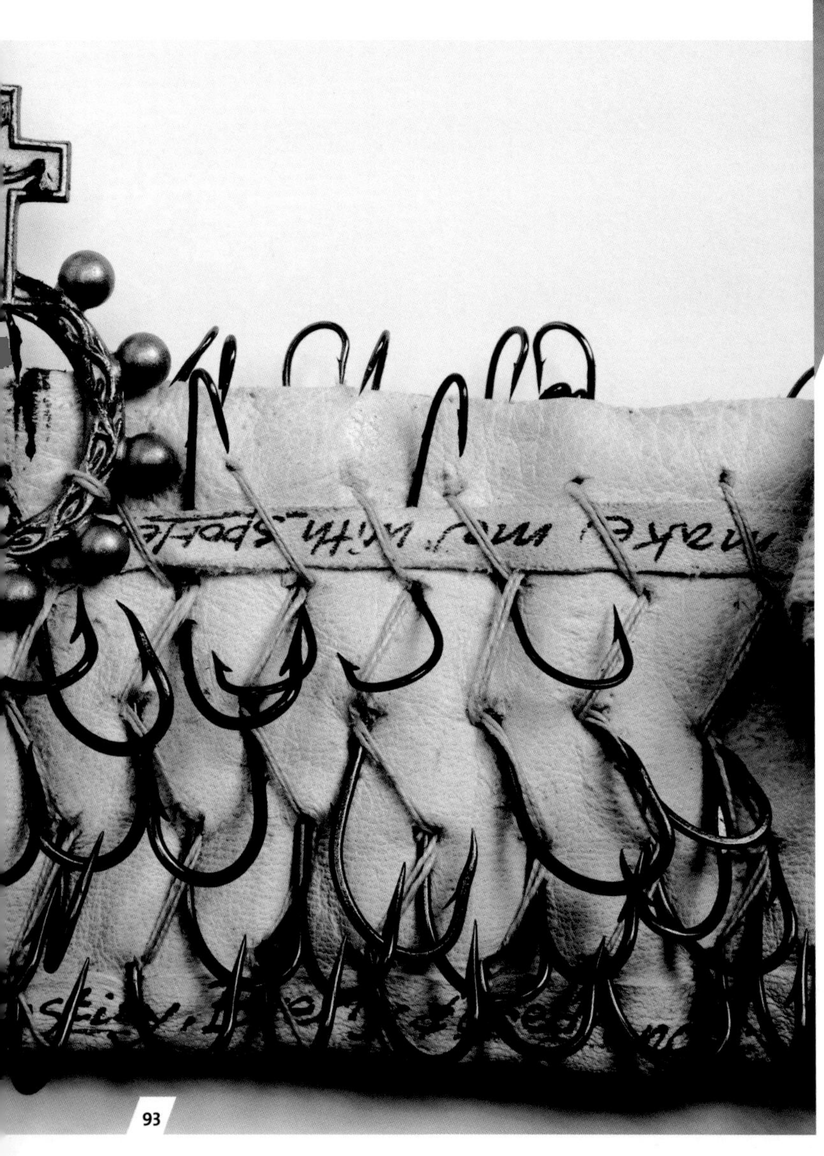

93

93. Rozanne Hawksley, *Penitence I: The Garter of Penitence* (detail), 2006–7. A leather garter laced with fish hooks is inscribed with the words: 'make me with spotless mind, pure heart and chaste body' – a prayer to St Joseph.

94. Denise Stanton, *Untitled 1* (detail), 2007. This hand-felted merino wool vessel incorporates a variety of techniques developed by the artist over the past seven years. One of a series of six vessels, it was inspired by 'the intriguing symbiotic relationships between fungi and their hosts, explored through the sensitive quality of textiles'.

95. Adele Zhang, *Illusion* (detail), 1999. Machine stitches control the patterns and the areas where texture is needed on this cloqué fabric, while a chemical reaction with lye-treated silk on cotton gauze causes shrinkage of various shapes and sizes. This provides flexibility but also control, allowing seamless fitting in wearable creations of any imaginable silhouette.

96. Val James, *Coat of Dreams* (detail), 2010. Traditional seams were eliminated in this coat, thus preserving the sheer quality of the fabrics. It is patterned in tonal colours and manipulated to introduce texture through free embroidery, reverse appliqué and twin-needle stitching.

97. American dressmaker, *Sleeveless chemise dress* (detail), mid-1920s. This three-tiered hem with alternating tabs was machine-embroidered with clear glass beads and rhinestones.

98. Jo Ann Stabb, *Swan Song: My Last Academic Plan Ever!* (detail), 2002. Recycled and reshaped industrial silk scraps cover the outside of this coat. Stamped inside are the following goals: 'Proposals of ideas; Revisit and Revision of ideas; Analysis of relevance; Integration of ideas and paradigms; Analysis of impact; Compression of ideas; Analysis of Critical MASS; Resource Allocation; RE-allocation of Resources; The BOTTOM LINE.' Dollar signs encircle the interior hem.

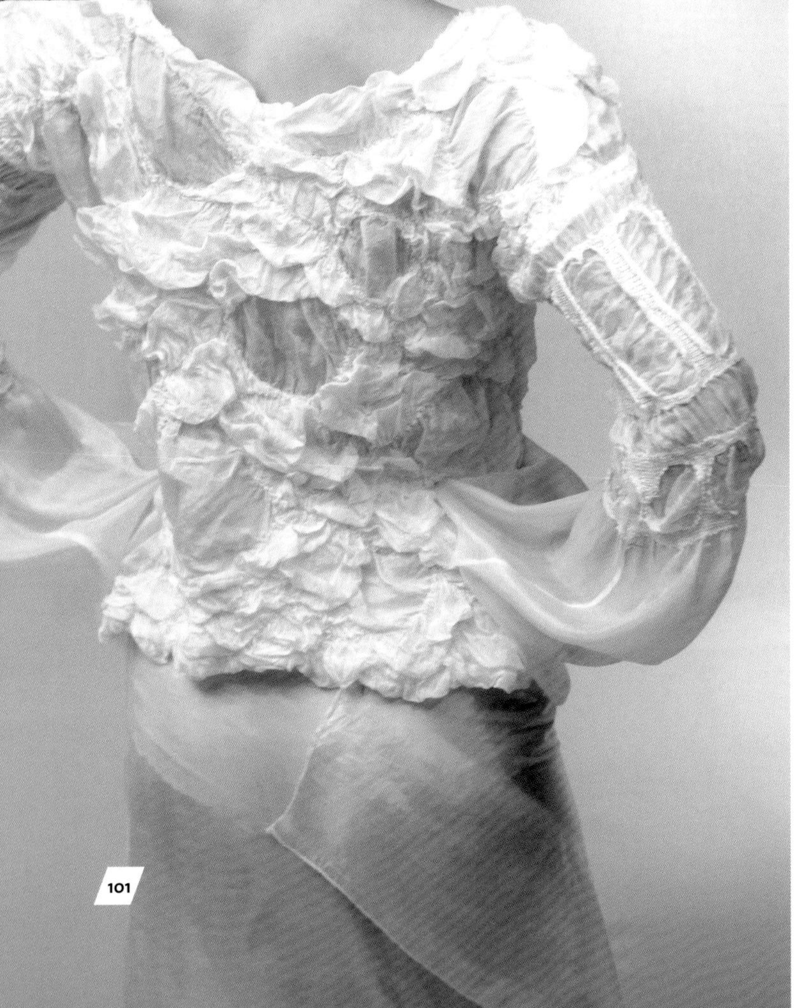

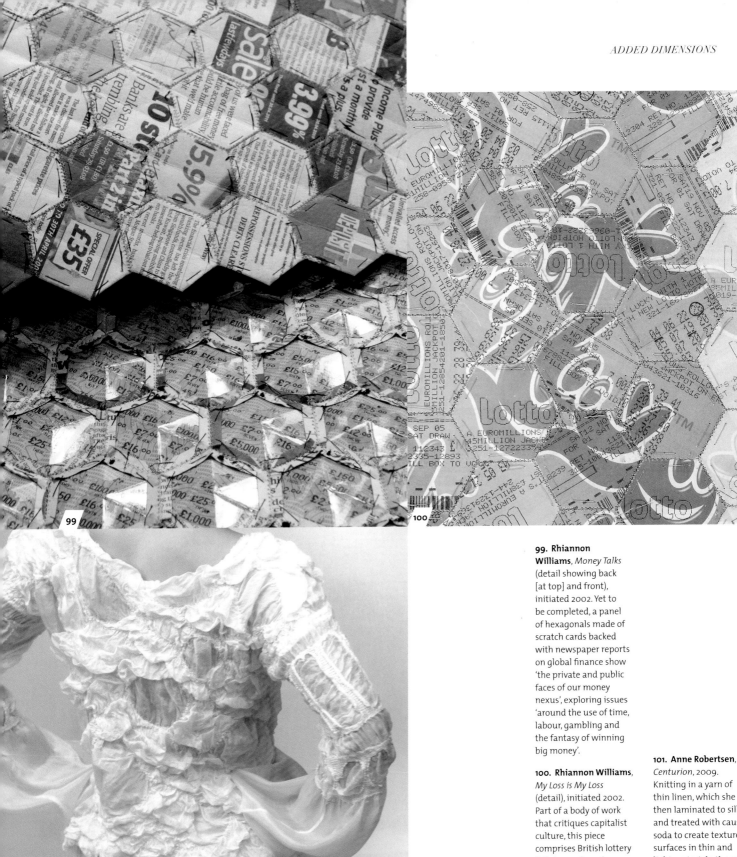

99. Rhiannon Williams, *Money Talks* (detail showing back [at top] and front), initiated 2002. Yet to be completed, a panel of hexagonals made of scratch cards backed with newspaper reports on global finance show 'the private and public faces of our money nexus', exploring issues 'around the use of time, labour, gambling and the fantasy of winning big money'.

100. Rhiannon Williams, *My Loss is My Loss* (detail), initiated 2002. Part of a body of work that critiques capitalist culture, this piece comprises British lottery tickets purchased every week. By 2011 the artist had spent over £4,500, and the work was 4.5 m (14 ft 9 in.) long. She says: 'the collection and slow accumulation of paper patches serve to dramatize consumer culture.'

101. Anne Robertsen, *Centurion*, 2009. Knitting in a yarn of thin linen, which she then laminated to silk and treated with caustic soda to create textured surfaces in thin and light materials, the artist used a knitting machine to get the jersey effect. She desribes herself as 'always exploring ways to find interesting surfaces, thin and light qualities, and wearable and comfortable elasticity'.

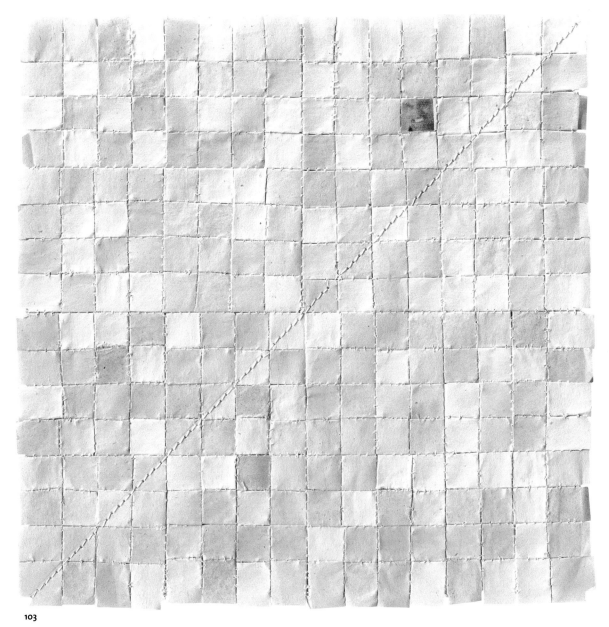

103

104

102. Deepa Panchamia, *1445 Pockets* (detail), 2005. Silk organza is manipulated through cutting, pleating and stitching, exploiting the material's transparency to emphasize the interaction between inner and outer spaces. Panchamia's intention is to produce 'delicate shadows and intricate tonal details that … intensify the linear motion and contours of the work'.

103. Jennifer Vickers, *Presence of Absence – 16 x 16* (detail), 2010. This is a section of a memorial patchwork quilt made of newsprint, hand- and machine-stitched, and backed with tissue. It contrasts blank squares representing the estimated number of civilians killed since the beginning of the Iraq War in 2003 with press images of the first 100 British military casualties.

104. Jane Clark, *Woven Light*, 2008. The darkness of black cotton warps and the brightness of fibre-optic thread wefts, woven in an undulating twill, provide essential contrasts: 'the handwoven and the electrical element – remove one of these and the piece has no substance. It is this dependence upon each other, this unity, that allows us to achieve.'

105. Barbara Shapiro, *Fragments II*, 1988. Handwoven silk has been coloured through shibori-dyeing, discharge, and with pigments, and then pieced to form a panel 86.4 cm (34 in.) square. The artist's wall pieces 'speak of historic textiles of many cultures, burnished with the patina of time'.

106. Ludwika Zytkiewicz-Ostrowska, *Blue*, 2007. A grid of squares, each composed of nine smaller *arashi* shibori-pleated and -dyed silk squares, forms this wall hanging. The module arrangement was imposed in order to control the shibori technique, through which the artist 'made order ... by means of direction, movement and value changes'.

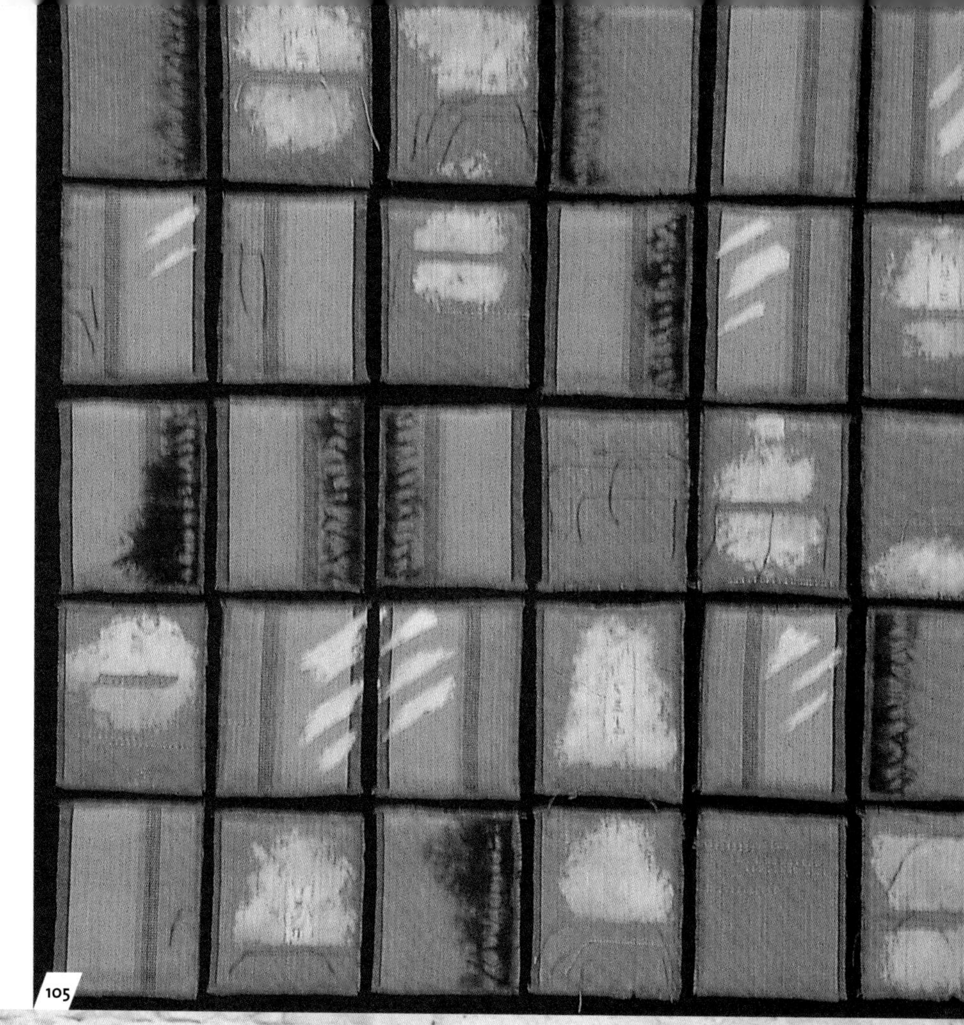

108

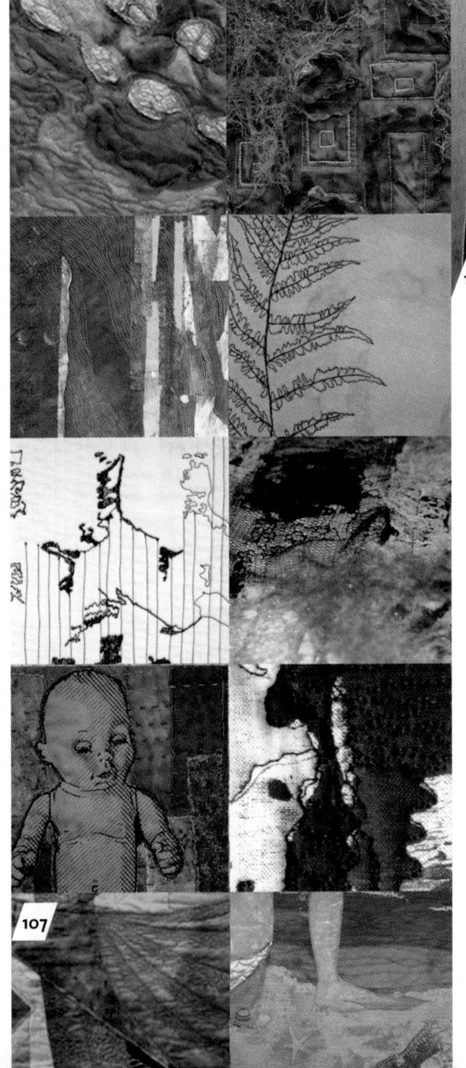

107. TeXui, *Group quilt*, 2011. TeXui is a group of ten Dutch fibre artists, founded in 2003. From left to right, starting at the top, the squares are by Jelly Dijkstra, Annette Jeukens, Rita Berghuis, Marjon Hoftijzer, Willy Doreleijers, Jacqueline de Jong, Elke Boesewinkel, Hanne Capel, Coby Brinkhuis and Marjon Hoftijzer.

108. Jennifer Shellard, *Project 2*, 2010. From a body of work focused on light and colour, investigating visual perception through time-based installations, handwoven textiles here reflect projected colours, engineered to change gradually while the eye adapts.

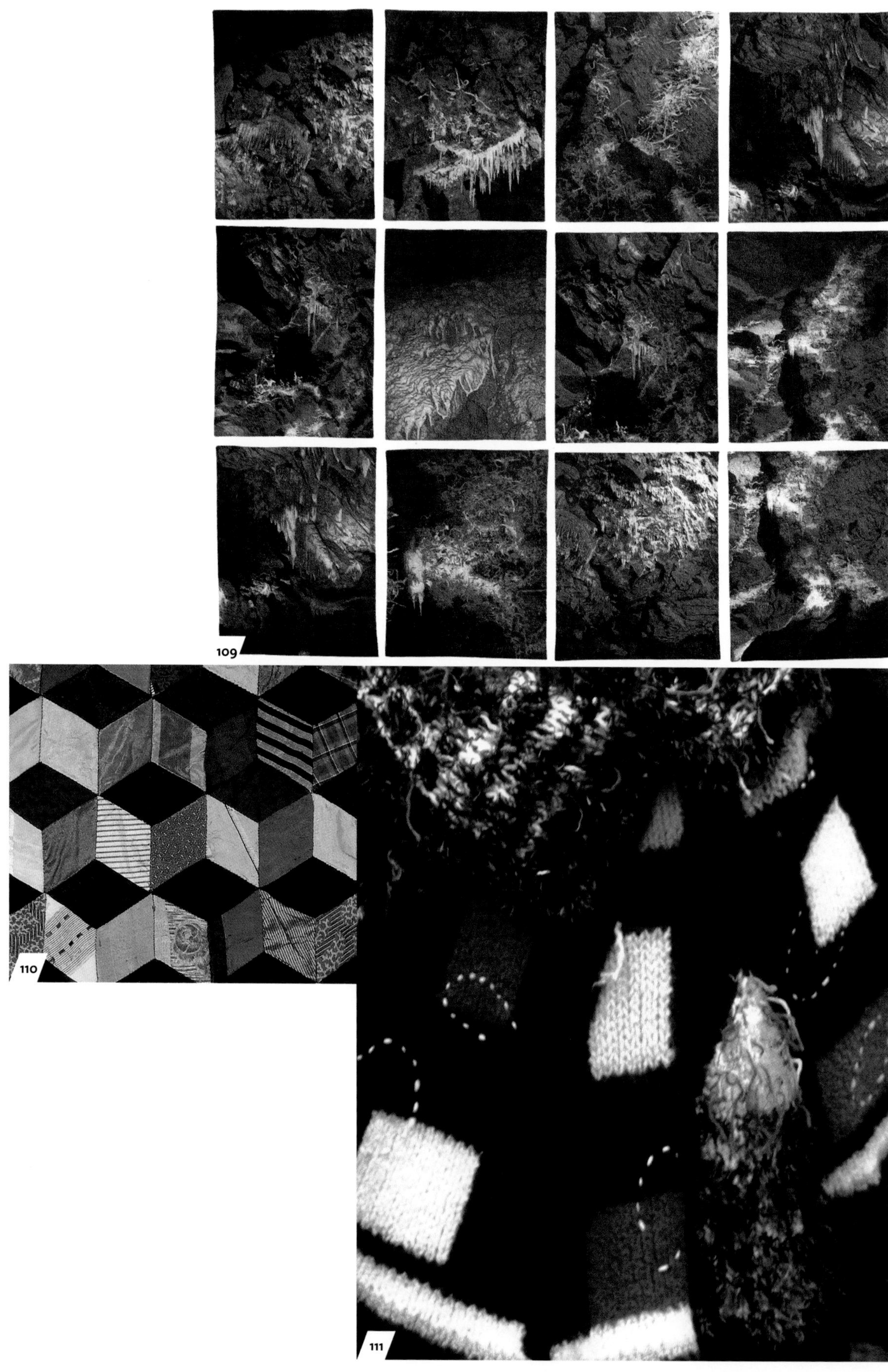
109
110
111

109. Susan Taber Avila, *Cave Stitchings*, 2009. Composed of twelve individual pieces of free machine stitching on digitally printed hemp backed with Ingeo (the trademark name for NatureWorks LLC's synthetic fibre made from corn), this work is roughly 147 cm (58 in.) square.

110. American quilter, *Pieced bedcover* (detail), *c.* 1870. Solid-coloured and printed silks are arranged in the 'baby blocks' or 'tumbling blocks' pattern.

111. Janet Lipkin, *Geometry* (detail), 2007. Hand-knitted gored short coat of wool and polyester yarn, felted and embroidered.

112. African Canadian artist (attributed), *Coverlet*, 1920s. Appliquéd coverlet using cotton seed sacking and recycled household textiles, mainly of wool. Arranged into fifteen squares and five 'slivers' of squares, it measures 127 × 203 cm (50 × 80 in.).

113. Shipibo Indian embroiderer, *Tubular skirt* (front detail), before 1968. From Pucalpa, Peru, the geometric design is formed of appliquéd strips of white and blue cotton and blue rickrack, with orange embroidery thread in chain and straight stitches completing the design.

114. French or English embroider, *Bed valance* (detail), late 16th century. Drawn work on fine linen, accented with green and peach-coloured silk embroidery.

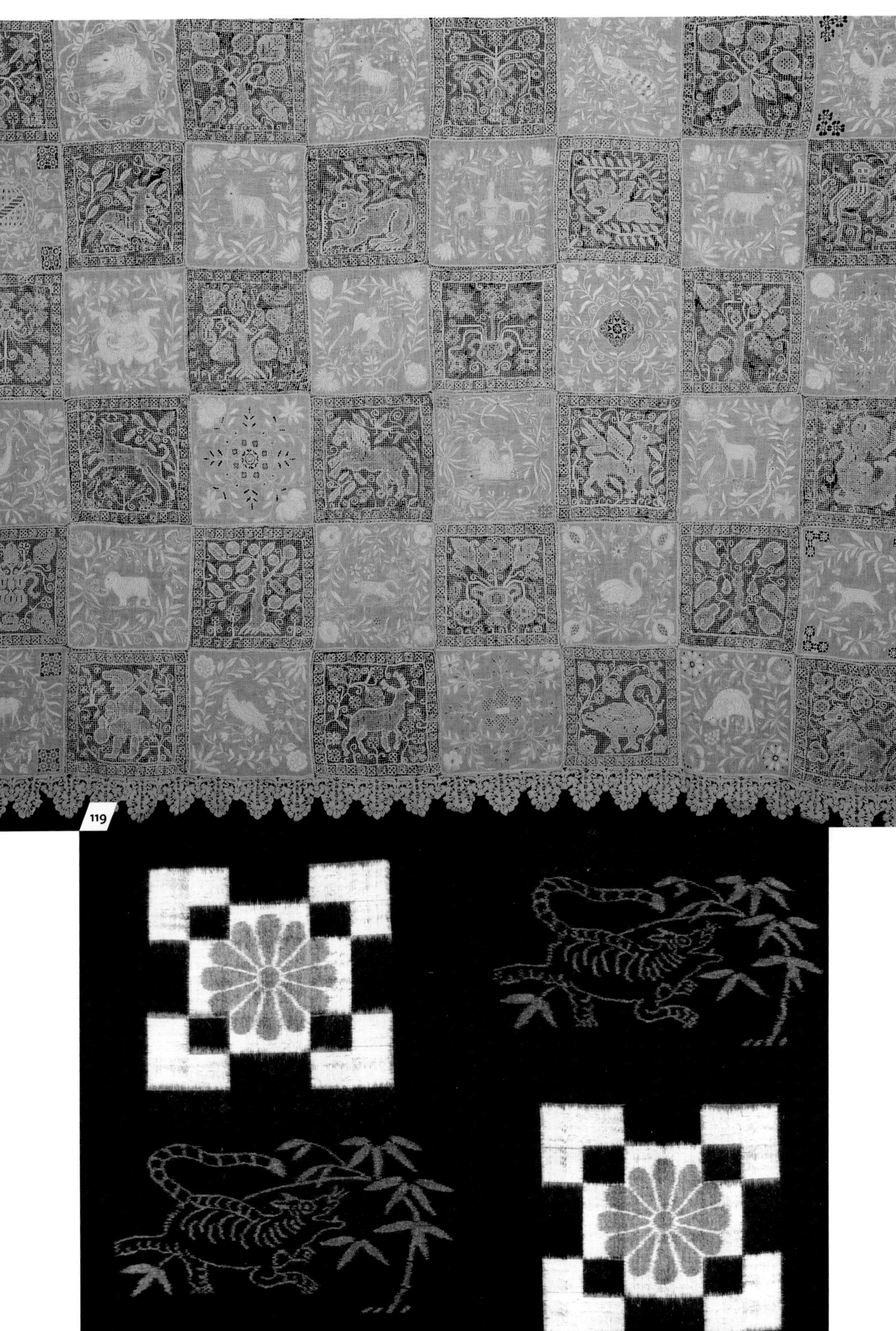

115. Persian embroiderer, *Presentation purse* (detail), 1890–99. This small purse is of overwrapped cut and drawn work on muslin, with a drawn work border. It was made to be given by a virgin bride to her mother; ultimately it was a gift to Sir Thomas Wardle from Caspar Purdon Clarke, then director of what was to become the Victoria and Albert Museum, London.

116. Pakistani embroiderer, *Wall hanging* (detail), before 1988. These bold blocks and their surrounding grid were produced using reverse appliqué.

117. American machine-lace manufacturer, *Bicentennial lace yardage* (detail), 1976. This 'patchwork' of imagery commemorating the United States Bicentennial was made on a Leavers lace machine, perfected in 1813.

118. Italian maker, *Table cover*, *c.* 1580–1600. Epitomizing the refinement and luxury of European furnishings of the period, four ornate needlace designs – all different – alternate with embroidered squares of *punto tagliato*, the Italian term for cutwork. The entire cloth is of linen.

119. French embroiderer, *Whitework coverlet*, 1600–25. Combining embroidery, lacis and cutwork, this composition of squares juxtaposes emblematic imagery representing mystical and mythical concepts.

120. Japanese weaver and dyer, *Futon cover* (detail), 20th century. Of seamed, narrow cotton cloths, the tiger and bamboo motifs appear as a result of indigo *kasuri* (weft ikat). The geometric shapes are double ikat.

121. American embroiderer, *Table carpet*, *c.* 1840–45. Appliquéd woollen squares have been joined together, their seams accentuated with couched cord. Here arranged symmetrically around the central motif, patterns such as these are also found on quilts and by this date were available in printed form.

122. Tibetan Buddhist maker, *Ritual patchwork*, probably 19th century. Here composed of 18th-century brocades, such patchworks were often found in Buddhist monasteries and were said to represent the absence of the Buddha. The act of stitching ritual textiles, like the copying of Buddhist scriptures, was considered a devotional pursuit. A literal translation of the word *sutra* (denoting the Buddha's teachings) is 'a stitch with intent'.

123

123. Dutch maker, *Patchwork coverlet*, *c.* 1795–1800. With the founding of the Dutch East India Company in 1602, Indian chintzes became plentiful in Holland. Here, examples from the 1770s and 1780s are combined with French printed cottons (featuring geometric and abstract patterns), which were the sole option after the Netherlands fell to French Revolutionary forces in 1794.

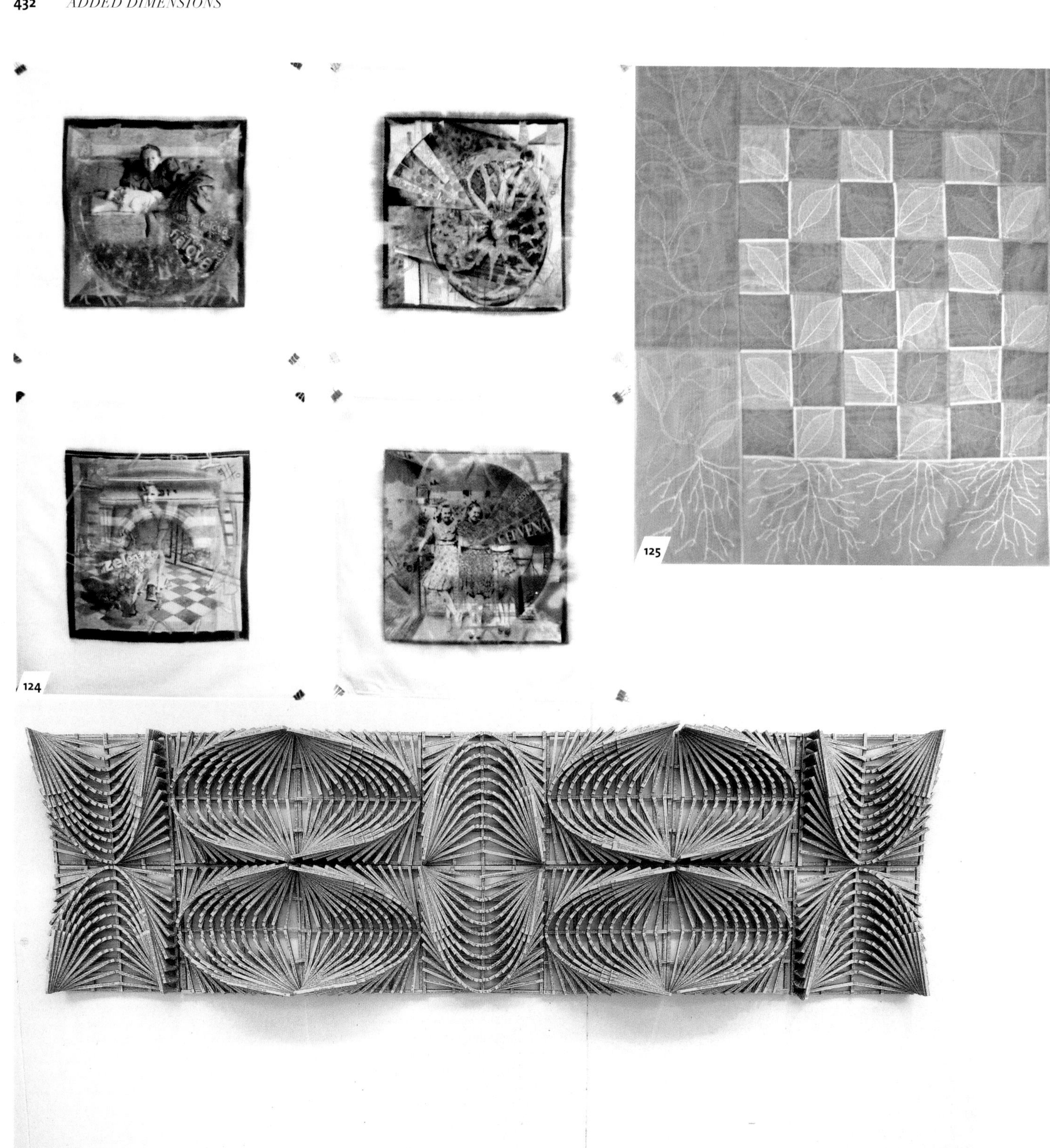

124

125

126

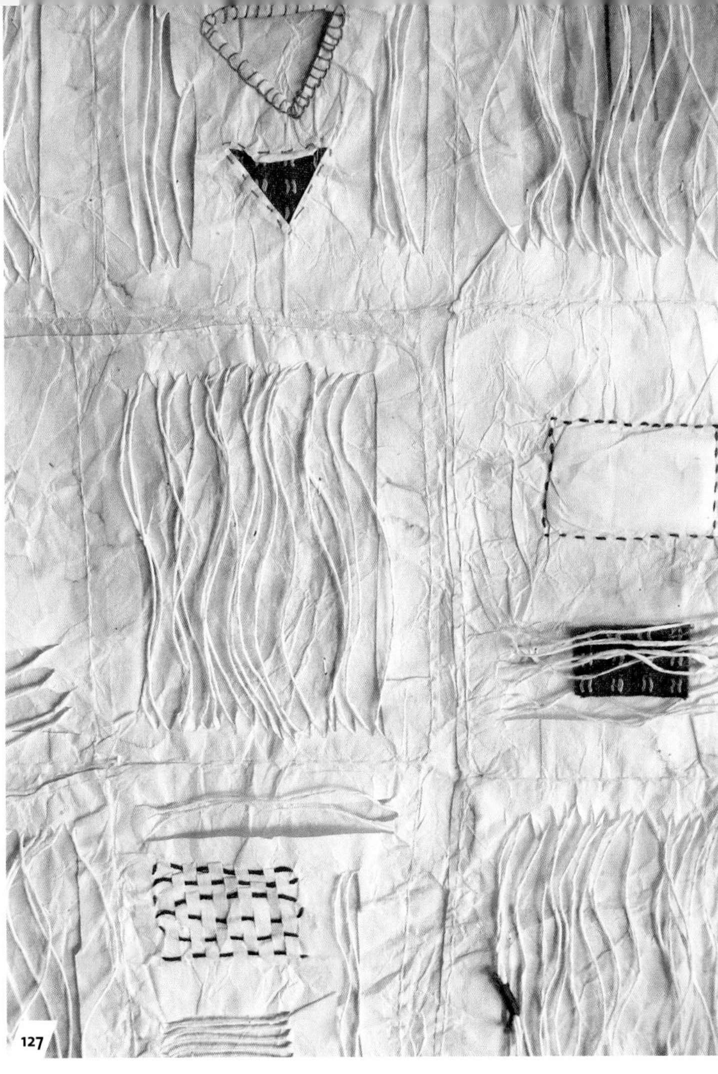

127

128

129

124. Leslie Nobler, *Prismatic Prague: 4 'Pages'*, 2010. Incorporating mixed media, digital art, transfer-printing, acrylic paint, dye and pencil on brocade, these panels 'reimagine priceless museum-quality objects .... The vast value of the art history, heritage and "soul" connected with these majestic, *unearthed* artefacts is so critical to making electronic art more "human" and more touchable.'

125. Nancy Crasco, *Growing Off the Grid*, 2009. Embroidering with silk organza and skeleton leaves, the artist cites the influence of Japanese *kesa* and Korean *pojagi*, both of which combine silk scraps into a single piece of cloth.

126. Mandy Gunn, *TEXT-ile Series, Tasmanian Story (For the Term of His Natural Life)*, 2011. This work is composed in part from cardboard constructions of collaged book text, taken from Marcus Clarke's 1874 novel about convicts in Australia, *For the Term of His Natural Life*. The remainder of the book was shredded and woven on a cotton warp into a scroll.

127. Sandy Webster, *Threadlines and Bloodlines* (detail), 2010. Webster made this work in memory of her mother and grandmother, who taught her to sew. *Threadlines* is composed of stitched and slit Thai *kozo* paper and a recycled dish towel.

128. Indian artisans, *Patchwork* (detail), before 1994. This pieced quilt, composed of a medley of recycled, primarily cotton materials, was purchased by Sandy Webster for her personal collection.

129. Gloria Hansen, *Squared Illusion 6*, 2007. Using silk fabrics, pastels, coloured pencils and fabric paint with machine-piecing and quilting, the artist explores visual ambiguities expressed in cloth and stitch.

130. Silke, *The Creation of Humanity According to the Popol Vuh*, 1993. The *Popol Vuh* (*Book of the People*) is a corpus of Pre-Columbian mythological-historical narratives from Guatemala's western highlands. Employing a range of stitch and appliqué techniques, this silk panel is 175 × 250 × 80 cm (69 × 98½ × 31½ in.).

131. Yderne, *Karen*, 2010. Made by a Danish quilt art group taught by Charlotte Yde, this depicts the writer Karen Blixen, best known for her book *Out of Africa*. Its members are Birgitte Aabye, Lisbet Borggreen, Kirsten Holm, Birgit Dam-Jensen, Evy Quistgaard and Hanne Stummann.

132. Cynthia Schira, *Jazz*, 2007. Made of cotton woven on a Jacquard loom in a tapestry-warp structure, with other materials collaged onto the top panel, this work, 264 cm (104 in.) wide, expresses the artist's fascination with visual notation methods or systems specific to different professions, whether musicians, weavers, architects or mathematicians.

133. Janet Haigh, *Safety Curtain – Burka Eyes* (detail), 2010. Hand- and machine-stitched faggoting and appliqué of silk, wool, cotton and rayon cloth combine with cut and engraved copper and vitreous enamelling to form this artist's thoughtful commentary on the burqa and individuality.

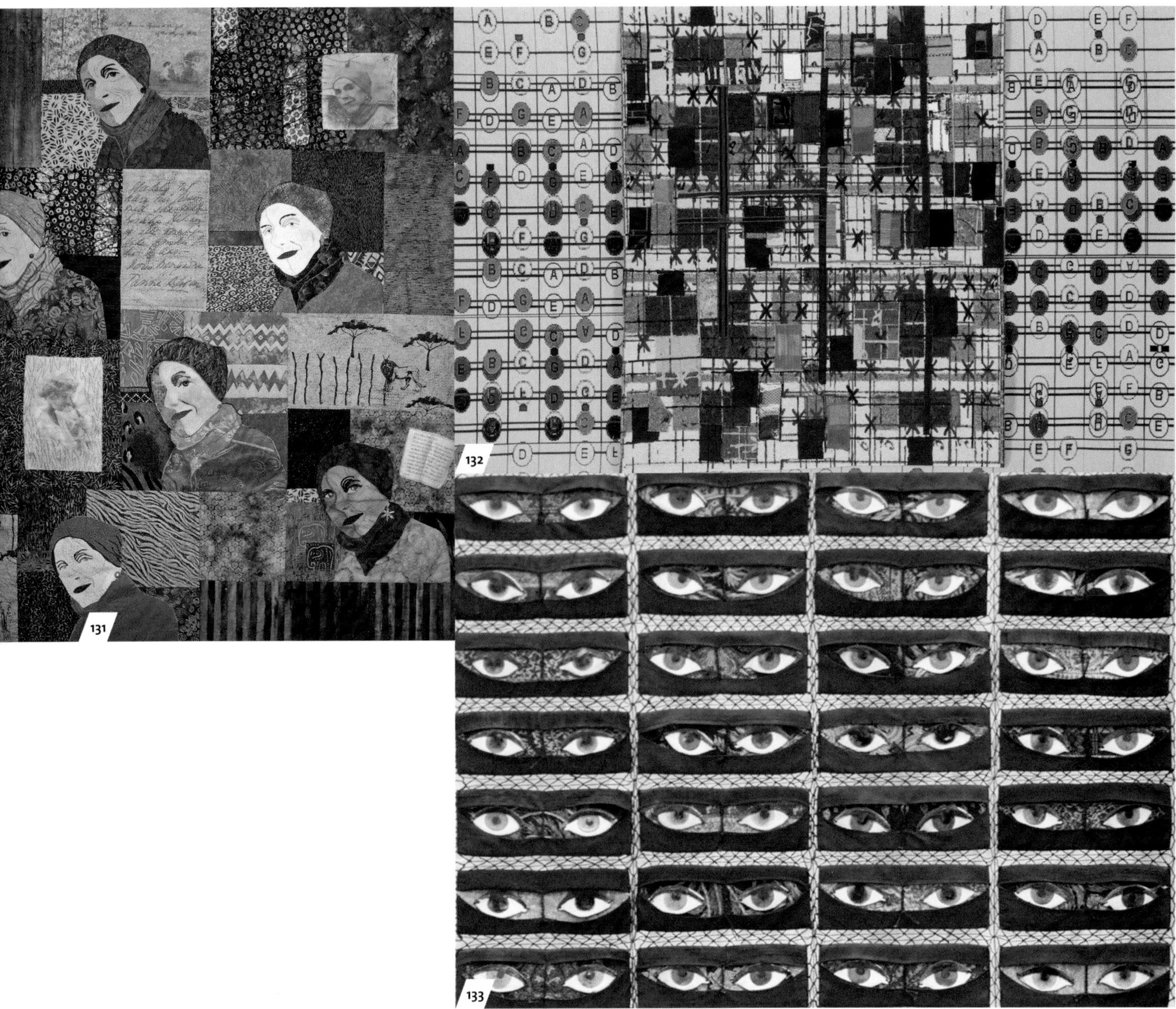

134 and 135. Rosemary Huggins, *The Poisoned Heart* (detail), 2011, and *Lady of Guadalupe* (135; detail), 2010. Influenced by the elaborate textiles of Mexico, the artist has incorporated mixed media, including materials collected from Oaxaca and Chiapas, into a hand-embroidered altar covering and machine-embroidered panel. The latter is a specific response to a street shrine to the Virgin of Guadalupe, housed in Mexico City.

134
135
136
137
138

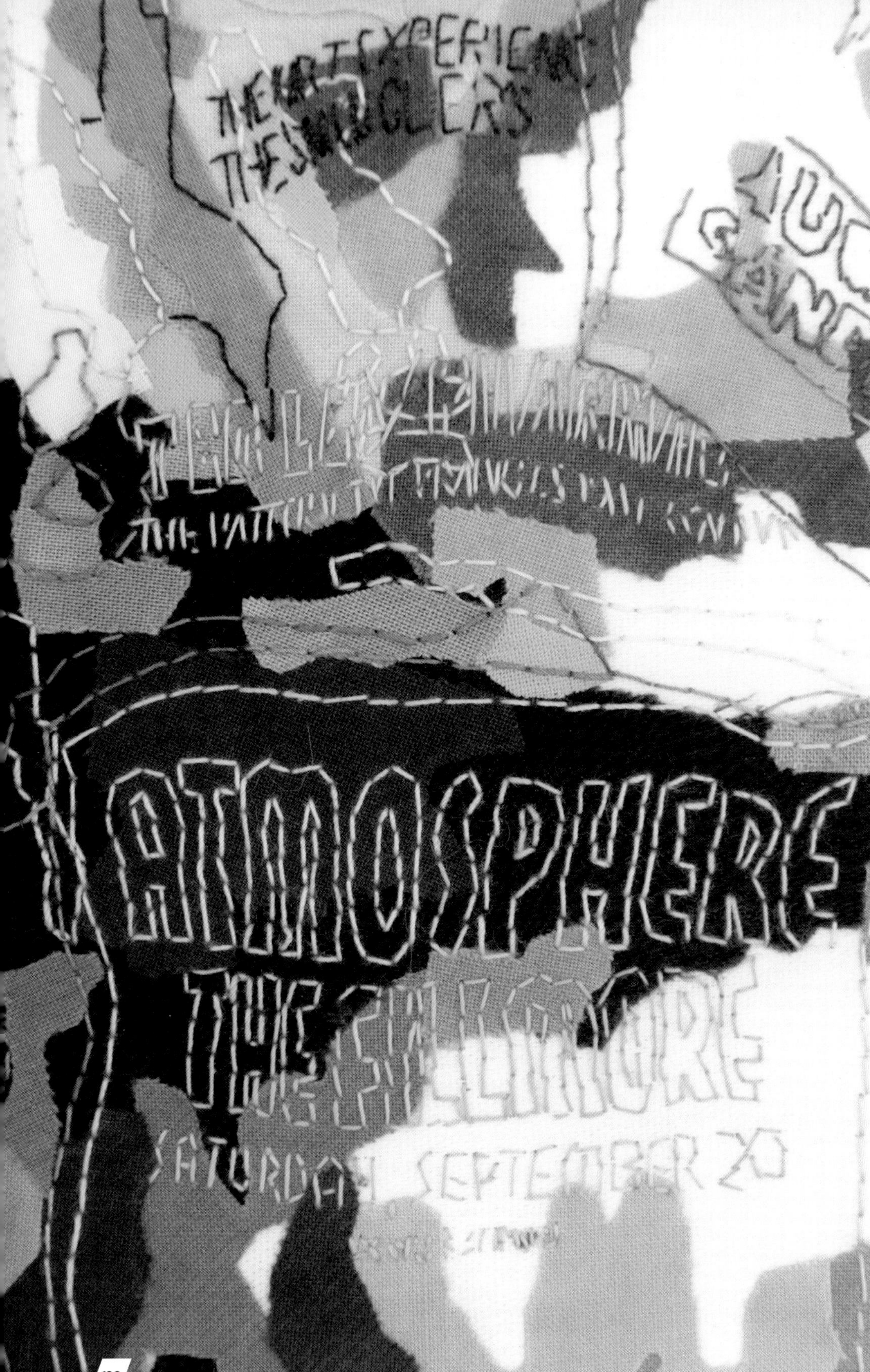

139

136. Tracy Jamar, *After Rain* (detail), 2002. Hand-hooked and appliquéd with machine-sewn accents on monk's cloth, this work is composed of fabrics and yarns of wool, cotton and synthetics, and glass beads. Many are repurposed personal items: 'Using the fabrics of everyday life to document an event, memory or image makes that which is personal public.'

137. Persian artisan, Rasht, *Domestic hanging or curtain* (detail), 19th century. On the Caspian Sea, Rasht had been a major centre of silk-trading and -weaving, but it gave its name to this form of appliqué of slightly felted wool, couched with cut-out details and over-embroidered. Most examples were exported to the western Caucasus and southern Russia.

138. Mexican embroiderer, *Lectern hanging*, *c.* 1730. This Passiontide hanging is densely worked with embroidery in polychrome silks and a variety of metallic threads. Completed with metallic braid, it measures 43.2 × 79.4 cm (17 × 31¼ in.).

139. Marty Jonas, *Vertical Litter* (detail), 2004. About 6 m (20 ft) long and 76.2 cm (30 in.) wide, this embroidered collage results from the artist's documentation of 'the unintentional art produced by years of anonymous contributors stapling advertising flyers to telephone poles'. The dyed, cut and collaged cotton fabrics have added details (distilled from photographs) hand-embroidered in silk.

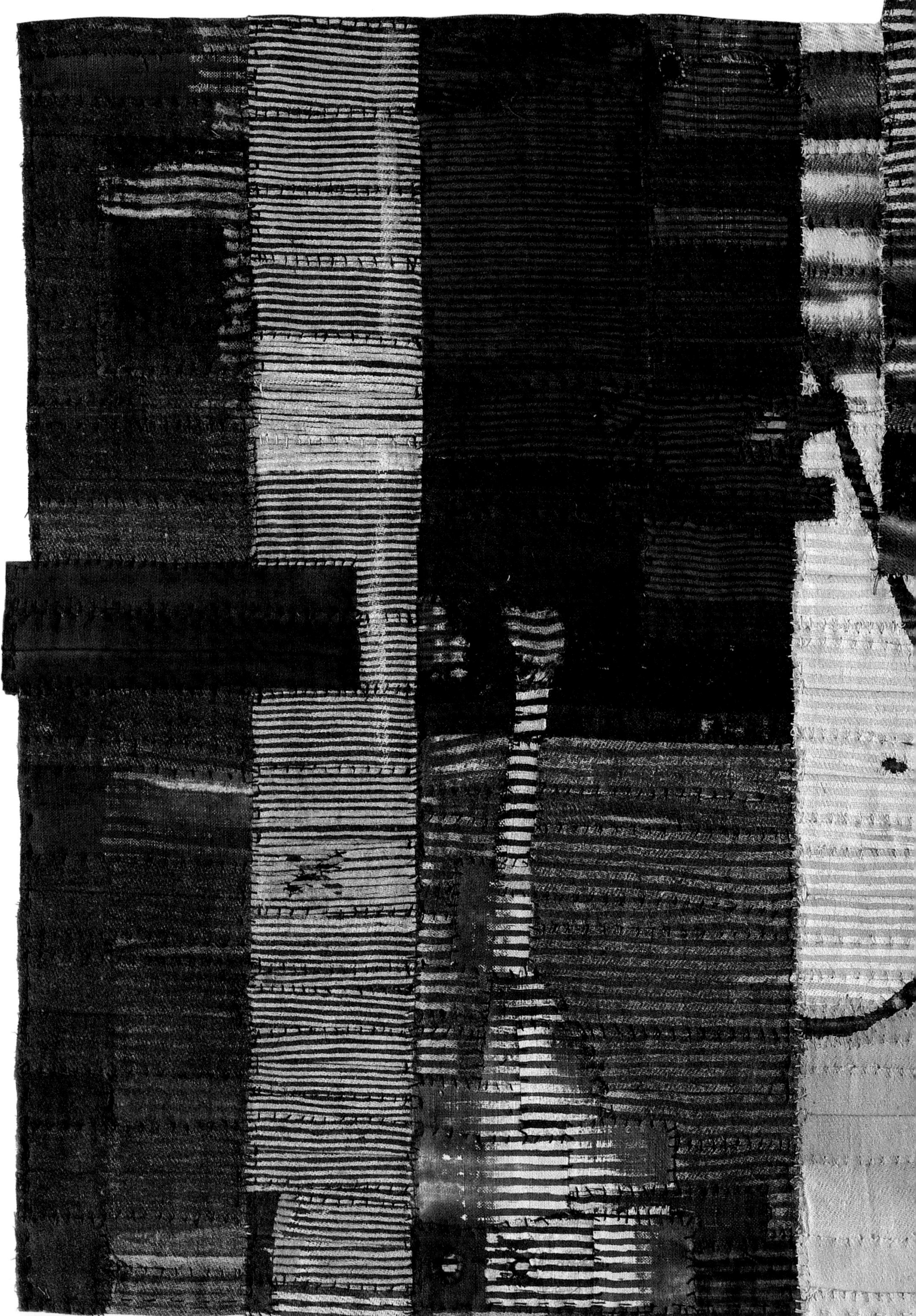

141

142

144

140. Matthew Harris, *Aoyama Window Cloth No. II*, 2009. This work was built in sections and constructed through a process of cutting, piecing and roughly stitching. Harris has made a deliberately imperfect cloth through tears, patches, darns and frayed edges, creating a visual jolt that gives the work a purposeful discordance.

141. Pauline Burbidge, *Under the Waterfall*, 2004. Layers of transparent, painted and pleated fine cotton fabrics were stitched and quilted by machine and hand to form this square panel. Burbidge was inspired to create this piece after walking under the waterfall in Watkins Glen, upstate New York.

142. Pauline Burbidge, *Applecross Quilt* (detail), 2007. Fine cotton and silk fabrics stitched, pleated, painted and quilted, both by machine and hand, capture both the landscape and the spiritual atmosphere that surrounds Applecross, which overlooks Skye on the north-western coast of Scotland.

143. Jun-ichi Arai, *Polyester/Heat Transfer*, 1980s. This polyester cloth, with multiple applications of gentle crush and heat-pressing with sheet-disperse dyes, illustrates Arai's innovations, which have contributed to the subsequent widespread use of this technique. Like his other textiles shown here, this example epitomizes Arai's marriage of craft and industry.

144. Jun-ichi Arai, *Crocodile*, 1980s. With a warp made of polyphenylene sulphide slit-yarn coated with aluminium, and a weft of wool, the cloth for *Crocodile* was partially shrunk through shibori (bound resist) and a heat-transfer treatment.

145. Jun-ichi Arai, *Nunome-gara (Cloth-eye pattern)*, 1982–83. A digitized design process and computer-Jacquard loom created this highly textured wool and acrylic cloth. Arai was the first to pioneer computerized Jacquard knit and weave machines, which facilitated the addition of supplementary warps and complex combinations of structure and materials.

146

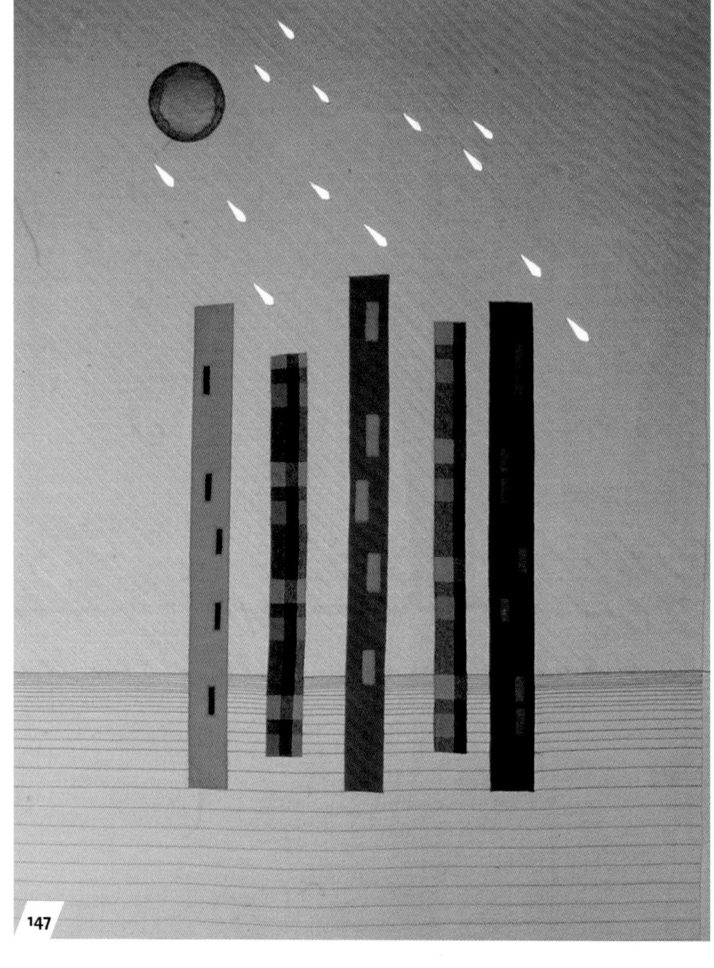

147

146. Greg Somerville, *The Blessings of One Mountain Day*, 2010. Using his own screen-printed fabrics, the artist here employed the Seminole technique, which involves piecing strips that are then cut and reassembled. The colours of this patchwork and appliqué embroidered quilt evoke autumn in Somerville's mountain home west of Sydney.

147. Margaret Wallace, *Total Eclipse*, 2004. This machine-appliquéd quilt is entirely of Australian wool fabric – some of it over fifty years old, including the grey ground, which the artist's mother bought from a Mr King 'who used to travel the country areas in his vintage Packard, with fabric-filled suitcases'.

148. Sue Hotchkis, *Ardwick*, 2011. Composed of cotton screen-printed with heat-expanding print medium and discharged, and of Kunin felt (made from 100% post-consumer recycled plastic bottles) coloured and distressed. These were free machine stitched in parts to capture 'the beauty caused by the passage of time, where exposure to the elements creates a harmony between the man-made and the natural'.

149. Els van Baarle, *Letters from a Friend*, 2007. This installation employs wax, dye and stitch on envelopes. The artist began the work shortly after the death of a friend, whose letters are contained in these envelopes.

148

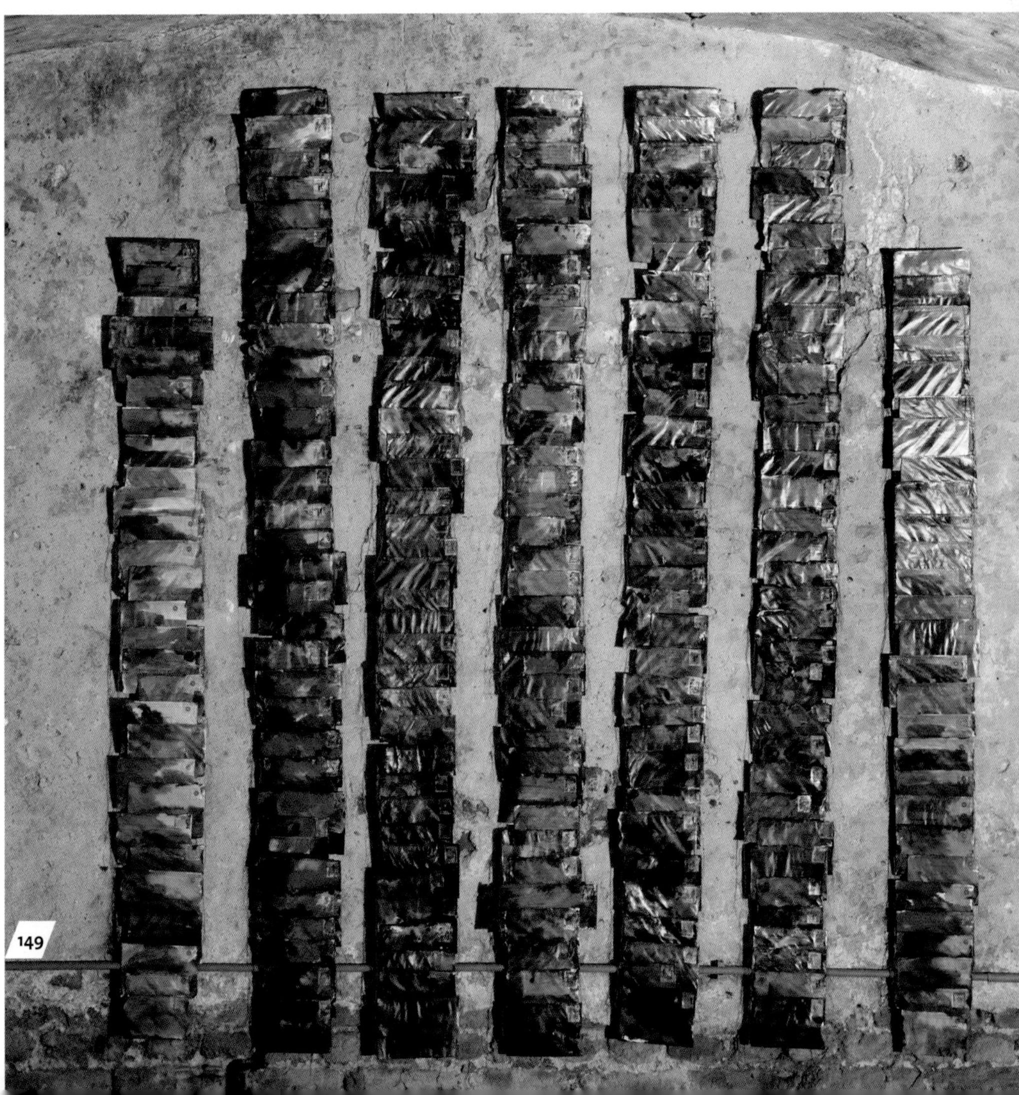

149

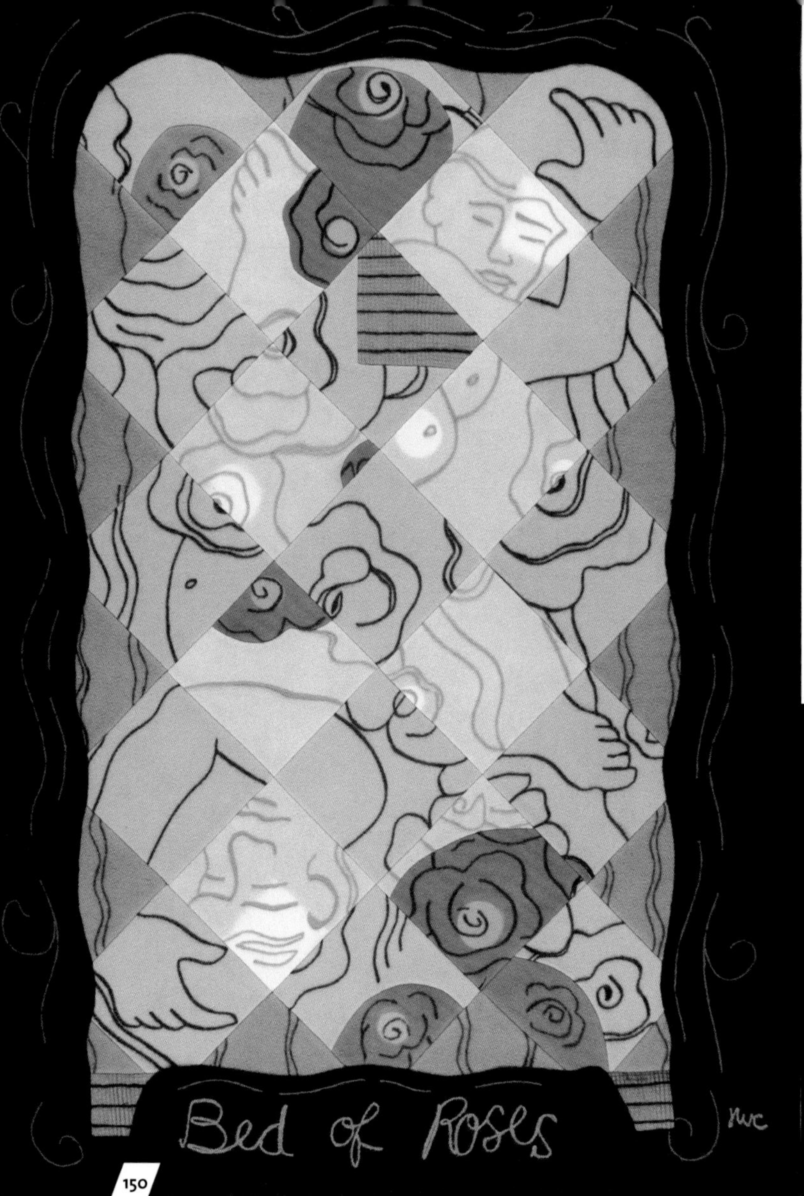

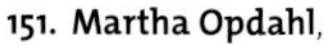

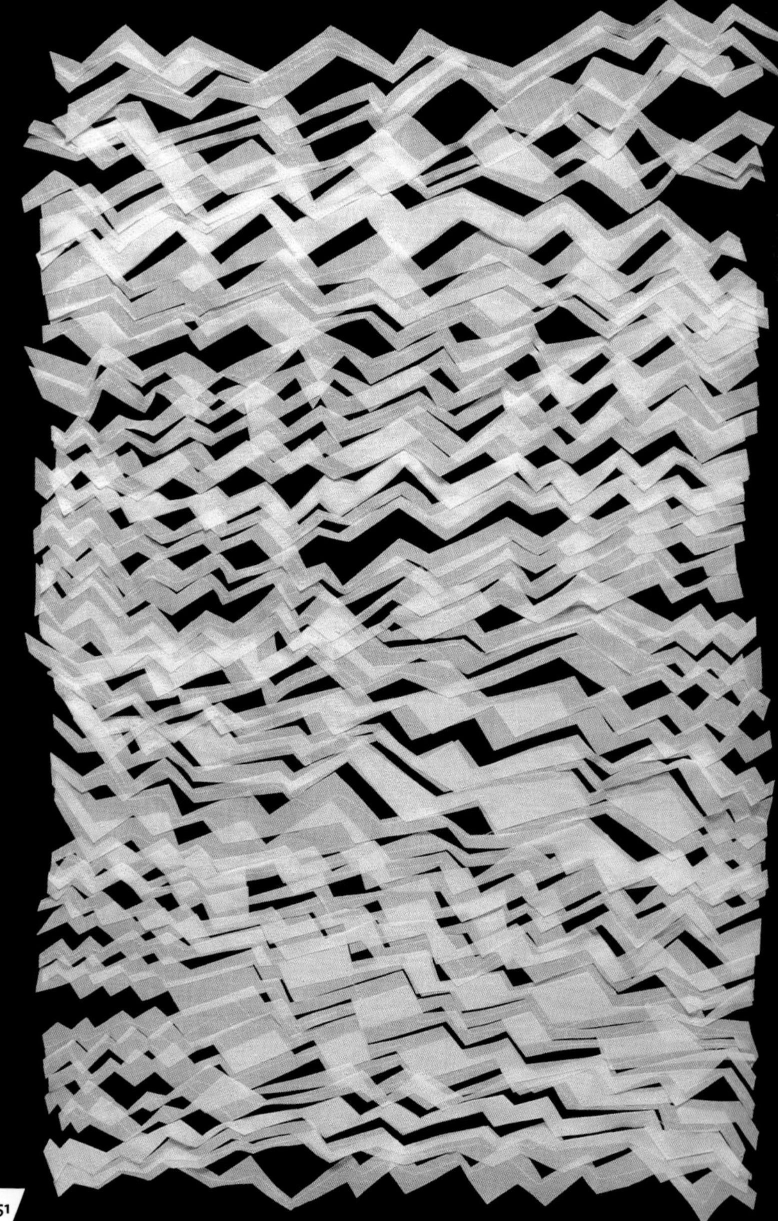

150. Jean Cacicedo, *Bed of Roses*, 1998. Incorporating a special process the artist has developed for wool fabrics, this work is composed of fulled woven wool, clamp resist-dyed, stitched, pieced and quilted. The imagery in this large panel evokes Cacicedo's training as a sculptor.

151. Martha Opdahl, *Construction #59*, 2008. Layered machine-embroidered cotton organdie is hand-sewn onto black acrylic, which is an integral part of the piece. It demonstrates a departure for Opdahl in terms of both technique and scale: she was previously known for her large tufted wool pieces, but this measures just 94 cm (37 in.) high.

152. Jean Cacicedo, *Layers of Meaning*, 2008. These panels, each 91.5 × 152.4 cm (3 × 5 ft) are of fulled woven wool dyed with pigments, pieced, stitched and quilted.

152

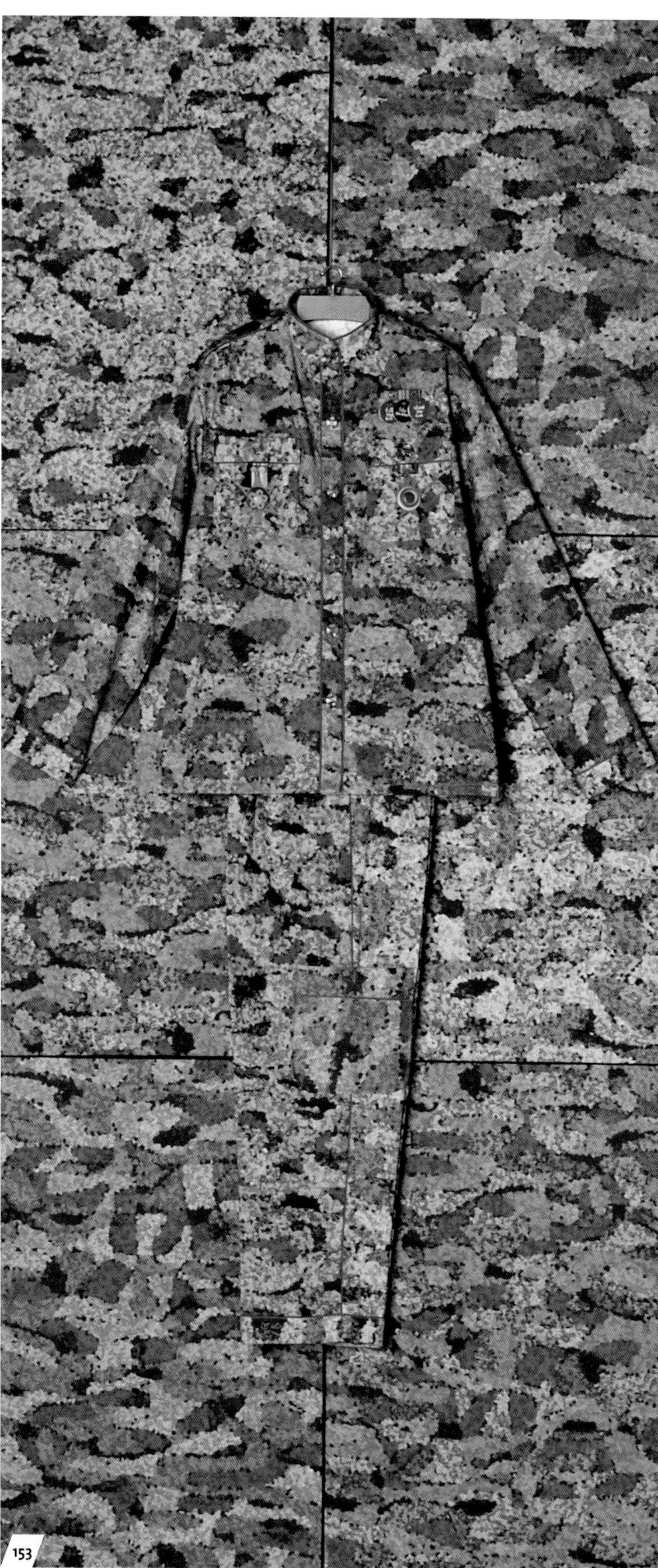

153. Annabelle Collett, *Neo Camo Installation* (detail), 2008. One of six panels of sewn and framed computer-designed and digitally printed fabric: Collett explains: 'Recently I have been looking at aspects of society through the notions of camouflage, ritual, comfort and difference. I incorporate various skills and media to make new imagery reflecting current concerns.'

154. Donna Jones, *Dancing to Sand Tunes* (detail), 2003. This is from a set of four panels portraying the beach where man-made marks are distorted and fade with the incoming tide. The cloth is 'snagged' by stitches onto handmade paper.

155 and 156. Lynette Douglas, *My Madiba Coat* (details), 2005. Made using appliqué, quilting and embroidery, this coat incorporates *isishweshwe* (traditional South African printed cottons, here by De Gama Textiles), including the reverse side, which bears the printer's stamp (155). One *isishweshwe* fabric made in honour of Nelson Mandela was cut to form a brooch showing Mandela's face (156).

157. Alvina Hall, *Lunette Landscape*, 2008. A shibori-pleated and bush-dyed reclaimed wool blanket, stitched over bush-dyed cottons and silks, captures the 'deeply eroded and evolving forms of the Lake Mungo Lunette [in New South Wales] and the histories this process reveals'.

154

155

156

157

158

159

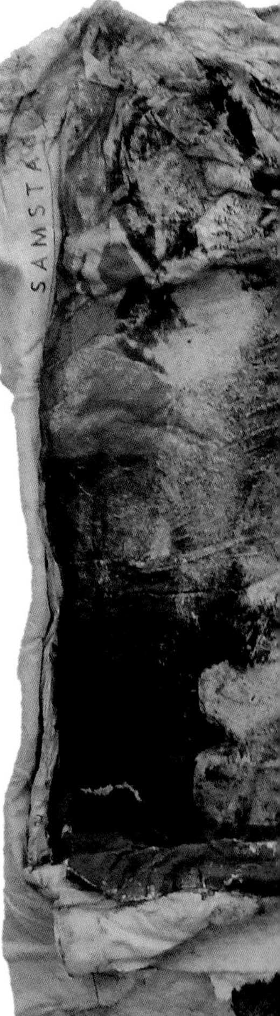

161

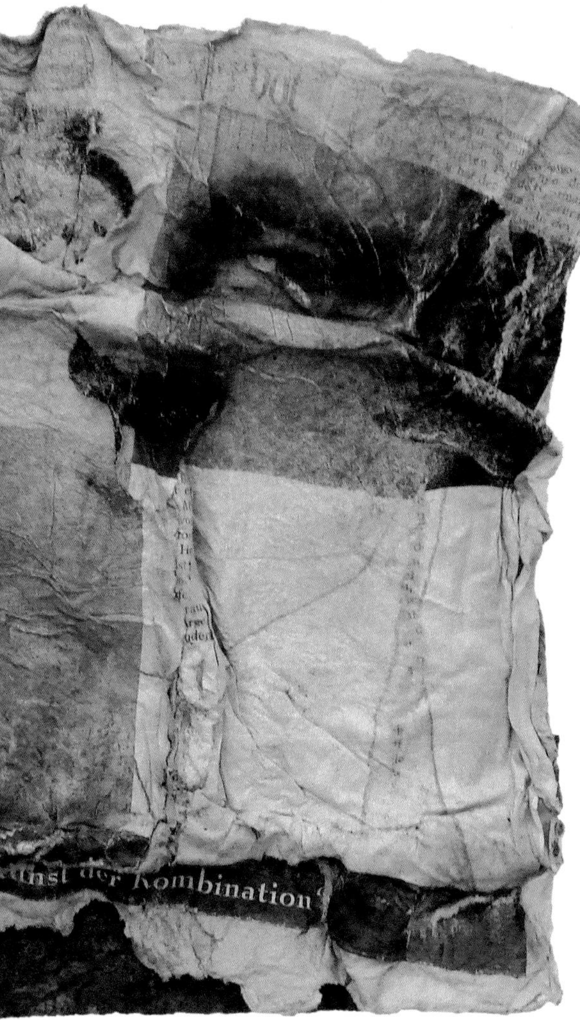

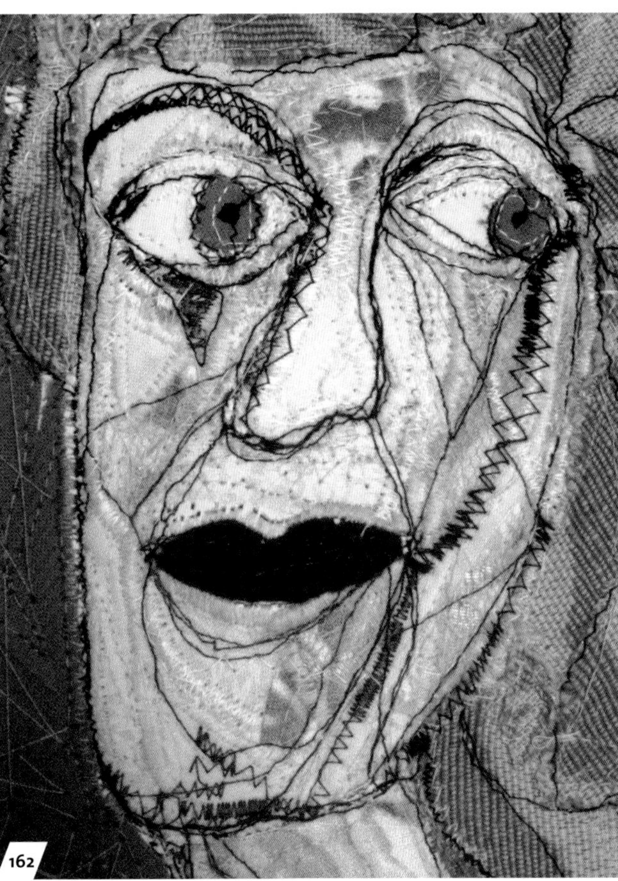

158. Susie Vickery, *Yak Butter Tea* (detail), 2007. This portrait employs hand embroidery and appliqué using Tibetan brocades and Tibetan aprons. It is of Aama, a Sherpa woman from the Mount Everest region of Nepal.

159. Jane McKeating, *'While I was gone – a counting book', Page 8*, 2010. Hand-stitched and digitally printed on frayed linen, this book, 20 cm (79 in.) square, depicts the artist's daughter's first eighteen years, with the reverse of each page recording McKeating's parallel journey.

160. Clairan Ferrono, *Through a Daughter's Eyes*, 2004. Repurposed clothing is machine-pieced, fused, appliquéd and quilted in a work capturing the artist's question: 'When my daughter was five she drew a portrait of me – all head and waving arms. Was this how she saw me?'

161. Rosmarie Reber, *Mona Lisa*, 2005. Exploring concepts of time, topicality and transcience, in art as in news, this work consists of silk compressed over forms created by car wheels passing over newspapers, deliberately positioned to be flattened and marked. They become symbols of the rushing tempo of our times.

162. Maria Holohan, *The Queen*, 2009. Drawing with cloth and stitch on card, the artist explores the dreams and nightmares of paranoid schizophrenia.

163. Ali Ferguson, *The Sideboard Drawer*, 2010. This drawer, filled with calico, gesso, vintage lace, haberdashery items, paper, wax, copper and found objects, is a tribute to the artist's ancestors and 'the skills that have been handed down to me', but also a recognition that 'some attitudes of previous generations are no longer appropriate'.

164. Rosalind Byass, *Postcard Home*, 2010. In a fabric collage created after a visit to Monet's garden, Byass worked heavy upholstery in machine stitching with overlaying and *broderie perse* ('painting' with printed textiles). Wool, wool batting and fragments of fine cotton threads were used for the dog's fur.

165. Larissa Murdock, *Fractions*, 2009. This hand and machine-stitched assemblage combines nappy liners, lumieres, recycled hijabs, digitally printed canvas, newspapers, shiva oil sticks and beads with embroidery and painting.

166. Maria Holohan, *God Knows What Time She Is*, 2010. The collaged and stitched cloth and mixed-media surface denotes the inability of humans to master their emotional environment. This work was a collaboration with the poet Hilda Sheehan, whose poem begins: 'God knows what time she is / Her face has stopped / A little hand points five.'

167. Uzbekistani artisan, *Tasselled hanging* (detail), before 1971. This elaborate silk and wool tassel with glass beads is, like the other objects illustrated here, from the Design Collection of the University of California, Davis.

168. Saudi Arabian artisan, *Asir-style woman's face mask* (detail), before 1982. This mask – constructed with hand-painted cotton, silver and aluminium ornaments, silver coins, cotton tassels and embroidery, plastic sequins, white glass seed beads, cotton string and a leather thong – was once in the possession of a wife of King Abdul Aziz.

169. Tunisian artisan, *Pouch*, before 1971. Tasselled and fringed recycled wool and cotton make up this pouch, which has wool yarn handles and two hollow bamboo rod 'liners'.

167

168

169

170. Persian artisan, *Wall hanging* (detail), early 20th century. This type of work came to be called *Rashti-duzi* (from the Rasht area of Persia), or 'rescht work'. Pieced, appliquéd (*tikeh-duzi*) and embroidered wool flannel (*mahout*) is embellished with silk chain stitch (*Golab-duzi*) and couching stitches.

171. Bai artisan, *Guobei* (detail), before 1995. This *guobei*, a type of baby-carrier unique to the Bai people – a minority group found in Yunnan Province, China – is embroidered in silk and acrylic yarns. Its central panel is appliquéd with quilted cotton and synthetic fabrics, plastic sequins and aluminium ornaments.

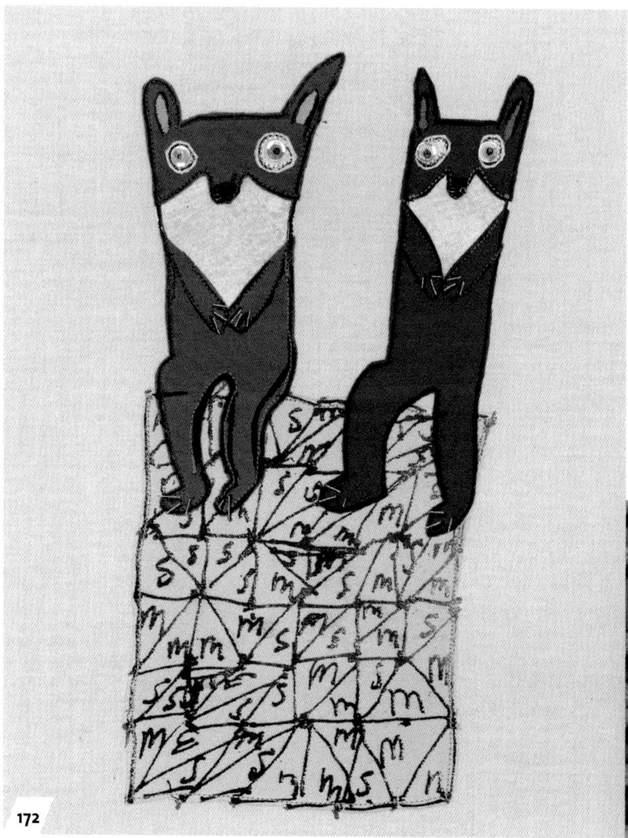

172. Rachael Howard, *Foxes on a Wall*, 2011. Spontaneous sketches, notes and scribbles are translated into screen-printed, appliquéd and embroidered narrative images, each 30 × 40 cm (11.8 × 15¾ in.).

173. Elizabeth Hinkes, *Pond Skaters*, 2005. Influenced by Cuna molas, Hinkes has used commercially made felt instead of cotton, machine-stitching through several layers before cutting sections away. 'The tactile quality of the fabric is of particular significance to me .... A chenille and crisp effect is created.'

174–181. Kuna Indian embroiderers, *Molas*, c. 1960s–70s. Molas are generally made entirely of cotton trade cloths; chain stitch is common to all of them, but stem, running and buttonhole stitches are also used, as well as decorative trimmings such as rickrack. These examples indicate the enormous variety of imagery possible. Some reflect outside influences, such as no. 174, which depicts a pair of gas canisters, while others show indigenous animals and people. Several of these were collected by Captain Kit S. Kapp during his expedition to Panama in 1970.

174

175

177

176

178

179

180

181

182. Miao artisan, *Small panel*, before 1988. Only 24 cm (9½ in.) high, this indigo-dyed cotton, batiked with geometric motifs, has hand-appliquéd brightly coloured cotton pinwheels.

183. Pia Welsch, *Oval no.50 – Fruitdrops*, 2009. Machine-pieced and machine-quilted from hand-dyed cotton poplins and satins, this work explores the concept of relentless repetition.

184. Ziazhai or Badaoshao artisan, *Chiubei-style woman's apron* (detail), before 1994. Black cotton twill has white cotton appliquéd in spiral, clover leaf, cross and stepped forms with polychrome silk satin stitches.

186

188

185

187

190

189

191

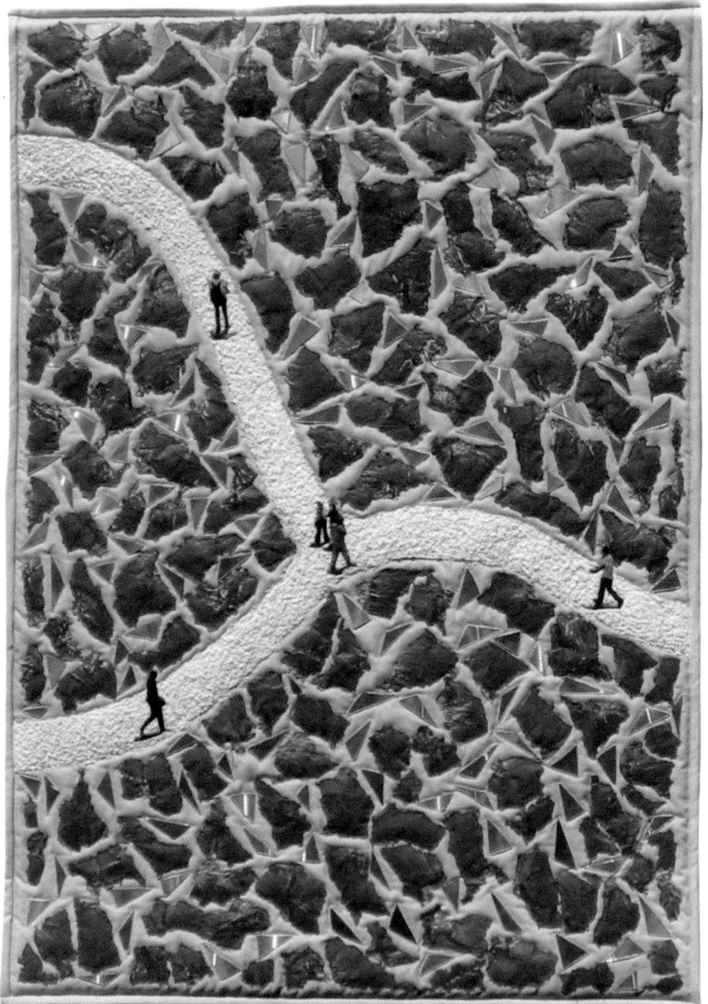

193

185. Greg Somerville, *Indra's Net No. 9*, 2009. Inspired by the Hindu myth that Indra's net encompasses the universe, this gift for Somerville's 21-year-old son employs screen printing, appliqué, embroidery, patchwork, quilting and shibori.

186. Yoshiko Katagiri, *Akane 381*, 2001. Hand-dyed sheeting, rayon satin, five kinds of silk *chirimen* (crêpe), *shiborizome* (tie-dyed silk), *ro* (a soft black silk), and an embroidered collar were hand-pieced, appliquéd, and hand-quilted. Katagiri's creation depicts 'scores of dragonflies turning the night sky to red'.

187. Katriina Flensburg, *By the Borderland IV*, 2008. Monoprinted, painted and machine-quilted on hand-dyed and commercial cottons, this piece reflects geographical and spiritual aspects of living in a 'grey zone' between several cultures.

188. Mohamed Dendon, *Tentmakers of Cairo appliquéd panel: 2007–11*, 2007. Made by men in Cairo's tentmakers' street for Western residents and employing traditional motifs such as the lotus in cotton layered onto a heavy canvas background, this and nos. 185–91 were among the international offerings on display at the Festival of Quilts, Birmingham, in 2011.

189. Yoshiko Katagiri, *Masoho 382*, 2004. Like *Akane 381* (186), this work is made of hand-pieced, appliquéd and hand-quilted panels.

190. Pia Welsch, *Oval 28 – Die Keimzelle (The Germ Cell)*, 2005. At 190 cm (75 in.) high, this hand-dyed cotton quilt is machine-pieced, embroidered and quilted, partly with a twin needle.

191. Irena Zemanova, *Lace* (detail), 2011. Made for the Czech Republic's annual Art Quilt Club exhibition in 2011, whose theme required the incorporation of lace.

192. Marty Jonas, *Ashby Avenue, Berkeley, CA*, 2004. Part of the artist's series of works that consider fly-posted telephone poles as urban installation art, this work is collaged with dyed and cut cotton fabrics in layers, with added details in hand embroidery. 'The result,' Jonas says, 'is an almost painterly translation that mimics the layered and fragmented character of the original street art.'

193. Marialuisa Sponga, *Blue Park*, 2010. On a three-layered cotton base, free machine stitched with transparent thread, 'heat-manipulated blue plastic from fruit crates takes on chromatic values of pure abstraction. CD fragments provide translucent effects. Photographs of human figures take a walk on white thread fragments.'

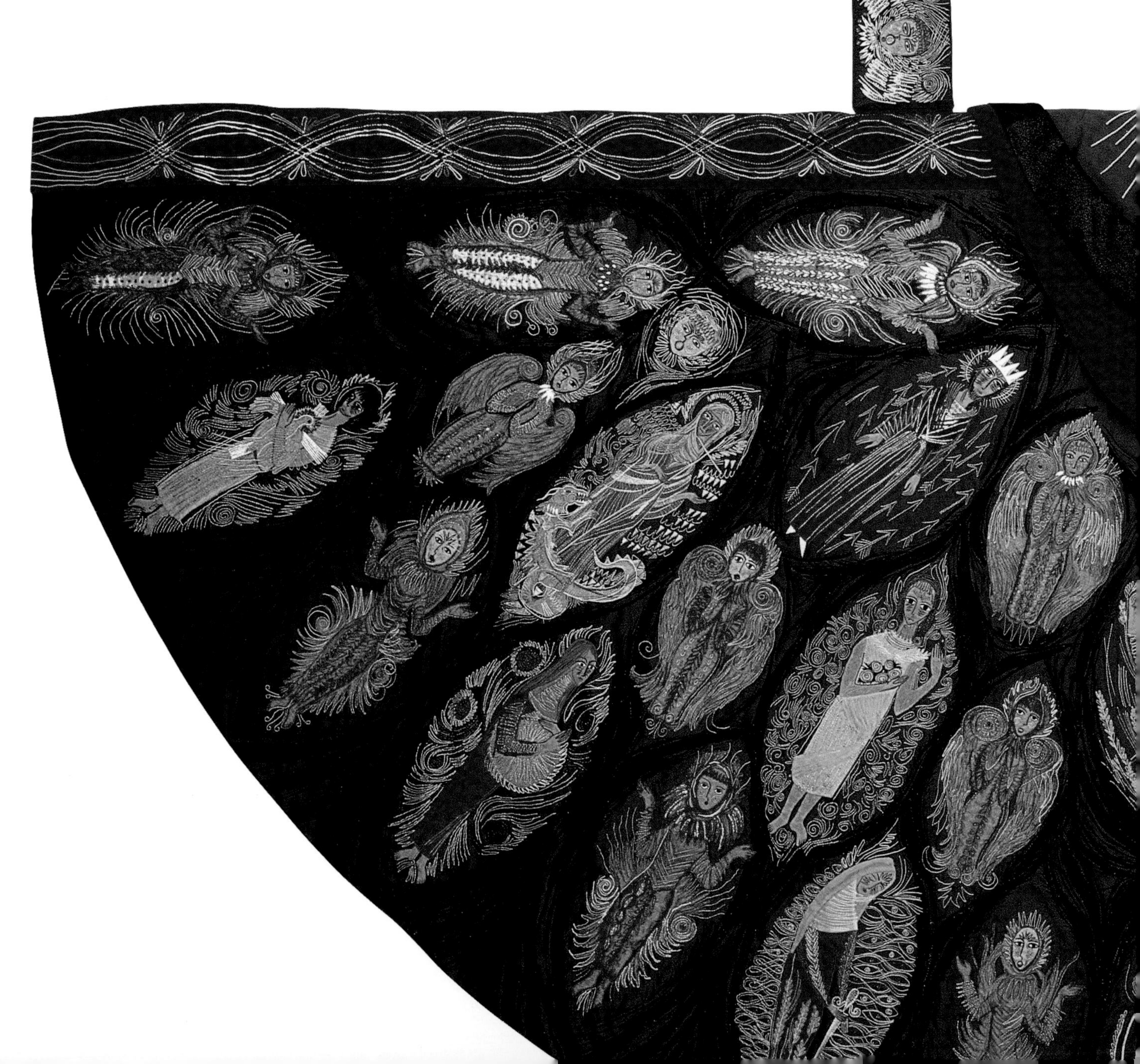

1

VI.

IMAGERY

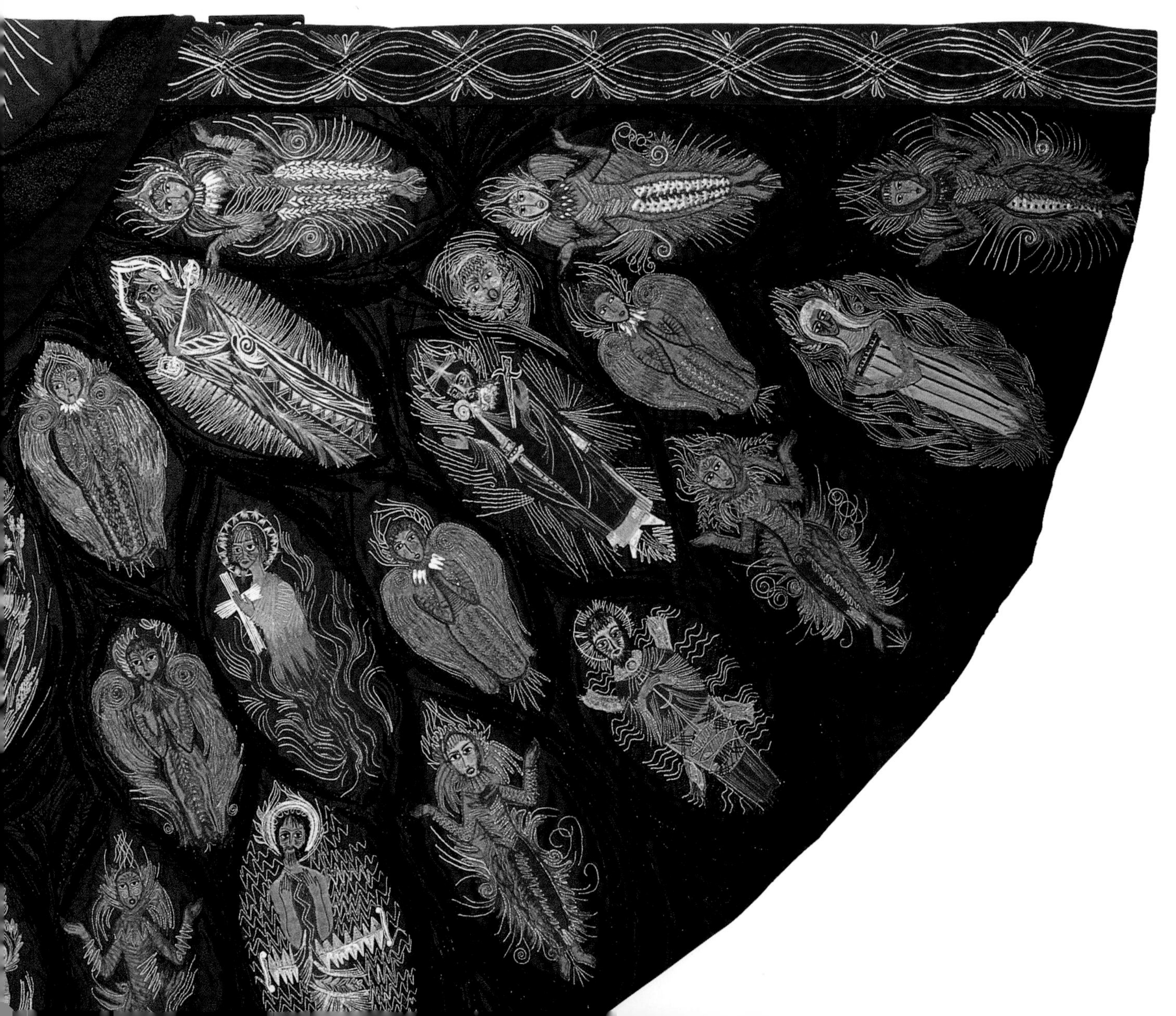

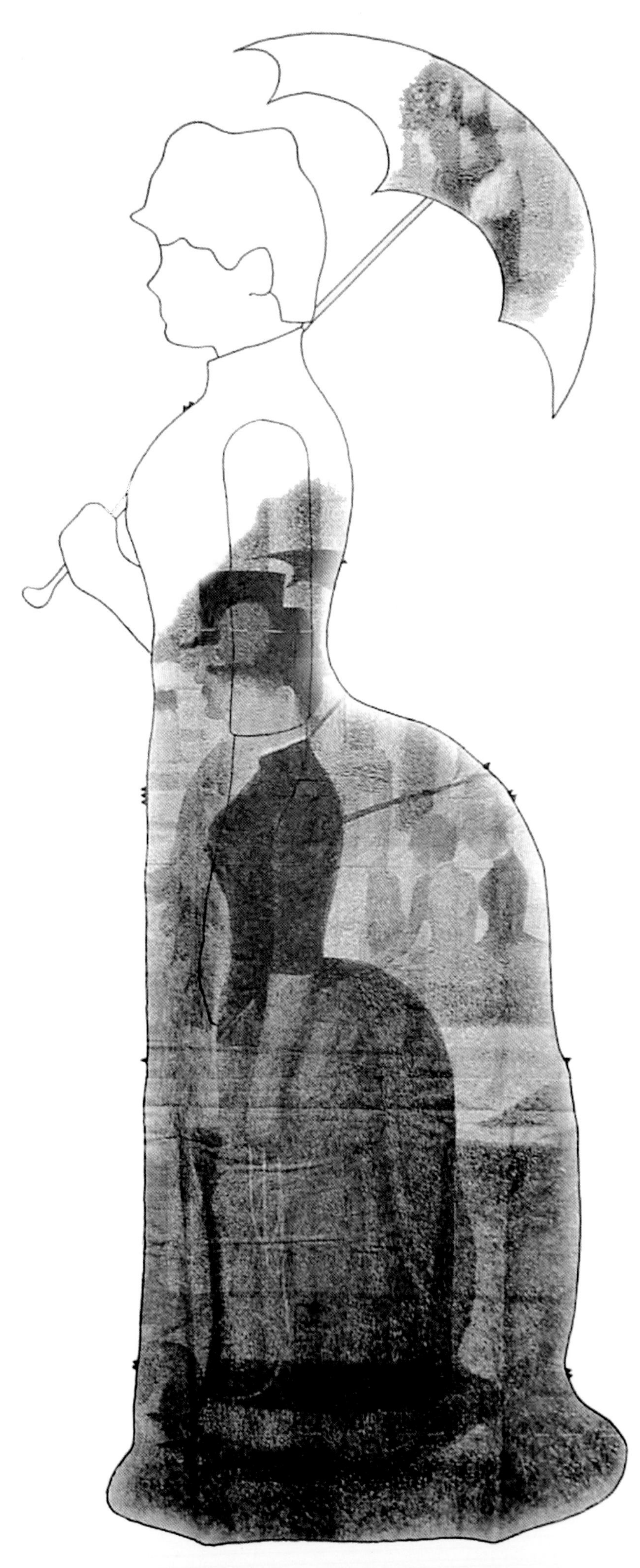

VI.

IMAGERY

Pictorial imagery is an element of textile art the viewer expects to find, despite the fact that it is only one aspect of this enormous field. Readers who have followed the text from the beginning will by now realize that one of my essential points is that textiles are three-dimensional objects within which structure, texture, insertions, additions, manipulations and movement can interact. In fact, it is more accurate to describe textiles not as a visual art, but as a sensory art, one that calls into play all of the senses: touch, sight, smell, sound and – for curious infants – taste. By activating so many receptors, textiles can even enhance the lives of people with disorders affecting brain and nervous system functions. Exemplifying this application is an 'Intelligent Textiles' sensory fabric that allows people with cerebral palsy to access a computer, and which knows where, how and when it is being touched. It was developed by Asha Peta Thompson and Stan Swallow; Thompson combined her skills of cloth design and fabric construction with Swallow's knowledge of electronics.

Textiles are equally important in shaping our ability to visualize, meaning that they help train the mind to imagine an internal representation, such as required when one reads a descriptive passage in a book (in studies of literature, this is simply called 'imagery') or needs to recall a route. A high level of 'visual imaging' – as this ability is called by cognitive psychologists – has been shown to be beneficial to planning and problem-solving, especially, and unsurprisingly, in art, design, technology and science; it facilitates the ability to retrieve information about physical relationships between objects, as well as their physical properties. Several studies have shown that women score much higher than men when tested for visual-imaging capacity, and, given how critical imagining, planning and problem-solving are in making textiles, this may go some way towards explaining why women are so successful in the textile arts. This conclusion certainly accords with the fact that, while men have often dominated the use of 'fully fledged' machines and mills, women have made many significant contributions during the exploratory stages of textile technologies, from screen printing to digital imaging over the past century alone.[1] In addition, visual imaging forms the basis of self-image, with which so many textiles can be associated. Aside

1. Susan Riley, *Hammersmith Cope*, 1968. Made by Beryl Dean and forty students at Hammersmith College for St Paul's Cathedral, London. Susan Riley, one of Dean's students, designed a number of ecclesiastical projects for Dean's embroidery classes, including this cope. The figures were machine-stitched individually and applied to the silk ground, then finished with metal threads, spangles and pearl purl. This piece required 5,000 hours to complete.

2. Jackie Langfeld, *Grande Jatte – Restricted Pattern*, 2009. This life-size inkjet print on dressmaker's tissue paper, tacked with cotton thread to calico, references Georges Seurat's painting *A Sunday on La Grande Jatte* (1884–86). The tightly restricting garment shape is a commentary on how self-image is often controlled by fashion and style today.

3

4

from those that express identity, many textiles are explorations of narrative and 'mapping', and this final chapter focuses on these three topics.

Identity

Just as the textiles we gather around us can become an exercise in finely judged or playful arrangement, they also reflect our identities, which is why the choice of a tie or a turban can speak volumes about a man **[35, 99]**. The equivalent statement piece for women – the scarf – can become a less individualistic choice when cultural expectations define its use, or a less surprising one where sartorial freedom is encouraged. Around the world, textiles still identify cultural ideologies, central among them, religious affiliations **[1, 20–24]**. The textile that announces its wearer's identity has been the subject of many studies, from the hierarchical symbolism of motifs in ancient Peruvian cloths to the design of the velvet that distinguished wearers as Venetian senators for nearly three hundred years **[3]**.[2]

Other textiles, such as the plaid, have managed to embrace multiple identities. Long associated with the Scottish tartan, plaid is also a pattern well known in the United States as a printed cotton called 'madras', which has been associated with informal wear – especially Bermuda shorts and golf clothing – since the 1960s **[37]**. The word 'madras' derives from the English name for the Indian city of Chennai, yet few on the golf course would recognize the textile's Indian roots, especially given its key role in the 'preppy' style of the 1980s. Among more elaborate patterns, perhaps the most multicultural is what is today popularly called 'paisley' **[25–34]**. Its origins lie in a stylized, pre-16th century Persian floral motif, or *buta*, that enriched large, sumptuous silk shawls or sashes. These were so desirable that by the 18th century Armenian merchants had already created alternative centres of production in Istanbul, Russia and Poland, creating one stylistic trajectory that can be followed through the Ottoman and Spanish empires, and the Hispano-Moresque diaspora. The same Persian *buta* pattern spread from Mughal India to Europe via the craze for luxury Kashmir shawls, evident by 1800. Not long afterwards, in order to meet European demand, variants of the patterns were being made in Russia, France and several cities in the United Kingdom, including Paisley, in Scotland. Paisley has been an element of the Western design vocabulary ever since, yet the term often associated with Scotland only by natives, such as Jill Kinnear, an emigrant from Scotland to Australia. Kinnear's work **[31, 36 and 39]** explores her interest 'in the role that traditional Scottish textiles – paisleys and, in particular, tartans – have played in the construction of a Scottish identity and mythology', and in the way that identity has 'migrated along with its mythologies to every corner of the world'.

In addition to the kilt, other Western fashions display subtle or overt markers of cultural allegiance that are often as dependent on the textile as on the tailoring. To give one example, the first company to become known for painterly fashion fabrics was Bianchini-Férier, which in 1912, some twenty years after it had been established in Lyon, contracted Raoul Dufy to provide exclusive designs **[4, 56, 59, 119, 132]**. Dufy's Fauvist coloured florals and geometric patterns, 'using blocks of opposing colors – the design created equally by the object and by the negative space enclosing it', encapsulated the youthful energy of the Jazz Age.[3]

5

Even after the Depression, when Dufy no longer supplied designs, Bianchini-Férier retained its characteristic style, and the company continued to be identified with high-spirited fashion, as evidenced by their designs from the late 1950s to the 1980s for Givenchy, Balenciaga, Pierre Cardin, Chanel, Nina Ricci, Dior, Féraud and Yves Saint Laurent, among others **[61–66]**. Many of these designs are now in the Design Library of New York and London, an extensive textile design archive. As the owner, Peter Koepke, says, 'We are very attracted to this period in 20th-century design because it remains so fresh and relevant to our clients today.'

To the same degree, textiles can be key to street styles – a point made by Melanie Miller's *Jeans, Baseball Cap, Sweatshirt* **[5]**, in which she exploits the capacity of the Schiffli machine to reproduce these items in stitch, pantograph-drawn at the side of the machine, to emphasize how today's ubiquitous and fashionable Western workwear relates to other commonly worn, simply-structured garments. Today street styles are so influential at all levels of fashion that blogs on the topic have been described as one of the 'great online phenomena of the past decade'.[4] The first such subculture to go global was the hippie movement, which crystallized at San Francisco's 'Be In' of 1967, and spread quickly throughout the United States and beyond. With the dissemination of hippie culture came the use of non-Western cloth and clothing, typically ancient in patterning and construction, which would have a lasting impact on the development of wearable art. (In its current form, wearable art is also indebted to artists working in and around the San Francisco Bay area, but it is global in scope: New Zealand's wearable art awards, held annually since 1987, are important, for example.) The assumption that textile artists will be aware of textiles of the past means that – in another contradiction typical of textiles – techniques and motifs rooted in one culture are individualized by artists in another. For instance, Jane Dunnewold, in a series of forty-eight *Etudes* she undertook as a meditation through making, incorporated

3. Venetian weaver, *Senatorial rank badge (stole)*, c. 1500. Introduced as part of a Venetian senator's garb in the 1400s, silk velvets with this design, created with two heights of pile, continued to fulfil the same role into the 18th century.

4. Raoul Dufy for Bianchini-Férier, *Cavaliers et Amazones (no. 8010)*, 1918. Drawing upon the tradition of French toiles, Dufy depicted historicized male and female riders. By using bold colours he created a contrapuntal over-pattern in this block-printed cotton.

5. Melanie Miller, *Jeans, Baseball Cap, Sweatshirt*, 2007. This multi-needle Schiffli embroidery on cotton comments on the transition from local to global and handmade to mass produced, and the attendant standardization of socially significant garments.

motifs found in non-Western textiles, including those with symbolic significance to Thai peoples [44]. She has nevertheless made these motifs her own, just as English-speakers seldom think of words such as 'ballet' or 'chauffeur' as foreign terms. As Dunnewold explains, 'there was a palpable rightness to revisiting my symbolic visual repertoire'.

The ability of textiles to signal visual distinctions or identities is astutely observed by many textile artists. James Fox, for example, in *men you been lookin'* [6], strives 'to convey ideas and questions about our expectations regarding gender roles, work, culture and other aspect of our social and personal lives'. By incorporating floral-patterned fabric into his piece, Fox plays with Western expectations and understandings of appropriate, or inappropriate, behaviour and garb. Obviously these expectations may well not be the same in other cultures and at other times, as is illustrated by comparing Fox's piece with a 19th-century Deccan shira [7], a south Indian cloth covering for a throne, or *simhasana*. One need not look over great distances or time spans to find such contrasts. Karen Taiaroa's *Whakaaria Mai (Show me)* reflects upon the continuous negotiation between the two cultures of New Zealand, the indigenous Maori and the white settlers, layering her work with family stories related to her mixed heritage [71, 72]. Taiaroa interweaves European and Maori narratives, imagery, symbolism and methodology 'to explore the similarities and misunderstandings that occur when two cultures come together,' adding her conclusion that 'cultures over time evolve rules to protect their members. These rules are handed on from generation to generation in narratives, songs and even games. Sometimes cultural rules are purposely and knowingly broken. And other times when cultures live alongside each other rules are broken and offence given through innocent ignorance.'

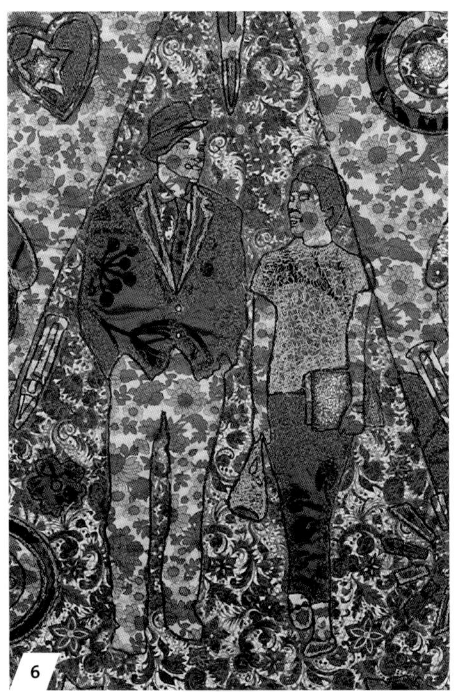
6

7

Textiles play no small part in handing down cultural rules. A group of painted bark panels, acquired in the Northern Territory of Australia in 1975, includes one that bears witness to their didactic capabilities: a warning depiction of a ritual execution. All except one of these works are by named artists: Jimmy Mijau Mijau, Peter Nambaraitj of Oenpelli, and Bardjaray of the Gumadeer River [75, 77, 78, 80]. They were acquired by G. Ledyard Stebbins and his wife, Barbara, shortly after he retired from the Department of Genetics, which he had been instrumental in establishing, at the University of California, Davis, in 1950. This is of no small import. Regarded as the botanical 'architect' of the evolutionary synthesis, as well as a passionate environmentalist, Ledyard through his work promoted both diachronic analysis (looking at change over time through common origins or causes, viewed as genetic relationships) and the more 'modern' synchronic analysis (comparing phenomena at any single point in time). One can imagine that his interest in origins allowed him to see Aboriginal art as a product of today, but also representing a living past, made modern because it remains meaningful. And that it does so is clear from the work of Eva Wanganeen [76] and Soraya Abidin [73], both of whom bring a contemporary approach to ancient imagery.

The combination of the diachronic and synchronic in textiles can be further explored by looking at a Japanese *kosode* dating from the 1800s [10]. Today in the collection of the Los Angeles County Museum of Art, this robe exemplifies the work of highly skilled silk-weavers of the Edo period. Additionally, it is linked

6. James Fox, *men you been lookin'* (detail), 2010. To represent the adaptations men have made in recent years, reverse appliqué with freehand machine embroidery is juxtaposed with potentially incongruous patterns. The work reflects the artist's personal experience of working in a range of fields, including engineering, art practice, and as the primary carer for his children.

7. Indian artisan, Sirhi, 1800–50. This Deccan *sirhi*, a cloth to cover a throne, or *simhasana*, is cotton painted with pigments and gold. It depicts the garb of fine silks associated with the southern part of India.

8. Japanese artisans, Kosode *fragment*, early 1700s. With a *rinzu* (silk-figured satin) ground, leaves of *kata kanoko* (imitation tie-dye) are set amid silk and metallic thread embroidery. This fragment and a companion kimono fragment (no. 9) were collected by Bella Mabury in 1917.

9. Japanese artisans, Katabira *fragment*, early 1700s. This summer-weight, unlined kimono has a ground of plain woven ramie and is embellished with *noribosen* (paste-resist dyeing), *kanoko* shibori (tie-dyeing), and silk and metallic thread embroidery.

10

to its American donor, Bella Mabury, who purchased it, along with other Japanese textiles **[8, 9]**, from Nomura Shojiro, a Kyoto antiques dealer, while she was travelling in Asia in 1917. More than the individuals it recalls, this *kosode* symbolizes a worldly cultural identity that Bella and three of her siblings – Carlotta, Eloise and Paul – nurtured for the city of Los Angeles by enriching the museum's collection. These four children of Josephine and Hiram Mabury, whose fortune was made in California banking and real estate, all contributed to the (then) Los Angeles Museum in various ways. Bella lent her significant collection of textiles in 1931, and then donated them eight years later, when Paul also gave the museum 'choice examples of the decorative arts', collected so that 'someday the masses might share in that which had always been [a] great source of pleasure and enrichment'. According to locals, these donations signified the moment when the museum ceased to be provincial.[5] A diachronic connection to the *kosode* under discussion is its illustration of one of the poems from *The Tales of Ise*. This collection of Japanese poetry has been famous since its compilation in the 9th century for representing a code of courtly behaviour understood by the cultural elite. And, at the time our *kosode* was made, this elite – and here is the significant parallel – had only just begun to include newly educated samurai. The robe depicts angular *yatsuhashi* (eight-plank bridges) in the iris-filled marshes of Mikawa Province, and anchors the idea of self-cultivation within Edo-period Neo-Confucianism. The imagery also links the garment to a wide range of other superbly crafted and widely collected Japanese objects, including illustrated books.

Narrative

The debate surrounding the question 'What is art?' is a narrative in itself, and one that is played out in the textile arts, in some cases quite literally. Tilleke Schwarz, for example, prefers to describe her work as a kind of visual poetry, with narrative elements used not to tell a story, but to invite the viewer to 'decipher connections or to create them'. Her incorporation of everyday, even banal, texts challenges hierarchies of taste and social order. The requisite deciphering is, of course, dependent on a fluency in the phraseology and symbolism used, which in this case includes motifs from traditional samplers. It is in this way that narrative and identity are intertwined – like the *kosode* discussed above, such art declares that 'I am what I know.' In her work *New Potatoes* **[101]**, Schwarz's inclusion of a section of a sampler references an older form of information transmission, one that was important before the availability of pattern books and has remained so ever since.

While pattern books for embroidery appeared in the 16th century, they remained relatively rare for a century more, and the ability to decipher stitched imagery depended on books of a different sort. Take, for example, an 18th-century depiction of Phaeton **[11]**, son of the mythological god Phoebus. Phaeton's reckless driving of his father's sun chariot caused severe cold when he veered away from the earth, and created deserts where the chariot came too near, leading Jupiter to strike Phaeton down with a thunderbolt. Although this myth is no longer widely familiar, it is a rather timely metaphor for the need to consider the consequences of our reckless self-indulgence. The work's maker, probably also its owner, would have expected its meaning to be clear to an 18th-century viewer, since the tale of

10. Japanese artisans, *Woman's* kosode, 1800s. Made of silk damask embroidered with silk and gold metallic thread embroidery, this textile depicts *yatsuhashi* (eight-plank) bridges among irises, referring to the famous iris marshes of Mikawa Province. The design also recalls a famous poem from the 9th century, *The Tales of Ise*, making it expressive of the traditional *miyabi* aesthetic of courtliness and refinement.

11

Phaeton was included in Ovid's *Metamorphoses*. Completed in AD 8, this Latin epic poem is said to have been the most read of all classical works during the Middle Ages. By the time this image of Phaeton was stitched, the poem was well known through a medieval French version called the *Ovide moralisé* (which influenced Chaucer), while Arthur Golding's English translation of 1565–67 was available to Shakespeare, who alluded to Ovid more than to any other author.[6]

In addition to mythological scenes, historical and biblical events dominate pictorial textiles from the Middle Ages until the 19th century. Importantly, embroideries, unlike tapestries, were of a scale that allowed them to be worked by an individual, and embroidery played a central role in the education of young women. During the 17th century, a needlework casket (an embroidery-covered box to hold needlework tools and threads) was the final demonstration of feminine proficiency **[106]**. These and many other embroideries of the period depict such strong women as Esther, an admired figure from the Old Testament whose heroic deeds saved the Jews from massacre.[7] The same story is found on a late 16th-century set of embroidered bed valances **[107]**, while another work, made by a late 17th-century embroiderer, depicts the Greek goddess Athena with her adopted child Erichthonius in his serpent form **[12]**. The goddess is associated with wisdom, virtue, civilization and strategy, and she is a patron of the arts and human endeavour (including weaving). Like the casket, these two pieces, featuring strong female figures, have passed through the New York textile dealership of Cora Ginsburg LLC, now overseen by Titi Halle. It is worth pausing here to note the influence of Ginsburg (née Kling, 1910–2003), who in 1929 married a noted antiquarian, joining his family's well-known antiques gallery when textiles

11. French embroiderer, *Needlework picture, c.* 1700–25. Worked in tent stitch in silk and wool, this scene depicts the Greek myth of Phaeton, best known through its telling in the second book of Ovid's *Metamorphoses*.

'were the stepchild ... so I took them under my wing'. Her particular passion was for 17th-century English embroidery (as well as 18th-century European costume, which formed the bulk of her substantial private collection), and 'gifted with an unerring eye, she made a profound and sustained contribution to a much undervalued, little studied area of the decorative arts and material culture'.[8] In other words, Ginsburg was skilled in the reading of textiles.

Textile narratives continue to draw upon mythologies, including those of the ancient world, such as Inge Norgaard's references to Norse myths in *Fimbulwinter* **[104]** and Marieta Toneva's *Life Source* **[81]**, inspired by 'the eternal struggle and the constant magnetism between good and evil, between light and darkness'. Other stories are more current and often contested, such as the myth of the patient woman, portrayed in Sue Dove's *Women Will Wait* **[105]**, or of women who constantly gossip and shop, as in Lilane Taylor's *Chatte Latte* **[103]**. Many such contemporary myths reflect concerns about power and its impact on gender stereotypes and relationships, and about the nature of existence. Using textiles to direct attention to life's struggles with these issues has an added frisson, given that textiles are so often a source of comfort. In his *Project Facade* **[83, 84]**, Paddy Hartley explores the impact of high explosives and heavy artillery used during the First World War, focusing his project around the story of Walter Yeo, a Plymouth sailor who was one of the first to receive ground-breaking corrective plastic surgery. Hartley explains that 'the battlefield casualties included an unprecedented number with horrific facial injuries – injuries so severe the men were commonly unrecognizable to loved ones and friends. Often unable to see, hear, speak, eat or drink, they struggled to reassimilate back into civilian life.' Pain, anxiety and the modern myth that there is a pill to fix any condition underscore Susie Freeman's and Dr Liz Lee's work *White Pain* **[13]**. The pills encased within a panel 24 m (26 yds) long are readily understood, as are the marks in

12. English embroiderer, *Athena*, late 17th century. Silk tent stitch is used to depict Athena's ermine stole, gown and shoes. The landscape is worked in queen stitch, and the white silk background in a fine trelliswork pattern.

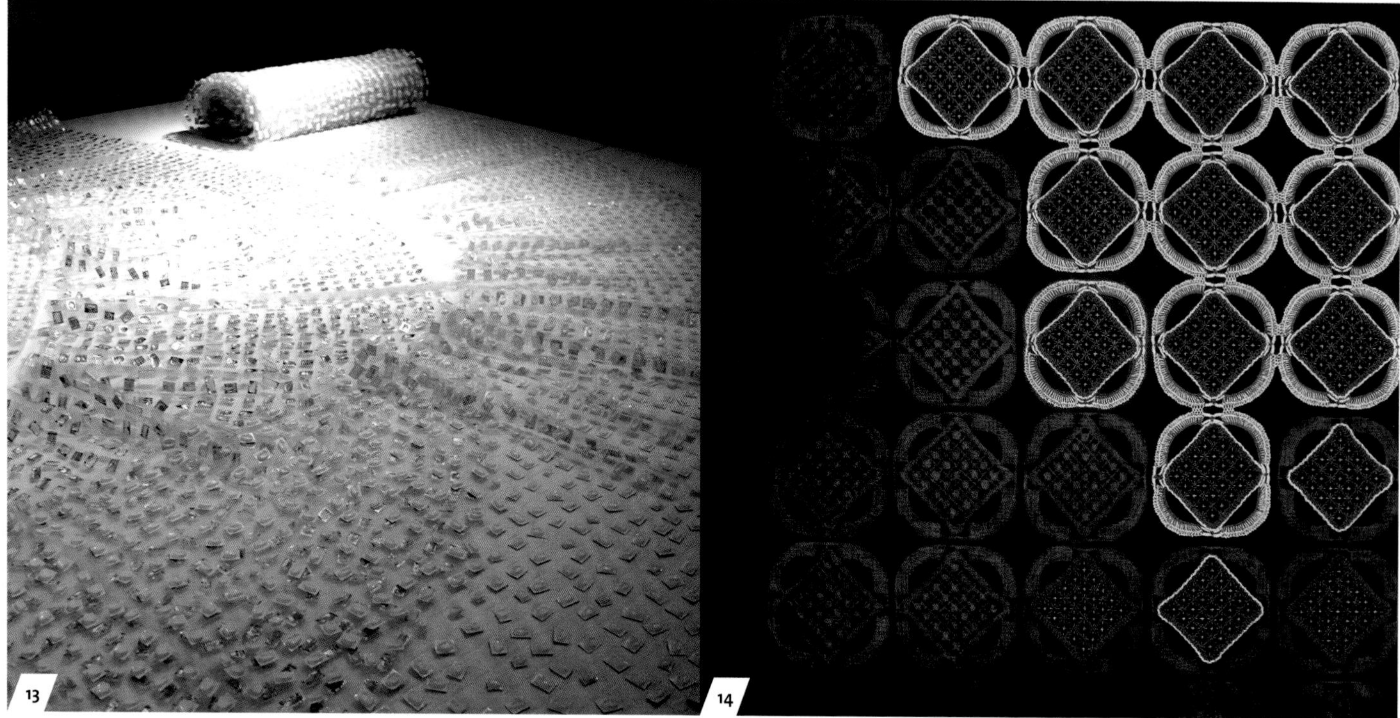

13. **Susie Freeman and Dr Liz Lee**, *White Pain*, 2007. This work is made from the packaging that remains after one man's lifetime of taking painkillers. The packets are encapsulated in a nylon monofilament pocket-knitted structure made using a hand-operated Swiss Dubied knitting machine. *White Pain* is 24 m (78 ft 9 in.) long.

14. **Elisa Markes-Young**, *The Strange Quiet of Things Misplaced #16* (detail), 2009. Young's complex and precise manipulation of wool, cotton and silk threads symbolizes a perfect memory, while acrylic, pencil and pastel 'shadows' of the same forms allude to memory loss.

Susie Krage's *Xs and Os* **[85]** – though it is still useful to have additional information about Krage, whose current work references circles of people and written communications, as well as the symbols for hugs and kisses. As she explains, 'having spent most of my married life overseas with my State Department husband and children, connections to my extended family and friends, both new and old, become important'. In contrast, some pieces require decoding. By creating a pattern that appears to fade away in *The Strange Quiet of Things Misplaced #16* **[14, 82]**, Elisa Markes-Young comments on a widespread concern, namely loss of memory. Nicky Schonkala's *Under My Skin* **[86]** is a personal narrative woven with 'stories of the past, present and future ... my physical location in central Australia and the continuing influence of this place on my life ... the influence of a lover ... my father's passing' – each in turn signalled by the patterns suggesting the skin of a Perentie (Australia's largest native monitor lizard), a 'Milky Way of freckles' and a genetic code.

Aside from panels and hangings, one cannot dismiss the narrative potential of yardage, every surplus length of which – either overtly or indirectly – is produced to become trade goods, to retain and communicate the sensibilities of the culture from which it originates, or to serve the tastes of distant consumers. This role is best seen through the study of patterns associated with regions where garments are made from uncut cloth (such as the *kanga*, sari, sarong, serape or shawl) or sewn into an untailored form such as the kaftan. West African batiks are a case in point. Although batik, a resist technique, has a long history in several African regions, it was the importation by Dutch traders of Indonesian batiks into Africa during the mid-1800s that created the appetite in Africa for lengths of cotton with complex crackled designs, typically in rich colours. A roller-printed variant (using two synchronized or duplex rollers to deposit wax

15

on both sides of the cloth simultaneously, based on a French method of printing banknotes) had been perfected during the 1830s and 1840s in a Belgian factory, Previnaire & Company. By the 1850s mass-manufacture of these types of cottons, especially for exportation, had developed in Switzerland, the Netherlands and England, leading to the terms 'real Dutch wax print' and 'Manchester batik' (both more appropriately known as 'print batik'). With or without the batik-like crackled ground, European manufacture, tailored to regional preferences within Africa, dominated supply until the 1960s, but in the post-colonial era factories in Nigeria and Ghana **[111, 113–17]** – as well as in Indonesia and, more recently, China – have supplied the demand among culturally authentic Africans everywhere.

The demand is such that the hand production of batiks has been reinvigorated by fair trade organizations such as Global Mamas, founded in Ghana in 2003. Batiks are now clearly essential to displays of personal identity throughout the African Diaspora, but the narrative of these cloths remains most potent in West Africa. According to the Global Mamas website, 'Prints range from abstract geometry to figurative images, and beyond. For many men and women, the patterns are a form of expression and even communication, announcing everything from their marital status and mood, to their political and religious beliefs.'[9] Heidi Chisholm, co-founder with Gareth Chisholm of the South African design collective Extra Fancy, designs exuberant patterns **[108–10, 112]** from her new base in Brooklyn, New York, celebrating what they refer to as Africa's 'super quirky crazy color culture clash style'.[10]

Other cultures narrate with cloth, too. Frances Ergen commissions headscarves and other textiles decorated with *oya*, to give work to the makers of this traditional Anatolian range of stitched edging and decorative techniques (including one said to be the origin of needlelace) **[15]**. She designs some scarf edgings

15. Anatolian lacemakers for Frances Ergen, London, *Oya*, 2010–11. Frances Ergen supports the makers of needlelace such as this by studying, sourcing, adapting and trading pieces of work from the Aegean and Anatolian regions.

herself, and others are part of the evolving local oeuvre: 'Due to family etiquette and traditions, certain subjects would inevitably be banned from conversation, so as this craft evolved, the ensuing symbolic language emerged accordingly – a secret communication between women. It is a form of expressing one's emotions ... through specific combinations of colours and designs; a fascinating source of unwritten female chat ... you could condemn your mother-in-law or express your passion for your new husband without being ridiculed by the whole of society.'[11]

16. **Maggi Toner-Edgar**, *Signpost Lace* (detail), 2006. This design for a textile derives from a sketchy mind map manipulated digitally. It was created while listening to Mary Schoeser's keynote address at Twisted Thread's 'Signpost to a New Space' conference in Harrogate in 2005. As Toner-Edgar says, 'my signature ... takes the harshness from the digital image [and] gives the digital a human touch'.

17. **Marie-Bonaventure Lebert for Hartmann et fils with Soehnée et Cie, Munster**, *Les Quatre Éléments*, c. 1810–18. This roller-printed cotton displays erudite imagery, including classical deities personifying the elements, typifying the renewed vogue for furnishings *à l'antique* during the Napoleonic period.

Of Time and Place

Bridging the gap between the narrative and the representation of time and place are 'toiles': a word that today signifies a cloth – typically of white or cream cotton – printed with scenes. The name comes from *toile de Jouy*, the fabric produced at the printworks in Jouy-en-Josas, near Versailles, where copperplate printing was added to their block-printing capabilities in 1770. The toile's distinctive feature was the single-colour application of a finely engraved image inspired by sources such as literature, opera or pastoral scenes. Despite the association of toiles with Jouy, they were produced in many locations both in and outside of France. The French themselves called them *toile d'Irlande*, because such tableaux on cloth were first chronicled in 1752, when copperplate-printed linen–cotton cloths were being printed by Theophilus Thompson and Francis Nixon in Ireland (and, soon afterwards, by Nixon in London). At least a century earlier the same technique had been used to print on silk, including images to be over-embroidered. Because silk is a protein fibre, it readily accepted the standard gall-based ink, but cotton and linen are cellulosics, so the gall matter first needed to be transformed into a dye. By the time this barrier was overcome, unadorned, engraved imagery on cloth spoke to a literate, world-aware consumer – an association it has never lost. Although toiles were occasionally enhanced by the addition of other colours through block-printing, most continued to be single-colour prints on a white or dyed ground. Toiles remained fashionable for furnishings until the 1830s, by which time they were roller printed **[17]**. Some did depict contemporary places and events, including military actions and even the copperplate printing of cloth itself, but many more toiles were produced in exotic *chinoiserie* and *indienne* styles or *à l'antique*, depicting subjects drawn from classical mythology. Block printers followed the fashion for toiles with more colourful variations of their own **[123–24]**.

As time elapsed, the 'isolated scene' format occasionally reappeared: updated, and true to the toile's original association with erudition, it incorporated visual references to major events or archaeological discoveries **[122, 133, 135]**. During the 1990s antique toiles were among the reserved, classical cloths that became sought out by both collectors and decorators. In the following decade a new breed appeared, referencing the originals in their limited colouration, placement of motifs and illustrative content, but recording modern life – our time, our places – with all their quirks and foibles. Jean Cacicedo's dyed, slashed and pieced woollen *Raincoat* **[137]**, for example, is a witty response to the weather in San Francisco. Digital production and design technologies have played no small part in this turn of events **[16]**. Naomi Ryder's *Cameo Pattern* **[134]**, for instance, is digitally printed with Photoshopped portions of her own embroideries.

17

Computer-aided production even makes it possible to produce drawings economically on an industrial Jacquard loom, as Jessica Smith has done **[121, 128–29]**. And although they, too, use digital capabilities, Paul Simmons and Alistair McAuley, who in 1990 founded Timorous Beasties in Glasgow, hand-screen print their influential toiles, stressing that the right technique must be used for each desired result **[125]**. Having been inspired by a toile in the Victoria and Albert Museum in London, Simmons and McAuley speak of their admiration for the sharpness of the original's imagery, of their quest for this kind of quality, and of their conviction that designing requires one to know how the final product is made.[12] In referencing the drawn line so directly and essentially being variations on historical illustrative media, such cloths encapsulate sensibilities of skill that are just as topical as their subject matter.

The 'print revolution' – the dominant cultural influence from the 1470s until the industrial revolution 300 years later – not only enabled innovative interactions between text and image, but also resulted in one of the most important markers of globalization, namely the wide availability of maps, which combined image and text. These were copperplate-printed on silk as well as paper, with optional additions, such as images of the four seasons, provided by those very same printers who printed patterns for embroiderers. The relationship between printing on paper and on yardage has remained significant since then, although it is often hidden (in the transfer of technology from newsprint production to textile printing, for example) or ephemeral, as in the unique production of a dress fabric by a Preston newspaper in 1897 to celebrate the Lancashire town's guild, founded in 1179 **[18]**. Hidden, too, were the 20th-century silk escape maps lining the jackets of parachute regiments in the Second World War. Of late, however, the development of digital printing has once again highlighted the relationship between paper and cloth, and at the same time satellite technology has transformed the concept of 'mapping', a term that today means far more than cartography and is widely applied to suggest both real and metaphorical connections. Topically, textiles have reflected this trend, too, not only in the textural mapping that transforms a flat computer graphic into one that appears three-dimensional, but also in the incorporation of map imagery itself. Among the several examples included here is one from Nancy Crasco's 'Weather Report' series **[159]**, which highlights climate change by interpreting commonly used adages about the weather, such as 'swimming against the tide', 'weathering the storm' or 'feeling under the weather'. As Crasco says, 'These phrases can be interchangeably used in connection with our personal lives or with life on our planet.'

Textile artists also use other kinds of mapping to consider dualities, ranging from abstract floor plans that question the interaction between the built and natural environment – explored in the work of Judi Fairburn and Dianne Finnegan (see Chapter V) – to observations of the more fleeting elements of terrain. Nicki Ransom asks in her *Footsteps II* **[145]**, 'What traces do we leave as we go about our daily lives? What evidence do we leave behind as we pass through – footsteps; a waft of air; a broken twig? Using the colours and textures of a footpath that ran alongside my house, this piece was part of a series that tried to reflect the subtle differences that occur after someone has passed by.' Norma Starszakowna explores the traces of humanity found on walls that have been rubbed, scarred,

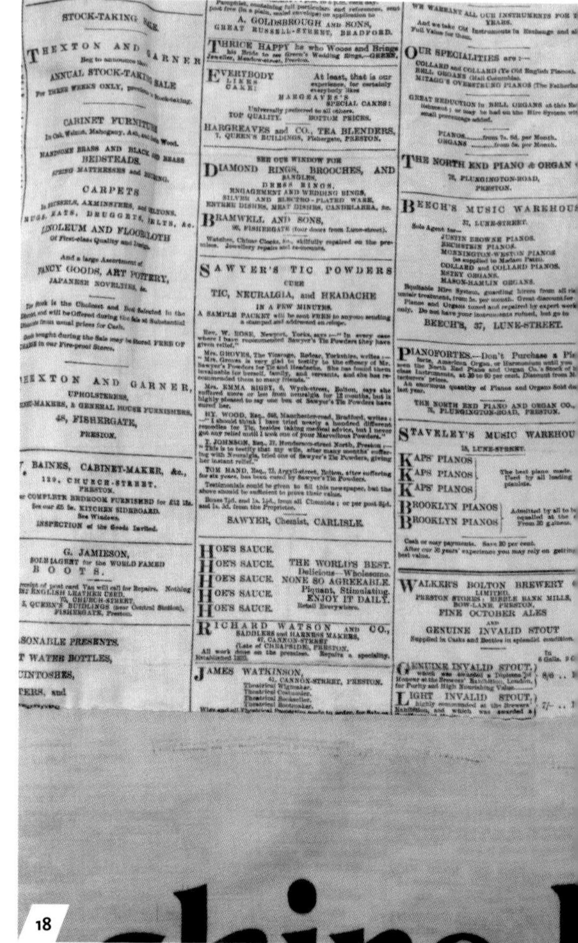

STOCK-TAKING

THEXTON AND GARNER

ANNUAL STOCK-TAKING SALE

CABINET FURNITURE

BEDSTEADS

CARPETS

LINOLEUM AND FLOORCLOTH

FANCY GOODS, ART POTTERY, JAPANESE NOVELTIES, &c.

THEXTON AND GARNER, UPHOLSTERERS, 48, FISHERGATE, PRESTON.

BAINES, CABINET-MAKER, &c., 129, CHURCH-STREET, PRESTON.

G. JAMIESON, BOOTS.

A. GOLDSBROUGH AND SONS, GREAT RUSSELL-STREET, BRADFORD.

THRICE HAPPY he who Wooes and Brings his Bride to see Green's Wedding Rings.—GREEN,

EVERYBODY LIKES CAKE!

HARGREAVES and CO., TEA BLENDERS, 7, QUEEN'S BUILDINGS, Fishergate, PRESTON.

DIAMOND RINGS, BROOCHES, AND BANGLES, DRESS RINGS, ENGAGEMENT AND WEDDING RINGS, SILVER AND ELECTRO-PLATED WARE,

BRAMWELL AND SONS,

SAWYER'S TIC POWDERS CURE TIC, NEURALGIA, and HEADACHE IN A FEW MINUTES.

SAWYER, Chemist, CARLISLE.

HOE'S SAUCE. THE WORLD'S BEST. Delicious—Wholesome. NONE SO AGREEABLE. Piquant, Stimulating. ENJOY IT DAILY. Retail Everywhere.

RICHARD WATSON AND CO., SADDLERS and HARNESS MAKERS, 47, CANNON-STREET

JAMES WATKINSON, 41, CANNON-STREET, PRESTON.

OUR SPECIALITIES are:—

PIANOS from 7s. 6d. per Month. ORGANS from 5s. per Month.

THE NORTH END PIANO & ORGAN 78, PLUNGINGTON-ROAD, PRESTON.

BEECH'S MUSIC WAREHOUSE 37, LUNE-STREET.

JUSTIN BROWNE PIANOS. BECHSTEIN PIANOS. COLLARD and COLLARD PIANOS. ESTEY ORGANS. MASON-HAMLIN ORGANS.

BEECH'S, 37, LUNE-STREET.

PIANOFORTES.—Don't Purchase a

THE NORTH END PIANO AND ORGAN CO., 78, PLUNGINGTON-ROAD, PRESTON.

STAVELEY'S MUSIC WAREHOU

KAPS' PIANOS KAPS' PIANOS KAPS' PIANOS

BROOKLYN PIANOS BROOKLYN PIANOS

WALKER'S BOLTON BREWERY LIMITED. FINE OCTOBER ALES AND GENUINE INVALID STOUT

GENUINE INVALID STOUT,

LIGHT INVALID STOUT,

18

18. Lancashire Daily Post, *Girl's fancy dress* (detail), 1897. Broadsheet and newspaper printers had contributed to the development of textile printing since the 17th century, and by the 19th century often produced 'novelty' silks such as this.

19. Helen Jones, *Luton Textile Archeology* (detail), 2011. One of two quilts made as part of a community project, this example presents the raw side, with participants' memories printed onto old sewing patterns and pinned in to create a collective narrative capable of constant change.

marked and overpainted, capturing the aged face of a place rather than of a single person **[152]**. The momentary quality of glinting light on a multifaceted glass edifice is Jane Freear-Wyld's subject matter **[153]**; Robina Summers observes the soon-to-be-gone frost **[150]**; and Teresa Poletti Glover preserves a fleeting reflection in a pool of water, which will never be the same again **[151]**. All of these works are reminders of life's temporary nature, able to be mapped only momentarily. Anne Morrell is similarly engaged in capturing the ephemeral mark **[158]**: *Make Tracks* refers to the short-lived signs of car wheels passing through mud, or of birds walking in the snow, and references the phrases associated with human endeavour, as in 'I've got to make tracks, I've got to get on'. Morrell adds, 'I love those marks as they leave a memory of what happened there – and then they in turn are gone'. Such mapping of memories, a core function of any saved, cherished textile, is an essential aspect of Helen Jones's project, *Luton Textile Archaeology* **[19]**. Jones asked participants to select a fabric and to match it to a personal recollection, to be incorporated into an installation that would present a positive vision for an English town suffering from economic decline and social tensions. She gathered fabrics from charity shops, rag recycling factories and other sources, and noticed that 'people were often surprised to find exact matches to fabrics or patterns from their past .... When the participants are interacting with the cloth through the haptic, visual ... and olfactory senses, powerful conscious and unconscious memories are triggered.' The final installation featured quilts left in a raw state and incorporated the participants' memories, which had been printed onto old sewing patterns and pinned in place – thus echoing the paper templates used in quilts of old. This final example draws together text, identity, narrative, and memories of times and places, illuminating their interconnections, which are so often integrated into textiles.

If the print revolution made imagery more widely available, and the Industrial Revolution made decorative products more affordable, the digital revolution has greatly increased virtual access to both. Has this devalued historical textiles? Judging from the statements of textile artists, the answer is 'no'. The artists seem even more aware of how important it is to have a first-hand acquaintance with models from the past. Has the digital revolution hindered textile artists today? Clearly not, as is illustrated by the vitality of fair-trade cooperatives and similar initiatives; when it comes to commissions, as Naomi Ryder points out, the internet is helpful, but the challenge is 'getting people to look at your portfolio instead of just your website'. Personal relationships remain crucial to success in this field, as in every endeavour, and it is telling that so many textiles today are a means of sharing one's identity and stories – the key to creating human bonds. It is especially significant that the topics of time and place have so strongly come to the fore in the past decade or so. The timing suggests that this is at least in part a response to the rise of the internet, in which there is no readily apparent chronology, nor evident geography. The virtual 'now' includes web content already twenty years old, and the use of a global service provider masks a user's location. Textiles, as the art most rooted in all of the senses, offer an antidote to the viral myth that skill is unnecessary, that knowledge need not be retained, and that the world can be understood through a two-dimensional image on a screen.

20. Ottoman imperial weaving workshop, *Silk lampas*, 1550–1600. Created during the artistic golden age of the Ottoman Empire, this silk incorporates threads of silver-gilt *lamella* wrapped around a silk core in a pattern devoid of representational motifs, in accordance with the Islamic beliefs of the Ottoman sultans.

21. Indian printer, Pha nung *fragment*, 18th–19th centuries. This painted and dyed garment cloth, worn by men and women, was made for the Siamese (now Thai) market. It incorporates Buddhist imagery, including supplicating *devas* and the Kirtimukha motif, the latter depicted in paler red against the rich mordant-dyed red ground.

22. A. W. N. Pugin, *Drummond*, 1850. Commissioned by J. G. Crace for the interior of Gawthorpe Hall, Lancashire – a Jacobean manor house redesigned by Sir Charles Barry (who as architect of The Houses of Parliament was to work with Pugin again) – this Gothic Revival design was originally block-printed at Bannister Hall, near Preston. Here it is a machine-woven tapestry produced today by Watts of Westminster.

23. Beryl Dean, *Queen of Heaven*, 1983. Incorporating small jewels and beads, this was worked in *or nué*, in which the modelling is the solely the result of the placement of couching stitches. Dean was regarded as the finest embroider in the UK in her day, and taught Constance Howard, after whom an embroidery research centre is named at Goldsmiths College, London.

24. Robyn Mountcastle, *Red Altar Fall*, 2005. Part of a series completed in 2010 for St Paul's Anglican Cathedral in Melbourne, this altar fall, tapestry-woven with wool, cotton and viscose on a weft of cotton seine twine, employs imagery and hues for Passiontide and other times in the liturgical calendar that call for red-violet vestures.

25

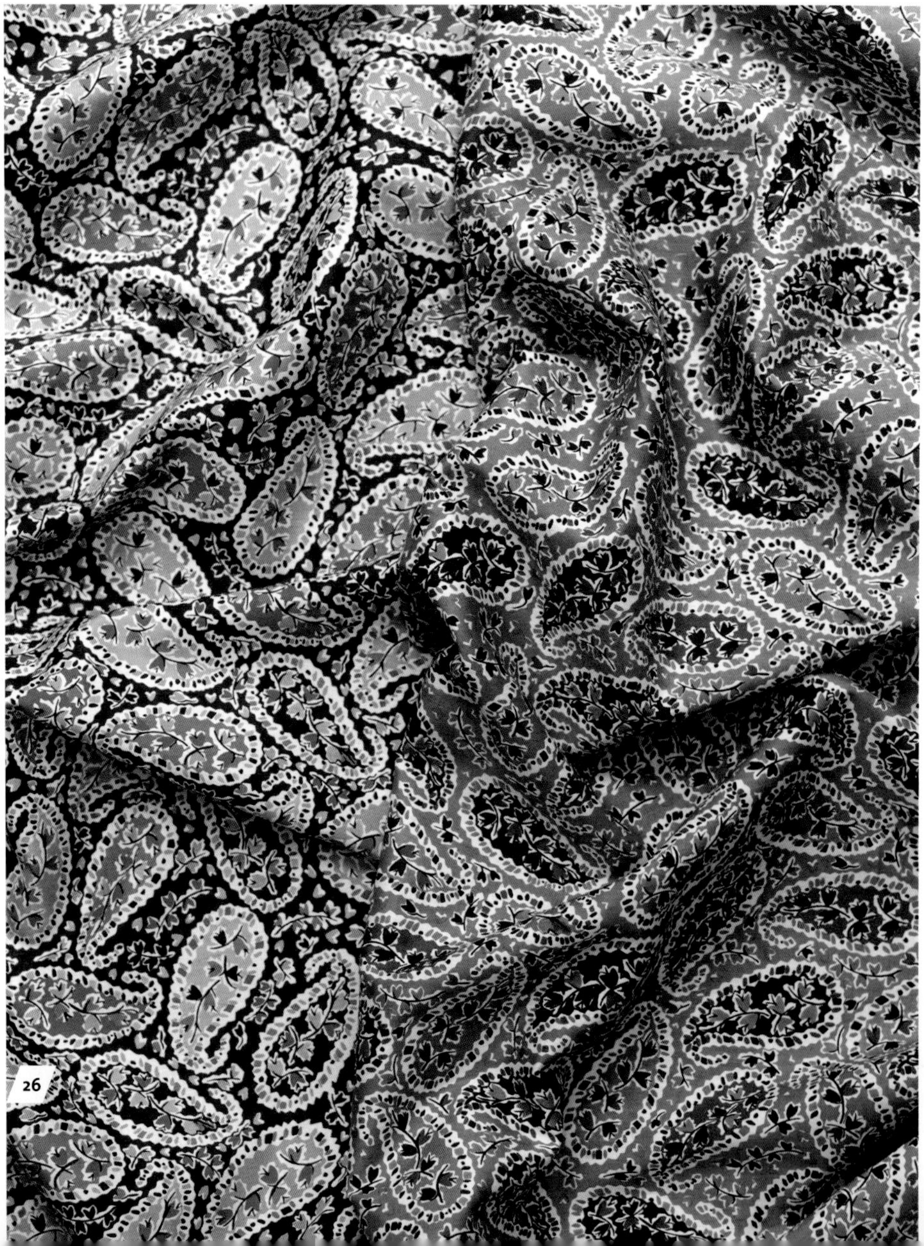

25. Kashmiri weaver, *Woman's shawl*, mid-1800s. Of cashmere (goat-fleece underdown), this large shawl (363 × 140 cm; 143 × 55 in.) was twill-woven with double-interlocking tapestry patterning, pieced and embroidered with wool.

26. Raymond Honeyman, *Small Paisley*, 1992 and 2008. Originally designed for the Liberty 1992 spring/summer range, the screen-printed cottons shown here were redrawn and recoloured for Liberty Japan in 2008.

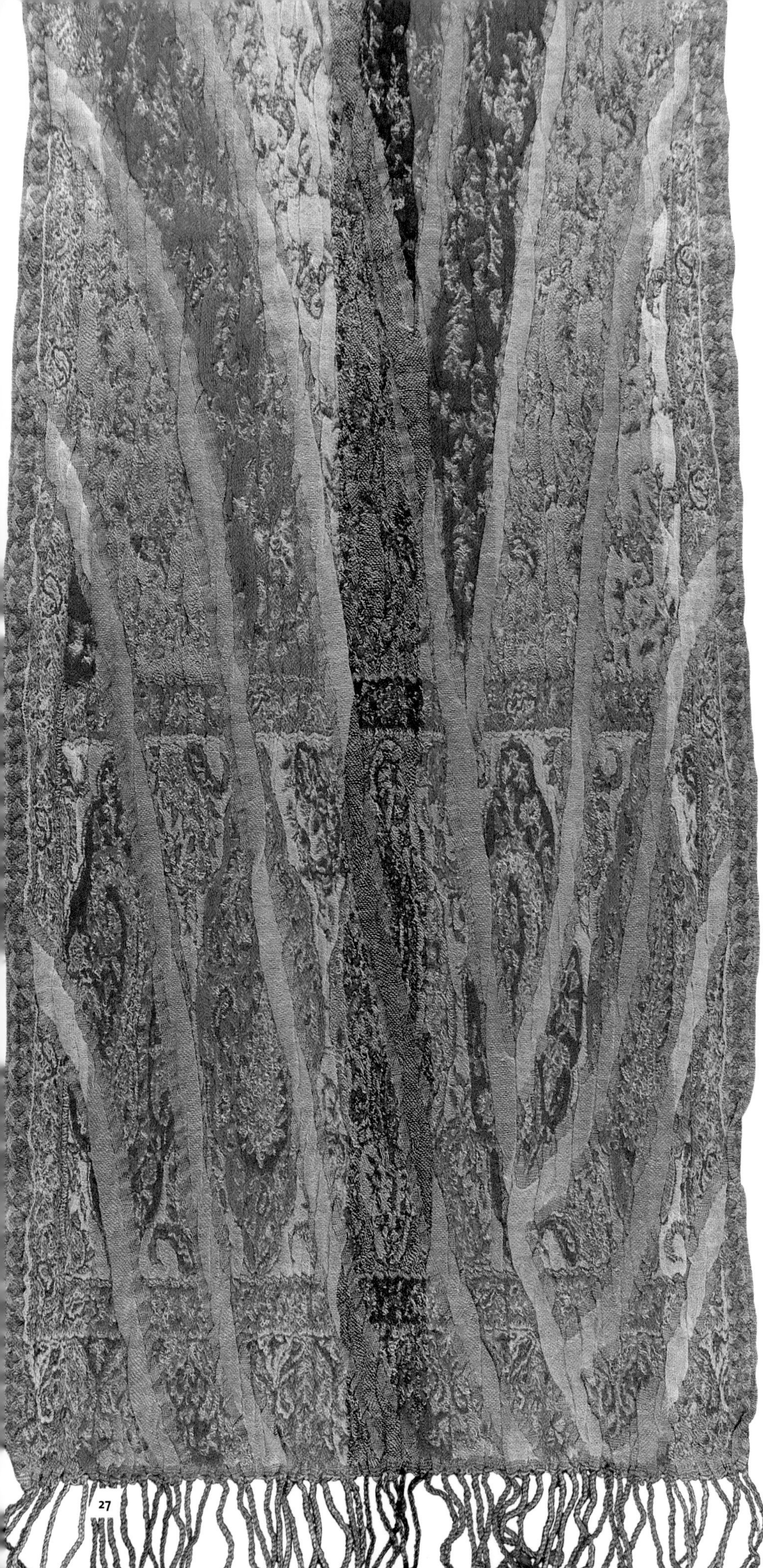

27. Indian manufacturer, *Long scarf*, *c.* 2000. This complex interpretation of the Kashmiri shawl is a rayon and acrylic double weave, with areas of single cloth (with floating wefts left unwoven behind) creating the crushed effects. The finely braided fringe, 6.4 cm (2½ in.) in length, reveals the colours of the warp threads.

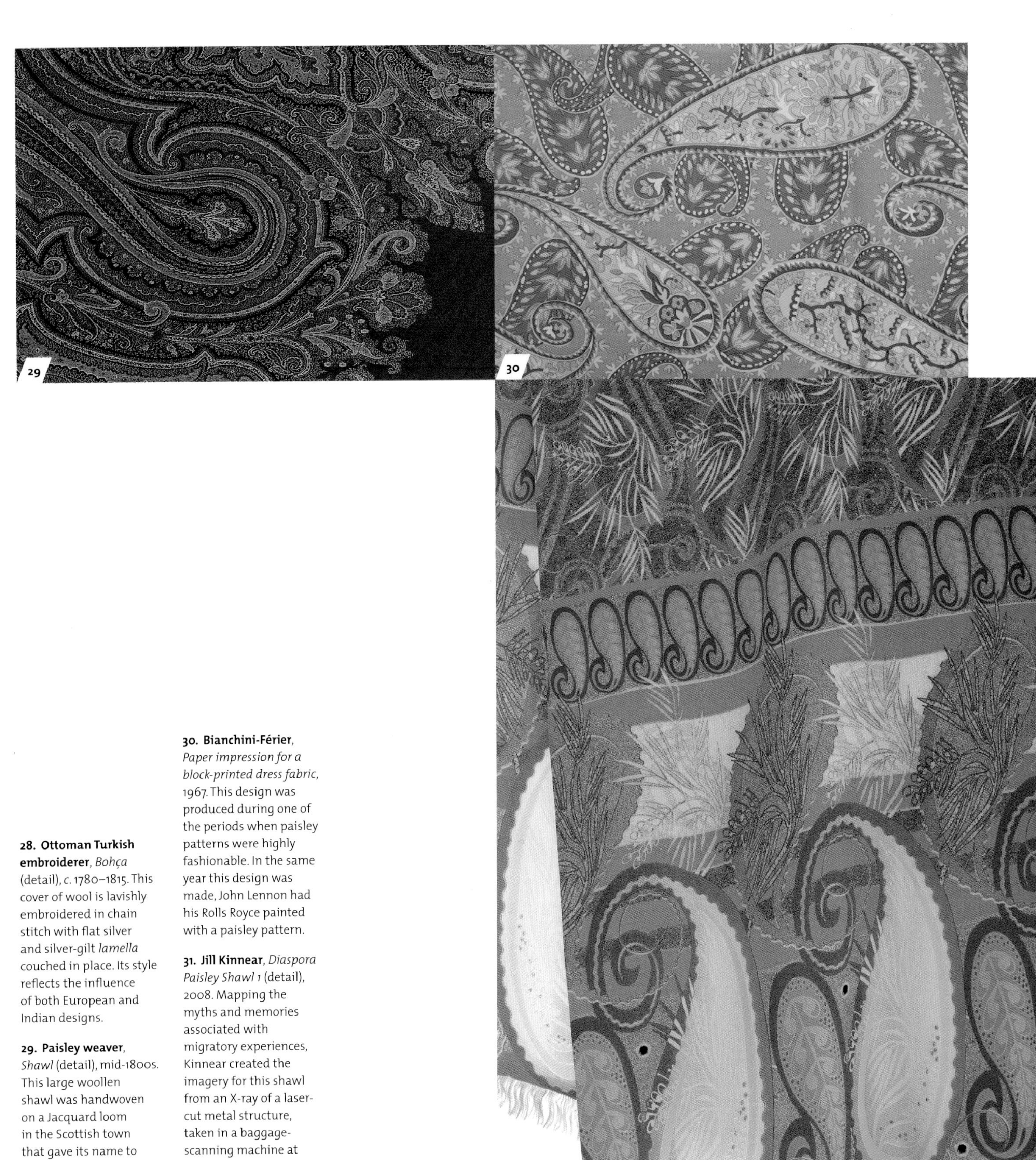

28. **Ottoman Turkish embroiderer**, *Bohça* (detail), *c.* 1780–1815. This cover of wool is lavishly embroidered in chain stitch with flat silver and silver-gilt *lamella* couched in place. Its style reflects the influence of both European and Indian designs.

29. **Paisley weaver**, *Shawl* (detail), mid-1800s. This large woollen shawl was handwoven on a Jacquard loom in the Scottish town that gave its name to *buta* patterns. This example employs the enormous, elongated motifs characteristic of European shawls of the period.

30. **Bianchini-Férier**, *Paper impression for a block-printed dress fabric*, 1967. This design was produced during one of the periods when paisley patterns were highly fashionable. In the same year this design was made, John Lennon had his Rolls Royce painted with a paisley pattern.

31. **Jill Kinnear**, *Diaspora Paisley Shawl 1* (detail), 2008. Mapping the myths and memories associated with migratory experiences, Kinnear created the imagery for this shawl from an X-ray of a laser-cut metal structure, taken in a baggage-scanning machine at Brisbane International Airport departure lounge, reconfigured and digitally printed onto silk crêpe de chine. (See also nos 37, 39.)

32. Sophie Pattinson, *Long shawl* (left), 2011. Pattinson has trained rural Bangladeshi women to embroider, creating a fairtrade export business that produces Pattinson's original designs as well those she has evolved from traditional patterns, exemplified by the screen-printed and stitched shawl on left, and a vintage embroidery from the Hazara Valley in northern Pakistan.

33. Kashmiri knitter, *Pair of wool stockinette stitch stockings*, 1800s or earlier. Lined with a layer of heavier knitted wool, stitched to hold it in place, such stockings were made to be worn indoors over pyjama trousers, without shoes. A similar pair was worn by Warren Hastings, the first governor general of India, from 1773 to 1785.

34. Lucknow artisans, *Sari* (detail), early 1800s. Fine plain woven cotton with cutwork is embroidered with Phanda knots, a variation of buttonhole stitches, as well as back and chain stitches.

34

35. Rajasthani dyer, Pagri, *c.* 1860s. This man's turban cloth, or *pagri*, is decorated in a complex type of tie-dye known as *laharia*. This is a wrap-resist process involving folding into accordion pleats widthwise, rolling diagonally and wrapping tightly with thread before each colour is dyed, resulting in symmetrical zig-zag or *grandadar* patterns.

36. Jill Kinnear, *Workshop of the Empire, a dress featuring Steel Tartan 1* (see no. 39), 2008. Made up from digitally printed single and triple silk georgette and silk shantung, this garment speaks of the role tartans have played in the construction of a Scottish identity and mythology. Both in its construction and pattern, the dress evokes 'empire'.

38

39

37. Indian printer and tailor, *Shirt* (detail), 1950s–60s. Made from a tie-dyed gauze-like turban cotton for the export market, this type of fabric became known in America as 'bleeding madras' after a principal centre of production, the Indian city of Madras (today Chennai). Locals there believe the pattern imitated the tartans worn by the Scottish regiments occupying southern India in the 1800s.

38. Persian weaver, *Sash*, 1690–1750. Woven for a nobleman, this silk brocaded with metal-foil threads employs an array of complex geometric and arabesque forms. They were sought after at home and abroad, particularly by Polish courtiers.

39. Jill Kinnear, *Steel Tartan structures*, 2008. These metal structures, each roughly 55 cm (21½ in.) square, were X-rayed to create the artist's own tartan textiles – analagous to the concept of the migratory or 'third' space. 'Like maps, the designs of tartan are linked to land, though not necessarily ancestral land. Their warps and wefts point east, west, north and south.'

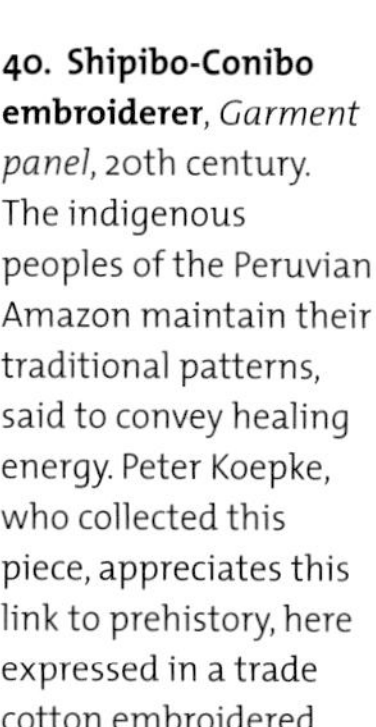

40. Shipibo-Conibo embroiderer, *Garment panel*, 20th century. The indigenous peoples of the Peruvian Amazon maintain their traditional patterns, said to convey healing energy. Peter Koepke, who collected this piece, appreciates this link to prehistory, here expressed in a trade cotton embroidered with modern thread.

41. Anne Woringer, *Le Labyrinthe de Pénélope*, 2009. Black linen patterned through *nui* (sewing-resist) shibori was hand-embroidered and quilted, then appliquéd onto 19th-century hemp.

42. Kuba weaver and embroiderer, *Kasai velvet*, *c.* 1950. The Kuba Kingdom, founded in the 17th century and today within Zaïre, maintains a tradition of male fibre-producers and weavers, and female dyers and embroiderers. Woven from raffia on an upright slanted loom, the pile is created from differing heights of stitched loops, cut open.

43. Candace Crockett, *Kuba Series #2*, 2002. Having studied Kuba cloths and developed an appreciation of their spontaneous and improvizational quality created through mutation and repetition, the artist has here chosen fine transparent white silk, printed layers of a basic image on it, changing its appearance through fabric manipulation and by adding and discharging colour.

40

41

42

43

44. Jane Dunnewold, *Etude 35 – Arabesque con Brio*, 2011. One of forty-five works resulting from a four-month commitment to create something every day, as a form of spiritual excercise, the direct and devoré patterns were taken from antique indigo pieces from Thailand. Incorporating hand-dyeing and -stitching, solvent (photocopy) transfers on silk were laminated to the background.

45. Shipibo-Conibo embroiderer, *Skirt panel*, 20th century. Both embroidered and painted, such patterns are attributed by the Amazonian Shipibo-Conibo to Ronin, the Great World Boa, who unites all designs on his skin. This panel is preserved in the Koepke Collection because 'The quality of the work serves to demonstrate the artist's level of thought and imagination.'

45

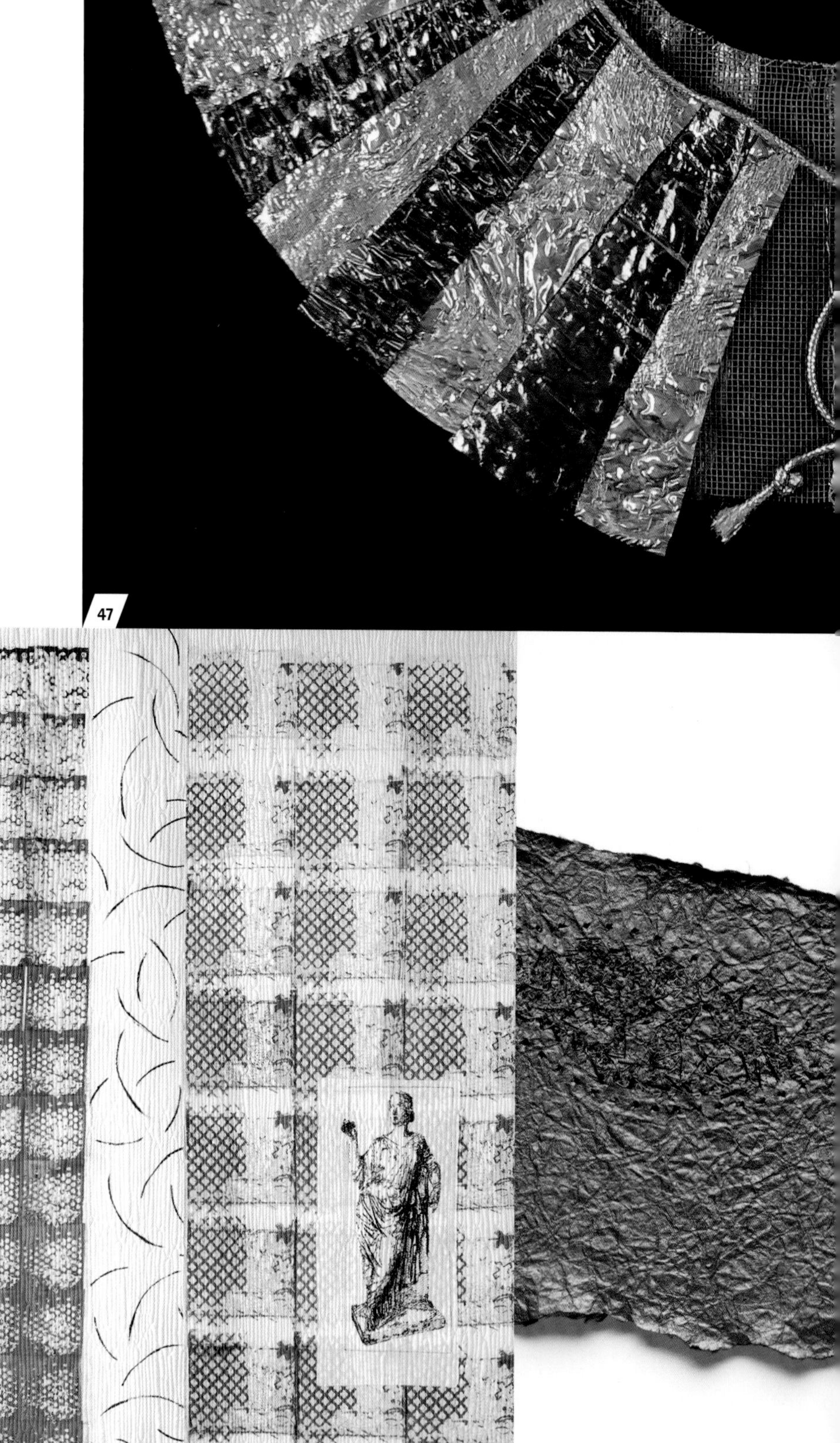
SHARIA VS DEMOCRACY
TEXTILE · FOLDS · BODIES
IS DIALOGUE POSSIBLE?

47

46

48

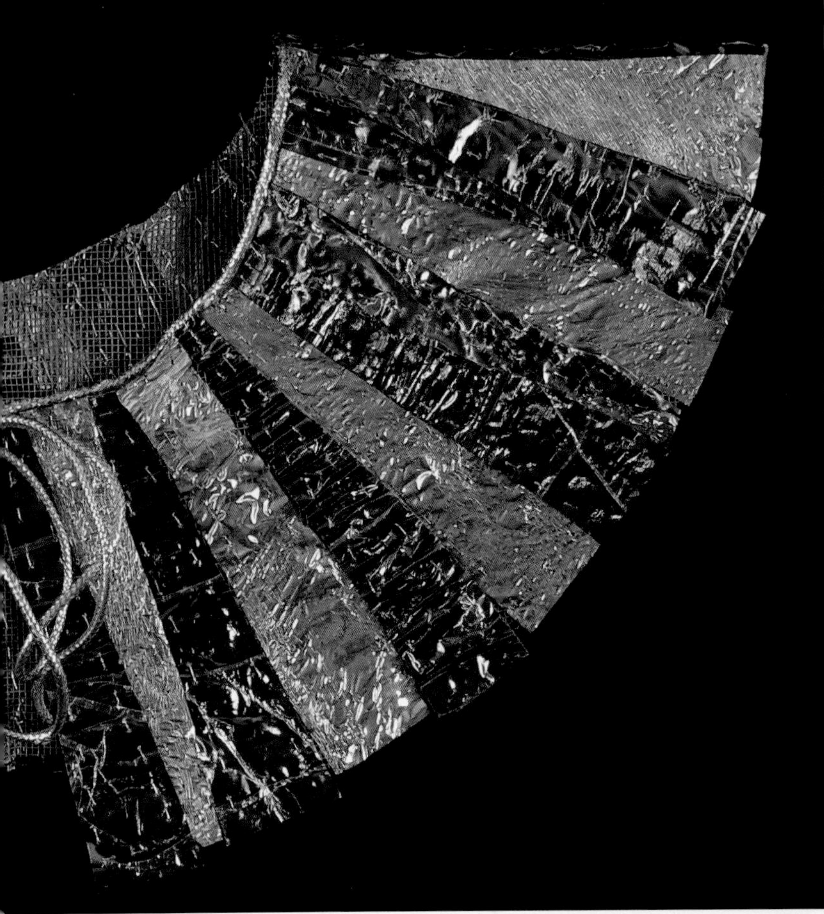

46. Charlotte Yde, *Dialogue 2*, 2010. This machine-quilted cotton panel (140 × 186 cm; 55 × 73¼ in.) with deconstructed screen printing, direct stamping, oil paint-stick, digitally programmed stitched drawings and letters reflects the artist's interest in the meaning of flowing-fabric clothing of other cultures and eras, here Muslim and Greco-Roman.

47. Jo Ann Stabb, *The Faux Egyptian Collar*, 1992. This work is constructed from strips of mylar and heat-modified plastics sewn/appliquéd to a base of plastic screening, with a tie of rayon 'rat-tail' cordage. Heat-modified plastics are blistered plastics and mylars that were uniquely made in Sausalito, California, not far from the artist's studio.

48 and 49. Dolores Slowinski, *Transmutation* (whole and detail), 2010. Part of the artist's 'Threadlines' series, this work of waxed-cotton embroidery floss on metallic *unryu* paper evokes the atomic-level process of changing lead into gold through the loss of three protons. It ponders the possibility that 'we may find that [the most profound] losses have been the means of our own transmutation from who we were to who we are and who we might become'.

50

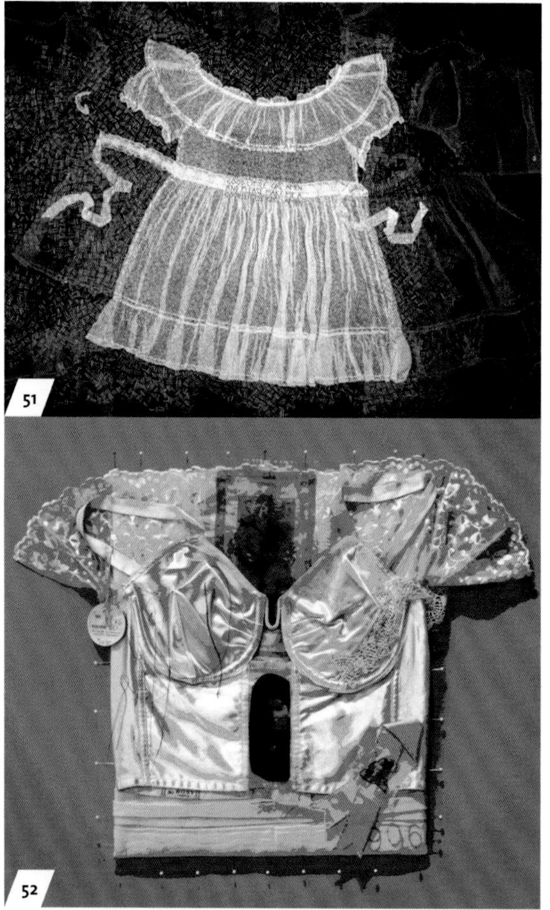

51

52

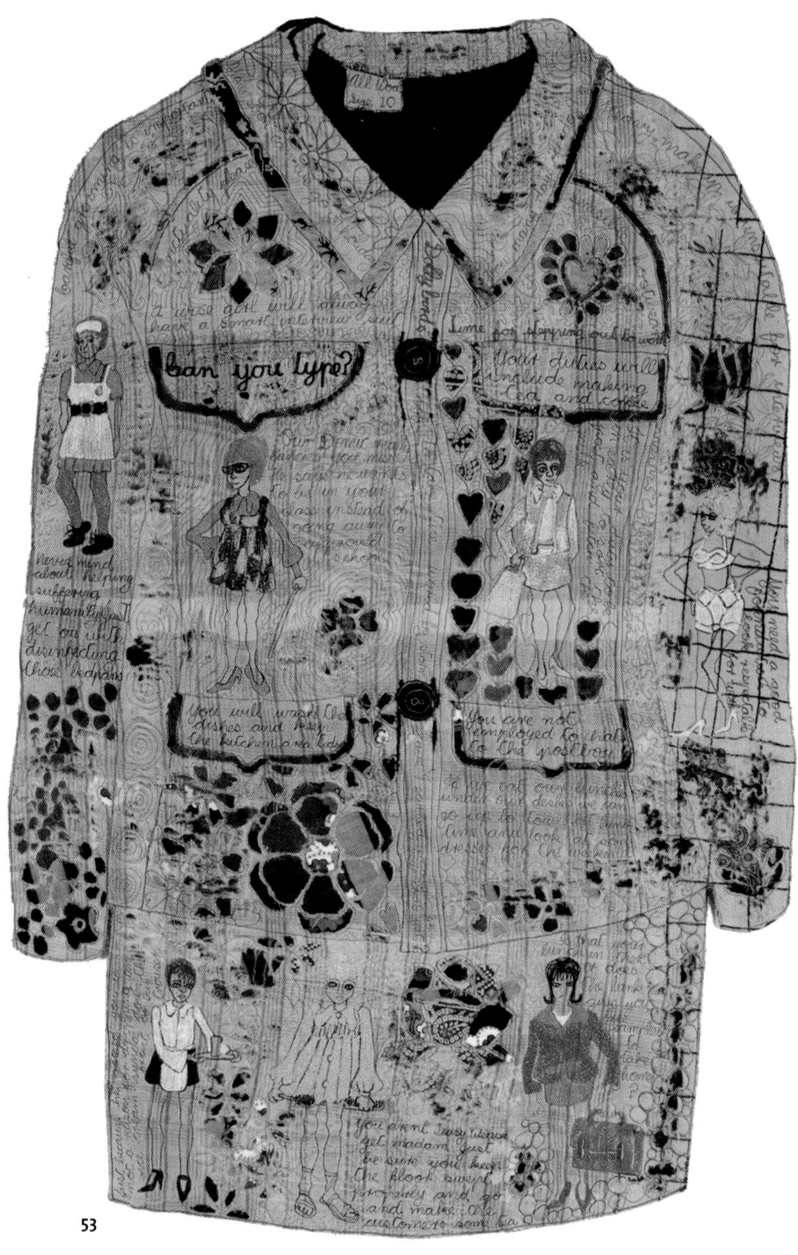

53

50 and 53. Val Jackson, *Room for a Workshop* and *Can You Type*, 2009. Layers of hand-dyed silks and lawns on a heavy felt base were embellished with free machine embroidery and reverse appliqué prior to distressing to expose the layers beneath. The process is intended to echo the way in which memory wears away and changes with the passage of time. Both pieces are from the artist's 'Rites of Passage' series and look at the high points of young adulthood. The use of old garments emphasizes the function of clothing and other possessions as markers of identity.

54

54. Elizabeth Brimelow, *461 Days – A Slice of My Life*, 2009. This is a stitched cloth, paper and card journal. As Brimelow says, 'each day I took a scrap of fabric and put it in the book, often with a small item of news … the weather, how my work was going, holidays, outings, family events and even winning the Ryder Cup'.

55. Allie Kay, *Voiceless* (detail), 2010. Silk strips are blanket-stitched into cut-outs in the linen. The poem is hand-embroidered between the lines of 'mouths', and the 'i's' are dotted with red beads.

55

51. Carolyn Nelson, *Self-Portrait as a Four-Year-Old*, 1976. Collage created from a partly deconstructed dress, made in 1948 (by the artist's grandmother) to wear while sitting for a portrait painting. Also incorporating hand-dyed silk organza and organzine thread, it visually contrasts the 'good little girl' who sits still with her much preferred freedom to move.

52. Maggi Toner-Edgar, *Inner Strength*, 2003. In a tribute to her sister's suffering and strength during a lost battle against cancer, the artist here represents the loss of femininity through a Parisian 1950s bustier and handmade 1920s' lace combined with images transferred to silk organza, and pins 'to show how our spirits were sewn together like a pin through cloth'.

56. Raoul Dufy for Bianchini-Férier, *Le Bon Ton*, 1920. Depicting the fashions of the day, this block print was intended for silk dress fabrics; here it is recorded on paper.

57. English manufacturer, *Cornely 'A' machine chain-stitched jumper* (detail), c. 1920. Visible on both the inside and the outside (below), fashionably vivid colours have been worked in fine wool onto vanishing muslin.

58. Alberto Fabio-Lorenzi for Bianchini-Férier, *Gouache design for 'Floral Bouquet'*, 1926–30. Lorenzi also designed fashion plates and other graphic works.

59. Raoul Dufy for Bianchini-Férier, *Les Arums*, c. 1919. Retaining its original glazing, this block-printed cotton is a furnishing fabric and had an accompanying wallpaper.

60. English manufacturer (attributed), *Hand block-printed cotton velvet*, c. 1913–23. In an amalgam of influential styles, the bluebell motif here echoes designs by the Weiner Werkstätte, while this type of rose is identified with the Glasgow School of Art, where Jessie Newberry used similar appliquéd roses in her embroideries.

61
62
63
64

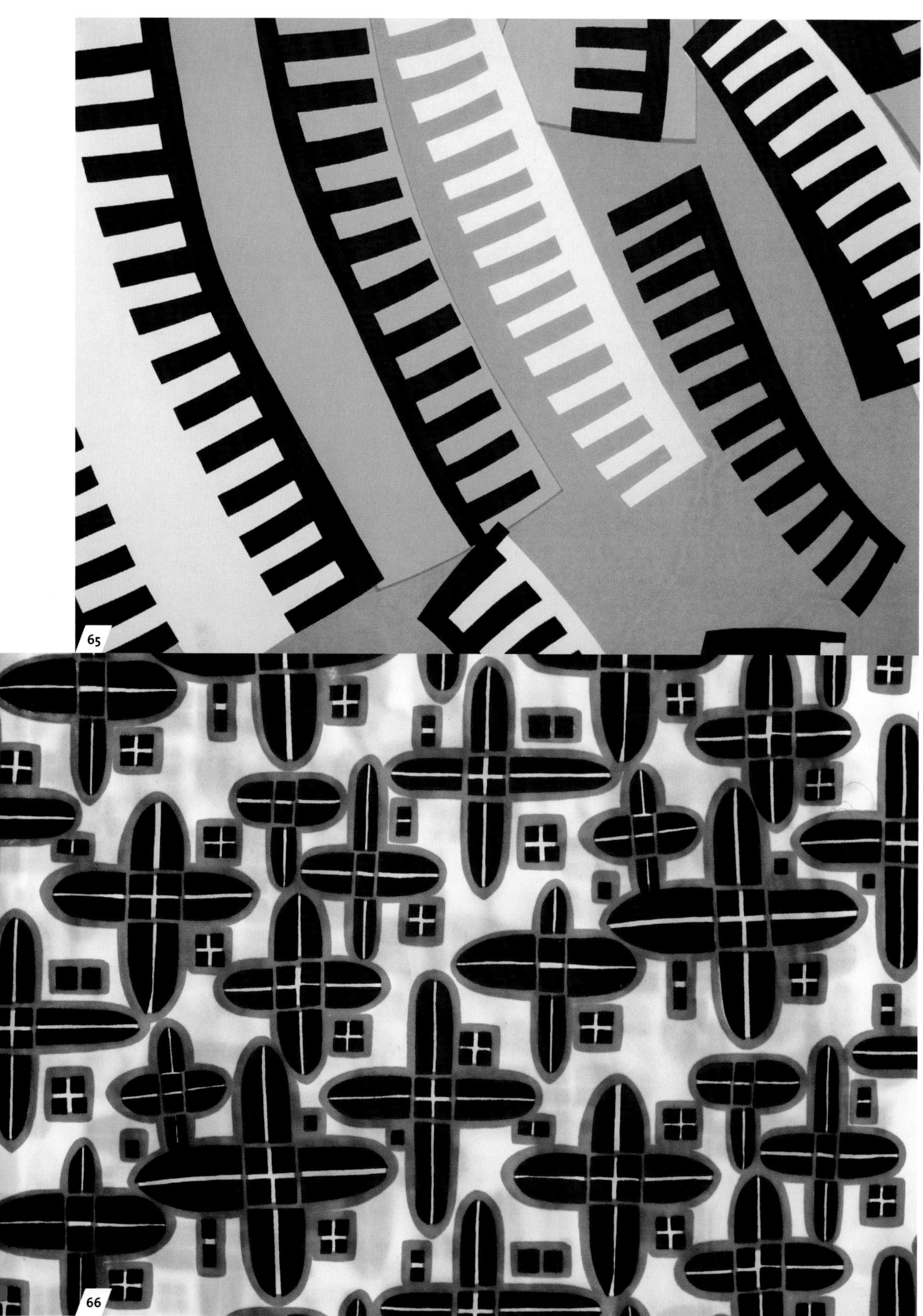

61–66. Bianchini-Férier, *Paper impressions*, 1961–81. Epitomizing this firm's continued production of painterly printed dress fabrics are six designs dated 1964 (61), 1980 (62 + 63), 1981 (64), 1967 (65) and 1961 (66).

67 and 69. Alfred Latour for Bianchini-Férier, *Hearts and Spades* and *Les Coquillages*, designed 1929. Both hand block-printed and launched in 1931 – the first on cotton and the second on linen – these form part of the first range to be designed by Latour, who succeeded Dufy as studio designer.

68. Dagobert Peche for the Weiner Werkstätte, *Block-printed linen*, 1911–15. Peche was a director of the Weiner Werkstätte and its most prolific designer until his death in 1923.

70. Robert Bonfils for Bianchini-Férier, *Leaves*, 1931. This cotton damask incorporates highlights of viscut, or laminated cellophane.

67
68
69
70

71

72

71 and 72. Karen Taiaroa, *Whakaaria Mai (Show me)* and *Consequences*, 2009. Screen printing, fabric paint, stamping, dye, appliqué and machine embroidery on a second-hand tablecloth. Working in layers by cutting and connecting pieces together, Taiaroa considers how oral narratives transfer cultural rules, prioritizing 'the different parts of the story using repetition, colour, light, compositional devices, and the size of motifs in the same way adjectives and verbs are used in narratives to enhance the impact of a story'.

73. Soraya Abidin, *Ride Me*, 2007. From the artist's 'Crazy Stitch Bitch' series, this work combines vintage Persian wool and metallic thread, hand-embroidered on a wool canvas to capture remnants of a dream Abidin had while travelling to Melbourne. As she says, 'to ride an ostrich is directly related to the spiritual freedom and psychological liberation felt during meaningful travel.'

74. Egyptian artist, *Panel*, 20th century. Painted on this coarsely woven, cream-coloured cotton is a Nubian ibex, a desert-dwelling goat that was common in ancient Egypt. The ibex is still considered a talisman of good fortune.

75. Peter Nambaraitj, *X-ray Crocodile*, c. 1975.
77. Bardjaray of Gumadeer River, *Man Getting Wild Honey*, c. 1975. These two bark paintings were both created by artists who were members of the Oenpelli tribe, Arnhem Land, one of the five regions in the Northern Territory, Australia.

76. Eva Wanganeen, *Bush Tucker*, 2007. Painting on silk with acid dyes and gutta resist has led this Aboriginal artist 'on a journey exploring the culture of the Arrente, Wirringu and Kokatha people, from whom I am descended. I continue to be inspired by what I learn and endeavour to pass on this knowledge through my art.'

78. Jimmy Mijau Mijau, *Kangaroo*, c. 1975.
80. Unknown artist, Goulburn Island, Northern Territory, *Ritual Execution Story*, c. 1975. Like the other two bark cloths shown here, these were collected by the geneticist G. Ledyard Stebbins and his wife, Barbara.

79. Tonga artist, *Tapa cloth*, 20th century. This South Pacific barkcloth is painted and stamped with pigments. It was imported into Hawaii by the Tonga Trading Company, founded in 1969 by Andrew B. White Sr., a former marine who became fluent in the Wallisian language during the Second World War and wished to gain fair prices for handmade Pacific Island objects.

81. Marieta Toneva, *Life Source*, 2010. Weaving with paper twine and fibre optics, the artist is here inspired 'by the eternal struggle and the constant magnetism between good and evil, between light and darkness'.

82. Elisa Markes-Young, *The Strange Quiet of Things Misplaced #16* (detail), 2009. Using acrylic, pencil, pastel, wool, cotton and silk on Belgian linen, the artist links her patterns and structure to the concept of collective consciousness, as well as to loss of memory, and thus identity. The work is a panel 110 cm (43¼ in.) square (shown in full on p. 472).

75

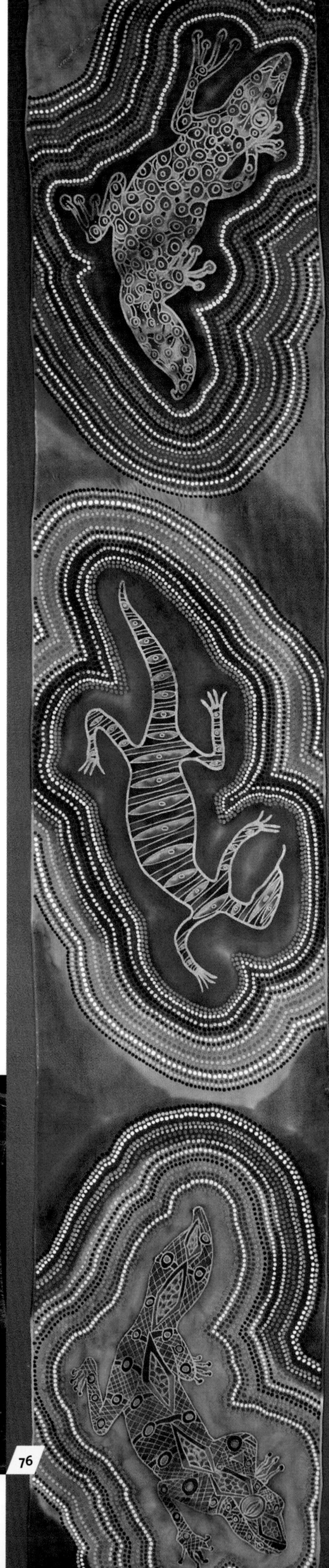
76

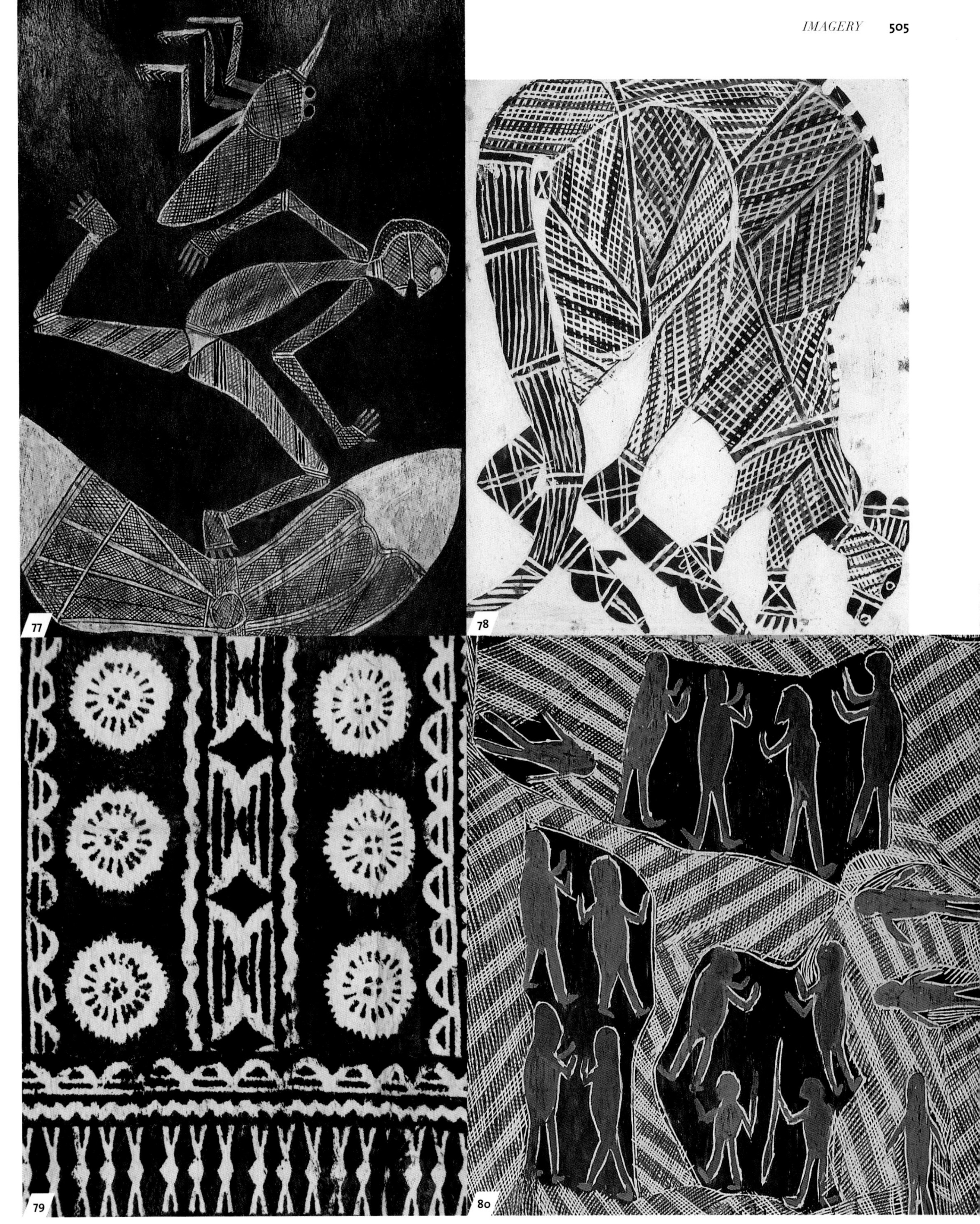
77
78
79
80

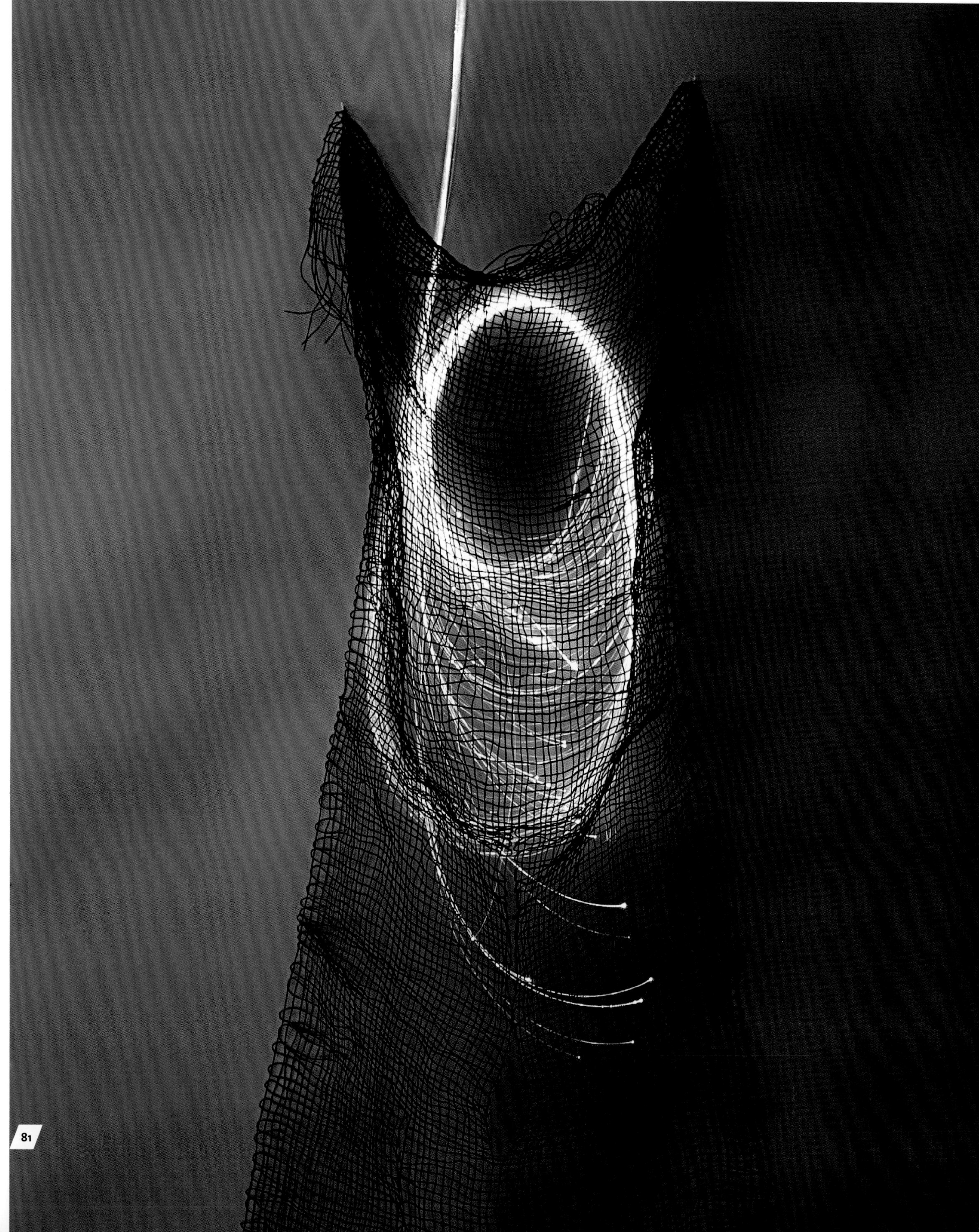

81

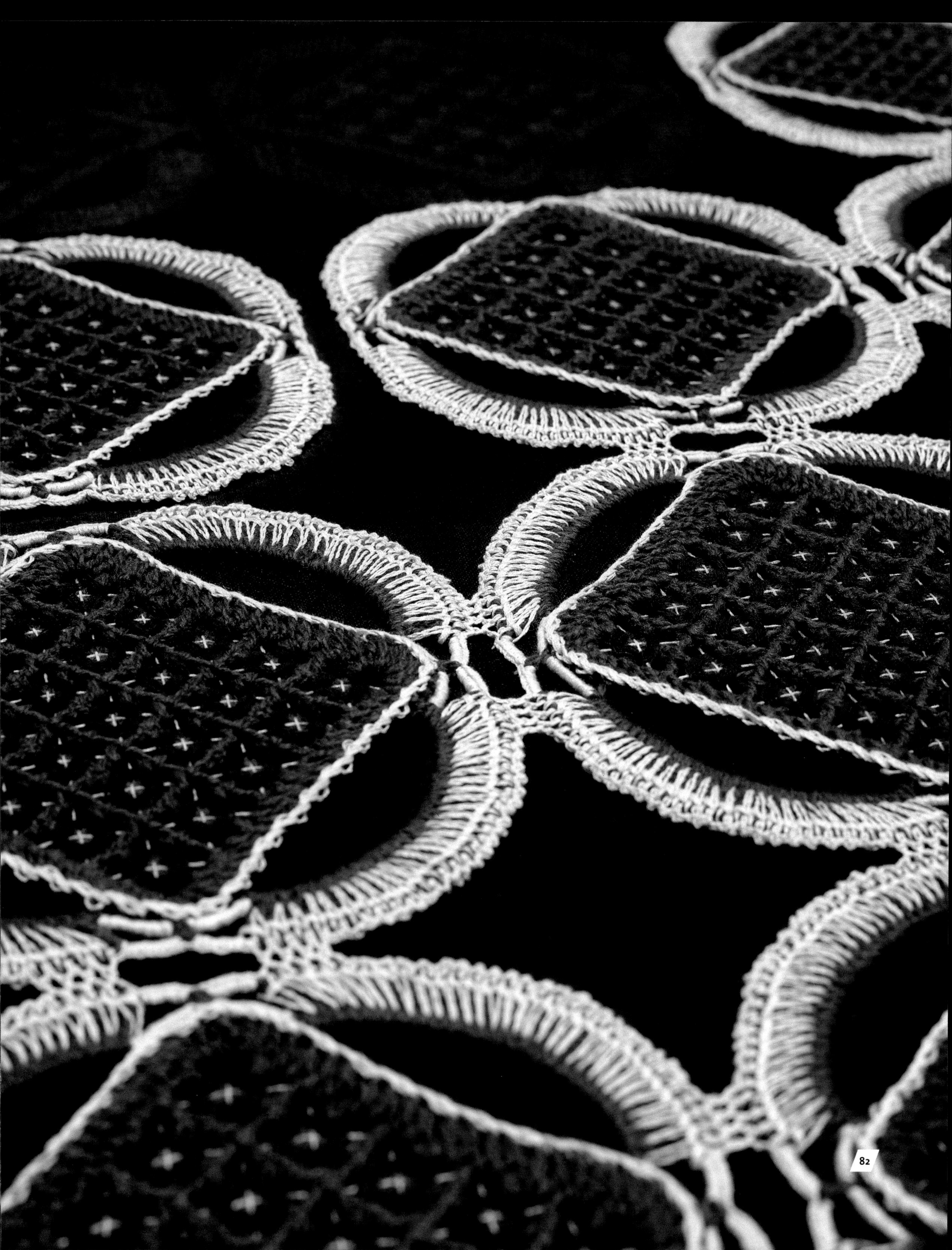

83
ENGLAND
DOGGER
BANK
LONDON
84

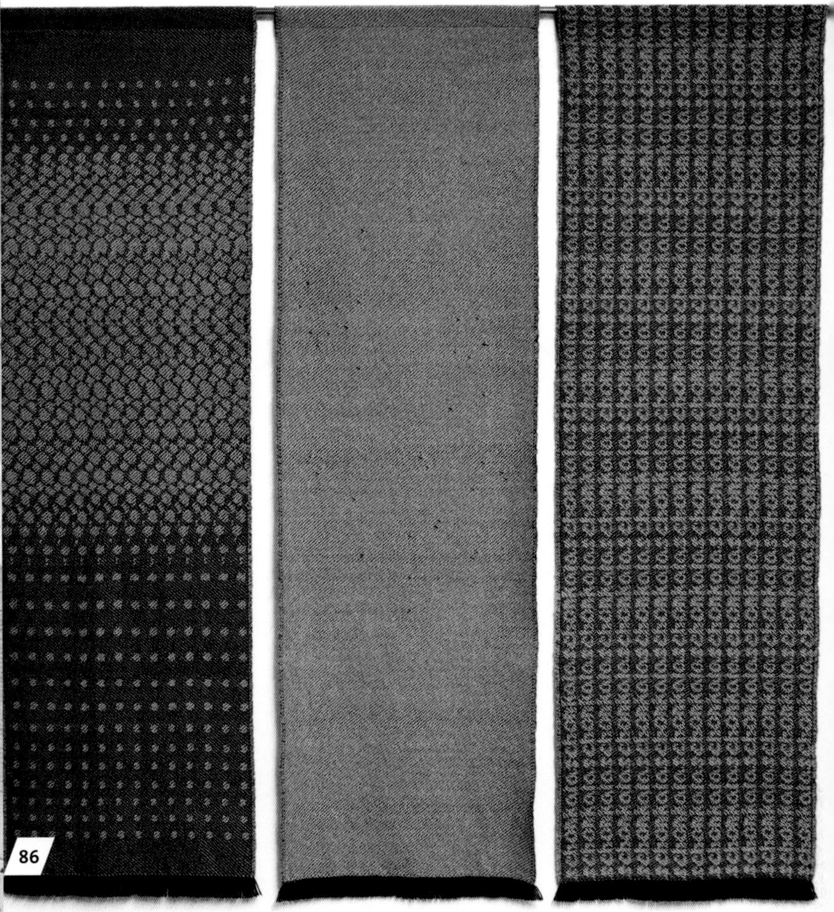

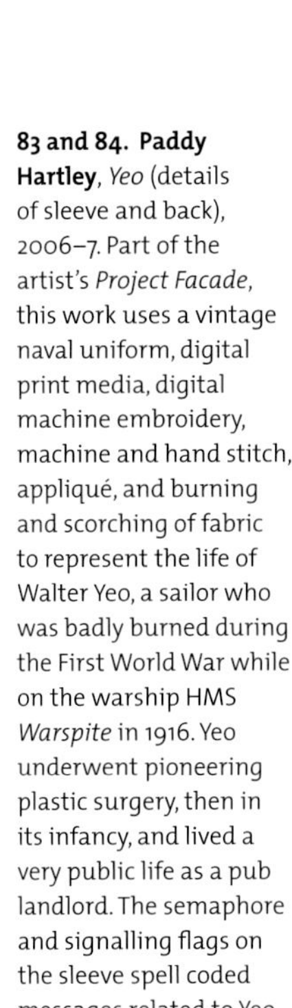

83 and 84. Paddy Hartley, *Yeo* (details of sleeve and back), 2006–7. Part of the artist's *Project Facade*, this work uses a vintage naval uniform, digital print media, digital machine embroidery, machine and hand stitch, appliqué, and burning and scorching of fabric to represent the life of Walter Yeo, a sailor who was badly burned during the First World War while on the warship HMS *Warspite* in 1916. Yeo underwent pioneering plastic surgery, then in its infancy, and lived a very public life as a pub landlord. The semaphore and signalling flags on the sleeve spell coded messages related to Yeo.

85. Susie Krage, *Xs and Os* (detail), 2010. Incorporating paper and metal-leaf lamination with screen printing on sheer polyester, this piece represents the importance of connections between distant family and friends, symbolized by the widely accepted symbols for hugs and kisses.

86. Nicky Schonkala, *Under my Skin*, 2011. The artist has created handwoven patterns in wool, and 'within each of these matrices embedded stories of the past, present and future . . . . Each woven panel is structurally a large grid or map, and the patterns created . . . form a secondary map that charts my experiences.'

87

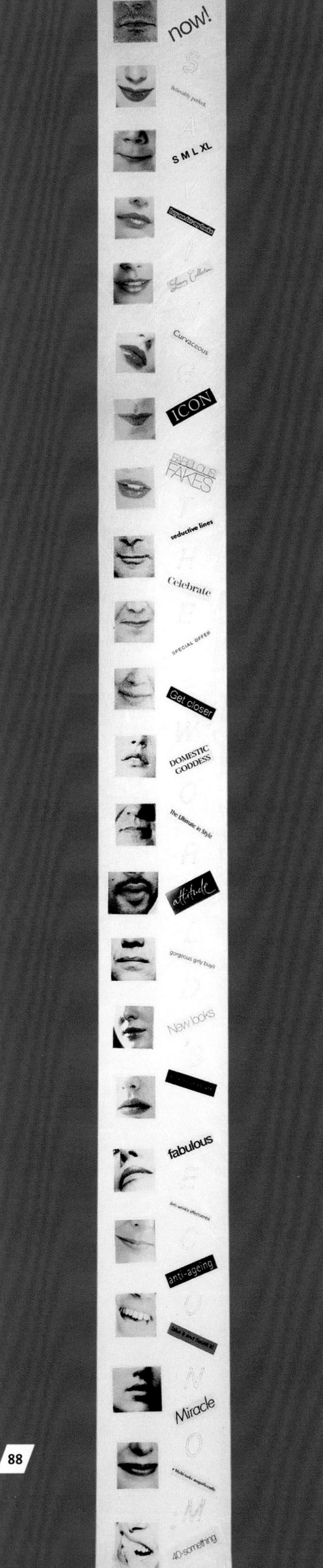

87. Bethan Ash, *Rosyn Coch (Red Rose)*, 2010. This improvizational cut-and-fused machine-stitched and -quilted cotton wall hanging takes its inspiration from the artist's love for her husband, a keen gardener, as well as for her son and old dog, Charlie, who died while this quilt was in the making – 'always at my side, and mostly getting in the way'.

88. Allie Kay, *Saving the World's Economy* (detail), 2009. A satirical look at advertising that urges us to spend so as to look and feel better. A Tyvek strip with windows cut out is filled with acetates printed from magazine advertisements, hand-stitched with invisible thread and inscribed with acrylic paint.

90

89 and 91. Jette Clover, *Letter Landscape 13*, 2008, and *White Wall 5*, 2009. Painting, screen printing, poster-paper lamination, collage and hand- and machine-stitching on cotton allow this former journalist to explore words and communication by collecting 'street memories'. Clover says: 'The fragments of text that I paint and print on my pieces are not meant to be contemplated for their meaning. They are there ...to be seen as representing the human need to state "I Was Here", from writing a blog, scratching on a rock or spray-painting an abandoned building, to making a quilt.'

90. Kay Kahn, *Portrait #3: The Flame*, 2009. Incorporating silks, cotton and paper, this complex surface has been developed through piecing, drawing, stitching, appliqué and quilting.

91

92

92. Jane McKeating, *Letter*, 2011. A page from the artist's 'Indian Whispers' collection, this work comprises layered linen and organza, both stitched and digitally printed. It express how time distorts memory: 'Cloth has a way of holding images differently from paper,' McKeating says. 'Very naturally old pieces become part of the new, just as the mind blends time, and presents images affected by the past and possibilities for the future.'

93. Allie Kay, *Exit Lines*, 2009. This quilt was inspired by the structures and surfaces of Daniel Liebeskind's Imperial War Museum North, in Manchester. It also articulates Kay's response to the futility of war in Afghanistan. The title is from a poem by Paul Muldoon, in which a single couplet reads: 'It's getting dark, but not dark enough to see / An exit wound as an exit strategy.'

94

93

94 and 95. Mirjam Pet-Jacobs, *And again 'The nights are white and black the days'* and *Change or Accept*, 2009. Two from eight in the artist's 'Mini-Solitude' series. Both employ dyeing, painting, hand and machine appliqué, machine embroidery and machine stitching. As Pet-Jacobs says, 'You have to come to terms with the good and bad things in life, accept them and let go of them.'

96. Anni Hunt, *Acquisition: A Pot of Gold* (detail), 2009. Made of painted, stamped and copper-foiled recycled paper pulp with a layer of silk organza to subdue the tones, and a collage of synthetic felt and silk-screened silk and hemp fabric, this is a vessel to contain 'all those finer treasures that one has acquired on life's journey'.

Mother

97. Catriona Faulkner, *Frida Forever*, 2011. In an homage to the artist Frida Kahlo and her imagination and strength of character, the artist has assembled and hand-stitched vintage or discarded treasures into place – 'selected pieces that I feel connect me to Frida in some way and explore aspects of her life and my own'.

98. Liza Green, *Spent Forces*, 2010. Bandage plastered and stitched to form a cartridge belt for recycled and found cartridges commemorates the lives of service men and women who have died in Afghanistan since 2001. 'I am acutely aware of the loss of life and severe injuries incurred by ordinary Afghan citizens. *Spent Forces* is also for them.'

98

LOVE is
the new
HATE
WING DENIES
CHANGE...
humans are the product of
WINDMILLS ARE OPPOSED BY SOME AS "AN EYESORE"
SECRETS
24946

99. Mulberry Neckwear Corporation, *Neckties*, 1996–2001. Founded in 1988 in California, Mulberry initially utilized hand-woven Thai silks. Among its successful licences was Grateful Dead neckwear, exemplified by some of these printed silk damask ties. Part of the proceeds were donated to the Rex Foundation, a charity founded by the band in 1983. All dating from 1996, the year after lead guitarist, Jerry Garcia died, these ties draw upon artwork by and for Garcia. Patterns include the Grateful Dead logo – a top view of a skull tattooed with a lightning bolt (above centre) – and motifs associated with various albums, meaning that those who could read the visual code could identify the wearer as a 'Dead Head'.

101

102

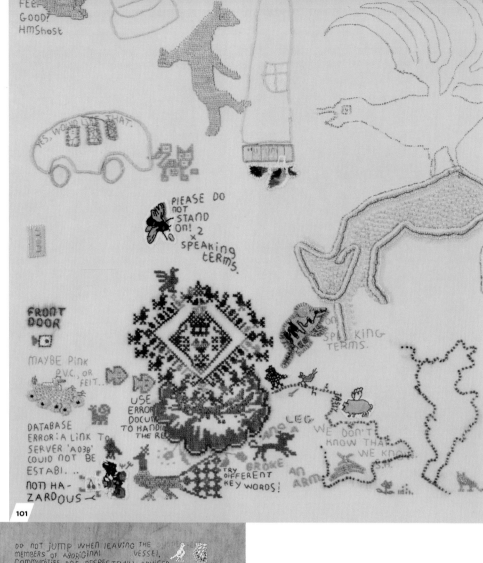

100. C. J. Pressma, *Secrets*, 2011. For this large machine-quilted panel measuring 264 × 188 cm (104 × 74 in.) the artist's photographs were collaged and inkjet-printed onto cotton.

101 and 102. Tilleke Schwarz, *New Potatoes* (detail), 2011, and *Count Your Blessings*, 2003. Silk, cotton and rayon threads, dyed by the artist, are worked mainly in cross and couching stitches in these two works on linen grounds. *Count Your Blessings* (no. 102) is an ironic record of trips to the US and Australia, including quotes from the Museum of Contemporary Art, Sydney, that justify its pictures of Aboriginals and the use of living goldfish in an installation – subjects sensitive in Austrialia.

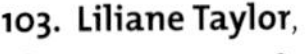

103. Liliane Taylor, *Chatte Latte*, 2008. By using appliquéd fray-edged recycled materials and free machine embroidery, the artist conveys the impression of a quick sketch preserving a just-observed scene.

104. Inge Norgaard, *Fimbulwinter*, 2006. This tapestry depicts the Norse myth of the cold and black three-year-long Fimbulwinter, during which one wolf will swallow the sun, another the moon, and the stars will fall. 'During this trial all morals break down and gods and giants destroy each other. Out of this, the new world as we know it emerges.'

105. Sue Dove, *Women Will Wait*, 2000. Hand-embroidering with stranded cotton, the artist uses 'the decorative elements of colour and pattern to create joyful, thoughtful images. All my work is a narrative on the stories of everyday life, semi-autobiographical.'

106

107

106. English amateur embroiderer, initials B. P., *Raised-work casket*, 1622. Incorporating a depiction of the biblical Esther and Ahasuerus in silk and metallic threads with seed pearls, this type of casket, made to contain personal items such as ink, paper and needlework tools, demonstrates the maker's mastery of embroidery.

107. French or English professional embroiderers, *Needlework bed valance* (detail), late 1500s. Part of a set of valances depicting the story of Esther and Ahasuerus, and worked in wool and silk tent stitch on canvas. The biblical figures are depicted in contemporary clothing.

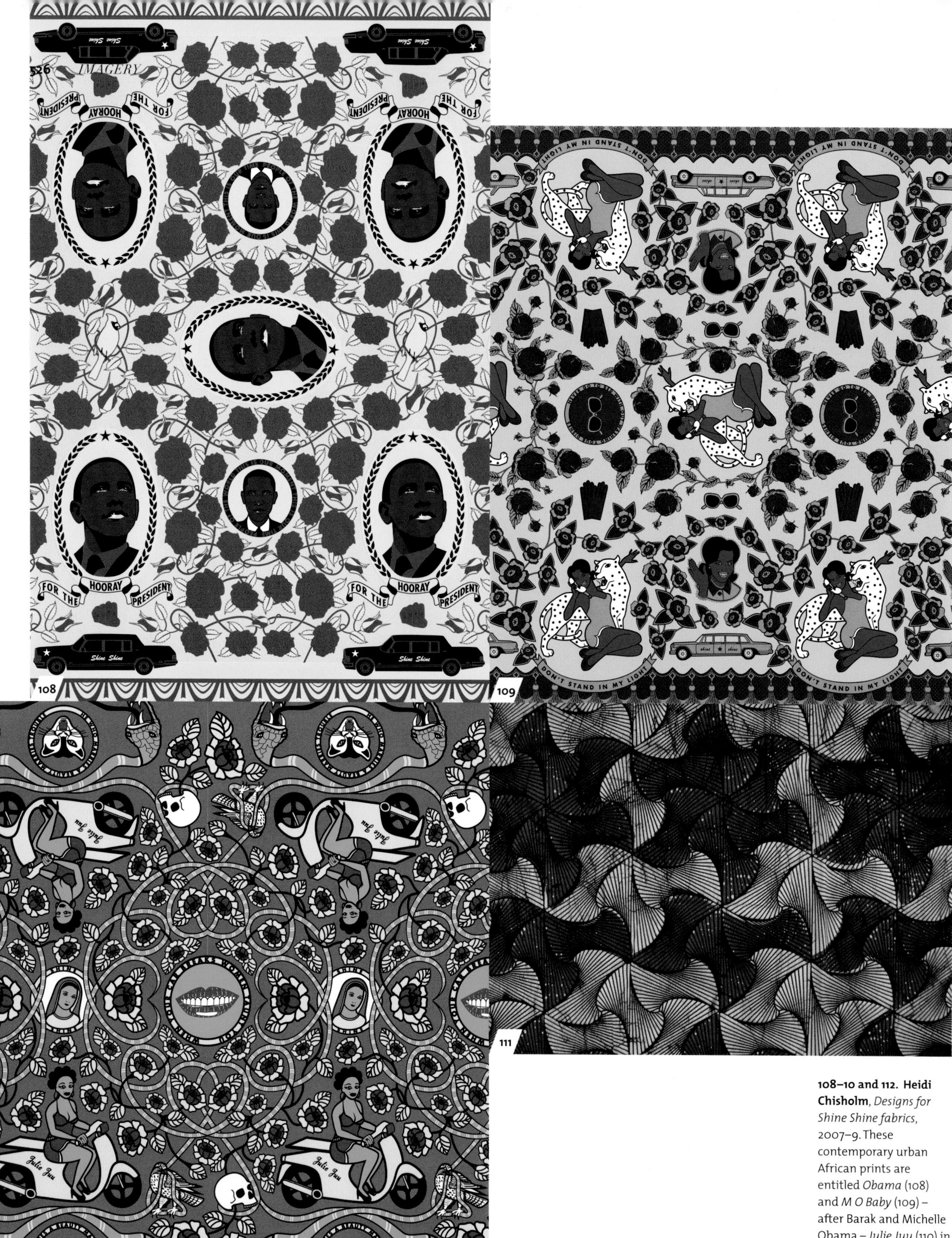

108–10 and 112. Heidi Chisholm, *Designs for Shine Shine fabrics*, 2007–9. These contemporary urban African prints are entitled *Obama* (108) and *M O Baby* (109) – after Barak and Michelle Obama – *Julie Juu* (110) in honour of the Ghanaian actress Abena Achiaa, and *Rosemary* (112). All are rotary printed.

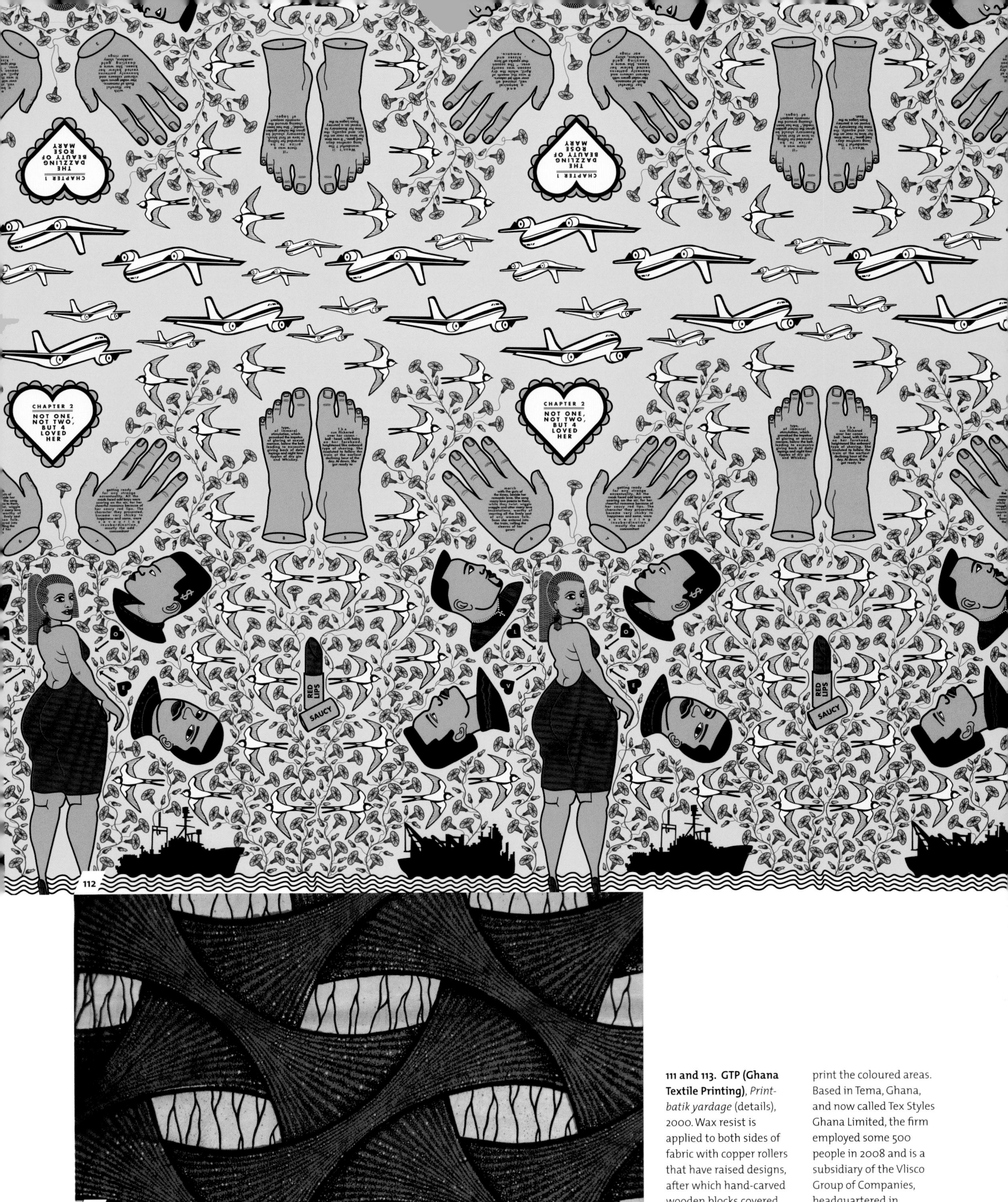

111 and 113. GTP (Ghana Textile Printing), *Print-batik yardage* (details), 2000. Wax resist is applied to both sides of fabric with copper rollers that have raised designs, after which hand-carved wooden blocks covered with felt are used to print the coloured areas. Based in Tema, Ghana, and now called Tex Styles Ghana Limited, the firm employed some 500 people in 2008 and is a subsidiary of the Vlisco Group of Companies, headquartered in Helmond, the Netherlands.

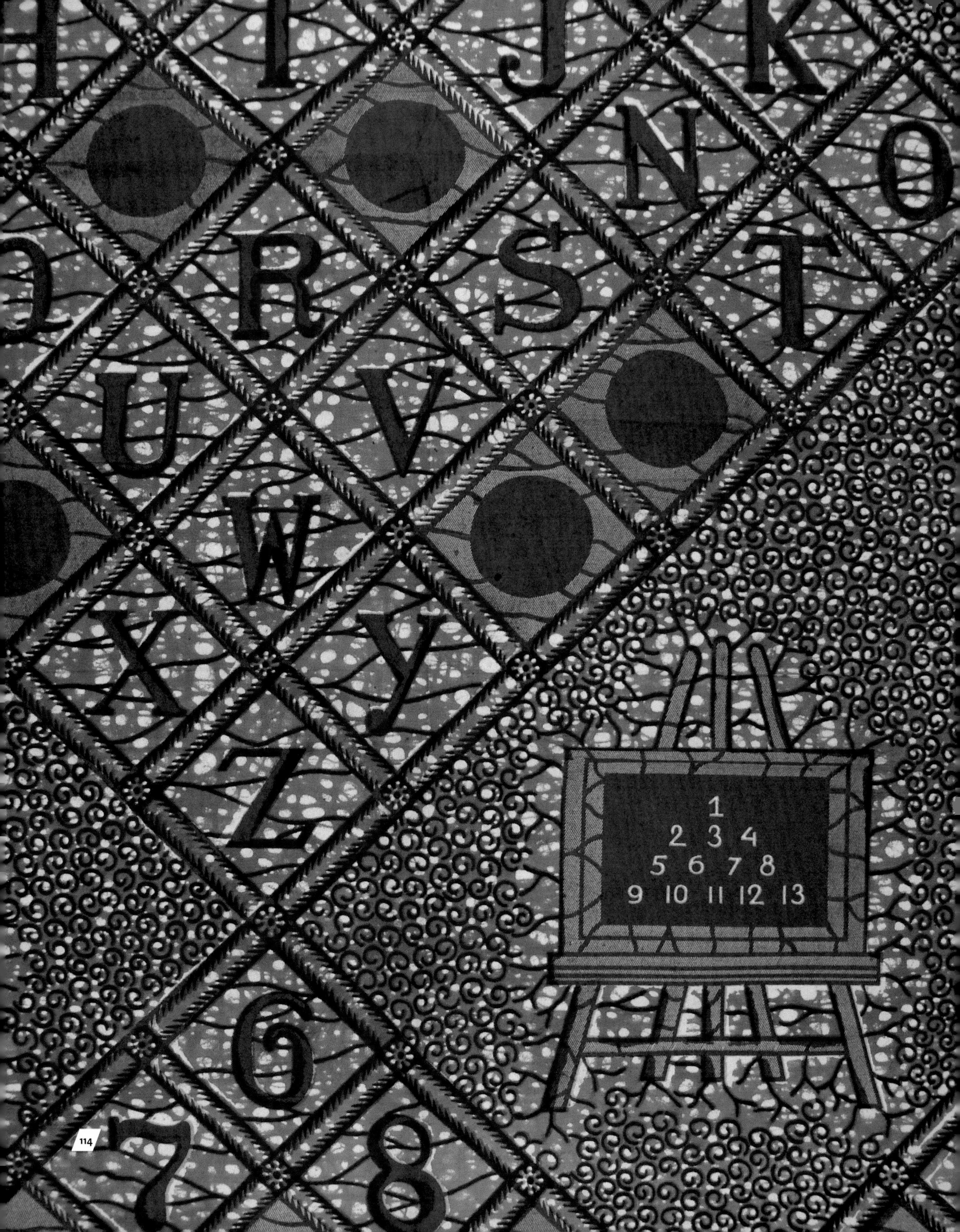

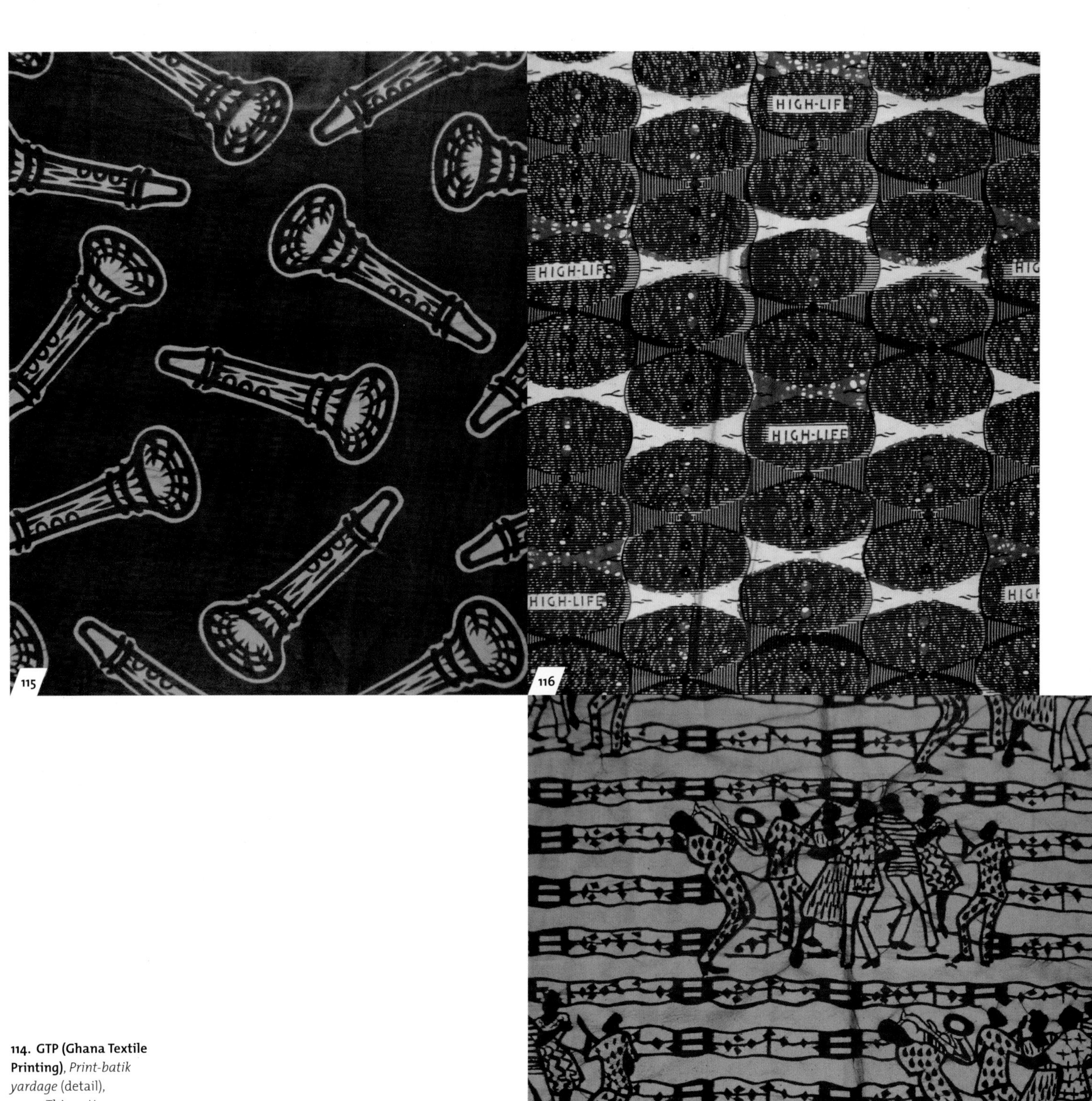

114. GTP (Ghana Textile Printing), *Print-batik yardage* (detail), 2000. This pattern, representing education, is one of the most popular designs worn by Ghanaian women, and is said to date from the early 20th century.

115 and 117. GTP (Ghana Textile Printing), *Print-batik yardage* (details), 2000. These blue and brown colourways were printed especially for the Nigerian market.

116. GTP (Ghana Textile Printing), *Print-batik yardage* (detail), 2000. The incorporation of the words 'high life' refers to a type of Malian music.

118 and 120. Cameroonian artisan, *Print-batik yardage*, before 1985. Part of the present-day Republic of Cameroon, in west Central Africa, was administered by the French from 1919 until 1960. During that period, the Compagnie Française pour le Développement des Fibres Textiles (CFDT) was responsible for the cultivation of cotton in the area.

118

119. Raoul Dufy for Bianchini-Férier, *La Jungle*, 1922. Here produced as a cotton ciselé (cut and uncut) velvet, this popular pattern was launched in 1922 for the year of the 'Exposition Nationale Coloniale de Marseille'. This exhibition displayed items from French South-East Asian colonies, such as Laos and Cambodia, as well as from France's vast African empire, encompassing Tunisia, Morocco, French Equatorial Africa, French West Africa, French Somaliland (now Djibouti), and the islands of Madagascar and the Comoros – thereby increasing the aesthetic influence of these countries on the arts of France.

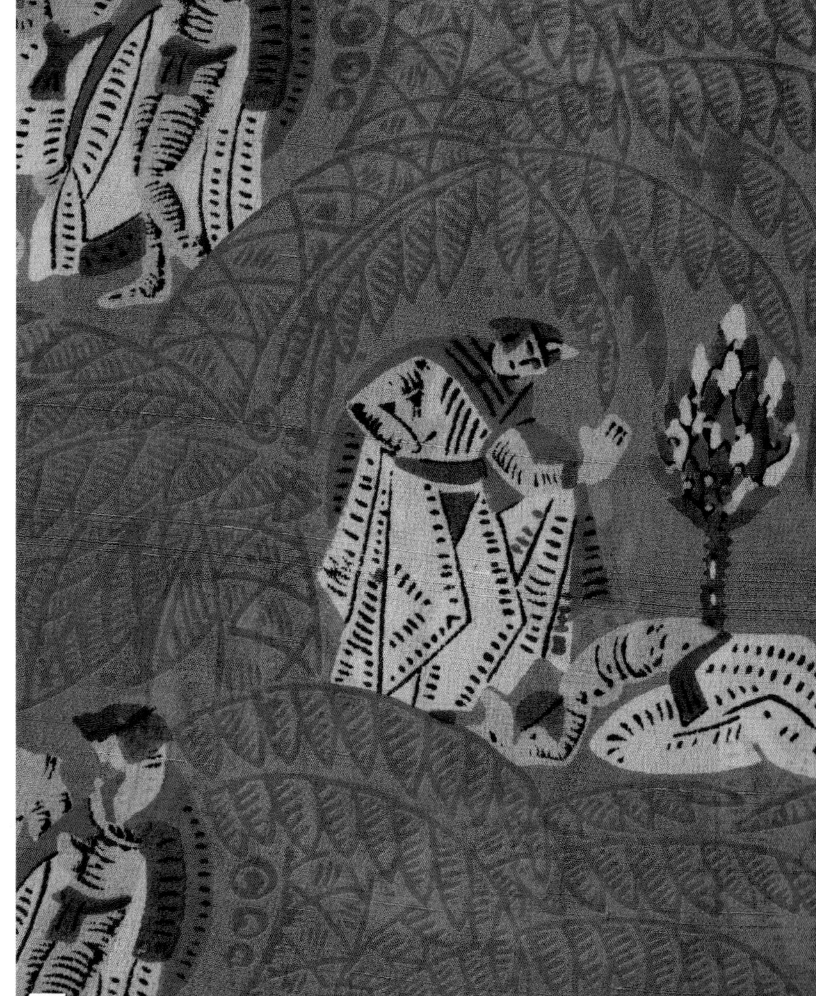

121. Jessica Smith, *Bizarre Dead Squirrel*, 2010. With an Egyptian cotton warp and rayon weft, this cloth was woven for the artist on an industrial Jacquard loom at Oriole Mill in Henderson, North Carolina. Smith creates historical schemes with a contemporary twist as part of her exploration of the digital: 'Industry can experiment with variety, while fine artists can explore mechanical production,' she notes.

122. English manufacturer, *Printed manmade-fibre dress fabric* (detail), mid-1920s. Howard Carter's discovery of the tomb of Tutankhamun in 1922 launched a craze for patterns containing Egyptian motifs. This fabric forms a dropped-waist garment, homemade in Lancashire, then the heart of England's textile printing industry.

123. Alsatian printer, *Block-printed scenic furnishing cotton,* *c.* 1775–95. With its scenes of merriment and tavern bearing the sign of a six-pointed star, this fabric may have been commissioned to celebrate reforms favourable to the Jewish community. Although this star was a longstanding sign of quality beer in the region, three-quarters of French Jews lived in rural Alsace, and inn-keeping was one of their permitted professions.

124. J. J. Pearman for Daniel Carling & Co., *Bannister Hall block-printed cotton border,* 1806. Bannister Hall Printworks near Preston, Lancashire, was the leading English printworks for woodblock furnishing chintzes. This scenic border, 23 cm (9 in.) in height, catered to the fashion for chinoiserie patterns.

125. Timorous Beasties, *London Toile*, 2005. Inspired by a love of London and its contrast of affluence and poverty, as well as by old toiles, the artists designed this fabric by 'separating the drawings, producing extra depth and texture by overlapping and leaving gaps in the artwork to create more tones where the inks overlap one another'.

126. Ivory Coast artist, *Korhogo cloth* (detail), 20th century. Named after the village of Korhogo, the design is an earth pigment that turns black after a period of time, painted on hand-spun strip-woven cotton canvas. The bird means freedom and the snake, earth's abundance.

127. Saul Steinberg, *Horses by Steinberg*, c. 1949–52. Hand-screen printed on polished cotton, this was one of several furnishing fabric designs supplied by Steinberg to Patterson Fabrics, New York. The Romanian-born artist became famous once he had settled in America, largely as a result of his thousand-plus illustrations for the *New Yorker*, the first appearing in 1941.

128 and 129. Jessica Smith, *South Beach Toile*, 2006, and *In Pursuit of Leisure*, 2004. A design and a cotton woven at a Belgian mill on an industrial Jacquard loom. Smith works on paper and with a computer, on which 'I design, produce, and "place" narrative patterns. These patterns have a historical reference, contemporary message and a subversive twist.'

125

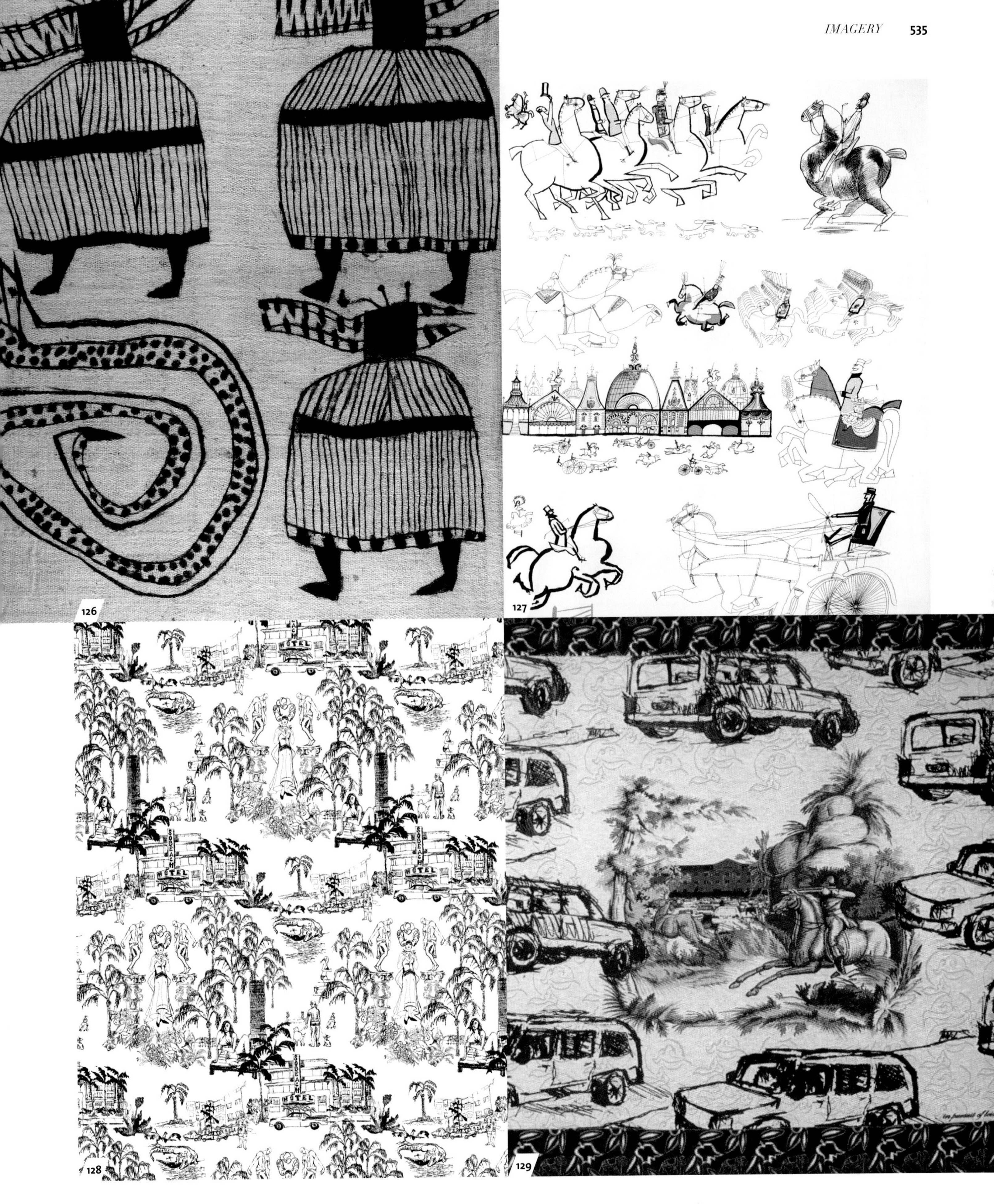

126

127

128

129

130. Robert Bonfils for Bianchini-Férier, *La Casbah*, 1934. A resist block print on silk, this scarf represents a centuries-old practice of commemorating political events on large silk squares (here measuring 67 cm, or 26½ in.). It was produced on the centenary of the French conquest of northern Algeria.

131. Japanese printer, *Yukata cloth*, 20th century. Used for informal summer kimonos, the indigo imagery was produced by *kataezone* (stencilled paste resist) and is based on scenes of Japanese nobility wearing court costume from the Heian period (749–1185).

132. Raoul Dufy for Bianchini-Férier, *Neptune*, c. 1920. Incorporating the initials of the firm and the location of its showroom, this hand block-printed linen was produced as part of the 'Toiles de Tournon' range.

133 and 135. Alberto Fabio-Lorenzi for Bianchini-Férier, *Jardinage* and *Table with Wine and Flying Cockatoos*, c. 1920. Both of these cotton damasks combine scenic elements with surrounding motifs in a manner typical of Modern classicism.

134. Naomi Ryder, *Cameo Pattern*, 2009–10. Ryder began by making freehand machine-embroidered line drawings that traced the activities of a friend from morning until evening, which she appliquéd to silk chiffon to create a curtain. This celebration of the events of everyday life was then photographed, scanned and digitally arranged to become a wallpaper design: 'I love using traditional skills alongside new technologies.'

133
134
135

136

136. Judith Content, *Precipice: La Briere series*, 2005. Content's quilted and appliquéd silk wall-piece derives its saturated, nuanced colours from the artist's use of discharge with her personal variant of the *arashi* shibori (pole-wrapping) technique, for which she uses wine bottles as an armature.

137

137. Jean Cacicedo, *Raincoat – San Francisco Bay*, 2000. Fulled, knitted wool, slashed, punched, dyed and pieced, forms this woman's coat. Inspired by personal myths and symbolic imagery, Cacicedo's work tells stories about physical and spiritual journeys.

138. Janet Twinn, *Half Light*, 2009. Composed of cotton dye-painted by the artist, machine pieced and quilted, this is from Twinn's 'Touchwood' series. Walking in the winter landscape of Surrey and the Cotswolds led her 'to investigate a completely new palette of earthy, terracotta hues'.

139. Ann Fahy, *Gathering*, 2009. This work is composed of linen, pleated on a smocking pleater and then dyed with Dylon dye in a microwave, backed and machine quilted. Fahy, who is based in Ireland, was inspired by a picture of charred tree stumps left by an Australian forest fire: 'When the stitching was removed and the pieces hung up, they started to take on personalities of their own.'

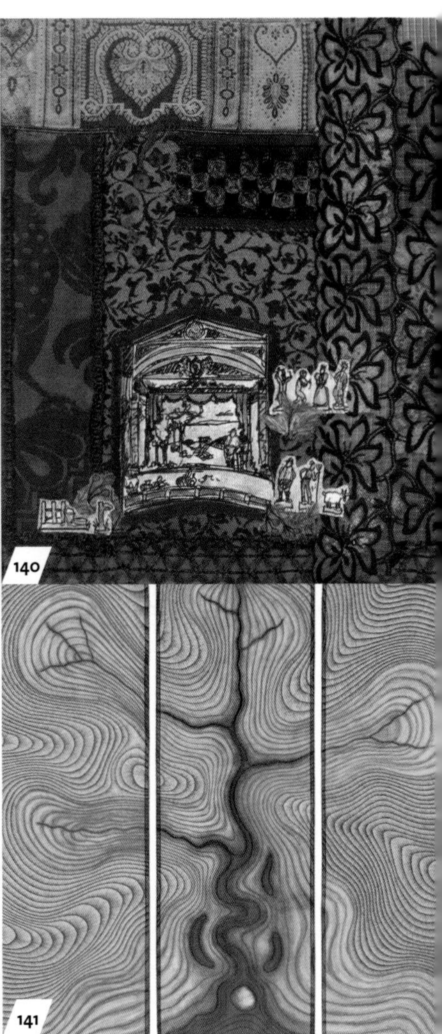

140. Diane Groenewegen, *Theatre Set*, 2011. Composed of remnants of a wool paisley shawl, Victorian checked silk fabric, Indian cloth embroidered with gold couching, vintage gold lace, silk brocade and 1950s nylon brown lace, this small work (roughly 14 cm or 5½ in. square) also incorporates screen printing and hand-colouring.

141. Dianne Firth, *Drainage Basin*, 2009. Informed by her training as a landscape architect and her observations of the relationship between nature and people, Firth created this machine-quilted triptych, 139 cm (55 in.) wide, employing a range of textiles, dyeing, painting and collage to highlight the issue of water conservation in Australia.

142. Cecilia Blomberg, *Moxee Tapestry* (detail), 2010. The result of a commission from the Washington State Arts Commission, this farmland scene was woven for Moxee Elementary School, based near Yakima in central Washington.

143. Elizabeth Brimelow, *Sole Bay*, 2007. Hand-painted, hand-dyed and hand-printed silk and cotton, machine- and hand-stitched and further embellished with appliqué and reverse appliqué form these sweeping abstract panoramas, inspired by the pebbles along a stretch of the Suffolk coast.

144. Cherilyn Martin, *It's the Stones that Speak VII*, 2009. Employing synthetic fabric, plastic, oil and acrylic paint, and other media, the artist uses fusing, machine stitching, hand-knotting and screen printing to create complex surfaces with hidden meanings: 'Underlying themes in my work deal with bereavement, loss and commemoration. I find inspiration in antiquity and in tactile remnants of the past.'

142

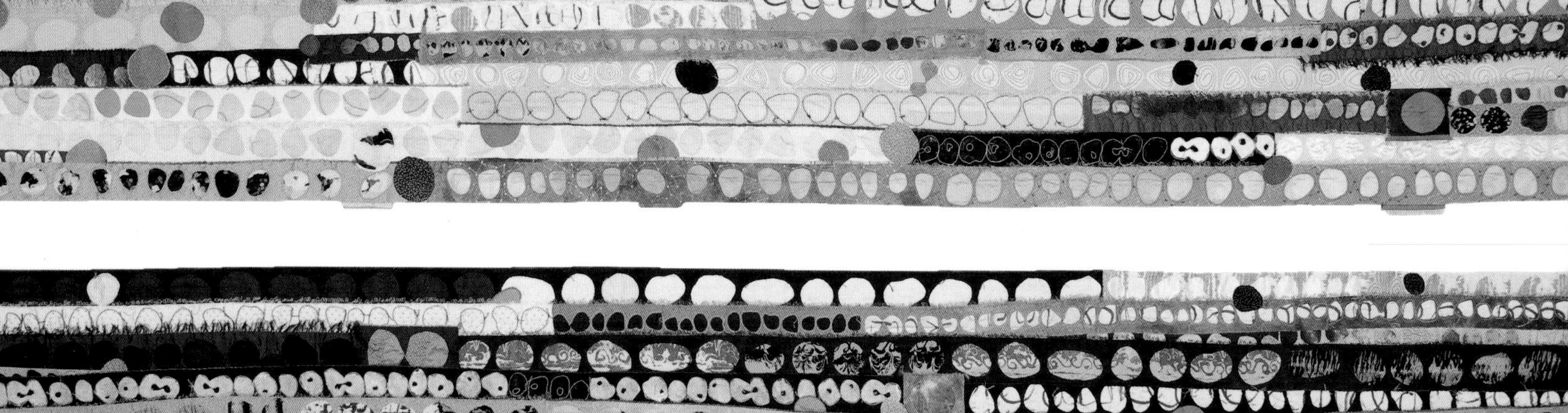

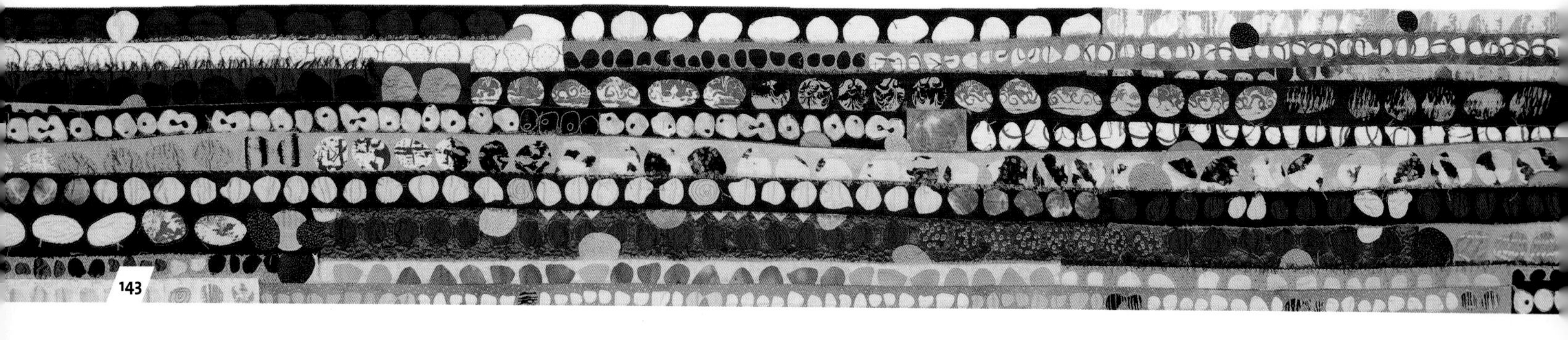

143

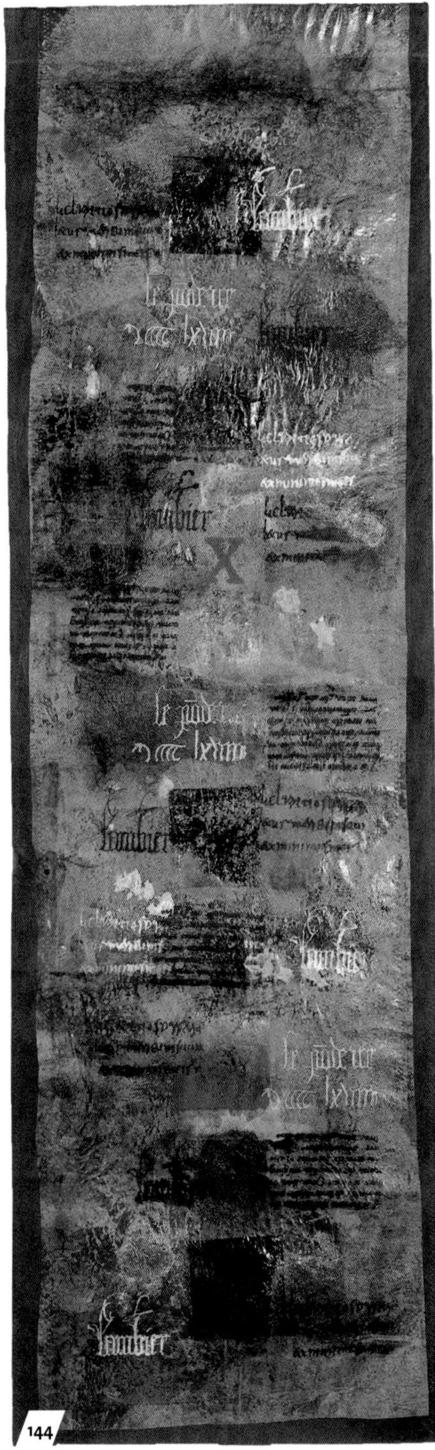

144

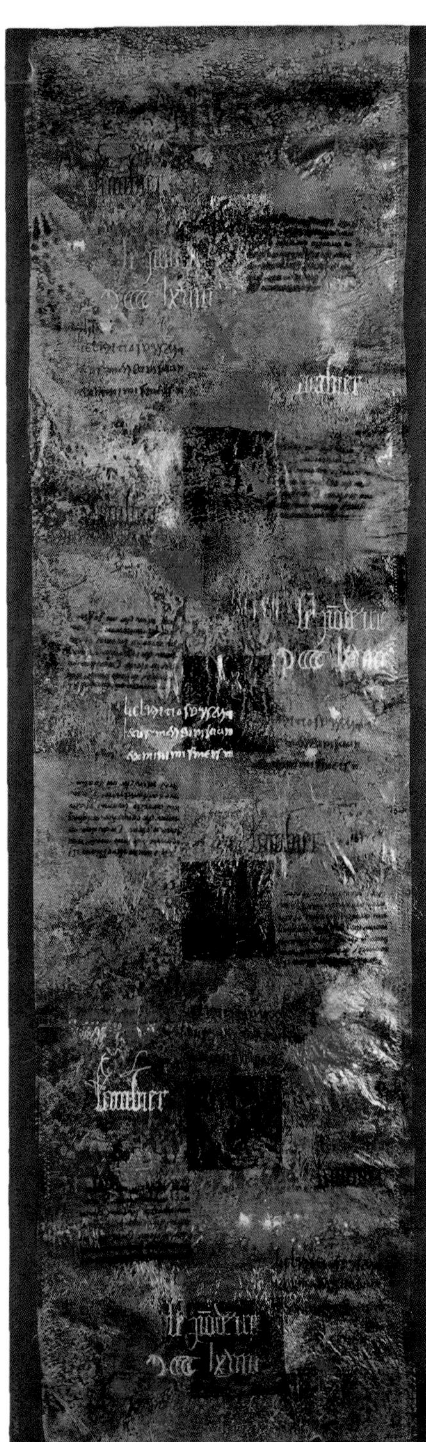

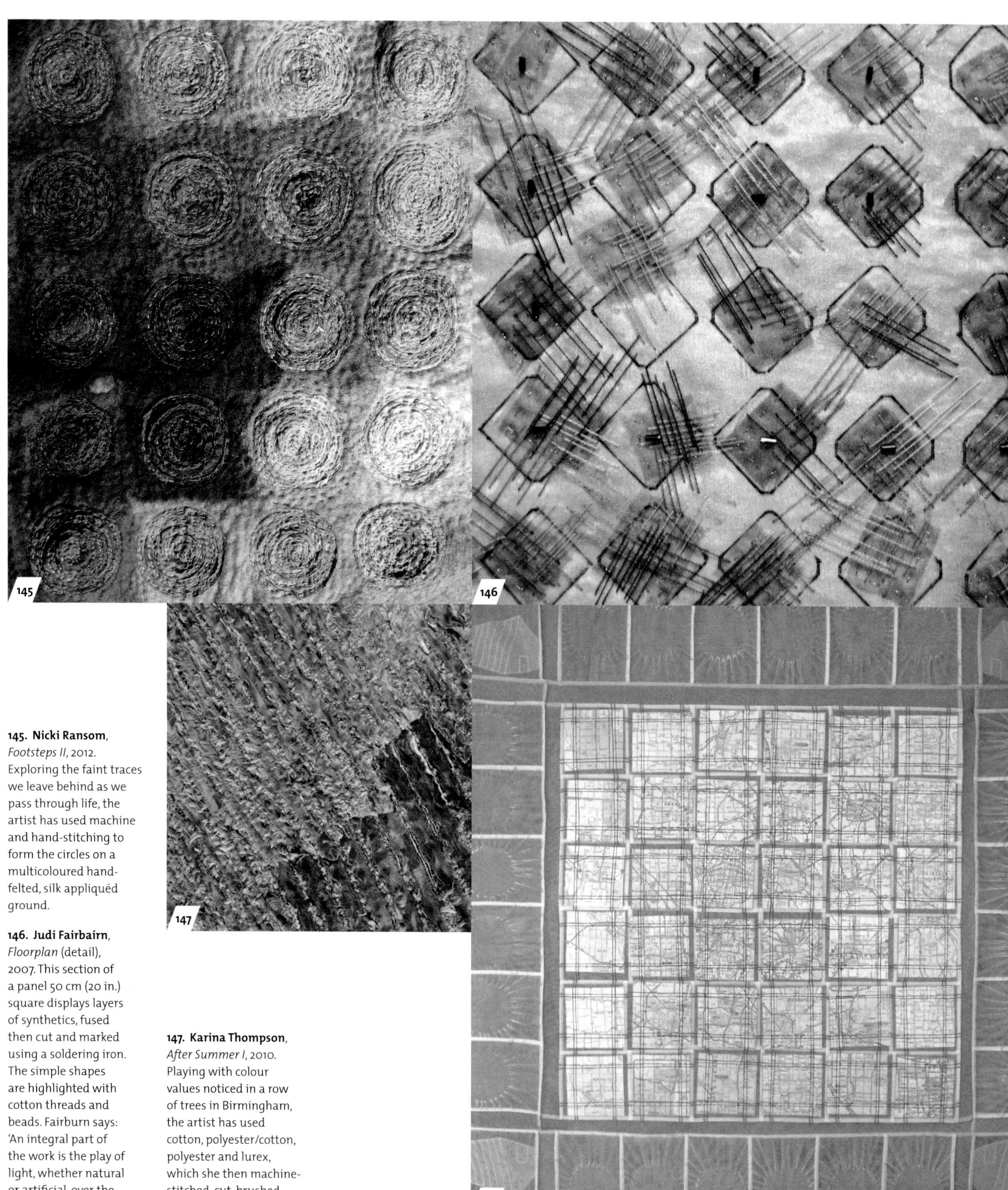

145. Nicki Ransom, *Footsteps II*, 2012. Exploring the faint traces we leave behind as we pass through life, the artist has used machine and hand-stitching to form the circles on a multicoloured hand-felted, silk appliquéd ground.

146. Judi Fairbairn, *Floorplan* (detail), 2007. This section of a panel 50 cm (20 in.) square displays layers of synthetics, fused then cut and marked using a soldering iron. The simple shapes are highlighted with cotton threads and beads. Fairburn says: 'An integral part of the work is the play of light, whether natural or artificial, over the surface.'

147. Karina Thompson, *After Summer I*, 2010. Playing with colour values noticed in a row of trees in Birmingham, the artist has used cotton, polyester/cotton, polyester and lurex, which she then machine-stitched, cut, brushed and appliquéd.

149

148. Nancy Crasco, *Living off the Grid*, 2008. For this piece, from a series using the image of pathways to represent strategies for reducing our carbon footprints, the artist has stitched silk organza, maps, and linoleum prints on silk using the construction of *pojagi* – Korean wrapping cloths pieced with thrice-stitched seams. This work is 66 cm (26 in.) square.

149. Inge Hueber, *Four Slices*, 2009. A mixture of home-dyed cotton and transparent organza was prepared for another project in 2006, but, in keeping with the tradition of recycling in quiltmaking, became pieces in their own right in 2009. 'Important for me in all my work are rhythm, colour and cloth. I feel very personal about my colours and built up my own range for over thirty years.'

150

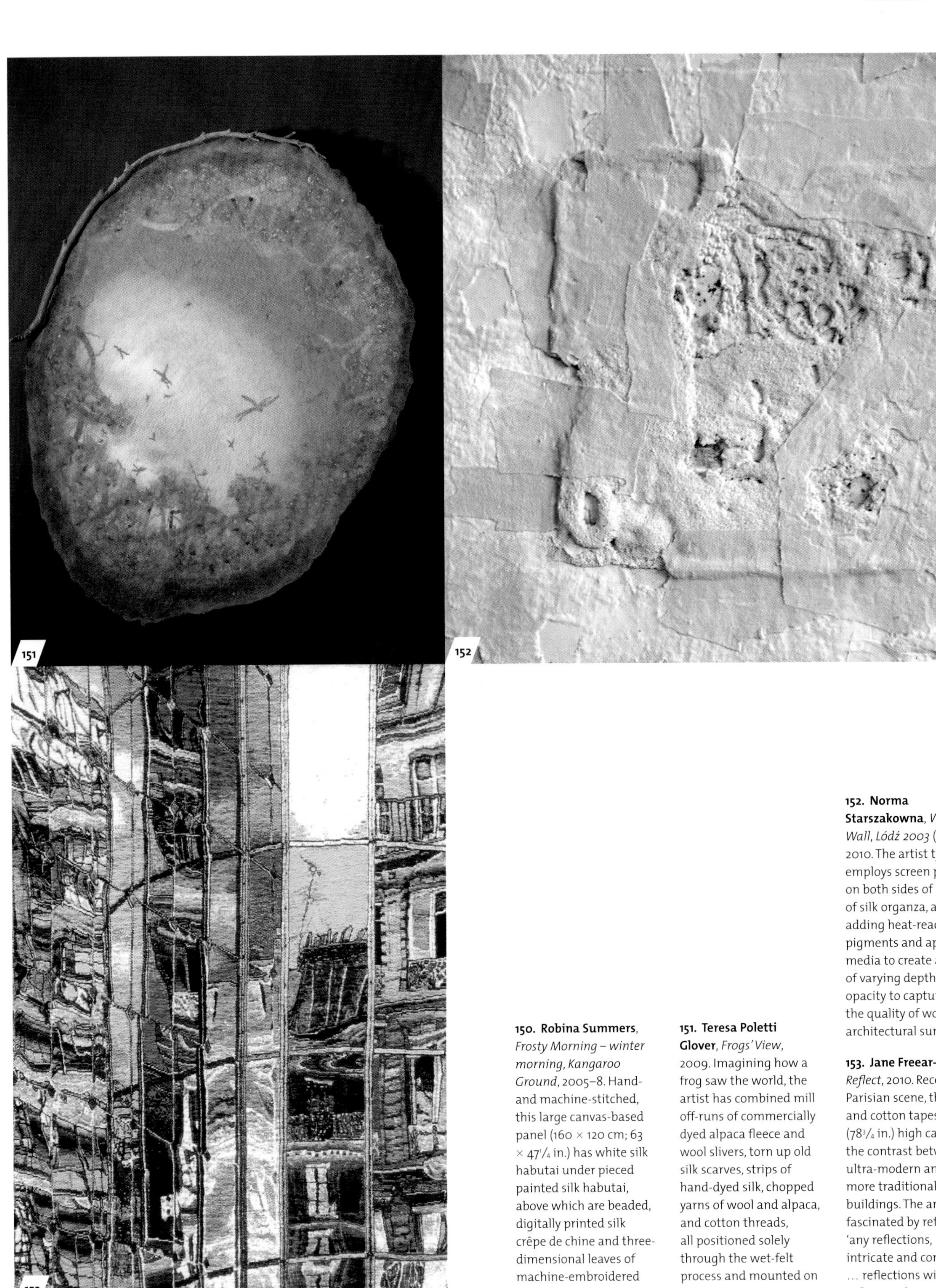

151

152

153

150. Robina Summers, *Frosty Morning – winter morning, Kangaroo Ground*, 2005–8. Hand- and machine-stitched, this large canvas-based panel (160 × 120 cm; 63 × 47¼ in.) has white silk habutai under pieced painted silk habutai, above which are beaded, digitally printed silk crêpe de chine and three-dimensional leaves of machine-embroidered painted silk.

151. Teresa Poletti Glover, *Frogs' View*, 2009. Imagining how a frog saw the world, the artist has combined mill off-runs of commercially dyed alpaca fleece and wool slivers, torn up old silk scarves, strips of hand-dyed silk, chopped yarns of wool and alpaca, and cotton threads, all positioned solely through the wet-felt process and mounted on a bush stick with wire.

152. Norma Starszakowna, *White Wall, Lódź 2003* (detail), 2010. The artist typically employs screen printing on both sides of a length of silk organza, as here, adding heat-reactive pigments and applied media to create a surface of varying depths and opacity to capture the quality of worn architectural surfaces.

153. Jane Freear-Wyld, *Reflect*, 2010. Recording a Parisian scene, this wool and cotton tapestry 2 m (78¾ in.) high captures the contrast between ultra-modern and more traditional stone buildings. The artist is fascinated by reflections, 'any reflections, intricate and complex … reflections within reflections'.

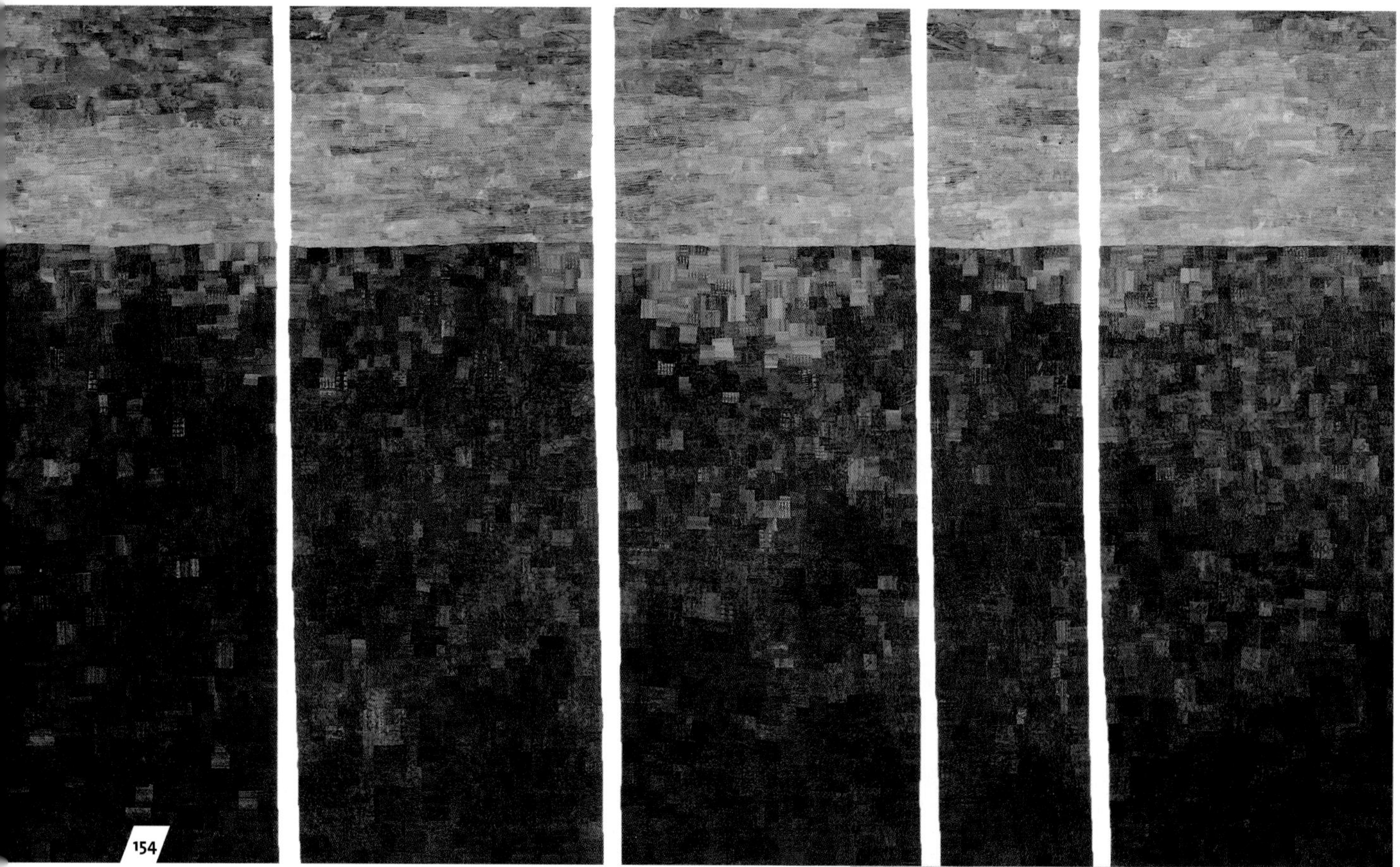

154

154. Dirkje van der Horst-Beetsma, *Frisian Landscape*, 2009. In these two quilted panels, inspired by the landscape of the artist's youth in the northern Netherlands, the sky is composed of pieces of hand-dyed cotton, silk and organza, while the land is entirely of print-batik cloths produced by Vlisco, Holland.

155. Sara Impey, *Process*, 2009. This hand-dyed, machine-quilted cotton wholecloth displays a text describing the artist's thoughts on the process of making and on the time taken, contrasting quilt-making with a digitally interactive choreographic performance. Each has lengthy gestational periods, but the processes and resulting artforms differ greatly.

156. Sandra Meech, *Meltdown 1*, 2010. This is the first in a series of pieces inspired by the breakdown of glaciers in arctic regions. Images taken in Iceland were collaged together and transferred to cloth in sections; the piece is layered and machine-quilted with copper metal and paint added to represent warmth in a cold landscape.

157. Jilly Edwards, *Around the Red Hills*, 2011. The memories and emotions evoked by travelling are distilled into this artist's tapestries, which use colour to capture her insights and responses to the landscape.

155

158. Anne Morrell, *Make Tracks* (detail), 2010. Stitched and smocked cotton captures the artist's interest in working through words as well as imagery. Here she includes tracks made by car wheels in the mud or birds walking in the snow, as well as a humorous reference with the phrase, 'I've got to make tracks.' She says: 'I love those marks as they leave a memory of what happened there – and then they in turn are gone.'

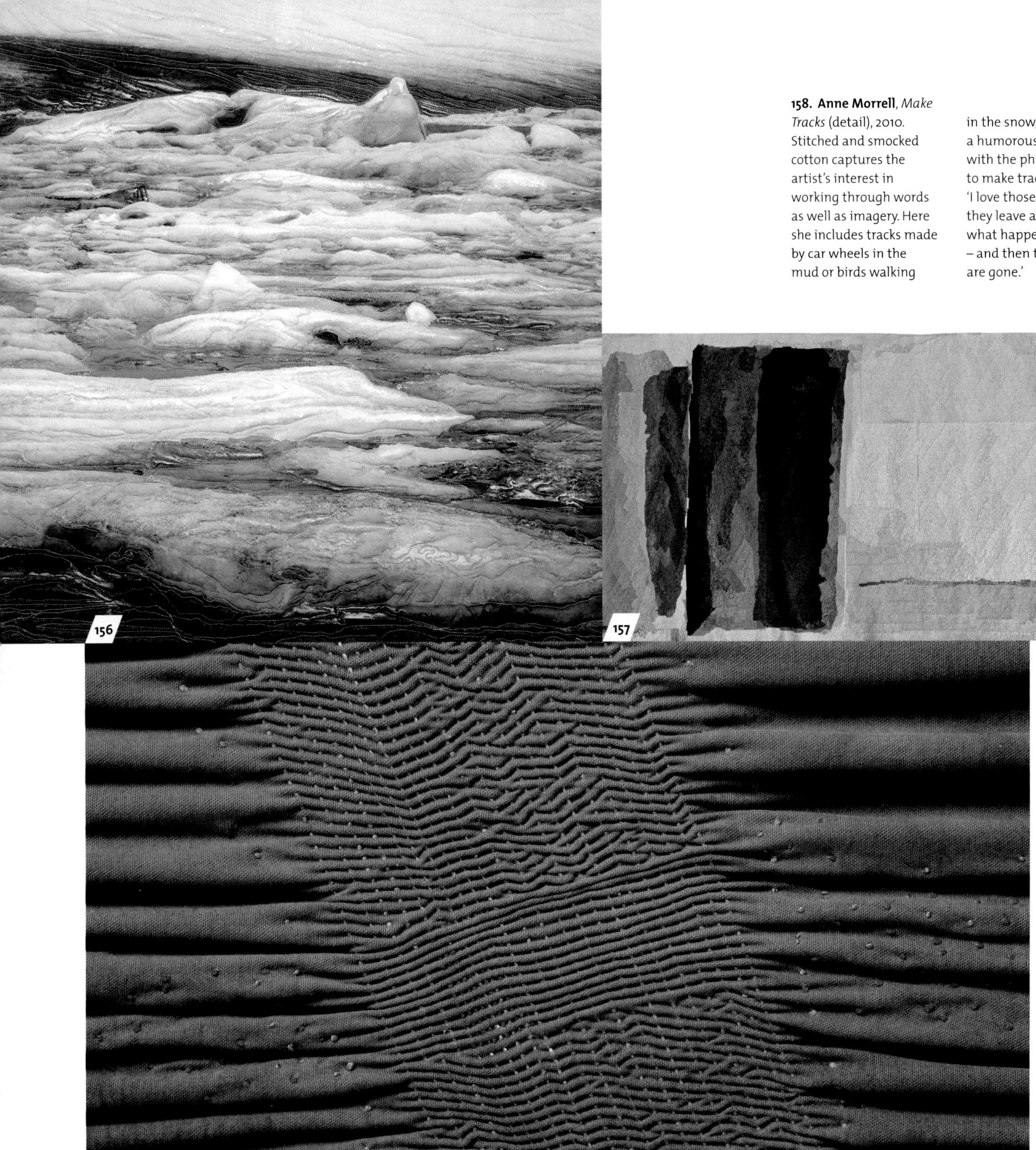
156
157
158

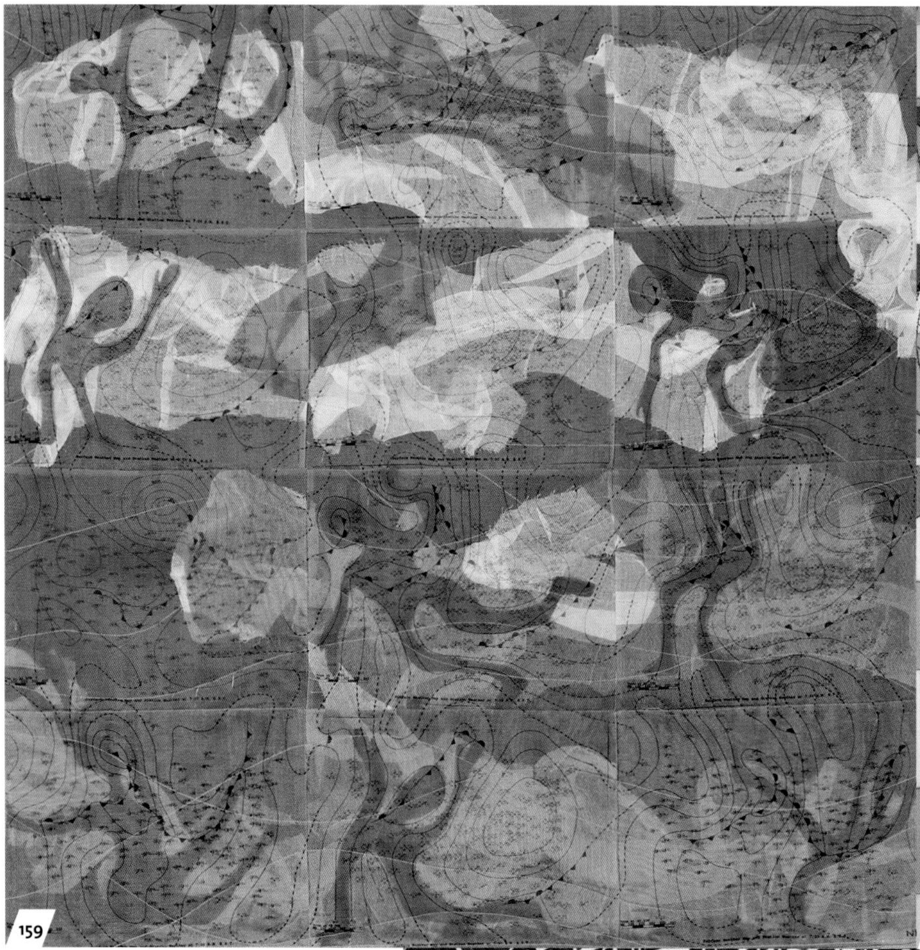

159. Nancy Crasco, *Under the Weather*, 2010. From the artist's 'Weather Report' series, which explores the problems associated with the use and misuse of natural resources, this *pojagi* embroidered panel employs US weather maps printed on cotton organdy, together with cheesecloth and silk organza.

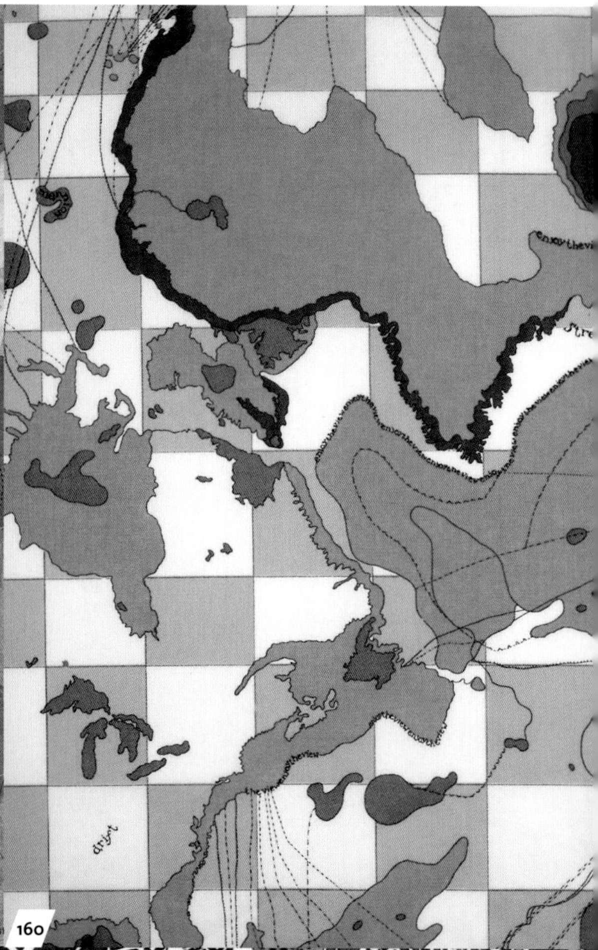

160 and 161. Emma Mawston, *Sydenham Palace* and *Mannion*, 2002. Mawston is head of design at Liberty Art Fabrics, where these dress fabrics were developed as part of a geographic collection for their spring/summer 2004 range.

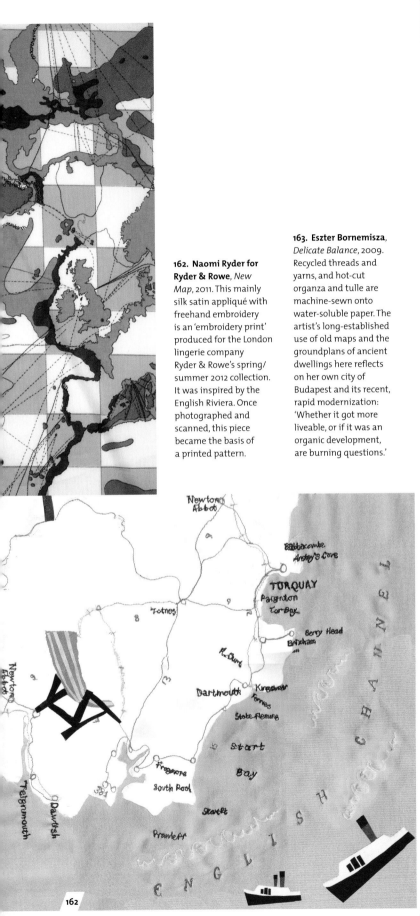

162. Naomi Ryder for Ryder & Rowe, *New Map*, 2011. This mainly silk satin appliqué with freehand embroidery is an 'embroidery print' produced for the London lingerie company Ryder & Rowe's spring/summer 2012 collection. It was inspired by the English Riviera. Once photographed and scanned, this piece became the basis of a printed pattern.

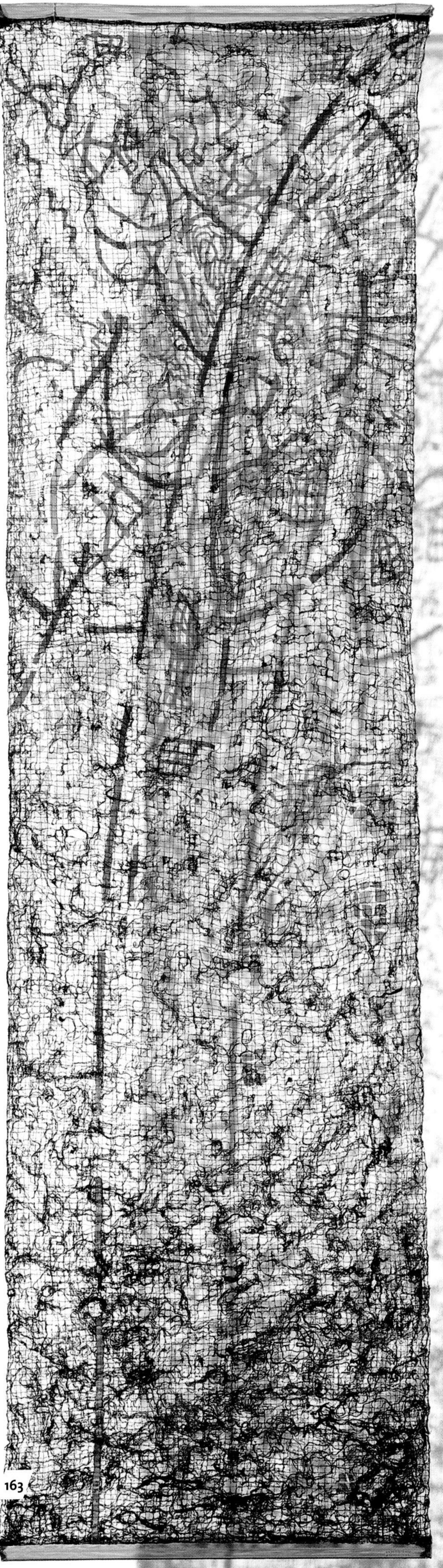

163. Eszter Bornemisza, *Delicate Balance*, 2009. Recycled threads and yarns, and hot-cut organza and tulle are machine-sewn onto water-soluble paper. The artist's long-established use of old maps and the groundplans of ancient dwellings here reflects on her own city of Budapest and its recent, rapid modernization: 'Whether it got more liveable, or if it was an organic development, are burning questions.'

164

165

166

164. Els van Baarle, *On The Road Again* (detail), 2010. Working onto maps, the artist has employed wax resists, screen printing and stitch to create seemingly charred surfaces.

165. Maggi Toner-Edgar, *Contribute to Knowledge*, 2006. A concept map used to record the artist's creative thoughts, this digital design, printed onto Vilene interfacing, is made up from the artist's own handwriting. It reads: 'Will they see embodied research' – a tongue-in-cheek remark, since this was a practice-based element of Toner-Edgar's PhD findings.

166. Dominie Nash, *Foliated Calligraphy*, 2009. Cotton and silk organza is assembled and embellished with machine appliqué, hand embroidery and deconstructed screen printing with fibre-reactive dyes – the latter made directly from large leaves through frottage, the rubbing technique, here done with pigment.

167. Fenella Davies, *Venice Light*, 2009. Using vintage sheeting, scrim, tissue, raffia, flashing and Japanese matting, this work, 236 cm (93 in.) wide, was hand-painted, bleached and collaged, with surface darning to connect the layers. It was designed to give a sense of place and mood, as the artist states: 'Implications of the past are a recurring theme – the traces of history and places – some definite, and some almost intangible.'

168

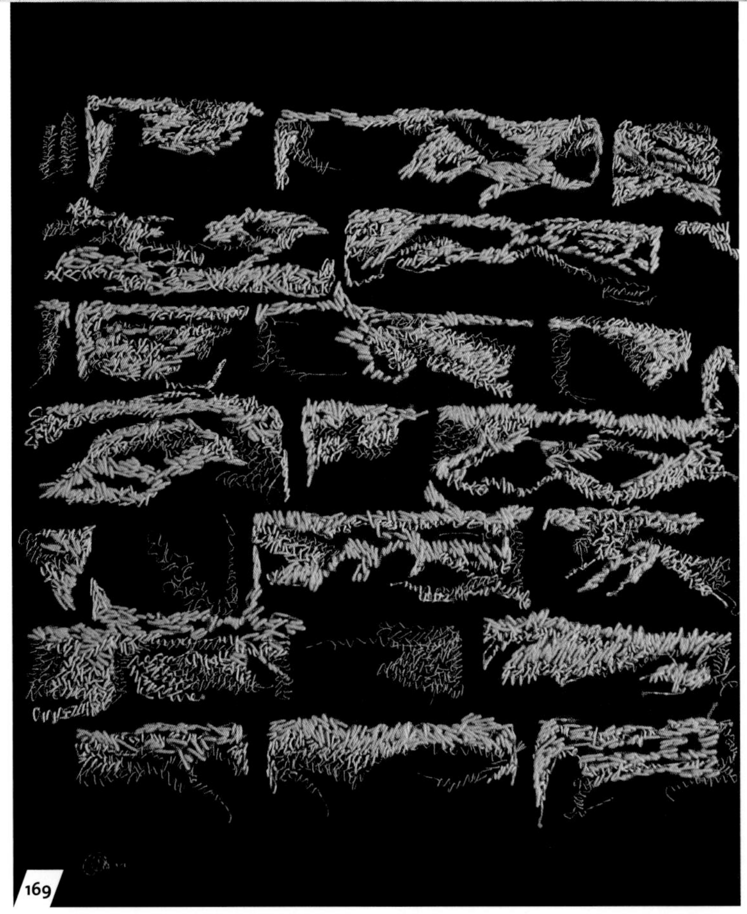

168. Bridget Ingram-Bartholomäus, *Under my Feet* (detail), 2010. Wool or wool-type fabrics – machine-appliquéd onto a background of mixed fabrics that have been strip-pieced, sometimes with the addition of pintucks – describe a path that leads nowhere.

169. Janelle Green, *Bricks of my Past*, 2011. Various yarns from the artist's 'historical stashes' were stitched on PVC gauze stretched over gessoed canvas to evoke the remnants of a brick chimney that formed part of the skeletal remains of her grandparents' house. The black ground denotes 'uncertainty in a past that hides many secrets'.

170. Maggi Toner-Edgar, *Double Ocho*, 2006. The crown of this hat is of digitally printed heavyweight vilene, trimmed with metallic ribbon and supporting a knitted steel-wire form tracing the path of the 'double ocho' tango step. Representing the creative thinking process and tensions between internal and external dialogues, the two strands also suggest the double helix of DNA.

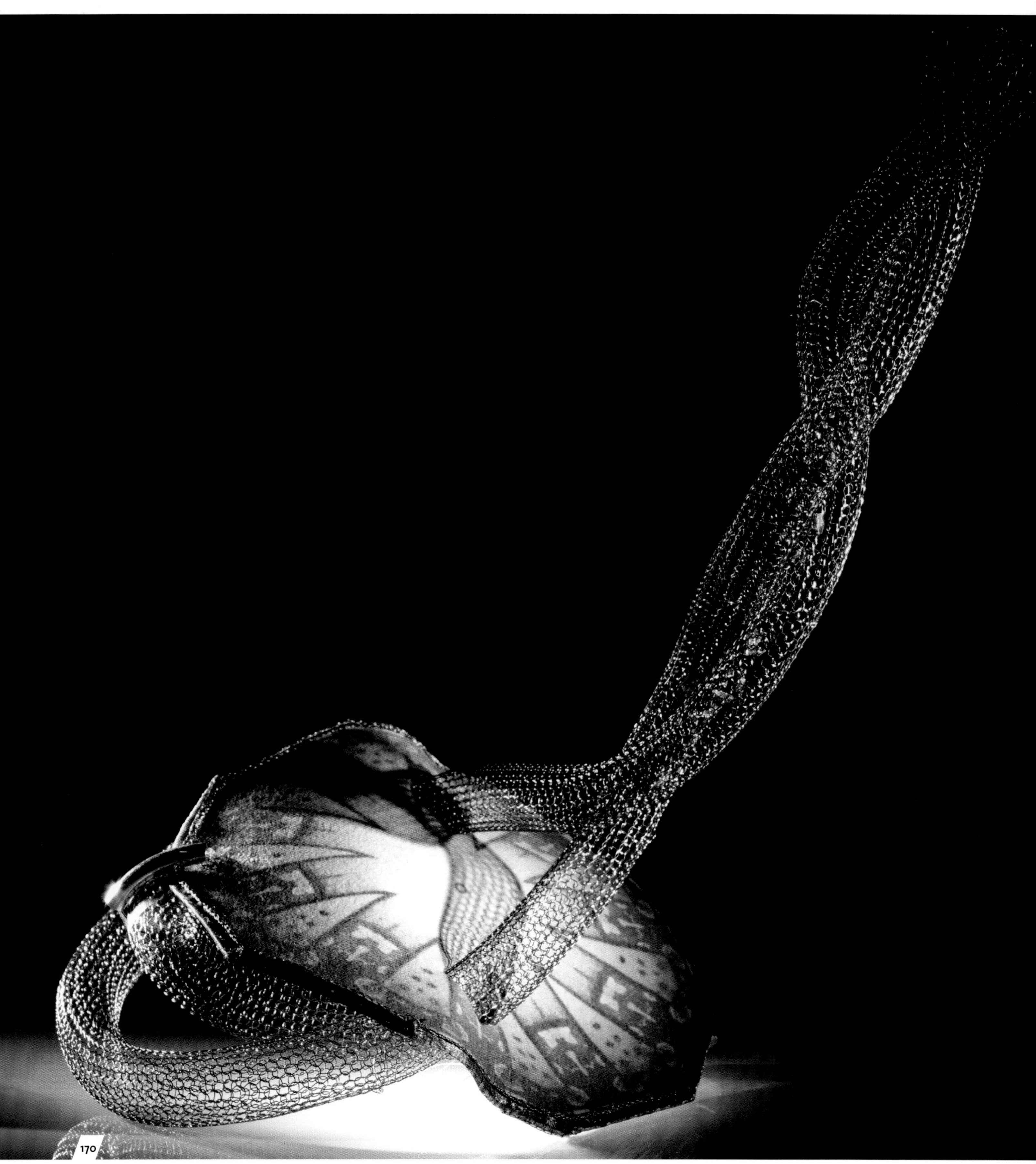

170

NOTES

CHAPTER 1

1. This had long been the case. See Tina Kane, *The Troyes Memoire: The Making of a Medieval Tapestry* (Woodbridge: Boydell Press, 2010), p. 49, for a discussion about a tapestry panel that was three times the cost of a painting in the 1450s.
2. See e.g. Gregory Battcock, *The New Art: A Critical Anthology* (New York: E. P. Dutton, 1966).
3. Hugh Kenner, 'Epilogue: The Dead-Letter Office' in Brian O'Doherty (ed.), *Museums in Crisis* (New York: George Braziller, 1972), p. 172.
4. See Judy Chicago, *The Dinner Party: From Creation to Preservation* (London: Merrell, 2007). This work was seen by over 1 million people in sixteen exhibitions and toured to six countries, but had no permanent home until 2007, when it was acquired by the Brooklyn Museum for its Elizabeth A. Sackler Center for Feminist Art.
5. Mary Schoeser, *World Textiles: A Concise History* (London: Thames & Hudson, 2003), pp. 194–213.
6. Lloyd Cotsen, 'Looking Behind My Eye', in Mary Hunt Kahlenberg (ed.), *The Extraordinary in the Ordinary: Textiles and Objects from the Collections of Lloyd Cotsan and the Neutrogena Corporation* (New York: Abrams, 1998), p. 11.
7. This and all further unnoted quotes come from interviews and correspondence undertaken by the author with the artists/collectors between March and November 2011.
8. Hans Schmoller, 'Panoply of Paper: On Collecting Decorated Papers', in *Paper Chase: An Exhibition of Decorated Papers from the Schmoller Collection* (Edinburgh: Edinburgh University Library, 1987), p. 2.
9. http://www.scribd.com/doc/33189555/Electronic-Text; http://www.e-text-textiles; http://www.electronicbookreview.com/public/e-t-t.html; both sourced 12 May 2012.
10. Marilyn Ferguson (1938–2008) was an influential American author, editor and public speaker, best known for her book *The Aquarian Conspiracy*, first published in 1980.
11. See Sherry Tuckle, *The Second Self: Computers and the Human Spirit* (London and Cambridge, MA: MIT Press, 2005), and Beverly Gordon, *Textiles: The Whole Story* (London and New York: Thames & Hudson, 2011), pp. 82, 227.
12. Donald A. Norman, *Things that Make Us Smart: Defending Human Attributes in the Age of the Machine* (Reading, MA: Perseus Books, 1993), pp. 3–17.
13. Jane Graves's text can be found at http://www.janegraves.org.uk/thesecretlives.htm, sourced 1 November 2011.
14. Caroline Till *et al.*, *Textile Futures* (exh. cat., London: Central Saint Martins, 2012), p. 7.
15. Esther Fitzgerald, *Seed and Spirit of Modernism: An Exploration Through Abstract Asian Textiles* (London: Esther Fitzgerald Rare Textiles), 2009, pp. 1–2, citing Tachman, *The Spiritual in Art* (1986).
16. Pam Meecham and Julie Sheldon, *Modern Art: A Critical Introduction* (London: Routledge, 2000), p. 160.
17. Fritz was the son of Leopold Iklé, founder of the famous Iklé Collection of textiles (Sammlung Iklé) at the Textilmuseum St Gallen, Switzerland.
18. The sociologist Richard Sennett describes this as 'craftsman-time' in *The Craftsman* (New Haven: Yale University Press, 2008), p. 251.
19. Ken'Ichi Iwaki, 'Preface' in *Sibyl Heijnen: Waving Space* (Tokyo: Gallery Le Bain, 2009), unpaginated.

CHAPTER 2

1. The beads were found in La Quina and the cordage in the Lascaux caves, both in south-western France. Early needles are associated with both the European Gravettian and the Eastern Gravettian cultures of roughly 26,000–20,000 BC, which included all mammoth-hunting peoples of Europe and Russia. Stringing and stitching were also done with very narrow strips of leather.
2. From the exhibition catalogue *Mika McCann* (Maui, Hawaii: Glassman Publicity, 1988), p. 1.
3. Todate Kazuko, 'Revitalizing Through Indigo: The Dye Art of Fukumoto Shihoko', trans. Meredith McKinney (exh. cat., Ibaraki, Japan: Tsukuba Museum of Art, 2009), unpaginated.
4. Ibid.
5. Jun Tomita's work can be found at http://www.browngrotta.com/Pages/tomita.php, sourced 19 November 2011.
6. See Xiaoming Tao, *Smart Fibres, Fabrics and Clothing* (Cambridge and Boca Raton, FL: Woodhead, 2001), and Terje A. Skotheim and John R. Reynolds (eds), *Handbook of Conducting Polymers* (London and Boca Raton, FL: CRC Press, 2007).
7. For further information on Norma Starszakowna see Mary Schoeser, *Portfolio Collection: Norma Starszakowna* (Brighton: Telos Art Publishing, 2005). All quotations are from correspondence with the artist.
8. From an interview Jun-ichi Arai gave to Paul Makovsky and Mary Murphy on 25 October 2004. See http://www.metropolismag.com/story/20041025/jun-ichi-arai-the-futurist-of-fabric, sourced 28 November 2011.
9. Ibid.
10. For more on the Solar Handbag, see http://www.diffus.dk/wordpress/?p=736, sourced 11 May 2012.

CHAPTER 3

1. Ed Rossbach, *Baskets as Textile Art* (New York: Van Nostrand Reinhold Co., 1973), p. 16.
2. Ed Rossbach, 'Ed Rossbach', in Rob Pulleyn (ed.), *The Basketmaker's Art: Contemporary Baskets and Their Makers* (Asheville, NC: Lark Books, 1986), pp. 15–16.
3. Ibid, p. 51.
4. Rossbach, *Baskets as Textile Art*, p. 124.
5. Pat Earnshaw, *The Identification of Lace* (Aylesbury: Shire Publications, 2009), p. 21.
6. Irene Emery, *The Primary Structures of Fabrics* (London: Thames & Hudson, 1994), p. 45.
7. Earnshaw, *Identification of Lace*, p. 22.
8. Desirée Koslin, 'Between the Empirical and the Rational', in Mary Schoeser and Christine Boydell (eds), *Disentangling Textiles* (London: Middlesex University Press, 2002), p. 196.
9. See http://en.wikipedia.org/wiki/Sampul_tapestry, sourced 26 October 2011.
10. Koslin, 'Between the Empirical', p. 197, and see Eric Broudy, *The Book of Looms: A History of the Handloom from Ancient Times to the Present* [1979] (Lebanon, NH: University Press of New England, 1993), and Richard Tapper and Keith S. McLachlan, *Technology, Tradition and Survival: Aspects of Material Culture in the Middle East and Central Asia* (London: Taylor & Francis, 2003).
11. Roger Hardwick, 'Peter Collingwood', http://ww.guardian.co.uk/artanddesign/2008/oct/25/1, sourced 26 October 2011.
12. Ibid.
13. http://longhouse.org/larsen.ihtml and http://longhouse.org/mission.ihtml, sourced 26 October 2011.

CHAPTER 4

1. Susanne Küchler and Graeme Were, *The Art of Clothing: A Pacific Experience* (London: Routledge), 2005, pp. xix–xx.
2. Marilyn J. Horn, *The Second Skin: An Interdisciplinary Study of Clothing* (Boston, MA: Houghton Mifflin, 1968), p.vii, crediting the study of the behaviour of clothing to George Hartmann.
3. http://www.surfacedesign.org/what-does-surface-design-mean-you, sourced 16 November 2011.
4. http://www.indianembassy.tj/en/economy/economy.php?id=14, sourced 12 November 2011.
5. See Brenda King, *Silk and Empire* (Manchester: Manchester University Press, 2005).
6. Helen Douglas, 'The Feel for Rugged Texture', in Mary Schoeser and Christine Boydell (eds), *Disentangling Textiles* (London: Middlesex University Press, 2002), p. 177.
7. Adolph Loewi advised Werner Abegg, whose collection, now preserved in the Abegg Stiftung, was to a large degree shaped by Loewi.
8. Leonardo da Vinci's fly spindle also allowed for the development of a circular multi-spindled throwing frame, and became the basis for many later continuous spinning machines. See http://www.museoscienze.org/english/leonardo/fusoaletta.esp, sourced 2 July 2012.
9. 'Transition and Resilience', *Textile Fibre Forum*, no. 68, 2002, p. 28.
10. See Lauren F. Hughes, 'Weaving Imperial Ideas: Iconography and Ideology of the Inca Coda Bag' in *Textile: The Journal of Cloth and Culture*, vol. 8, July 2010, pp. 149–78, for a detailed analysis of the patterns on later Andean textiles.
11. Ruthie Petrie, 'Rozsika Parker', http://www.guardian.co.uk/world/2010/nov/21/rozsika-parker-obituary, sourced 15 November 2011.
12. Judy Barry, 'The Pleasures of the Machine-stitched Mark', in Alice Kettle and Jane McKeating (eds), *Machine Stitch: Perspective* (London: A&C Black, 2010), pp. 23–24.
13. See Anita Feldman and Sue Pritchard, *Henry Moore Textiles* (London: Lund Humphries: 2008).
14. Printing on jersey required duplicate screens (fine and larger mesh) for some colours. For the challenges of printing on jersey, see Liz Arthur (ed.), *Robert Stewart: Design 1946–95* (London: Glasgow School of Art Press / A&C Black, 2003), p. 96.

CHAPTER 5

1. Colleen E. Kriger, *Cloth in West African History* (Lanham, MD: Rowman AltaMira, 2006), pp. 81–83.
2. For the Swiss textile scholar Alfred Bühler, who continued to make important contributions to the wider field of ethnographic textiles until his death in 1981, see Robyn J. Maxwell, *Textiles of Southeast Asia: Tradition, Trade and Transformation* (Rutland, VT, and Tokyo: Tuttle Publishing, 2003). For other discussions of the collection of such textiles, see Jack Lenor Larsen, *The Dyer's Art: Ikat, Batik, Plangi* (New York: Van Nostrand Reinhold Co., 1976) and Jonathan C. H. King, *First Peoples, First Contacts: Native Peoples of North America* (Cambridge, MA, Harvard University Press, 1999), the latter discussing the British Museum collections.
3. Margot Schevill, Janet Catherine Berlo and Edward Bridgman Dwyer, *Textile Traditions of Mesoamerica and the Andes: An Anthology* (Austin, TX: University of Texas Press, 1996), p. 5.
4. *Hali*, nos 123–25, 2002, p. 62.
5. http://shiboriorg.wordpress.com/members/analisahedstrom/, accessed 22 November 2011.
6. Linda Eaton, *Quilts in a Material World: Selections from the Winterthur Collection* (New York: Abrams, 2007), pp. 164–67, citing Ruth Finley, *Old Patchwork Quilts and the Women Who Made Them* (Philadelphia: J. B. Lippincott, 1929), p. iv, and the fact that Henry du Pont owned a copy of this volume.
7. The exhibition 'American Pieced Quilts' was drawn from the collection of Jonathan Holstein and Gail Vander Hoof, and inspired Faith and Stephen Brown to begin collecting quilts, leading to several exhibitions and publications. See, for example, http://americanart.si.edu/pr/library/2000/09/amish/ and Faith and Stephen Brown, *Amish Abstractions: Quilts from the Collection of Faith and Stephen Brown* (Petaluma, CA: Pomegranate Communications, 2009).
8. See Gwen Marston, *Mary Schafer: American Quilt Maker* (Ann Arbor, MI: University of Michigan Press, 2004), p. 64, for the prizes won by Schafer at the first Association exhibition.
9. Hannah B. Higgins, *The Grid Book* (Cambridge, MA: MIT Press, 2009), p. 277, citing Howard Gardner's influential *Frames of Mind: The Theory of Multiple Intelligences*, first published in 1983, in its tenth edition by 1993, and available as an e-book by 2011.
10. Richard Sennett, *The Craftsman* (New Haven and London: Yale University Press, 2008), pp. 14–15.
11. Mary Lloyd Jones in *The Festival of Quilts 2011* (exh. cat., August 2010), p. 9.
12. *The Connoisseur*, vols. 17–19, pp. 200–201 available at http://books.google.co.uk/books?id=PYweAQAAMAAJ&q=stumpwork&dq=stumpwork&hl=en&ei=egPTTvOqFcv48QPwheTlDw&sa=X&oi=book_result&ct=result&resnum=3&ved=0CEEQ6AEwAjgU, sourced 27 November 2011.
13. Margaret Jourdain, *The History of English Secular Embroidery* (New York: Dutton & Co., 1912), p. 156.
14. Captain Kapp led nine Explorers Club Flag expeditions to Central and South America, and published numerous books on his studies of the indigenous cultures. See http://www.explorers.org/index.php/about/about_the_club. Other active collectors were Bob and Marianne Huber in the late 1960s; in 1973 they filmed a documentary on *mola*-making and the Kunas. See http://www.mola-museum.com/about_us.html, sourced 21 November 2011.
15. Yosi Anaya, Universidad Vericruzana, 'Welcome to World Textile Art': http:///www,wta-online.org, sourced 27 November 2011.
16. Ibid.
17. Audrey Walker, extract from *The World of Embroidery Magazine*, 1993, in *Mary Cozens-Walker: Objects of Obsession 1955–2011, A Pictorial Autobiography* (Ipswich: Healeys Print Group, 2011), p. 27.
18. Jennifer Harris, extract as above, p. 41.

CHAPTER 6

1. For the relationship between women and machines, see Sadie Plant, *Zeros + Ones: Digital Women + The New Technoculture* (London: Fourth Estate, 1998).
2. See, for example, Lauren Finley Hughes, 'Weaving Imperial Ideas: Iconography and Ideology of the Inca Coca Bag' in *Textile: The Journal of Cloth and Culture*, vol. 8, no. 2, July 2010, pp. 148–179, and Lisa Monnas, *Merchants, Princes and Painters: Silk Fabrics in Italian and Northern Paintings 1300–1550* (London and New Haven: Yale University Press, 2009).
3. Whitney Blausen, 'Bianchini-Férier', http://www.fashionencyclopedia.com/Ba-Bo/Bianchini-F-rier.html, sourced 23 January 2012.
4. According to Yvan Rodic, 30 September 2009, blogs 'have become a core reference tool for fashion houses and designers who monitor them for global inspiration and to learn how trends are being adapted on the street – and all without leaving their desks'. From http://www.thecoolhunter.co.uk/fashion, sourced 3 July 2011.
5. Thomas L. Scharf (ed.) 'LACMA's Founding Collectors: The Mabury Family', http//www.sandiegohistory.org/journal/85winter/100htm, sourced 18 August 2011. See also Iwao Nagasaki, 'The Migration of Japanese Textiles to America', and Sharon Takeda, 'The Bella Mabury Collection of Japanese Textiles', in Dale Gluckman *et al.*, *When Art Became Fashion: Kosode in Edo-Period Japan* (Los Angeles: Los Angeles County Museum of Art, 1992).
6. The Golding edition and that by George Sandys (1621, revised 1632) influenced Milton, Dryden and Pope. See Helen Hackett, 'England looking outwards in the 16th and 17th centuries': http://www.ucl.ac.uk/european-institute/highlights/england, sourced 6 November 2011.
7. For further information, see Melinda Watt and Andrew Morrall (eds), *English Embroidery from the Metropolitan Museum of Art, 1580–1700: Twixt Art and Nature* (New Haven and London: Yale University Press, 2008).
8. Michele Majer, 'Cora Ginsburg: Biography' (unpublished paper, 2011), citing (re 'step-child') the *Philadelphia Inquirer*, 25 September 1988, p. 6-F.
9. http://www.globalmamas.org/Info/36-.aspx, sourced 25 January 2012. Global Mamas is supported by Women in Progress (WIP), an international non-profit organization.
10. Extra Fancy can be found at http://www.extrafancyco.com/index.php?/infoo/aboutpress/, sourced 23 January 2012.
11. http://www.francesergen.com/, sourced 7 November, 2011.
12. http://www.vam.ac.uk/channel/things/textiles/timorous_beasties/, sourced 8 November 2011.

FURTHER READING

BIBLIOGRAPHIES, DICTIONARIES AND GENERAL HISTORIES

Anawalt, Patricia Rieff, *The Worldwide History of Dress* (London and New York: Thames & Hudson, 2007)

Annual Textile Bibliography (Textile Society of America and Magrath Library, University of Minnesota): http://www.textilesociety.org/publications_bibliography.htm

Barber, Elizabeth, *Prehistoric Textiles* (Princeton, NJ: Princeton University Press, 1992)

Bibliographica Textilia Historiae: On The Textile Literature (The Center for Social Research on Old Textiles [CSROT]) http://egressfoundation.net/egress/index.php?option=com_content&view=article&id=68&Itemid=343

Bibliography, Early Modern Dress and Textiles Research Network: http://www.earlymoderndressandtextiles.ac.uk/bibliography/

Burnham, Dorothy K., *Warp and Weft: A Textile Terminology* (Toronto: Royal Ontario Museum, 1980)

Eicher, Joanne B. (ed.), *Berg Encyclopedia of World Dress and Fashion*, vols 1–10 (New York: Oxford University Press, 2010)

Emery, Irene, *The Primary Structures of Fabrics: An Illustrated Classification* (Washington, DC: The Textile Museum, 1980)

Geijer, Agnes, *A History of Textile Art* (London: Pasold Research Fund, 1979)

Harris, Jennifer (ed.), *5,000 Years of Textiles* (London: British Museum Press, 2010)

Jenkins, David (ed.), *The Cambridge History of Western Textiles* (Cambridge: Cambridge University Press, 2003)

Johnson, Donald C., *Agile Hands and Creative Minds: A Bibliography of Textile Traditions in Afghanistan, Bangladesh, Bhutan, India, Nepal, Pakistan and Sri Lanka* (Bangkok: Orchid, 2002)

Kennett, Frances, *Ethnic Dress: A Comprehensive Guide to the Folk Costume of the World* (London: Reed International, 1995)

McIntyre, J. E. and P. N. Daniels (eds), *Textile Terms and Definitions*, 10th edn (Manchester: The Textile Institute, 1995)

Montgomery, Florence, *Textiles in America 1650–1870: A Dictionary Based on Original Documents* (New York and London: WW Norton, 1984)

Randall, J. L and E. M. Shook, *Bibliography of Mayan Textiles* (Guatemala City: Museo Ixchel de Traje Indigena de Guatemala, 1993)

Schoeser, Mary, *World Textiles: A Concise History* (London and New York: Thames & Hudson, 2003)

Seiler-Baldinger, Annemarie, *Textiles: A Classification of Techniques* (Washington, DC: Smithsonian Institution Press, 1994)

Siegelaub, S. (ed.), *Bibliographica Texilia Historiae* (Amsterdam and New York: International General, 1997)

The Textile Museum, *An Introduction to Textile Terms* (Washington, DC: The Textile Museum): http://www.textilemuseum.com/PDFs/TextileTerms.pdf.

Tilke, Max, *Costume Patterns and Designs: A Survey of Costume Patterns and Designs of All Periods and Nations* (London: A. Zwemmer Ltd, 1956)

Tortora, Phyllis and Robert Muhel, *Fairchild's Dictionary of Textiles*, 7th edn (New York: Fairchild, 1996)

Trench, Lucy (ed.), *Materials and Techniques in the Decorative Arts: An Illustrated Dictionary* (London: John Murray, 2000)

Wyatt, Neal *et al.*, 'Recommended Core Bibliography of Textile and Clothing Resources for Academic and Public Libraries', *Reference & User Services Quarterly*, vol. 47, no. 4, 2008 (American Library Association)

TECHNIQUES

Abegg, Margaret, *Apropos Patterns: For Embroidery, Lace and Woven Textiles* [1978] (Riggisberg: Abegg-Stiftung, 1998)

Anderson, Clarita, *American Coverlets and their Weavers: Coverlets from the Collection of Foster and Muriel McCarl (Williamsburg Decorative Arts Series)* (Columbus, OH: Ohio University Press, 2002)

Black, Sandy, *Knitwear in Fashion* (London: Thames & Hudson, 2005)

Cason, Marjorie and Adele Cahlander, *The Art of Bolivian Highland Weaving: Unique, Traditional Techniques for the Modern Weaver* (New York: Watson-Guptill Publications, 1976)

Earnshaw, Pat, *The Identification of Lace* [1980] (Oxford: Shire Publications, 2009)

Earnshaw, Pat, *Lace Machines and Machine Laces* (London: Batsford, 1986)

Eaton, Linda, *Quilts in a Material World: Selections from the Winterthur Collection* (New York: Abrams, 2007)

Fisch, Arlene, *Textile Techniques in Metal* (Asheville, NC: Lark Books, 2001)

Gillow, John and Brian Sentance, *World Textiles: A Visual Guide to Traditional Techniques* (London: Thames & Hudson, 1999)

Harvey-Brown, Stacey, *Woven Shibori* (Stoke-on-Trent: The Loom Room Publications, 2010)

Huli, Alastair and Jose Luczyc-Wyhowska, *Kilim: The Complete Guide* (London: Thames & Hudson, 2000)

Kadolph, Sara J., *Textiles*, 11th edn (Upper Saddle River, NJ: Prentice Hall/Pearson, 2010)

Kettle, Alice and Jane McKeating (eds), *Machine Stitching: Perspectives* (London: A&C Black, 2010)

Kraatz, Anne, *Lace: History and Fashion* (London: Thames & Hudson) 1989 [originally in French as *Dentelles* (Paris, Éditions Adam Biro, 1988), translated by Pat Earnshaw]

Larsen, Jack Lenor, *Interlacing: The Elemental Fabric* (New York: Kodansha America, 1987)

Levey, Santina , *Lace: A History* (London: Victoria & Albert Museum; Leeds: W. S. Maney, 1983, reprinted 2001)

Marinis, Fabrizio de', *Velvet: History, Techniques, Fashion* (Milan: Idea Books, 1994)

Marshall, John, *Make Your Own Japanese Clothes: Patterns and Ideas for Modern Wear* (Tokyo and New York: Kodansha International Ltd, 1988)

Milanesi, Enza, *The Carpet: Origins, Art, and History* (Ontario: Firefly Books Ltd, 2002)

Morrell, Anne, *The Techniques of Indian Embroidery* (London: Batsford Ltd, 1994)

Paine, Sheila, *Embroidered Textiles: A World Guide to Traditional Patterns* (London: Thames & Hudson, 2010)

Phillips, Barty, *Tapestry* (London: Phaidon, 1994)

Pritchard, Sue, *Quilts 1700–2010: Hidden histories, Untold Stories* (London: Victoria & Albert Museum, 2010)

Richards, Ann, *Weaving Textiles That Shape Themselves* (Ramsbury: The Crowood Press, 2012)

Rossbach, Ed, *Baskets as Textile Art* (New York: Van Nostrand Reinhold Co., 1973)

Rutt, Richard, *A History of Hand Knitting* (London: Batsford 1987; repr. Interweave Press, 2003)

Saint-Aubin, Charles Germain de, *Art of the Embroiderer* [Paris: 1770], facsimile edition by Nikki Scheuer (trans.) and Edward Maeder (Los Angeles: Los Angeles County Museum of Art, 1983)

Sentance, Brian, *Basketry: A World Guide to Traditional Techniques* (London: Thames & Hudson, 2007)

Sherrill, Sarah, *Carpets and Rugs of Europe and America* (New York, London and Paris: Abbeville, 1996)

Wada, Yoshiko, *Memory on Cloth: Shibori Now* (Tokyo: Kodansha International Ltd, 2002)

Wada, Yoshiko *et al.*, *Shibori: The Inventive Art of Japanese Shaped Resist Dyeing: Tradition, Techniques, Innovation* [1983] (Tokyo, New York and London: Kodansha International Ltd, 2012)

Yoshioka, S. *et al.* (eds), *Tsutsugaki Textiles of Japan: Traditional Freehand Paste Resist Indigo Dyeing Technique of Auspicious Motifs* (Kyoto: Books Nippan, 1987)

FIBRES AND DYES

Arthur, Liz (ed.), *Seeing Red: Scotland's Exotic Textile Heritage* (Glasgow: Collins Gallery, 2007)

Balfour-Paul, Jenny, *Indigo* (London: British Museum Press, 1998)

Chenciner, Robert, *Madder Red: A History of Luxury and Trade* (London: Routledge Curzon, 2000)

Delamare Françoise, *Colour: The Story of Dyes and Pigments* (London: Thames & Hudson, 2000)

Garfield, Simon, *Mauve: How One Man Invented a Colour That Changed the World* (London: Faber, 2000)

Gittinger, Mattiebelle, *Master Dyers to the World: Technique and Trade in Early Indian Dyed Cotton Textiles* [1982] (Washington, DC: The Textile Museum, 1997)

Handley, Susannah, *Nylon: The Story of a Fashion Revolution* (Baltimore: The Johns Hopkins University Press, 1999)

Kasselman, K.D., *Natural Dyes of the Asia Pacific Region* vol. 2 (London: Studio Vista, 1997)

Larsen, Jack Lenor *et al.*, *The Dyer's Art: Ikat, Batik, Plangi* (New York: Van Nostrand Reinhold Co., 1976)

Mairet, Ethel, *Vegetable Dyes: Being a Book of Recipes and Other Information Useful to the Dyer* (London: Faber & Faber, 1916; 6th edn 1938 available at http://www.gutenberg.org/files/24076/24076-h/24076-h.htm)

Ponting, Ken, *A Dictionary of Dyes and Dyeing* (London: Bell & Hyman, 1981)

Riello, Giorgio and P. Parthasarathi (eds), *The Spinning World: A Global History of Cotton Textiles, 1200–1850* (Oxford: Oxford Uinversity Press/Pasold Research Fund, 2011)

Rivers, Victoria, *The Shining Cloth: Dress and Adornment that Glitters* (London: Thames & Hudson, 1997)

Sandber, Gosta, *The Red Dyes: Cochineal, Madder, and Murex Purple* (Asheville NC: Lark Books, 1998)

Schoeser, Mary, *Silk* (New Haven and London: Yale University Press, 2007)

Yafa, Stephen, *Cotton: The Biography of a Revolutionary Fiber* (New York: Viking, 2005)

AFRICA

Bouttiaux, Anne-Mari, *African Costumes and Textiles: From the Berbers to the Zulus* (Milan: 5 Continents Editions, 2008)

Gillow, John, *African Textiles: Colour and Creativity Across a Continent* (San Francisco: Chronicle, 2003)

Kriger, Colleen E., *Cloth in West African History* (Lanham, MD: Rowman AltaMira, 2006)

Lagamma, Alisa and Christine Giuntini, *The Essential Art of African Textiles: Design without end* (New York: Metropolitan Museum of Art, 2009)

Lamb, Venice and Alastair Lamb, *Sierra Leone Weaving* (Hertingfordbury: Roxford Books, 1984)

Mack, John, *Malagasy Textiles (Shire ethnography)* (Princes Risborough: Shire, 1989)

Picton, John (ed.), *The Art of African Textiles: Technology, Tradition, and Lurex* (London: Lund Humphries, 1995)

Ross, Doran, *Wrapped in Pride: Ghanaian Kente and African American identity* (Los Angeles: Fowler Museum of Cultural History, 1998)

Spring, Christopher and Julie Hudson, *North African Textiles* (London: British Museum Press, 1995)

ASIA AND THE PACIFIC

Barnes, Ruth and Mary Hunt Kahlenberg, *Five Centuries of Indonesian Textiles* (London: Prestel, 2010)

Clark, Ruby, *Central Asian Ikats* (London: V&A Publishing, 2007)

Conway, Susan, *Thai Textiles* (London: British Museum Press, 1992)

Corrigan, Gina, *Miao Textiles from China* (London: British Museum Press, 2001)

Debaine-Francfort, Corinne and Abduressul Idriss, *Keriya, mémoire d'un fleuve: Archéologie et civilisation des oasis du Taklamakan* (Suilly-la-Tour: Éditions Findakly, 2001)

Harvey, J., *Traditional Textiles of Central Asia* (London: Thames & Hudson, 1997)

Gibbon, Kate Fitz and A. Hale, *Ikat Silks of Central Asia: The Guido Goldman Collection* (London: Laurence King/ Alan Marcuson, 1997)

Gittinger, Mattiebelle, *Splendid Symbols: Textiles and tradition in Indonesia* [1979] (Singapore and New York: Oxford University Press of South East Asia, 1990)

Gittinger, Mattiebelle and H. Leedom Lefferts, *Textiles and the Tai Experience in Southeast Asia* (Washington, DC: The Textile Museum, 1992)

Gluckman, Dale and Sharon Takeda, *When Art Became Fashion: Kosode in Edo-Period Japan* (Los Angeles and New York: Weatherhill, 1992)

Gonick, Gloria and Ichiko Yonamine, *Splendor of the Dragon: Costume of the Ryukyu Kindgom* (Los Angeles: Craft and Folk Art Museum/Okinawa Prefectural Museum, 1995)

Hamilton, Roy, *From the Rainbow's Varied Hue: Textiles of the Southern Philippines* (Los Angeles: Fowler Museum of Cultural History, 2002)

Jackson, Robert D., *Imperial Silks: Ch'ing Dynasty Textiles in the Minneapolis Museum of Art* (Minneapolis: Art Media Resources, 2000)

Kahlenberg, Mary Hunt and Valérie Berinstain, *Asian Costumes and Textiles: From the Bosphorus to Fujiyama – The Zaira and Marcel Mis Collection* (Milan: Skira, 2001)

Kawakami, Barbara F., *Japanese Immigrant Clothing in Hawaii 1885–1941* (Honolulu: University of Hawaii Press, 1993)

Lipton, Mimi and Cyril Barrett (eds), *The Tiger Rugs of Tibet* (London: Thames & Hudson, 1989)

Neich, Roger and Mick Pendergrast, *Traditional Tapa Textiles of the Pacific* (London: Thames & Hudson, 1997)

Tagwerker, Edeltraud, *Siho and Naga – Lao Textiles: Reflecting a People's Tradition and Change* (New York: Peter Lang, 2009)

Watt, James C. Y. and Anne E. Wardwell, *When Silk Was Gold: Central Asian and Chinese Textiles* (New York: Metropolitan Museum of Art/Abrams, 1997)

Zhao, F., *Treasures in Silk: An Illustrated History of Chinese Textiles* (Hong Kong: ISAT/Costume Squad, 1999)

EUROPE AND NORTH AMERICA TO 1985

Atterbury, Paul and Clive Wainwright, *Pugin: A Gothic Passion* (New Haven and London: Yale University Press, 1994)

Buruma, Anna, *Liberty & Co. in the Fifties and Sixties: A Taste for Design* (Woodbridge and New York: Antique Collectors' Club, 2008)

Campbell, Thomas P., *Tapestry in the Renaissance: Art and Magnificence* (New York: Metropolitan Museum of Art, 2002)

Clark, Robert and Andrea Belloli (eds) *Design in America: Cranbrook Vision, 1925–50* (New York: Abrams, 1983)

Coatts, Margot *A Weaver's Life: Ethel Mairet 1872-1952* (London: Crafts Council, 1983)

Constantine, Mildred and Jack Lenor Larsen, *The Art Fabric Mainstream* (New York: Van Nostrand Reinhold Co., 1981)

Constantine, Mildred and Jack Lenor Larsen, *Beyond Craft: The Art Fabric* (New York: Van Nostrand Reinhold Co., 1973)

Endrei, Walter, *The First Hundred Years of European Textile Printing* (Budapest: Akademiai Kiado, 1998)

German Renaissance Patterns for Embroidery: A Facsimile Copy of Nicolas Bassee's New Modelbuch of 1568 (Austin, TX: Curious Works Press, 1994)

Gerstein, Alexandra (ed.), *Beyond Bloomsbury: Designs of the Omega Workshop 1913–19* (London: Courtauld Gallery/ Fontanka, 2009)

Hanson, Viveka, *Swedish Textile Art : Traditional Marriage Weavings from Scania (The Nasser D. Khalili Collection of Swedish Textile Art)* (London: Kibo Foundation 1996)

Hardy, Alain-René, *Art Deco Textiles: The French Designers* (London: Thames & Hudson, 2006)

Hiesinger, Kathryn and George Marcus, *Design Since 1945* (Philadelphia: Rizzoli, 1983)

Jackson, Lesley, *Alastair Morton and Edinburgh Weavers: Visionary Textiles and Modern Art* (London: V&A Publishing, 2012)

Jones, Owen, *The Grammar of Ornament* [1856] (London: A&C Black, 2008)

Kachurin, Pamela Jill, *Soviet Textiles: Designing the Modern Utopia* (Boston, MA: MFA Publications, 2006)

King, Brenda, *Dye, Print, Stitch: Textiles by Thomas and Elizabeth Wardle* (Brenda King, 2009)

Klein, Bernat, *Eye for Colour* (London: Collins, 1965)

Koike, Kazuki (ed.), *Issey Miyake: East Meets West* (Tokyo: Heibonsha, 1978)

McFadden, David and Lotus Stack, *Jack Lenor Larsen: Creator and Collector* (London: Merrell, 2004)

Miller, Lesley E., 'Jean Revel: fine artist, designer or entrepreneur?', *Journal of Design History*, vol. 8, no. 2, 1995, pp. 79–96

Monnas, Lisa, *Merchants, Princes and Painters: Silk Fabrics in Italian and Northern Paintings 1300–1550* (New Haven and London: Yale University Press, 2008)

Parry, Linda, *Textiles of the Arts & Crafts Movement* [1998] (London: Thames & Hudson, 2005)

Parry, Linda, *William Morris Textiles* (London: Weidenfeld and Nicolson, 1983)

Rehman, Naheed Jafri Sherry, *The Kashmiri Shawl: From Jamawar To Paisley* (Ahmedabad: Mapin Publishing, 2006)

Robertson, Kay, *2,000 Years of Silk Weaving: An Exhibition Sponsored by the Los Angeles County Museum in collaboration with the Cleveland Museum of Art and the Detroit Institute of Art* (New York: E. Weyhe, 1944)

Rothstein, Natalie, *Silk Designs of the Eighteenth Century* (London: Thames & Hudson, 1990)

Rowe, Ann P. and Rebecca A. T. Stevens, *Ed Rossbach: 40 Years of Exploration and Innovation in Fiber Art* (Asheville, NC: Lark Books, 1990)

Schoeser, Mary, *Marianne Straub* (London: Design Council, 1984)

Schoeser, Mary, 'A Secret Trade: Plate-printed textiles and dress accessories, *c.* 1620–1820', *Dress: The Annual Journal of the Costume Society of America*, vol. 34, 2007, pp. 49–59

Staniland, Kay, *Medieval Craftsmen: Embroiderers* (Toronto: University of Toronto Press, 1991)

Scott, Katie and Cherry, Deborah (eds), *Between Luxury and the Everyday: Decorative Arts in Eighteenth-Century France* (Oxford: Blackwell, 2005)

Talley, Charles, *Contemporary Textile Art: Scandinavia* (Stockholm: Carmina, 1982)

Troy, Virginia Gardner, *Anni Albers and Ancient American Textiles: From Bauhaus to Black Montain* (Aldershot and Burlington, VT: Ashgate, 2002)

Troy, Virginia Gardner, *The Modernist Textile: Europe and America, 1890–1940* (London: Lund Humphries, 2006)

Volker, Angela and Ruperta Pichler, *Textiles of the Weiner Werkstätte, 1910–1932* (London: Thames & Hudson, 1994)

Watt, Melinda and Andrew Morrall, *English Embroidery in the Metropolitan Museum 1580–1700: 'Twixt Art and Nature* (New York: Metropolitan Museum of Art, 2009)

Yefimova, Luisa V. and Tatyana S. Aleshina, *Russian Elegance: Country and City Fashion from the 15th to the early 20th Century* (London: Vivayas Publishing, 2011)

INDIAN SUBCONTINENT

Ames, Frank, *Woven Masterpieces of Sikh Heritage: The Stylistic Development of the Kashmir Shawl 1780–1839* (Woodbridge and New York: Antique Collectors' Club, 2010)

Askari, Nasreen and Liz Arthur, *Uncut Cloth: Saris, Shawls and Sashes* (London: Merrell Holberton, 1999)

Askari, Nasreen and Rosemary Crill, *Colours of the Indus: Costumes and Textiles of Pakistan* (London: Merrell Holberton, 1997)

Barnes, Ruth, *Indian Block-Printed Textiles in Egypt: The Newberry Collection in the Ashmolean Museum* (Oxford: Clarendon Press, 1997)

Christi, Rta Kapoor *et al.*, *Handcrafted Indian Textiles: Tradition and beyond* (New Delhi: Roli Books, 2004)

Crill, Rosemary, *Chintz: Indian Textiles for the West* (London: V&A Publishing, 2008)

Crill, Rosemary, *Indian Ikat Textiles* (London: V&A Publishing, 1998)

Edwards, Eiluned, *Textiles and Dress of Gujarat* (London: V&A Publishing, 2011)

Gillow, John and Nicholas Barnard, *Indian Textiles* (London: Thames & Hudson, 2008)

Guy, John, *Indian Textiles in the East: From Southeast Asia to Japan* (London: Thames & Hudson, 2009)

Konieczny, M. G., *Textiles of Baluchistan* (London: British Museum Press, 1979)

Mason, Darielle *et al.*, *Kantha: The Embroidered Quilts of Bengal from the Sheldon and Jill Bonovitz Collection and the Stella Kramrisch Collection of the Philadelphia Museum of Art* (New Haven: Yale University Press, 2009)

Paine, Sheila, *Embroidery from India and Pakistan* (London: British Museum Press, 2001)

Weir, Shelagh, *Palestinian Costume* (Austin, TX: University of Texas Press, 1989)

NATIVE AND LATIN AMERICA

Braun, Barbara (ed.), *Arts of the Amazon* (New York and London: Thames & Hudson, 1995)

Cordry, Donald and Dorothy Cordry, *Mexican Indian Costumes* (Austin, TX, and London: University of Texas Press, 1968)

Crawford, Morris de Camp, *Peruvian Textiles* [1915] (Charleston, NC: Nabu Press, 2010)

Freeman, Roland, *Communion of the Spirits: African-American Quilters, Preservers, and Their Stories* (Nashville, TN: Thomas Nelson, 1996)

Harless, Susan E. (ed.), *Native Arts of the Columbia Plateau: The Doris Swayze Bounds Collection* (Bend, OR: The High Desert Museum/Seattle & London: University of Washington Press, 1998)

Her Many Horses, Emil (ed.), *Identity by Design: Tradition, Change, and Celebration in Native Women's Dresses* (New York: Harper Collins/The National Museum of the American Indian, Smithsonian Institution, Washington, DC, 2007)

Perrin, Michael, *Magnificent Molas: The Art of the Kuna Indians* (Paris and London: Flammarion,1999)

Rowe, Anne P. *et al.*, *Costume and Identity in Highland Ecuador* (Seattle: University of Washington Press, 1998)

Rowe, Anne P. and J. Cohen, *Hidden Threads of Peru: Q'ero Textiles* (Washington, DC: Merrell, 2002)

Sawyers, Alan, *Early Nasca Needlework* (London: Laurence King, 1997)

Sayer, Chloe, *Costumes of Mexico* (Austin, TX: University of Texas Press, 1985)

Sheville, Margot, *Maya Textiles of Guatemala: The Gustavus A. Eisen Collection, 1902* (Austin, TX: University of Texas Press, 1979)

Scheville, Margot B., *Evolution in Textile Design from the Highlands of Guatemala* (Berkeley, CA: Lowie Museum of Anthropology, University of California, 1985)

Scheville, Margot B. *et al.* (eds), *Textile Traditions of Mesoamerica and the Andes: An Anthology* (Austin, TX: University of Texas Press, 1996).

Vavalle, J. A. and J. A. G. Garcia (eds), *The Textile Arts of Peru* (Peru: Integra AFP, 1999)

NEAR AND MIDDLE EAST

Erickson, M., *Textiles in Egypt 200–1500 AD in Swedish Museums* (Gottenburg: University of Gottenburg, 1997)

Fluck, Cacilia and Gisela Helmecke (eds), *Textile Messages: Inscribed Fabrics from Roman to Abbasid Egypt* (Leiden, Boston and Tokyo: Brill, 2006)

Frances, Michael and Rupert Waterhouse, *Great Embroideries of Bukhara* (London: Textile and Art Publications, 2000)

Gervers, Veronika, 'The Influence of Ottoman Turkish Textiles and Costume in Eastern Europe: with particular reference to Hungary', *History, Technology, and Art Monograph 4* (Toronto: Royal Ontario Museum, 1982)

Gillow, John, *Textiles of the Islamic World* (London: Thames & Hudson, 2010)

Hoskins, Nancy Arthur, *The Coptic Tapestry Albums: and the Archaeologist of Antino* (Seattle: University of Washington Press, 2004)

Krody, Sumru Belgar, *Flowers of Silk and Gold: Four Centuries of Ottoman Embroidery* (Washington D.C: The Textile Museum/London: Merrell, 2000)

Noever, Peter, *Fragile Remnants: Egyptian Textiles of Late Antiquity and Early Islam* (Ostfildern: Hatje Cantz, 2006)

Paine, Sheila, *Embroidery from Afghanistan* (London: British Museum Press, 2006)

Palace of Gold and Light: Treasures from the Topkapi, Istanbul (Chicago: University of Chicago Press, 2001)

Raby, J. and A. Effeny (eds), *Ipek: The Cresent and the Rose: Imperial Ottoman Silks and Velvets* (London: Azimuth, 2001)

Raven, Maarten J. *et al.*, *Pharaonic and Early Medieval Egyptian Textiles – Collections of the National Museum of Antiquities at Leiden* (Turnhout: Brepols, 2002)

Scarce, Jennifer, *Women's Costume of the Near and Middle East* (London: Unwin Hyman, 1987)

Stauffer, A., *Textiles of Late Antiquity* (New York: Metropolitan Museum of Art, 1995)

Taylor, Roderick, *Ottoman Embroidery* (New York: Interlink, 1997)

Taylor, Roderick, *Embroidery of the Greek Islands* (New York: Interlink, 2002)

Wearden, Jennifer and Patricia L. Baker, *Iranian Textiles* (London: V&A Publishing, 2010)

AFTER 1985

Information on monographs and exhibition catalogues can be found by consulting the websites listed in 'Resources'. The following titles provide an overview of the development of art textiles since the mid-1980s and are therefore listed chronologically.

Tsurumoto, Shozo (ed.), *Issey Miyake Bodyworks* (Tokyo: Shogakukan, 1983)

Rhodes, Zandra and Anne Knight, *The Art of Zandra Rhodes* [1984] (London: Michael O'Mara, 1995)

Parker, Rozsika, *The Subversive Stitch: Embroidery and the Making of the Feminine* [1984] (London: IB Tauris, 2010)

Dale, Julie Schafler, *Art to Wear* (New York: Abbeville Press, 1986)

Chloe Colchester, *The New Textiles* (London: Thames & Hudson, 1993)

Holborn, Mark, *Issey Miyake* (Cologne: Taschen, 1995)

Schoeser, Mary, *International Textile Design* (London: Laurence King, 1995)

Wada, Yoshkio and Rebecca Stevens, *The Kimono Inspiration: Art and Art-to-Wear in America* (Washington, DC: The Textile Museum, 1996)

Brackman, Barbara, *Patterns of Progress: Quilts in the Machine Age* (Seattle: Gene Autry Western Heritage, 1997)

Braddock, Sarah and Marie O'Mahony, *Techno Textiles: Revolutionary Fabrics for Fashion and Design* (London: Thames & Hudson, 1999)

McCarty, Cara and Matilda McQuaid, *Structure and Surface: Contemporary Japanese Textiles* (New York: Museum of Modern Art/Abrams, 1999)

Sato, Kazuko, *Issey Miyake Making Things* (Paris: Fondation Cartier pour l'art contemporain/Zurich: Scalo, 1999)

Stevens, Rebecca, *Technology as Catalyst: Textile Artists on the Cutting Edge* (Washington, DC: The Textile Museum, 2002)

Aimone, Katherine Duncan, *The Fibrearts Book of Wearable Art* (Asheville, NC: Lark Books, 2004)

Leventon, Melissa, *Artwear: Fashion and Anti-Fashion* (Fine Art Museum of San Francisco/New York: Thames & Hudson, 2005)

McQuaid, Matilda, *Extreme Textiles: Designing for High Performance* (New York: Cooper-Hewitt, National Design Museum, 2005)

Braddock, Sarah and Marie O'Mahony, *Techno Textiles 2: Revolutionary Fabrics for Fashion and Design* (London: Thames & Hudson, 2007)

Millar, Lesley, *Cloth and Culture Now* (Canterbury: University College for the Creative Arts, 2007)

Cole, Drusilla, *Textiles Now* (London: Laurence King, 2008)

McFadden, David Revere *et al.*, *Radical Lace and Subversive Knitting* (Woodbridge and New York: Antique Collectors' Club, 2008)

Monem, Nadine (ed.), *Contemporary Textiles: The Fabric of Fine Art* (London: Black Dog, 2008)

Colchester, Chloe, *Textiles Today: A Global Survey of Trends and Traditions* (London: Thames & Hudson, 2009)

Quinn, Bradley, *Textile Designers at the Cutting Edge* (London: Laurence King, 2009)

Hunh, Shu and Joseph Magliaro, *By Hand: The Use of Craft in Contemporary Art* (New York: Princeton Architectural Press, 2010)

Off the Wall: The World of Wearable Art (Nelson, New Zealand: Craig Potton Publishing, 3rd edn 2011)

Moriyama, Professor Akiko, *Arai Jun-ichi: Tekisutairu bankakyou – Jun-ichi Arai: The Dream Weaver* (Tokyo: Bigaku Shuppann, 2012)

Further Reading compiled with the assistance of Jo Ann Stabb

RESOURCES

DESIGNERS, ARTISTS AND MANUFACTURERS

Soraya Abidin www.dickidin.com.au
Jackie Abrams www.jackieabrams.com
Nadia Albertini www.nadiaalbertini.com
Brigitte Amarger www.brigitteamarger.com
Sonja Andrew s.andrew@manchester.ac.uk
Janice Appleton www.janiceappleton.com
Lucy Arai www.lucyarai.com
Patricia Armour www.tapestryartist.co.nz
Bethan Ash www.bethanash.co.uk
Christine Atkins www.christineatkins.net
Jenny Balfour-Paul j.a.balfour-paul@exeter.ac.uk
Jo Barker issuu.com/michaeldancer/docs/jobarker_14
Margaret Barnett mabarnett1@bigpond.com
Mary Barron www.visualarts.net.au/gallery/maryelizabethbarron
James Bassler gail.martin.gallery@att.net
Daniela Bauer www.a-hat.de info@a-hat.de
Joan Beadle J.Beadle@mmu.ac.uk
Linda Behar www.lindabehar.com
Trish Belford and Ruth Morrow www.tactilityfactory.com
Boisali Biswas www.boisalibiswas.com
Patricia Black www.patricia-black-artwear.com
Sandy Black www.fashion.arts.ac.uk/research/staff/a-z/professorsandyblack
Cecilia Blomberg www.ceciliablomberg.com
Lisbet Borggreen lisbit@net.telenor.dk
Eszter Bornemisza www.bornemisza.com
Silke Bosbach www.silke-bosbach.de
Neil Bottle www.neilbottle.com
George-Ann Bowers gabowers@earthlink.net
Melanie Bowles www.tedresearch.net
Michael Brennand-Wood www.brennand-wood.com
Cheryl Bridgart www.bridgart.com
Elizabeth Brimelow ebrimelow@Hotmail.com
Ann Brown annbrownart@gmail.com
Caroline Brown www.carolinebrownarttextiles.com
Hilary Buckland thebucklands@iinet.net.au
Pauline Burbidge www.paulineburbidge-quilts.com
Rosalind Byass rosalindbyass@hotmail.com
Jean Cacicedo www.jeancacicedo.com
Elizabeth Calnan www.elizabethcalnantextiles.com
Sarah Campbell www.sarahcampbelldesigns.com
Vanda Campbell vanda.campbell@virgin.net
Nigel Cheney www.nigelcheney.com
Heidi Chisholm www.heidichisholm.com
Joanne Circle jocircle@telus.net
Jane Clark www.jointworks.co.nz
Marian Clayden www.marianclayden.com
Jette Clover www.jetteclover.com
Candiss Cole www.candisscole.com
Annabelle Collett yayadesign@mail.com
Carole Collett carolecollett.com
Vishna Collins vishnacollins@optusnet.com.au
Dana Connell www.wolfdesignsonline.com
Judith Content judithcontent@earthlink.net
Janet Cooper www.janetcooperdesigns.com
Mary Cozens-Walker www.marycozenswalker.co.uk
Nancy Crasco www.nancycrasco.com
Fiona Crestani f.crestani@sbg.at
Candace Crockett crockett@sfsu.edu
Margaret Frances Crowther margaretf.crowther@virgin.net
Bailey Curtis www.baileycurtis.com
Lotte Dalgaard lotte.dalgaard@pc.dk
Naseem Darby www.naseemdarbey.com
Fenella Davies www.fenelladavies.com
Ulla De Larios www.ulladelarios.com
Diffus Design www.diffus.dk
Lynette Douglas www.beautifulhats.biz
Sue Dove suedove55@hotmail.com
Dovecot Studios, Edinburgh www.dovecotstudios.com
Hil Driessen www.hildriessen.com
Jane Dunnewold www.complexcloth.com
Jilly Edwards www.jillyedwards.co.uk
Andrea Eimke www.atiu-fibrearts.com
Elegant Additions, Inc. www.elegantadditionsinc.com/general.php
Andrea Ellis www.texperience.fr
Erin Endicott www.erinendicottart.com
Sharon Epstein sharon@sharonepsteintextiles.com
Frances Ergen www.francesergen.com
Dawn Zero Erickson www.dawnzeroerickson.com
Ann Fahy www.quiltart.eu
Judi Fairbairn www.odysseytextileart.co.uk
Jennifer Falck Linssen www.jenniferfalcklinssen.com
Christopher Farr www.christopherfarr.com
Catriona Faulkner www.catrionafaulkner.com
Ali Ferguson www.aliferguson.co.uk
Clairan Ferrono www.fabric8tions.net
Anne Field www.annefield.co.nz
Diane Finnegan www.diannefinnegan.com.au
Dianne Firth craftact.org.au/portfolios/textiles
Katriina Flensburg www.katriinaflensburge.se
Sara Forzano www.gladraglabel.ch
James Fox www.jamesfoxtextileartist.co.uk
Jane Freear-Wyld www.janefreear-wyld.com
Susie Freeman www.pharmacopoeia-art.net
Christina Frey ch-kd.frey@t-online.de
Alex Friedman alexfriedmantapestry.com
Linda Friedman-Schmidt www.lindafriedmanschmidt.com
Shihoko Fukumoto web.kyoto-inet.or.jp/people/shihoko
Fran Gardner www.frangardner.intuitwebsites.com
Caren Garfen www.carengarfen.com
Frances Geesin www.francesgeesin.com
Amy George www.amyrrgeorge.com
Urusula Gerber-Senger www.ursula-gerber.ch
Preeti Gilani www.gilani.com
Teresa Poletti Glover www.feltart.com.au
Lucy Goffin www.lucygoffintextiles.co.uk
Doria Goocher doriadesigns@gmail.com
Janelle Green nelstoyandbookhaven@bigpond.com
Linda Green www.studiogreen.me
Liza Green lizagreen.blogspot.com
Julia Griffiths Jones www.juliagriffithsjones.co.uk
Erika Grime sites.google.com/site/sokjova1/
Diane Groenewegen www.atasda.org.au
Gabriele Grohmann www.grohmannberlin.de
Carole Anne Grotrian www.caroleannegrotrian.com
Mandy Gunn www.mandygunnart.com
Guarav Jai Gupta contact@akaaro.com
Lois Hadfield loisilk@sbcglobal.net
Janet Haigh www.janethaigh.wordpress.com
Havva Halaceli www.havvahalaceli.blogspot.com
Alvena Hall alvenah@senet.com.au
Hand & Lock www.handembroidery.com
Gloria Hansen www.gloriahansen.com
Matthew Harris www.matthewharriscloth.co.uk
Lyn Hart www.desertsongstudio.com
Paddy Hartley www.paddyhartley.com
Stacey Harvey-Brown www.theloomroom.co.uk
Beth Hatton www.bethhatton.net
Ellen Hauptli www.ellenhauptli.com
Rozanne Hawksley www.rozannehawksley.com
Ana Lisa Hedstrom www.analisahedstrom.com
Cecilia Heffer www.fibre2fashion.com
Sibyl Heijnen www.sibylheijnen.com
Robert Hillestad rhillestad@inebraska.com
Elizabeth Hinkes www.odysseytextileart.co.uk
Pat Hodson www.pathodson.co.uk
Maria Holohan www.axisweb.org/artist/mariaholohan
Raymond Honeyman raymondhoneyman@yahoo.com
Jan Hopkins janhopkinsart@blogspot.com
Dirjke van de Horst-Beetsma dirkje.artquilt@xs4all.nl
Sue Hotchkis susanhotchkis@yahoo.co.uk
Rachel Howard www.rachaelhoward.com
Inge Hueber www.ingehueber.de
Valerie Huggins v.huggins962@btinternet.com
Lynn Hulse www.ornamentalembroidery.com
Annie Hunt www.annihunt.com
Marie-Laure Ilie www.marilorart.com
Sara Impey www.quiltart.eu
Bridget Ingram-Bartholomaus quilts@bridgetIngram-bartholomaeus.de
Louisa Jane Irvine www.louisajane.net
Anne Jackson www.annejackson.co.uk
Val Jackson valstitch@gmail.com
Tracy Jamar www.tracyjamar.com
Val James val.ron@optus.net.au
Silvia Japkin Szulc japkin2@gmail.com
Marty Jonas www.martyjonas.com
Helen Jones textilearchaeology@virginmedia.com
Yoshiko Katagiri daifukuquilt@yahoo.co.jp
Allie Kay kay.allie22@gmail.com
Christine Keller www.christinekeller.net
Mo Kelman www.mokelman.com
Alice Kettle www.alicekettle.com
Kay Khan www.kaykhanart.com
Jill Kinnear www.jillkinnear.com
Joanna Kinnersley-Taylor www.joannakinnerslytaylor.com
Sheila Klein www.sheilaklein.com
Susie Krage skrage2@att.net
Padmaja Krishnan www.transitdesign.in/blog
Tracy Krumm www.tracykrumm.com
Jackie Langfeld www.jackielangfeld.co.uk
Anne Leon www.anneleon.com
Ruth Levine studiolevine@gmail.com
Bette Levy www.pyrogallery.com
Liberty Art Fabrics www.liberty.co.uk
Hillu Liebelt www.hilluliebelt.com
Janet Lipkin www.janetlipkin.com
Mary Lloyd Jones www.marylloydjones.co.uk
K. C. Lowe www.kclowe.com
Josette Luyckx and Marie Paine www.mariejosette.com
Heather Macali www.heathermacali.com
Janine McAullay-Bott www.aritja.com.au
Martha McDonald marthalmcdonald.blogspot.com
Jane McKeating www.62group.org.uk
Althea McNish www.mcnishandweiss.co.uk
Pat Maloney patmaloney93@aol.com
Ptolemy Mann www.ptolemymann.com
Elisa Markes-Young www.zebra-factory.com
Ruth Marshall www.ruthmarshall.com
Cherilyn Martin www.cherilynmartin.com
Paula Martin www.performingdesign.com.au
Vicki Mason www.vickijewel.com
Katherine Maxwell www.katherinemaxwell.com
Sandra Meech www.sandrameech.com
Melba www.maningrida.com
Nancy Middlebrook www.nancymiddlebrook.com
Melanie Miller www.artdes.mmu.ac.uk/profile/miller
Eleri Mills www.thackeraygallery.com
Mariana Minke www.textile-design-studio.com
Claudia Moeller www.claudiamoeller.com
Pat Moloney patmaloney93@aol.com
Julie Montgarrett jmontgarrett@csu.edu.au
Cathy Moon www.camoon.com.au
Samantha Morris sammorris23@gmail.com
Alison Morton alison.theweaver@gmail.com
Robyn Mountcastle ramountcastle@bigpond.com

Mungo www.mungo.co.za
Larissa Murdock murdock48@gmail.com
Dominie Nash www.dominienash.com
Carolyn Nelson www.carolynnelsonart.com
Nithikul Nimkulrat www.inicreation.com
Leslie Nobler www.leslienobler.com
Sara Nordling www.sanordling.com
Inge Norgaard www.ingenorgaard.com
Nuno Works Warehouse www.nunoworks.com
Catherine O'Leary www.catherineoleary.com.au
Loretta Oliver lorettaoliver@wordpress.com
Clyde Olliver www.clydeolliver.com
Martha Opdahl www.marthaopdahl.com
Maria Ortega www.mariaortega.com
Quico Ortega www.cdmt.es
Oriole Mill www.theoriolemill.com
Christine Paine christine.paine@tideline.net
Deepa Panchamia www.deepapanchamia.com
Sabine Parge sabine.parge@gmail.com
John Parkes johnparkesjp@yahoo.com.au
Tim Parry-Williams www.transitionandinfluence.com/gallery/timparrywilliams.html
Teresa Paschke www.teresapaschke.com
Sophie Pattinson www.sophiepattinson.com
Hilary Peterson hilary.peterson@skymesh.com.au
Sadhana Peterson web.me.com/sadhana/sadhanas_site/sadhana_peterson.html
Mirjam Pet-Jacobs www.mirjampetjacobs.nl
Errol Pires errolsan@yahoo.com
Michael Pollard www.michaelpollard.co.uk
Astrid Polman www.astridpolman.nl
Denise Prefontaine denise.p@mymts.net
Lars Pressier larspressiertextiles@blogspot.com
C. J. Pressma www.cjpressma.com
Della Reams www.dellareams.com
Rosmarie Reber www.rosreber.ch
Mary Restieaux maryrestieaux@btinternet.com
Heike Reul www.kunstgewand.de
Ann Richards acostall@yahoo.com
Lesley Richmond www.lesleyrichmond.com
Chinami Ricketts chinami@rickettsindigo.com
Rowland Ricketts rowland@rickettsindigo.com
Anne Robertsen annerobe@hotmail.com
Kathryn Round www.tedresearch.net
Naomi Ryder www.naomiryder.co.uk
Ryder & Rowe www.ryderandrowe.com
Kyoko Sakurabayashi kiyokosaku@hotmail.com
Christine Sawyer sawyers37@talktalk.net
Karin Schaller schallerkarin@hotmail.com
Cynthia Schira www.cynthiaschira.com
Jakob Schlaepfer www.jakobschlaepfer.com
Ann Schmidt-Christensen asc.cph@firkant.net
Kim Schoenberger www.kimschoenberger.com
Nicky Schonkala nickshonk@hotmail.com
Stephanie Schulte steph_s_22@hotmail.com
Amanda Schwartz www.mmu.ac.uk
Tilleke Schwarz www.tillekeschwarz.com
Judith Scott www.judithscott.org
Ken Scott www.kenscott.it
Nalda Searles naldasearles1@bigpond.com
Anne Selby www.anneselby.com
Margo Selby www.margoselby.com
Barbara Shapiro www.barbara-shapiro.com
Rose Sharp-Jones www.rosesharpjones.co.uk
Jessica Shellard j.shellard@fashion.arts.ac.uk
Jenine Shereos www.jenineshereos.com
Melanie Siegel www.msiegel.ca
Silke www.silke.com.ar
Adrienne Sloane www.adriennesloane.com
Dolores Slowinski www.doloresslowinski.com
Jessica Smith www.domesticelement.com
Tricia Smout www.triciasmout.com.au
Greg Somerville www.gregsomerville-performingdesign.blogspot.com
Mandy Southan www.mandysouthan.co.uk
Marialuisa Sponga www.sponga.com
St Jude's Gallery www.stjudesgallery.co.uk
Jo Ann Stabb jcstabb@ucdavis.edu
Denise Stanton www.denisestanton.co.uk
Norma Starszakowna starszakowna@hotmail.com
Stehli Seiden, Switzerland www.stelhiseiden.ch
Sue Stone www.womanwithafish.com
Janet Stoyel www.clothclinic.co.uk
Edwina Straub www.edwinastraub.com
Reiko Sudo reiko@nuno.com
Eun-Kyung Suh suh1021@hotmail.com
Robina Summers robina.summers@gmail.com
Evette Sunset evettesunset@hotmail.com
Flora Sutton www.florasutton.com.ar
Susan Taber-Avila www.suta.com susan@suta.com
Karen Taiaroa kmtaiaroa@gmail.com
Lilane Taylor www.lilanetaylor.com
Sass Tetzlaff www.sasstetzlaff.co.uk
Kariina Thompson www.karinathompson.co.uk
Asha Peta Thomson asha@intelligenttextiles.com
Timorous Beasties www.timorousbeasties.com
Pilar Tobón www.pilar-tobon.com
Jun Tomita web.me.com/juntomita.textile
Maggi Toner-Edgar www.toneredgar.com
Marieta Toneva www.marietatoneva.se
Tonga Trading Company www.hawaiiandiscovery.com
Janet Twinn www.janettwinn.com
Michiko Uehara www.michiko-uehara.jp
Els Van Baarle www.elsvanbaarle.com
Gerda Van Hamond www.gerdavanhamond.blogspot.com
Anton Veenstra tontoaine@gmail.com
Jennifer Vickers jennifer.vickers@hotmail.co.uk
Susie Vickery www.susievickery.com
Yoshiko Wada www.yoshikowada.com
Yvonne Wakabayashi www.yvonnewakabayashi.com
Margaret Wallace wallacemk@bigpond.com
Carole Waller www.carolewaller.co.uk
Lois Walpole www.loiswalpole.eu
Eva Wanganeen www.evawanganeen.com.au
Jessica B. Watson www.jessicabwatson.com
Watts www.watts1874.co.uk
Sally Weatherill www.sallyweatherill.co.uk
Sandy Webster www.sandywebster.com
Pia Welsch www.pias-quilt-werkstatt.de
Angelika Werth www.angelikawerth.ca
Anne-Marie Wharrie www.wharrie.com
Ilka White www.ilkawhite.com.au
Kath Wilkinson www.kathwilkinson.com
Hilary Williams/The Silk Route www.thesilkroute.co.uk
Rhiannon Williams r.c.williams@derby.ac.uk
Marie-Therese Wisnioski www.artquill.blogspot.com
Cygan Wlodzimierz www.cyganart.art.pl
Dana Wolf www.wolfdesignsonline.com
Deirdre Wood woodwarp@hotmail.co.uk
Anne Woringer www.quiltart.eu/anneworinger.html
Izabela Wywra wyrwa.iza@op.pl
Tatyana Yanishevsky www.knitplants.com
Charlotte Yde www.yde.dk
Irena Zemanova www.praguepatchworkmeeting.com
Adele Zhang azhang@ucdavis.edu
Ludwika Zytkiewicz-Ostrowska www.ludwikazytkiewicz.com

COLLECTORS, COLLECTIONS, DEALERS, GALLERIES AND GROUPS

Artitja Fine Art Gallery www.artitja.com.au
Ashikaga Museum of Art, Japan www.watv.ne.jp/~ashi-bi
Australian Forum for Textile Arts www.tafta.org.au
Austrian Museum of Applied/Contemporary Art, Vienna www.mak.at
Bianchini-Férier Archive www.design-library.com
BPK Photo Agency, Berlin www.bpk-images.de
Braintree District Museum www.braintree.gov.uk/Braintree/leisure-culture/BDMS/Museum
Centre De Documentació i Museu Tèxtil, Terrassa, Spain www.cdmt.es
Central Saint Martins Museum and Contemporary Collections, London www.csm.arts.ac.uk/museum
Constance Howard Resource and Research Centre in Textiles, Goldsmith's College, London www.gold.ac.uk/constancehoward/archive
Cooper-Hewitt, National Design Museum, New York www.cooperhewitt.org
Crafts Study Centre, Farnham www.csc.ucreative.ac.uk
Design Collection, University of California at Davis www.designmuseum.ucdavis.edu
Design Library, New York and London www.design-library.com
Donald Brothers Archive, Heriot-Watt University, Edinburgh archiveshub.ac.uk/features/textiles-donaldbrothers.html
Embroiderers' Guild www.embroiderersguild.com
European Textile Network www.etn-net.org
Royal Albert Memorial Museum and Art Gallery, Exeter www.rammuseum.org.uk
Esther Fitzgerald www.estherfitzgerald.com
Francesca Galloway www.francescagalloway.com
Cora Ginsburg LLC www.coraginsburg.com
Gothenburg Museum of Art, Sweden konstmuseum.goteborg.se
Joss Graham www.jossgraham.com
Titi Halle www.coraginsburg.com
Handweavers' Studio and Gallery, London www.handweavers.co.uk
Harris Museum and Art Gallery, Preston www.harrismuseum.org.uk
International Quilt Study Center and Museum, Nebraska www.quiltstudy.org
Robert Hillestad Textiles Gallery, University of Nebraska-Lincoln textilegallery.unl.edu
Kanazawa College of Art, Japan www.kanazawa-bidai.ac.jp
Peter Koepke pk@designlibrary.com
Jack Lenor Larsen, Longhouse Reserve, East Hampton www.longhouse.org/Larsen.ihtml
Margo Lewers, The Penrith Regional Gallery & The Lewers Bequest www.penrithregionalgallery.org
Liberty Archive, Liberty Art Fabrics www.liberty.co.uk
Los Angeles County Museum of Art www.lacma.org/art/collection/costume-and-textiles
Loughborough University, School of the Arts Textile Research Group www.lboro.ac.uk/departments/sota/research/groups/textile
Ethel Mairet Collection, Crafts Study Centre, Farnham www.csc.ucreative.ac.uk/
Manchester Metropolitan University www.mmu.ac.uk
Gail Martin Gallery gail.martin.gallery@gmail.com
Metropolitan Museum of Art, New York www.metmuseum.org
Museum of Art, Rhode Island School of Design, Providence www.risdmuseum.org
Museum of Cultures, Basel www.mkb.ch
Museum at Fashion Institute of Technology, New York www.fitnyc.edu/museum
Museum of Modern Art, New York www.moma.org
Okawa Museum, Kiryu, Japan www.kiea.jp/OkawaMuseum.html
Philadelphia Museum of Art www.philamuseum.org
Powerhouse Museum, Sydney, Australia www.powerhousemuseum.com
Ruthin Craft Centre, Wales www.ruthincraftcentre.org.uk
The Silver Studio Collection, Middlesex University, London http://archiveshub.ac.uk/contributors/museumofdomesticdesignandarchitecture.html
Peta Smyth www.petasmyth.com
Studio Art Quilts Associates www.saqa.com
Surface Design Association www.surfacedesign.org
TED www.tedresearch.net
Takasaki Museum of Art, Japan mmag.pref.gunma.jp
Texui www.texui.nl
Twisted Thread www.twistedthread.com
Victoria & Albert Museum, London www.vam.ac.uk
Warner Textile Archive, Braintree www.warnertextilearchive.co.uk
Weiner Werkstätte Archive www.backhausen.com
Winterthur Museum, Wilmington, Delaware www.winterthur.org
World Shibori Network www.shibori.org
World Textile Association www.wta-online.org

ACKNOWLEDGMENTS

It has been a privilege to sift through thousands of images of current textiles, most generously submitted by the artists for consideration. My thanks go to all who did so, including those whose work could not be included. Some artists also gave assistance in securing images from others: Sara Impey, Claudia Moeller, Julie Montgarrett, Christine Paine, Ann Richards, Adrienne Sloane, Pilar Tobón and Charlotte Yde. Special mention must be given to Anne Morrell and Tim Parry-Williams, without whom the global breadth of images would have been reduced. Several organizations also played a critical role in securing images, particularly Anna Baptiste and Andrew Salmon of Twisted Thread, Philip Hughes and Jane Gerrard at the Ruthin Craft Centre, the Australian Forum for Textile Arts, the European Textile Network, the Surface Design Association and the World Textile Association.

Others whose help I'm pleased to acknowledge are fellow archivists, curators and historians: Anna Buruma at Central Saint Martins and Liberty; Alan Cook of the Cummersdale Design Collection, John Davis at Manchester Metropolitan University, Linda Eaton at Winterthur, Stephanie Murfin and Caroline Alexander at the Harris Museum, Lynn Felsher Nacmias at FIT, Sharon Takeda at LACMA, and Adele Zhang at the UCD Design Museum. I am especially grateful for the expertise of Dale Gluckman and Eva-Lotta Hansson, and for the time and information given to me by the collectors and dealers Esther Fitzgerald, Francesca Galloway, John Gillow, Titi Halle, Kay Robertson and Roddy Taylor. Lynn Hulse, Sandy Rosenbaum and Jo Ann Stabb were facilitators *extraordinaire*, both contributing their own knowledge and enabling access to interviews with others.

The many challenges presented during the production of this book were overcome with the able assistance of the team at Thames & Hudson. And without the incredible focus and organizational skills of my own assistant, Diane Mackay, it would not have been possible. Over the course of the many months it has taken to prepare this volume, many others too numerous to mention offered valuable encouragement and insights; my gratitude goes out to them all.

PICTURE CREDITS

The author would like to thank the following sources for their kind permission to reproduce the photographs in this book. Every effort has been made to seek permission to reproduce these images. Any omissions are entirely unintentional and details should be addressed to the author. Museum accession numbers are given where appropriate.

Abbreviations:
BDM: The Warner Archive at Braintree District Museum; **BF**: © The Design Library; **CSM**: Central Saint Martins College of Art and Design, Museum and Contemporary Collections; **FIT**: The Museum at The Fashion Institute of Technology, New York; **Fitzgerald**: Esther Fitzgerald Rare Textiles; **Galloway**: Francesca Galloway; **Ginsburg**: TiTi Halle, Cora Ginsburg LLC; **Harris**: The Harris Museum & Art Gallery, Preston; **HW**: Herriot-Watt University, Edinburgh; **LACMA**: Los Angeles County Museum of Art; **MAK**: Austrian Museum of Applied/Contemporary Art, Vienna; **MMU**: Visual Resources Centre, Manchester Metropolitan University, photography Steven Yates; **RCC**: Ruthin Craft Centre; **Smyth**: Peta Smyth Antique Textiles; **PRG**: The Penrith Regional Gallery & The Lewers Bequest; **Stabb**: Collection of Jo Ann Stabb, all photographs by Barbara Molloy; **TT**: Twisted Thread; **UCD**: Design Collection, The School of Design, University of California, Davis, all photographs Barbara Malloy; **Winterthur**: The Winterthur Museum, Delaware.

With the exception of those listed below, all images are courtesy of and copyright the Artist.

p. 2. Ginsburg; **pp. 4 & 5** Sue McNab; **pp. 6 & 7** Galloway; **p. 8** Jeremy Addington; **p. 10** BPK/Museum für Asiatische Kunst, Staatliche Museen zu Berlin/Iris Papadopoulos; **p. 12** Schoeser

1.2 Andrew Stone; **1.3** 2000.41.07 UCD; **1.5** Ginsburg; **1.6** Petronella Ystma; **1.7** Stabb; **1.8** Sally Edwards; **1.9** Dr John Cooke; **1.12** Galloway; **1.13** Eva Fernandez; **1.14** Charles Frizzell; **1.15** M.91.184.144 LACMA; **1.16** Ginsburg; **1.17** M.77.70.4 LACMA; **1.18** Science Museum; **1.19** Ginsburg; **1.20** Stabb; **1.21** 2001.07.19 UCD; **1.22** Fitzgerald; **1.23** Longevity, London; **1.24** Ginsburg; **1.25** Bruce Sojka Grime; **1.26**, **1.27** Fitzgerald; **1.28** 2002.20.14 UCD; **1.29** M.2000.2 LACMA; **1.30** 1993.14.01 LACMA; **1.31** 1989.02.52 UCD; **1.32** 2002.20.20 UCD; **1.33** Stabb; **1.34** 2000.41.13 UCD; **1.35** 2000.41.14 UCD; **1.36**, **1.37** Ginsburg; **1.38** © Dovecot Studios Archive; **1.39** Fitzgerald; **1.40** PRG; **1.41** 2001.10.05 UCD; **1.42** 2000.44.06 UCD; **1.44** Fitzgerald; **1.45** RCC; **1.46** VanEijsden NL; **1.47** Andra Nelki; **1.48** Lynn Hulse; **1.49**, **1.50**, **1.51** Fitzgerald; **1.52** BDM; **1.53** Ginsburg; **1.54** RCC; **1.55** Stabb; **1.56** PRG; **1.57** Fitzgerald; **1.58** John Nollendorfs; **1.60** Anna Blackman Photography; **1.61** Ginsburg; **1.62** Stabb; **1.63** 1994.20.92 UCD; **1.64** 1996.08.01f UCD; **1.65** Stabb; **1.66** 1986.01.06 UCD; **1.67** 1992.05.04 UCD; **1.68** 1986.04.01 UCD; **1.69** Stabb; **1.70** Ginsburg; **1.72** Karen Philippi; **1.73** Edward Field; **1.74** Johannes Kuhnen; **1.76** Tim Benko; **1.78** M.Yusef; **1.79** M. Bouscaren; **1.80** William King; **1.81** Greg Somerville; **1.84** Natalija Brunovs; **1.85** Dewi Tannatt Lloyd; **1.86** Lynne Ewings/Artist; **1.87** Joupvan Houdt; **1.89** Christian Capurro; **1.90**, **1.91** M.39.2.392 & M.39.2.16 LACMA; **1.92** Ginsburg; **1.93** Lyn Hulse; **1.94** 1996.08.17 UCD; **1.95** M.55.12.49 LACMA; **1.96** 1994.16.05 UCD; **1.97** 1995.35.09 UCD; **1.98** 1989.02.51 UCD; **1.99** 1995.23.01 UCD; **1.100** 1989.02.49 UCD; **1.101** 1989.02.56 UCD; **1.102** Lyn Hulse; **1.103** 1999.30.08 UCD; **1.104** Fitzgerald; **1.105** M.55.12.45 LACMA; **1.106** Tessa Holding; **1.107** Galloway; **1.108** Stabb; **1.109** 2001.07.03 UCD; **1.110** c19782 Harris; **1.111** Lyn Hulse; **1.112** Fitzgerald; **1.113** 1989.04.01 UCD; **1.114** Liberty Ltd; **1.115** Fitzgerald; **1.116** Ginsburg; **1.117** Ziggie Bergmann; **1.118** 185 Harris; **1.119** 2003.04.02 UCD; **1.120** Maja Kihlstedt; **1.121** Fitzgerald; **1.122** Ian Hobbs; **1.123** BarryShapiro; **1.125** Lucy Barden; **1.126** George Skevos Karpathakis; **1.128** YAM; **1.129** © Atelier Silke Bosbach 2011; **1.132**, **1.133** Ginsburg; **1.134** M. Kluvanek; **1.135** A385266 LACMA; **1.136**, **1.137** Ginsburg; **1.138** Schoeser; **1.139** Ginsburg; **1.140** Visual Winds Studio, New York; **1.141** Gene Lee

2.1 Robert Diamante; **2.3** D. S. Walsh; **2.4** Stabb; **2.5** Sharon Reisdorph; **2.6** Courtesy of Gail Martin Gallery; **2.9** Timothy Fuss, www.pixelwave.com; **2.11** Stabb; **2.13**, **2.14** © Paddy Hartley, All rights reserved; **2.15** Barry Shapiro; **2.16** Ron Geesin; **2.17** Andy Taylor; **2.18** Lisbeth Holton; **2.19** 1995.18.01 UCD; **2.20** Ginsburg; **2.21** Victor France; **2.22** 1989.04.03a UCD; **2.23** Eva Fernandez; **2.24** Lee Fatheree; **2.26** Lyn Hulse; **2.27** 1969.03.14 UCD; **2.28** 1992.08.01 UCD;

2.29 1991.18.1 UCD; **2.30** 282000.25.01 UCD; **2.32** Pharmacopaeia Art; **2.33** Schoeser; **2.34** Peter Volicek; **2.35** Sue McNab; **2.37** Gerhardt Heindersburger; **2.38** Joe Mackay; **2.39** 1990.1.45 UCD; **2.40** 1990.1.46 UCD; **2.41** Stabb; **2.42** 2001.06.01b UCD; **2.43** 1991.15.17b UCD; **2.44** Stabb; **2.45** Al Sim; **2.46** Amaya Gálvez Mendez; **2.47** Kandi Terrar; **2.48** 1976.02.04ab UCD; **2.49, 2.50** Ian Hobbs; **2.54** Takao Oya, Japan; **2.56** Nao Yagi; **2.57** Kenji Nagai; **2.59** 1988.02.07 UCD; **2.60** 1988.02.27 UCD; **2.61** 1988.02.34 UCD; **2.62** 1989.02.12 UCD; **2.63** 1988.12.13 UCD; **2.64** 2000.29.34a UCD; **2.65** 1988.02.36 UCD; **2.66** 2000.29.23a UCD; **2.67** 1988.12.16 UCD; **2.68** Greg Somerville; **2.69** Maj Lundell; **2.70** Courtesy Gail Martin Gallery; **2.71** Dawghaus Studio; **2.72** 1976.02.09 UCD; **2.73** Mike Hodson; **2.76, 2.77** Galloway; **2.78, 2.79, 2.80, 2.81, 2.82** © Claudia Moeller; **2.85** 1991.15.11 UCD; **2.87, 2.88, 2.89, 2.90** © The Tactility Factory; **2.91, 2.92** Ron Geesin; **2.93** Richard Sargent; **2.94** Galloway; **2.95** 1994.22.04 UCD; **2.96** 1995.35.08i UCD; **2.97** Rod Buchholz; **2.100, 2.101** David Caras; **2.102** Ginsburg; **2.103** Ginsburg; **2.104** 2001.07.02 UCD; **2.105** 1995.35.30a UCD; **2.107** Sharon Reisdorph; **2.108** © MAK; **2.112** 2001.07.32 UCD; **2.113** Stabb; **2.114** Ginsburg; **2.115** 1995.19.02 UCD; **2.116** Don Tuttle; **2.117** 1991.18.02 UCD; **2.118** Andra Nelki; **2.119** Stabb; **2.120** Andy Taylor; **2.121** P. Havakort, NL; **2.122** Philip Cohen; **2.123** Richard Walker; **2.124** Terence Bogue; **2.126** Dr Ellak von Nagy Felsobuki; **2.127** Takashi Hatakeyama; **2.128** Glenn Hudson; **2.129** Takashi Hatakeyama; **2.130** Stabb; **2.131, 2.132** Jakob Schlaepfer; **2.133** Alexandra Manczak; **2.135** Peter Becher; **2.137** Al Karevy; **2.138** Lisbeth Holten; **2.139** 1999.13.01side UCD; **2.140** 1989.02.58 UCD; **2.141** Frank Vinken, Essen; **2.143** Dewi Tannatt Lloyd; **2.146** Jason Ingram; **2.147** © S. Heijnen, NL

3.1 Takao Oya, Japan; **3.2** Chee-Heng Yeong; **3.3** 1988.02.63 UCD; **3.4** 1988.02.69 UCD; **3.5** 1988.12.21 UCD; **3.6** Stabb; **3.7** Quico Ortega, Centre de Documentació i Museu Tèxtil, Terrassa, Spain; **3.8** 1989.02.03 UCD; **3.9** 1989.12.19 UCD; **3.10** Jenny Kühn, Berlin; **3.11** 1976.01.86 UCD; **3.12** Encyclopaedia Destructica; **3.13** 1986.04.15 UCD; **3.14** John Matthew Deepak; **3.15** Stabb; **3.16** M.71.52 LACMA; **3.17** M.81.69(3) LACMA; **3.18** M.55.57.1 LACMA; **3.19** Schoeser; **3.20** 1996.08.23 UCD; **3.21** Ginsburg; **3.22** Ginsburg; **3.23** Marie Clews; **3.24, 3.25, 3.26** Ginsburg; **3.27** 2001.07.22 UCD; **3.28** 1992.08.08 UCD; **3.29** 1992.08.10 UCD; **3.30** 1999.30.03 UCD; **3.31** FXP Photography; **3.33** RCC; **3.34** Dana Davis Photography; **3.35** Kate Cameron; **3.36** Joachim Rommel, bild-media, Lochgau; **3.37** Ginsburg; **3.39** Douglas Peck; **3.42** Ken Yanoviak; **3.45** Quico Ortega, Centre de Documentació i Museu Tèxtil, Terrassa, Spain; **3.49** This Way Design; **3.50** Paul Pavlou; **3.51** Dana Davis Photography; **3.53** 1988.02.64 UCD; **3.54** 1988.02.46 UCD; **3.55** 1988.12.17 UCD; **3.56** Fitzgerald; **3.57** 1987.02.03 UCD; **3.58, 3.59** John Matthew Deepak; **3.60, 3.61** Joe Mackay; **3.62** 1988.12.06 UCD; **3.63** 1989.02.19ab UCD; **3.64** 1989.02.11 UCD; **3.65** 1989.02.10 UCD; **3.66** 1989.02.26ab UCD; **3.67** 1989.02.22 UCD; **3.68** 1989.02.30 UCD; **3.69** 1989.02.05 UCD; **3.70** Stabb; **3.71** 1989.02.15 UCD; **3.72** 1988.02.67 UCD; **3.73** 1989.02.07 UCD; **3.74** 1988.12.12ab UCD; **3.75** 1988.12.15 UCD; **3.77** 1986.04.12 UCD; **3.78** 1988.12.15 UCD; **3.79** Ginsburg; **3.81** Stabb; **3.82** 1987.02.22 UCD; **3.83** 1990.1.29a,b UCD; **3.85** Takao Oya, Japan; **3.88** George Schiffner; **3.91** S. Mackrill; **3.92** Rowland Ricketts; **3.94** 1986.02.09 UCD; **3.95** Juho Huttenen; **3.96** H. R. Rohrer; **3.97** Joe Low; **3.98** RCC; **3.99** Sue McNab; **3.100** RCC; **3.101, 3.102** Tal Wilson; **3.104** Rod Buchholz; **3.105** Al Karevy; **3.110** Barry Shapiro; **3.112** Bruce Sojka Grime; **3.113** Larry Barns; **3.114** M.55.12.6 LACMA; **3.116** 96.121.1FIT; **3.117** John Woodin; **3.120** Ginsburg; **3.122** Stabb; **3.123** Galloway; **3.124** 1995.35.15a UCD; **3.125** Ginsburg; **3.126** Tyler Robbins; **3.127** Schoeser; **3.128** Roberto Zanello; **3.129** Barry Shapiro; **3.131** 1988.13.13ac UCD; **3.133** Stabb; **3.134** 1995.30.01 UCD; **3.135** 1991.15.02 UCD; **3.136** 1992.03.08e UCD; **3.137** 1992.08.16a; **3.138** M.81.69(2) LACMA; **3.139** M89.176.4 LACMA; **3.140** M.39.2.467 LACMA; **3.141** 1995.35.08k; **3.142** 1991.15.12a; **3.143** 1990.23.03 UCD; **3.144** Ginsburg; **3.145** Stabb; **3.146** 1994.16.15 UCD; **3.147** 1996.11.112 UCD; **3.148** 1996.11.176 UCD; **3.149** Ginsburg; **3.150** Daiju Goto; **3.153** Ginsburg; **3.154** Ginsburg; **3.155** 1987.02.26 UCD; **3.156** Smyth; **3.157** 1997.15.10 UCD; **3.158** 1995.35.08h UCD; **3.159** 1992.18.01 UCD; **3.160** 1995.35.08j UCD; **3.161** 1997.15.17 UCD; **3.162** Liberty Ltd; **3.163** 1991.09.3 UCD; **3.164** 1994.20.54e UCD; **3.165** 1994.20.46 UCD; **3.166** 1994.20.54b UCD; **3.167** 1994.20.61 UCD; **3.168** 1994.20.103ab UCD; **3.169** 1994.20.104 UCD; **3.170** 1994.20.59 UCD; **3.171, 3.172** © The Artist and Artitja Fine Art; **3.173, 3.174** Joe Ofria; **3.175** Paul Pavlou; **3.179** Barbara Bellingham; **3.180** 1992.12.26 UCD; **3.181** M.58.7 LACMA; **3.187** Galloway; **3.188** Stabb

4.1 Luke Watson; **4.2** Parallax Photography; **4.3** Liberty Ltd; **4.4** Galloway; **4.5** Stabb; **4.6** Mark Lee; **4.7** Donald Brothers Archive; **4.8** A.H.946 LACMA; **4.10** John Nollendorfs; **4.11** M.72.68.7 LACMA; **4.12** Ginsburg; **4.13** Melanie Gordon; **4.14** James Austine; **4.15** DSC7218 MMU; **4.16** Joe Low; **4.18** Stabb; **4.19** 1999.19.2 UCD; **4.20** Liberty Ltd; **4.21** Schoeser; **4.22** Logan Mclain; **4.23** 2005.70.1_01FIT; **4.24** Schoeser; **4.25** www.DPFstudio.com; **4.27** Lyn Hulse; **4.29, 4.30, 4.31** Hand & Lock; **4.32** Smyth; **4.33** c190Harris; **4.34** Schoeser; **4.36** Phillipa Swan; **4.37** Lyn Hulse; **4.38** Roland Straub; **4.39** Ginsburg; **4.42** 1989.02.13 UCD; **4.43** Stabb; **4.44** Joe Mackay; **4.45** M.55.12.27 LACMA; **4.46** Ian Hobbs; **4.47** 2002.12.01 UCD; **4.48** Stabb; **4.49** 2007.05.06; **4.50** 1990.12.12; **4.51** 2000.41.31; **4.52** 1990.12.13 UCD; **4.53, 4.54, 4.55** Stabb; **4.56** Stabb; **4.57** 2002.20.10 UCD; **4.58** 1992.08.02 UCD; **4.59** Ginsburg; **4.60** 1991.13.02 UCD; **4.61, 4.62** Ginsburg; **4.63** Bob Elbert; **4.64** M.89.176.3 LACMA; **4.65, 4.66, 4.67** BDM; **4.69** Ginsburg; **4.70** Stabb; **4.71** Ginsburg; **4.73** Mike Hodson; **4.74** Liberty Ltd; **4.75** Mike Hodson; **4.76** 1995.35.07 UCD; **4.77** 2005.36.1_01FIT; **4.79** 1990.3.2 UCD; **4.80** 1994.16.09 UCD; **4.81, 4.82** Ginsburg; **4.83, 4.84** Liberty Ltd; **4.85, 4.86** Ginsburg; **4.87** Fitzgerald; **4.88** Jakob Schlaepfer; **4.89** Fitzgerald; **4.91** Dewi Tannat Lloyd; **4.93, 4.94** Kenji Nagai; **4.95** 2005.6.1.1A_01 FIT; **4.96, 4.97** Michael Pollard; **4.98** Geoffrey Carr; **4.99** Richard Sargent; **4.101** Tom Van Eynde; **4.102** Bob Elbert; **4.104** Andrew Brown; **4.105** Ginsburg; **4.106** Richard Stewart; **4.107** © St Jude's; **4.108** © Sarah Campbell; **4.109** 1965.01.05 UCD; **4.110** Ginsburg; **4.111** Liberty Ltd; **4.112** Stabb; **4.113** 2001.10.04; **4.114** Galloway; **4.115** Smyth; **4.118, 4.119** Ginsburg; **4.120** 1992.12.29c UCD; **4.121, 4.122** Ginsburg; **4.123** Schoeser; **4.124, 4.125, 4.126, 4.127** BF; **4.128** DSC7234 MMU; **4.129, 4.130** Lyn Hulse; **4.131** Stabb; **4.132** 1997.01.01; **4.133** 1997.01.03; **4.134** 1997.01.08; **4.135** 1997.01.10b; **4.136** 1997.01.10a; **4.137** 1997.01.09; **4.138** 1997.01.12b; **4.139** 1997.01.13; **4. 140** 1997.01.12a(8x) UCD; **4.142** Peter Mennim; **4.143, 4.144** Kenji Nagai; **4.145** M.79.48 LACMA; **4.148** TB Studio; **4.149, 4.150, 4.151, 4.152, 4.153, 4.154, 4.155, 4.156, 4.157** (9x) CSM; **4.158** Joe Low; **4.160** MMU; **4.161** Andrew Stone; **4.164** 1995.31.02 UCD; **4.169** Stephen Thornton; **4.170** Stefan Pahi; **4.171** Rob Mostert, Netherlands; **4.172** Stephen Yates; **4.173** Mike Buick; **4.174, 4.175** Ginsburg; **4.178, 4.179, 4.180, 4.181** (4x) Liberty Ltd; **4.182** Harris; **4.183** 1996.24.04 UCD; **4.184** Liberty Ltd; **4.185** Ginsburg; **4.186** 1988.15.70 UCD; **4.187, 4.188** Ginsburg; **4.189** Peter Vorlicek; **4.190** David Caras; **4.191** Larry Grawel; **4.192** Joe Low; **4.193** M.82.105.2 LACMA; **4.194, 4.195** Ginsburg

5.1 Ginsburg; **5.2** 1992.03.12 UCD; **5.3** Ginsburg; **5.4** 1997.15.07a UCD; **5.5** Stabb; **5.7** 1988.12.49 UCD; **5.8** Eddie Jozefiak; **5.9** Photographix; **5.10** 1969.056930124 Winterthur; **5.11** DSC6903_1_ MMU; **5.12** Ginsburg; **5.13** Galloway; **5.14** TT; **5.15** 2006.01.01b UCD; **5.16** Maria Gabriela Ferrer; **5.17** Chris Marchant; **5.18** 2000.41.06 UCD; **5.19** 2000.41.05 UCD; **5.20** 1986.10.01 UCD; **5.21** Ginsburg; **5.22** 2001.01.01 UCD; **5.23** Stabb; **5.24** Stabb; **5.25** Stabb; **5.26** 2004.06.09; **5.27** Stabb; **5.28** 2010.04.246 UCD; **5.29** Collection of Julie Schaffer Dale; **5.30** Chris Franklin; **5.31** 1999.30.05 UCD; **5.32** Stabb; **5.33** 1999.14.02 UCD; **5.34** 1995.04.07a UCD; **5.35, 5.36, 5.37, 5.38** Fitzgerald; **5.39** Joe Mackay; **5.40** Roger Clayden; **5.42** Clyde Oliver; **5.43** M75_50_1_2 LACMA; **5.44** Courtesy Gail Martin Gallery; **5.47** Stabb; **5.48** Schoeser; **5.49** Stabb; **5.50** S. Mackrill; **5.51** Stabb; **5.52** Jakob Schlaepfer; **5.53** Ole Akjoj; **5.54** Schoeser; **5.56** Nadine Elhage; **5.60** © Atelier Silke Bosbach 2011; **5.61** Craig Potton; **5.62** Sharon Reisdorph; **5.63** Don Hildred; **5.64** James Dewrance; **5.65** Chris Arend; **5.66, 5.67** Don Tuttle; **5.68** This Way Design; **5.69** Chee Heng Yeong; **5.70** Al Sim; **5.71** Susan Fan Brown; **5.73** Takashi Hatakeyama; **5.57** Peterde Ronde; **5.76** Wendy McEahern; **5.78** Nicholas Watt; **5.79** Lucy Barden; **5.80** Anna Blackman Photography; **5.82** 2002.08.01c UCD; **5.83** Joe Mackay; **5.84** Myles Prangnell; **5.86** Ginsburg; **5.87** Reeve Photography; **5.88** Eva Fernandez; **5.90** Visual Winds Studio, New York; **5.91** Reeve Photography; **5.92** Ken Rowe; **5.93** Dewi Tannatt Lloyd; **5.95** Zhang UCD; **5.96** Karen McKenzie; **5.97** 1990.19.1 UCD; **5.98** Stabb; **5.99, 5.100** Sally Edwards; **5.101** Simen Korsmo Robertsen; **5.102** Sing Lo; **5.104** Tony Clark; **5.105** Don Tuttle; **5.109** Lee Fatheree; **5.110** 1989.11.01 UCD; **5.111** Barry Shapiro; **5.112** Fitzgerald; **5.113** 1985.01.52 UCD; **5.114** Ginsburg; **5.115** Galloway; **5.116** 1988.15.40 UCD; **5.117** 2000.29.16 UCD; **5.118** Ginsburg; **5.119** Fitzgerald; **5.120** 2000.25.15; **5.121** Ginsburg; **5.122** Fitzgerald; **5.123** Ginsburg; **5.124** Keli Dougherty; **5.130** Colección Acevedo, Buenos Aires; **5.131** Lisbet Borggreen/Lars Hansen; **5.132** Neil Keach; **5.134** Clint Eley; **5.137** Lyn Hulse; **5.138** M.85.96.2 LACMA; **5.140** Peter Stone; **5.141** Luke Watson; **5.142** Keith Tidball; **5.147** Andrew Brown; **5.149** Joup Van Houdt; **5.150** David E. Leach; **5.151** Michael Cavanagh, Bloomington, IN; **5.152** Roger Mulky; **5.153** M. Kluvanek; **5.154** RCC; **5.155, 5.156** Emil von Maltitz; **5.157** M. Kluvanek; **5.159** Steve Yates; **5.160** Tom Van Eynde; **5.161** Roberto Zanello; **5.163** Paul Ferguson; **5.164** John Brash; **5.167** 1989.02.59; **5.168** 2000.25.06; **5.1 69** 1988.13.01; **5.170** 1991.15.23; **5.171** 2001.14.01 UCD; **5.174** 2000.03.06; **5.175** 2000.03.07; **5.176** 2000.03.11; **5.177** 2000.03.02; **5.178** 2000.03.01; **5.179** 2000.03.03; **5.180** 2000.03.13; **5.181** 2000.03.10; **5.182** 1988.12.64 UCD; **5.183, 5.190** Klaus Herzberger; **5.184** 1995.08.03 UCD; **5.186, 5.188, 5.189, 5.191** TT; **5.193** Giancarlo Sponga

6.1 The Beryl Dean Archive, reproduced by permission of the Dean and Chapter of St Paul's Cathedral/The Executors of the Beryl Dean Estate; **6.2** Sudir Hood; **6.3** M.79.8.6 LACMA; **6.4** Galloway; **6.6** David Taylor Photography; **6.7** Galloway; **6.8** M.39.2.262 LACMA; **6.9** M39.3.240 LACMA; **6.10** M39.2.9 LACMA; **6.11** Peta Smyth Antique Textiles; **6.12** Ginsburg; **6.14** Christopher Young; **6.17** Ginsburg; **6.18** tc866 Harris; **6.20** Galloway; **6.21** Ginsburg; **6.22** Watts of Westminster; **6.23** Iveta Olejkova, by kind permission of Elizabeth Elvin; **6.24** Tim Gresham; **6.25** 60_46_12_2 LACMA; **6.26** Liberty Ltd; **6.27** Stabb; **6.28** Galloway; **6.29** 1989.01.04 UCD; **6.30** © The Design Library; **6.31** Don Hildred; **6.32** Joe Mackay; **6.33** M75.4.22; **6.34** M83_105_27_2 LACMA; **6.35** Ginsburg; **6.36** Don Hildred; **6.37** 1986.04.17 UCD; **6.38** Galloway; **6.39** Don Hildred; **6.40** © Peter Koepke; **6.41** Bruno Jarrett; **6.42** Fitzgerald; **6.44** Dawghaus Studio; **6.45** © Peter Koepke; **6.47** Stabb; **6.49** R. Hensleigh; **6.50, 6.53** David Heke, Chester; **6.55** Daragh Muldowney Dulra Photography, Ireland; **6.56** Galloway; **6.57** MMU; **6.58** Galloway; **6.59** Ginsburg; **6.60** Fitzgerald; **6.61, 6.62, 6.63, 6.64, 6.65, 6.66** © The Design Library; **6.67, 6.68, 6.69, 6.70** Galloway; **6.71, 6.72** Allan Cox; **6.73** Tony Dick; **6.74** 2001.07.29; **6.75**1986.05.02; **6.77** 1986.05.04; **6.78** 1986.05.08; **6.80** 1986.05.09; **6.79** 1999.09.32 UCD; **6.82** Christopher Young; **6.83, 6.84** © 2000 Paddy Hartley, All rights reserved; **6.85** Fred Krage; **6.86** Peter Carroll; **6.88** Daragh Muldowney Dulra Photography, Ireland; **6.89** TT; **6.91** Pol Leemans, Belgium; **6.90** Wendy McEahern; **6.92** Mary Stark; **6.94, 6.95** Foto Studio Leemans NL; **6.97** HelenExcell; **6.99** 2001.14.03,.09,.15,.12,.04,.10,.07,.04,.13 UCD; **6.101** Rob Mostert, Netherlands; **6.102** MMU; **6.106, 6.107** Ginsburg; **6.111** 2000.35.21 UCD; **6.113** 2000.35.20; **6.114** 2000.35.25; **6.115** 2000.35.16; **6.117** 2000.35.17; **6.116** 2000.35.24 UCD; **6.118, 6.120** 2006.01.05 a&b UCD; **6.119** Fitzgerald; **6.121** Charlie Ribbon Photography; **6.122** tc1049 Harris; **6.123** Fitzgerald; **6.124** Ginsburg; **6.125** TB Studio; **6.126** 2006.01.03b UCD; **6.127** Ginsburg; **6.130** Galloway; **6.131** Stabb; **6.132, 6.133, 6.135** Galloway; **6.136** James Dewrance; **6.137** Barry Shapiro; **6.138** Michael Wicks; **6.139** Daragh Muldowney Dulra Photography, Ireland; **6.141** David Paterson; **6.143** Michael Wicks; **6.144** Visual Photography Design, NL; **6.147** Richard Battye for River Studio Photography, Birmingham; **6.149** Roland Hueber, Germany; **6.150** Tony Summers, Upfront Pictures; **6.151** Kristal Gilmour; **6.152** Andy Taylor; **6.154** www.DPFstudio.com; **6.155** Peter Evans Photography; **6.156** Michael Wicks; **6.157** Michael Pollard; **6.158** Mei Lim; **6.159** Susan Byrne; **6.160, 6.161** Liberty Ltd; **6.162** Naomi Ryder for Ryder & Rowe Co.; **6.163** Tihanyi & Bakos; **6.164** Joup van Houdt; **6.166** Mark Gulezian/Quicksilver Photographers; **6.169** Angela Coombs-Matthews; **6.170** Roger Lee

INDEX

Page numbers in *italic* refer to illustrations.